DON WAREHOUSE

The
Complete Diary
of a Cotswold Parson

The Complete Diary of a Cotswold Parson

The Diaries of the Revd. Francis Edward Witts

1783-1854

in 10 volumes

Edited by Alan Sutton

Volume 2

The Curate and Rector

Diaries covering the Period

1806-1825

AMBERLEY

The Complete Diary of a Cotswold Parson

Volume 2

The Curate and Rector

First published 2008 by
Amberley Publishing
Cirencester Road
Chalford
Stroud
Gloucestershire
GL6 8PE

ISBN 978-1-84868-001-2

The illustration on page 2 is detail from the churchyard, Cirencester, taken from *Delineations of Gloucestershire*.

Typesetting and origination by Amberley Publishing
Printed in England by Asterim Limited
Bound in Scotland by Hunter & Foulis

Contents

Ferdinando Tracy (1659–82) = (1680) Katherine Keck

John Tracy (1681–1735) = Anne (d. 1761), da. of Sir Robert Atkyns of Sapperton

Anthony Tracy-Keck (d. 1767)
= (1736) Susan Hamilton (1706–55)
da. of James, 4th Duke of Hamilton

Anne Tracy (1701–63)
= John Travell (1699–1762)

Henrietta Charlotte (1742–1817)
= (1774) Edward Devereux (1741–83)
12th Viscount Hereford

Susan (1746–1835)
= (1771) Francis Charteris (1749–1808)
Lord Elcho, M.P.

Anne (1738–1826) d. unm.

Frances (1735–1767) d. unm.

Ferdinando (1740–1809) = Martha Rollinson (1741–80)

Francis (1728–1801) d. unm.

Catherine (1742–1804) d. unm.

Agnes (1747–1825) = Edward Witts (1746–1816)

Martha (176?–1839)
= 1 John Buxton (1756–98)
= 2 William Whalley (177?–1845)

see separate pedigree below

Jane (17??–97)
= 1 William Naper (1749–91)
= 2 Sir Henry Rycroft (17??–1846)

James Lennox William Naper (1791–1868)
= Selina Skipwith (d. 1880)

Jane Naper (1792–1853)
= (1815) Sir George Cornewall (1774–1835)

Francis (1783–1854)

George (1785–1823)

Edward (1786–94)

- Edward Witts (1649–1688) = Jane Hinton of Aldbourne
  - Edward Witts (1650–1715) = (2) Miriam Adams
    - Edward Witts (1676–1736) = Sarah Broome
      - Edward (1701–54)
        - Broome (1738–69) = Elizabeth London (1738–1837)
          - Broome Philips (1767–1845) = Jane Lake
            - Jane (1810–55) = James Currie Duncan
            - Emma (1812–99) = R. Allen
            - Broome Lake (1812–61) = Maria Dickson
            - William Frederick (1818–84) = Ellen May Witts
            - Maria (1822–1904) = John Edward Woodroffe
          - Edward London (1768–1841) = Ann Parrott
          - Maria Amelia (1769–1830) = A. Rodick of Wellingborough
            - Edward London
            - Henry
            - Unnamed boy
            - Unnamed girls
      - Richard (1705–55) = Jane Parish
        - Richard Parish (1748–1828)
      - George (1710–16)
      - Broome (1713–68) = Apphia Anthony (1713–60)
        - *see pedigree on page 8*
      - John (1707–30)
      - Mary (1703–04)
      - Sarah (1715–66) = Thomas Hunt

Broome Witts = Apphia Anthony
(1713–68) (1713–60)
1741

Broome (1744–1827) = Amelia London (1742–1832)

Apphia (1743–1840)
= 1 (1770) Col. Joseph Peach (d. 1770)
= 2 (1772) Thomas, 2nd Baron Lyttelton (1744–1779)

Sarah (1745–1834) = Edward Stone
- Sarah = Charles Shard

Edward (1746–1816)
see Agnes Travell on page 6

Richard (1747–1815) = Martha Steere (1755–1815)
- Lee Steere (1774–1832) = Sarah Harrison
  - five children (died young)
- Richard (1775–1834)
- Eliza (1777–1829) = Mr Daniell
  - George (18??–1823)
  - Sophy
  - Eliza

John (1751–1816) = A. Townson (d. 1811)
- John (1777–1857)
- Ann (1775–1839)
- Apphia (1781–1859)

George (b. & d. 1751)

Anthony (1749–52)

Alice (1742–1800) = Thomas Williams

List of Illustrations

Anderson. *Shropshire: Its Early History and Antiquities*, John Corbett Anderson, 1864.
Bigland. *Historical, Monumental and Genealogical Collections, relative to the County of Gloucester; printed from the original papers of the late Ralph Bigland.* 1791.
BOTT. *The Book of the Thames*
CMAG. Cheltenham Museum and Art Gallery.
Corry. *The History of Bristol*, John Corry, 1816.
Crapelet. *Souvenirs de Londres en 1814 et 1816*, G. A. Crapelet, Paris, 1817.
DG. *Delineations of Gloucestershire*, J. & H. S. Storer and J. N. Brewer, 1826.
Evans. *The History of Bristol*, John Evans, 1816.
Glover. *The History of the County of Derby*, Stephen Glover, 1829.
GN. Stiftung Weimarer Klassik, bestand: Goethe-Nationalmuseum.
HCA. *The History of Calwich Abbey*, Mary Teresa Fortescue, 1915.
Knight. *Old England a Pictorial Museum of Regal, Ecclesiastical, Baronial, Municipal and Popular Antiquities*, Charles Knight, 1845.
Lee. *History of the Town and Parish of Tetbury*, Alfred T. Lee, 1857.
Martineau. *A Complete Guide to the English Lakes*, Harriet Martineau, 1855.
PE. *Picturesque Excursions*, Arthur Freeling, *c.*1840.
Papworth. Papworth's *Select Views of London*,1816.
PTRT. *Picturesque Tour of the River Thames.*
Rudder. *A New History of Gloucestershire*, Samuel Rudder, 1779.
Rutter. *Delineations of the North Western Division of the County of Somerset*, John Rutter, 1829.
WFP. Witts Family Papers.

The codes in italics at the end of each illustration relate to the catalogue of the Alan Sutton Image Archive.

12. Bachelor of Arts, Oxford; Rudolph Ackermann. *A History of the University of Oxford, its Colleges, Halls and Public Buildings*. 1813. *B0930-19*
13. Long Ashton Church. *C0101-03*
14. New Park; drawn by J. P. Neale, engraved by F. Mansell. *B0326-16*
15. Stert, Wiltshire. *WFP F393. B1017-30*
16. Urchfont Church. *WFP F393. B1017-24*
17. Plan, probably Urchfont Parsonage. *WFP F393. B1017-21*
18. Urchfont Church, 20 August. *WFP F393. B1017-19*
19. Sketch of house WFP F393. *B1017-18*
20. Stonehenge. *WFP F393. B1017-25*
21. Stonehenge. *WFP F393. B1017-26*
22. Stonehenge. *WFP F393. B1017-27*
23. Urchfont Church. *WFP F393. B1017-20*
24. Sketch of bridge and house, *WFP F393. B1017-23*
25. Charles Mayo, 1750-1829; line illustration from *A Genealogical Account of the Mayo & Elton Families*. Charles Herbert Mayo, 1908. *B1015-01*
26. Sketch of house. *WFP F393. B1017-23*
27. Cottage in Wiltshire. *WFP F393. B1017-29*
28. Salisbury 1798; Francis Jukes after Edward Dayes. *B1121-05*
29. Huntsman and dogs leaping hurdle; etching by Henry Alken, published in his *Scraps from the Scrap Book of Henry Alken*, London, 1821. *B1228-15*
30. Map of Wiltshire south-east of Devizes; from *The Ancient History of Wiltshire* by Sir Richard Colt Hoare, 1812-1821. *B1007-03*
31. Cow with bell. *WFP F393. B1017-28*
32. Map of Wiltshire south-west of Devizes; from *The Ancient History of Wiltshire* by Sir Richard Colt Hoare, 1812-1821. *B1007-04*
33. West View of Stonehenge, published by W. Miller, Albemarle Street, London, 1 January 1812; from *The Ancient History of Wiltshire* by Sir Richard Colt Hoare, 1812-1821. *B1007-02*
34. View of Bath showing the South Parade, bridge etc.; from *The Beauties of England & Wales*. *B0325-14*
35. Bromsgrove Church. *WFP F393. B1017-22*
36. Letter from Francis to Margaret, 1 February 1808. *WFP F470. B0926-21*
37. The Piccadilly Nuisance, Dedicated to the Worthy Acting Magistrates of the District, (29 December 1818); George Cruikshank (1792-1878). *B0324-24*
38. Berkeley Square; *Papworth. A1210-29*
39. British Institution, Pall Mall; published 1 April 1808 at R. Ackermanns Repository of Arts, 101 Strand. *B0324-18*
40. Cross-section of Barker's Panorama at Leicester Square. *B1020-04*
41. Covent Garden Theatre 1808, prior to the fire in September. *B1020-01*
42. After the opera; illustration by George and Robert Cruikshank for Pierce Egan's *Life in London*, 1821. *A0914-02*
43. Rodborough Manor; T. Way, Lithographers, London. *B0809-01*
44. Huntsman and dogs at inn; etching by Henry Alken, published in his *Scraps from the Scrap Book of Henry Alken*, London, 1821. *071228-08*
45. Lansdown Crescent, built by John Palmer; engraving by A. Woodroffe *c.*1820. *B0403-07*

84. Windermere, Water Head; Pyne, after James Baker, lithograph, 1853. *B1121-11*
85. Lakes View; drawn by T. L. Aspland and engraved by W. Banks, *Martineau. A0704-12*
86. Windermere from near Rigg's Hotel; drawn and engraved by W. Banks. *Martineau. A0704-20*
87. Pencil sketch view near Ambleside; by Francis Witts. *WFP F393. B1019-11*
88. Rydal Water; drawn by T. L. Aspland and engraved by W. Banks, *Martineau. A0704-19*
89. Derwentwater; drawn by T. L. Aspland and engraved by W. Banks, *Martineau. A0704-23*
90. Windermere from Lowwood Hotel; drawn and engraved by W. Banks, *Martineau. A0704-13*
91. Windermere from near Storrs; drawn by T. L. Aspland and engraved by W. Banks, *Martineau. A0704-14*
92. Coniston from the wood above Bank Ground; drawn by T. L. Aspland and engraved by W. Banks, *Martineau. A0704-15*
93. Wastwater; drawn by T. L. Aspland and engraved by W. Banks, *Martineau. A0704-22*
94. Vale of Keswick; drawn by T. L. Aspland and engraved by W. Banks, *Martineau. A0704-18*
95. Grasmere from Red Bank; drawn by T. L. Aspland and engraved by W. Banks, Harriet *Martineau. A0704-16*
96. Grasmere from Loughrig Fell; Pyne, after James Baker, lithograph, 1853. *B1121-08*
97. Derwentwater; Pyne, after James Baker, lithograph, 1853. *B1121-07*
98. Pencil sketch of waterfall; by Francis Witts, *WFP F393. B1019-09*
99. Skiddaw; Pyne, after James Baker, lithograph, 1853. *B1121-09*
100. Honister Crag; drawn by T. L. Aspland and engraved by W. Banks, *Martineau. A0704-21*
101. Upper Reach of Ullswater; drawn by T. L. Aspland and engraved by W. Banks, *Martineau. A0704-17*
102. Keswick; Pyne, after James Baker, lithograph, 1853. *B1121-10*
103. Brougham Hall. *B1227-20*
104. Distance travelled, page 1, 1817. *WFP F523. B1017-09*
105. Distance travelled, pages 2 & 3, 1817. *WFP F523. B1017-08*
106. Leicester Abbey; *Knight. A0916-111*
107. Mrs. Siddons. *B1121-64*
108. Taking Amusement; drawn and etched by Richard Dagley, published in *Takings, or, the Life of a Collegian*, 1821. *B1230-05*
109. James Gillray cartoon on the topic of gout. *B1025-14a*
110. The Bath Races; from *The Comforts of Bath*, Thomas Rowlandson, 1798. *B0324-19*
111. Admiral Sir James Saumarez. *A0930-32*
112. Bath Abbey Church; *Knight. A0916-110*
113. Sir Richard Colt Hoare; from *The Ancient History of Wiltshire* by Sir Richard Colt Hoare, 1812-1821. *B1007-05*
114. The Interior of the Concert Room; from an engraving by J. C. Nattes, 1806. *B0403-02*
115. Ornamental cottage at Banwell; *Rutter. B0721-09*
116. Illustration from Manuscript diary. *WFP F308. B1101-01*
117. Worlebury Camp; *Rutter. B0721-01*
118. Weston old Church; *Rutter. B0721-02*
119. Weston-super-Mare; *Rutter. B0721-03*
120. Congresbury Church; *Rutter. B0721-04*
121. Congresbury Parsonage; *Rutter. B0721-05*
122. Monastic barn at Worle; *Rutter. B0721-06*
123. Brean Down and Black Rock; *Rutter. B0721-11*
124. Uphill Church; *Rutter. B0721-12*

Introduction

In January 1806 Francis Edward Witts was twenty-two years old and heading towards his twenty-third birthday. His parents, Edward and Agnes, were living on very restricted means and his younger brother, George, had recently been commissioned into the Royal Artillery.

Francis had nearly finished his studies at Wadham College, Oxford, and was in search of a vocation. He had wanted to make his career in the diplomatic service and in 1801 he had been successful in obtaining a position as secretary to the British Minister in Copenhagen, but this had been brought to a premature end by the Battle of Copenhagen, and all further attempts to find similar employment were fruitless. He had toyed with banking and the law, but attempts at securing appropriate patronage came to nothing, notwithstanding the best endeavours of family and friends. For the past few years he had been viewing the Church as a viable alternative, and, with his favoured choice closed to him, he now sought a suitable curacy with which to commence his clerical career.

Francis and his parents lived a peripatetic life. Ever since Edward's bankruptcy in 1796 the family had moved from place to place, usually in lodgings, but occasionally staying with relatives and friends. The practice in recent years had been to take a tenancy in Clifton, which they sub-let at a profit in the summer months, during which time they would tour their wealthy acquaintances, always with a stop-over of several weeks with their particular friends John and Harriet Granville of Calwich Abbey in Staffordshire. Despite their slender means, the family only stayed in fashionable places, usually the watering-holes of Clifton, Bath and Cheltenham. In the autumn of the previous year (1805) they had stayed for several weeks at Tunbridge Wells. Now, at the start of 1806, they were back at their main base, 2 Boyce's Buildings in Clifton.

During the summer of 1805, after their usual visit to Calwich, the family had stayed for a while at Buxton in Derbyshire, with the hope that Francis might find the waters efficacious in easing his rheumatism. During this visit the family became acquainted with a wealthy widow, Jane Backhouse, and her daughter, Margaret. Agnes was astute enough to recognise the potential of this; although not as well connected as the Wittses, the Backhouses were a very respectable mercantile and banking family. Margaret was not a beauty, and seems to have been quiet and retiring, but marriage was a business and Francis had little hope of inheriting or earning sufficient money to support the sort of life that he would have wanted to lead. From this acquaintanceship the connection was fostered and during the autumn negotiations were entered into. On 4 December 1805 Francis travelled north to spend some time with Mrs Backhouse and Margaret, not returning until 8 January 1806. Unfortunately, no record has survived from this period, apart from fleeting references in Agnes' diary, recording the receipt and despatch of letters to and from her beloved son.

Volume Two of *The Complete Diary of a Cotswold Parson* covers the period January 1806 to February 1825. For 1806 and 1807 we have a reasonable amount of information, but then Francis Witts appears to have fallen out of the habit of maitaining a diary. The period 1808 to 1819 is very sparse on detail and only a few travel journals survive. Information for what happened within the family for most of this time has been extracted from the diaries of Agnes Witts. From January 1820 Francis took up his pen once more and, with occasional breaks, continued his dairy until his death in August 1854.

Francis first visited Urchfont in Wiltshire in June 1806 and finally took up his curacy there in August of that year, Edward and Agnes residing with him. In 1808 he married Margaret Backhouse and in the same year his uncle, Ferdinando Tracy Travell, died. In 1809 he succeeded to his late uncle's living at Upper Slaughter in Gloucestershire, at which point Edward and Agnes settled in Cheltenham. In 1811 Margaret gave birth to a girl, who died two weeks later. In 1813 she successfully bore their second and only surviving child, Edward Francis, who would eventually follow in his father's footsteps as rector of Upper Slaughter.

The diary for 1806 commences on 14 January. Francis Witts was back at Clifton and divided his day between visiting and religious studies, intermixed with his search for a curacy: *17 Jan 1806: wrote to the Revd. B. Port respecting the Curacy of Ham.* On the same day, following much religious reading, he found time for entertainment: *at a ball in Bristol in honour of the Queen's birthday — the room not extremely crouded, but the dancers often incommoded; a great medley of genteel & vulgar, handsome and ordinary; but the Select gained a great addition to Mrs. Gould's party, whose accession rendered our Clifton set far superior to any other party.*

The Clifton set and the social whirl into which Francis threw himself is very clearly illustrated in the entry for 21 January. Late in the afternoon he set off for Stoke in a hackney carriage for a dinner with some of the most illustrious members of the south Gloucestershire county set, which also had the benefit of including his college friend William Dowell. After a quick ride back he also managed to attend a dance on the same evening:

Tuesday Jan. 21st ... Wrote upon business to Mr. Edwd. Horne the Solicitor, & a letter upon general subjects to my friend Round. Mounted a hackney between four & five to repair to Capt. Webb's at Stoke, where a large & pleasant party were assembled, & most hospitably & handsomely entertained. His dinner excellent; his Madeira & Claret delicious. Besides my excellent friend Dowell, whom I had infinite pleasure in again seeing, we had Col. Kingscote, Sir Will. Guise, & Sir Henry Lippincott, Major Durbin, Capt. Cooke, Mr. Probyn, Messrs. P & J. Baillie, & Mr. Foster. By a rapid ride home I contrived to reach a dance at Lady Teresa Dease's, before ten o clock, where I danced with a Miss Holford from Cheshire in obedience to Lady Teresa's Commands, with Miss Dease, & with my amiable friend Miss Gould. The party was very numerous, perhaps, too crowded, but upon the whole was pleasant, and the supper good. Had much pleasant conversation with Lord Fingal, a man of great sense & moderation, the excellent Lady Ford, Mrs. Gould, Mr. Baggot, Mr. Probyn &c. Received an obliging letter from Mr. B. Port, declining the proposition which I had made to him.

This lengthy extract has been given to demonstrate the typical mix of Francis' life at this time: study, enjoyment and job-seeking. What the proposition made to Bernard Port was is unknown, but presumably he was hoping he might step into a vacant curacy when he had been ordained—the connection being that Port was the nephew of the family friend John Granville. As for the enjoyment, the result of the previous evening's entertainment was a hangover: *Wednesday Jan. 22nd ... Rose very late, by dissipation so unhung as not to sit down to study, thus lengthning a vacation I had no idea once of granting to myself.*

The same situation occurred the following day, when social events impinged on his time, affecting his conscience: *Thursday Jan 23d: ... Read part of the Bish. of London's 21st. Lecture, but was prevented from a more exact adherence to the rules of Study I had prescribed to myself by my other Engagements.* In fact, this theme of self-criticism for dissipation and neglect of studies repeats itself throughout this particular diary.

Edward and Agnes were concerned at the youthful dissipation demonstrated by Francis, and it seems clear that Agnes was worried about his attitude to the young ladies of Clifton when they were in negotiations with the Backhouses. After much socialising and constant self-criticism for neglecting his studies, a family argument arose:

25 Feb. ... An unhappy domestic contest in the morning dejected & dispirited me: if all the reproaches made against me were well founded, my punishment was as merited as it was severe: if I be not so lost as was represented my tendencies to vanity & self-esteem received at least a salutary check. ... Wrote to Mr. Travell upon business. Received a letter from the Revd. Mr. Cumberland, which reduces to a shadow my expectations of the Curacy of Ampney; perhaps Providence does not esteem me as yet worthy to labour in the vineyard.

Perhaps it was the receipt of the letter from the Revd Mr Cumberland that sparked the dispute. The letter to Mr Travell was to his maternal uncle, Ferdinando Tracy Travell, the rector of Upper Slaughter—one of those busy in the search on behalf of Francis. Agnes did not note the event in her diary, but she did record her beloved son's twenty-third birthday the following day. As for Francis, following on from the family discord, his birthday was a day of some circumspection:

Wednesday Feb. 26: A stormy, windy, cold day, one violent shower. The day appointed for a general national fast; not less a day of humiliation to me as the twenty third anniversary of my birth; the witness of resolutions broken before they were well uttered, of contrition momentary as the sounds, which expressed it.

In March there was a breakthrough. Francis wrote to enquire about a vacancy advertised in the Bath newspaper, and was subsequently interviewed for the position:

Wed 12 March: Called upon the Revd. G. Smith respecting an advertised Curacy; found an elegant young man of congenial taste; his own Curacy not actually promised but under treaty; unpromising too, near Devizes, & I have the next refusal. As he pointed out another extremely eligible, Coome Hay, in Somerset, with a pleasant furnished Parsonage &c. so he obligingly accompanied me on a visit to the Rector, Mr. Merewether, Walcot Parade; doubts entertained, that a family in treaty for the House will take it otherwise. I consider my prospect favourable.

There is an interesting coincidence here, for at that time, and indeed later on, it seems that the families did not realise that there was a connection. It appears that George Smith's uncle, John Smith of Combe Hay (173?–1775; M.P. for Bath) married Anne Tracy, a second cousin twice removed to Francis Witts. The Smith family were centred on Combe Hay and Steeple Ashton, and it was through George Smith's connections that he knew about the Combe Hay opportunity; an act, it seems, of selfless generosity. Thus began an unhappy working relationship, for, although the first meeting was promising, time would eventually prove that the two young men could not work together.

While these opportunities were unfolding, social life in Clifton went on as before, and, notwithstanding the negotiations between the Wittses and Backhouses, Francis did not feel it to be improper to indulge in mild flirtation, which turned to embarrassment when a few strands of gossip were related to him during an evening party: *Friday March. 14th ... to a party at Mrs. Vane's, numerous & hot; played speculation with the young people, sitting by & chatting with Cecilia Wolseley all the Evening, who told me many a secret of my own, which I had no notion were in her keeping: not sorry when the Carriages were announced.*

On 17 March Francis returned to Oxford, but first visited the Revd Mr Merewether:

... After an affectionate leave of my Parents, & an early breakfast, set off in the Oxford Mail, having changed my birth on account of the weather. My society throughout not numerous, still less select. Instead of breakfasting at Bath visited Mr. Mereweather respecting the Curacy & Parsonage of Coombe Hay; he is not disinclined to treat with us, & I delegated the whole business to my Father, whom I led him to expect in a few days. Took some refreshment at Didmarton, & dined at Cirencester, where I wrote a few lines to my Father indicating the event of my visit to Mr. Mereweather ...

Edward and Agnes duly fell in with their son's request, and on 21 March they set off in a post-chaise for Combe Hay, where they stayed for three hours with Mr Mereweather, finalising the terms.

In Oxford Francis met up with all of his old acquaintances and prepared himself for his first day of determining his future on the 24th. For some reason there is a gap in the diary between 22 March and 18 June. After 22 March there is a half-page gap, and then the following page picks up once more in Clifton. Due to this gap we have little knowledge of what was going on. From the diaries of Agnes Witts we learn that Francis returned and took up his duties at Combe Hay, but in only two weeks—and before the family had actually removed from Clifton—the old rector was dead, and one of the few duties undertaken by the new curate was to bury him. With immediate effect Agnes recorded Francis taking up negotiations with George Smith and on 26 May he assisted Smith, the vicar of Urchfont, in his Whitsun duties. Agnes met George Smith the following day and thought well of him: *... Mrs. Langhams made me an early visit and Mr. Smith a very long one much conversation about his House in Erchfont an agreeable Gentlemanlike man ...*

Then, on 28 May, the two young men set off on a jaunt into Devon. The diaries of Francis pick up again on 18 June 1806, by which time Edward and Agnes had moved into temporary accommodation in Richmond Terrace. How the Devon trip went we do not know, although it appears there was some discord, for once back in Clifton Francis received a letter from Smith which was not to his liking: *19 June ... Received an unpleasant letter from Smith which afterwards gave me considerable uneasiness.* The following day all of this worry was forgotten as Francis enjoyed an evening which well expresses his youthful exhuberance:

Friday June 20th. About eight went with the Salters to Mrs. J. Auriol's fête champêtre, the Gardens very prettily arranged with festoons of coloured lamps & a Marquee the Band of the Mid'sex Militia &c. Danced upon a sloping green with the two Salters. A good supper within doors. Very pleasant; chiefly with the Goold party, the Salters, Jessop, Adair &c. Walked with the Goolds round the Hill, stargazing, at two in the morning: after which Adair, Jessop, & myself forced Mrs. Salter's Castle, & made her & the Girls give us breakfast, we helping to light the fire, boil the kettle &c., & after seeing the sun rise retired to bed by four o clock.

What Edward and Agnes made of this is unknown and was not recorded in Agnes's diary, but Francis recorded some element of parental displeasure: *Saturday June 21st. ... Sad domestic uneasiness consumed great part of the afternoon.*

From this point on the problems with parents and Smith were catalogued, but notwithstanding the misgivings, negotiations were eventually completed:

Monday June 23d ... Made a fruitless call upon Smith at Glocester House ... Walked upon the Mount with Smith discussing particulars relating to his House ... After dinner, joined a party at the Goolds for Ashton, the usual set, R. Adair excepted, with the addition of Jessop & Captn. Fallon. The walk, strawberries &c. pleasant enough. Mrs. Goold gave us a supper afterwards & Mary Goold sang delighfully. Found my Parents much exasperated at my having accepted the Invitation to Supper, & retired miserable ... 28 June After an early breakfast proceeded with my Parents in a chaise to view Erchfont ... upon our arrival at the Castle Inn Devizes we looked at some comfortable lodgings in case we should want them, took a late dinner, & afterwards walked through beautiful fields to Mr. Sutton's handsome Seat, New Park; after strolling still more through the Town; retired to bed early.

This was the first visit to see Urchfont. Presumably by this time the difficult negotiations with Smith were beginning to become resolved—at least to the extent that Francis would view the place and take a service there, for the following day he preached at Stert for the first time:

Sunday June 29: As beautiful a day as the preceding. After breakfast pursued the road to Erchfont; opposite Stert Chapel quitted the chaise & my Parents to do duty there; preached to them a Sermon instilled Life a Journey. Received with politeness by Mrs. Jacques, Miss Gale &c. Afterwards walked across beautiful fields to Erchfont, where my Father & Mother were busily exploring the Vicarage, & better pleased with it than I had hoped.

It was not yet all over, for two days later there was still uneasiness as to whether or not a successful conclusion could be reached. In the end, after more sleepless nights and difficult conversations, the concluding negotiations took place at Urchfont over the weekend of 5 and 6 July. Francis had bought a horse in the spring, and he was now in the process of buying a gig, but in the meantime he drove a rented cart on his way to meet Smith:

Saturday July 5: Very fine day. Rode to Bath after breakfast. After baiting there, harnessed my Grey in a Taxed Cart, & drove him to Erchfont; passed the Evening unpleasantly with Smith ... After a late breakfast & coming to a conclusion with Smith, walked to Stert, called upon Mrs. Jacques; performed the Afternoon Duty at the Chapel, preaching upon the neglect of GOD's Salvation to a good congregation.

Little is known of the Jaques family, but presumably Mr Jaques was the other curate, for there were two churches to be served: Urchfont and Stert. George Smith had been vicar since 1802, and his predecessor was George Jaques, who had held the living since 1773. Presumably curate Jaques was the late vicar's son. George Jaques, junior, was also curate at All Cannings, a position he had held since 1789. The actual nature of these various curacies is a little confusing; an entry in October does little to remove this confusion: *18 Oct 1806 ... being administered at Erchfont Church by Jaques, I took his duty at All Cannings & Ashlington ...*

On 14 July 1806 Edward and Agnes moved from Clifton, taking lodgings in the Market Place, near the castle, in Devizes. In August they were away travelling while much of the refurbishment was being done to the vicarage at Urchfont, then, on 17 September, Francis at long last collected his mother to take her to Urchfont, while Edward walked from Devizes—probably due to the gig being full—for Edward and Agnes were now also to live at the vicarage with their son.

William Dowell, Francis Witts's closest friend, was ordained on Sunday 14 September, and the following week he joined his friend at Urchfont and preached the sermon. This might, perhaps, have been a dry run, for between 15 November and 14 December Francis left his curacy in the hands of Dowell while he went to Beck House, near Settle, Yorkshire, on a visit to Mrs Backhouse and Margaret.

During the time when he was getting acquainted with his parishioners and the local farmers and gentry, Francis was writing letters on numerous matters of business. Some were on behalf of his brother, George. Francis had taken on the task of dealing with his brother's troublesome creditors and his correspondent Adamson appears to have been a lawyer or an agent in this matter. The problems relating to George's debts rumbled on for a number of years and many of the letters from Francis to his uncle, Ferdinando Tracy Travell, and other members of the family were on this painful subject. As for the letters to Horne, they appear to have been part of the marriage settlement preparations, Horne being an attorney for the Witts family.

On 19 February 1807 Francis headed to London for the purpose of his ordination, which he recorded in very scant form, returning by 25 February. There is then a gap until 8 March, but during all of this time his lack of social activity was replaced by what he referred to as '*promiscuous reading*,' much of it aimed at a composition of his own on the history of duelling. During February, March and April he was heavily involved in this project and on Friday 24 April he packed up his manuscript and sent it off—and this is the last we hear of it.

On 22 May Francis met Miss Carter, and from then on they met quite frequently for a number of weeks. From 2 June until July he referred to her in his diaries as HMC. Why did he feel it necessary to use initials? Was he feeling guilty about his familiarity with Miss Carter? How did this leave matters with Margaret Backhouse: was he having second thoughts? There can be little doubt that the Backhouse connection was primarily driven forward as a business connection, but were there ever moments when he was in serious doubt about a loveless marriage? We shall never know, but the diary entries are certainly enigmatic and there is much that might be read between the lines.

Miss Carter appears to have been a house guest of the Butcher family and Francis seems to have taken every opportunity of meeting her. He called on the 26th, they walked on the 28th, etc. Then there is a gap in the diaries between 10 and 23 June—perhaps it was too painful to write anything? We know from the diaries of Agnes Witts that Francis was around. We also know from the diaries of Agnes Witts that Miss Carter called at the vicarage regularly during those two weeks. Then there is silence and Miss Carter is not referred to again until July, when there is one tiny, enigmatic entry: *Thursday July 9th: Beautiful summer weather, very warm. H.M.C.—Finished a Sermon as yesterday.* And that is the very last we hear of Miss Carter. Temptation had come, but had also departed before too much serious damage was done.

There is a gap in the diaries covering the period 4 September to 5 December. From the diaries of Agnes Witts the known sequence of events is as follows:

2 September 1807: Edward and Agnes Witts lodged at 3 Richmond Terrace, Clifton. 7 September 1807: Edward and Agnes were at Cheltenham when Francis arrived: ... *at my Sisters door our Dear Franks cheerful face made us happy ... 16 September 1807: ... went early with Frank for an hour to Mrs. Timbrells in spite of a very bad cold ...* 8 October 1807: the family travelled to Birmingham, Francis parting from his parents at Bromsgrove to proceed northwards the next day. 9 October 1807: Edward and Agnes reached Calwich Abbey to stay with the Granvilles. *24 October 1807: ... wrote an important letter to Frank ... 29 October 1807: ... received a long letter from Frank ... 19 November 1807: ... doubly oppressive to me from the idea that my Dear Son was begin his journey from Yorkshire ... 21 November 1807: ... before tea arrived our Dear Frank in health and safety after a perilous journey ... 22 November 1807: ... to church where Frank performed the whole of the service ... 24 November 1807: ... a tolerable mild fine day sufficiently so for the two Ports & Frank to set out for the Doveridge coursing party which they were to take up their quarters ...* 28 November 1807: the family arrived at Hanbury to stay with their old friend the Revd William Burslem: *29 November 1807: ... Frank performed all of the service ... 4 December 1807: ... at Gloucester we joined our Servant who had set out the day before when Frank & he got into the gig wch. had been painting at a coachmakers, & rejoined us at Froster Inn 11 miles further where we dined and slept.*

During his absence in the north Francis had been covered in his curacy by Mr Williams of West Lavington. No record has been found of him, but presumably he was an unemployed 'guinea' curate.

Once back at Urchfont, family life continued as before. On 30 January 1808 Francis wrote to the Bishop of Salisbury in relation to his vicar, and on 6 February George Smith wrote to him: *Received a letter from Smith, my Vicar, from Chippenham, whither he seems to be come with a view of dislodging me; painful enough ...* And then, two days later, the young men met, but in a civil enough manner to dine together: *Monday Feb. 8. White Hart Inn—Chippenham: ... Repaired to the White Hart; whence to Smith's lodgings. Dined with him, & held a long conversation upon business, leading, I presume, to my finally leaving Erchfont at the expiration of my term.*

What the term was is not clear, but it would seem as if its end was imminent as an immediate search for another curacy commenced. On 15 February he received information from Hampshire respecting one such opportunity. A week later and Francis was in London, summoned by his Bishop, whom he met on the 23rd:

... Called early on the Bp. of Sarum, by whom I was handsomely received, & conversed not unsatisfactorily on the subject of my engagement with Smith ... Thursday Feb. 25: ... Cold & raw weather, being a hard frost. Called upon the Bishop of Salisbury & made most satisfactory arrangements in my business with his Lordship.

It appears from this that after earlier exchanges with the bishop where Francis had been deemed to be at fault, the tables were turning and on 7 March Francis recorded receiving a letter illustrative of Smith's unreasonable behaviour: ... *Heard from Smith in Town; an embarrassing letter, which required a letter to the Bishop of Salisbury* ... but not all was well in this tedious affair, for Smith appears to have worked on the bishop and on 16 March Francis recorded a less favourable letter: *Received a very unpleasant letter from the Bishop of Sarum, subversive of his former promises. Replied to it.*

By 1 April matters were coming to a conclusion and Francis met Smith's attorney, William Salmon, in Devizes, which Francis referred to as a '*painful business*'. At this point in the diary some leaves have been cut out, and this clearly happened at the time, for when starting afresh on the new recto page, he wrote the year—an unusual occurrence. It may have been that he let his temper betray itself in relation to Smith and later regretted what he had written and removed it. Two weeks later another twist in the tale developed with the visit to Urchfont of Smith's patron: *Monday April 18th: ... Dr. Dodsworth, the Canon of Windsor, my Vicar's Senile & Patron, called early & conferred with us two hours, on his road from Devizes to Salisbury; apparently, a genteel, but crafty man ...*

On 25 April the bishop wrote summoning Francis to Salisbury the following day. The meeting eventually took place at eight o'clock on the 27th, and Francis felt it went well.

On 1 May 1808 life for Francis took a different turn:

Sunday May 1st.—Bell Inn Gloucester.— Left Erchfont at nine o clock, giving morning Service at Stert; to the Jaques's before, at the Gales after Church, no Sermon, but a Sacrament. Rode off before twelve with Will. Wood as far as Rowde, passed through Chippenham without stopping dined at Spencer's at Malmsbury. Pursued my way through Tetbury & Minchin-Hampton, by Bownham House to the Fleece Inn at Rodborough. Left there my Horse & Dog & took a fast trotting Hack to Gloucester. Arrived at that place by nine, where I had the happiness to meet my friends, Mrs. Backhouse, Miss Richardson & my beloved Margaret. Supped & retired.

In just one day many thoughts must have passed through the mind of the young curate. Going through Malmesbury his attention must have strayed back three and a half years, when he and his closest friend, William Dowell, passed through and stayed overnight on their walk from Oxford to Clifton. And then, just a few miles further at Bownham House, there was his old home, which he had left at the age of ten following his father's continued financial problems—leading thereafter to a five-year stay in Edinburgh. From Bownham House he would have seen the old Bear Inn across the road, and then turned down Bear Hill and right onto the Bath Road to the Fleece at Rodborough—another familiar spot from his childhood. Then in the hackney he would have taken the same vale road as in his childhood when he was at school at Elmore—and all of this on the way to see his future bride and mother-in-law. The following day, with his party, he retraced his way to Rodborough to collect his horse and his dog, and then left Mrs Backhouse's carriage to mount his own horse and to lead the party to Bath, to meet his parents in their comfortable lodgings. Francis continued his diary for another few days and then on Friday 6 May it came to an abrupt end, not to be re-started until January 1820.

For the next eleven years most of the detail that can be gleaned for the lives of Francis and Margaret comes from the diaries of Agnes Witts. Travel diaries were kept and most appear to have survived, but for day-to-day life the detail is lost.

On 30 May 1808, Francis Witts married Margaret Backhouse at Dowry Square Chapel in Bath. The service was conducted by the Revd William Burslem. The young couple appear to have returned to Urchfont, while Edward and Agnes Witts remained in Bath until 8 June, when they went to Cheltenham.

On 17 June Agnes recorded: ... *visited* ... *old Mrs. Timbrells* ... The underlining is by Agnes to emphasise the point. She and Edward were assiduous in cultivating the old ladies who had the power of presentation to the living at Upper Slaughter.

On 28 June 1808 Francis and Margaret arrived in Cheltenham from Wiltshire. On 13 July 1808 they headed back to Urchfont, leaving Edward and Agnes at Cheltenham. Francis recorded the trip in a rather ebullient and literary fashion. The 'Route from Cheltenham to Erchfont' was certainly written in a different, experimental style, and between that and his next journal, a journey into Craven written in June 1809, we only have short pieces of information from Agnes Witts.

On 27 September 1808 Ferdinando Tracy Travell died. Without wasting a day, Agnes called on the Timbrell sisters to press the claim of Francis to the living of Upper Slaughter. At first it did not go well, but by 8 October it was resolved in Francis's favour and the elder Timbrell sister called on Agnes to confirm their positive decision. Francis appears to have left Urchfont for good on 23 November 1808, presumably glad to be away from the troublesome vicar, George Smith.

The events of the next seven months are rather sketchy, and again filtered through the diaries of Agnes Witts. The remainder of November 1808 and much of December were taken up with plans for Upper Slaughter. For Christmas and the first three months of 1809 the young couple were in Yorkshire. The reason for the extended stay is not recorded. Francis arrived back in Gloucestershire in early April, but at least for the time being he was by himself. They then settled into the rectory and by June were back in Craven once more. It was not until the end of June that their normal routine in Upper Slaughter was set to begin, and on 27 June Agnes visited the place, her first visit since the painful times of 1793.

During that same summer George was to be a guest at Upper Slaughter for a few weeks. The next three years are all from the pen of Agnes and the narrated events are mostly of painful domestic happenings, for it appears that Margaret had two, if not three, miscarriages prior to giving birth to a baby girl in the spring of 1811, but the premature child only survived for about twenty days. Agnes visited in the summer, but she found Mrs Backhouse and her aged father rather a burden: *15 August 1811: walk'd towards L. Slaughter before dinner being the last day before the departure of Dr. Moorhouse & Mrs. Backhouse the cheerfulness of the party in general was rather forced ...*

In the mix of daily life an important event took place in January 1812, for Francis Witts was appointed as a magistrate, and he took his place at the Sessions for the first time on 12 January

1812. For the remainder of his years Francis was to hold a prominent position in public life.

For August 1812 there is another surviving travel journal. This starts on 3 August as the couple take a trip into the north. Francis recorded Warwick Castle and Lichfield in detail, visiting them when they stayed with the Granvilles at Calwich. From there a ten-day trip to Buxton allowed them to take the waters and on about 20 August they arrived at Beck House, Yorkshire, where they remained until November.

On 2 March 1813 Margaret at long last gave birth to a healthy child, Edward Francis. Agnes did not visit her new grandson for two months as Mrs Backhouse remained at the rectory for a good while, and it seems that Agnes was reluctant to call while she was still in residence.

Francis Witts was to receive a welcome addition to his income in June 1814 when he became rector of Stanway, a living in the gift of Agnes's cousin, Lady Hereford. From this point on, Francis was a frequent visitor to Stanway, where Charles Keysall was his curate. During this same year, George Witts returned from overseas and spent from the early summer until December either at Upper Slaughter or at Cheltenham. This was to be almost the last visit the family would enjoy from George, for he afterwards returned to Malta and died on board ship in his eventual attempt to return to England in 1823. He was buried at sea. During this extended visit of George, Francis did not see that much of his brother, as from August to November there was another extended stay in Yorkshire. During this northern visit his parishioners at Upper Slaughter were looked after by George Wellford. A 'flashback' of 10 September 1824 provides some of the detail:

Our old friend Mr. Wellford came on a visit to us. I must retrace a little his history. He is the son of some very old and intimate friends of my Uncle Broome Witts, & as such was introduced to me by him in 1814, when Mr. Wellford, at a more advanced age than is usual, was about to enter into the Church. His views had in earlier life been directed to trade, which he had quitted from a desire to enter into the Church, although his family were dissenters. He had consequently gone to Exeter College. I was able to forward his wishes, & oblige my Uncle, by giving him a title for orders on this living, and he resided here in the Rectory house, as Curate, during a visit of three months, which we made in Yorkshire.

Little is known of the years from 1814 to 1816 apart from diary entries made by Agnes Witts. In January 1815 George had been visiting Upper Slaughter and he returned to Cheltenham on 7 January. On 9 January Francis was inducted to Stanway. On 14 January Richard Witts, uncle to Francis, died in London.

By February George was in Portsmouth awaiting a ship to take him to rejoin his regiment. In March Francis was writing long letters to his mother from Bath, during what was probably another trip to recoup the health of Margaret. On 4 May Francis and Margaret, together with Mrs Backhouse, arrived for a two-week visit to Cheltenham.

In June Edward and Agnes spent much time at Stanway and on 14 August they left Cheltenham for a stay at Upper Slaughter. During all of this time Agnes was receiving letters from, and sending letters to, George at Sicily, Genoa and Marseilles.

On 23 October 1815 Agnes recorded that Miss Currer, a relation of Margaret's, was staying at Upper Slaughter and on that day Miss Currer, Francis and Margaret dined at Mr Pole's at Wick Hill, and that '*old Derby & Joan prefer'd staying at home*'

On 19 December 1815 Francis and Margaret visited Cheltenham and two weeks later

Francis went to Malvern to visit Lady Lyttelton and his poor uncle John Witts, who was dying. He died three days later on 4 January 1816. Francis then went back to Cheltenham and he and Margaret returned home to Upper Slaughter on 25 January. By 20 June Edward and Agnes finally decided to rent Belle Vue Place, the house in which they both eventually died, and on the following day they left Cheltenham for a visit to Upper Slaughter.

On 25 June 1816 Frederick Aston, Francis's pupil, had '*a display of moderate fireworks at night*' and the following day Agnes '*amused the Youth with a game at the Royal game of Goose*.' On 28 June Lady Lyttelton arrived at Upper Slaughter, and the following day left to visit her brother Broome at Cookham Grove.

In August 1816 Francis and Margaret paid a visit to Lady Lyttelton at Malvern, and, as it turned out, were not to revisit until the spring of 1825.

After an illness of several months, Edward Witts died on 26 December 1816, and in the following summer Lady Hereford also died. The two events, especially the former, changed the life of Agnes in a radical manner. Stanway had gone to Francis Charteris, Lord Elcho, later to become 6th Earl Wemyss, but his mother, Lady Elcho, first cousin to Agnes, now took up a regular residence at Stanway and Agnes was as frequent a guest there as she had been in Lady Hereford's time.

The summer of 1817 also saw another extended journey in the north for Francis and Margaret, this time it was a tour of the Lake District, undertaken between 30 August and 14 September. As usual, Francis maintained a travel journal, written in a rather tedious style, as if for the benefit of others.

At a similar period the following year, Francis left Upper Slaughter for Beck House on 30 August, arriving on 5 September. The trip appears to have been for business, as he travelled alone, but he again kept a detailed travel diary, this time rather more informative than literary.

At last, after a gap in regular diary-keeping of a little under twelve years, Francis Witts took up his pen once more in January 1820. The diary starts on 5 January with an account of a journey to Bath. It may well have been that this journey was the catalyst that restarted the regular record-keeping, particularly as it coincided with the start of a calendar year. The visit was for the purpose of improving the poor health of Margaret, but it also became a healthy social event, much to the taste of Francis. The couple returned on 5 February to Upper Slaughter, but happily the record-keeping continued. The visit also coincided with the death of the Duke of Kent and of his aged brother King George III. Perhaps this momentous change of dynasty may also have had an effect on the diary habit. The events in France and on the Continent in general were also conducive to record, and the Cato Street Conspiracy added sensationalism. In fact, the events of 1820 provided much that was worth setting down for posterity and much space is given over in the diary to recording national and international news.

In April Francis Witts recorded some interesting snippets of his magisterial work and clearly demonstrated his Tory and social stance. He was the leading advocate of the erection of a hand-mill in the Northleach House of Correction as a means of increasing the deterrent effect of incarceration. His entry for 11 April 1820 is censorious of an attempt to effect change in the social order: *The news from the manufacturing districts is again very alarming; though happily the promptitude & energy of the Magistracy supported by a strong military force & the loyalty of the better sort have succeeded in suppressing the most daring revolutionary attempts.*

During the years when Francis Witts did not maintain his diaries, we know from references in the diaries of Agnes that he took pupils to supplement his income. This need was reduced after he acquired the living of Stanway and by 1820 it virtually came to an end with one particularly useless and disappointing pupil, Thomas Saumarez, the second son of the eminent Admiral Sir James Saumarez, who lived and studied at the rectory from August 1819 to July 1820. One of his early pupils had been Frederick Aston, the son of the new tenant at nearby Eyford Park. Agnes Witts recorded her opinions of the family with approbation: *5 June 1811: ... new tenants at Eyford Park Mr & Mrs Aston ... 20 June 1812 ... Mr. Aston and his fine boy Frederick drank tea ...* The fine boy ended up being tutored by Francis and he held as high a regard for the youth as his mother. Frederick Aston eventually went up to Oxford, but, as Agnes recorded, he was a frequent visitor at the rectory during his vacations: *19 June 1817: ... Frederick Aston spent the evening here just arrived from Oxford ...* In January 1820 Francis and Margaret had met the Astons in Bath, for by this time Mr Aston had relinquished the Eyford tenancy which he had held from 1811 to 1817 during Vernon Dolphin's minority, and in May Francis had the pleasure of recording a visit from his protégé:

19 May 1820: My young friend Frederick Aston arrived from his Brother-in-law's, M^r. Watkins's, Berkley near Frome, to pass ten days with us. His recent creditable examination for his Bachelor's degree has released him for the present from academical labours, and, while it makes him tread as on air, cannot but give me, as his former tutor, cause of sincere satisfaction.

In the near future this satisfaction took on a more practical form when Charles Keysall relinquished the curacy at Stanway, enabling Francis to appoint his friend. Agnes recorded her own pleasure: *24 November 1821: ... Mr. F. Aston the new curate from Wood Stanway ... 25 November 1821: Much pleased with Mr. Aston's manner of performing ...* The underlining was Agnes's manner of emphasis.

This friendship lasted throughout the life of the diarist and there was always a strong bond between the two men. Throughout the early years of the diaries in particular there are countless references and much mutually agreeable socialising. One particularly self-satisfied entry occurs on Friday 30 November 1838, when Francis Witts felt he had scored a double win, for on the one hand he has managed to elevate his friend, and at the same time freed up the curacy of Stanway for his own son:

An important letter from the Bp. of Gloucester acquainting me that he has given the living of Northleach to my Curate Aston, being glad out of his poor patronage so to provide for a deserving Clergyman who has discharged the duties of Curate in his diocese with credit for 17 years. The appointment is very much to his Lship's honour and in conformity with a resolution expressed by him, publicly and privately to reserve his minor preferments to praiseworthy clergymen who have been long curates in his diocese. How far I may have been indirectly instrumental to the appointment I cannot say. But in a conference with Holt, the Bishop's private secretary in Oct. 1837, prior to my Son's ordination, when regretting that I could not place E.F.W., as Curate at Stanway, because I ought not to attempt to displace F. Aston, who had so long served my cure with comfort and satisfaction to all parties, Holt dwelt on the Bp's design of appropriating his smaller patronage to men of Aston's class, and offered to take an opportunity of mentioning him favourably to the Bp.

The early summer of 1820 was given over to the exciting news about Queen Caroline, made particularly relevant to Francis by the fact that one of the Queen's chief advisors was his childhood friend Henry Brougham. The situation was even more relevant to Agnes Witts in that she still maintained a strong friendship and regular correspondence with Henry's mother, Eleanor. At the same time, and of more importance to the family, was news from George. With his eminent friends, the Pellews, he had joined the diplomatic expedition to Constantinople:

4 July 1820: We derived much satisfaction to-day in the receipt of a letter from my Brother. It appears, that the news of his promotion to the rank of Captain in the Royal Artillery, which places him on half pay, was brought to him at Malta, by his friend the Hon. Captn. Pellew, a son of Lord Exmouth, commanding the Revolutionnaire. That officer was conveying to Constantinople, Mr. Frere, the Diplomatist; to hold the situation of Minister Plenipotentiary to the Porte, in the Interval between the departure of Sir R Liston the actual Ambassador, & the arrival of his successor, Lord Strangford. Captn. Pellew having warmly pressed George to accompany him & Mrs. Pellew, who sails with her husband on the Voyage, two short hours sufficed him to prepare for his departure, obtain the General's leave, & bid farewell for a time to the Island, where he has so long been on active service. A fortnight brought them to the end of their cruize, and the Palace of the British Embassy. Nothing can be more animated & interesting than my Brother's sketch of the voyage, country & society: nor are many better calculated to appreciate & describe such scenes.

In family matters Francis Witts showed that he could care very deeply on one level, but he was not a man of compassion when it came to crimes committed by what he regarded as the lower orders. Towards the end of the summer he was in Gloucester, house-hunting for his mother-in-law, when he called at the prison to visit a sheep stealer:

Monday 21 August 1820: ... visited the County Hall, & Gaol. At the latter I had an interview with Jos. Palmer, a Sheep Stealer, whom I had committed & who had been tried, sentenced & left for execution: tho' found guilty on the clearest & most direct evidence, this hardened young man, persisted in denying his crime, & at the same time, that he had every reason to believe, that he would be hanged on the following Saturday: nor did my admonitions appear to affect him more than other exhortations, which had been addressed to him.

There are few points in the diaries when their author demonstrated his own potential for fallibility. Fourteen years after the incident in Gloucester prison there occurred the murder of Mr Rens, and the subsequent attempt by Francis Witts to have two loose characters of Stow, Cox and Clifford, convicted for the crime; even when they were proved innocent he showed no remorse at the likelihood that he may have sent them to the gallows for a crime they did not commit. He had no doubt that Joseph Palmer was guilty, but what if the persistent denial was because Palmer was innocent? We shall never know.

On the following day this Francis and Margaret set off on a short summer tour, leaving Palmer to his fate. Two days later the diary comes to an end—not unusual for the narratives of the various family tours, which start off with detailed descriptions and then peter out. Nothing survives for the period 24 August 1820 to 4 September 1822—a gap of more than two years. The diaries then commence once more with a change in style.

At some point in the early summer of 1822 we know that Francis visited his uncle, Broome Witts, at Cookham Grove, accompanied by Margaret, but the exact dates are uncertain.

From the diaries of Agnes Witts it appears that Edward started at school in Bath in January 1822, and at the same time Margaret was there once again taking the waters for her health. In September 1822 the diaries begin again, but this time the tone, the style and the content is subtly different, and with a few variations here and there this is the style that continues until Francis Witts's death thirty-two years later. Why there was a gap of two years is difficult to explain, but with previous travel narratives the same situation had occurred, with a detailed narrative fading away to nothing. What the precise catalyst was for this re-starting is not clear.

As for the content, there is nothing of particular note. Affairs at Stanway were recorded when Agnes and Lady Elcho were in residence. On the family front Francis's cousins, Anne and Apphia Witts, were staying at Gloucester and so there were several meetings. Apart from this, the diary consists mainly of magisterial business intermixed with national news and literary comment. Francis enjoyed *Waverley* and from an early date noted the commonly held belief that the author was Sir Walter Scott. In fact, Scott's anonymity became more transparent as the novels followed one another, and as early as 1815 he was invited to dine with the Prince Regent, who wanted to meet the author of *Waverley*. Other books are reviewed by the diarist; the anonymous (at the time) publication of *The Confessions of an English Opium Eater* was considered by him possibly to come from the pen of a Lake Poet.

At the very end of 1822 Francis Witts detailed a long and tedious disagreement with one of his chief parishioners, Vernon Dolphin, with regard to his reneging on previously agreed contributions to the cost of repairs to the church and of new pews. Francis and his mother had been very friendly with Vernon Dolphin's uncle, John Dolphin, curate of Lower Slaughter for many years. In fact, there was a tie between the families, John Dolphin and Ferdinando Tracy Travell both having married Rollinson girls. The disagreement was therefore embarrassing and distressing. Three months later John Dolphin arrived on a visit to his nephew and called at the rectory; the diarist was rather disappointed, but not surprised, that Vernon Dolphin had given his uncle a rather selective account of the disagreement. The affair was not mentioned in the diaries again, but rumbled on until a mediation was arranged by third parties on 17 February 1824. The two men then met, shook hands, and Vernon Dolphin invited Francis and Margaret Witts to dinner.

In May 1823 a twelve-day visit into Yorkshire was necessary for family affairs in relation to Mrs Backhouse's business matters. While there, Francis Witts met the new tenant of Beck House, a Mr Wood, who ran a paper manufactory. As usual, the journey was narrated in fascinating detail.

On Friday 4 July a letter from Malta brought news of George. Francis had not seen his brother since 1815 and the family was looking forward to welcoming him home, but the news, concerning his health, was alarming. As a result, Francis headed off to London on Monday 7 July to meet the army agents, Greenwood & Cox, and afterwards called on the Pellews, who were in town. Whilst in London he caught up with family and friends and the three days were a whirlwind of activity as he marvelled much at the changes that had taken place since his last visit. The fears that had been entertained about George were well founded, for on 13 August the mournful news arrived that he had died at sea on his way back to England:

... Soon after the receipt of this mournful information, I mounted my horse for Stanway to impart it to my poor Mother, to tell her, I was her only surviving child. The stroke was heavy, but borne with resignation, & not without acknowledgment of the wisdom & mercy of Providence.

The death of George affected Francis in several ways, one of which was introspection. Eleven days later, on his wife's birthday, he made more mention of her than at almost any other time in his diaries. Margaret was quiet, sickly and not a beauty, but there was undoubtedly a strong bond between them which he felt now during his time of mourning:

24 August 1823: My dear wife's birth-day. She was born in 1786. GOD be thanked, that of late her delicate health seems rather re-established. I can never be sufficiently grateful for her constant affection, warm participation in my pleasures and griefs, anxiety to make me comfortable. She is a pattern to wives in her judicious care of her family, kind heartedness to her poor neighbours, and prudence in her own expences. I have to thank GOD for an union with a woman of virtuous & religious principles, good sense, and amiable temper. These qualities adorn the wife & the mother.

Much of the diary is rather tedious, but occasionally a few indiscretions creep in, mixed with humorous asides or moralistic critique, and also with occasional allusions to social class. All of these come in to the entry for 6 September 1823 when Francis was a guest at Stanway, visiting his mother and Lady Elcho. Lady Rossmore must have been a good size for him to comment upon it, for neither Francis nor his mother might have been referred to as slim:

I found a large party of ladies at Stanway house: besides Lady Elcho, my mother & Miss Church, were there the excellent Sisters my cousins Guydickens; also the old, witty, intrusive Countess of Cork & Orrery ... This dowager without mercy quarters herself on her country friends during the Summer, returning the civilities received by invitations to eccentric fetes, and odd parties at her house in town during the London Season. Miss Vernon, more than a septuagenarian, was another guest: formerly a maid of honour to Queen Charlotte & sister to the notorious Lady Grosvenor; a corrected character, it is said, ladylike in manner, but a bitter foe of old Cork & O: animosity not unfrequently exploding between them. Lastly on the preceding evening had arrived my fair & fat cousin Lady Rossmore, Lady Elcho's youngest daughter, from Ireland, where she had left her Lord, but attended by her stepdaughter Miss Westenra, a round insipid girl of twenty. Lady R. retains her wit, volubility, warmth of colouring in narrative, good opinion of her-self, & strong prejudices & partialities; does she repent in her secret soul of an union with a Peer of doubtful character & ruined fortune? and do the style & title of Irish Baroness compensate for Irish embarrassments, law suits & shifts? I doubt it.

The following week Francis Witts was visiting his Aunt Travell in Cheltenham, and a visitor from Italy was one of the guests, a circumstance which lent itself to a lengthy passage and, undoubtedly, mixed with his current introspection, less than a month after the news of George's death, took him back to his youthful days in Weimar:

Thursday Sept. 11. Our evening circle was increased by the addition of Mr. & Mrs. Rosenhagen, & their guest M. Costantini ... a learned Italian, has been a traveller in most parts of Europe, and I boldly collected all my French to converse with him: nor was I unrewarded, for I found in him much eloquence, right sentiments, & extended information on literary subjects; both as to the Literature of his own country and that of France & Germany; nor is he illversed in that of England, though he does not attempt to converse in our language. His fortunes have, I apprehend, been impaired in the revolution ... M. Costantini resided at one period at Berlin, & the charms of the lovely & virtuous Queen of Prussia seem to have impressed him in the same manner as all those, who have moved within the sphere of her attractions. Never vision more beauteous walked this earth than this hapless Queen, when I saw her in the Court of Weimar in the summer of 1800, where with her respectable consort, her sister, the handsome & clever Princess of Tour & Taxis, & a brilliant suite, the little metropolis of the Duchy was graced with these illustrious visitors. Nor should I fail to mention the good and prudent, the simple minded, wise & virtuous Duchess of Weimar, whose sober dignity & calmness subdued even the ferocious insolence of Buonaparte in the hour of arrogance. M. Costantini spoke of her with the respect, which her character ever excites, of the Literary ornaments of Weimar, the old Wieland, composing in his cabinet amid wreaths of smoke, issuing from his Pipe, the highly gifted Goethe, vain of the little splendour of his post of Secretaire d'Etat pour les affairs etrangeres ...

The following day, still in Cheltenham, a tea-table guest at Aunt Travell's was the sister of Francis Beaufort, of later fame as the man who devised the wind-strength scales still in use today: *Another of Mrs. Travell's guests, was a Miss Beaufort, sister of Captain Beaufort of the Royal Navy, who has been engaged in surveying and laying down on the charts the coast of Southern Anatolia.*

One of Francis Witts's favourite pastimes was music, and in his youth he took every occasion to visit the opera or to listen to concerts. In rural Gloucestershire this opportunity was much reduced and the hundredth anniversary of the Three Choirs Festival was not an occasion to be missed. On 17 September he was asked to stand as one of the clerical stewards—a great honour, but he made some play out of his diffidence and reluctance, for, in point of fact, it gave him the opportunity for further mixing at what he would have considered the appropriate level in society:

... I had not been long in the Cathedral, before I was given to understand by Mr. Pettat, as representing Mr. Huntley, that it was wished, that I should undertake the office of clerical Steward at the next Music meeting. I had anticipated such an application, & from the uncertainty always attendant on such celebrities, whether the company will be sufficiently numerous to pay the expences, or whether in the case of a dearth of company a heavy surplus would not be left for the Stewards to pay, I had almost determined to decline the office. But it was strongly pressed upon me, and I was so unwilling, that it should appear, that I was averse to act with Mr. Dolphin, who is appointed one of the Lay Stewards, that after some deliberation I promised to act as Clerical Steward at the next Triennial anniversary ... My colleagues will be the Hon. Mr. Moreton, eldest son of Lord Ducie, the Hon. James Dutton, eldest son of Lord Sherborne, Vernon Dolphin; Mr. Bankes Prebendary of Gloucester and Son-in-law of the Lord Chancellor, & Mr. Bowles, of Bremhill, Wilts, & Rector of Dumbleton in this Diocese; the Sonneteer, & Author of various poems, essays, occasional sermons &c. Three years will add, perhaps, a little steadiness to the very juvenile lay stewards, but their connections, at least as to two of them, will certainly insure a numerous attendance of opulent & fashionable visitors: the same will be the case as to my clerical colleagues, and I have reason to expect, that in Mr. Bankes I shall find an able co adjutor in the arrangements for the Music &c.

By coincidence, the diaries around this period provide much useful material, for it is in a throwaway line of 3 October 1823, when Francis met a nephew of his former employer in Copenhagen, Sir William Drummond, that we hear that the original plans in 1800 had been to visit Vienna following the short stay in Dresden:

... *From Weimar we repaired to Dresden, in which beautiful & interesting city we passed several weeks. My appointment as secretary to Sir W.D. made a change in our projected tour towards Vienna &c.: and the whole of our party bent their course with me to Copenhagen, remaining there till the following spring, when on the rupture with the Danes, we repaired to Britain, on board the Kite Sloop of War, dispatched from the fleet for that purpose.*

In fact, much of the retrospective work in building the life profile of Francis Witts and his family comes from such snatches as this, filling in gaps in the diaries or supplying family information not available elsewhere.

On 8 October Francis Witts was an overnight guest at Batsford Park, the home of Lord Redesdale, a highly influential peer and past Lord Chancellor. The occasion is well documented by the diarist, who wrote of the nobleman in appropriately deferential terms and who clearly enjoyed the event and the occasion for further social development. Patronage was not expected from this quarter, but he well knew that good connections were essential if the possibility of patronage was to appear at some point in the future, and every opportunity was taken to consolidate his position through the magistracy, the Church and his extended family connections. One such family connection, which was negative rather than positive, was to come to light on 1 November when the rupture occurred between Captain Edward Parry and Miss Emily Browne. The latter had, it appeared, been guilty of a youthful indiscretion, eloping with a boy gardener. The two had been chased, caught and speedily separated, but the damage was done, and, in a similar manner to Mr Wickham and Lydia Bennett in Jane Austen's *Pride and Prejudice*, the social expectations of the day were unforgiving. Emily was second cousin once removed to Francis Witts.

Having lost his brother in the summer, Francis was now having concerns about his mother. From several sources we know that Agnes was overweight, but the diary of 25 November is specific:

My Mother left us for Cheltenham. Her birthday was on the 23^d. she was then 75 years old. Since she has been with us this time, she has never breathed the outward air, and so has avoided the cough often so troublesome to her. Her breathing is at times very bad, and her general health very fluctuating. Her great size makes all motion unpleasant to her, and her want of exercise causes a tendency to sleep in her chair. Her hearing & memory are both impaired, and her spirits droop much in the want of cheerful and varied society.

Prior to this, Agnes was generally a very active person with a great appetite for walking and general exercise, but by 1823 she was evidently much less physically active. She did, however, have an extremely active mind and demanded company and cards to avoid boredom. Even on this day, after returning from Upper Slaughter to her home in Cheltenham, she was busy socialising, as her own diary records: *Nov 25th: I left Upper Slaughter between 11 & 12, to return to my long separated home, was securely seated before some of my kind neighbors came in to welcome me, as Mrs. Cooke, Mrs. Devonsher, Miss Delancey & Mrs. Bittamore. Well tired by night.*

Agnes Witts was taken severely ill on 21 December and Francis discovered this on his arrival at Cheltenham two days later to prepare for the funeral of Mrs Judith Lightbourne, patroness of the living at Upper Slaughter. The illness of Agnes lasted until 26 January, when she recorded in her diary that was once more able to take up the pen. The funeral of Mrs Lightbourne resulted in an extremely long and detailed account of his dealings with his patroness and provides much illuminating information.

On 6 February 1824 the reports from the House of Commons provided an opportunity for Francis to expound on the subject of slavery, and he was prompted to comment that:

The well meant, but injudicious and rather fanatical urgency of Messrs. Wilberforce, Buxton & others, forming a strong party in & out of the House of Commons, to advance from the abolition of slave trading to an emancipation of the slaves, and the resolutions of parliament in the last session, that an amendment of their state & improvement in education, religion and morals should be cautiously enterprized, with a view to their emancipation at a distant period, when their advancement in civilization shall entitle them to enjoy the privileges of freedom without danger to themselves or others, have been so artfully misrepresented to the Negroes, partly, as it would seem, thro' the Methodist Missionaries settled in the islands, as to lead them to conclude, that their emancipation was decided on in the Mother country, but withheld wrongfully from them by their Masters & the public authorities in the colonies …

He went on to advocate that the responsibility for education should be left to a new bishopric of the Church of England, and his tenor seems to indicate that he was in sympathy with the slave owners:

They complain, that the treatment of Slaves has been grossly misrepresented in the speeches and pamphlets of Messrs. Wilberforce &c., and that, on the contrary, the Slaves are generally treated with kindness, so much as to place them in the scale of comforts on a par with, or even above the English labourer. Undoubtedly, there has been great misrepresentation; still there is room for much improvement; & that should be imparted, not, as Messrs. Wilberforce & Co. would wish, by missionaries, representatives of sectarian Interests both in & out of the Church, but by a systematic introduction of a visible church Establishment under one or more Bishops, presiding over a more numerous body of Clergy, who shall devote their talents & zeal to the inculcation of sound principles of religion & morals, educating the lower orders both black & of mixed colour …

In addition to his thoughts on slavery, the Tory magistrate was also unbending in his view that prison should be an uncomfortable and irksome place. On 10 March 1824 he visited Gloucester gaol to supervise the tread-mill, the installation of which he had warmly advocated:

I visited the Gaol, where the arrangements for the tread-mill are fully completed, by the paving the Court in which it is erected, building sheds to shelter the Turnkeys superintending the work, & the prisoners when off the wheel, particularly by the erection of separation boards between each prisoner at work, which totally precludes conversation at the work, but requires also that each prisoner should tread on the same spot during the whole of the period allotted to him on the wheel. This, perhaps, as rendering the work more irksome, is desirable; unless the boards be found in warm weather to exclude air too much, or limit too much the vibration of the prisoner's body when at work.

As a magistrate Francis Witts took a hard line with dissolute behaviour, but if the person imbibing more than was appropriate came from a higher social position then a more sympathetic tone would be adopted. In the diaries one of the clearest instances of this was in the sudden death of Winchcomb Hicks, where drunkenness was translated into a 'disordered stomach making him very unsteady.' The event occurred on 31 March 1824, following the dinner to celebrate Francis's friend, Thomas Lloyd Baker, being installed as High Sherriff of Gloucestershire:

... The hilarity of the evening was, however, exchanged for a strong feeling of gloom by a melancholy accident, which befel M^r. W. H. Hicks, son of H. Hicks of Eastington, an eminent clothier, and esteemed Magistrate, as he was setting out to ride home about nine o clock. Though he appeared quite sober, when he left the party, the outward air had the effect on a disordered stomach of making him very unsteady, & bewildered him, insomuch, that he was found on the Bristol road, a little beyond the Spa, fallen from his horse & almost dead. It appears, that he fell on his head, that a sharp stone in the road cut his temporal artery, & that he bled to death ... Winchcomb Hicks was unmarried, a young man of considerable expertness in commercial pursuits, & much beloved in his family. From sudden death, Good Lord, deliver us!

One recurring theme throughout the diaries relates to the health of Margaret Witts. She had always been delicate and it appears she had several miscarriages before giving birth to their first child, a girl, in 1811. This child only lived for a few weeks and the sole surviving child was Edward, born in 1813. The entry for Saturday 1 May 1824 is typical: *Leaving my wife with her Mother, in the hope that with change of air, and more genial weather, her health will be recruited, I set off for Upper Slaughter, summoned, as usual, by the duties of my profession, and purposing to remain, as a bachelor, there, for a fortnight.*

As a Tory magistrate, Francis Witts took a conventional and hard line in the administration of justice and with regard to his own views on the social order, but in other respects he was enlightened and looked at progress with enthusiasm. One particular example was with the revolution of steam power, and he took a great interest in technological developments. The meeting of the Foss and Cross turnpike commissioners on 6 May 1824 gave him an opportunity to record his thoughts:

At a meeting of the Commissioners of the Foss and Cross Turnpike roads to-day, at which I presided, a proposition was made by M^r. James, Engineer of the Stratford & Moreton Railway, for diverting a portion of the Turnpike road, near Moreton, as a mutual accommodation. At the same time this gentleman communicated much information on the subject of rail roads, with which he is connected, either in progress or in agitation ... These are sanguine schemes, but in the present redundance of capital, funds for the execution may be found, and they are more deserving of support than Columbian or Peruvian or Mexican loans, or than many other bubbles of this stock-jobbing age. Besides, the power of steam, and the new discoveries in science and mechanics, render easy and cheap schemes, which even *a few years since would have been considered hopeless. The tram waggons now may be made to travel without horses by steam, and are so worked both in Yorkshire & Northumberland. M$^{r.}$ James gave me a sketch of such an engine, followed by and connected with a travelling supply of water for the boiler; steam is generated, the chimney of the moveable engine puffs out smoke, and away they go with a whole string of waggons laden with coal or other commodities towed at their rear ...*

One of the interesting strands in the early diaries is the dispute with the Revd I. Baillie. The two men were good friends to begin, but a few years later it all went wrong. The very first reference to their meeting is given on 15 September 1825: ... *M$^{r.}$ Baillie, Curate to M$^{r.}$ Rice at Great Risington, & private Tutor, to one of his younger sons, Henry, with his pupil, dined with us to-day. M$^{r.}$ Baillie was Wellford's predecessor in the Curacy of Bray.*

Many interesting characters appear on the pages of the diaries. One larger-than-life character was the famous bibliophile Sir Thomas Phillipps of Middle Hill. Francis Witts had a low opinion of the collector and derided his pedigree. Even so, in years to come he was not slow to take advantage of the bibliophile and lent a large amount of money on mortgage to the baronet. Their first meeting was at a dinner party at Stanway on 2 November 1824:

Sir Thomas and Lady Phillipps, from Middle Hill, M$^{r.}$ & M$^{rs.}$ S. Gist, two Miss Gists, & M$^{r.}$ W. Gist, & M$^{r.}$ Wynniatt joined the dinner party. Sir T.P. was lately created a Baronet; he cannot boast of being an hereditary gentleman; his father, the first owner of Middle Hill of his name, raised himself from menial employments to considerable wealth by successful enterprize in the most money making times of the cotton manufactory. He retired to his native parish, Broadway, where & in the adjacent villages he had realized his property, when he left his Lancashire speculations to others, & the present Baronet is the offspring of an illegitimate union. His wife is daughter of a Gen$^{l.}$ Molyneux, who has now for some years lived at Cheltenham, of Irish extraction & possessing many of the characteristics of his country, not very rich, not very prudent, not very select in his society. The Lady of Middle Hill has no greater pretensions to legitimacy than her spouse, and is a boisterous dame strongly contrasting with her Lord's reserve. He is an Antiquary, book collector; who has yet perhaps still more experience to buy than he has yet paid for, but report says, much trash has already been foisted upon him ...

The Hunt family were distant relations to Francis Witts, but not by ties of blood. Sarah Witts, great-aunt to Francis, that is, sister to his paternal grandfather, was also great-aunt to Thomas Welch Hunt, being married to Thomas Hunt, brother to Thomas Welch Hunt's grandfather, Edward. In short, it was not an especially close relationship. On 30 December 1824 Francis first heard of the murder of Thomas Welch Hunt near Naples. This was to be an unfortunate event in the life of Francis Witts, for in a few years' time he was rather foolishly to accept executorship of the will of Mrs Mary Hunt and, through a complex series of events, become embroiled in a tedious business that was still not resolved at the time of his own death in 1854. In fact, the Hunt executorship is a sorry presence throughout the diaries, and the event triggering this was Thomas Welch Hunt's murder:

A very melancholy event has happened to M$^{r.}$ T. Welsh Hunt, late High Sheriff for Northamptonshire, and his wife, one of the Northamptonshire Ishams. M$^{r.}$ T. W. Hunt is a distant relation of mine, a very respectable young man, of good fortune, and only married about half a year ago. I met him in the autumn of 1823 at his aunt's, M$^{rs.}$ M. Hunt's, at Gloucester. He had been abroad before his marriage, *and repaired thither immediately after his union with his bride. They were at Naples: and on the 3$^{d.}$ Inst. had gone with an English Party to visit the celebrated ruins of Pæstum. Returning from thence, M$^{r.}$ Hunt's carriage was attacked by three brigands, to whom he surrendered an inconsiderable sum of money, protesting he had no more abut him, and even asking for some small coins back to pay necessary demands on his return to Naples. The banditti persisted, that he had more money in his possession, and required him to deliver it up, with a threat of firing at him; he rejoined, that they dared not shoot, as it was in the day light; scarcely had he uttered the words, when a shot was fired, & the contents of the piece lodged in the heart of M$^{r.}$ Hunt, & in the lungs of his wife. The Banditti horror-struck, or aware of the approach of travellers, fled without rifling their victims, & some English Officers, belonging to a vessel of war in the bay of Naples, who had been on the same excursion, soon found the wounded sufferers. They were conveyed to the wretched inn at Pæstum; such poor aid, as the miserable, almost savage, country affords, was procured; an English Surgeon was brought from Naples; but all in vain, poor M$^{r.}$ Hunt survived only two or three hours, and his wife died on the following day ...*

The problems of the end of 1824 saw no let up in the New Year, for on 1 January 1825 Francis was summoned to Stanway by a letter from Miss Church, where his mother was dangerously ill. She was within a day or so removed to her home in Cheltenham to be cared for by her own doctor, but it was to no avail and she died on 9 January. Francis was now an orphan:

Death rapidly advanced during the night and morning, and at mid-day my beloved Mother breathed her last. She went off gently, & the last fearful struggle past, her features resumed the usual placidity, and lost the distortion, which for some days had disfigured them. Thus am I at length bereft of Father, Mother & Brother! GOD's will be done! GOD be thanked for the blessings still left to me, an excellent wife & promising child. Great reason have I to speak well of my departed Parent. She was a most affectionate wife & mother, a well principled Christian, warm in her friendships, strong in point of judgment, well informed, had an extensive knowledge of life, and in her best days, even to a late period, shone in society & conversation. She was 76 years of age, having been born in 1748. Nov. 22. She was last survivor but one of the numerous family of John Travell Esq$^{r.}$ of Swerford, in Oxfordshire, her Mother being one of the many daughters of John Tracy Esq$^{r.}$ of Stanway. My beloved Parents had experienced much misfortune in middle life by a reverse of fortune; but activity of mind, mutual attachment, and love for their children upheld them buoyant on the waves of distress, and GOD be blessed, that it has been in my power to comfort & succour them in their declining years: this will be my consolation when I reflect on the death bed twice witnessed in this house, when I deposit the aged widow's remains by the side of the coffin containing those of her affectionate and indulgent husband ...

The funeral nine days later was a distressing time for Francis and he felt every distress with great pain—the unfeeling, vulgar curate, the gaping crowds:

Tuesday Jan. 18: A most gloomy wet morning after a stormy night was congenial to the depression of my spirits. My Mother's great nephew, William Whalley, arrived from Swerford to breakfast at nine o clock, but it was half past 10 AM. before we could reach the Church. The Service was performed by the Curate, a vulgar unfeeling man: his careless manner, his uncouth pronunciations, and coarse appearance were all forbidding. Crowds of curious spectators flocked round the coffin & vault; but all was curiosity, no sympathy was visible; most trying is this appearance of indifference; and equally so the suppressed voices of the assistants, as they lowered the coffin through the narrow mouth of the vault, grating against the top of the arch, and at length deposited beside the last inmate of the dark abode. At length my tender Mother reposes by the side of her beloved & indulgent husband; eight years of widowhood have been passed; now both are numbered with the dead. As to myself the burst of suppressed grief is passed, and the lassitude of sorrow remains; but I cannot and ought not to lose sight of the blessings still reserved to me by a gracious Providence, an affectionate wife, a promising child, and ample provision of earthly comforts.

Francis had now lost his father, his brother and finally his beloved mother. The relationship between Agnes and her first born son had been extraordinary and from his birth to her own death Agnes had worshipped the boy to the exclusion of her two other sons. At the end of this volume two, with the loss of his mother an important chapter closes in Francis's life.

Witts Family Papers F304

Journal.—

Tuesday Jan 14th.—Clifton.

Clear weather interrupted by one or two heavy storms. Studying St. Matthew's Gospel with the excellent Lectures of Bishop Porteus; examined the latter part of the 16th. and the 17th. Lecture.[1] Read an animated Charge of Massilon translated by the Revd. T. St. John, upon Zeal.[2] Waited upon Mrs. Chollet, who recounted her narrow escapes from assassination in the West Indies. Called upon the good Mrs. Monro & Mrs. Newnham. Found Mrs. Gould's family at home with the beautiful Miss O'Callaghan of Cheltenham, & made an agreeable visit; went down to Barry's Library in Bristol & returned with the conversible Miss A Wilkinson. Great part of the Evening was dedicated to the study of Nowell's Catechism, upon the Topic of Prayer. At nine o clock repaired to the Assembly Rooms; joined Mrs. Gould's party &c. Danced & had much pleasant conversation with the beautiful Miss Gould, no less handsome in person, than cultivated in mind. Danced also with the pleasing Miss Roberts; conversed much with Capt. Webb.— |

Wednesday Jan. 15th.—

Stormy weather, much rain falling, and great wind. Occupied in the forenoon with the 18th. of Bishop Porteus's Lectures on St. Matthew, and a fine charge of Massilon, on being called to the Ministry, concluding with a noble prayer. Passed more than an hour in interesting conversation with my admirable friend Mrs. Carrick and a short time in poor Mr. Townsend's sick room. After dinner sat for a quarter of an hour with Mr. Port and his Daughter; the Evening was dedicated to the study of Nowell's Catechism, upon Prayer, in general, & the Lord's Prayer, in particular. Alone; my Father & Mother having an engagement.—

Thursday Jan. 16.—

A stormy Day; unceasing torrents of rain prevented my accompanying Miss Port to Bath, as had been my intention. Studied the Bishop of London's 19th. Lecture during the forenoon. Made a round of visits, found Lady Ford, Mrs. Roberts's & Mrs. Salter's families at home, & entered with them into various conversation. Passed a domestic Evening, during great part of which I pursued the Examination of the Lord's Prayer in Nowell's Catechism, & continued a Sermon previously begun.— |

---

1. Beilby Porteous, Bishop of London, Lectures on the Gospel of St Matthew (1802).
2. A Translation of the Charges of Massillon, translated T. St. John (1805), — based on the essays and sermons of Jean-Baptiste Massillon, Bishop of Clermont.

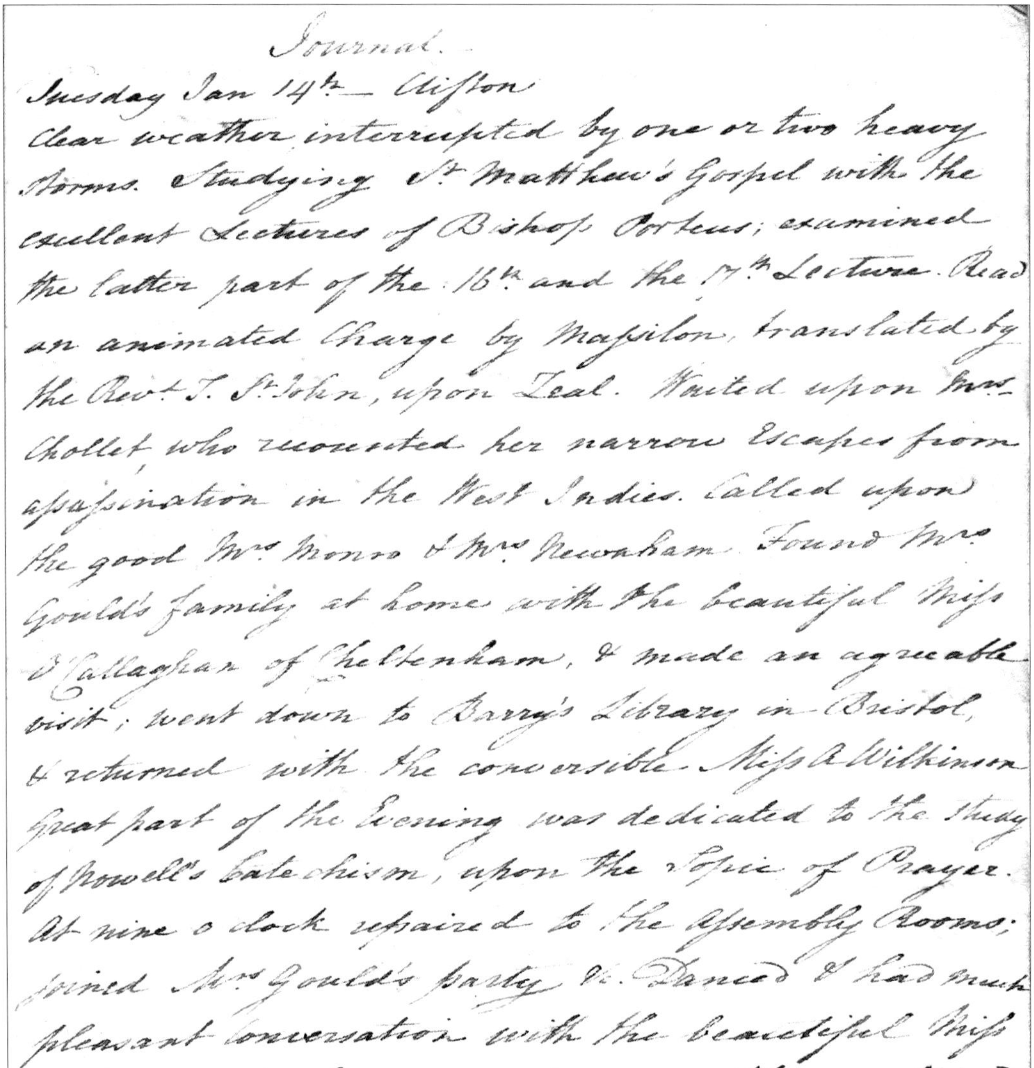

Journal.

Tuesday Jan 14th — Clifton

Clear weather interrupted by one or two heavy storms. Studying St Matthew's Gospel with the excellent Lectures of Bishop Porteus; examined the latter part of the 16th and the 17th Lecture. Read an animated Charge by Massilon, translated by the Revd T. St John, upon Zeal. Waited upon Mrs Chollet, who recounted her narrow Escapes from assassination in the West Indies. Called upon the good Mrs Monro & Mrs Newnham. Found Mrs Gould's family at home with the beautiful Miss O'Callaghan of Cheltenham, & made an agreeable visit; went down to Barry's Library in Bristol, & returned with the conversible Miss A Wilkinson. Great part of the Evening was dedicated to the study of Nowell's Catechism, upon the Topic of Prayer. At nine o clock repaired to the Assembly Rooms; joined Mrs Gould's party &c. Danced & had much pleasant conversation with the beautiful Miss Gould, no less handsome in person, than cultivated in mind. Danced also with the pleasing Miss Roberts; conversed much with Capt. Webb.—

Friday Jan. 17th.—

Fine clear weather, a happy change. Pursued my study of St. Matthew with the Bishop of London's 20th. Lecture and wrote to the Revd. B. Port respecting the Curacy of Ham. Walked to Bristol, to the Library, conversed with Mr. Foster, Mr. Plunkett, Dr. Davis & Mr. Newnham, walked round the Hill, called upon the agreable Miss Macbride. Did not intermit the study of Nowell upon the Lord's Prayer, though preparing for the Ball at Bristol in honour of the Queen's Birthday. Went down in a postchaise with my Mother & Mr. Ryan; joined Mrs. Salter &c. Danced with Miss Ford and Miss Salter; the room not extremely crouded, but the dancers often incommoded; a great medley of genteel & vulgar, handsome and ordinary; but the Select gained a great addition in Mrs. Gould's party, whose accession rendered our Clifton set far superior to any other party. Had much Conversation with Captn. Webb, Mrs. O Callaghan the beautiful Mother, her sweet Daughter, Miss Gould and her Aunt &c. Returned late without accident or fatigue. |

Saturday Jan. 18th.—

A promising morning terminated in a day of almost unceasing rain; & boisterous Wind. Accompanied Ryan in the Morning to Queen Square, where the Garrison fired a feu de joye in commemoration of her Majesty's Birthday. The rain that fell obstructed the view, & deterred many genteel persons from making their appearance. In hopes of a cessation of the Rain loitered at the Library, at the Billiard Table, and Bush Coffee House. Came to Clifton in a Hackney Coach. Ryan made us a visit. My body so fatigued & my head so confused by yesterday's dissipation, that I did not venture upon any serious study, merely dipping into the Monthly Review for December, & two Volumes of Asiatic Researches.

Sunday Jan. 19th.—

Fine weather; no rain; partial sunshine, drawing forth most whom the preceding bad weather had confined. To Morning Service at Dowry Square Chapel. Mr. Humphries officiated. He preached admirably upon Cor. 10. 31. Considering religious forms under the heads of public, ~~private~~ domestic & private as tending to the Glory of GOD, the utility & comfort of Man. Conversed with the Newnhams, walked a little | with the Roberts's, for a long time with the Junr. Garden, a sensible pleasant young Man, with his Father, with the Salters &c. I am concerned to state, how small a portion of this Day was appropriated to suitable study or avocations. Recd. a letter upon business from Mr. Travell. Passed great part of the Evening at the Dowager Countess Fingal's where a very numerous Circle was assembled. Introduced to the Earl & Countess Fingal,[3] engaged in various Conversation with the Roberts's, O Callaghans, Dewe's, Dr. Carrick, Hon. R. Plunkett &c.

Monday Jan. 20th.—

Incessant rain with a constant boisterous wind all day long. Sallied forth early after breakfast to the Box Office of the Theatre Bristol to procure places for Mrs. Salter & her party; found Mr. Newnham upon the same errand, returned with him to Clifton with much political & serious

3. Arthur James Plunkett, Earl of Fingall, (1759-1836), his wife was Frances Plunkett, née Donelan, (1766-1835). Plunkett was the leader of the Irish Roman Catholics in their agitation for relief from political disabilities.

conversation by the way. M$^{r.}$ C. Roberts called upon us in the forenoon. Made a very pleasant call upon M$^{rs.}$ Salter and her young Ladies. Received another letter upon business | from Mr. Travell, and wrote one upon the same subject to M$^{r.}$ Dawkins. Began a letter to Round. At an early hour in the Evening Lady Ford's Coach came to convey my Mother and myself with M$^{rs.}$ & the Miss Salters & Miss Ford to the Play. The Duenna was represented;[4] Don Carlos by Incledon, whose vulgarity quite subdues the effect his Notes might produce. The Characters cast as formerly. Incledon afterwards sang Sally in our Alley & ~~af~~ in the Entertainment the Bay of Biscay o! the Farce was the Lock & Key. An Interlude, a Dance alluding to the Victory of Trafalgar completed the amusements of the Evening. I was seated between Miss Ford & Miss Salter, with the latter of whom particularly I had much amusing conversation.

Tuesday Jan. 21$^{st.}$—

Better weather, though very indifferent, a thick fog, & dirty beyond bearing. Walked upon Richmond Terrace with M$^{r.}$ C. Roberts. Caught a transient glimpse of my friend M$^{rs.}$ Carrick. Wrote upon business to M$^{r.}$ Edw$^{d.}$ Horne the Solicitor, & a letter upon general subjects to my friend Round. Mounted a hackney between | four & five to repair to Cap$^{tn.}$ Webb's at Stoke, where a large & pleasant party were assembled, & most hospitably & handsomely entertained.[6] His dinner excellent; his Madeira & Claret delicious. Besides my excellent friend Dowell, whom I had infinite pleasure in again seeing, we had Col. Kingscote, Sir Will. Guise,[5] & Sir Henry Lippincott,[7] Major Durbin, Cap$^{tn.}$ Cooke, M$^{r.}$ Probyn, Mess$^{rs.}$ P. & J. Baillie, & M$^{r.}$ Foster. By a rapid ride home I contrived to reach a dance at Lady Teresa Dease's, before ten o clock, where I danced with a Miss Holford from Cheshire in obedience to Lady Teresa's Commands, with Miss Dease, & with my amiable friend Miss Gould. The party was very numerous, perhaps, too crouded, but upon the whole was pleasant, and the supper good. Had much pleasant conversation with Lord Fingal, a man of great sense & moderation, the excellent Lady Ford, M$^{rs.}$ Gould, M$^{r.}$ Baggot, M$^{r.}$ Probyn &c. Received an obliging letter from M$^{r.}$ B. Port, declining the proposition which I had made to him.—[8] |

Wednesday Jan. 22$^{nd.}$—

An improvement in the weather, dry above but extremely dirty under foot. Rose very late,

---

4. *The Duenna*, a play written by Richard Brinsley Sheridan in 1775.

5 Edward Webb, (1779-1839). Edward was the son of Edward Webb, (1730?-1795) of Cote House, Westbury-upon-Trym, M.P. for Bristol in 1780 who was a Gloucester merchant and brewer, also owning cloth mills near Stroud. Edward junior was privately educated and then joined his brother John in Bengal where he was a writer in the East India Company's service. He returned to England in 1801 and by 1803 was a Captain in the North Gloucestershire Militia. The following year (1807) he married Jane Mary Catherine Guise, the sister of Sir Berkeley William Guise, a reforming Whig, who in 1811 successfully contested the county as the candidate of the independent gentlemen. Edward Webb went on to become M.P. for Gloucester, 1816-1832.

6. Sir Berkeley William Guise, (1775-1834) of Highnam Court, Gloucestershire. Guise was M.P. for Gloucestershire, 1811-1832, Gloucestershire East, 1832-34. The family had estates at Elmore Court and Rendcombe. He died unmarried.

7 Sir Henry Cann Lippincott, (1776-1829). Henry succeeded to the baronetcy on the death of his father in 1780, and in this respect he was similar to his friend Edward Webb whose father had also died when he was very young. At about this time (1806) Henry had either just sold, or was about to sell Stoke House, illustrated above. He matriculated at Oriel College, Oxford in 1794 and thereafter appears to have had an undistinguished career. He did not marry, but father an illegitimate son, (Edward Cann Lippincott, born *c.* 1828). The only other point of notoriety was that he was tried for rape in 1810. He died at his home in Portman Square, London.

8. The curacy at Ham.

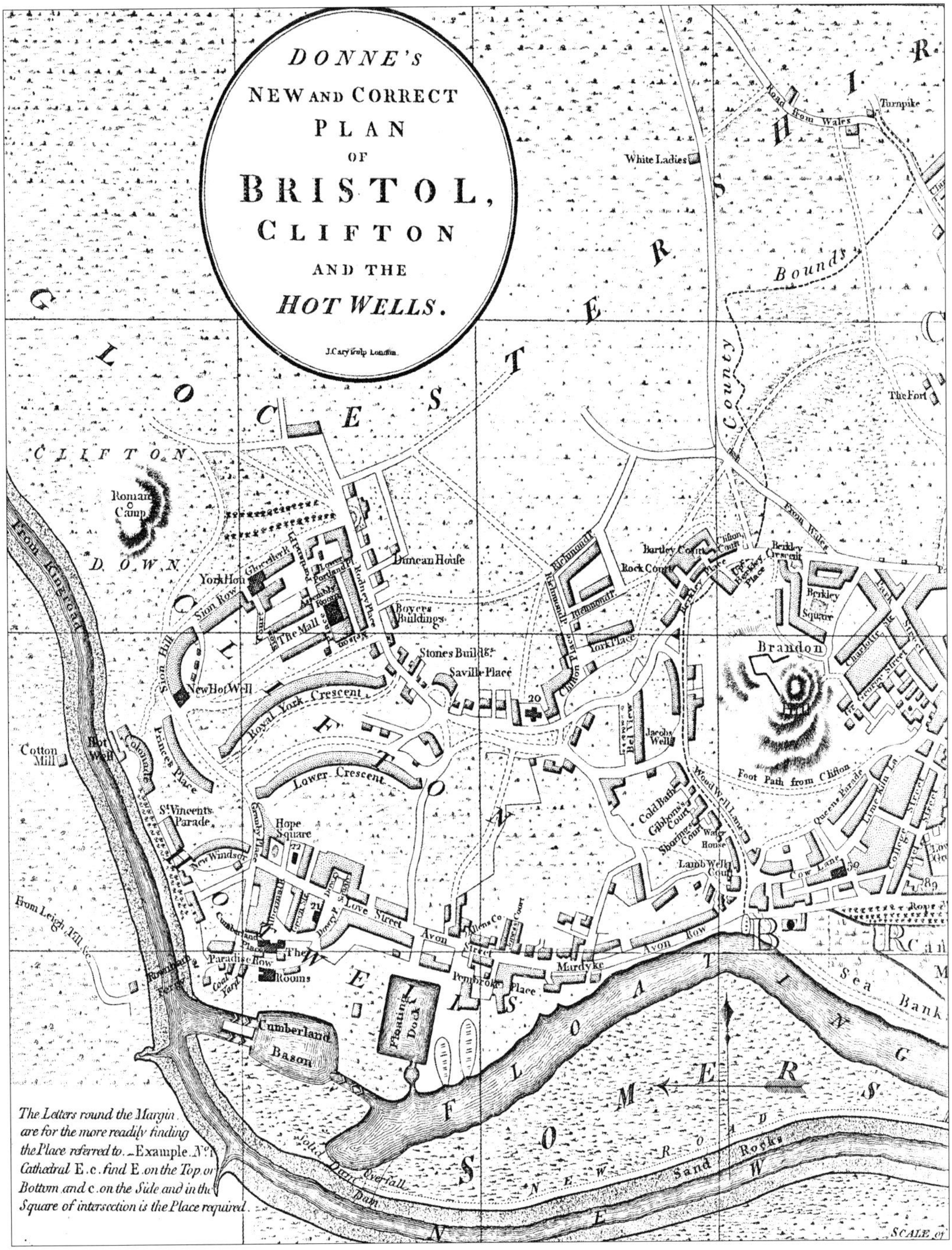

1. Map of Clifton in 1800.

2. Stoke Bishop.

by dissipation so unhung as not to sit down to study,[9] thus lengthning a vacation I had no idea once of granting to myself. Called upon Mr. Townsend, walked with Charlotte & Jane to Bristol. At the Library, reading the King's Speech. Upon my return to Clifton called upon the admirable Lady Wolseley and her amiable Daughter Cecilia; the poor Mother scarcely recovered from a complicated fracture in her arm. Walked with Mrs. & the Miss Salters till dinner. Read the first Volume of a new Novel by Surr entitled a Winter in London.[10] Late in the Evening joined a party at the Dow. Countess Fingal's; had a good deal of pleasant conversation with Lord Fingal, Dr. Carrick, Mr. Gould, a remarkably pleasant man, Mr. James Bagot, the Newnhams &c.

Thursday Jan 23d.—

Still fine weather, a milder air & pleasant sun. Read part of the Bish. of London's 21st. Lecture, but was prevented from a more exact adherence to the rules of Study I had prescribed to myself | by my other Engagements. Dowell & his handsome friend Mr. Gwynn called, &

9. Unhung. The Oxford English Dictionary does not list the word in this context, but it was probably university slang. The term 'hangover' did not come into use until early in the twentieth century — and probably not unconnected with the usage given in this diary entry of 'unhung'.

10. Thomas Skinner Surr, *A Winter in London; or Sketches of Fashion* (1804).

3. High Street, Bristol

brought me an invitation to Cote. Called with my Mother upon the Miss Carlyons, whose drawings in the Stile of M$^{r.}$ Jos. Barker & M$^{r.}$ Hewlett afforded me pleasure in examining. The landscapes were executed in a chaste, grave style. Called upon M$^{rs.}$ Salter & her Daughters, & with my Mother upon M$^{rs.}$ J. Auriol. Received with great sorrow the rumour of the great M$^{r.}$ Pitt's decease.[11] Dined, passed the Evening and slept at my friend Dowell's, where I met with the usual hospitable reception. The party was completed by the agreeable M$^{r.}$ & M$^{rs.}$ Gwynn & M$^{rs.}$ Brown. Played two Rubbers at Whist in the Evening.

Friday Jan. 24$^{th.}$—

Boisterous wind throughout the Day: rain violent in the morning. Our party separated after breakfast M$^{r.}$ & M$^{rs.}$ Gwynne to Bath, M$^{rs.}$ Dowell drove M$^{rs.}$ Brown to Redlands, whither William accompanied me, & whence I escorted M$^{rs.}$ Brown to Park Street, William & M$^{rs.}$ D. taking the road towards Winterborn. To the Library. Found upon | my return to Clifton a delightful letter from my beloved Margaret, & M$^{r.}$ Parris calling upon my Father & Mother, conversing agreeably. M$^{r.}$ Hawes called & obligingly promised to assist my Enquiries for a Curacy. M$^{rs.}$ J. Auriol also made a short visit. Called upon M$^{r.}$ Port, who is confined by the Gout. Learnt the confirmation of the deplorable intelligence, which was anticipated yesterday. Walked with C. Roberts. In the Evening studied part of the Bishop of London's

11. William Pitt the younger, (1759-1806), Prime Minister from 1783 to 1801 and from 1804 until his death. He was disliked by the Whigs and radicals, but he had turned away from the traditional aristocratic support for the Tories to embrace the more serious-minded gentry, who had long felt excluded from politics.

4. Residence of Gustavus, a pencil sketch by Francis Witts.

21st. Lecture & experienced how difficult it is to emerge from indolence in study to diligence. Received a Letter upon business from Mr. H. Dawkins. Began Carr's Northern Summer an amusing Tour through Denmark, Sweden, Russia & Prussia.[12]

Saturday Jan 25th.—

Remarkably fine weather, sun shining, prospect clear. Concluded the Bish. of London's 21st. & studied part of his 22nd Lecture. Mr. Port & Mr. C. Roberts called. To the Library at Bristol. Made a short visit to the Goolds, the Mother & Daughter as usual receiving me most pleasantly. Perambulated | the Hill, walked a little with Mrs. OCallaghan, Miss C. Salter &c. Read the 2nd. Vol of Surr's entertaining novel, the Winter in London. Drank Tea and supped very pleasantly at Mrs. Salter's. A very small party; only Lady & Miss Ford, Captn. & Mrs. Otway and another Gentleman besides ourselves. Played at Loo.—

Sunday Jan. 26th.—

Rain had fallen during the night, & incessant snow came down from 10 o clock till the Evening. Ventured to Dowry Square Chapel, alone; Mr. Hawes officiated, and preached upon the Passion of Revenge. Continued Carr's Northern Tour. Read a Charge by Massilon, highly impressive, upon Reflection on the success of our Ministry. Concluded the 22nd. & studied the 23d. of Bishop Porteus' admirable Lectures. Read a memoir, illustrative of

12. Sir John Carr, *A Northern Summer, or Travels round the Baltic, through Denmark, Sweden, Russia, Prussia and part of Germany.* (1804).

some points in the Cabirian & Elensinian Mysteries by a reference to Oriental Mythology, apparently apposite & instructive.—We passed a domestic Evening. |

Monday Jan. 27$^{th.}$—

A dreary wintry prospect & snow or sleet falling incessantly throughout the Day; according to D$^{r.}$ Carrick, who keeps a register of the weather, so much snow has not fallen within the same time at Clifton for four years. Finished the 24th & last of Bishop Porteus' Lectures & with it the 2$^{nd.}$ Vol. Read a noble Charge by Massilon on Solicitude for the Salvation of Souls. Continued Carr's amusing Northern Tour. D$^{r.}$ Carrick called upon us in the forenoon. Defied the weather in the Evening to repair to a Rout & dance given by M$^{rs.}$ McCausland, which would have been more pleasant, if I had known more of her guests & there had been fewer children. We were accompanied by M$^{r.}$ C. Roberts. I danced with Miss M. Morse, M$^{rs.}$ J. Auriol, M$^{rs.}$ Parris & Miss Binden. Conversed with C. Roberts, Ryan, the Hon. D. Ruthven &c.—

Tuesday Jan. 28$^{th.}$—

The snow still laying on the ground & with a very | piercing air sleet falling the greater part of the Day.—Studied Nowell's Catechism upon the Lords Prayer and the Sacraments, particularly, Baptism. Wrote a letter to Dowell at Oxford respecting an advertisement in the Oxford Journal for a Curacy.—To Bristol. To the Library: conversed with M$^{r.}$ Plunkett, M$^{r.}$ J. Bagot, Barry &c. Walked with my Father thro' various parts of Bristol & returned over S$^{t.}$ Michael's Hill. Continued Carr's Northern Summer, an amusing, but inaccurate publication: finished Surr's interesting Novel, a Winter in London, continued the Homicide. Finished a Sermon on the Attributes of the Deity, which I have long been employed about. Passed my Evening alone; my Father & Mother drank Tea & supped at M$^{r.}$ Port's, an invitation I readily waved, but so great is the Empire of habit over me, that it required an effort to ~~the~~ resist the Temptation of going to the Ball at the York House. It is only seclusion from constant Society, that can give a relish for domestic duties & Comforts.—

Wednesday Jan 29$^{th.}$—

A very hard frost, & fine wintry weather, snow still upon the ground. Read M$^{rs.}$ Charlton's Homicide.[13] Wrote a long letter to my beloved Margaret. Called upon M$^{rs.}$ Salter, where I found M$^{rs.}$ & Miss Becher, and upon M$^{rs.}$ OCallaghan. Afterwards to Bristol, where I met & conversed with a variety of people; to the Library &c. Read Carr's Northern Summer, & some articles in the Monthly Review for August last. Began a voluminous work, Owen on the Hebrews.[14] D$^{r.}$ Owen a contemporary of Cromwell, is the most esteemed of the Puritans for his Learning and piety: his opinions were independent, he was ejected from Oxford for non-conformity. Read the Editor's (M$^{r.}$ E. Williams's) preface, the life of the author & the 1$^{st.}$ Exercitation to shew that the Epistle to the Hebrews is canonical. Passed a domestic Evening.—

---

13. Mary Charlton, *The Homicide*. (1805).
14. John Owen, *An Exposition on the Epistle to the Hebrews; with preliminary exercitations*, ed. Edward Williams DD (1790).

Thursday Jan. 30th.—

The same kind of fine wintry weather, beautiful sun, & hard frost. Studied two Exercitations of Dr. Owen, one proving St. Paul to be the Author of the Epistle to the Hebrews, the other showing the time when it was written, and the occasion of | it. Mrs. Salter called in the forenoon. Two letters upon business to Mr. Horne & Mr. Travell confined me so much, that I had barely half an hour's enjoyment of the beautiful weather; though much mortified by the being detained, I believe it were better for me oftener to experience such little disappointments; I allow them to weigh upon me too much. Called for a quarter of an hour upon Mr. Port. Walked a little with Robt. Garden, Mr. Gillibrand &c. In the Evening my Father & Mother left me, & went to make up a Rubber for Mr. Port. Read several articles in the Monthly Review for August last. Continued Carr's Northern Summer. Finished Mrs. Charlton's Homicide. Read an Essay in the Asiatic Researches upon Hindu Religious Ceremonies.

Friday Jan. 31st.—

Similar fine weather for the Season. Studied an Exercitation by Dr. Owen on the Identity (Oneness) of the Christian Church; shewing it to be the same Church, differently modified, of which Abraham was made partaker by Faith. Wrote to Mr. | Matthews upon business. Walked with my Mother to Bristol and consumed all the morning there. At the Library, conversing with Mr. Plunkett &c. Dined en famille with the Garden Family, giving them every information respecting Oxford, & the settling of their Son there. Began the 1st. Vol. of Dallas's Morlands, having finished the three last, an inverse rule of proceeding, allowable in Novels.—[15]

Saturday. Feb. 1st.—

Some snow had fallen in the night, and a thaw which succeeded the morning frost, made the ways very dirty. Rose with a severe head-ach and cold in the head. Finished Carr's amusing but inaccurate Tour in the North. When my headach was sufficiently abated, studied an Exercitation of Dr. Owen's upon the Jewish Writings, their method of dividing the H. S. their Massora, oral Law, Talmud &c. To Bristol, R. Garden accompanying me part of the way. After I had returned from the Library &c. walked with the Salter Party in the Mall, where the N. Glocester Militia were inspected by Gen. Champagné. Finished the 1st. Vol. of Dallas's Morlands, and began Mrs. Bennet's new but ponderous & ill written Novel "Vicissitudes | abroad".[16] Studied Dr. Nowell's Catechism upon the Lord's Supper. Passed a domestic Evening.

Sunday Feb. 2nd.—

A very cold, frosty Day: very sharp air & very muddy ways. At Dowry Square Chapel Mr. Humphries preached with great eloquence & fervour upon the advantages of institutions for public worship. Returned to Clifton with Mrs. Salter & Mrs. Becher. Called upon the amiable Mrs. Carrick, whom I found slowly recovering from a severe attack of illness, Mrs. Ramsay & the little Northumbrian Charges with her. After a very pleasant visit, joined the Salter party, but left them rudely & abruptly, fancying I spied a disinclination to my making one of their Cortége on the Mall, where the Middlesex Band was playing. Blamed

15. Robert Charles Dallas, *The Morlands. Tales Illustrative of the simple and surprising.* (1805).
16. Agnes Maria Bennett, *Vicissitudes Abroad; or, the Ghost of my father.* (1806).

myself afterwards for venturing to interpret a look & gesture, & for allowing my temper to be ruffled and suspicion raised; but the circumstance impressed upon my mind doubts of the propriety of my assiduities in that Quarter, which still | possess me. I must be more guarded, & less susceptible. Joined Col. Napier, to whom I was introduced, & his Sisters, & walked with them to the Wells. Though my solitude in the Evening was uninterrupted, my Father & Mother being at Lady Fingal's, I trifled my time away most scandalously, making progress only in Mrs. Bennet's very indifferent Novel. May the next week's records compensate for the Errors of this Day.—

Monday Feb. 3d.—

A gloomy day, bitterly cold; freezing very hard, and a heavy snow falling after six o clock in the Evening. Studied Dr. Owen's Exercitation on the Messiah, the deliverer from Evil, which was too long for one Day's labour. Called upon Col. Napier, but found only his Mother & elder sister at home. Walked to Bristol, and to the Library &c. Read an excellent Charge by Massilon upon Solicitude to suppress Vice. With great difficulty reached Mrs. Ames's party as the Horses could hardly find a footing in the snow & at first refused the Hill. A very large Circle assembled, but I enjoyed myself but little | in consequence of the rudeness always shewn me by the three young Men of the House. Dancing to a limited time occupied the young people, who were sent home supperless before twelve, but we had much difficulty in getting back, in consequence of the perilous night. Danced with Miss Smith, Miss Russel, Miss Monck, & Miss Wolseley. Conversed with Mrs. Dowell, E. Webb, G. Monck, &c.—

Tuesday Feb. 4th.—

Milder weather, a fog, and thaw dissipated the snow quickly: heavy rain came on in the Evening and night. Finished Dr. Owen's Exercitation on the Messiah, the Deliverer from evil. Called upon my excellent friend Mrs. Carrick, where Col. & the Miss Napiers paid a short visit. Called at Sir W. Wolseley's;[17] all the good trio at home & Lord Kilwarden with them uttering anything but the words of wisdom.[18] We had the satisfaction of hearing from my Brother from Bremen; he is oppressed by Rheumatism in consequence of his busy movements in Germany, but in hope of soon returning. Began a Tour in Italy by Kotzebue in the style of his former Tours. | Continued Mrs. Bennet's Novel Vicissitudes. Supped at Mrs. J. Auriol's; besides ourselves, the Lady & her Husband, Gillibrand, the notorious Mr. Stackpole & his wife & a Mr. Jenner formed the party. Mr. & Mrs. Frampton & Mrs. & Miss Vandeleur had gone before supper. No great amusement for me, while the rest played at Cards, but the supper was merry, & I had a wide scope for observation.—

Wednesday Feb. 5th.—

Rain falling in the forenoon, the air damp & thick but mild. Studied an Exercitation of Dr. Owen's upon the appearances of the Messiah under the Old Testament. Wrote a long letter to my Brother on the Continent, & to Matthews, the Solicitor, upon business. Mr. Port called in the forenoon. Called upon the Salters, and made a pleasant visit to the young Ladies, Mrs.

---

17. Sir William Wolseley, (1740-1817).
18. John (Wolfe), Viscount Kilwarden and Baron Kilwarden of Newlands, (1769-1830).

Salter not being returned from Bath; met at their house Cap^tn. and M^rs. Otway. Called upon M^r. Townsend's family, various individuals of which I saw, & my Father joined me there. Learnt from his paper the positive arrangement of the New Ministry, in which the Grenville party have | four Cabinet Ministers, the Foxites five, & the Addington Party two. Passed a domestic Evening, as I declined going to a Concert, Ball &c. at Alderman Daubeny's at Redland to which I had been invited.[19] Read a Charge of Massilon's upon a good Example, very impressive; studied Nowell upon Sacraments, & completed his admirable & well written Catechism. Transcribed part of a Sermon on the Divine Attributes. Did not entirely desert M^rs. Bennet's Vicissitudes.

Thursday Feb. 6th.—

A brilliant morning proved a gloomy close day with a good deal of rain. Read two capital Charges by Massilon on the Excellence of the Ministry, and on the manner, in which the Clergy ought to conduct themselves among men of the World. Read a Memoir in the Asiatic ~~Society~~ Researches upon the Hindu Chronology. Visited the Salters, & passed an hour very pleasantly with them. Left my Card with M^rs. Salter for Lady Teresa Dease: sat for near an hour with my friend M^rs. Carrick and her sweet little protegée. A letter from | M^rs. Backhouse to my Mother gave charming accounts of my Margaret. Studied an Exercitation of D^r. Owen upon the present belief of the Jews concerning the Messiah. Passed a domestic Evening. Continued Kotzebue's Travels to Italy. Heard from Dowell, who gives a very bad account of the Health of our poor friend Evans.

5. View of Clifton.

19 Alderman George Daubeney, (1742-1806) was infamous from his incompetent handling of the Bristol Bridge riots in September 1793 when ten people were killed. To his credit he was among the signatories of a 1788 petition for the abolition of the slave trade, even though his family had investments in sugar refining. He also owned the glasshouse and was Mayor of Bristol in 1786. He was also a M.P. for Bristol.

Friday Feb. 7

A very brilliant morning, and a fine mild though dirty day, but that there were two very heavy showers of rain about two o clock.—Continued Mrs. Bennet's Vicissitudes. Studied an Exercitation of Dr. Owen, wherein he proved the Messiah long since come; from Jacob's prophecy of the Shiloh, & Haggai's prophecy of the glory of the second Temple. Called upon my dear friend Mrs. Carrick before I walked to Bristol, to the Library &c. Walked a little way afterwards with Mrs. Salter & Captn. Port. Began J. G. Vossii Disputatio Theologiea de Sacramentium vi et Efficacia. Studied §1–18. a very logical work. Heard from Mr. E. Horne; a letter upon business. My Mother being confined by a severe Cold could not accom- | -pany my Father to make up a rubber at Captn. Port's: I did not leave her. Entered upon Jos. Lancaster's Improvements in Education,[20] & was much pleased with the independent & simple style, by which he recommends himself to notice.—

Saturday Feb. 8th.—

A great deal of rain had fallen during the night, more fell in the forenoon, the day was more gloomy than bright, & more rain fell in the Evening. Continued Mrs. Bennet's Vicissitudes, and Lancaster's Impro ve ments. Studied part of an Exercitation by Dr. Owen, in vindication of Daniel's prophecy of 70 Weeks. Lady Ford & her Daughter called, & I had the pleasure of meeting them again at my friend Mrs. Carrick's. whom I looked in upon before I went to Bristol, where I repaired to the Library as usual, & whence I betook myself to a Bookstall in Bridewell lane, where for a small Sum I provided myself with four Treatises by the Author of the Whole Duty of Man, Archb. Synge's Gentleman's Religion,[21] Barrow's Sermons,[22] & Taylor's Holy Living & Dying.[23] The last for Mrs. Carrick. The whole lot | cost four shillings. I passed a ~~domestic~~ solitary Evening as my Father & Mother repaired to a party at Mrs. Sheridan's, reading Kotzebue's Italian Tour, & the Monthly Review for January. Read also a Charge by Bish. Massilon on the prudent behaviour of the Clergy.—

Sunday Feb. 9.

After heavy rain during the night, a lowring morning was followed by a fine clear day, except a heavy shower between three & four. Read a charge by Massilon on the Duty of visiting the sick & two devout little tracts, the Christian's Daily Devotion, and the Way of Living by a rule and Method, a sermon upon Eccles. 3.1. At Dowry Square Chapel Mr. Humphries officiated & gave a very good Sermon upon the parable of the Sower & the Seed. Walked a little before Chapel & after with Col. & Miss A. Napier. Called upon Mrs. Salter, in pursuance of whose injunction to enlist for her approaching Dance two more beaux, I called upon Colonel Napier: walked a little with Miss Ford, for a long time in very interesting Conversation with Mr. Newnham. In the Mall, where the Band played (the RWMM) walked a little with | Mr. Probyn of the North Gloc. Mil., whom also I pressed into Mrs. Salter's service; called upon Mrs. Roberts's family & made a very agreeable visit. Thus I passed the

---

20. Joseph Lancaster, (1778-1838), *Improvements in Education, as it represents the industrious classes of society.* (1805).

21. Edward Synge, Archbishop of Tuam, *A Gentleman's Religion and the grounds and reasons of it.* (1703).

22. Isaac Barrow, *Twenty-two Sermons on various subjects.* (1798).

23. Jeremy Taylor, Bishop of Down and Connor, (1613-67), *The Rule and Exercises of Holy Living and Dying.* (1663 and at least thirty editions up to the time of the diary).

6. The Exchange.

morning in a far too dissipated manner; no meditation, no deliberation; & thus was unhung for any valuable purpose in the Evening. How necessary is a constant guard upon my truant Imagination! Passed the Evening domestically: Read some articles in the Appendix to the Monthly Review, & visited Mr. Port's bedroom, whom I found very ill, his son with him.

Monday Feb. 10.—

Beautiful mild weather. Transcribed part of my Sermon upon the divine attributes. Thoroughly ashamed of a day of shameful idleness for at an early hour Mr. Newnham accompanied me to Bristol, where I passed several hours, searching with him for Old Divinity. Walked a little with Mrs. Newnham & S. Townsend with Miss Smiths, with Miss Macbride, with my friends the Salters &c. Did little in the afternoon but pursue Mrs. Bennet's interesting tho' ill written Novel Vicissitudes. To a small dull party at Lady Wolseley's, where I conversed chiefly with Cecilia Gillibrand, George Goold &c. Continued Kotzbue's Tour.—

Tuesday Feb. 11th.—

Beautiful mild weather, one very heavy storm falling in the afternoon. Finished transcribing the Sermon upon the Attributes of GOD. Continued Mrs. Bennet's Vicissitudes. Mrs. Chollet made a visit to us in the forenoon. Called upon poor Mr. Port, whom I found better, tho' very low.—Walked to Bristol, to the Library &c. Called upon a Mr. Cumberland, respecting a Curacy near Cirencester, on which I could not definitively settle. Learnt the faithless seizure of Hanover by his Prussian Majesty. Called upon Mr. Townsend, who was pretty well. Had the satisfaction of knowing, by a letter from my Brother, that he is safely arrived from the

Continent in Yarmouth roads.[24] Dined with Lieut. Col. Napier at his Mother's in S$^{t.}$ Vincent's Parade, the young Ladies & Major Patton formed our party, which was pleasant enough. Accompanied them to the York House Ball; danced with Isabella Salter, & Cecilia Wolseley, our Tea party consisted of M$^{rs.}$ Salter, her young Ladies, Ryan, M$^{rs.}$ Chollet & my Mother; conversed much | with M$^{rs.}$ J. Auriol, M$^{rs.}$ Gillibrand, M$^{rs.}$ Salter & others. Passed the Evening pleasantly, how profitably or innocently I am deterred from examining, but I hope, the time is not far distant, when a profession will mark distinctly the path, & guard me effectually against all temptations to desert it.

Wednesday Feb. 12$^{th.}$—

Very beautiful weather, till rain fell in the Evening and night. Read a very curious funeral Sermon by Bish. Jer. Taylor; continued Kotzebue's tour in Italy & M$^{rs.}$ Bennet's Vicissitudes. Walked with my Father & Mother, Miss Macbride, Col. Napier &c. Called upon M$^{r.}$ Carlyon, a very respectable Cornish Gentleman, upon the Salters repeatedly, in the hopeless business of procuring them a beau, upon Lady Wolseley & Cecilia &c.—About nine o clock repaired to M$^{rs.}$ Salter's, carrying Col. & Miss Ann Napier, besides whom I introduced ~~Mr. Brigs!~~ M$^{r.}$ Probyn; long before the dancing began, & very tedious; conversed with Lady Ford, M$^{rs.}$ Roberts, M$^{rs.}$ OCallaghan, C. Wolseley &c. When all were assembled, the Room presented a goodly shew, | & had not Lord Kilwarden taken a liberty by bringing M$^{r.}$ Stacpoole, uninvited, M$^{rs.}$ Salter would have nothing to regret. Indeed every body was perfectly pleased. Danced with the beautiful Miss OCallaghan, with Isabella Salter, Cecilia Wolseley & Miss Ford. Much of the arrangement was delegated to me, I presided at supper at one of the Tables, where the Goold party, the Adairs & Cecilia made my office very pleasant. Formed a little quiet Circle after the Ladies were gone, Gillibrand, Geo. Gould, M$^{r.}$ Leslie, M$^{r.}$ Adair, Napier & myself. Kept up the dancing till four o clock in the Morning.

Thursday Feb. 13$^{th.}$—

The same kind of beautiful weather. After a very late breakfast began to alter a Sermon of D$^{r.}$ Jer. Taylor upon Immortality. Continued M$^{rs.}$ Bennet's Vicissitudes & read some articles in the Monthly Review. To Bristol, to the Library &c., & walked with Col. Napier & Major Patton upon the hill. Walked also with Miss Upton, & with the Salter party, with whom I had left my Card. Visited with a head-ach, | a fair tax for my dissipation yesterday. Passed the Evening most agreeably in intimate conversation with my dear friend M$^{rs.}$ Carrick; the good Doctor with us great part of the Evening & the Enthusiast, D$^{r.}$ Bridges for a short time.

Friday Feb. 14$^{th.}$—

Rain had fallen copiously during the night, & came down heavily in the forenoon, the rest of the day was fine & mild. Continued Kotzebue's Tour, M$^{rs.}$ Bennet's Vicissitudes & read some articles in the Monthly Review & Appendix. Continued to adapt a sermon from D$^{r.}$ Jer. Taylor. To Bristol, to the Library &c. Walked with Col. Napier & Major Patton, in Town, & upon the Hill, also with the beautiful Miss OCallaghan. Received a welcome letter from my lovely Margaret. Read a Charge by Massilon upon the pernicious effects of avarice

24. George Witts' regiment had been involved in the expeditionary force to Germany which had been inconclusive and ineffective.

7. The Hotwell House seen from the Rocks at Clifton.

in the Clergy. Passed a domestic Evening. Studied the remainder of D^r. Owen's Exercitation upon Daniel's prophecy of 70 weeks.—

Saturday Feb. 15th.

Fine weather, excepting one heavy hail storm about ½ past three o clock. Continued M^rs. Bennet's | Vicissitudes & Kotzebue's Travels. Employed in altering a Sermon from Bish. Jer. Taylor. Wrote letters on business in my Father's name to M^r. Stormonth & to M^r. Elrige. Walked to Bristol, to the Library, to Lansdown's &c. Caught a transient glimpse of my friend M^rs. Carrick. Passed a domestic Evening. Studied an Exercitation, wherein D^r. Owen answers the Evasions of the Modern Jews respecting the prophesies of the Messiah, and part of another to prove, that Jesus of Nazareth is the promised Messiah. Read also a Charge of Bish. Massilon upon Gentleness & mildness.—

Sunday Feb. 16th.—

A dark & rather stormy day; showers in the forenoon, & heavy rain in the Evening. At Dowry Square Chapel in the morning; M^r. Hawes officiated & delivered a sermon on the Salvation of those, who believe, and the condemnation of those, who do not. Returned from Chapel with M^r. Garden, walked to Bristol with DeMauny, returned with him & ~~Ryan,~~ Robins walked on the Mall, where the band played; for a short time | with the Salters, also with the Smiths; afterwards with M^rs. Carrick & for some time with M^r. Roberts. All this lounging upon such a day deserves the severest reprobation. In the Evening my Mother attended Countess Fingal's party, my Father & myself remained at home. I arranged various papers &c.

Monday Feb. 17th.

A very fine day, rather cold. Finished Mrs. Bennet's ponderous novel, & continued Kotzebue's Italian Tour. Studying the alteration of a sermon from Bp. Jer. Taylor. Walked with my Mother & Mrs. Roberts. With Robins in Bristol & to Clifton, with Mr. & Mrs. Newnham, with my Father; called with him upon Lady Wolseley & Cecilia. Passed a domestic Evening. Read a fine Charge of Bish. Massilon upon constancy in Prayer. Studied the conclusion of Dr. Owen's Exercitation to prove Jesus Christ of Nazareth, the Messiah.

Tuesday Feb. 18th.—

A hoar frost in the morning & thick fog; the remainder of the day cold, raw & gloomy. Continued Mr. Jos. Lancaster's Improvements &c. Completed | the alteration of a sermon ~~by~~ from one by Dr. Jer. Taylor. Read an excellent Sermon upon Wisdom by Dr. Js. Barrow. Accompanied my Mother to Bristol. To the Library, Red School &c. Walked a little upon the Hill. Dined at the worthy Dr. Carrick's to meet Mr. Jessop, a very ingenious & pleasing young man, superintendant of the improvements upon the harbour, Son of the celebrated Engineer. Our trio & quartette in the Evening as pleasant & instructive, as it must always be in such refined Society. Began a novel entitled the Confessions of the Nun of St. Omer.[25] —Called in Bristol upon Mr. Cumberland.—

Wednesday Feb. 19th.—

Dull weather, but not unpleasant. Continued Kotzebue's Tour in Italy & C. Dacre's Confessions of the Nun of St. Omer. Transcribed a sermon upon the Immortality of the Soul: began to alter from Dr. Js. Barrow a sermon upon Wisdom. Several gentlemen &c. called, whom I did not see; Mr. Cumberland's Brother, the Minister of Driffield visited me about the Curacy of Ampney, which I hope to procure. The Revd. Mr. Cumberland a very pleasant & obliging man. Walked to Bristol | with his Brother, to the Library &c. Walked upon the Hill for a short time with Caroline Salter & Mary Ford. Passed a domestic Evening. Studied a dissertation of Dr. Owen, answering the objections of modern Jews to the Christian Faith, & began another laborious discussion of the Priesthood of the ~~Jews.~~ Messiah.

Thursday Feb. 20th.—

A dull day with a tendency to rain. Finished C. Dacre's Confessions of the Nun of St. Omer's, continued Kotzebue's Travels in Italy, & Jos. Lancaster's Improvements in Education. Transcribing a Sermon upon the Immortality of the soul & adapting a discourse on Wisdom from Dr. Js. Barrow. Wrote to my beloved Margaret. Walked to Bristol with the Hon. R. Plunkett. In Bristol at the Library &c. On my return to Clifton passed a very agreeable half hour visiting Mrs. Salter & her amiable Daughters. A domestic Evening. Studied the conclusion of an elaborate & abstruse Exercitation by Dr. Owen upon the Priesthood of the Messiah—Received a very polite amusing letter | from Mr. V. Jones Junr. from Dresden.—

Friday Feb. 21st.—

A dull, cold, cheerless, day~~s~~, rain in the Evening. Continued Kotzebue's Tour and Jos. Lancaster's Improvements &c. Transcribed part of a Sermon on the Immortality of the Soul,

---

25. Charlotte Dacre, *The Confessions of the Nun of St. Omer. A Tale.* (1798).

8. Bristol from St Augustine Back.

& studied the alteration of another upon Wisdom from Dr. Barrow.—Wrote to Mr. Horne upon Business. Accompanied my Father to Bristol: left my card there with Mr. Wright, to the Library &c.: returned with Mr. Newnham; sat for half an hour with my amiable friend, Mrs. Carrick; in the Evening my Father & Mother were engaged abroad; I studied a very abstruse Exercitation by Dr. Owen upon the necessity of the Priesthood of Christ; & perused J.G. Vosii de Sacramentorium vi et Efficacia §18–24.—

Saturday. Feb. 22nd.—

A windy day, but in general clear & sunny; one heavy shower. Continued Lancaster's Improvements &c. Transcribed part of a Sermon on the Immortality of the Soul & continued to adapt a discourse of Dr. Barrow's on Wisdom. Wrote upon business to Mr. Dean | the sword Cutler, & Mr. Matthews. To Bristol; walked with Mr. Wright to the ruins of the Iron Bridge over part of the Canal, which fell as it was erecting two days ago & wounded severely several Workmen. To the Library &c. Walked with Mrs. Salter & Isabella on the Hill. In the Evening studied part of an Exercitation by Dr. Owen on the Kingdom of Christ. To a Rout at Mrs. J. Auriol's; hot, crouded, & tolerably pleasant. Conversed chiefly with Cecilia Wolseley & Miss Smith.

Sunday Feb. 23d.—

Dull weather; Two or three showers; a very mild atmosphere. At Dowry Square Chapel: Mr. Humphries officiated, & preached a very fine Sermon on the decay of Christian Piety. Wrote letters upon business to George & Mr. Horne. To the Post Office, Bristol, walked a little with Robins; afterwards upon the Hill for a longer time with the Salters &c. The Roberts's called upon us. Passed a domestic Evening. I am ashamed to say, I did nothing more than arrange a few unimportant papers. |

Monday. Feb. 24th.—

A pleasant mild day without sun; a tendency to haze. Continued Mr. Jos. Lancaster's Improvements & Kotzebue's infamous Tour in Italy. Finished transcribing a Sermon upon the Immortality of the Soul, & continued the alteration of another upon Wisdom from Dr. Js. Barrow: Read a fine Charge by Massilon upon Study & Knowledge in the Ministry. Made a fruitless call at Cote; walked with the Salter party; called upon Mr. Townsend. Finished an interesting Exercitation of Dr. Owen upon the Lordship of Christ. Passed a domestic Evening.

Tuesday. Feb. 25th.—

Beautiful mild weather, not quite without sun; An unhappy domestic contest in the morning dejected & dispirited me: if all the reproaches made against me were well founded, my punishment was as merited as it was severe: if I be not so lost as was represented my tendencies to vanity & self-esteem received at least a salutary check.[26] Walked to Bristol, to the Library &c. Conversed with Mr. Plunkett &c. Walked a little on the Hill with my Mother. Wrote to Mr. Travell upon business. Received a letter from the Revd. Mr. Cumberland, which reduces to a shadow my expectations of the Curacy of Ampney; perhaps Providence does not esteem me | as yet worthy to labour in the vineyard. Continued Mr. Jos. Lancaster's Improvements, & altering a Sermon upon Wisdom from Dr. Js. Barrow. To a York House Ball at the usual late hour. Had the mortification of dancing two dances with a very deformed Lady, Miss Stables, at Mr. & Mrs. Roberts's particular desire. Danced one afterwards with my friend Mary Goold. Conversed with the Salters, Ryan, Tyler, Goold & Gillibrand party, Robin, Miss Holford, the Poetess,[27] the Roberts's &c. Very crouded & warm.

Wednesday Feb. 26.—

A stormy, windy, cold day, one violent shower. The day appointed for a general national fast; not less a day of humiliation to me as the twenty third anniversary of my birth; the witness of resolutions broken before they were well uttered, of contrition momentary as the sounds, which expressed it. An accident in Dowry Square Chapel having filled it with Smoke, I attended Divine Service at St. Augustine's, where Mr. Brocklesbank's bad delivery & Elocution were compensated by a forcible & sensible Discourse | upon Prov. 14. 34. Wrote letters upon business to Mr. Horne & a Mr. Robinson, an Attorney in Charter House Square. To Bristol again, to the Post Office, Bush &c. Walked with Robins, the Ch. deMauny, Mr. Kelly, Mr. Sheridan, all of whom I ought to avoid; walked with the Salters &c. for a little; with Cecilia Wolseley & Miss Goold for a moment &c. In the Evening my Father & Mother joined a party at Mrs. Auriol's in York Place; I dreamt away the Evening in a sad degrading manner. Finished Mr. Jos. Lancaster's Improvements &c. & began a refutation of some parts of them by Mrs. Trimmer.[28] —

Thursday Feb. 27th.—

Stormy weather, extremely windy, & showery. Continued Kotzebue's Travels in Italy. Wrote

26. Agnes Witts makes no reference to this domestic contest in her diary, and it may have been Edward who challenged Frank's lack of attention to his clerical studies and questioned his social activity. The letter from Mr. Cumberland presumably arrived early, sparking off this discord.
27. Margaret Holford, *Gresford Vale and other poems*. (1798).
28. Sarah Trimmer, *A Comparative View of the new Plan of Education*. (1805).

upon business to Mr. Matthews upon general topics to Dowell. Mr. Port called upon us. To Bristol, to the Bank, Library, Lansdown's &c. Walked back with the elegant George Goold, afterwards upon the Hill a little with Caroline Salter & with Ryan. In the Evening went early to Mrs. Pennington's | much talked of assembly. Accompanied my Father & Mother, Mrs. Cary & Miss Stafford. Till the arrival of the Parties, with whom I was more particularly intimate, conversed much & pleasantly with Mr. Bridges of C.C.C. an immense croud, heat intolerable & dancing very fatiguing; but every body resolved to be amused, four Rooms open; two for Cards; one for Dancing, another for retiring to: refreshments bad, served out some sandwiches & Porter after a considerable effort. Conversed chiefly with Geo. Goold, & all the rest of his family, the Salters, Col. Napier, Cecilia Wolseley, Mary Ford, Miss Bradby, Mr. Bridges &c. Danced with Mary Goold, Isabella Salter, & Miss Roberts. Heard from Mr. Horne upon business.

Friday Feb. 28th.—

An extremely fine pleasant day. Enervated by the dissipation of the preceding night, rose late & had neither inclination nor time to apply to severe studies. Col. Napier called upon us. I visited, with him the Wolseley family; walked with him to & in Bristol. Learnt the News of the capture of the Cape of Good Hope,[29] returned from Bristol with Mr. | Sheridan, called in Gloucester Row & sat very pleasantly with Mary Ford & Isabella Salter. Walked with Miss OCallaghan & Miss Goold on Richmond Terrace. Wrote a letter, chiefly upon matters of taste to Willson. At a late dinner at Mr. Robert's very pleasant: a family party with the accession of the Revd. Mr. Barlow prebendary of Bristol, brother to the Governor-General of India. Heard from Mr. Horne upon business.—

Saturday March 1st.—

A dark but fine day, no Sun, but the air mild. Began R. Cumberland's memoirs of himself: a very entertaining work.[30] Finished the alteration of a Sermon from Barrow upon Wisdom. Walked to the Wells, called upon Mrs. Pennington. Called also upon the Goolds & Roberts's. In the Evening drank Tea with Mr. Port; a party of Savoyards playing German Tunes, who had fixed themselves in Sr. J.J.W. Jervis's Hall called me forth for an hour's Walk by moonlight, & thus promoted my disposition to idleness. |

Sunday March 2d.—

Beautiful weather, rather windy but extremely pleasant. To Bristol Cathedral, where Mr. Humphries chanted the Service & the Revd. Mr. Barlow, Prebendary, preached moderately upon Prayer. Walked a little with the Wolseleys, a good deal at various times with the

29. The Cape had been in British hands in 1795, but was relinquished in 1803. On 19 January the British returned again and seized the colony from the Netherlands East Indies Company. It remained a British colony until incorporated into South Africa in 1910. It was a strategic point on the route to the east.

30. Richard Cumberland, *Memoirs, written by himself. Containing an account of his life and writings interspersed with anecdotes & characters of several of the most distinguished persons of his time.* (1806). This work was of particular interest to Francis Witts as Edward and Agnes knew the dramatist well, and his daughter, Lady Elizabeth Bentinck was a close friend and correspondent with Agnes. Frank had been introduced to Cumberland the previous autumn in Tunbridge Wells.

9. The Overfall Dam near the floating dock and Cumberland Basin.

Goolds; called upon Mrs. Gillibrand; walked with the Roberts's, O'Callaghans, Salters &c. on the Mall, where the Band played, crouds of fashionables. Heard from Mr. Travell upon business. Continued Cumberland's Memoirs & Mrs. Trimmer's reply to Jos. Lancaster's scheme of Education. Passed the Evening most pleasantly & supped at the Goolds; besides the family party & myself, no one but Lord Ruthvan,[31] a great deal of pleasant Conversation & music: Mary Goold singing in a very superior style. A good supper & Mrs. Gillibrand conveyed Ruthvan & myself to our respective homes about midnight. |

Monday March 3^d.^—

Cold & windy weather, a tendency to rain & clouds of dust. Began a Sermon upon 1 Pet. 3. 14. Continued Cumberland's Memoirs. Wrote upon business to Horne, a letter of Congratulation to Mrs. Timbrells, who have gained their Cause,[32] & a letter to Round respecting my intended visit to Oxford, in answer to one, which I received from him. To Bristol: to the Fair &c.: joined Mr. Kelly. In the Evening to a Route at Mrs. Roberts's, pleasant enough, as I conversed a great deal with the Salters, Fords, Webbe, &c.—About forty persons, the whole well conducted: Miss Roberts & Miss Ford playing upon the Piano.—

---

31. Lord Ruthven (not Ruthvan) was a subsidiary title of the Earls of Carlisle — the Howard family. Who exactly this individual was is not known, but it was not the eldest son, George Howard, as he took the title Viscount Morpeth. The family tended not to use the Ruthven title after 1819 when John Polidori published a successful novel *Lord Ruthven* where the fictional lord was a vampire!
32. The Timbrell sisters were attempting to prove their case to succeed to the Tracy estate at Sandywell. This was important for Frank and Agnes as the sisters now owned the advowson of Upper Slaughter and would have the right of the presentation to the living following the death of Ferdinand Travell. Edward and Agnes Witts had been visiting the Timbrell sisters in Cheltenham since the previous summer, trying to win favour as relations to the Tracy family.

Tuesday March 4th.—

Very fine congenial weather; a slight tendency to rain. Continued a Sermon upon 1. Pet. 3. 14.—Finished Cumberland's Memoirs & Mrs. Trimmer's reply to Mr. Jos. Lancaster's Improvements. Had great pleasure in visiting my friend Mrs. Carrick after her return from a visit to her Father's. To Bristol, the Library &c. Walked back with Newnham. Walked the Wolseleys. | With my friends, the Salter's upon the Downs. Idled my time away in the Evening shamefully. My Father & Mother visiting the Miss Stables's.—

Wednesday March 5th.—

A cold, rather raw, gloomy day. Continued a Sermon upon 1 Pet. 3. 14. To Bristol; to the Library &c. Called upon Mr. Barlow, the Prebendary, who very obligingly gave me his advice respecting an application to the Bish. of Bristol for Ordination. Walked upon the Downs & under the Rocks &c. to the bason intended for a floating dock, to view the Mechanism of the Pumps & Steam Engine with Mr. Jessop. Walked with the young Lady Salters & my Mother. Continued Kotzebue's Italian Tour. Began a pretty simple tale, Lucy Ormond. Read some articles in the Monthly Review for February. My Father & Mother had an engagement at Captn. Fallon's. I profited little by having the Evening quite to myself. |

Thursday March 6th.—

A hoar frost in the morning, beautiful weather followed. Wrote to the Bish. of Bristol, to request from his Lordship a private ordination or letters Demissory. Wrote to Cruttwell the Bath Printer respecting a Curacy advertised. Paid a short visit to my friend Mrs. Carrick. Walked to Bristol, to the Library, to Bedminster Iron Bridge &c. Walked with Cox & Ryan upon the Hill. Had a letter from Napier to excuse his visiting Lady Wolseley. Received a charming letter from my beloved Margaret. Finished Kotzebue's Travels in Italy. Read several articles in the Monthly Review. Repaired in the Evening to a party at Lady Wolseleys, numerous & warm, but visiting so congenial a family must always be pleasant. Conversed a great deal with the amiable Cecilia, with Harriet Port, Mrs. J. Auriol, Plunkett, Port, Cox &c.

Friday March 7th.

Not ~~fi~~ so fine a day as the preceding; less Sun & a more gloomy atmosphere. Transcribing a Sermon upon Wisdom, composing another | upon 1. Pet. 3. 14. Walked to Bristol; afterwards upon the Hill &c. with Cox & Ryan, & with my charming friends the Goolds. Begun a new & pretty Novel, Eversfield Abbey, which seduced far too much of my attention.[33] Visited Miss Wilson's route, which was numerous & not unpleasant. Conversed in the usual animated manner with the amiable Cecilia till placed for the remainder of the Evening at a Speculation Table by the side of the frigid Miss Scott: amused myself as well as I could for the rest of the Evening; some of the most notable personages were little Miss Stranbenzee, Mrs. J. Auriol &c.—

Saturday March 8.—

No sun but a very fine mild spring day. Transcribing a Sermon upon Wisdom. Calling upon my friend Mrs. Carrick for a short time. Accompanied my Mother upon a long walk to visit

---

33. Mary Belson, *Eversfield Abbey*: a novel by the authoress of *the Aunt* and *the Niece*. (1806).

M^rs. Dowell, at Cote, who was not at home; I did the honours of the House & Garden. Walked a short way with M^rs. Gillibrand & Miss OCallaghan. Heard from M^r. Cruttwell of Bath, with a direction to a Rev^d. Smith No. 6 | Westgate Buildings, to whom I wrote respecting a Curacy advertised in the Bath Chronicle.[34] Finished Eversfield Abbey, a pretty, moral, novel. Began the 1st. Vol. of Sir W. Jones's Works.[35] Drank Tea & passed the Evening pleasantly at M^rs. Salters, meeting the Hon. M^rs. Yorke & Miss Bradby, Lady Ford & Miss Ford, M^rs. Otway, & M^r. Cox. Played successfully in partnership with Isabella at Loo.—

Sunday March 9th.—

True March weather. The Day, in general cold & raw, two or three heavy hail showers, part of the morning clear & fine, snow & sleet falling in the Evening. To Dowry Square Chapel in the Morning M^r. Hawes officiated, & preached without animation upon Eph. 5. 14. Walked to Bristol; afterwards in the Mall with the Salter party &c. Passed a domestic Evening except, that M^r. Port & Harriet called for an hour after Tea. From a volume of Tracts, read three sensible & earnest Essays by different anonymous old authors 1st. Plain Directions for studying the H.S. 2nd. An Earnest Persuasion to the Serious observance of the Lord's Day. 3. A regular Method of governing a family. A Serm. from Josh. 24. 15. last part. Read an Essay upon the Art of Preaching by M. Reybaz:[36] & | Thoughts upon the Composition of a Sermon as adapted to the Church of England by the Rev^d. The. S^t. John, & a prayer for those, who enter upon the Ministry, all excellent, & subjoined to the R.T. S^t. J's translation of the Charges of Massilon.

Monday March 10th.—

Perfectly according with the Season, alternate hail & snow storms, & cold cheerless weather. Finished a Sermon upon the Relation of Piety & Happiness. Received a letter from Round, upon my coming to Oxford, & respecting two Curacies, which I answered, & wrote a letter to a person at Brackley, respecting a Curacy advertised in the Oxford Journal. To Bristol, to the Post, Library, Sale of Books in Union Street &c. Called & passed nearly an hour with M^rs. Salter & her Daughters. Reading Barrow's Sermons. At six o clock went to the Play; joined the Goold & Gillibrand party, sat by M^rs. Gillibrand & her humorous Spose: conversed much with them all & with Jessop: amused with the play, Shakespeare's Twelfth Night; some characters infamously represented, Sir Andrew Aguecheek by Mallinson, Malvolio by Lovegrove, Viola by Miss Fisher passably well acted. A broad | Pantomime, Harlequin Asop followed, whimsical enough, displaying with effect the activity of its producer, Gomery. Returned in Gillibrand's Voiture.

---

34. There was a coincidence here that Francis Witts was unaware of, for the young Revd. Smith was eventually to marry a distant relation of his, Anne Tracy, the daughter of Charles Hanbury and Henrietta Susannah Tracy. This was the very first communication to his future rector.
35. The theological, philosophical, and miscellaneous works of William Jones 12 vols. (1801).
36. Étienne Salomon Reybaz, *A Letter on the Art of Preaching.* (1805).

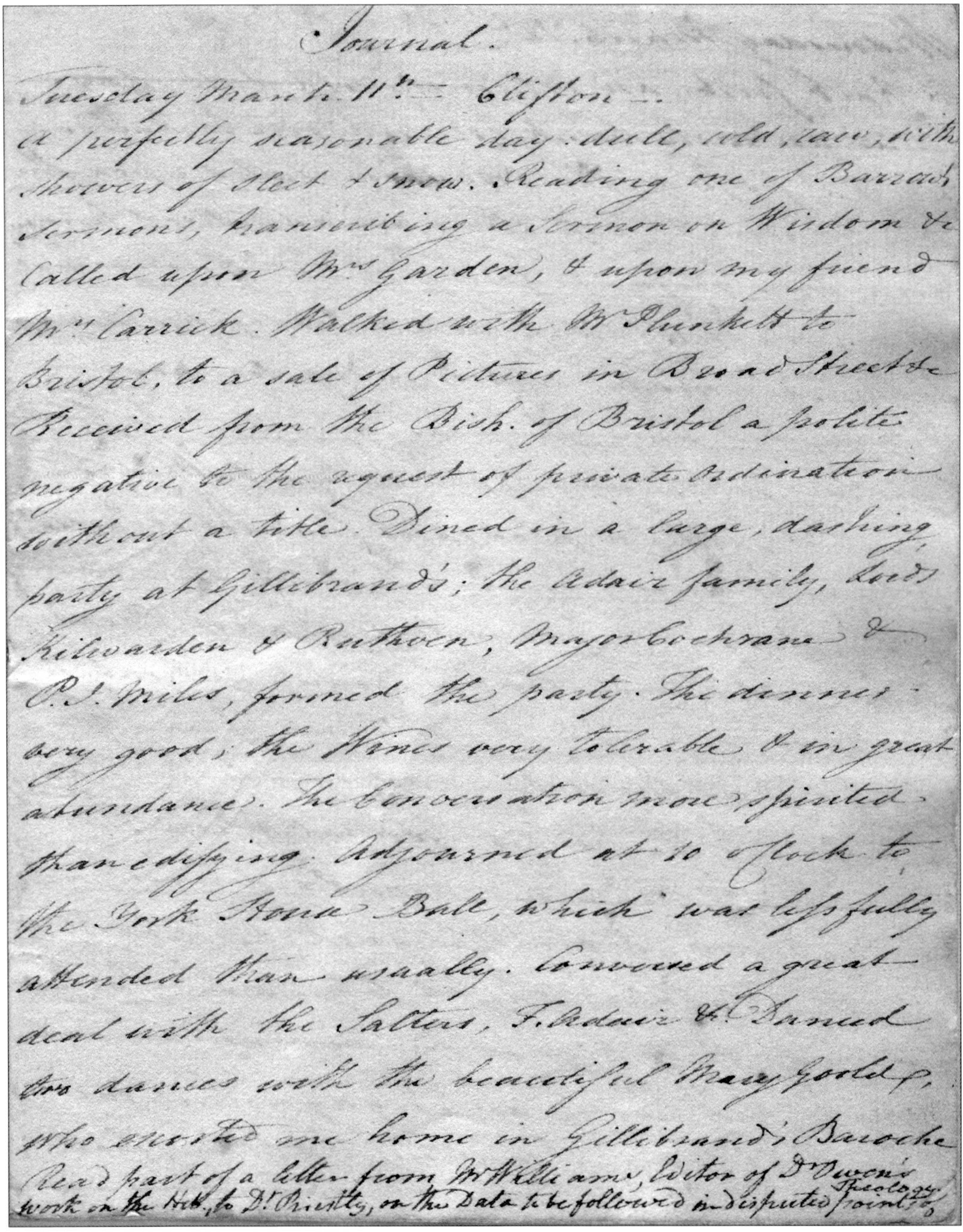
Journal.
Tuesday March 11th — Clifton —
A perfectly seasonable day: dull, cold, raw, with
showers of sleet & snow. Reading one of Barrow's
Sermons, transcribing a Sermon on Wisdom &c.
Called upon Mrs Garden, & upon my friend
Mrs Carrick. Walked with Mr Plunkett to
Bristol, to a sale of Pictures in Broad Street &c.
Received from the Bish. of Bristol a polite
negative to the request of private ordination
without a title. Dined in a large, dashing
party at Gillibrand's; the Adair family, Lords
Kilwarden & Ruthven, Major Cochrane &
P. J. Miles, formed the party. The dinner
very good; the Wines very tolerable & in great
abundance. The Conversation more spirited
than edifying. Adjourned at 10 o'clock to
the York House Ball, which was less fully
attended than usually. Conversed a great
deal with the Salters, F. Adair &c. Danced
two dances with the beautiful Mary Goold &c.
who escorted me home in Gillibrand's Barouche.
Read part of a letter from Mr Williams, Editor of Dr Owen's
work on the Heb., to Dr Priestley, on the Data to be followed in disputed Theology points &c.

Witts Family Papers F305

1806

N°. 2 |

Journal

Tuesday March 11th. Clifton—

A perfectly seasonable day: dull, cold, raw, with showers of sleet & snow. Reading one of Barrow's sermons, transcribing a Sermon on Wisdom &c. Called upon Mrs. Garden, & upon my friend Mrs. Carrick. Walked with Mr. Plunkett to Bristol, to a sale of Pictures in Broad Street &c. Received from the Bish. of Bristol a polite negative to the request of private ordination without a title. Dined in a large, dashing party at Gillibrand's the Adair family, Lords Kilwarden & Ruthven; Major Cochrane & P. J. Miles, formed the party. The dinner very good; the Wines very tolerable & in great abundance. The conversation more spirited than edifying. Adjourned at 10 o clock to the York House Ball, which was less fully attended than usually. Conversed a great deal with the Salters, F. Adair &c. Danced two dances with the beautiful Mary Goold, who escorted me home in Gillibrand's Baroche. Read part of a letter from Mr. Williams, Editor of Dr. Owen's work on the Heb., to Dr. Priestly, on the Data to be followed in disputed points of Theology. |

Wednesday March. 12th.—

A hard frost, an extremely cold, dull, day. After an early breakfast, rode over to Bath, where I passed the forenoon. Called upon the Revd. G. Smith respecting an advertised Curacy; found an elegant young man of congenial taste; his own Curacy not actually promised but under treaty; unpromising too, near Devizes, & I have the next refusal. As he pointed out another extremely eligible, Coome Hay, in Somerset, with a pleasant furnished Parsonage &c. so he obligingly accompanied me on a visit to the Rector, Mr. Merewether, Walcot Parade; doubts entertained, that a family in treaty for the House will take it otherwise. I consider my prospect favourable. Called upon Mrs. Napier, the Colonel, & the young Ladies, & upon Mrs. Moncaster. Returned home to dinner, with a head-ach, & very fatigued. (histerne venas inflatus Jaccho.) Unable to join the Party at Lady Wolseleys in the Evening. My Father & Mother not having an engagement, we were all at home.[1] I continued a little of Leo. X. |

---

1. It would seem that with mother and father at home, there was domestic pressure on Frank staying in also. Agnes writes: *Severe wind & strong inclination to snow. Frank rode early to Bath & return'd to Dinner half starved.*

Thursday March. 13.—

A fine day, but rather dull & cold: a slight snow falling in the Evening. To Bristol. Conversed with Mr. Barlow respecting Curacies &c. to the Library &c. Walked back with Cox & Ryan. Wrote a letter to my dearest Margaret, and another requesting a remittance to meet me at Oxford to Mr. Travell.[2] Assisted my Mother in writing to Col. Leigh, the Patron of Coombe Hay, requesting his sanction in my Treaty with Mr. Merewether. Walked upon the Hill with my Father & Mother. In the Evening they had an engagement, which I did not accompany them to; at home I read part of a Sermon by Barrow, the conclusion of Mr. William's letter to Dr. Priestly, & a letter by the same to Mr. David Levi, recommending to the Jews the Study of Dr. Owen's Exposition. Continued Roseve's Leo. X.—

Friday March. 14th.—

Snow upon the ground in the ~~E~~ morning, more than one shower of rain during the course of the day. Began altering a sermon upon Honour from Dr. Barrow. Copying part of another upon Wisdom. | Replied in general terms to the Bishop of Bristol's letter. Called for half an hour upon my friend Mrs. Carrick. Walked to Bristol with Ryan, where Cox joined us; both Gentlemen called upon us. Continued Roseve's Leo. X. At an early pleasant family dinner with Mr. Garden, where our family was met by Mr. Coote. Adjourned from there to a party at Mrs. Vane's, numerous & hot; played speculation with the young people, sitting by & chatting with Cecilia Wolseley all the Evening, who told me many a secret of my own, which I had no notion were in her keeping: not sorry when the Carriages were announced.

Saturday March. 15th.—

A fine clear frost in the morning; afterwards a beautifully mild luminous day. Breakfasted tête-à-tête in unreserved free conversation with my friend Mrs. Dowell, respecting the trying subject of William,[3] poor Fred. Daubeny's untimely Death,[4] &c. She brought me from Cote to Clifton in her Carriage. I walked a little with Robins; to Bristol with Cox, to the Library &c.Mr. Rimington accompanied us back. Walked for some time with Mrs. Salter; paid a very | pleasant visit to Mrs. Goold & Mary; walked a little with Mr. Port, & farther with Miss Upton. Continued Reseve's Leo X. Passed an extremely pleasant afternoon in a small party at ~~Mrs~~ Lady Ford's; Mrs. & Miss OCallaghan, Mrs. Salter & Isabella, Honble. Mr. Yorke, Cox, & the Miss Stables. Every interval between the Music of Miss Ford upon the Piano, Miss M. Stables upon the Harp in a very superior style, & Miss OCallaghan very moderately ~~support~~ singing, was filled with pleasing & intimate conversation with Isabella, Lady Ford, Mrs. Salter &c.—

Sunday March 16th.—

Constant moist weather from morning till night, and extremely dirty. At the Cathedral in the forenoon with Robins. Mr. Foster performed the Service & Mr. Barlow preached upon the Image of GOD as the model of man. Passed an hour with my amiable friend Mrs. Carrick.

2. Frank was still receiving his twice-yearly payment from his uncle Ferdinand towards his university education at Oxford.
3. William Dowell was Frank Witts' closest friend. What the problem was is unknown.
4. Frederick Daubeny, (1776-1806). Little is known of this friend other than he was from Westbury-on-Trym, close to Cote. Frank had met him at a dinner party at Cote on 21 January 1805 and chatted with him at Ashe's concert at Bristol on 29 November 1805.

10. College Green.

Called afterwards upon Mrs. Gillibrand, & Mr. Robert's Family. Occupied in preparations for my departure tomorrow for Oxford. To the sombre Conversazione at the Dowr. Countess Fingal's, which | was enlivened to me by the presence of many of my favourites, as the Goolds, Gillibrand's & Salters. Conversed, as usual, at great length & with much interest with Isabella Salter, Mary Goold, Gillibrand &c. Besides these Fouchet, Mrs. J. Auriol, Col. Baillie, Miss Buggins &c. were present.

Monday March. 17th. Oxford. Wadh. Coll.

Heavy rain, when I left Clifton, which never ceased till it changed into heavy sleet & snow upon the Glocestershire Hills, which hardly intermitted the whole way. After an affectionate leave of my Parents, & an early breakfast, set off <u>in</u> the Oxford Mail, having changed my birth on account of the weather. My society throughout not numerous, still less select. Instead of breakfasting at Bath visited Mr. Mereweather respecting the Curacy & Parsonage of Coombe Hay; he is not disinclined to treat with us, & I delegated the whole business to my Father, whom I led him to expect in a few days. Took some refreshment at Didmarton, & dined at Cirencester, where I wrote a few lines to my Father indicating the event of my visit to Mr. Mereweather. | Took some refreshment at Farringdon, & slept great part of the way to Oxford. Upon arriving at College, I found very indifferent rooms provided for me, but patiently settled myself in them.

Tuesday March. 18.—

Very indifferent weather, a mist throughout the day, at one time very heavy rain. Breakfasted with my excellent but indolent friend Dowell,[5] where I was met by Dr. Price, & Round;

5. Perhaps this was the problem. William was not attentive to his studies.

Trevenen also called in. Accompanied Round to Mr. Clarke's, the Collector's at St. John's, who fixed my first day of determining for the 24th. my second is on the 26th. Called upon Round; walked a little with Alford & Paget; visited the Bodleian Library, skimmed Strutt's Sports, Pegge's Curialia,[6] read some sonnets of Petrarea &c. but was driven to college by the cold. Transcribed arguments to be used in the Schools. Walked round the Parks with Prower. Called upon Michell. Dined at Dr. Price's, meeting Stevens, Round, & a Mr. Latham of B.N.C. a pleasant party. Played two rubbers at Whist & was winner.

Wednesday March. 19.—

A dull damp morning, but the weather improved & the day became very fine. Received a letter with | a remittance from Mr. Travell, to which I replied. Wrote to my Parents. Breakfasted at Dr. Price's, meeting Dowell. Walked a little with Michell & with Worsley. At the Convocation was presented for determination by Mr. Rogers, conversed with Bright, Hall & Sir C. Pegge. Sat for a few minutes with our poor dying Warden. Called upon Round & with him left a card for Lady Pegge. Had the pleasure to meet Robt. Garden in High St. with whom, having driven over from Bampton, I strolled all the forenoon. Called unsuccessfully upon Hankey at the Star & upon McCausland in Peckwater. Dined in the Balliol Hall with Round, adjourning afterwards to the Junr. Common Room, where Gamlin, Wilson & a Merton man, Mr. Burney, Grandson of the Historian of Music,[7] & Godson of Parr, formed a very agreeable party. Accompanied Round & Burney to the Music Room, where the sorry attractions of Mr. Miller, Mrs. Salmon & a Mr. FitzMaurice ~~a~~ on a vile squeaking Union Pipe, had collected a tolerably full room. Lindley great as usual, the others not above mediocrity, & the Piper, thanks to good taste, fairly hissed off the field. Conversed with Sir. J. Riddell, Priest, More, Trevenen, Micklem, Jenkins, Round, Burney &c. |

Thursday March. 20th.—

Rather a raw, unpleasant, dull, day. Breakfasted at the Coffee House. Called upon Dr. Price, & upon Dowell. Walked with the latter to the Town Hall, where the band of the German Heavy Dragoons, resting at Oxford upon their march to Ireland were playing, Joined by Trevenen; visited Angelo's fencing school in the Town Hall;[8] conversed with Sir James Riddell. Called upon Round, walked with Dowell & Trevenen to Joh. Pullen's tree, with Trevenen to his rooms, & with him & Dowell to the Fencing school, where L. C. Hamilton distinguished himself, & to Sadler's. Wrote to Mrs. Dowell upon the prospect of William's Examination.[9] Dined in the Hall, conversing with Worsley. Read after dinner in my room alone Potter's Translation of the Choephoroi of Æschylus.[10] At Chapel in the afternoon. Lounged a little with Prower. At seven o clock visited the Music Room, Mr. FitzMaurice's Pipe was well supplied by the German Band, the other performers as on the former night. Several of the German Officers present; I had much conversation with one | of them in his

---

6. Samuel Pegge, *Curialia, or an historical account of some branches of the Royal Household.* (1791).
7. The grandfather was Charles Burney, (1726-1826), he was the author of *The present state of music in France and Italy* among many other works. He was the father of the novelist Frances Burney, (1752-1840).
8. Henry Angelo, (1752-?).
9. One is left wondering if William knew about this letter to his mother?
10. Robert Potter, *The Tragedies of Aeschylus translated into English verse.* (1777).

11. Watercolour of Henry Angelo's fencing academy

own language: a very pleasant young man. Conversed with Round, Trevenen, Stacie, the More's, Darke, Burney, Marsh, Priest, Cabbell &c.—

Friday March. 21st.—

A fine day, but the air cold: at night rain came on. Breakfasted with Dr. Price, meeting Dowell, with whom I lounged till the Bodleian was opened, where I read Horace Walpole's Tragedy of the Mysterious Mother,[11] skimmed other of his productions, & amused myself with Faujas de St. Fond's Tour in England.[12] Looked into the Examining School, walked with Adams & with Worsley round Ch. Ch. Meadow. Dined in the Hall. Occupied after dinner till time to repair to Sir C. Pegge's in arranging Papers. A very large male Party to Cards & Supper at the Knights: I played three rubbers unsuccessfully; of the party were Stevens & his Wife, Matthias of B.N.C., Budd of C.C.C., Marsh, Marshall of Ball. Dr. ~~B~~ Price, Michel, Simmons, Round, Dr. Cooper, Mr. Jebb, Mr. Davis &c.— |

Saturday March 22nd.—

Damp under foot, but otherwise very fine weather. Breakfasted with Dr. Price. Called upon Hastings, went with him in quest of a liceat first to Merton then to Worcester College. Passed two or three hours in the Bodleian, skimming a variety of books. Called upon Dowell. Walked with Round: with Michell round the Parks. Dined in the Common Room; Michell, Rogers, Price, Dr. Cooper, Stevens & Hall formed the party, which was pleasant enough. Came off victorious after two rubbers at Whist. |

There is a gap in the manuscript diary here. The remainder of this page is left blank and on the verso the diary takes up again, this time back in Clifton.

---

11. Horace Walpole, *The Mysterious Mother, a tragedy in five acts and verse.* (1768).
12. Faujas de St. Fond, (1741-1819), *Voyage en Angleterre en Ecosse et aus Iles Hébrides.* Paris, 1797.

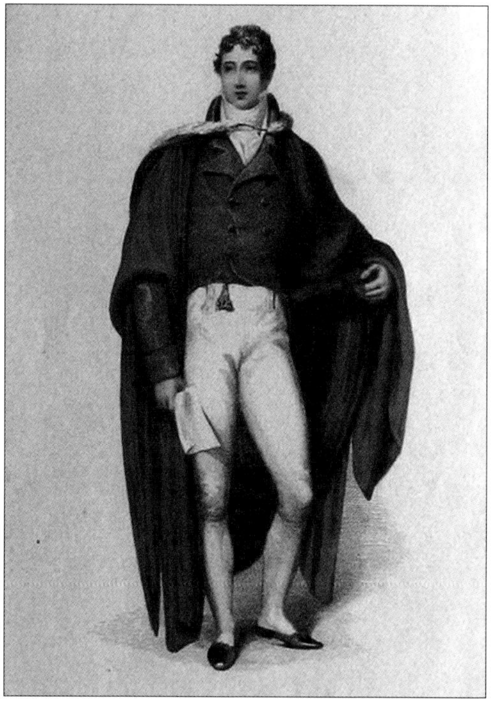

12. *Bachelor of Arts, Oxford.*

On 21 March 1806 Agnes records that she and Edward Witts set off in a postchaise for Bath to discuss with the Revd. Mereweather Frank taking the curacy with her and Edward taking the house. The discussions appear to have gone well. On 16 April Agnes records . . . the close of it made delightful by the arrival of Frank on his new Grey Horse. On 21 April Frank set off early for Combe Hay and arrived home late. On 23 April Frank set off for London with the hope of getting ordained. On 29 April Agnes records receiving a letter to the effect that Frank was ordained on Sunday (27 April 1806). On 2 May Frank returned home, but there was then much discussion on hearing of the death of the poor rector, Revd. Mereweather. Then a sequence of entries which speak for themselves: 3 May 1806: . . much occupied in setting Frank off for Bath to be in readiness to go over to Combhay on Sunday to do his duty both there and at Foscote . . . 7 May 1806: . . . Quite a broiling hot day, ill-suited to dear Frank's fatiguing ride to Comb hay and back to bury the poor old Rector . . . 11 May 1806: . . . Frank left us very early in the morning to serve his Churches & proceed into Wiltshire . . . 13 May 1806: found our Dear Son returned full of credentials relative to the Curacy in Wiltshire . . . 18 May 1806: . . . went in a postchaise thro' Bristol to Ashton Church for the satisfaction of hearing our beloved Frank do the duty there for Lewis, a trying, agitating pleasure but much gratified by his performance . . . 24 May 1806: . . Dear Frank went early into Wiltshire to give some assistance to Mr. Smith in his Whitsunday Duty . . . 26 May 1806: . . . found our dearest Frank but lately come home driven by Mr. Smith . . . 27 May 1806: . . . Mrs Langhams made me an early visit and Mr. Smith a very long one much conversation about his House in Erchfont an agreeable Gentlemanlike man . . . 28 May 1806: . . . our Dear Frank left us after Breakfast to accompany Mr. Smith in a little jaunt into Devonshire . . . 14 June 1806: . . . & to Dinner arrived at last our beloved Frank to our no small joy.

Clifton. 16 Richmond Terrace
Wednesday June 18th.—

Beautiful summer weather. Before & after breakfast strolled upon the Terrace & with Mr. Deacon. Read part of Bishop Burnet's Pastoral Care.[13] Copied part of a Sermon, I had prepared upon Wisdom. Rode over the Downs. Walked a little. In the afternoon to Bristol. To

13. Gilbert Burnet, Bishop of Salisbury, (1643-1715), *Discourse of the Pastoral Care.* (1692, 12th edition 1805).

13. Long Ashton Church

the library &c. In the Evening at a very pleasant party at M^rs. Goold's: much conversation & singing Mary Goold delightfully in voice, & Mary Ford, playing very correctly. The Auriols, M^rs. Rowe, Garden, Adair &c. of the Party. Reading Butcher's Excursion from Sidmouth to Chester,[14] & M^rs. Temple's novel Ferdinand Fitzormond.[15] Wrote to M^r. Matthews.—

Thursday June 19th.

A similarly beautiful day. Walked a little on | the Terrace after breakfast. Wrote to Lady Lyttelton; read Burnet's Pastoral Care, transcribed part of a Sermon. Received an unpleasant letter from Smith which afterwards gave me considerable uneasiness. Called upon Miss Hume & I walked with W. Deacon &c. In the Evening, strolled to Bristol, on the Hill &c. with the Goold party, Garden & Adair, Mrs. & Mr. Deacon, the Salters &c.—

Friday June 20th.

A continuation of the same fine weather. Walked before breakfast on the Hill &c. with Robt. Garden. Wrote to Smith. Walked on the terrace after breakfast ^with the Salters. Studied Burnet's Pastoral Care & copied part of a Sermon; Called without success upon M^rs. Carrick; walked with Robt. Adair. Studied Bonnycastle's Astronomy.[16] About eight went with the Salters to M^rs. J. Auriol's fête champêtre, the Gardens very prettily arranged with festoons of coloured lamps & a Marquee the Band of the Mid'sex Militia &c. Danced upon | a sloping green with the two Salters. A good supper within doors. Very pleasant; chiefly with the Goold party, the Salters,

---

14. Edmund Butcher, *An Excursion from Sidmouth to Chester, in the summer of 1803, in a series of letters to a lady.* (1805).
15. Mrs Temple, *Ferdinand Fitzormond: or, the Fool of Nature.* (1805).
16. John Bonnycastle, *An Introduction to Astronomy, in a series of letters from a preceptor to his pupil in which the most useful and interesting parts of the science are clearly & familiarly explained.* (1786).

Jessop, Adair &c. Walked with the Goolds round the Hill, stargazing, at two in the morning: after which Adair, Jessop, & myself forced Mrs. Salter's Castle, & made her & the Girls give us breakfast, we helping to light the fire, boil the kettle &c., & after seeing the sun rise retired to bed by four o clock.—Read Mrs. Temple's romantic novel Ferdinand Fitzormond.

Saturday June 21st.

Rather cooler, but as fine weather as ever. Walking upon the Terrace before & after breakfast, first with R. Adair. Reading Burnet's Pastoral Care & transcribing a Sermon. Called in vain upon the Salters, & with pleasure upon the Goolds. Walked with R. Garden to Bristol to the library &c., calling upon Mr. & Mrs. Auriol by the way. Called again upon the Goolds. | Sad domestic uneasiness consumed great part of the afternoon.[17] Rode across the Downs; walked with R. Garden, the Goold's &c. upon the Hill, retired, well fatigued.—

Sunday June 22d.

A beautiful day, less sultry than usual. Accompanied my Mother to Clifton Church, where J. W. Humphrey officiated, & preached an excellent discourse upon the Jewish Dispensation. Mrs. Roc called after Church. Called upon the Gardens: walked upon the Hill with my Father & R. Garden, where the Middlesex band were playing. Read Grant's Poem upon the Restoration of learning in the East, very good. The Garrison was inspected before Gloucester Row in the Evening; my Father & myself were joined by R. Garden, & joined the Salters &c. After a quarter of an hour's visit to Lady Fingall, joined the Goolds & walked for the remainder of the Evening in their suite, | two military bands playing. Wrote to a Mr. Morgan respecting a Readership at Ludlow.

Monday June 23d.—

A continuance of the same fine weather. Walked after breakfast upon the Terrace with my Mother. Made a fruitless call upon Smith at Glocester House. Read Burnet's Pastoral Care. Walked upon the Mount with Smith discussing particulars relating to his House. Rode a little upon the Downs. After dinner, joined a party at the Goolds for Ashton, the usual set, R. Adair excepted, with the addition of Jessop & Captn. Fallon. The walk, strawberries &c. pleasant enough. Mrs. Goold gave us a supper afterwards & Mary Goold sang delighfully. Found my Parents much exasperated at my having accepted the Invitation to Supper, & retired miserable.[18]

Tuesday June 24th.—

A very windy day & colder. Read Burnet's Pastoral Care. Great uneasiness respecting our Treaty with Smith. Walked with my Father to call upon him at Glocester House in vain. Had a long conversation with him ~~before~~ on the Downs afterwards. Found Mrs. Carrick visiting | when I came in again. Walked with my Mother. Transcribed a sermon. In the Evening accompanied Mrs. Carrick, Dr. Nott, & Captn. Bradshaw to Miss Bethells, where we met Miss M. Boycott & drank Tea, with a Sullabub & strawberries & cream in Dr. Nott's Hayfield afterwards. Pleasant enough.—

17. Nothing mentioning any discord is recorded in the diary of Agnes.
18. Agnes mentions that Frank was with Mr. Smith much of the morning and with the Goold party at Ashton eating strawberries. She does not mention discord or exasperation or any words at all.

Wednesday June 25$^{th.}$—

The day warmer & cloudy. Wrote a few lines to George. Walked after breakfast upon the Terrace with my Mother. To Bristol, to the Library &c. Wrote a note to Smith. Rob$^{t.}$ Garden called. With him called upon the Goolds. Called also upon the Miss Bethells. Walked with R. Garden. After dinner employed in breaking in my grey horse in a hack Post Chaise. Walking with Rob$^{t.}$ Garden & his Father. Drank Tea with their family. Afterwards walked with the Goolds. & the Knours & Miss Ford. Two Bands performing: one upon Richmond Terrace, the other on Gloucester Row.

Thursday June 26.

A propitious rain after a season of great drought. | Called upon Smith in the forenoon. Finished transcribing a Sermon: Christian Virtue the Parent of Happiness. Read Burnet's Pastoral Care. Finished Ferdinand Fitzormond; began a novel of La Fontaine translated by Isabelle de Montolieu authoress of Caroline de Lichfeld Marie Menzikof & Fedor Dolgorouki.[19] —

Friday June 27.—

A good deal of rain fell: some clear intervals. Called upon Smith soon after breakfast. Walked to the top of the Hill with D$^{r.}$ Bridges, called upon M$^{rs.}$ Carrick & upon the Goulds. Rob$^{t.}$ Garden called upon me. Finished Burnet's Pastoral Care. Rode a little upon the Hill; R. Garden walking by my side & sitting with me afterwards. To a large, pleasant party at Lady Ford's; the Miss Nevilles & Mary Ford playing, conversed with the Goolds, Adairs, Salters, Cox, Miss Ford &c.—

Saturday June 28$^{th.}$ —

A beautiful fine summer's day. After an early | breakfast proceeded with my Parents in a chaise to view Erchfont; at Bath, where we first halted, made an unsuccessful call upon M$^{rs.}$ Bates, but meeting George Rashleigh walked over the Town with him: upon our arrival at the Castle Inn Devizes we looked at some comfortable lodgings in case we should want them, took a late dinner, & afterwards walked through beautiful fields to M$^{rs.}$ Sutton's handsome Seat, New Park; after strolling still more through the Town; retired to bed early. Began Shee's Rhymes on Art.[20] —

Sunday June 29.—

As beautiful a day as the preceding. After breakfast pursued the road to Erchfont; opposite Stert Chapel quitted the chaise & my Parents to do duty there; preached to them a Sermon intitled Life a Journey. Received with politeness by M$^{rs.}$ Jacques, Miss Gale &c. Afterwards walked across beautiful fields to | Erchfont, where my Father & Mother were busily exploring the Vicarage, & better pleased with it than I had hoped. After looking over it again into the antique Church &c., returned to Devizes, & after dinner, returned to Bath, where we arrived before nine o clock at the Elephant & Castle & retired after taking some Tea.—

---

19. Auguste La Fontaine, (1759-1831), *Marie Menzikof et Fédor Dolgorouki*. London, 1804.
20. Sir Martin Archer Shee, (1769-1850), *Rhymes on Art; or the Remonstrance of a Painter . . . including strictures on the state of the arts, criticism, patronage, and public taste*. (1805).

14. *New Park.*

Monday June 30th.—

A great deal of drizzling rain & some heavy fell, till the Evening, which proved fine. Mrs. Bates gave us a very handsome breakfast, after which my Father & myself explored the different Coachmakers for Gigs, respecting one of which we called upon Mr. Meyler in the Grove. Returning to take leave of Mrs. Bates & afterwards went to the Elephant & Castle to dine, & about ½ past five pursued the well known Route to Bristol & Clifton, where we arrived unhurt; though part of our Equipage was injured by the Bristol pavement. Found | an unsatisfactory reply respecting the Ludlow Readership.—

Tuesday July 1st.—

Very fine weather, though rather cold for the Season. Called upon George Rashleigh at the New Inn, & upon Smith. Walked to Bristol &c. with Geo. Rashleigh. With my Father & Mother in the Evening, which was worn by considerable uneasiness respecting Smith's affair &c.—

Wednesday July 2nd.

Very fine weather. Rode over to Bath & returned to dinner. Walked alone chiefly in the Evening a little with Mr. Deacon, Mrs. & Miss Venour, & the Goolds. Uneasy all day; this affair with Smith disturbing me.—

Thursday July 3d.

Extremely fine. Called upon Smith after breakfast. Much contentious conference & uneasiness respecting his business. Walked to Bristol to the Library &c. In the Evening, walked | alone, & with my Father & Mother, Mrs. Hamilton &c. – Began Scott's Sir Tristram.[21] —

---

21. Sir Walter Scott, (1771-1832), *Sir Tristram.* (1803).

15. Stert, Wiltshire; a sketch by Francis Witts.

Friday July 4th.—

Very fine weather. Visited Smith for an hour or two after breakfast. Walked with my Mother. In the Evening walked to Bristol, & upon the Terrace, the band playing & with Miss Macbride.

Saturday July 5.—

Very fine day. Rode to Bath after breakfast. After baiting there, harnessed my Grey in a Taxed Cart, & drove him to Erchfont; passed the Evening unpleasantly with Smith.—

Sunday July 6.

Much rain had fallen in the night but the day was fine. After a late breakfast & coming to a conclusion with Smith, walked to Stert, called upon Mrs. Jacques; performed the Afternoon Duty at the Chapel, preaching upon the neglect of GOD's Salvation to a good congregation. Returned to Bath in the Evening | & after a walk retired to sleep at the Elephant & Castle.

Monday July 7.—

A very rainy forenoon, the remainder of the day fine. Left Bath on horseback for Clifton where the day cleared, came the upper Road. Walked with my Father & Mother before dinner. Afterwards to Bristol, to the Coachmakers &c.—Began transcribing a Sermon of Dr. Horne's upon Repentance.

Tuesday July 8th.— |

After the above date, the half page remaining on this verso is blank. The facing recto commences at the top of the page with the date 17 July 1806.

During this period we have information from Agnes Witts. She is packing both 'at home' meaning Richmond Terrace, and in Boyces Buildings. It appears that they retained the lease and were sub-letting. Agnes is then packing to send items off to Devizes. On Saturday 12 July Frank set off in his new gig to do his duty at Urchfont the following day. On 14 July Edward and Agnes followed in 'Thomas's carriage' stopping a few hours at Bath for shopping. On arriving at Devizes, they met Frank and settled into lodgings in Market Place. The following day Frank was the greater part of the day with Mr. Smith at Urchfont.[22]

Devizes. Thursday. July 17$^{th.}$ 1806.—

A very showery forenoon, & fine evening. Wrote to M$^{r.}$ Travell. Rode to Erchfont; met & conversed with the Revd. G. Jacques by the way. Arranging matters with Smith. After dinner took a walk upon the London Road with my Father & Mother, returning by New Park.

Friday July. 18$^{th.}$—

Heavy showers, the intervals long & fine. Rev$^{d.}$ M$^{r.}$ Mayo called in the forenoon. Left my cards with M$^{rs.}$ Hillier & at D$^{r.}$ Spaldings. Rode to Stert Cottage & walked from thence with M$^{r.}$ & M$^{rs.}$ Jacques four miles to Stoke to dine with M$^{r.}$ Mayo. A very hospitable reception; the Rectory good, but the Village & Country indifferent. The party consisted besides ourselves of $^{Revd.}$ M$^{r.}$ Lucas, M$^{rs.}$ Mayo, three Miss Hilliers, & a Miss Ferrals. Walked back to Stert & reached Devizes after dark.— |

Saturday July 19$^{th.}$—

Rather a cloudy day, but without rain. Rode to Erchfont to settle matters with Smith. Found Jacques there who assisted us. In the Evening drove my Mother upon the London Road as far as Bishop's Cannings & back.—

Sunday July 20$^{th.}$—

Fine weather. Pursuing my clerical duties at Stert & Erchfont, preaching upon the Excellency of Patience. Called of course upon M$^{rs.}$ Jacques & Smith. A late dinner at D$^{r.}$ Spalding's: he a plain man of sense, his Lady very eccentric, his Daughter insignificant, met by a Miss A. Taylor, other Company to Tea, particularly, M$^{rs.}$ Hillier & her interesting Daughter nearly blind, M$^{rs.}$ Carrick's cousin whom I conversed with for a long time.—

Monday July 21$^{st.}$—

Very heavy showers of rain, & some thunder with bright intervals. Transcribing from D$^{r.}$ Coneybeare a Sermon upon the Division of Mankind into rich & poor. Wrote to my Uncle Witts. Dined with the Jacques's at Stert | Cottage, meeting M$^{r.}$ Compton of Erchfont & Newbury, an honest, plain man, his wife & sister. A good plain dinner, wine, beer, pipes of tobacco.

Tuesday July 22$^{nd.}$—

A fine day, but heavy rain late in the Evening. Rode to Erchfont in hopes of ~~a st~~ arranging matters with Smith but a sudden dispute made one quickly return, & occasioned two letters to & from him to me & one to & from Jaques. Walked a little with my Father & Mother.

22. The gap in the diary is somewhat compensated for by entries in the diary of Agnes Witts.

Continued a Sermon begun yesterday. To a rout at Dr. Spaldings: a large party, the Hostess more garrulous than ever; I principally conversed with Mr. Mayo & Miss H. Hillier, a very interesting creature. Was introduced to a Miss Tylee, & to Mrs. Sutton of New Park, Sister to Lord Sidmouth,[23] a very lady like person, who with her Daughter & Miss Estcourts[24] were the most pleasing persons in appearance in the circle. Some bad music upon a worse instrument.

Wednesday July 23d.— |

An inclination to reign all the morning; very heavy rain at night. Rode over to Smith to make future arrangements; an odious occupation; continued modelling a Sermon from Dr. Coneybcare. Confined in the Evening by the rain. Began the Revd. Mr. Lucas's Infernal Quixote, a novel.[25] –

Thursday July 2~~2nd~~4

A violent thunderstorm & other showers during the day. Passed the greater part of the day with Smith at Erchfont. Examining Wyndham's Wilts & Lloyd's Thesaurus Ecclesiasticus.[26] –

Friday July 25th.

Fine weather: little or no rain. Wrote in my Father's name to Sir John Callander, & to Mr. Horne & Mr. Adamson. Called in vain ~~upon~~ with my Father & Mother upon Mrs. Sutton at New Park. Drove my Mother a very pretty drive to Pottern a very pretty village. Finished my Sermon from Dr. Coneybeare. Passed the Evening pleasantly at Mrs. Hillier's meeting a Family party & Mr. Mayo. |

---

23. The sister was Eleanor Addington, she married James Sutton of New Park, Wiltshire in 1771. He died in 1801. Henry Addington, later Lord Sidmouth, was Speaker in the House of Commons during the 1790s and a favourite of the King, who appointed him Prime Minister in 1801 after Pitt and Castlereagh had resigned over Irish Catholic Emancipation. Later he became Chancellor of the Exchequer and was made a viscount in 1805. His most noteworthy measure as Chancellor was an attempt to deal with the effects of widespread poverty by funding the building of over one hundred churches in urban areas. Sidmouth became Home Secretary in the Castlereagh administration from 1812 to 1822, and was one of the most repressive holders of that office. He supported the actions of a government, reviled by liberals and radicals, by creating an intricate network of spies, informers and agents provocateurs. Shelley in *The Mask of Anarchy* (1819) depicted his intellectual and emotional dishonesty as

    Clothed with the Bible, as with light,
    And thc shadows of the night,
    Like Sidmouth next, Hypocrisy
    On a crocodile rode by.

    Another sister of Addington's, Susan, married Bragge Bathurst of Lydney Park in Gloucestershire and became the mother of one of Frank Witts' closest communicants and friends — Charles Bathurst. *See* Biographical Index.
24. Eleanor the second daughter of James and Eleanor Sutton married in 1800 Thomas Grimston Bucknall Estcourt, (1775-1853), originally Estcourt, near Tetbury, Gloucestershire and later of New Park near Devizes, Wiltshire. The Miss Estcourts were presumably his sisters. Estcourt was M.P. for Devizes, 1805-1826 and Oxford University, 1826-1847.
25. Charles Lucas, *The Infernal Quixote. A Tale of the Day.* (1801).
26. John Lloyd, *Thesaurus Ecclesiasticus: an improved edition of the Liber Valorum, containing a valuation of all the livings in England and Wales.* (1788).

16. Urchfont Church; a sketch by Francis Witts.

Saturday July 26th.—

Very fine weather. Received a letter from Willson. Rode over to Erchfont to settle matters with Smith, from whom I parted without regret, as he set off for Andover. Conversed a little with Jaques, upon the road. Walked with my Father & Mother in the Evening through the fields to Devizes & back.

Sunday July 27th.—

Very fine weather. After breakfast drove my Father to Erchfont, where the morning service was. Preached upon the division of mankind into rich & poor. Making some arrangements at the Vicarage. Walked to Stert, & called as usual on Mrs. Jacques, & performed the Evening duty there. Walked in the Evening with my Father & Mother in the fields. Began to model from Dr. Coneybeare a Sermon upon the faith of Abraham.

Monday July 28th.—

A beautiful day, except one short & violent thundershower. Accompanied my Mother in the Gig, to call upon the Jaques's at Stert, who received us very handsomely. Proceed to Erchfont Vicarage to arrange various matters. In the Evening walked with my Father to the Green. Continuing a Sermon upon the faith of | Abraham. Began Mrs. Trimmer's Guardian of Education.[27]

Tuesday July 29th.—

Very fine weather. Wrote to Margaret, to Mr. Travell, & to Willson. Continued to model a Sermon from Dr. Coneybeare. Called with my Mother upon Mrs. J. Tylee, a very pleasant little woman. Mrs. & Miss Spalding called. Walked, with my Father &c. In the Evening took a long walk in the fields with my Father & Mother.

27. Sarah Trimmer, *The Guardian of Education*, 5 vols. (1802-6).

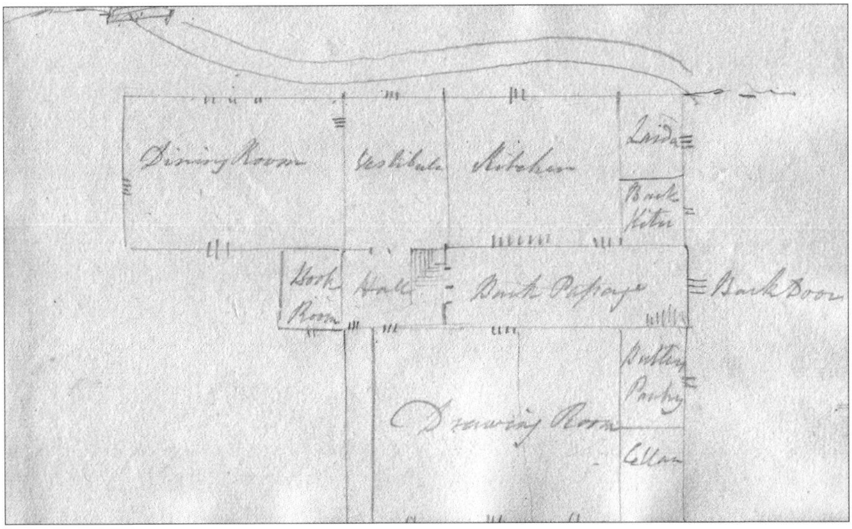

17. Plan, probably of Urchfont Parsonage; a sketch by Francis Witts.

Wednesday July 30$^{th.}$—

A very fine forenoon: a good deal of rain in the Evening. Heard from M$^{r.}$ Witts of Cookham, & from Travell. Wrote to M$^{r.}$ Witts. Drove my Mother to Erchfont, where we made various arrangements. Finished modelling a Sermon from D$^{r.}$ Coneybeare upon the Faith of Abraham. Walked a little in the Evening.

Thursday July 31$^{st.}$—

A very fine day. Received two letters from M$^{r.}$ Horne. Wrote one to George & to M$^{r.}$ Adamson.[28] Drove my Father to Erchfont, to make arrangements there. Walked in the Evening in the fields with my Father & Mother.

Friday Aug. 1$^{st.}$—

A dull day with many showers, & misty rain. Drove my Mother to Erchfont, making arrangements. Walking alone in the Evening. |

Saturday Aug. 2$^{nd.}$—

Very stormy & showery weather. Drove my Mother to Erchfont to arrange various matters there. Walked in the Evening to the woods, a very pretty picturesque scene.—

Sunday Aug. 3$^{d.}$—

Very fine weather. Drove my Father as far as Stert upon the road to Erchfont, the morning Service at the former place, called upon M$^{rs.}$ Jaques as usual, walked to Erchfont, making arrangements, & doing the Evening duty, at both places preaching upon the

28. Who Mr. Adamson was is unknown, but he appears to be a lawyer and also appears to be wrapped up in George's affairs. In 1810 Frank had the difficult job of paying off some of George's creditors, and it was a Mr. Adamson that he dealt with. For Edward Horne, *see* 6 August 1807 below.

Faith of Abraham. Mrs. Hillier drank tea with us. Commenced altering a Sermon from Dr. Coneybeare upon the Vanity of human things.—

Monday Aug. 4th.—

Very fine weather. Made a circuitous walk to Erchfont over the fields, but returned the direct footpath. Making arrangements there & christening a child. Wrote to Mr. Horne, Mr. Higgins, & Mr. Collins, Canal, Salisbury. Preparing a Sermon upon the Vanity of human Pursuits. Passed a very pleasant Even. at Mrs. J. Tylee's: Mrs. Gent, Mrs. Hillier, & Miss Tylee besides ourselves; walked to Newlands, Mrs. Gent's beautiful grounds & gardens.— |

Tuesday Aug 5th.—

A fine forenoon, a dull afternoon, showery in the Even. towards sunset fine. At an early hour my Father & Mother left me upon a visit to Mr. Ram's in Berks.[29] Received a letter from Mr. Travell. Drove John to Erchfont to make various arrangements. Continued to model a Sermon upon vanity from Dr. Coneybeare. Took a long walk in the Evening.—

Wednesday Aug. 6th.—

A fine day, excepting a trifling shower in the afternoon. At Erchfont, whither I rode; to arrange matters, thence through Cherrington & Patney to Dirchamstoke to call upon Mr. Mayo: called upon his Sister, him I met upon my return to Devizes, & was introduced to Mr. Higginson of Rowde. Wrote part of a Sermon upon the Vanity of human things. Took a pleasant walk in the Even. under Roundway Hills.

Thursday Aug. 7.—

A little rain in the morning, otherwise a very fine day. Heard from my Mother. Wrote to her. Called upon Mrs. Hillier, Mr. C. Tylee &c. Finished transcribing a Sermon upon vanity from Dr. Coneybeare. After an early dinner rode over to Erchfont to attend a funeral. Drank Tea. Upon my return at Miss Tylee's with their family party Mr. & Mrs. Gent, Mr. W. Wood &c. Walked in Mrs. Sutton's beautiful woods, passed the Evening very pleasantly.

Friday Aug. 8.—

Very fine weather. Reading in the forenoon. Proceeded | to dine at Mr. Compton's at Erchfont, calling in the Gig at Stert, to take up Miss Biggs. Arranging matters in the Vicarage. Met the Jaques's at Mr. Compton's, & a very hospitable reception. Interred a Corpse, the oldest inhabitant of the Village, aged 83. Supped at Mr. Jaques's & reached my lodgings later than usual.

Saturday Aug. 9.

A very fine but sultry day. Walked to Erchfont to overlook my workmen & returned to dinner. Passed the Evening at Mrs. Gents. Tea, walking & supper, very pleasant, the Tylee Family, Mrs. Sutton, Mrs. Shields & daughter formed the party.—

---

29. Mr. Ram was Abel John Ram, the man who stole Frank's first love, the delectable Fanny Port. John Granville had adopted his niece Fanny, and the Granvilles were also present at the Ram's house at Burnham, near Maidenhead.

Sunday. Aug. 10.—

A fine & a warmer day than yesterday. Rode to Erchfont, performed the morning duty there, & walked to the Evening Service at Stert. Preached upon the Vanity of human things. Sent John back to Devizes with my horse & accepted of an invitation to a family dinner with the Jaques's: Mr. & Miss A. Gale called in the Evening. Walked back to my Lodgings at nine o clock.—

Monday Aug. 11.

Beautiful weather for the Harvest. Heard from my Mother. Received a call from Mr. Higginson. Began to remodel a Discourse of Dr. Coneybeare's upon the Moral Infirmity of Human Nature. Rode to Erchfont to overlook my Workmen. Found a note | from my Friend Jem Evans who had called en passent while his horses were baiting at the Bell. Dined at Dr. Spalding's, Mr. Spalding his Brother an elegant & agreeable man. The Dr. & his wife highly ridiculous. Mr. Gaisford, & Mr. C. Mayo made up the party. In the Evening walked with the Ladies & Mr. J. Maynard to the very pretty Gardens of the latter at the Brow. Returned by nine after some sad singing by Miss Spalding.

Tuesday Aug. 12.—

Very fine weather. Wrote to my Mother. Heard from Mr. Adamson. Transcribing part of a Sermon upon the Moral Infirmity of Man from Dr. Coneybeare. Mr. Gaisford called upon me. Rode to Polshot to call upon Jem Evans, who ~~was~~ is on a visit there at Dr. Skinner's. Meeting the Dr. his Spouse & Son with Miss Skinner going an airing to Seend, accepted their invitation to return to dinner: in the meantime rode back to Devizes, & called upon Mrs. James Gent a pleasant visit. Received very handsomely by Dr. Skinner & his family (one Son & three Daughters) & passed a pleasant Day: in the Evening Mr. & Miss Skinner & Jem indulged us with several interesting pieces of Haydn & Handel.—Returned at the close of the Evening.—

Wednesday. Aug. 13.—

Very showery weather. In vain expected friend | Jem to pass the day with me. Called in vain on Mr. Gaisford. Drove John to Erchfont, calling on Mrs. Jaques by the way. Transcribing from Dr. Coneybeare part of a Sermon upon the Infirmity of the Moral Nature. Took a long & pleasant walk in the Evening towards Rowde &c.—

Thursday Aug. 14.

Showery weather. Early Jem Evans gave me the pleasure of his Company to breakfast; we then walked over the Canal & thro' Mrs. Sutton's Woods. I afterwards drove him over to Erchfont, & thence to Mr. Richard's, the Rector of little Cheverel where he was to dine, the road laying thro' Eastcott & East Lavington, returned thro' Pottern to Devizes a beautiful drive to dinner. Heard from Margaret & received a letter upon Parish business, which I answered. Continued to model from Dr. Coneybeare a Sermon upon the moral weakness of human nature. Took a long walk to Allington &c. in the Evening.—

Friday Aug. 15.—

Very fine weather. Finished modelling a Sermon on the Moral Infirmity of human nature by Dr. Coneybeare. Called upon Mrs. Hillier. | Walked to Erchfont, to make arrangements.

Called at Sturt Cottage by the way. Dined with the J. Tylee's a very pleasant party Mr. C. Mayo & his Sister, Mrs. Newman Mr. Neat, Mrs. C. Tylee, Mr. & Mrs. Gent & Mrs. Hillier, & Mr. Thomas. Walked with the Ladies in the afternoon. Listened for half an hour to the band. Supped with the same party & Mr. W. Salmon.—

~~Sunday~~ Saturday Aug. 16.

Very fine weather. After an early breakfast drove my friend Jem Evans to Erchfont & afterwards part of the way over the Plain when he joined the Doctor & his Lady. I returned to Erchfont to ~~make~~ give directions & found Jaques there, whom I drove to Stert, & returned to Devizes to dinner. Heard from my Mother, wrote to a Creditor of George's,[30] & a letter upon parish business. Walked to the Summit of Roundway Hills in the Evening.

Sunday. Aug. 17th.—

Very fine weather. After breakfast sallied forth on horseback to perform the morning duty at | Stert, where I preached as afterwards at Erchfont upon the moral Infirmity of human Nature. Called of course upon Mrs. Jaques & her Sister &c. Returned to dinner at Devizes. Wrote to my Mother. Walked in Mr. Heathcote's woods &c. Mr. Gaisford called in the Evening. Began a Sermon; the Considerations excited by a plentiful harvest.—

Monday Aug. 18th.—

Very fine weather. Called upon Mrs. & Miss Spalding. Walked to Erchfont to inspect workmen. In the Evening walked upon the London road &c.—Continuing a Sermon begun yesterday.

Tuesday. Aug. 19.—

A sultry morning, & in the Evening a most tremendous storm: thunder & lightning awful from six till 12 o clock. Drove John over to Erchfont to arrange matters.—

Wednesday. Aug. 20th.

~~Very fine~~ Showery weather. Rode early to Erchfont to marry a couple. Mr. Jaques paid me a visit. Walked in the Evening upon Roundway Hill.

Thursday Aug. 21st.

~~Very fine~~ Showery weather. Drove John to Erchfont, halting at Stert to marry a Couple, & calling upon the Jaques's. Called upon the Messrs. Salmons. Walked in the Evening towards Pottern.— |

18. Urchfont Church 20 August; a sketch by Francis Witts.

30. It appears that George was having difficulty with debts at this early point, and this is probably connected with Adamson.

Friday Aug. 22nd.—

Very fine weather. Received a letter from my Mother, & wrote to Margaret. Heard also from Smith. Finished a sermon: reflections excited by a plentiful Harvest. Mrs. Hillier called upon me; as also Mr. Skinner with his friend Mr. Clarke. Called at Mrs. J. Tylee's meeting Mr. J. Tylee & Charles Mr. Barrie, Mrs. Hillier & Harriet, Miss Tylee &c. Went to the Bear to see the boys of the Club at dinner: The bear Club an excellent Charitable Institution to which I was elected a Member at the Dinner in the Town Hall, which was very good, more than 80 of the Gentlemen of the Town & neighbourhood present.[31] The Venison remarkably well flavoured & drest. Conversed chiefly with Gaisford, C. Tylee, Tom Tylee, Alfred Wyatt &c. Drank tea & supped with Mrs. Hillier, meeting Mrs. J. Tylee, Miss H. Tylee, Charles Tylee, Alfred Wyatt &c. Walked a little in the Evening.—

Saturday Aug. 23d.—

Very fine weather. Drove John to Erchfont to make arrangements for my removal thither. Finished a Sermon upon the Harvest.— | Wrote to my Mother. Met & conversed a little with Mrs. Jaques. Dined with Gaisford unpleasantly enough, meeting young Grubbe. Drank Tea & supped at Mr. J. Tylee's, walking with the party in the Interval. Miss Tylee, C. Tylee, Alfred Wyatt, Mrs. Hillier & Harriet, Mr. Maurice & Miss M. Gibbs. Very agreeable.—

Sunday Aug. 24.

Very fine. Rode to Erchfont to morning Service. Preached there & at Stert a Discourse the Reflections excited by a prosperous Harvest. Called on the Jaques's of course. Dined with John Gale & excellent man, though suffering from a wrist disorder. John Thomas called in. Left them soon & took a walk by moonlight after my return to Devizes.—

Monday Aug. 25th.—

Very fine weather. Preparing to leave Devizes for Erchfont, where I came in the Evening to sleep. Called upon Mrs. Hillier & Harriet. Walked a little about the town. Had a visit from F. Mereweather from Calne, who called with me upon Gaisford &c. Walked about the Town with me & | with Alfred Wyatt & C. Tylee. Dined at the Elder Mr. Tylee's, very pleasantly meeting Mereweather Mrs. Tom Tylee, her Husband, Alfred Wyatt &c. Accompanied the Ladies some part of the way upon their walk, & then drove John over with me to Erchfont, where things were made tolerably comfortable for me.—

Tuesday Aug. 26.—

Very wet weather: rain falling in very heavy showers with little intermission & during the night. Writing a Funeral Sermon upon the Death of a young man knocked on the head in a quarrel by his fellow servant. Called upon the Jaques's & Gales. Heard from my Mother.

Wednesday Aug. 27.—

Rain falling in showers throughout the day; the intervals fine. Transcribing a funeral Sermon. Rode to Devizes upon various Errands. Called upon my friends the Hilliers. Met there Miss

31. The Devizes Bear Club dated back to 1664 and also had a charity school.

19. Sketch of house, probably Urchfont Parsonage, by Francis Witts.

H. Tylee. Met & Conversed with Miss Tylee, Mrs. Lediard, Alfred Wyatt, Charles Tylee, W. Butcher &c. Wrote to my Mother. The funeral of poor Simon Hall came on in the Evening for which at the desire of the Club I preached a funeral Sermon.—

Thursday Aug. 28.

Showery weather, but rather finer. Began a Sermon upon Anger. Mr. W. Butcher called upon me. Never left | my own premises.—

Friday Aug. 29th. —

Still showery, but less wet. Composing a Sermon upon anger. Not off my own premises, till dinner time, when I repaired to W. Butchers, to meet Captn. Hayward of Cliff Hall & a friend of his. Moderately agreeable. Staid to supper.—

Saturday Aug. 30th.

Rather showery, but less rain than of late. Rode through Eastroft & Lavington to call upon Captn. Hayward at Cliff Hall, & returned thro' West Lavington & over the downs.—

Sunday Aug. 31st.—

Very fine weather: only a very sight sprinkling of rain. Morning Service at Stert discoursed upon Anger. Sat with Mrs. Jaques as usual. Evening Service at Erchfont. Walked to Stert & back.

Monday Sep. 1st.—

Fine weather. Jaques called upon me. I walked with him to Stert & thence to Devizes to accelerate workmen. Heard from my mother.

Tuesday Sep. 2d.—

Very fine weather. Rode upon the Plain. Gaisford called. A funeral in the Evening.

Wednesday Sep. 3d.

Gloomy showery & cold. Composing a Sermon upon the Love of our Neighbour. Walked in the fields in the forenoon.

Thursday Sep. 4th.—

Extremely wet, violent showers, very frequent. Wrote to my Mother. Rode to Devizes to hurry workmen. | Called at Mrs. Hillicrs.

There is a strange occurrence in the diary here. The next fours days he has written 'Dec.' instead of 'Sep'. Unusually, he has not gone back and crossed them through. At the bottom of the page he corrects himself and reverts to 'Sep.' The problems with the workmen were clearly playing on his mind.

Friday Dec. 5.—

Fine weather. Walked in the fields towards Patney &c.—Wrote to Mr. Travell.—

Saturday Dec. 6.—

Fine weather. Finishing a Sermon upon love to our neighbour. Heard from my Mother. A funeral at Stert & drank Tea in the Evening with the Jaques's.—

Sunday Dec. 7.—

A fine day, though rather cold except a heavy storm at night. Morning Service at Erchfont & Evening at ~~Deviz~~ Stert, preached upon the love of our neighbour. Dined at Jaques's.

Monday Dec. 8.

Very fine weather. But a violent storm about four o clock. Rode across the Plain to Stonehenge, which gave me very great pleasure, took more than one sketch of it. To Amesbury where is an ancient Seat of the D. of Queensbury pleasant enough, where Gay under the protection of the Dowager Duchess wrote. Returned wet thru' & tired to dinner and went early to bed.

20. Stonehenge; a sketch by Francis Witts.

21. Stonehenge.

Tuesday Sep. 9$^{th.}$—

Very wet all the morning, yet rode to Devizes to hurry workmen & carry letters to the Post to my Mother & M$^{r.}$ Matthews. Heard from the former | & wrote a second letter & heard from Margaret. Composing a second discourse upon Love of our Neighbour. Walked about in the Evening.

Wednesday Sep. 10$^{th.}$—

Several heavy showers during the day. Never left the premises. Composing a Sermon upon the love of our Neighbour. Wrote in the Evening to my Father.

Thursday Sep. 11$^{th.}$—

A Showery morning but fine afternoon & Evening, tho' cold. Busy in the House & Gardens &c. M$^{r.}$ Mayo called upon me. Walked in the Evening over to Jaques & smoked, drank tea, & supped with him.—

Friday Sep. 12$^{th.}$—

Beautiful weather. Rode to Eastcott, to the dwelling House of the late M$^{r.}$ Axford to join the cavalcade upon ~~Mr.~~ occasion of his burial. The gentlemen assembled were Mess$^{rs.}$ Lancaster, Burges, Smith, Sainsbury &c. Preceded the Hearse & mourning Coach to the Grave after taking refreshment. Buried a child afterwards. Lancaster dined with me. Rode over to Devizes to the Castle to meet my dear Parents. Had the chagrin to find my Father much indisposed: in consequence of which slept there.

Saturday Sep. 13$^{th.}$—

Very fine weather. After breakfast returned | to Erchfont leaving my Father much better. After writing to M$^{r.}$ Travell, & Mess$^{rs.}$ Edwards, returned to Devizes & back in the Evening.

22. Stonehenge.

Sunday Sep. 14th.—

Very fine weather, but cold in the afternoon. Morning Service at Stert, & afternoon Service at Erchfont: at both preached upon the Love of our Neighbour & sat with Mrs. Jaques between; at home in the Evening.—

Monday Sept. 15.

Very fine weather, but rather cold. Drove over early to Devizes. Wrote to Mr. Dry, whom I had heard from. Brought my Mother to Erchfont to make arrangements & conveyed her back. Returned to dinner. (Called in the forenoon, upon Mrs. Hillier & Harriet, met Miss M. Gibbs &c.) Wrote to Margaret.

Tuesday Sept. 16.

Very fine weather. Composing a Sermon upon our relative Social Duties. Never left the Premises.—

Wednesday Sept. 17.

Beautiful weather. Composing a Sermon upon our relative social Duties. Drove to Devizes to reconduct my Mother to Erchfont. My Father walked & they took up their abode in the Vicarage for the first time. Jaques & a Mr. Jones of Enford, Steward for the Widows & Orphans of the Clergy of the diocese, called. Rode & walked a little in the Evening. |

Thursday Sept. 18th.—

Fine forenoon, & wet afternoon. Composing & transcribing a Sermon upon our relative Duties to individuals. Never left the premises.

Friday Sept. 19.

Symptoms of rain in the morning, but fine weather afterwards. Transcribing a Sermon upon our relative Duties to individuals. Drove my Mother to Devizes upon various

Errands. Heard from Mr. Travell, & Dowell, who gives me hope of seeing him at Devizes tomorrow. Walked in the Evening.

Saturday Sept. 20.—

Very fine weather. Finished transcribing a Sermon. Variously employed in the Morning. After an early dinner, drove to Devizes to meet & bring Dowell, who arrived by the London Coach to my great satisfaction, obliged to lodge him at the Village Inn.

Sunday Sept. 21.—

Equally fine weather. My Dear Friend indulged me with a Sermon of my own upon human life, being his first exhibition since his ordination by the Bish. of Bristol ~~lately~~ last Sunday, extremely well. My Father too indisposed | to go to Church. I read prayers. During the interval, before we walked to Stert, Mrs. Poore of Wedhampton, & her Sister, Mrs. Smith, Mrs. Legge, & Miss Frusler called upon my Mother at Stert, Dowell read prayers, & I preached upon the duty of Children to parents. Visited Mrs. Jaques of course. After dinner took a walk with Dowell in the Fields.

Monday Sept. 22.—

Very fine weather. Dowell resolved to return & I conveyed him by ½ past 7 to Devizes, whence he departed in the Coach. Composing a Sermon upon our relative duties to individuals. Walked a little in the Evening with my Mother.—

Tuesday Sept. 23d.—

Beautiful weather after a little morning rain. Composing a Sermon upon our relative duties to individuals. Drove my Mother upon the Andover road; extremely pretty, by Wedhampton, Conock, Cherrington, Marden, Charlton, nearly to Ruttsall.

Wednesday Sept. 24.—

Very fine weather. Rode to the Clergy meeting at Devizes held annually for the purpose of raising a fund for the orphans & widows of the Clergy of the County of Wilts, to which I subscribed my quota. Conversed chiefly with Ward of Bradford Dr. Skinner, Ledyard, C. Mayo, &c. met Mrs. Hillier &c. Heard from Willson.—

Witts Family Papers F306

Journal.—

Thursday Sept. 25. Vicarage, Erchfont, Wilts.

Very fine weather. Walked with my Father & Mother to pay a morning visit to Mrs. Poore of Wedhampton, and her Sister, Mrs. Smith, the former my parishioner; the walk pleasant, the place comfortable, the Lady's manners agreeable. Married a couple in the forenoon.—

Friday Sept. 26.—

Very fine weather. Wrote to Mr. Travell, and a letter upon George's business. Drove my Mother to Devizes; called upon Mrs. Hillier, besides whom & Harriet we met Miss Gibbs: walked with M^rs.^ & Miss Spalding, with whom I had an explanation respecting an alteration in the Lady's verses falsely attributed to me. Wrote to Mr. Gaisford upon the same subject.

Saturday Sept. 27.—

Very fine weather. Mrs. Butcher called.

Sunday Sept. 28th.—

Very fine weather. Drove my Mother to morning service at Stert, where I preached upon the Duties of subjects to their lawful Governors. Called upon Mrs. Jaques & Miss Gale. Baptized a child. At the | Evening service here preached upon the Duties of children to parents. Walked with my Father & Mother in the Evening.

23. Urchfont Church; a sketch by Francis Witts.

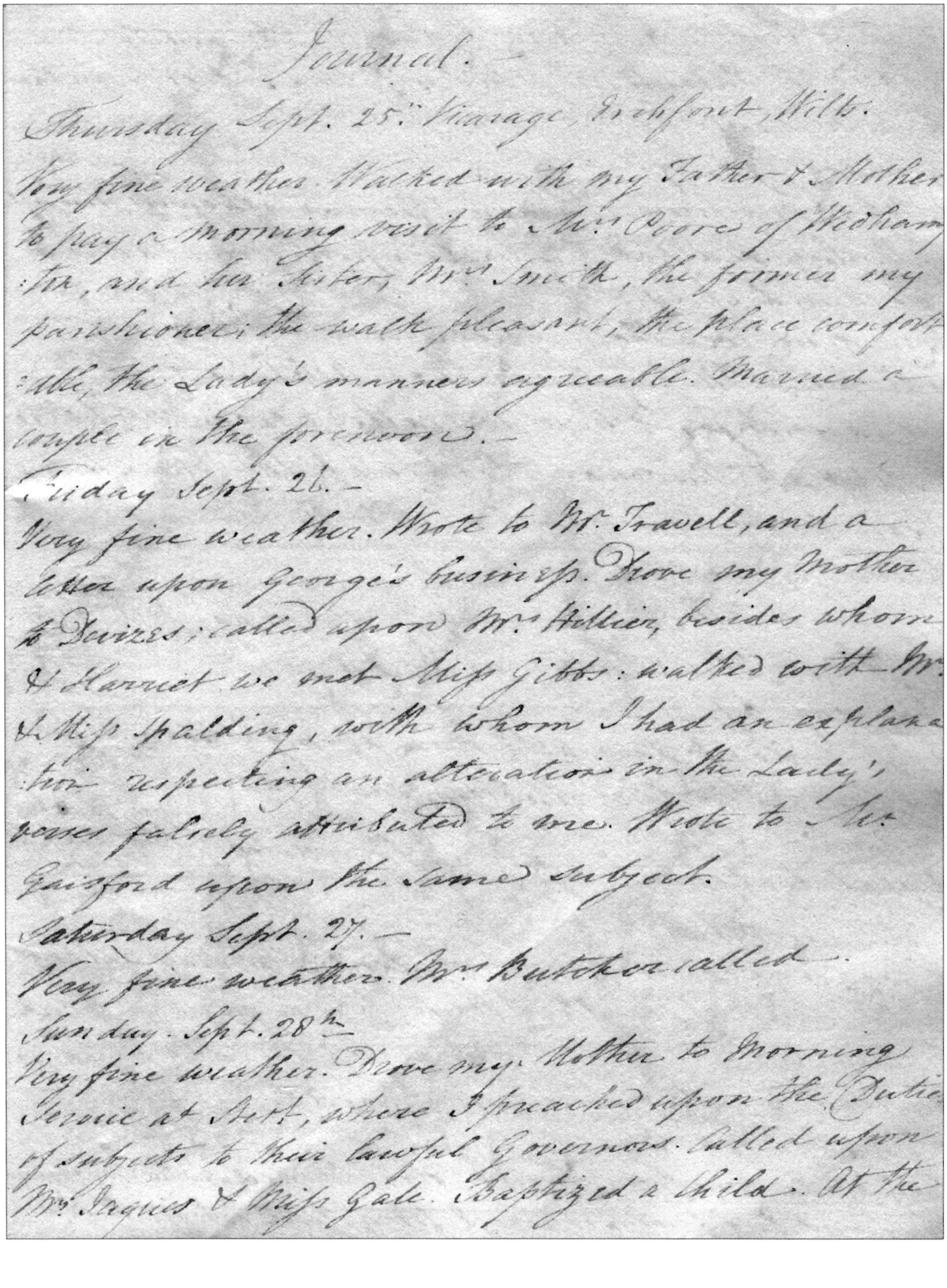

Journal.—

Thursday Sept. 25th Vicarage, Urchfont, Wilts.

Very fine weather. Walked with my Father & Mother to pay a morning visit to Mrs Poore of Wedhampton, and her Sister, Mrs Smith, the former my parishioner; the walk pleasant, the place comfortable, the Lady's manners agreeable. Married a couple in the forenoon.—

Friday Sept. 26.—

Very fine weather. Wrote to Mr Travell, and a letter upon George's business. Drove my Mother to Devizes; called upon Mrs Hillier, besides whom & Harriet we met Miss Gibbs: walked with Mrs & Miss Spalding, with whom I had an explanation respecting an altercation in the Lady's pews falsely attributed to me. Wrote to Mr Gaisford upon the same subject.

Saturday Sept. 27.—

Very fine weather. Mrs Butcher called.

Sunday. Sept. 28th

Very fine weather. Drove my Mother to Morning Service at Stert, where I preached upon the Duties of subjects to their lawful Governors. Called upon Mrs Ingles & Miss Gale. Baptized a child. At the

Monday Sept. 29.—

A foggy morning, & heavy & frequent showers throughout the day. Walked to Devizes upon several errands.

Tuesday Sept. 30.—

Very fine weather. Called upon the Jaques's & rode with Mr. Jaques through Ashlington to All Cannings where we called upon Mr. Davis & Mr. & Mrs. Newman, looked at the Church &c. Heard from Margaret.

Wednesday October 1.—

Very fine weather after a foggy morning. Drove my Mother to Devizes after various errands.

Thursday Oct. 2.—

A less brilliant day, with rain at night. Rode for two hours thro' Cherrington, Marden &c.

Friday Oct. 3d.—

A good deal of rain fell in the course of the day.

Saturday Oct. 4.

A foggy morning: a good deal of rain falling in the course of the day. Wrote to Margaret. Rode to Market Lavington, returned over the plain. Received a letter from Mr. Travell.

Sunday Oct. 5.—

Fine mild weather, though overclouded. The morning service at Erchfont, where I preached upon the | Duties of subjects to their lawful Governors. Evening service at Stert where I preached upon our duties to Spiritual Pastors & Masters. Called as usual upon Mrs. Jaques.—

Monday Oct. 6.—

Beautiful weather. Wrote to Mr. Travell & Mr. Edwards of Bristol upon business, & to Major Sandby respecting a Servant. Drove my Mother to Devizes & transacted various necessary matters. Met & conversed with Mr. & Mrs. J. Tylee, Mrs. Hillier & Harriet &c.

Tuesday Oct. 7th.—

Very fine weather. Drove to Devizes; after transacting some business, repaired to Mr. John Tylee's to dinner, whither my Father & Mother soon came, where we had a very pleasant party, Mrs. Hillier & Harriet, Mr. Gent, Mr. Gaisford, & in the Evening Miss Tylee. My Father & Mother slept at Mr. Tylee's, Mr. Gent accomodated me in his house.

Wednesday Oct. 8.—

Very pleasant weather. Before breakfast walking in Gent's gardens in the town with him & old Tylee &c. Breakfasted with the John Tylee's very pleasantly. My Father walked home, before I drove home my Mother, we walked a pleasant party through Newlands &c. I conversed almost wholly with Harriet Hillier & felt grieved to part for perhaps a very

24. Sketch of bridge and house; by Francis Witts.

long time from so interesting, sensible & unfortunate a young woman. Mrs. Hillier & her Daughter set out for Ireland upon Friday. Wrote to Dowell. |

Thursday Oct. 9.

A dull & cold forenoon: the afternoon more pleasant. Set out after an early breakfast to call upon Frank Merewether at Calne: Rode through Devizes to call at the Post, over Roundway Hill & Buckhampton Downs, by Blackford Street & Blacklands to Calne a manufacturing Town, & Borough, not inconsiderable, with a church of handsome exterior, the gift of wch. is with the Canvas of Windsor. A canal comes up to the Town. My acquaintance was not at home: returned by the Turnpike road to Devizes, within sight of Bowood, & Hands House, near Bromham, & through Rowde; met in Devizes, a Mr. Jollife of Ashton, whom I accompanied upon his journey to Conock Gate whence I returned to Wedhampton with Mrs. Poore & Mrs. Warrener. Walked with my Father & Mother.

Friday. Oct. 10.—

Very fine weather. Rode to Market Lavington, West Lavington, & Littleton upon one or two errands. Jaques called in the forenoon.—

Saturday Oct. 11.

Dull weather, & more cold. Walked with my Father & alone: not far from the Village.—

Sunday. Oct. 12.

Very fine weather. Drove my Mother to Stert to the morning service, where my Father met us, having walked; I preached a Sermon upon the shortness of human life: called upon Mrs. Jaques. A very large | Congregation in the afternoon at Erchfont, being the Feast; I preached upon the Duties owing to Teachers & spiritual Pastors.—

Monday Oct. 13.

Very fine weather. Christened three Children. Rode by Crookwood through intricate lanes to Devizes upon various errands. Met M^r. J. Tylee & M^rs. J. Tylee. Upon my return met Jaques & walked with him & with Lediard & another Gentleman. Called at Jaques's, he walked on with me to the Bell. Wrote to Smith.

Tuesday Oct. 14.—

Stormy weather. Rain at distant intervals, & in the Evening. The mid-day very fine. Gardening all the forenoon—

Wednesday. Oct. 15.

A mild & dull day. Walked to Devizes upon various errands. Heard from Dowell. Jaques called in the forenoon. Wrote letters upon business to M^r. Adamson & to Horne. Called in the morning upon M^rs. Compton.

Thursday Oct. 16.

Very cold, windy & hazy. Rode over the plain & returned by the Andover Road.—

Friday Oct. 17.

Very fine weather. Drove my Mother to Devizes upon various errands. Called upon M^rs. Spalding & her Daughter. In the Evening wrote to George.

Saturday Oct. 18.—

A fine cold day. Walked with my Father & Mother in the village. Drove my Father upon the Andover Road as far as Rushall.

Sunday Oct. 19.—

Very fine cool weather. The Sacrament being administered at Erchfont Church by Jaques, I took his duty at All Cannings & Ashlington, twice at the former place & once at the latter. Repeating twice the same | Sermon upon Repentance. Called upon Davis & Jacob Giddings, an opulent farmer at Ashlington. Returned home to dinner at nearly six o clock.—

Monday Oct. 20th.

The morning very fine, very heavy rain for an hour at mid-day, the Evening lowring. Wrote to Barry at Bristol. Rode to Devizes to the Green Fair, of sheep, cattle, horses, cheese, &c. not very amusing; conversed with Davis &c. Had various errands to make out. Called upon M^rs. Jaques at Stert upon my return.—

Tuesday Oct. 21.

Very heavy rain had fallen in the night & early in the morning & continued in heavy showers throughout the day. M^r. Butcher called. Did not leave the premises.

Wednesday Oct. 22.

Very hard rain had fallen in the night, & continued during the morning, with hardly intermitting showers throughout the day. Rode to Devizes upon various errands. Met by the way the Rev^d. — Foster Minor Canon of Bristol upon his road to his living at Marden; rode from Musteed into Devizes with William Wood. Mrs. Butcher in the Evening gave a rout & supper, at which were present our family the Comptons & Legges: not very unpleasant.

Thursday Oct. 23.

Very fine weather. Walked with my Father & Mother, & called upon one or two Parishioners. Drank tea, played cards, & supped at Mrs. Legges, meeting the Butchers & Comptons & played at Commerce, not wholly disagreeable.

Friday Oct. 24.

A very hard hoar frost early. The day wonderfully fine. After | an early breakfast accompanied Compton upon horseback across the plain to Netheravon the seat of Mr. H. Beech M.P. for Cirencester, to be present at one of his Coarsing meetings. The House spacious & very pleasantly situated upon the edge of the plain. The stables and kennels in the highest perfection. Received very handsomely by Mr. Beech,[1] his Son, Lady & Daughter, walked with the Master round his garden where, in a very short space, we ~~met~~ saw probably more than 100 Hares together. At twelve we took the field with 10 or 11 brace of Greyhounds, more than 20 Gentlemen present, amongst whom were Mr. Pickering & his Lady, Mr. E. Poore, Mr. Dyke, Mr. Gibbs, &c. The sport was admirable, being upon the fallow lands & adjacent Downs, we coursed 12 or 15 hares, most of which afforded excellent sport, & I rode as hard as most people, enjoying it extremely. Leaving off sport at 4 we reached Erchfont before 6 o clock.

Saturday Oct. 25.

Cold damp weather, & a tendency to rain. The Revd. Mr. Peck & Mr. Brabant called. Received a pleasant letter of invitation from C. Mayo, which I answered.—

Sunday Oct. 26.

Very fine weather. Jaques undertook the Sacrament duty at Stert & the afternoon duty at Erchfont, in consequence of which I took his duty at All cannings & Ashlington, where I preached the Discourse, which I have entitled Life a Journey. Mr. Davis absent from home. Called upon Mr. Newman's pleasant family at Cannings & upon Jacob Giddings at Ashlington. Returned to a late dinner & found Mr. & Mrs. Jaques & their neice dining at the Vicarage. Not sorry, when they took their departure. |

Monday Oct. 27.—

Very fine weather. Wrote to Mr. Travell upon business & to Margaret. Drove my Mother to Devizes upon various errands. Met & conversed with Mr. Jaques, Mrs. J. Tylee, Mrs. & Miss Spalding, Chs. Mayo &c.

Tuesday Oct. 28.—

Indifferent showery weather. Met a party to Tea & Supper at Mr. Compton's, the Legg's, Butchers, Mr. W. Keetch & ourselves. Played at Commerce, not unpleasantly. Heard from George.

---

1. This is the same Mr. Hicks Beach that Frank referred to during his walk from Oxford to Clifton in December 1804 when accompanied by William Dowell.

Wednesday Oct. 29.

25. *Charles Mayo, 1750-1829.*

Very fine weather. Dr. & Mrs. & Miss Spalding called upon us & we proceeded together to dine at Mr. C. Mayo's at Stoke, where we made a very agreeable visit. A Postchaise from Lavington conveying us very conveniently. Met Mr. Townsend, R. of Pewsey, & author of a Journey in Spain,[2] Revd. Mr. Pyke, & the Spaldings. Conversed a great deal, & mostly upon literary & political subjects with Mr. Townsend & Mr. Mayo.[3]

Thursday Oct. 30th.—

Very fine weather. Drove my Mother to Littleton to call upon Mrs. Tinker, the road through Lavington being very bad drove round by Devizes & Pottern, the latter part very beautiful. Found Mrs. T. & her whole family of seven daughters at home: the eldest a sweet girl. A Mrs. South with them. Heard from Margaret, Mr. Travell, & Smith.

Friday Oct. 31st.—

A finer day than the appearance of the morning prognosticated: Rain (a little) at night. Miss Tylee called. | Mrs. Compton's, Mrs. Butcher's & Mrs. Legg's families met at the Vicarage to tea, cards & supper; not unpleasant.

Saturday Nov. 1st.

A tendency to rain, but upon the whole a mild & not unpleasant day. Wrote to Mr. Travell, Smith, Cruttwell & Limebeer. Rode to Devizes, called upon the Jaques's at Stert, & upon Miss Tylee; various errands in Town.

Sunday Nov. 2nd.—

A very stormy & rainy forenoon, & very showery afternoon. The morning service at Erchfont, the Evening at Stert. Rode to the latter, calling upon Mrs. Jaques, at both preached upon Wisdom.—

---

2. Joseph Townsend, (1739-1816). Townsend was the vicar of Pewsey but also well known in his time as a physician and geologist. It was in Townsend's house, 29 Pulteney Street, Bath, in 1799 that the noted geologist William Smith dictated to another clerical geologist Revd. Benjamin Richardson, the first chart of geological strata and the fossils they contained. As for Townsend, his tour through Spain in 1791 he published *A Journey Through Spain in the Years 1786 and 1789*, which dealt comprehensively with "topography, mineralogy, soils, agriculture, finance and manners" shocked by the swarms of beggars that he met Townsend was impressed by the fact that population in Spain was visibly growing faster than resources, with dire results for health.

3 Charles Mayo, (1750-1829). Mayo was rector of Huish near Marlborough from 1775 and then succeeded his father, John Mayo as rector of Beechingstoke (Stoke), in 1779, holding both livings until his death. It was at 'Stoke' only two miles from Urchfont, where the diarist met and dined with him. Charles Mayo was said to be a man of great simplicity of character, and was thought to bear a considerable resemblance to Dr. Syntax. As an instance of his absence of mine the story is told that a friend met him one day, deep in thought, walking from Devizes to Beechingstoke with his horse's bridle hung over his arm, from which the beast had flipped its head, without the owner, who had been leading it, becoming aware of its escape, until aroused from is reverie.

Monday Nov. 3$^{d.}$—

The morning very showery, the afternoon fine. Wrote to Margaret.

Tuesday Nov. 4$^{th.}$—

A dull damp day. Wrote to Dowell. In pursuance of an invitation dined with the Mayor & Corporation of Devizes upon occasion of the Election of Members for the Town; M$^{r.}$ Smith & Mr. Estcourt being re-elected.[4] Met a very large & select party & dined at ½ past four in the Town Hall. Conversed chiefly with the M$^{r.}$ Salmons, F. Merewether, M$^{r.}$ Estcourt, M$^{r.}$ C. Lucas, Compton, Jaques &c. As I had my Gig I brought the latter home to save his exposing himself & literally dropped him at his own door.

Wednesday Nov. 5$^{th.}$—

Very fine weather. Drove Mother to Wedhampton in the l vain hope of visiting M$^{rs.}$ Poore, afterwards upon the plain.

Thursday Nov. 6.

Very fine weather. Received two letters from Horne.

Friday Nov. 7.—

Very fine weather. Wrote to Horne. Drove my Father to Devizes upon various errands. Met & conversed with M$^{r.}$ & M$^{rs.}$ J. Tylee, C. Tylee, Miss Tylee, M$^{r.}$ & M$^{rs.}$ M. W. Salmon, Ch. Mayo, M$^{rs.}$ & Miss Spalding &c.

Saturday Nov. 8.—

Very fine weather. Rode to Lavington, Littleton &c. Heard from Dowell.—

Sunday Nov. 9.

Very fine weather. The morning service at Stert whither I rode, calling of course upon M$^{rs.}$ Jaques, the Evening at Erchfont, to which M$^{rs.}$ Tinker's family came, calling upon us, namely M$^{r.}$ & M$^{rs.}$ Tinker, M$^{rs.}$ South, & the two elder Miss Tinkers. Preached at both places upon Contentment, as enforced by the consideration of GOD's unlimited Bounty & his absolute sovereignty.

Monday Nov. 10.

Dull, but fine weather. Drove my Mother to Devizes upon various errands.—

Tuesday Nov. 11.

A dull cold day. M$^{rs.}$ Jaques called.—

Wednesday Nov. 12.—

Very foggy till the Evening. Exercised myself & my Horse upon the plain.

---

4. Joshua Smith, (1732-1819), of Erlestoke Park, near Devizes. Thomas Estcourt, (1748-1818), of Estcourt House, near Tetbury, M.P. for Cricklade, 1790-1806. Estcourt was the father-in-law of Mrs. Sutton's daughter, Eleanor.

26. *Sketch of house; by Francis Witts.*

Thursday Nov. 13th.

Mild fine weather. Drove my Father to call upon Mrs. Poore, & at Mr. Peck's at Rushall; found neither at home. Received letters from Margaret, Mr. Travell & | Dowell.

Friday Nov. 14th.—

A wetting fog throughout the day. Wrote to Margaret & Dowell. A man of business called to search the register. Rode to Devizes upon various errands.—

Saturday Nov. 15.—

A mild day with a tendency to rain. Drove my Mother to Devizes upon various Errands.— From this till the 14th of December was engaged in a visit at Beck House &c.[5] |

Dec. 14. Sunday.

Very wet weather. Morning service at Erchfont: preached there & at Stert upon the attributes of the Deity: called upon Mrs. Jaques.—

Dec. 15th. Monday.

Very wet. Rode to look at a Horse for Dowell. Commenced a Sermon upon the Day of Judgment. Wrote to Dowell, Smith, Horne, Mr. Travell, &c. Called upon the Leggs.

---

5. Frank made a visit to Beck House in Yorkshire to visit Mrs. Backhouse and Margaret. It was the first time they had seen each other since the 7 June 1805. William Dowell stood in for Frank at Urchfont and Stert. Frank left Stert after performing the duty there on his way to Gloucester, proposing to sleep at Gloucester. John the servant returned home in the gig the following day, after having dropped his Master at Gloucester where he was to take the coach. William Dowell arrived in the evening of Saturday 22 November. Agnes records 'a very good sermon from our young friend ...' Dowell arrived each of the two subsequent Saturdays — 29 November and 6 December, the next Saturday, 13 December, saw the return of the lover from Yorkshire.

27. Cottage in Wiltshire; a sketch by Francis Witts.

Dec. 16. Tuesday.

Less wet. Never left the premises & variously engaged. Received a letter from my beloved Margaret.

Dec. 17. Wednesday.—

Very damp, but no decided rain. Rode to Devizes upon various errands.—Wrote to my sweet Margaret.

Dec. 18. Thursday.—

Very damp & now & then rain. Rode to Stert. Called upon Jaques.

Dec. 19. Friday.—

Sunshine & fine open weather. Wrote to M[r.] Horne &c. Drank tea plaid cards & supped at Butcher's: M[rs.] & Miss Legg, Miss Smith, two Brothers of Butcher & ourselves made the party.—

Dec. 20. Saturday.

Very boisterous weather particularly in the afternoon, which confined me to the House. Wrote to M[r.] Adamson.— |

Dec. 21. Sunday.

The forenoon extremely wet & boisterous: the afternoon finer. Morning service at Stert. Called as usual upon M[rs.] Jaques. Preached both there & in the Evening at ~~Stert~~ Erchfont upon the Day of Judgment.

Dec. 22. Monday.—

Damp weather. Rode to Wedhampton & called upon M[rs.] Poore.—

Dec. 23. Tuesday.

Very damp & rainy weather. Heard from Mr. Horne. Never left the premises. Mr. Butcher, his wife, brother Charles & Miss Smith, met Mrs. & Miss Legg to tea, cards & supper at the Vicarage.

Dec. 24. Wednesday.—

A wet morning & very fine afternoon. Rode thro' Cherrington, Patney, Ashlington &c.

Dec. 25th.—Thursday.—

A dull day with some rain. Morning service at Erchfont & Evening at Stert. Preached at both a Sermon adapted to the occasion. Heard from Mr. Travell.—

Dec. 26. Friday.—

A very fine winter's day. Drove my Mother upon the Devizes Road.—

Dec. 27. Saturday.

Very fine weather: hardly a symptom of rain. Drove my Mother to call upon Mr. Warrener at Conock & Mrs. Poore at Wedhampton. Heard from Margaret. |

Dec. 28 Sunday.

Very fine weather. The morning service at Stert, where I called as usual upon Mrs. Jaques, the afternoon at Erchfont: preached at both a Sermon adapted to the close of the year.—

Dec. 29 Monday.

A rainy morning, afternoon fine. Rode & called upon the Jaques's. Wrote to Margaret.—

Dec. 30th.—Tuesday.—

A damp morning & fine afternoon. Walked, but not far from the village.

Dec. 31st. Wednesday.

A north east wind & cold day: rain in the afternoon. Rode to Devizes. Called upon Mr. J. Tylee; met & walked with Thring. |

1807

Vicarage Erchfont.

Thursday. Jan. 1st.

A hoar frost, clear & pleasant weather. Transcribed part of a Sermon upon Contentment as enforced by the Considerations of GOD's general & particular providence. Prepared for the compilation of another upon the Conversion of St. Paul. Studied Millar's Historical View of the English Government, the Saxon æra.[6] Walked with my Father & Mother & alone. Called upon

6. John Millar, (1735-1801), *An Historical View of the English Government.* (1801).

two Villagers. Received a letter upon business from Mr. Travell. Compiling a chronological view of English Architecture from the publication, entitled Essays on Gothic Architecture, being those of the Revd. J. Milner, the Revd. — Bentham, Dr. Warton & Captain Grose.[7]

Friday Jan. 2d.

A strong hoar frost, cold & hazy weather: but a fine winter day. Wrote letters upon business to Mr. Travell & Mr. Horne. Drove my Mother to Devizes. Called at | different shops; without meeting them upon Mrs. Spalding & Mrs. James Gent: found Mrs. J. Tylee at home, with the Revd. Michael Wyatt & Miss Anstie. Conversed with Mr. Brabant, Mr. Wood &c. Had a funeral & a churching upon my return. Began Mad. de Genlis Novel, rash Vows for the second time. Busy on the same architectural studies as upon the preceding Evening. Began also some notes respecting the Alien Priories & their possessions.

Saturday Dec. 3d.—[8]

A hoar frost, & very fine day. Transcribing a Sermon as upon Thursday. Accompanied my Father upon a walk to call upon Mrs. Tinker's family at Littleton, where we were very pleasantly received by a house overwhelmed by sickness. Went by Sander's Lane, returned through Lavington, Easterton & Eastcott. Reading Mad. de Genlis Rash Vows. Marking Extracts from Millar upon the English Government &c.—

Sunday. Dec. 4.—

A cold day, a suspension of the Frost. Undertook Jaques's Duties, as he performed the Sacrament duty at Erchfont. Rode to All-cannings by Cherrington & Patney, preached a Sermon containing Reflections | adapted to the Commencement of a year; the same at Ashlington, where I found there was little hope of Jacob Gidding's life. Called upon Mr. Newman's family at Cannings. After an Evening service there by candle light, returned, rather fatigued to a late dinner. Read Mad. de Genlis Rash Vows &c.—

Monday Dec. 5.

A frost in the morning, suspended during the day, renewed at night. Transcribing a Sermon, as upon Saturday. Finished Mad. de Genlis Rash Vows. Drove my Mother to call upon Mrs. Jaques & Miss Gales.—

Tuesday Dec. 6.

A hard frost & very fine weather. Reading Millar's Historical View. Transcribing a Sermon as yesterday. Composing another upon the Conversion of St. Paul. Walked to Easticott to call upon Leonard Tinker, who could not see me. Making Extracts from Millar &c.—

Wednesday Dec. 7th.—

A hard frost, & fine weather. Transcribing a Sermon upon our Duty to our neighbour.

---

7. *Essays on English Architecture*, (1802).
8. From Saturday 3 January through to Thursday 8 January Witts writes 'Dec.' instead of 'Jan' and does not correct his manuscript even after he realises the error.

Compiling another as yesterday. Rode to exercise my horse as far as Wedhampton. Read Millar's Historical View. Made Extracts from Millar &c.—

Thursday Dec. 8th.—

A frost, but upon the decline & a dull day. Transcribing | & composing Sermons as yesterday. Studying Millar's Historical View, & Abbé Fleury's Manners of the Israelites.[9] Mrs. Sutton called but I did not see her.—In the Evening looking over old papers.—

Friday Jan. 9th.—

A thaw, the forenoon fine the afternoon misty. Transcribing & compiling Sermons as yesterday. Rode to Devizes: executed some Commissions: called upon Mr. W. Salmon. In the Evening looking over old papers. Reading Millar's Historical View.—

Saturday Jan. 10th.—

A cold day, rather thick, without frost. Transcribing a Sermon as yesterday, & preparing to compose another upon the Ministry of St. Paul. Studied Millar & the Abbé Fleury. Examined old papers, prepared for Sunday's duty, made Extracts from Millar &c.—

Sunday Jan. 11th.—

A very unpleasant day, raw & a thick fog. Undertook Jaques's duty, as ~~yester~~ Sunday last. After morning service at All cannings, where I preached upon Wisdom, christened a new born infant in the Mother's room. At Ashlington, met Mr. Brabant &c. & found Jacob Giddings greatly recovered, & almost out of danger. Preached there as at Allcannings, whither I returned to the Evening service, and reached home to a late dinner considerably fatigued.

Monday Jan. 12th.—

A cold, but not very damp day. Transcribing a Sermon | as upon Saturday, & composing another upon the Ministry of St. Paul. Churched a woman & christened her child. Studied Millar. Wrote to Margaret. Made extracts from Millar &c.—

Tuesday Jan. 13th.—

Fine but cold & windy. Transcribing a Sermon upon the Conversion of St. Paul. Arranging Books &c. Drove my Father to Devizes upon various Errands. Began the Nun & her Daughter a novel.[10]Arranging Letters, & making Extracts &c. in the Evening. Suffered by a head ach.—

Wednesday Jan. 14th.—

A frost in the morning. Snow began falling about 11 in the forenoon, continued without interruption till 5 in the afternoon, when it laid very deep. Engaged from 11 to 4 in attending the funeral of the late Mr. L. Tinker from Eastcott to West Lavington, which was handsome & expensive, but the weather was extremely unfavourable. Among the Gentlemen present

---

9. Abbé Claude Fleury, *The Manners of the Israelites*. First published in French in 1681, an English language edition was published in Newcastle in 1786.
10. Helen Craik? *The Nun and her Daughter; or, Memoirs of the Courville Family.* (1805).

were Mess$^{rs.}$ D. & B. Compton, Williams, William Tinker, Smith, Garent, Sainsbury &c. Read the Nun & her Daughter. Making Extracts in the Evening.—

Thursday Jan. 15$^{th.}$—

A very hard frost in the morning seemed to promise a duration of the snow; but a thaw rapidly came on attended with heavy rain in the Evening. Transcribing a Sermon as upon Tuesday, & composing another as upon Monday. ~~Wrote~~ Read the Nun & her Daughter & Fleury's Manners of the Israelites. Buried a Corpse. | Making Extracts from Millar &c. in the Evening.—

Friday Jan. 16$^{th.}$—

Very fine mild weather, with some sunshine. The snow entirely dissipated by the Rain & thaw. Transcribing & composing Sermons, as yesterday. Rode to Devizes, had a passing conversation with M$^{rs.}$ John Tylee, Miss Tylee, Bernis, D$^{r.}$ Compton &c. Called at Ekkelhampton to enquire after Jacob Giddings, of whom I heard a good report from his Daughter. Read the Nun & her Daughter. Millar's Historical view, from which I made some extracts and arranged some papers.

Saturday Jan. 17$^{th.}$—

A rainy morning & Evening: the interval fine. Transcribing & composing Sermons as yesterday. Finished the Nun & her Daughter. Studied Millar's Historical View. Began Sir W. Forbes's Life of D$^{r.}$ Beattie.[11] Preparing for Sunday's duty & arranging Papers.—

Sunday Jan. 18$^{th.}$—

Fine weather, & cold. The morning service at Erchfont. Preached a Sermon upon Contentment, enforced by the Consideration of GOD's general & particular providence. M$^{rs.}$ Legg & Miss Legg called. At Stert called upon M$^{rs.}$ Jaques as usual; prepared for visiting Salisbury tomorrow, during the Evening; began Clara Reeves Memoirs of Sir Roger de Clarendon,[12] I read the Life of D$^{r.}$ Beattie.

Monday Jan 19$^{th.}$

A frost in the morning; cold weather; turned to rain which after two o clock was unremitting. Visited Salisbury; driving a Parishioner's Son thither to | school; the road over the plain dull & cold, but good, although little passing. Took Hay & water at the Druid's Head, a solitary Public House the only habitation, except the turnpike gate, between Erchfont & Salisbury; the approach & coup d'oeil of the city & Old Sarum &c. are fine. A moderate Inn & stabling; called upon M$^{r.}$ Bowsher the Bp's. Register, respecting the nomination business without much success. Called at D$^{r.}$ Evans's where I was not admitted;[13] passed an hour & half very much to my satisfaction in viewing the Cathedral; perambulated the Close & other parts of the Town in the Evening by moonlight. Dined alone & passed a solitary Evening.—

---

11. Sir William Forbes, *An Account of the Life and Writings of James Beattie.* (1805).
12. Clara Reeve, (1729-1807), *The Memoirs of Sir Roger de Clarendon.* (1793).
13. The father of Jem Evans, Frank's college friend.

28. Salisbury.

Tuesday Jan 20th.—
A fine morning, the noon cold & stormy. After breakfast again surveyed the Cathedral & Close, & part of the Town, the Square & the Council House very handsome. St. Thomas's Church Gothic of a very rich style, the rest of the Town I thought poor, & the Canals apparently neither ornamental, nor convenient. Returned to Erchfont to dinner over the Plain. Met John Davis upon the road. Read Clara Reeves Sir Roger de Clarendon, & Sir W. Forbes's life of Dr. Beattie. Preparing a letter respecting my nomination to the Bishop of Salisbury. Heard from my friend Round. |

Wednesday Jan 21.—
A day of unceasing rain, which in the Evening turned to Snow, but not heavy. Finished a letter to the Bishop of Salisbury, wrote to Round, & to Mr. Travell. Read the Memoirs of Sir Roger de Clarendon, & Sir W. Forbes's life of Dr. Beattie, from which I made Extracts in the Evening &c.

Thursday Jan 22.—
A slight morning frost, almost unceasing rain & snow till Evening, but the latter dissolving. Finished composing a Sermon upon the Ministry of St. Paul. Finished Sir Roger de Clarendon. Began Mad. de Genlis Historical Novel—Mad. de Maintenon. Continued Sir W. Forbes's life of Beattie. Made Extracts from it &c. in the Evening.

Friday Jan 23d.—
A frost in the morning & very fine winter day. Transcribing a Sermon upon the Conversion of St. Paul. Preparing for another upon the Powers of Conscience. Rode to Eastcott, & called

29. Huntsman & dogs.

upon the Widow Tinker, & to Littleton upon M^rs. Tinker, her Daughters &c. where I made a pleasant visit. Read Mad. de Maintenon, the Life of D^r. Beattie, & Voltaire's Philosophie de l'Histoire.[14] Arranged papers & began to remodel my foreign journal.[15]

Saturday Jan. 24.

A hoar frost, not out of the ground till near one o clock, a very | fine day. After breakfast rode to meet M^r. Edwards's Foxhounds with Butcher & Keetch near Kingston's Copse; for two hours the scent laid very bad & one fox was lost in Cover. M^r. Tinker, M^r. Edwards, M^r. Eldridge &c. present. Miss Tinker, M^rs. Hayward &c. surveying the progress of the hounds. Found at last in Park Copse & had a noble burst, across two turnpike roads right an End almost without check to Stoke Park; where we lost Reynard in M^rs. Smith's plantations. Very hard riding, bad leaps, & heavy country: but the Grey did wonders. Recovering the fox was found impossible, & I left the party with Butcher, returned thro' the beautiful village of Stoke & by M^r. Smith's elegant Mansion, thro' little Chiverell, Littleton &c., & home by Lodge Lawn. Received a letter from the Bishop of Sarum; read D^r. Beattie's life & la Philosophie de l'Histoire; prepared for tomorrow's duty & remodelled my foreign Tour.

Sunday Jan 25th.—

A frost, & thick wetting fog till sunset. The morning service at Stert, preached upon the Conversion of S^t. Paul. Called as usual at M^rs. Jaques's: preached the same Sermon in the Evening at Erchfont. Remodelling my foreign Journal in the Evening.—

---

14. Voltaire, (François Marie Arouet), (1694-1778), *Philosophie de l'Histoire*, (1770).
15. The Journal was the narrative of the tour in Germany, 1798-1800, *Witts Family Papers, F156*.

Monday Jan. 26.—

A hoar frost in the morning; afterwards a very fine day. Wrote to Bishop Douglas. Rode to Devizes, called upon Miss Tylee, with whom I found M^rs. J. Tylee & M^rs. Gent. Made a pleasant visit. Conversed with | Jaques &c. In the Evening remodelled my foreign Journal &c. Read Voltaire Philosophie de l'Histoire.—

Tuesday Jan. 27.

A cold east wind, but no frost. Transcribing a Sermon upon the Ministry of S^t. Paul: compiling another upon the Power of Conscience. Walked in the Village & near it. Read Sir W. Forbes's Life of D^r. Beattie. In the Evening remodelled my foreign Journal. Heard from Margaret.

Wednesday Jan. 28.—

A frosty morning: a tendency to rain in the afternoon; a dull day. Transcribing a Sermon & composing another as yesterday. Walked to the foot of Redhorn hill. Read Sir W. Forbes's Life of D^r. Beattie. Remodelled my foreign Journal.—

Thursday Jan 29th.—

A foggy, raw day. Finished Sir Will. Forbes's Life of D^r. Beattie. Received an adverse letter from Bishop Douglas, & a letter from M^r. Travell. Remodelled my foreign journal.—Rode for an hour in the forenoon upon the plain &c.—

Friday Jan 30th.—

No frost but a cold morning; the day improved as it advanced. Wrote to Margaret, & to Smith. Rode to Devizes, conversed with Jaques, M^rs. J & Miss Tylee, M^r. W. Salmon &c. Heard from Dowell. Read Voltaire's Philosophie de l'Histoire. Transcribed a Sermon as Wednesday. Remodelled my foreign journal &c..

Saturday Jan. 31st.—

A very fine winters day. More than one storm passed over | our heads, a shower fell in the afternoon, & heavy rain in the Evening. Drove my mother to Devizes, after having written to M^r. Travell & M^r. Horne. Heard from M^r. ~~Harr~~ ^Adamson upon business. Called upon Miss Tylee. Conversed with M^r. Ledyard &c. Read Voltaire's Philosophie de l'Histoire: began the Life of Lord Herbert of Cherbury.[16] Prepared for to-morrow's duty & remodelled my foreign journal.

Sunday Feb. 1st.—

A little snow had fallen during the night, & a very hard frost commenced; the day was very cold, but the sun shone. Read a reflection of Sturm, & three Papers in the Spectator of Addison's &c.[17] Morning service at Erchfont: preached upon the Ministry of S^t. Paul,

16. Edward Herbert, Lord Herbert of Cherbury, (1583-1648). The work was autobiographical but contained much of interest from the early seventeenth century. It was first published in 1764.
17. Joseph Addison, (1672-1719). The papers by Addison in the *Spectator* were published between 1711 and 1714. The extracts read may have been *Pleasures of the Imagination.*

& at Stert in the afternoon; called upon Mrs. Jaques. Finished the Life of Lord Herbert of Cherbury. Began Storch's Picture of Petersburgh.[18] Remodelling my foreign journal.

Monday Feb. 2d.—

A very hard frost. A tendency to snow which subsided in heavy & constant rain till the Evening. Similar Employments before breakfast as yesterday. Composing a Sermon upon the duties of Parents to Children. Wrote to Mr. Travell & to Mr. Adamson. Read Storch's Picture of Petersburg. Remodelled my foreign journal.

Tuesday Feb. 3d.—

A morning frost: a tendency to snow in showers, but clear weather with sunshine till the Evening when some rain fell; & at night the sky was clear. Employed before breakfast in the same routine. Composing a Sermon ~~expand~~ as yesterday. Walked in the Village & to the | foot of Redhorn Hill. Read Storch's Picture of Petersburg. Prepared myself for the duty of visiting the sick by reading the Comment upon the Visitation by Comber & the first visit in Dr. Mants Enlarged office for the Visitation. Making notes for my essay on Duelling from Lord Herbert of Cherbury's Life.—

Wednesday Feb. 4th.—

A very raw cold day, much small rain; & the weather extremely unpleasant. Engaged before Breakfast as usual. Had much satisfaction in visiting an aged & sick woman at farmer Pyle's, to pray with her.—Composing a Sermon, as yesterday. Buried a poor boy, who had lost his life by a neglected fracture of the skull. Read Storch's Picture of Petersburg. Collected notes for my Essay on Duelling. Read the second Visit of the Sick, in Dr. Mant's Office of Visitation. Remodelled my foreign journal.—

Thursday Feb. 5.—

A violent storm early in the morning; the day cold & raw with a tendency to rain, which fell in the Evening. At my usual early occupations. Visited & prayed with a poor sick woman. Rode to Devizes, where I had several errands: particularly as commissioner to the Administration of Leonard Tinker's Effects, which took me to Mr. W. Salmon's where I met W. Tinker, Danl. Compton &c. Also met & conversed there with Mr. Estcourt, Salmon Junr., Eldrige, Tom Tylee &c. In the Evening wrote to George. Finished my Sermon upon the Duties of Parents. Made extracts from the Life of Lord | Herbert of Cherbury.—

Friday Feb. 6th.

Very raw, unpleasant weather: a frost in the morning; a tendency to rain, which was confirmed in the afternoon. Transcribed a Sermon upon the Duties of Parents. Called upon Mrs. Poore & her sister Mrs. Smith at Wedhampton, whither I walked. Baptized an infant. Made collections for the Essay on Duelling & read Storch's Picture of Pertersburg.—

Saturday Feb. 7.—

A sprinkling of snow & a hard frost early; the day very cold & raw. Mr. Tinker called early

18. Henry Storch, *Picture of Petersburgh*, from the German. (1801).

to tempt me hunting; but without success. Transcribed a Sermon as yesterday. Called upon Daniel Compton, rode upon discovery through Marden, Stoke, Wilcot &c. Read a Sermon of D^r. Blair's upon the true honour of man. Made collections for my Essay on Duelling, & preparations for tomorrow's duty. Read Storch's Picture of Petersburg.—

Sunday Feb. 8.—

A most turbulent, cold rainy morning: the afternoon less wet. Fulfilled my customary morning task. The morning service at Stert; preached upon the duties of Parents. Called upon M^rs. Jaques, with whom I found Miss Hitchcock. At Erchfont, preached the same Discourse, christened a child, & churched the Mother. Reading Storch's ~~History~~ Picture of Petersburg, the 2^d. Vol. of Mad de Maintenon by Mad. de Genlis, part of Mant's Visitation Office, & began Lord Lyttelton's Life of Henry the 2^d.—[19]

Monday Feb. 9. |

A very rainy & stormy day throughout, much wind & very cold. My avocations before breakfast as customary. Read Mad. de Genlis Mad. de Maintenon. Prepared for writing a Lent Sermon upon Meditation. Baptized an infant & visited one or two villagers. Read Millar's Historical View & Lord Lyttelton's Life of Henry the 2^d.—

Tuesday Feb. 10.—

A day without rain, but very cold, & a strong Northwest wind; much rain in the Evening. Pursued my customary Morning Exercises. Compiling a Sermon as yesterday. Rode upon the plain. Received letters from M^r. Travell, M^r. Horne, M^r. Dawkins & Margaret. Read Mad. de Genlis' Mad. de Maintenon, Millar's Historical View, & Lord Lyttelton's History of the R. of Henry the 2^d. Visited in the forenoon Dame North.

Wednesday. Feb. 11.—

A strong wind, & cold air with a tendency to rain. At my customary morning avocations. Compiling a Sermon as yesterday. Wrote to Messrs. Dawkins & Horne. Dined at Wedhampton not unpleasantly with M^rs. Poore & M^rs. Smith.

Thursday. Feb. 12.

Very fine weather. Well employed in the morning as usual. Finished a Sermon upon Meditation. Wrote to M^r. Travell. Rode to Devizes. Heard from Smith & M^r. Travell. Read Millar & Lord Lyttelton.

Friday Feb. 13th.

A fine day, but rather cold. Wrote to Bishop Douglas. Drove my Mother as far as Uphaven. Strolled about the premises. Transcribing my Sermon upon Medi- | -tation. Read Lord Lyttelton.

---

19. George, Lord Lyttelton, (1708-1773). *History of Henry II* . (1767). George, 1st Lord Lyttelton was the father-in-law of Frank's aunt, Apphia, Lady Lyttelton.

Saturday Feb 14th.

Fine weather, though cloudy & rather cold, having been a slight frost in the morning. Transcribing a Sermon as yesterday: Walking near the village & calling upon our neighbour Gilbert. Read Storch's Picture of Petersurg. Preparing for tomorrow's duty.

Sunday Feb. 15th.—

Very fine weather. The morning service at Erchfont, where I had nearly forty Catechumens & churched a woman: I ~~also~~ preached upon the duty of Meditation. Mrs. Tinker of Littleton & her two daughters were among my congregation & called upon us after Church. At Stert called upon Mrs. Jaques, preached the same Sermon, & dined with the Gales meeting Mr. Jaques, Dimond &c. A funeral in the Evening. Read some of Sterm's reflections, of Storch's Petersburg, and began Gersner's Gedichte. Heard from Mr. Adamson & Mr. Auriol.—

Monday Feb. 16.

Misty in the morning and afternoon; the midday & Evening fine. Wrote to Mr. Auriol & to Dowell. Drove my Mother to call upon Mrs. Poore. Read Gersner's Gedichte. Began Dr. Dodd's Novel: the Sisters. Read Lord Lyttleton's Henry the 2d. Finished a Sermon upon Conscience.—Read Storch's Picture of Petersburg.—

Tuesday Feb. 17.—

A fine day, but overclouded & cold, with a slight tendency to rain: snow & heavy rain came on at night. Preparing a Sermon for the Fast day. Read Dr. Dodd's sisters, Gersner's Gedichte &c. Walked to Stert. Called upon the Gales & Mrs. Jaques. Received letters from Mr. Hodgson, Sec. to the Bp. of Salisb. & Mr. Horne, the former summoning me | to ordination in Town Sunday next. Wrote to Margaret & to Hatchett's; compiling in haste my Fast day Sermon.—

Wednesday Feb. 18.—

After a tempestuous night a very hard frost, & slight snow: the day clear & sunny, but very cold, in the afternoon a slight inclination to Snow. Rode forth to get Erchfont served during my absence & a testimonial to shew the Bp. Accomplished the former by calling upon Mr. Lancaster at Patney, the latter by waiting upon Jaques, Lediard, & Higginson. Heard from Mr. Travell. Dined at Mr. Tinker's at Littleton & passed the Evening very pleasantly, going in the Lavington Chaise, met Mr. & Mrs. Richards, Mr. Bafret, Mr. Bernard, Mr. Eldridge &c. Cards in the Evening & Miss Tinker very handsome.

The next day I repaired to Windsor & London for the purpose of ordination, which being accomplished, I returned to Erchfont upon Wed. Feb. 25. |

Sunday March 8.—

The weather less cold, & more sun. Morning Service at Erchfont. Preached upon false Conscience. Catechized & christened an infant. The same Sermon at Stert. Called upon Mrs. Jaques: dined at John Gale's, their own family & Miss Gabrielle, Mr. Dimond, & John Thomas in the Evening; pleasant enough.

Monday March 9th.—

A hard frost; then rain, sleet & snow & cold northwind great part of the day. Composing a Sermon upon the Prophetic Character of Christ. Visiting Samuel Plank a devout man, a cripple, who had written to beg to see me. Walked to the foot of Redhorn Hill. Read Tristram Shandy &c.[20] Made Sermon notes from Bourdaloue. Wrote to Margaret.—

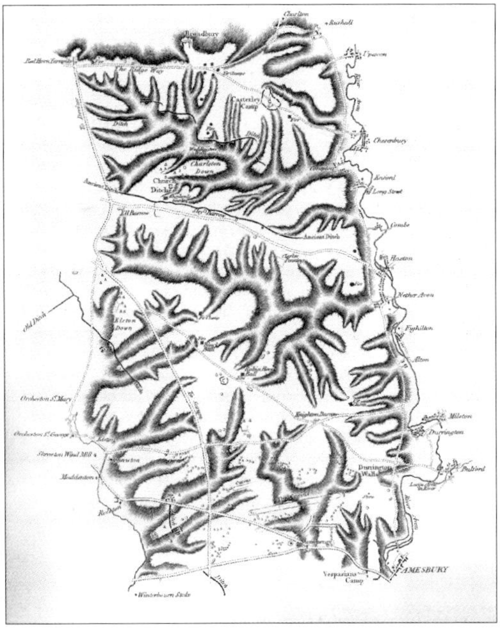

30. Map of Wiltshire south-east of Devizes showing Red Horn turnpike in the top left corner.

Tuesday Mar. 10th.—

Very cold, frosty & flittering hail & snow. Composing a Sermon as yesterday. Reading Tristram Shandy. Mr. C. Tylee, & Miss Tylee called; the latter bringing me a letter from my dear friend Mrs. Carrick with a present of Mr. George Herberts little tract a Priest to the Temple, most acceptable. Walked to the foot of Red Horne Hill. Heard from Ch. Whalley, Mrs. Travell, Mr. Smith &c. Reading Mr. George Herbert's work.—

Wednesday Mar 11th.—

Extremely cold, north East wind, frost &c. Composing a Sermon as yesterday, & preparing one upon the Sacrament. Walked to the foot of Red Horn Hill. Read the Priest to the Temple,[21] Tristram Shandy, the Gipsy Countess,[22] Mr. Dobson's Memoirs of Chivalry[23] &c.

Thursday Mar. 12th.—

Cold & sunny; upon the whole a fine day. Composing a Sermon upon the Sacrament. Finished Mr. Dobson's Mem. of Chivalry. Called upon Mrs. Jaques at Stert whither I I walked. Called in the Evening upon Samuel Plank. Received letters from Round & Evans; read Tristram Shandy, the Gypsey Countess &c.—

Friday Mar. 13th.

Cold, but after mid-day sunny & fine. Transcribing a Sermon upon the Prophetic Character of Christ, & preparing for another upon Christian Humility. Rode to Devizes on various Errands. Wrote to Evans & Mr. Granville. Read Tristram Shandy, the Gypsey Countess &c.—

20. Laurence Sterne, (1713-1768) *The Life and Opinions of Tristram Shandy, Gentleman.* (1759-1768).
21. George Herbert, *A Priest to the Temple.* (1652).
22. Elizabeth Gunning, (Elizabeth Campbell, Duchess of Argyll), (1733?-1790), *The Gipsy Countess.* (1799).
23. Susannah Dobson, *Memoirs of Ancient Chivalry,* (1784).

Saturday Mar. 14th.—

A dull cold morning, the afternoon bright & finer. Transcribing a Sermon upon the Prophetic Character of Christ. Reading Mr. G. Herbert's Tract a Priest to the Temple. Walked in the fields.—

Sunday Mar. 15.

Weather such as yesterday. Walked to Stert to perform the morning duty, catechized & preached upon the Prophetic character of Christ. Called upon Mrs. Jaques. Preached the same Sermon at Erchfont in the Evening, catechized & buried a Corpse. Read Mr. G. Herbert's Tract & part of a Journal on the Queen of Louis 14th.

Monday Mar. 16.—

Cold weather, northwest wind, & flitting snow. Wrote to Mrs. Carrick & Mr. Horne. Composed part of a Sermon upon the Sacrament. Rode to Devizes. Called upon Mr. Ledyard & Mr. John Tylee. Read Tristram Shandy, Voltaire's Pucelle d'Orleans &c.—[24] |

Tuesday Mar. 17.—

Fine weather, but some flitting snow. Finished a Sermon upon the Sacrament. Mr. D. Jones of Conock called upon us. Walked in the fields & read La Pucelle d'Orleans, the Gipsey Countess &c.—

Wednesday Mar. 18th.—

Showery weather, the first day of spring. Revising a Sermon upon Prayer & Confession in sickness. Began another upon the Death of Christ, compiled from Archb. Wake's Commentary on the Catechism. Reading La Pucelle d'Orleans, Gersner's Idyllen, the Gipsey Countess &c.—Walked with my Father to Kingston's Copse &c.—Botanizing.—

Thursday Mar. 19.—

Fine weather, but the wind cold & the morning frosty. Compiling a Sermon as yesterday. Reading La Pucelle d'Orleans. Finishing the Gipsy Countess. Walked in the Fields. Botanized.—

Friday Mar. 20th.—

An early frost, the day very fine. Began Mounteneys Demosthenes.[25] Reading La Pucelle d'Orleans &c. Drove my Mother to Devizes. Various errands. Called upon Mrs. John Tylee. Conversed with several persons. Heard from Mr. Horne. Transcribing a Sermon upon the Lord's Supper.

Saturday March 21st.—

Early a fog & moist, the day very warm & sunny. Mounteney's Demosthenes. Transcribing a Sermon upon the Lord's Supper. Botanizing. Walked a little in the garden &c.— |

---

24. Voltaire, *La Pucelle d'Orleans.* (1762).
25. Richard Mounteney, *Demosthenes logoi elektoi.*

Sunday Mar. 22d.—

A moist fog early, which cleared to a very fine warm sunny day. Reading a funeral oration by Bossuet upon Marie Therese Q. of Louis 14. done by Flechier upon La Marechal de Tureau. Began Thomas à Kempis. Looked into Mr. Travell on the Lessons. Morning Service at Erchfont, catechised, christened & churched. Preached upon the Lord's Supper. Walked to Stert: met Tinker & Bernard at Mrs. Jaques. Catechised & preached upon Confession & Prayer in Sickness.—

Monday Mar 23d.

A cold north East wind, but the day sunny, after a morning frost. Read Mounteney's Demosthenes. Wrote to Mr. Horne; drove my Father to Devizes upon various Errands. Botanized. Finished a Sermon upon the Death of Christ. Read La Pucelle d'Orleans &c. Heard from Margaret.

Tuesday Mar 24th.—

Cold east wind, & sun. Composing a Sermon upon the Resurrection of Christ. Wrote to Smith. Botanized. Walked in the garden &c. Finished Tristram Shandy. Read La Pucelle d'Orleans, Gersner's Idyllen &c. Transcribed a Sermon upon the Death of Christ. Read Clark's History of Knighthood.[26]

Wednesday March 25th.— |

A cold easterly wind, but dry & sunny. Read Gersner's Idyllen. Finished La Pucelle d'Orleans. Morning prayers at Erchfont being the Wednesday before Easter. Walked to Wedhampton to enquire after Mrs. Poore. Called upon Samuel Plank. Botanized. Transcribed a Sermon upon the Death of Christ. Composed one upon the resurrection of Christ. Began Beattie's Minstrel.—[27]

Thursday March 26.—

A cold wind, the early part of the day fine, the rest raw and cloudy. Transcribed a Sermon upon the Death of Christ. Composed another upon the Resurrection of Christ. Morning Prayers at Erchfont. Walked in Eastcott field &c. with my Father & Mother. Read Beattie's Minstrel, & Gersner's Idyllen. Prepared for the Duties of the ensuing day.—

Friday March 27.—

A damp day; with some rain & wind. Finished a Sermon upon the Resurrection of Christ & transcribing it. Read Gersner's Idyllen. Morning Service at Erchfont & a Sermon upon the Death of Christ being Good Friday. Churched a woman. Evening service at Stert with the same Sermon. Called upon Mrs. Jaques & the Gales. Walked thither. Administered the Sacrament in the Evening to S. Plank &c. Read Clarks History of Knighthood.

Saturday March 28th.—

Cold, windy, & dull weather. Studied Demosthenes. Trans- | -cribed a Sermon upon the Resurrection of Christ. Had Prayers at Erchfont. Called upon Mr. Jones. Walked in the fields & botanized. Finished Beattie's Minstrel, read Gersner's Idyllen. Preparing for Duty tomorrow.—

---

26. Hugh Clark, *History of Knighthood.* (1784).
27. James Beattie, (1735-1803), *The Minstrel.* (1771-4).

Sunday Mar. 29th.—

Easter day. Cold, raw, & Easterly wind. Reading Jer. Taylor upon the Lord's Supper, & Comber's Companion to the Common Prayer.[28] Morning service at Erchfont. Preached upon the Resurrection of Christ. Administered the Sacrament to 24 persons, the first time publicly. Walked to Stert; called upon Mrs. Jaques, preached the same sermon to a large Congregation.

Monday Mar 30th.—

Cold weather, but finer: still an Easterly wind. Married a Couple & churched a woman in the forenoon. Rode to Devizes upon sundry Errands. Reading Beattie's Poems & began la Dot de Suzette.[29] Altering a Fast Sermon. Reading Clark's History of Chivalry.

Tuesday March 31st.—

A more seasonable day of showers, though the rain cold, the Wind westerly. At a vestry inspecting Parish Accounts great part of the forenoon. Did not quit the premises. Read la Dot de Suzette. Wrote to Margaret.

Wednesday April 1st.—

A severe wind from the N.E: snow, rain & falling weather throughout the day. Wrote to Margaret, Mr. Bazley (Bristol) Mr. Lancaster &c. Rode to Devizes upon Errands. Reading Noble's Memoirs of the Cromwell | family.[30]

Thursday Ap. 2d.

A snow covered earth in the morning, showery & in the intervals sunny, but the wind cold; did not leave the premises. Reading the ~~Life~~ Memoirs of the Cromwell Family.—

Friday Ap. 3.—

A hoar frost, Snow or cold rain occasionally falling, otherwise fine. Preparing a Sermon upon Decision of character. Reading the ~~Life~~ Memoirs of Cromwell Family. Walked upon the plain. Botanizing.—Promiscuous Reading in the Evening.

Sat. Ap. 4th.—

A hoar frost, & very fine weather followed. Preparing for the Duties of the morrow. Studying Geography. Various reading, as of Gersner's works &c.—

Sunday Ap. 5th.—

A frost in the Morn. & very fine weather. Matins & Sacrament at Stert to a very small Congregation. Called upon Mrs. Jaques. Evening service & crouded Church at Erchfont. Read Caleb Williams & Archb. Wake on the Catechism. Walked to & from Stert.—

---

28. Thomas Comber, Dean of Durham, *A Companion to the Common Prayer.* (1684).
29. Joseph Fiévée, (1767-1839), *La Dot de Suzette, ou Mémoires de Mde. De Senneterre, par elle-même.* Paris, (1798).
30. Mark Noble, (1754-1827), *Memoirs of the Protectoral Family of Cromwell.* (1787).

Monday Ap. 6th.—

Beautiful weather after a hoar frost.—Drove my Mother to Devizes Various Errands. ~~Called upon~~ conversed with C. Tylee, Jaques &c. Read Caleb Williams & various other occupations.— |

Tuesday April 7th.—

Very fine weather. Began the Alcestis of Euripides.[31] Gardening in the forenoon. Began a Sermon upon decision of Character. Preparing an Essay on Duelling in the Evening. Reading Clark's Orders of Knighthood.

Wednesday April 8.—

Extremely warm & fine. Preparing a Sermon upon decision of character. Drove my Mother to Littleton & West Lavington; made a long call upon the Tinkers. Read Ah! quel Conte![32] very amusing. Preparing my Essay on Duelling by various reading. Began to compose it.

Thursday April 9th.—

Beautiful weather. Composing a Sermon upon decision of Character. Gardening, great part of the forenoon. Reading Ah! quel Conte—Received a letter from Thring. Preparing & writing my Essay on Duelling in the Evening.

~~Wednesday~~ Friday April 10th.—

Genial rain early. Cloudy & a strong W. wind afterwards. Composing a Sermon upon Decision of Character. ~~Calling~~ Rode to Devizes for the paper &c. Reading Ah! quel Conte: Preparing for my Essay upon duelling.

Saturday April 11th.

Very windy, cloudy, but no rain; not so warm.—Transcribing a Sermon upon Decision of Character. Gardening great part of the forenoon. Read- | -ing Ah! Quel Conte! Did not leave the premises.—

Sunday April 12th.

A High wind, & fine day. Altering a Sermon from Dr. Conaul, upon circumspection. Morning Service, Christening & Churching at Erchfont, preached upon Decision of Character. After Church 38 Catechumens appeared in our garden to receive each a cake as a Reward for their regularity & perfectness. Walked to Stert, found Mrs. Newman, Miss & Master Newman, Mr. F. Gibbs, & young Lambert, with Mrs. Jaques, preached the same Sermon; botanized, & read Ah! Quel Conte.

Monday April 13th.—

Very early, a fine piercing rain: heavy showers twice or thrice during the day, at other times very fine & pleasant. Compiling a Sermon upon Circumspection of Conduct. Rode

31. Euripides, *Alcestis*. This was Euripides first surviving play, first performed in Athen, 438BC. The edition being read is unknown.
32. Claude Prosper Jolyot de Crébillon, (1707-1777), *Ah! Quel Conte! Conte Politique, et Astronomique*. Brussels, (1754).

31. Cow with bell; a sketch by Francis Witts.

to Devizes upon different Errands. Wrote to Mr. W. W. Salmons. Read Ah! quel Conte &c. Called upon Mrs. Legg & Miss Frusler.—

Tuesday April 14.—

Very fine weather. Writing my essay upon Duelling.—Drove my Mother to call upon Mr. Jones & Mrs. Warrener at Conock & upon Mrs. Poore at Wedhampton. Read Ah! Quel Conte & Marianne Vie de Marchioness.—

Wednesday April 15.—

Cloudy, stormy, cold, & Easterly wind. Writing my essay upon duelling. Reading La Vie de Marianne.[33] Walking in the fields & Botanizing. Calling upon Mrs. Crook & praying with John Marlen's wife.

Thursday April 16.—

Cold weather, & Easterly wind. Transcribing a Sermon upon | Circumspection. Reading La Vie de Marianne. Rode to Devizes upon several Errands. Heard from Margaret.

Friday April 17.—

In the morning, the Ground covered with snow. Storms of snow & hail throughout the day. Visited poor Marlen's wife. Transcribing a Sermon upon Circumspection. Composing my Essay on Duelling. Reading Gersners Idyllen &c.—

Saturday April 18.—

A very cold north wind, & fleeting snow storms after a morning's frost. Transcribing a Sermon upon Circumspection. Drove my Mother in the Gig to Devizes on various Errands. Read Gersners Idyllen. Visited Marlen's Wife. Read Noble's Memoirs of the House of Cromwell.

33. Pierre Carlet de Chamblain de Marivaux, (1688-1763), *La Vie de Marianne.* (1745).

Sunday Apr. 19th.—

Cold wind but clear weather. Walked to Stert to perform the morning duty, preached on Circumspection; called upon Mrs. Jaques. Evening service with the same Sermon at Erchfont. Buried a Corpse in the Evening. Reading Memoirs of the Marchioness of L.V.

Monday Apr. 20.—

Similar cold & clear weather. Called to pray with Marlen's Wife. Rode to Devizes Fair &c. Conversed with the Tylees, Wood, Keetch, Jaques, Tinker &c. Wrote to Margaret.— |

Tuesday April 21st.

The same cold wind & ungenial weather. Preparing & composing my Essay on Duelling. Reading an History of Duelling, translated from the French. Working in the Garden.—

Wednesday April 22d.—

Trifling rain in the morning and in the Evening, early & late. Wind Easterly, a point to the South, still cold. Prayed with John Marlen's Wife. Finished my Essay & began transcribing it. Walked to Redhorn Hill &c. in the Even. with my Father to see young Skyscrapers. Reading Noble's Memoirs of the Protectorate House of Cromwell.

Thursday Apr. 23d.—

A change in the wind to south & round to the west; transcribing my Essay; making extracts from a Book on Farraday, reading Memoirs of the Marchioness L.V. & of the Cromwell Family. Drove my Mother to visit Mrs. L. Mayo, whom with her brother we found at home.—

Friday April 24th.

A mild & much finer day than many previous. Transcribing my Essay. Giving the sacrament to John Marlen's Wife &c. Miss Tylee called; also Jaques. Sent off my Essay.[34] Reading Memoirs of the Marchioness L.V &c.

Saturday Apr. 24th.—

Fine summer weather. Began Polyæni Stratagemata.[35] Began composing a Sermon upon GOD a Creator Ruler & Benefactor. Rode with Mr. D. Jones to Devizes. Gardening in the Evening. |

Sunday April 25th.

Very delightful weather. Studied Valerius Max.[36] Morning service at Erchfont, preached a Sermon "Christian Virtue, the parent of happiness. Walked to Stert; called upon Mrs. Jaques.

---

34. Nothing more was ever heard of the *Essay on Duelling*. Did he send it to a publisher? No copy exists in the Witts Family Papers.

35. Polyaenus. *Polyæni Stratagemata*. Polyaenus, a Macedonian lived at Rome in the second century AD. When the Parthian War broke out (162-5) Polyaenus, too old to fight in the campaign, dedicated to the emperors Marcus Aurelius and Lucius Veras a work called Strategica, or Stratagemata, an historical collection of stratagems and maxims of strategy written in Greek and strung together in the form of anecdotes.

36. Valerius Maximus is known as the compiler of a large collection of historical anecdotes entitled *De Factis Dictisque Memorabilibus Libri IX*, arranged under different heads, the sayings and doings of Roman worthies, kept distinct in each division from those of foreigners.

Preached the same sermon. Mrs. L. Mayo among my Congregation. Began Stavorinus's Voyage to the East Indies[37] & read Dr. Halifax Bp. of Gloucester Vindication of Bp. Butler: with Bp. Butler's primary Visitation Charge.—

Monday Apr. 26th.

The weather equally fine. Studied Polyænus. Composing a Sermon as on Saturday. Drove my Mother to Devizes. Wrote to Round. Worked in the Garden. Read Bp. Halifax's Analysis of Bp. Butler's Moral Theory, Stavorinus's Voyage & began the Winter in Bath.—[38]

Tuesday Apr. 27th.

Cloudy, but genial warm weather. Studied Valerius Maximus. Composing a Sermon as yesterday. Walked towards Crookwood, Kingston's Copse &c. Visited at Mr. Butchers in the Evening & supped. Miss C. Goodman a very nice naïve girl. A Miss Stevens &c. |

Wednesday April 29th.—

Very sultry, scorching weather with a little air. Read Polyænus. Married a Couple: Miss C. Goodman & Miss Stevens called & went to the wedding. To Devizes. To the Clergy meeting. Conversed with Mr. Jones, Mr. Brereton &c. Called upon the Tylees. Gardening in the Evening & finishing a Sermon as yesterday. Read the Winter in Bath.—

Thursday April 30th.—

Very sultry, the wind Easterly. Sun & dust very oppressive. Studied Val. Max. Drove my Mother to Devizes, where my Father meeting us, we passed a fire at Mr. Salmon's Office, several parcels of Land to difft. Purchasers.[39] Read Stavorinus's Voyage. Buried a corpse in the Evening.

Friday May 1st.—

Very beautiful weather. Studying Polyænus. Transcribing a Sermon, entitled GOD a Creator & Ruler. Botanizing. Walking in the fields beyond Lydeway. Reading Stavorinus's Voyage to the East Indies & Kelly's Memoirs of a Magdalen, or History of Louisa Mildmay.[40] Drove my Mother in the Evening upon the Andover Road | & called at Mrs. Warrener's at Conock.

Saturday May 2d.—

Cloudy, sun at intervals, a tendency to rain, much lightning at night. Studied Valerius Maximus. Finished transcribing a Sermon. Rode to Lavington, & in the Copses &c. speculating. A funeral in the Evening. Read the History of Louisa Mildmay &c.

Sunday May 3d.—

A fine dew & cooler Day; sunny & fine till Evening, when rain fell. Morning Service at Stert. Preached a Sermon entitled GOD a Creator & Ruler. Visited Mrs. Squires.

---

37. Johan Splinter Stavorinus, *Voyages to the East Indies.* (1798).
38. *The Winter in Bath.* The author of this work is anonymous, but also wrote *The Corinna of England, and a Heroine in the Shade,* and *The Banks of the Wye.*
39. The 'fire' sale in this sense was a sale at reduced prices to raise money quickly.
40. Hugh Kelly, (1739-1777), *Memoirs of a Magdalen, or the History of Louisa Mildmay.* (1767).

Preached the same Sermon at the afternoon Service at Erchfont. Two funerals in the Evening. Reading Louisa Mildmay & the Marchioness of L.V.—

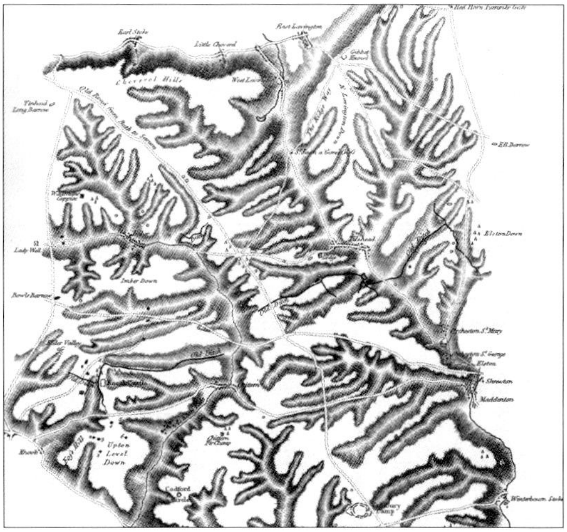

32. Map of Wiltshire south-west of Devizes. Red Horn turnpike is to the top right. Urchfont is fractionally north-west to the turnpike, just off the map.

Monday May 4th.—

Very fine rain had fallen during the night; the day was hazy, the wind Easterly & at times rain fell through a cold Atmosphere. Rode to Devizes upon several errands. In the Evening Mrs. Warrener & Mrs. L. Mayo, Mr. Mayo & Mrs. Jones visited us to tea. Walked | with my Father & the Gents. back as far as Lydeway.

Tuesday May 5th.—

After a night of fine rain the day was showery & seasonable. Composing a Sermon upon the Duty of frequently attending the Lord's Supper. Walked in the Evening to Red Horn Hill &c. Heard from Margaret.—

Wednesday May 6th.—

A day of very fine rain in almost constant showers. Read Memoirs of the Marchioness L. V. Mr. Jones called in a post chaise to convey me to the Election Dinner at Devizes Mr. Smith & Mr. Estcourt being re-elected. Very pleasant & agreeably. Conversed with Mr. Long M.P.[41] Estcourt, Revd. M. Wyatt, Tinker, Dr. Hill, Dr. Spalding &c. Tea & coffee at Mr. W. Salmon's. Wrote to Horne.—

Thursday May 7.—

Cold wind & showery weather, much heavy rain. Composing a Sermon upon the Immortality of the Soul. Rode with Butcher over his Upland Farm. Reading &c. |

Friday May 8th.—

Very showery weather. Transcribing a Sermon upon the Duty of frequently attending the Lord's Supper, after having finished it in the forenoon.—Did not leave the premises.—

Saturday May 9th.—

A great deal of rain fell. Transcribing a Sermon as yesterday. Rode through Eastcott Eastetton &c. Heard from Horne.—

---

41. Richard Godolphin Long, (1761-1835). M.P. for Rood Ashton, Wiltshire, 1806-1818. Henry Hunt of Chisenbury, who criticised the choice of Long to replace Ambrose Goddard as county member in 1806 described Long as follows: 'Mr Richard Long of Rood Ashton was a fox-hunting country squire, without any other qualification to be a Member of Parliament than that of belonging to an ancient family of the county, in fact, he was proverbially a man of very inferior knowledge, remarkable only for being a stupid country squire.'

Sunday May 10$^{th.}$—

Rain early in the morning, little or none afterwards; but the Day gloomy and the air raw. Read Stavorinus's Voyages to the East Indies. Morning service at Erchfont & preached upon the necessity of frequently attending the Lord's Supper. Rode to Stert, called upon M$^{rs.}$ Jaques, as usual. Preached there upon the Immortality of the Soul. Wrote to Margaret. Read Bishop Wilson's Introduction to the Lord's Supper.

Monday May 11$^{th.}$—

Finer weather, at intervals delightful; some showers, particularly at night. Preparing a Sermon upon the descent of the Holy Ghost. Reading Bp. Wilson's Introduction, & Stavorinus's Voyages. Wrote to M$^{r.}$ Travell. Drove M$^{r.}$ Jones, upon | whom I called at Conock to the nomination of his cousin Rich Long, & H. P. Windham Esq$^{r.}$, for the County at Devizes. Conversed with Jaques, M$^{r.}$ Richards, M$^{rs.}$ H. Beech, J. Tylee, &c.

Tuesday May 12$^{th.}$—

Very rainy without much intermission. Compiling a Sermon as yesterday. Walking to Redhorne Hill &c. Read Stavorinus's Voyages.

Wednesday May 13$^{th.}$—

Showery weather. Finishing the Sermon on the descent of the Holy Ghost. Began Miss Lee's Life of a Lover[42] & Mackenzies Voyages across the N.W. Continent of America.[43] Walked before dinner & rode afterwards. Called upon the Leggs.—

Thursday May 14$^{th.}$—

Very showery weather. Heavy rain at intervals & extremely dirty. Transcribing the Sermon finished yesterday. Walked to Redhorn Hill. Reading the Life of a Lover & Mackenzie's Voyages. Called without meeting them upon the Comptons.—

Friday May 15$^{th.}$— |

After a night of rain, the weather recovering. Wrote to M$^{r.}$ Horne. Rode to Devizes upon various Errands. Reading the Life of a Lover & Mackenzie's Voyages.—

Saturday May 16.—

Cloudy, ungenial weather. But fine enough to drive my Mother to call upon M$^{rs.}$ Poore at Wedhampton, with whom we met M$^{rs.}$ Smith. Walked botanizing in the fields. Gave the Sacrament to Sam$^{l.}$ Plank &c.—Transcribing my Sermon & preparing for tomorrow.

---

42. Harriet Lee, *The Life of a Lover.* (1804).
43. Alexander Mackenzie, (1763-1830). *A Narrative or Journal of Voyages and Travels through the North-West Continent of North America in the Years 1789 & 1793.* (1802). In an interesting twist of history, Mackenzie's voyages across North America were recognised by Napoleon as a means by which he could embark on a re-conquest of Canada. He arranged for the book to be smuggled from England and translated into French. Mackenzie's description of the West Canada river system was so precise, that Napoleon languishing in prison, gave orders to Bernadotte, his key Marshall, to lay out a new plan to retake New France. Mackenzie thus became an unwitting accomplice by providing the navigational details to invade Canada via the Mississippi from New Orleans.

Sunday May 17.—

Very fine weather. Genial & beautiful. Whitsunday. Morning service at Erchfont & Sacrament. Christened a child. Evening service at Stert. Called upon M$^{rs.}$ Jaques as usual. Preached at both upon the Descent of the Holy Spirit upon the Apostles. Read the Life of a Lover &c.—

Monday May 18$^{th.}$

Very fine weather. Preparing a Sermon upon the duty of an inoffensive conduct. Began & finished it. Drove my Mother to Devizes. Called upon Miss Tylee. Christened five children in the Evening.— |

Tuesday May 19$^{th.}$

Beautiful weather, but the wind cold. Transcribing a Sermon upon the Duty of an inoffensive conduct, which I ~~read~~ preached after the Morning Service to an immense croud, being the Feast of the Erchfont Club; a very gay day: the whole procession with their flags & music paid by the Comp^{t}. of a Visit. Walked upon the Plain & after dinner rode. Read the Life of a Lover. Heard from M$^{r.}$ Travell.

Wednesday May 20$^{th.}$—

A very cold morning & beautiful noon, the Evening again cold. Wrote to M$^{r.}$ Travell. Rode to Devizes by Lavington & Littleton; called upon M$^{rs.}$ & Miss Tinkers. Various Errands at Devizes. Beginning a Sermon upon the Holy Trinity. Reading the Life of a Lover.

Thursday May 21$^{st.}$—

Strong wind, sunny weather. Composing a Sermon on the Trinity. Finished the Life of a Lover. Worked in the Garden. M$^{r.}$ & M$^{rs.}$ Compton, M$^{r.}$ & M$^{rs.}$ Tinker with their two daughters, & the Rev$^{d.}$ M$^{r.}$ White of Jeffont came to us to tea & supper, & staid till near twelve.

Friday May 22$^{d.}$—

Very windy, but very fine weather. Composing a Sermon | as yesterday. Rode upon the plain with the Butchers & Miss Carter. Read Tuckey's Voyage to New Holland &c.[44] M$^{r.}$ Butcher Sen$^{r.}$, M$^{r.}$ & M$^{rs.}$ W. Butcher, Miss Carter, M$^{rs.}$ Poore, M$^{rs.}$ Smith & Miss Legg drank tea & supped with us.—

Saturday May 23.

Beautiful weather. Busy in finishing a Sermon on the Trinity. Walked & botanized. In the Even. drove my Mother on the Plain. Finished Tuckey's Voyage. Read Mackenzie's.

Sunday May 24.

Trinity Sunday. Heavenly weather, but extremely warm. Rode to Stert, preached a Sermon upon the Trinity, & administered the Sacrament. Evening service at Erchfont, preached the

---

44. James Hingston Tuckey, (1776-1816). *An Account of a Voyage to establish a Colony at Port St. Philip in Bass's Strait, on the south coast of New South Wales in His Majestie's Ship Calcutta, in the years 1802,3,4.* (1805).

same Sermon to a large Congregation, Mr. Jones, the Tinkers, Comptons &c.—A funeral in the Evening. Walked in the fields. Began the invisible Enemy a Romance.[45] Wrote to George.

Monday May 25.—

A very hot gloomy day. Rain in the Evening. Began altering a Sermon from Dr. Adams upon keeping the Commandments. Drove my Mother to Devizes. ~~Called on~~ Conversed with Ledyard, Mrs. Poore &c. Heard from Margaret & Mrs. Carrick. Walked to the 5 | Elms in the Evening; also had a funeral. Read the Invisible Enemy &c.—

Tuesday May 26th—

A Showery growing Day; cold in the Evening. Continuing a Sermon as yesterday. Called upon the Butchers. Gardening. Walked to the foot of Red Horn Hill.

Wednesday May 27th.—

A very fine day. Cold in the Evening. Gardening all day. Drove my Mother in the Evening on Lydeway to Wedhampton &c. Wrote to Mr. W. W. Salmon. Walked to the 5 Elms.—

Thursday May 28th.—

No rain till the Evening, but the weather cold tho' not unpleasant. Continuing a Sermon as Tuesday. Rode to Lydeway. Gardening & walked in the Evening with Mrs. Butcher & Miss Carter.—

Friday May 29th.—

Till the afternoon fine, but cool: about three a storm of thunder & lightning & rain all the Evening. Rode off early on a visit to W. Thring, at Great Sutton, two miles beyond Heytesbury, about twelve miles from Erchfont over the plain; found my way very well by observing the various landmarks. | Heytesbury a lively village & the country pretty. Sir W. Acourt's a pleasant place Great Sutton Parsonage an old Abbey, I presume retired, & well wooded: The village large & clean.[46] Walked with my friend, & rode with ~~my~~ his Father, through the villages of Longbridge Deverell &c., to the Marquis of Bath's beautiful sheet of water & splendid Park & grounds at Longleat; returned thro' Warminster, Bishopstow &c.; the roads good & Country pretty enough. Dined & slept. Dr. & Mrs. Thring very civil.

Saturday May 30th.—

Incessant hard rain & violent hurricane throughout the day. Staid at Sutton in expectation of a change till 1 o clock; then rode home at the risk of my life across the plain. Wet through long before I reached Erchfont & almost cut to pieces by the wind. Head ached, sleepy & after finishing a Sermon went early to Bed.

---

45. Thomas Pike Lathy, *The Invisible Enemy.* (1806).

46. William Davison Thring, (1782-1854). Thring was at Wadham with Frank Witts. The property of Sir William A'Court would have been of interest to Witts as they were at Weimar together, although A'Court studied under M. Mounier at the Belvedere. A'Court was Secretary to the Legation at Naples, 1801-7, so at this point he would have been away from home.

Sunday May 31st.

Cold, lowring weather; a tendency to rain.—Morning service at Erchfont. Preached upon keep- | -ing the Commandments; the same at Stert where I met the Miss Williams's & Miss Newman at Gales. Drank tea at W. Butcher's &c.—

Monday June 1st.—

Cold weather, and almost unceasing rain throughout the day. Composing a Sermon upon tenderness to the brute Creation. Wrote to Margaret. Read Mackenzie's Voyages. Began Le Chevalier's Voyage de la Propontide &c.[47]

Tuesday June 2d.

Finer weather, but still not hot. Composing a Sermon as yesterday. Walked to Wedhampton called on Mrs. Poore & Mrs. Smith. Called on Mrs. W. Butcher. Walked in the Evening; met Legg. Lounged with HMC.[48] Drove my mother round Etchilhampton Hill &c. in the Gig.

Wednesday June 3d.

Very fine weather. Composing a Sermon as yesterday. Drove my Father to Devizes. Called upon Mrs. Tylee. Walked to the 5 Elms. Read Le Chevalier's Voyage & the Invisible Enemy. Wrote to Mr. Walsh of Oxford. Poor Joseph Legg died.

Thursday June 4th.—

Very fine weather. Finished the Composition of a | Sermon, as yesterday.—Walked with Mrs. Butcher & H.M.C. in the fields. Heard from Smith &c. Drove my Mother to tea at Wedhampton with Mrs. Poore, Mrs. Smith still there. Read Le Chevalier's Voyage, the Invisible Enemy &c.—

Friday June 5th.—

Very fine weather. Transcribing a Sermon upon tenderness to the Brute Creation. Mrs. Butcher & HMC made a long & pleasant morning visit. Walked with them & drank tea en famille. Singing &c. Gardening.—

Saturday June 6th.—

After a night of rain the morning dull & cloudy. Showers during the day which prevented our visiting Miss Tylee in the Evening. Walked a very little. Gardening. Wrote to Smith &c. Transcribing a Sermon as yesterday. The Evening being without rain rode with HMC thro' Cherrington, Patney, Ashlington &c. & back by Lydeway.—

Sunday June 7th.—

A dull & misty morning with a tendency to rain. Walked before breakfast with HMC. Morning Service at Stert. Preached upon the Duty of shewing tenderness to the Dumb

---

47. Jean Baptiste Le Chevalier, *Le Voyage de la Propontide et du Pont-Euxin.* (1790).

48. HMC was Miss Carter. Why did Frank Witts feel it necessary to use initials? Was he feeling guilty about his familiarity with Miss Carter?

animals. As I returned met & walked with Mrs. Butcher & HMC. Evening service & the same Sermon at ~~Stert~~ Erchfont. Walked in the Evening with my Father alone. Read Glencore Tower.[49] |

Monday June 8th.—

Cool weather & more clouds than sun: a tendency to rain, which fell in the Evening. Walked before Breakfast with HMC. Attending poor Joseph Legg's funeral &c. M. Lavington 1 Hearse 11 Coach. Mr. Smith. Apoth. the Father Brother & myself. Mr. Williams met us at the Church yard wicket: Walked before & after dinner. Read Glencore Tower, Voyage de la Propontide & Life of Secker &c.

Tuesday June 9th.—

Windy, cloudy weather, in the Evening a short violent thunderstorm. Composing a Sermon upon the Duties we owe to ourselves. Gardening. Drove my Mother in the Gig, but were arrested in our progress by the Visit of Miss H. Tylee. Walked to Erchfont Marsh &c. Walked in the Evening to Eastcott with HMC. Reading Voyage de la Propontide & Tissot's Life of Zimmerman.[50]

Wednesday June 10th.—

A good deal of rain fell during the day, which was dull & lowring. Occupied about parish business & composing a Sermon as yesterday. Gardening, called at Butcher's &c. Wrote to Mr. Horne. Rode to Devizes. Walked with H.M.C. read Voyage de la Propontide—Soldiers Love & Sailor's Friendship[51] —M.G. Lears's Feudal Tyrants &c. — |

Tuesday June 23d.—

Very fine weather without a burning sun.—Composing a Sermon upon the Miracles of Christ. Visiting John Willis at Redhorne struck with a Palsy. Called upon Mr. Compton. Drove my Mother upon the Andover Road in the Evening & called upon Mrs. Warrener with whom we found Mrs. Poore & Mrs. Smith. Read La Perouse's Voyage.[52]

Wednesday June 24th.—

Very fine weather. Composing a Sermon as yesterday. Drove my Mother to call upon Mrs. Sutton at New Park. Very handsomely received by Mrs. S. & Mrs. Estcourt, found there Mrs. Sutton of Devizes, Mrs. Shield, & Miss Haraland the House, Grounds & Gardens very handsome. Called in Devizes at the Post & upon Miss Tylee. Rode in the Evening upon the Plain. Called upon the Comptons. Read La Perouse's Voyage & Mrs. Sheridan's Nourjahad.[53]—

---

49. *Glencore Tower* was anonymous. It was advertised in the *Morning Chronicle* of 28 August 1806, 2 volumes, 12mo. At eight shillings. Available from Minerva Office, Leadenhall Street.
50. Tissot, *Traité de l'Expérience en Général et en Particulier dans l'Art de Guérir.* A life of Johann Georg Zimmerman, one of the most prominent physicians of his time, and also a prolific writer.
51. Anna Maria Porter, *A Sailor's Friendship, and a Soldier's Love.* (1805).
52. Jean Françoise Galaup de la Pérouse, (1741-1788). *Voyage en Terre de Feu.* (1785-6).
53. Frances Sheridan. *The History of Nourjahad,* (1767).

Thursday June 25th.

Very fine weather. Composing a Sermon as yesterday. Rode to Redhorn to visit John Willis. In the Evening rode in Crookwood &c. |

Friday June 26.—

Beautiful weather. Accompanied my Father in the Gig to Stoke Park &c. Finished & began to transcribe a Sermon as yesterday. Mrs. Jones called. Walked in the Evening. Wrote to Mr. Horne.

Saturday June 27.—

Very glorious weather. Transcribing a Sermon as yesterday. Rode to Redhorn to Willis. Walked in the Evening.

Sunday June 28th.—

Beautiful weather. Morning Service at Erchfont. Mrs. Poore called. Preached on the Miracles of Christ. Same Sermon in the Evening at Stert. Called on Mrs. Jaques & Mrs. M. Giddings drank tea &c.

Monday June 29th.

Beautiful weather, though rather overclouded. Began composing a Sermon upon the Future Happiness of the Righteous. Gardening. Read La Perouse, Feudal Tyrants &c. In the Evening drove my Mother to drink tea at Mrs. C. Mayo's at Beeching Stoke; met Mrs. J. Gent, Miss H. Tylee, Mr. & Mrs. Lancaster.— |

Sunday July 5th.—

Fine summer weather. Showers lightly fell in the Evening. Reading Acerbi's Travels in Sweden, Finland and Lapland.[54] Morning service at Stert whither I rode, called upon Mrs. Jaques, & preached upon the future happiness of the righteous. Conversed with Miss A. Gale. Evening duty at Erchfont: preached the same Sermon. Mrs. Poore called. Walked with my Father late. Met & conversed with Messrs. Compton & Smith.

Monday July 6th.

Beautiful weather. The Evening not too hot. Reading Acerbi's Travels. Writing to Margaret. Rode to Devizes. Drove my Mother to Conock to drink tea with Mrs. Warrener; my Father walked & met us.

Tuesday July 7th.—

Equally fine weather without any other inconvenience than dust. Began modelling a Sermon upon the sublime motives & principles of Christianity from Dr. Adams. Began Bish. Warburton's | Julian.[55] Dr. Hill & his son called. Drove my Mother to Eastcott & Littleton where we respectively visited Miss Compton & the Tinkers. Heard from Mr. Travell & wrote to him.

---

54. Guiseppe Acerbi, (1773-1846), *Travels through Sweden Finland and Lappland to the North Cape n the years 1798 and 1799.*

55. William Warburton, (1698-1779). Warburton was Bishop of Gloucester, 1759-1779.

Wednesday July 8th.—

Beautiful Summer Weather. Cool air & hot sun. Preparing a Sermon as yesterday. Read Warburton's Julian. Drove my Mother to Devizes. Called upon Mr. & Mrs. John Tylee. Gardening & walked in the Evening.—

Thursday July 9th.—

Beautiful summer weather, very warm. H.M.C.—Finished a Sermon as yesterday. Read Warburton's Julian. Visited John Dunford. Began Corn. Nepos.[56] Read Acerbi's Travels. In the Evening drove my Mother to Stert to drink Tea at the Gales. My Father walked; met the Jaques's, Clare, Brabant, Mr. Ward &c.—

Friday July 10th.—

Extremely warm, but very fine weather. Read Warburton's Julian. Wrote to Horne. Studied Cor. Nepos. Visited W. Willis. Gardening. Wrote to Smith. Finished Acerbi's Travels.—

Saturday July 11th.—

Clouded weather, inconsiderable showers, heavy wind, fine Evening. Read Warburton's Julian. Studied Cor. Nepos. Rode to Stert in the Evening. Gardening.— |

Sunday July 12th.

Very fine weather; the wind still rather high. Morn. service at Erchfont preached upon the sublime motives & Principles of Christianity: the same Sermon in the afternoon at Stert. Called upon Mrs. Jaques as usual. Wrote to Mr. Horne: heard from Mr. Travell.—

Monday July 13th.—

Very warm & cloudy: two very heavy storms fell after mid-day. Rode off early to Bath to meet Mr. H. Ginder upon Acct. of Edwd. Purbridge. Detained at Devizes, till the Bank was open: transacted my business & other errands at Bath: called upon Mrs. Bates: dined at the Elephant Inn, drank tea at Alford & reached home before ten o clock.

Tuesday July 14th.—

Very close warm weather. Cloudy & showery. Began a Sermon on the due observance of the Sabbath: Reading Bligh's Voyage to the South Sea.[57] Churching two women. Drove my Father to dine at Jaques's. Met the Comptons of Erchfont & Eastcott. The three ladies came in the Lavington Chaise. Good dinner and welcome. The Gales drank tea, Miss Anne & Miss Gabriel.— |

Wednesday July 15th.—

Weather cloudy, threatening rain, without any warm with a light wind: Read Captn. Bligh's Voyage. Wrote to Mr. Travell. Drove my Mother thro' Lavington, Worton, & Seend to

---

56. Cornelius Nepos, (*c.*100-24BC). Nepos was a Roman biographer. Supposedly he was born at Hostilia, a village in Cisalpine Gaul, not far from Verona. His simple style of writing made him very popular fro Latin studies. The precise work referred to here is unknown.

57. William Bligh, (1754-1817), *A Voyage to the South Sea,* (1792). Bligh is more famous as being the harsh captain of HMS Bounty in which the mutiny took place in 1789.

Devizes to dine at M[rs.] John Tylee's. My Father walked & met us. Miss Tylee completed the party. Very pleasant. Heard from M[rs.] Horne. Drove home by nine o clock.

Thursday July 16th.—

Similar weather; more sun than on the preceding day. Composing a Sermon as Tuesday. Read Foster's Observations on a Voyage round the World.[58] Gardening. M[rs.] Legg & Miss Thurles called late.

Friday July 17th. 1807

Very fine weather: though overclouded, a pleasant wind stirring. Finishing & transcribing a Sermon as yesterday. Read Haller's Usong.[59] also Forster's Observations. Gardening &c. M[r.] & M[rs.] Jaques, Miss Diggs & Miss Gabriell drank tea with us. Walked part of the way back with them to Stert.—

Saturday July 18th.—

Cloudy weather with intervals of very hot sun. Rode early to Devizes. Heard from Margaret & from Ginder. Transcribing a Sermon as yesterday. Reading Lathom's Novel, Human Beings.[60] — l

Sunday July 19th.

Cloudy weather, & warm, but the day fine, excepting one shower in the Evening. Morning Service at Stert. Called upon M[rs.] Jaques, met there Miss Biggs. Preached upon the due observance of the Sabbath. The same Sermon in the afternoon at Erchfont, M[rs.] Poore also called upon us. Miss Thurles, & M[rs.] M. Giddings also drank tea & passed the Evening with us. Read Human Beings.

Monday July 20th.—

Cloudy, warm & showery, the Evening fine. Began composing a Sermon upon reading the Holy Scriptures & other Books of Piety. Reading Warburton's Julian. Working in the Garden. Reading M[rs.] Hutchinson's life of Col. Hutchinson[61] & Human Beings. Spent the Evening and supped at M[rs.] Leggs. Meeting the Comptons of both families & a Miss Hart from Corsham, who played & sung not ill.

Tuesday July 21st.—

Very fine summer weather. Continued a Sermon as l yesterday. Finished Warburton's Julian. Began Gerard's Pastoral Care. Also began Constance de Lindensdorff.[62] Read M[rs.] H. life of Col. Hutchinson. Rode upon the plains. The Leggs drank tea with us with Miss Hart.—

---

58. J. R. Foster, *Observations Made During a Voyage Around the World,* (1778).

59. Albrecht von Haller, (1708-1777). *Usong.* (1771). Haller was a Swiss born anatomist and physiologist. *Usong* is a philosophical romance, a departure from his usual writings.

60. Francis Lathom, *Human Beings.* (1807).

61. Lucy Hutchinson, *Memoirs of the Life of Colonel Hutchinson,* Lucy Hutchinson was a well-educated Puritan officer's wife. She wrote the life of her husband, John Hutchinson, between 1664-1670, but in fact the work also contains a very descriptive account of the state of the country at the time and remains a standard work.

62. Francis Lathom, *Constance de Lindensdorff.* (1807)?

Wednesday July 22d.

An extremely hot, sultry day, ending in short thunderstorms towards night, without much explosion or lightning. Wrote to Margaret. Drove my Mother to Devizes. Called upon the Tylees, & pleasantly received Mrs. Smith a very attractive young woman. Read Constance de Lindensdorff—Mrs. H. life of Col. Hutchinson, Bougainville's Voyage &c.[63]

Thursday July 23d.

The weather cloudy, & in the Evening less warm than usual; a tendency to rain, very little fell during the day, but heavily at night. Composing a Sermon as yesterday. Reading Gerard's Pastoral Care, Life of Col. Hutchinson & Constance de Lindensdorff. Heard from George. Drove my Mother to Wedhampton, my Father walked; drank tea with Mrs. Poore, Mrs. C. Mayo, called there also.—

Friday July 24th.—

Hot & cloudy with frequent & some heavy showers; | some distant thunder. Transcribing a Sermon as yesterday. Wrote to Mrs. Heard & Sir Edward Smith. Read Constance de Lindensdorff &c. In the Evening drove my Mother to tea and supper at Mrs. R. Compton's at Eastcott. Besides the family party met the Jaques's, Mary Gibbs, & Leggs. The Evening was fine & we returned home late.

Saturday July 25th.—

The forenoon was alternately wet & dry; many showers fell. The Evening was fine & pleasant. Transcribing a Sermon as yesterday. Finished Constance de Lindensdorff. Read Gerard's Pastoral Care, & Life of Col. Hutchinson. Heard from Mrs. Travell. Drove to Stert after dinner to fetch Miss Gibbs to a party at our house. Mrs. Jaques walked. Found Mr. Mayo on our return. The rest of the party were the two families of Comptons & Leggs: all staid supper but Mr. Mayo.—

Sunday July 26th.—

Very heavy & constant rain from an early hour in the morning till mid day: the afternoon & Evening very fine. Morning service at Erchfont & a Christening. Preached upon neglecting the Salvation of GOD. At Stert called as usual upon Mrs. Jaques. Miss Gibbs there. Preached upon the duty of an inoffensive conduct. | Read Gerard's Pastoral Care & Bougainville's Voyage.

Monday July 27th.—

Very fine weather. Continuing an incomplete Fast Sermon: Reading Gerard's Pastoral Care & Bougainville's Voyage. Went in the Lavington Chaise to dine at New Park, where we found a most pleasant reception from Mrs. Sutton & Mr. & Mrs. J. Estcourt Norhangers; only Mr. Estcourt Senr. & his Lady & two Daughters & a Miss Matthews. Music by Mrs. J. Estcourt & Miss C. E.—a very agreeable visit. Returned by ten o clock.

---

63. Louis-Antoine de Bougainville, (1729-1811), *Voyage autour du Monde.* (1771).

Tuesday July 28$^{th.}$—

Weather very fine & pleasant. Finishing a Sermon as yesterday. Read Gerard's Pastoral Care. Life of Col. Hutchinson & Bougainville's Voyage. Drove my Mother in the Evening to Conock. Drank tea with M$^{rs.}$ Warrener. Met M$^{rs.}$ Poore. Strolled a little afterwards with Mark Giddings.

Wednesday July 29$^{th.}$—

A dull gloomy forenoon, the afternoon & Evening wet with very heavy rain. Transcribing a Sermon as yesterday. Read Gerard's Pastoral Care. Life of Col. Hutchinson. Bougainville's Voyage. Duchess of Marlborough's Account of her Conduct.[64] Wrote to M$^{r.}$ Horne & to Round. |

Thursday July 30$^{th.}$—

Cloudy weather, threatning for rain, which fell in one heavy storm. Drove my Father to Devizes on various Errands. Met & conversed with M$^{r.}$ Estcourt. M$^{rs.}$ Poore drank Tea with us. Walked in the Evening to the foot of Red Horn Hill. Read Bougainville's Voyage & the Duchess of Marlborough's Vindication of her Conduct.

Friday July 31$^{st.}$—

From an early hour in the morning till 5 oclock P.M. almost incessant rain. The Evening fine. Transcribing a Sermon as yesterday. Wrote to George. Read Gerard's Pastoral Care, Forster's Observations made on a Voyage round the World & some Odes of Horace. Walked in the Evening to the foot of Redhorn Hill.

Saturday Aug. 1$^{st.}$—

After one morning shower, the remainder of the Day was fine, drying, with a light wind, & warm. Arranging Sermons. Read Gerard's Pastoral Care. Visited Matt. North & his Dame. Read the life of Col. Hutchinson. Heard from Smith. Walked in the Evening with my Father & Mother to the 5 Elms. Read a few Odes of Horace.

Sunday Aug. 2$^{d.}$—

Very fine summer weather: clear & warm. Morning service at Stert, preached upon reading the bible & | books of Piety. Called upon M$^{rs.}$ Jaques, as usual. Evening Service with the same Sermon, a Christening & Churching at Erchfont. Walked with my Father & Mother in the Evening. Read Warner's Northern Tour.[65] Col. Hutchinson's life. Began Malthus on Population.[66]—

Monday Aug. 3$^{d.}$—

Very fine weather for the beginning of harvest, which will in a day or two be general. Altering a Sermon from D$^{r.}$ Conant on the Inveteracy of Sin. M$^{rs.}$ Smith & Miss Tylee called,

---

64. Sarah Jennings Churchill, Duchess of Marlborough, (1660-1744), *An Account of the Conduct of the Dowager Duchess of Marlborough, From Her First Coming to Court, to the Year 1710. In a Letter from Herself to my Lord.* (1742).

65. Richard Warner, (1763-1857), *A Tour through the Northern Counties of England, and the Borders of Scotland.* Bath, Crudwell. (1802). See below, *Characters of Bath*.

66. Thomas Robert Malthus, (1766-1834), *An Essay on the Principle of Population.* (1798).

33. West View of Stonehenge.

my Mother returned with them to Devizes in the Chaise, I drove the Gig & brought her back after doing some Errands. Wrote to Mr. Travell. Studied Gerard's Pastoral Care. Read Warner's Northern Tour.

Tuesday Aug. 4th.—

Fine weather excepting one or two storms of rain. Finished altering a Sermon as yesterday. Studied Gerard's Pastoral Care: Visited Mrs. Crook. Finished the life of Col. Hutchinson. Heard from Margaret. Wrote to Mrs. Carrick. Walked to Foxley Corner. Finished Warner's Northern Tour. Read Malthus on Population & Neumann's Gesundbrunnen.[67]—

Wednesday Aug. 5th.—

A strong tendency to rain, which fell in a trifling | degree twice in the forenoon but was withheld by the wind. More small rain came down in the Evening. Drove my Father to Stonehenge. Transcribed a Sermon finished yesterday. Read Neubeck's Gesundbrunnen, Malthus on Population, &c.—

Thursday Aug. 6th.—

The morning & forenoon damp with small rain, the early part of the Evening fine, later heavy rain. Transcribing a Sermon as yesterday. A Gentleman from Mr. Horne brought us various deeds to sign.[68] Studied Gerard's Pastoral Care. Read Neubeck's Gesundbrunnen, Malthus on Population. Walked in the Evening with my Father & Mother in the field.

---

67. Valerius Wilhelm Neubeck (not Neumann, 1765-1850), *Die Gesundbrunnen, Ein Gedicht in vier Gesängen.* (1798).
68. What these deeds relate to is unclear. It is possible that it was early legal planning for his future marriage to Margaret Backhouse and Mr. Edward Horne was been acting for the Witts family on this matter.

Friday Aug. 7th.—

The morning of doubtful appearance after a night of rain; much continued to fall thro'out the day. Revising Sermons. Reading Neubeck's Gesundbrunnen. Rode after breakfast to attend Visitation at Lavington found Archd. Daubeny with many Clergymen, Messrs. Key, Spencer, Smith, Prince, Jones, Basset, Richards, Dr. Skinner, Williams, Rogers &c. &c. Service read in consequence of an error by the Archdeacon, no Sermon, but an Excellent Charge delivered by him relating to the state of the Church Establishment as endangered by the late attempts to introduce a liberty of conscience, inconsistent with the principles of the constitution as established at the Reformation | & Revolution.[69] Dined 7 in number very indifferently. After dinner appointed one of the Stewards of the Pottern Division of the Wilts Clergy Orphan Charity. Mr. Wood of Swainswick, my Colleague. Rode home with Mr. Jones of Enford.

Saturday Aug. 8th.—

Very fine weather quite restored from its former & late moisture. Wrote to Horne, Margaret & Ginder. Rode with my letters to Devizes. Met & conversed with Mr. & Mrs. Jaques. Walked a little in the Evening. Revising Sermons &c. Finished die Gesundbrunnen.

Sunday Aug. 9th.—

Very fine weather, apparently settled. Morning Service at Erchfont. Preached upon the Inveteracy of Sin. Mrs. Poore called. Evening Service at Stert with the same Sermon. A large Congregation being Stert feast. Dined at John Gale's, meeting the Miss Gabriells, Mr. Brabant, & Miss Goodman very pleasantly. Began Dutens Memoires d'un Voyageur qui se repose. A Christening at each Church.—

Monday Aug. 10th.—

The weather, though somewhat cloudy, very fine—Began a Sermon upon GOD considered as a Benefactor. Read Dutens Memoirs d'un Voyageur qui se repose, Malthus on Population. Drove my Mother to Devizes. Called on Mrs. Hill, & Miss Tylee. Had some conversation | with Higginson, Wynne &c. Had previously called at Erchfont on poor John Kite. Heard from Sir Edwd. Smith.—

Tuesday Aug. 11th.

Doubtful, cloudy weather: a tendency to rain chiefly during the Evening: at night some very heavy rain fell. Read Dutens Memoires: composing a Sermon as yesterday. Mrs. Poore, Mrs. Warrener & Miss Lancaster & Dr. & Mrs. Hill & their son Charles drank tea with us. Walked late to Foxley Corner.—

Wednesday Aug. 12th.—

Very fine weather. Composing a Sermon as yesterday. Read Dutens Memoires. Visiting John Dunford & John Kite. Began Turnbull's Voyage to the Pacific Ocean.[70] Wrote to Dowell.

---

69. This probably refers to the works of John Aikin, (1747-1822). Aikin edited the *Monthly Magazine* from 1796 to 1807 and was a leading advocate of liberty of conscience.
70. Alexander Turnbull, *A Voyage to the Pacific Ocean.* (1784).

Thursday Aug. 13th.—

An inauspicious morning after heavy rain in the night. The day cloudy but the Evening very fine. Composing a Sermon as yesterday. Reading Turnbull's Voyage. Heard from Mr. Horne. Drove my Mother in the Evening to drink tea at Jaques's; met Mr. Tirrip A. Gale: Miss Gabriell's, Miss F. Goodman & Mr. Wood.

Friday Aug. 14.—

The Day very fine & warm, but cloudy after a violent night of heavy rain. Some also fell in the afternoon & Evening. Reading the Scriptures &c. Wrote to Mr. Horne & to Gaisford. Called & left my card | for the Revd. Mr. Rogers at Lavington. Proceeded in my ride by Worton to Poulshot, called upon Dr. Skinner & his son, received subscriptions to the Clergy Fund, returned thro' Devizes. Met & conversed with Mr. Wood. Passed the Evening at Mark Giddings's where were Charles Giddings's wife & daughter.—

Saturday Aug. 15th.—

Very fine weather, but very warm and occasionally overclouded. Reading the Scripture &c. Transcribing a Sermon as yesterday. Walked in the afternoon with my Mother: looked in upon John Kite. Read Turnbull's Voyage to the Pacific Ocean.

Sunday Aug. 16th.

Very fine summer weather. Morning service at Stert preached a Sermon, entitled GOD a Benefactor—Called upon Mrs. Jaques, as usual. Evening service & the same Sermon at Erchfont. Sundry Parishioners drank tea with us, Mrs. M. Giddings, Mr. Jones's wife the Widow Jones, C. Giddings' Wife & Daughters.—Began upon the 2d. Part of the Sermon preached in the morning.

Monday Aug. 17th.—

Beautiful but very warm weather. Left home early upon an expedition to Fonthill House Sale. Proceeded first across the Plain to Filshead Lodge George —— Esqr. to solicit subscriptions to the | Clergy Fund. Filshead Village is seated in a valley formed by the undulations of the plain. The Lodge formerly, an inconsiderable hunting Box is now a consequential place, tolerably well wooded, surrounded with younger plantations & bordered every way by downs of turf, or valuable arable land. The roads very bad & the neighbourhood worse. Pursued my route towards Chilten Windmill, making an unnecessary diversion to the side of Shrewton; pursued a track from the former place which led me into the Warminster & Salisbury Road, & the Village of Codford, situated with several others in a rich Valley upon the little river Wily. Leaving Codford by Stockton & crossing over Stockton Hill, by midday had a view of Mr. Beckfords fine plantations & place at Bishops Fonthill. The original house was shorn of its wings in a square edifice well situated in a valley at the foot of various wooded elevations in a noble park near a fine sheet of water. Its most eccentric owner having erected an abbey upon | the summit of the loftiest eminence on his Estate, has consigned the Mansion with all its excellent & valuable furniture to public auction.[71]

71. William Beckford, (1760-1844). Beckford was one of the most fascinating men of his age; wealthy, intellectual,

This had collected crouds of every degree from the Lord & Lady to the Broker: I took the advantage of walking through the superb suite of rooms, which are furnished in the most magnificent style; oriental alabaster & rich mosaic tables, splendid hangings, tables & furniture of every description. The paintings &c. chiefly attracted my notice & among those in particular, some beautiful drawings—one of Exeter Cathedral by D. E. Cort—Ruins a magnificent production of Robart of the French Academy—The fifth plague of Eygpt a splendid production of Turner.—Romney's Masterpiece, the Gypsey from Shakespeare's Midsummer's Night Dream "The Fairy land keeps not the Child of me", &c. the principal figure the portrait of a delicious Griselle, maid & mistress of the Artist. | An admirable View in Venice—by Canaletto—a sweet morceau of Leon. da Vinci our Saviour & S^t. John—naked infants, kissing each other delicate & peaceful—a most beautiful Cabinet picture of the Nativity by Ludov. Caracci, a groupe most admirably formed, with a most sweet effect of light of unique excellence.—S^t. Jerome & the angel Guerchino very fine.—A beautiful portrait—Gonzales—Spanish Grandee on Horseback—Two beautiful sea pieces a calm & a storm by Vernet—Charity & Nymph curious, & the attitude of the latter charming by Raphael—Two N. Prussians—the Woman taken in Adultery & the Magdalen washing our Saviour's feet, the latter especially splendidly fine—The Grand Statue of Bacchus antique—a magnificent production—And the Hebe of Moite of Paris—delicate & charming. A great deal of valuable Porcelain. Leaving this magazine of splendor passed over various downs to the village of Usley | & Deptford Inn where I had the pleasure to meet & dine with an acquaintance the Rev^d. M^r. Pulsford of Wells: returned home late in the Evening by Shrewton, Maddington, Tilshead &c.—

Tuesday Aug. 18th.—

Very fine, but very sultry weather. M^r. Rogers the Vicar of Lavington made a long morning visit. M^r. & M^rs. Legg & Miss Trusler, M^r. & M^rs. Butcher drank tea played cards, supped with us.—

Wednesday Aug. 19th.

Very beautiful summer weather. Very hot. Composing a Discourse upon GOD a Benefactor. Finished Turnbull's Voyage to the Pacific Ocean. Rode in the Evening on Lidelexey.[72]—

Thursday Aug. 20th.—

One heavy shower about midday, otherwise very fine. Finished the Composition of a Sermon as yesterday. Rode through Eastcott, Easterton, Lavington &c. M^rs. Poore passed the Evening with us. Walked with her to Foxley Corner & Home.

---

cultured and exotic. In 1781 he inherited vast wealth from his father. Byron referred to him as 'England's wealthiest son.' Beckford became infatuated with the very young William Courtenay and the later exposure of his love letters led to a scandal that essentially ruined his life. As a social outcast he led a solitary eccentric life. He was acquainted with Voltaire, was visited by Nelson (through the Hamilton connections on his mother's side). He was an avid collector of fine works of art and books and a writer of some repute, his gothic novel, *Vathek* being his best known work. He pulled down much of Fonthill House, and this diary entry relates to the sale of furniture at that time. Beckford spent much of his wealth creating his gothic fantasy Fonthill Abbey. In later life he moved to Bath, and build Fonthill Tower at Lansdown.

72. Lidelexey — the first reference to the name of Frank's grey.

Friday Aug. 21st.—

Extremely fine weather, but very sultry in the former part of the day. Transcribing a Sermon finished yester- | -day. Rode to Devizes upon various errands; conversed with Mr. Jones, Mr. & Mrs. Jacques, Willm. Woods, &c. Heard from Margaret, Horne & Gaisford. Replied to the two latter. Passed the Evening and supped at the Comptons, meeting the Leggs & Butchers; & Mrs. Bodman.

Saturday Aug. 22d.—

After a shower of rain early, the day very fine. Transcribing a Sermon as yesterday, wrote to Mrs. Travell. Rode to Lavington & W. Lavington called upon Mr. Williams at the latter place with whom I agreed to do my Erchfont Duty during my approaching absence & called after there upon Mr. Halliday for his subscription to the Clergy meeting.[73] In the afternoon accompanied my Father & Mother in the Lavington Chaise to Littleton. Drank tea & supped at Tinkers, the young Ladies absent [_____][74] the Comptons, Mrs. Smith, Mrs. Edwards, Mrs. Saunders &c.—

Sunday Aug. 23d.

Very fine weather, though extremely warm. Morning Duty at Erchfont, where I preached the second part of "GOD a Benefactor." Mrs. Poore, Mrs. Compton, & Mrs. Bodman called. Evening service at Stert. Called as usual upon Mrs. | Jaques. Began Memoires of M. de Brinboc.[75] Finished transcribing the Sermon, which I preached.—

Monday Aug. 24th.—

Very fine weather, overclouded & not so warm. Once or twice a tendency to rain. Read Memoires of M. de Brinboc. Wrote to M Smith. Drove my Mother to Devizes. Called upon Mrs. J. Tylee, & Miss Tylee, conversed with Barwis, C. Tylee &c. Wrote to Margaret on her Birth-day.—

Tuesday Aug. 25th.

Very fine warm summer weather. Finished letter to Margaret. Began the 2d. Vol. of Warner's Northern Tour. Rode thro' Lavington to Little Cheverill. Called with Mr. Royce on Mrs. Richards. Called on the Roger's. Mr. & Mrs. J. Tylee & Charles, drank tea & passed the Evening with us.

Wednesday Aug. 26th.—

Very beautiful weather. Drove my Mother to Conock & Stoke, called upon Mrs. Warrener, Mrs. Jones, Mrs. & Miss L. Mayo: Met at the two Houses Dr. Hill & Mrs. Collins. Drank tea at Mrs. Poores, whither I drove my Mother—Wrote to Mr. Horne. Read Warner's Northern Tour.— |

---

73. An expedition was being planned for Yorkshire. It appears that William Dowell, to whom Frank had written on 12 August had not yet replied.

74. Word indecipherable.

75. *Memoires of M. de Brinboc.* An anonymous novel. (1805).

Thursday Aug. 27th.

Very fine warm weather, a heavy storm in the Evening with thunder & lightning. Rode to collect subscriptions for the Clergy Charity through Cheriton, Patney, Stoke, Wilcot, Rushall, &c. [______] [______][76] Clarke tho neither at home. Heard from Dowell. Began Brewster's Secular Essay.[77]—

Friday Aug. 28th.—

Symptoms of rain, after heavy morning rain the Evening very fine—Rode to Devizes & returned with Daniel Compton.—Read Brewster's Secular Essay &c. Walked in the Evening to the foot of Redhorn Hill.—

Saturday Aug. 29th.—

Fine weather with local & passing showers. Rode to Devizes to the Bank. Heard from Mr. Horne & Mr. Travell. Wrote to the latter. Conversed with Mr. Wood &c. ~~Walke~~ Rode home with Jaques, who called upon us. Walked in the Even. to the bottom of Redhorn hill.—

Sunday Aug. 30th.

Fine weather, but a fresher air, & a slight tendency to rain. Morning service at Stert. Preached upon the duty of Repentance. Visited Mrs. Jacques as usual. Wrote to Mr. Travell. At Erchfont afternoon service. Preached upon the Immortality of the Soul. Mrs. Poore, Miss Truslee & Mrs. Legg called. Wrote to Mr. Auriol & Mr. [__________].[78] |

34. View of Bath showing the South Parade, bridge etc.

---

76. Two words indecipherable.
77. John Brewster, *A Secular Essay Containing a Retrospective View of Events Connected with the Ecclesiastical History of England, during the Eighteenth Century.* (1802).
78. Name indecipherable.

Monday Aug. 31$^{st.}$

Weather very fine. After an early breakfast accompanied my Parents to Bath. I rode, they went in the Lavington Chaise. Called at the Post at Devizes without success. Saw Alfred Wyatt & C. Tylee. At Bath repaired to the Elephant & Castle. Visited my Taylor & Bootmaker &c. Dined at the Inn. Passed the Evening & supped at M$^{rs.}$ Bates's.

Tuesday Sep. 1—

Beautiful weather. Breakfasted at M$^{rs.}$ Bates. Shopping & calling on M$^{rs.}$ Drew in Pulteney Street. Left Bath at two for Erchfont. My Father & Mother go to Clifton tomorrow. Five hours riding home. Dined at John Rocks at Clifford. Read Brewster's Secular Essay.—

Wednesday Sept. 2$^{d.}$—

Very fine weather. Rode by Upavon to Manningford & back. Called at M$^{rs.}$ Giffard's for the Rev$^{d.}$ M$^{r.}$ White's Subscription to the Clergy in vain. Called on D$^{r.}$ Wells. I Wrote to Betsey Nash—M$^{rs.}$ Legg & her family party, viz Braham, Strace, her Mother, M$^{r.}$ & M$^{rs.}$ Kennedy &c. visited me after Dinner. Drank tea & supped at M$^{rs.}$ Legg's. Butchers &c.

Thursday Sep. 3$^{d.}$—

Equally fine weather. Called upon several villagers. Dined with M$^{rs.}$ Poore at Wedhampton. Called at Miss Lewis's. Heard from M$^{r.}$ Travell & John Auriol.—

There is a gap in the diaries covering the period 4 September to 5 December. From the diaries of Agnes Witts the known sequence of events is as follows:

2 September 1807: Edward and Agnes Witts lodge at 3 Richmond Terrace, Clifton. 7 September 1807: Edward and Agnes are at Cheltenham when Francis arrives: . . . 'at my Sisters door our Dear Franks cheerful face made us happy' . . . 16 September 1807: . . . 'went early with Frank for an hour to Mrs. Timbrells in spite of a very bad cold' . . .

35. Bromsgrove Church; a sketch by Francis Witts.

8 October 1807: The family travelled to Birmingham, Francis parted from them at Bromsgrove to proceed northwards the next day. 9 October 1807: Edward and Agnes reached Calwich Abbey to stay with the Granvilles. 24 October 1807: . . . 'wrote an important letter to Frank'; 29 October 1807: . . . 'received a long letter from Frank'; 19 November 1807: . . . ' doubly oppressive to me from the idea that my Dear Son was begin his journey from Yorkshire'; 21 November 1807: . . . ' before tea arrived our Dear Frank in health and safety after a perilous journey';

22 November 1807: . . . ' to church where Frank performed the whole of the service'; 24 November 1807: . . . ' a tolerable mild fine day sufficiently so for the two Ports & Frank to set out for the Doveridge coursing party which they were to take up their quarters'; 28 November 1807: The family arrived at Hanbury to stay with their old friend Revd. William Burslem: 29 November 1807: At Hanbury: . . . 'Frank performed all of the service'; 4 December 1807: . . . ' at Gloucester we joined our Servant who had set out the day before when Frank & he got into the gig wch. had been painting at a coachmakers, & rejoined us at Froster Inn 11 miles further where we dined and slept.'

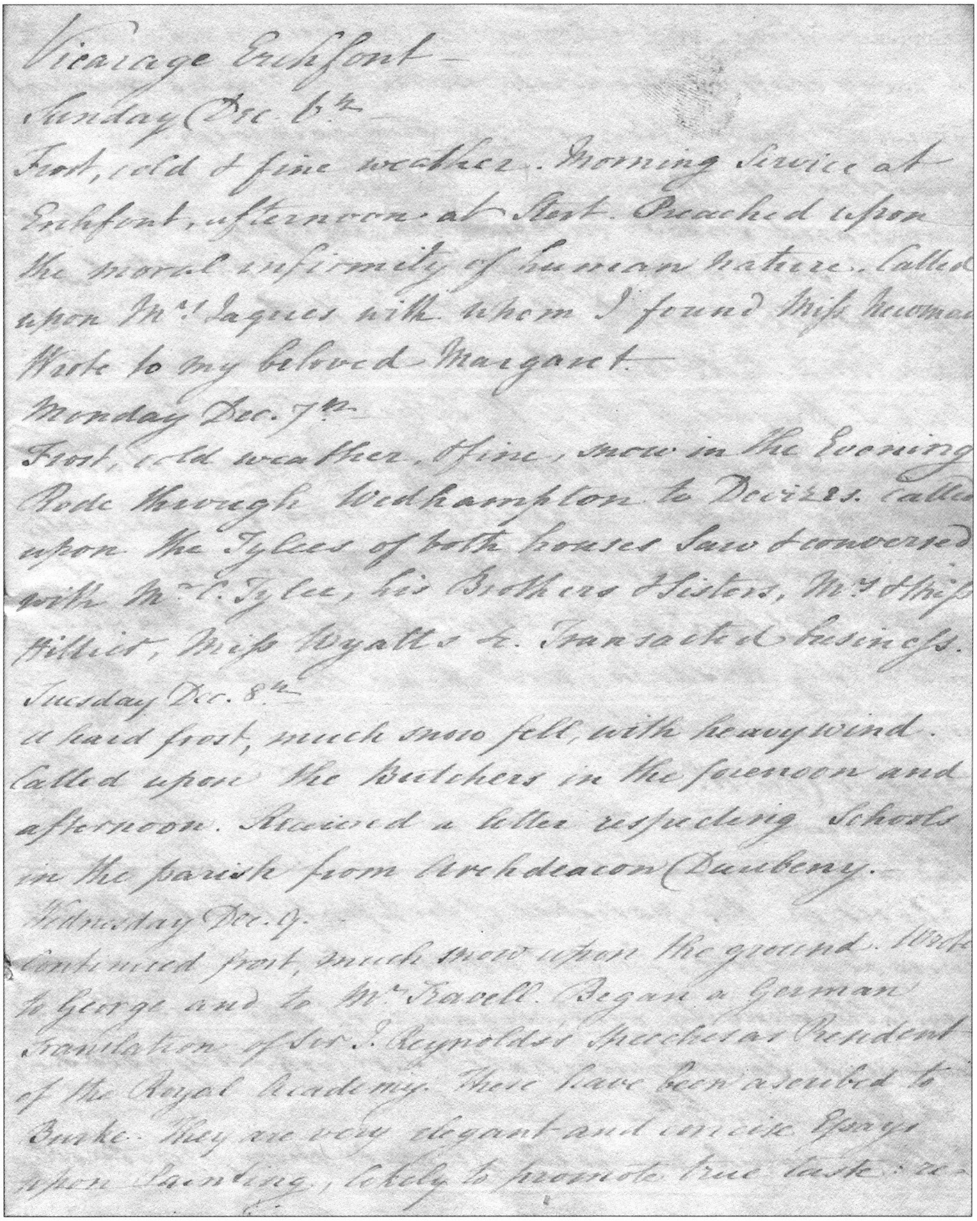
Vicarage Erchfont —
Sunday Dec. 6th
Frost, cold & fine weather. Morning Service at Erchfont, afternoon at Stert. Preached upon the moral infirmity of human nature. Called upon Mrs Jaques with whom I found Miss Neeman
Wrote to my beloved Margaret.
Monday Dec. 7th
Frost, cold weather, & fine, snow in the Evening. Rode through Wedhampton to Devizes. Called upon the Tylees of both houses saw & conversed with Mr C. Tylee, his Brothers & Sisters, Mrs & Miss Hillier, Miss Wyatts &c. Transacted business.
Tuesday Dec. 8th
A hard frost, much snow fell, with heavy wind. Called upon the butchers in the forenoon and afternoon. Received a letter respecting Schools in the parish from Archdeacon Daubeny.
Wednesday Dec. 9.
Continued frost, much snow upon the ground. Wrote to George and to Mr Fravell. Began a German translation of Sir J. Reynolds's Speeches as President of the Royal Academy. These have been ascribed to Burke. They are very elegant and concise Essays upon Painting, likely to promote true taste: re-

Witts Family Papers F307

Vicarage Erchfont—
Sunday Dec. 6th.—

Frost, cold & fine weather. Morning service at Erchfont, afternoon at Stert. Preached upon the moral infirmity of human nature. Called upon Mrs. Jaques with whom I found Miss Newman. Wrote to my beloved Margaret.

Monday Dec. 7th.

Frost, cold weather, & fine, snow in the Evening. Rode through Wedhampton to Devizes. Called upon the Tylees of both houses. Saw & conversed with Mr. C. Tylee, his Brothers & Sisters, Mrs. & Miss Hillier, Miss Wyatts &c. Transacted business.

Tuesday Dec. 8th.

A hard frost, much snow fell, with heavy wind. Called upon the Butchers in the forenoon and afternoon. Received a letter respecting schools in the parish from Archdeacon Daubeny.

Wednesday Dec. 9.

Continued frost, much snow upon the ground. Wrote to George and to Mrs. Travell. Began a German translation of Sir. J. Reynolds's Speeches as President of the Royal Academy. These have been ascribed to Burke. They are very elegant and concise Essays upon Painting, likely to promote true taste: re- | -commending industry and labour, and valuable to every class of Students, from the many excellent general principles, which they involve.

Thursday Dec. 10.

Frost and snow, but not piercingly cold. Walked to Stert and Devizes. Called on Mr. & Mrs. Jaques, walked with the latter into town. Called upon Miss Hillier, where I met Miss C. Wyatt, Miss S. Hughes, & Miss H. Tylee. Buried a corpse, christened a child, churched a woman. Heard from my beloved Margaret. Read Sir J. Reynolds, and began an eventful novel by the favourite writer, Mrs. Hunter, of Norwich: family annals or Worldly Wisdom;[1] written in the cause of integrity and virtue.

Friday Dec. 11th.—

A gradual thaw, and mild weather. Wrote to the Bishop of Salisbury respecting the State of Schools in the parishes of Erchfont & Stert. Studied Cicero de Oratore, full of admiration

1. Rachel Hunter, *Family Annals, or Worldly Wisdom.* (1807).

at his inimitable suavity and elegance of diction & thought. Continued Family Annals & Sir Josh. Reynolds.—

Saturday Dec. 12th.—

A thaw, which rendered the roads more practicable, | but the air was moist. Rode to W. Lavington: called on Mr. Williams, Mr. Hallilay's family, our future neighbours at Wedhampton, and Mrs. Tinker. Called in vain on Mrs. Rogers. Continued Cicero de Oratore, delighted with the urbanity of his Style. Continued Sir Josh. Reynolds. Glad to find many of my previous notions upon similar subjects confirmed by his.—

Sunday Dec. 13th.

Fine open weather for the season. Morning service at Stert, preached there and at Erchfont upon the Excellency of Patience: called upon Mrs. Jaques, as usual. In the Evening began to remodel a discourse from Dr. Jones's Vol. of Sermons, entitled "GOD is our Father". Began to read Prior's Poems; his Dedication to one & Eulogium of another Dorset, I read with distrust, but it contains some fine writing, many of his poems are highly humorous, & in his verse there reigns an enviable terseness & elegance.[2]

Monday Dec. 14th.—Antelope Inn Salisbury.—

Extremely fine open weather. Left Erchfont before dawn, on horseback, to repair to Salisbury, where I arrived to breakfast, at the Antelope Inn. Transacted business with Dodsworth the verger and | Agent for my Vicar, a lively good natured man with some good paintings. Walked over the Episcopal Palace & Grounds, repaired to Collins' Book-shop &c. At the moment of my projected return met Col. Cooper of the 2nd. Som. Mil. quartered in the Town. Could not refuse the pressing invitation of an old friend. He introduced me to his friends Col. Edm. Bastard & his son, the former member for Dartmouth, very pleasant men,[3] also the Adjutant, Mr. Eyre & Miss Eyre &c. Walked with Cooper &c. At the Mess our party was increased by six German L'Dr. Officers, upon their return from Copenhagen, intelligent polite men with whom I conversed much in their own tongue. An excellent dinner, wine in abundance, and retired late.

Tuesday. Dec. 15th. Vicarage Erchfont

A hard frost, & fine weather. Before breakfast saw our German guests depart. At Cooper's breakfast table, the Bastards, Adj. B. & myself.—At the Parade in the Close. Walked with Fouward. Left my friend between one & two o clock. At home to dinner. Heard from Round. Began Mrs. Sheridans old novel Sydney Bidulph, in | the Richardsonian Style, but tolerably interesting.[4] Read Prior's Poems.—

Wednesday Dec. 16th.—

A raw day, without frost. Wrote to my beloved Margaret. Rode to Devizes. Called upon the

---

2. Matthew Prior, (1664-1721).
3. Edmund Bastard, (1758-1816) of Sharpham nr. Totnes, M.P. for Dartmouth, 1787-1812. Edmund Bastard, (1784-1834) of Kitley, nr. Plymouth, M.P. for Dartmouth, 1812-1816, and Devon 1816-1830.
4. Frances Sheridan, *Memoirs of Miss Sydney Biddulph*.

Hilliers, met Ch. Tylee & Michael Wyatt, called on John Tylee, whose infant is deplorably ill, called upon Mr. Tylee & his daughter, met & conversed with various acquaintance, Jaques, Eldridge &c. Rode home with Mrs. Butcher.—A funeral & churching. Read Prior's Poems & Mrs. Hunter's Wordly Wisdom.

Thursday Dec. 17.

An unpleasant, raw, foggy day. Called upon Mrs. Butcher, Mrs. Legg, John Sainsbury, a wretched object, John Dunford, Harry Snook, Mrs. Crook, Matthew North &c. Read Mrs. Hunter's Novel & Prior's Poems. Received a letter from my beloved Margaret.[x]

Friday Dec. 18th.—

A still more unpleasant, & foggy, raw day than the preceding. Rode to Devizes upon various errands. Saw & conversed with Miss Hillier, John Gale &c. Called upon Mr. Lediard. Heard from Mr. Travell. Finished Mrs. Hunter's Novel: & read Mrs. Sheridan's Sidney Bidulph.—

[x] Began a Sermon for Xmas day from a Vol. of Mr. Newton. Also entered upon the study of Hammond's Practical Catechism. |

Saturday Dec. 19th.

A raw, unpleasant day: a thick fog. Never left the house: Remodelling a Sermon as on Thursday. Studied Hammond's practical catechism, the author a Divine of Profound learning. Continued Cicero de Oratore—Read Mrs. Sheridan's Sidney Bidulph, a very affecting Tale.

Sunday Dec. 20th.

Very cold, being a hoar frost & thick rime. Morning service at Erchfont. Preached upon the division of mankind into rich & poor. The same was repeated in the afternoon at Stert, where I was with Mrs. Jaques as usual. A funeral in the afternoon. Read Sidney Bidulph, a most pathetic Tale.

Monday Dec. 21st.

A similar hoar & rime as on the preceding days, the atmosphere being very dense. Finished new-modelling the Sermon mentioned on Saturday. Visited poor John Sainsbury. Rode to Devizes, conversed with Gaisford, Burton &c. Wrote to my beloved Margaret. Read Sidney Bidulph.

Tuesday Dec. 22.—

Fine clear day, a hard hoar frost. Transcribing a Sermon finished yesterday. Jaques, his wife & neice called upon me. Studied Hammond's Practical Catechism. Wrote to Horne. Read Sidney Bidulph. Nursed a Cold, staying all day at home. |

Wednesday Dec. 23d.—

A fine forenoon, being clear & a hard hoar frost; in the afternoon the wonted cold rime returned. Transcribing a Sermon as yesterday. Rode to Devizes, returned in my Gig lately repaired. Conversed with Mrs. Jaques &c. Read Sidney Bidulph, & began ~~Mrs.~~ Domestic Scenes, a novel from the German by the authoress of Agnes de Lislein, our old acquaintance

Mad de Wohlzogen,[5] Wife to one of the Chamberlains of the Duke of Weimar. Studied Hammond's Practical Catechism.—

Thursday Dec. 24th.

A thaw rendered the surface of the ground very moist; but it still continued extremely cold. Finished transcribing a Sermon as yesterday. Projected another on the nature of the Gospel Covenant. Visited three sick & poor old men, John Sainsbury, William Bailey, & Francis Hayter: called upon William Jones & Charles Giddings at Uphill. Finished that most interesting novel, Sidney Bidulph. Studied Hammond's Practical Catechism & Cicero de Oratore.

Friday Dec. 25th. Christmas day.

A very fine winter's day, sun without frost. Morn. Service at Erchfont with a Sacrament; preached upon the Darkness of former ages contrasted with the light of Christianity. Evening service and the same Sermon at Stert. Called as usual upon the Jaques's. Read Domestic Scenes.— |

Saturday Dec. 26th.—

Rain had fallen during the night; the day was damp & misty, but mild; more rain fell in the Evening. Began a Sermon upon the nature of the Gospel Covenant. Studied Hammond's Practical Catechism, upon Faith; Administered the Sacrament to Matt. North's Wife, & Samuel Plank;—Heard from Dowell & from my beloved Margaret. Studied Cicero de Oratore. Read the October Edinburgh Review.[6]

Sunday Dec. 27.

Very fine mild weather. Morning Service at Stert where I preached upon the duty of frequently attending the Sacrament, which I also administered. The Evening service at Erchfont, where I preached a Sermon, named All is Vanity, where I also churched two women & christened a child. Read the last Edinburgh Review.

Monday Dec. 28th.

Violent wind with gusts of rain, which fell heavily during the Evening and night. Preparing a Sermon as on Saturday. Studied Hammond's Practical Catechism on Faith, & Sandiland's single Sermon on Faith and Works. Read the last Edinburgh Review. Began & ended the Marquis de Salvo's interesting narrative of his Flight & Rescue of the Heroic Mrs. Spencer Smith, a French Prisoner, by a daring & hairbreadth Escape from Brescia, thro' Tyrol, | Saltzburg, Austria, Bohemia, Gallicia & Livonia to England. Wrote to my beloved Margaret. Read Domestic Scenes.—

5. Karoline von Wolzogen, *Domestic Scenes.*
6. This is the first mention of the *Edinburgh Review*. The magazine was started in 1802 by Francis Jeffrey as a literary and political review and was a strong supporter of the Whig party and laissez-faire politics. One of its most influential editors and contributors was Henry Brougham who Frank Witts knew very well. Agnes Witts was a very close friend of Henry Brougham's mother, Eleanor. Undoubtedly Frank would have been interested in the reviews and would have been quietly fascinated with what the bright young lawyer was now doing, but he would have deplored the politics.

Tuesday Dec. 29th.—

Very violent wind attended with heavy rain, yet not so much as yesterday, but falling in storms: the Evening & former part of the night serene, the latter heavy rain. Working at a Sermon as yesterday. Visiting John Sainsbury. Read Domestic Scenes. Studying Sandiland's single Sermon on Faith and Works & Hammond's Practical Catechism. Finished the topic of Faith. Read Priors Henry & Emma, much beautiful versification. I can not avoid thinking Johnson's Critique too severe, the poem was not meant to convey an exalted moral.

Wednesday Dec. 30th.—

A fine winter's day, open & milder, one gust of rain in the afternoon. Continued composing a Sermon, as yesterday. Jaques called. Rode with him part of his way home, then thro' Wedhampton to Conock; & called upon Jones & his Aunt Warriner. Christened a child privately.—

Thursday Dec. 31st.—

A fine morning, ending in a turbulent & rainy day; much rain in the Evening and night. Finished the Sermon upon the Nature of the Gospel Covenant; being the first part. Studied Hammond's Practical Catechism upon | Hope, the Love of GOD & Charity. Read Prior's Poems & Domestic Scenes. Studied Cicero de Oratore. Buried poor Francis Hayter.

1808.

Friday Jan. 1st.—

Very beautiful, mild, open, weather; a gust of rain in the afternoon; heavy rain in the night. Transcribing a Sermon finished yesterday. Reading Domestic Scenes. Dined at Jaques's meeting Miss A. Gale & Miss M. Gabriel; very unpleasant & dull.

Saturday Jan. 2d.—

The Day very fine, open, & mild: in the Evening heavy rain. Transcribing a Sermon as yesterday. Rode to Etchelhampton: Jacob Giddings absent, sat with his Daughter. Read Domestic Scenes. Heard from my dearest Margaret.

Sunday Jan 3d.—

Very fine weather, being a frost (hoar) clear & sunny. Morning Service at Erchfont with a Christening & Churching. Preached upon the nature of the Gospel Covenant. Afternoon Service at Stert; called upon Mrs. Jaques; preached the same Sermon. Dined with the Gales, meeting Mrs. Jaques, John & Alfred Thomas, John Grant, Mr. Hayward, Mrs. Newell, Miss Gabriell's & Miss A Biggs. A pleasant visit & much instructive conversation. Began Anna Maria Porter's interesting novel, the Hungarian Brothers.[7]— |

7. Anna Maria Porter, *The Hungarian Brothers.* (1807).

Monday Jan. 4th.

A frost, fine weather throughout the day, but rain at night. Began composing the second part of the Sermon compleated last week. Visited John Sainsbury. Continued A.M. Porter's fascinating novel, the Hungarian Brothers. Wrote to my beloved Margaret.

Tuesday Jan. 5th.—

A day of very heavy rain almost without interval: the Evening not so wet. Composing a Sermon as yesterday. Studying Hammond's Practical Catechism: Reading Domestic Scenes.

Wednesday Jan. 6th.—

A very fine forenoon, which turned to gloom and a little rain in the afternoon. Finished composing a Sermon as yesterday. Read Domestic Scenes. Drank tea & supped without pleasure at the Butchers, met Mrs. Butcher of Sharcot & a Miss Daisy B—.

Thursday Jan. 7th.—

A dull day, mild & obscure, without rain. Preparing for the compilation of another Sermon from Mr. Jones, the Witnesses of the Being & Goodness of GOD. Studying Hammond's Practical Catechism. Heard from my beloved Margaret & Mrs. Dodsworth. Read Domestic Scenes.— |

Friday Jan. 8th.

Thick fog, without moisture, not cold. Transcribing the Sermon finished Wednesday. Compiling as yesterday from Dr. Jones. Administered the Sacrament privately at John Sainsbury's. Visited William Baily. Finished Mad. de Wohlzogin's domestic Scenes. Began Coxe's Tour in Monmouthshire.[8] Wrote to Mrs. Dodsworth.—

Saturday Jan. 9th.—

Mild weather, in the forenoon a thick fog, clearing afterwards to a fine day. Transcribing a Sermon as yesterday. Rode to Beching Stoke: called on Mr. Mayo & his sister. Read Prior's Poems. Read Coxe's Tour in Monmouthshire.—

Sunday Jan. 10th.—

Fine mild forenoon, rather misty afterwards.—Morning service at Stert. Preached the second part of the Sermon on the nature of the Gospel Covenant, as also at Erchfont. Called on Mrs. Jaques & the Gale's. Churched a woman at Erchfont. Read Coxe's Tour in Monmouthshire.

Monday Jan. 11th.—

Fine open weather. Rode to Devizes, conversed with Mrs. Tylee. Read Coxe's Monmouthshire. Wrote to my beloved Margaret. Compiling a Sermon, as on Friday.— |

Tuesday Jan. 12th.

Fine open weather. Rather colder. Compiling a Sermon as yesterday. Walked with my

8. William Coxe, An Historical Tour of Monmouthshire. (1811).

Father & Mother. Called on Dame North. Read Coxe's Tour in Monmouthshire—Studied Hammond's Practical Catechism.—

Wednesday Jan. 13th.—

Fine weather; clear & sunny, but rather cold. Wrote to Mr. Travell. Drove my Father to Devizes. Saw & conversed with some of the Tylees &c. Finished the Compilation of a Sermon as yesterday.

Thursday Jan. 14th.—Devizes.

Extremely boisterous, cold, rainy weather: Sleet & hard frost at night. Composing a Sermon upon Christian Humility. Transcribing one finished yesterday. Read Hammond's Practical Catechism. Accompanied my Father & Mother in a Chaise to Devizes Assembly. Drank tea, supped & slept most agreeably at John Tylee's. Met Miss Tylee. The Ball began at 8 & ceased at one. Conversed with the Tylee family, the Salmons, the Tinkers, the Spaldings, Mr. Rogers, Mr. Banvis, W. Wood, Eldridge, Macfarlane, Brabant, H. Merewether, Miss F. Goodman &c. On the whole a pleasant meeting.

Friday Jan. 15. Vicarage, Erchfont.

Very hard frost, intensely cold. Breakfasted most | pleasantly at Mr. John Tylee's: ~~visite~~ called upon Mrs. Hill, & the other Tylee Family: conversed with the Miss Tylees, Charles Hill, &c.—Heard from my beloved Margaret. Read Coxe's Tour in Monmouthshire. Transcribing a Sermon as yesterday; for we returned home to dinner. My Father walked; I drove my Mother in the Gig.—

Saturday Jan. 16.—

A very hard frost, rather yeilding after midday. Resumed at night with a sprinkling of snow. Transcribing a Sermon as yesterday. Read Coxe's Tour in Monmouthshire. Heard from Mr. Dodsworth.

Sunday Jan 17th.—

A very hard frost, & cold weather. Snow sprinkled on the ground; the roads very slippery. Morning service at Erchfont. Preached a Sermon, intitled the Witnesses of the Being and goodness of GOD. The same in the Afternoon at Stert; visited Mrs. ~~Gale &~~ Jaques, where I found the Miss Hughes's; pleasant young women. Read the Miseries of Human Life;[9] a very humorous production of Mr. Beresford of Merton College, but cui bono?[10] Continued the third volume of that interesting novel, the Hungarian Brothers.

Monday Jan. 18th.

Hard frost, very clear & cold weather. Composing a Sermon upon Humility. Mrs. Butcher called. Reading | the Miseries of Human Life. Finished the Hungarian Brothers. Wrote to my beloved Margaret & to Horne.

---

9. James Beresford, *The Miseries of Human Life.* (1806).
10. Cui bono — good for whom, or whom benefits?

Tuesday Jan. 19th.—

The frost going, the day cold & dull. Composing a Sermon as yesterday. Wrote to Round. Read the Miseries of Human life, & Coxe's Travels in Monmouthshire. Mrs. Legg called in the morning.

Wednesday Jan. 20th.—

A slight frost; very fine weather. Finished the composition of a Sermon upon Humility. Visited John Sainsbury. Read Coxe's Tour in Monmouthshire.

Thursday Jan. 21st.—

Very hard frost, some snow fell in the middle of the day; otherwise very fine. Beginning another Sermon upon Attachment to the World. Transcribing the Sermon finished yesterday. Read Coxe's Monmouthshire. Dined very agreeably at Mr. Mayo's of Beching Stoke; met Mr. Dyke, Mrs. Dyke Poore, Mrs. W. Dyke & Mr. Brabant. A pleasant ride home.

Friday Jan 22d.—

Very hard frost & fine winter's day. Composing a Sermon upon Attachment to the World. Read Coxe's Tour in Monmouthshire & finished the Miseries of Human Life. Baptized an Infant. Walked to All Cannings to bury a corpse for Mr. Jaques in his absence at Bath. Called at Etchelhampton on Jacob Giddings, & on the Newmans at Can- | -nings; not at home to dinner till six o clock.—Transcribing a Sermon as yesterday.—

Saturday Jan 23d.

A thaw, falling weather at times, moist & raw atmosphere. Transcribing a Sermon as yesterday. Finished Coxe's Monmouthshire. Heard from my beloved Margaret & Horne.

Sunday Jan 24th.—

In the forenoon, a fog, which clearing up the weather became very fine, but heavy rain fell at night. Morning Service at Stert: preached upon Christian Humility; called upon Mrs. Jaques & the Gales; at Erchfont in the afternoon preached the same Sermon, & christened a Child. Read Horsely Curteis's verbose & bombastic Romance, St. Botolph's Priory,[11] & Mr. Raymond's interesting Memoirs of the Poet Dermody.[12]

Monday Jan. 25th—

Early frost, hardly giving throughout the day, some showers of sleet; but in general clear & fine. Read the Report of the African Institution, formed for the laudable purpose of civilizing the natives of that conduct. Composing a Sermon upon Attachment to the World. Rode to Devizes. Called at John Tylee's. Saw him, Mrs. & Miss Tylee &c. Called at the Gale's & Jaques's. Buried a Corpse at Stert & another at Erchfont. Read the Memoirs of Dermody & St. Botolph's Priory. Wrote to my beloved | Margaret & to Horne.—

---

11. T. H. J. Curteis, *St. Botolph's Priory, or the Sable Mask.* (1806).
12. J. Grant Raymond, *The Life of Thomas Dermody, interspersed with pieces of original poetry.* (1807).

Tuesday Jan. 26$^{th.}$—

Hard frost, very fine weather. Composing a Sermon as yesterday. Visited John Sainsbury. Walked to the foot of Redhorn Hill, & with my Father. Learnt the melancholy tidings of poor Lord Elcho's death on the 20$^{th.}$ Inst. Read S$^{t.}$ Botolph's Priory, & Raymond's Life of Dermody.—

Wednesday Jan 27$^{th.}$—

A morning frost; about midday Snow beginning to fall, turned to rain for the afternoon. Finished the Composition of a Sermon, as yesterday. M$^{rs.}$ Sutton & M$^{rs.}$ Estcourt called. Read the life of Dermody & S$^{t.}$ Botolph's Priory.—

Thursday Jan. 28$^{th.}$—

Very windy, & cold, rain falling in frequent heavy showers. Composing a Fast Sermon from Cowper's Expostulation. Transcribing a Sermon finished yesterday. Completed the Memoirs of the unfortunate & vicious Dermody. Read S$^{t.}$ Botolph's Priory till I was choked with bombast: read no more. Read Prior's Poems. Heard from my beloved Margaret.

Friday Jan. 29$^{th.}$

A slight frost in the morning: the air cold & wind high. Compiling a Sermon upon GOD our Father from D$^{r.}$ Jones. Transcribing a Sermon as | yesterday. Rode to Devizes. Read Prior's Poems. Read a Report of the American Quaker's rational attempts to civilize the native Tribes.—

Saturday Jan. 30$^{th.}$

Rain had fallen during the night, & continued abundantly, though not unintermittingly through the day. Transcribing a Sermon as yesterday. Compiling a funeral Sermon from D$^{r.}$ Jones, for a Sermon to be preached at the funeral of Rob$^{t.}$ Pile, Monday. Read the Edinburgh Review, last number. Wrote to the Bishop of Sarum respecting my engagements with Smith.

Sunday Jan 31$^{st.}$

Open, cloudy, but mild weather. Morning Service at Erchfont. Preached upon Attachment to the World & churched a woman. Afternoon Service at Stert. Called upon M$^{rs.}$ Jaques & the Gales. Preached the same Sermon. Began Essai sur la vie du Grand Conde Par Louis de Bourbon, Prince de Condé, son quatrième Descendant. Finished a funeral Sermon begun yesterday. Wrote to M$^{r.}$ Dodsworth.

Monday. Feb. 1$^{st.}$—

An open mild rain, at times with a tendency to rain. Transcribing a Funeral Sermon finished yesterday. Read Essai sur la vie du Grand Condé, an interesting & well written biography of a very won- | -derful man. Assisted at the Funeral of R. Pile, attended by the members of the Club & an immense croud: preached a Funeral Sermon. Wrote to my beloved Margaret.

There are few surviving letters to Margaret from Francis. Those that do survive were clearly kept by Margaret for some reason or other and now sit in the Witts Family Papers catalogued as F470. This letter is the only 'love letter' that survives from before their marriage. It is made more difficult to read by being cross-hatch written. Interestingly Margaret has annotated some letters in this sequence as being 'from Frank', clearly showing that she referred to him as 'Frank' rather the common convention of the time 'Mr. Witts'. The letter is postmarked 3 Feb 1808.

Miss Backhouse
Beck House
Settle

Vicarage Erchfont
Feb 1st 1808

My Dearest Margaret,

My first solicitude now is to relieve your mind of any anxiety which my black seal & paper may have occasioned, for though we sincerely lament the loss of an old & agreeable friend, yet he was not so near to me as to excite any very strong regret in you; however, I am sure, had he survived, he would have been pleased to have learnt that I was made happy in marriage & had he lived to have known you, you would with me have regretted his loss. I speak of poor Lord Elcho, Earl of Wemyss' Son, the husband of my mother's first cousin, in age he corresponded with that of my Mother & there was always much intimacy between us. He was a very handsome generous man not endowed with great talents, but very agreeable, his family numerous & chiefly daughters, all variously married, but one this Girl, his wife & son, with my Brother, attended him in his last illness, being an inflammation on the lungs, carried him off in a fortnight. His daughter, Augusta Charteris, had written to my Mother ten days before, mentioning his illness, the intimation of it came from George last Wednesday, who had never left him from his first attack till he breathed his last, except to get Physicians from Edinbro! for he died at his Seat, Amisfield, near Haddington, within half a mile of my Brother's Barracks, who was indeed always as it were domesticated with them. His Father, between 80 & 90, is a hardhearted avaricious Man, & had till very lately, always kept him very low, for his rank, in income; but of late had given him this fine Seat & adequate Income, in which they were hardly settled. He is a great loss, & having always lived on a confined income, & contracted great debts, it would have seemed a more prosperous lot , if he had lived to enjoy for a few years the immense wealth annexed to his Father's title. I was under particular obligation to him for his introducing me to the diplomatic station I formerly held, & for his peculiarly friendly partiality. He will be a great loss to George, who was also a favourite with them all.

When I sat down to write, I did not mean to postpone this long my heartfelt thanks for your very affectionate letter of the 24th from which, as usual, I derived great pleasure that, which preceded it, was not the less welcome , for its omissions perhaps, peculiarly dear, because it shewed me, that even in the enjoyment of gay society, your heart turns to me, since I am too much delighted by the hope to doubt, that your heart always guides your pen. I derive this idea from what I feel within myself. It gives me satisfaction to learn Miss Richardson's recovery, I hope she will soon be well enough to visit you, that some earnest arrangements may be made for your Southern Journey; I do not say; as you did, in your last letter but one, <u>for your leaving home</u>, for I hope, that was a lapse, & that, in approaching my residence, with our parents hopes, you think rather, that you are going home. Willing she give Smith & his friends every fair chance, (since writing to the Bishop is tantamount to exposing his vices & incapacity,) I waited one week longer in expectation of hearing from some of the crew: but that being frustrated, I yesterday dispatched a very plain statement to the Bishop, told him I considered myself unhandsomely used, represented Smith as unable to do his own duty, expressed, that I deemed my compensation for duty inadequate, & concluded by requesting him to make such arrangement as he thought fit between us. Thus I have no further to attend to their caprice, but leave all to the Bishop's arbitration their silence & illiberality has occasioned this Exposure, & they must abide by the consequences. You talk of my having been displeased by some despondence of yours, as to the displeasure, I certainly recollect nothing of it, & suspect it to be a fancy of your own, I rather think, you will very seldom excite that feeling in me, &, certainly, not for a duration; I never was vexed with you for anything but exposing yourself without a wrap to the Cold & night air. My last gigantic Dispatch was of unusual importance; the more I think upon the subject, the more I am satisfied of the propriety of immediately investigating the true power you have over that Estate, & I hope you will comply with my suggestions on the subject. I cannot help thinking also, that it would be wise to entrust the Preparing of the Settlement to Mr. Hartley earlier than is proposed, under the chance of any formalities rendering its execution a work of longer duration than we expect. I am peculiarly pleased at the idea, that I seem to be winning on your Grandfather's good graces, by the proof that he often speaks of me; if that is a sign of esteem, I am certain you could not come into a family, which loves you more than mine; since from real partiality, & out of indulgence to me, my Father & Mother incessantly converse of you, & anticipate with delight the moment when they shall salute you as their Daughter.

What you write & do is so infinitely more important than what occurs to me, that I usually defer to the last the record of my operations since I last wrote, & though you tax me with not being minute, I assure you, I mention almost every trivial occurrence so extremely uniform is our method of passing time, & as for our general habits I have already amply described them by word of mouth I have not stirred from the village since I wrote excepting one morning's ride to Devizes: nor have seen any one, excepting M^rs. Sutton of New Park, and her Daughter, M^rs. Estcourt, Wife of the Member who were here. Preaching seems to have been my chief occupation, & you must impute it to that, if you find this a stupid letter, since I have been haranguing a Congregation of between 500 & 600 at the funeral of a common parishioner, member of a Club, who always pay for a Sermon for each member, who dies. Such is the paucity of our engagement & the unchequered train of employment in a Wiltshire village far from unpleasant to me, but I fear it may disappoint you. Yet as I shall heed no seclusion; when you partake my retirement, I hope my society will be no less a compensation to you. My Father & Mother beg their love to you; pray remember us kindly to your Mother, & never cease to believe me your affectionate & sincere

F. E. Witts

Tuesday Feb. 2^d.—

Very stormy weather, many violent showers fell in the course of the day. Began the composition of a Sermon demonstrating the Christian Service to be reasonable. Transcribing

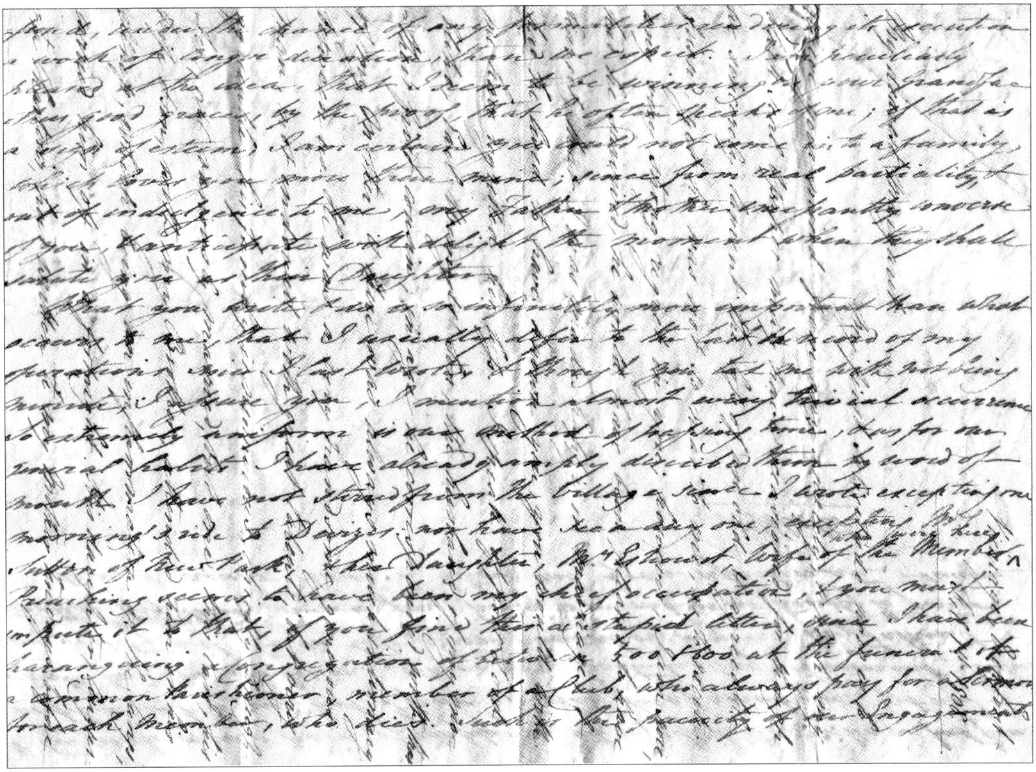

36. Letter from Francis to Margaret, 1 February 1808

the Funeral Sermon preached yesterday. Read Essai sur la vie du Grand Condé. Began Mountville Castle a Novel by Brewer.[13]

Wednesday Feb. 3d.—

A tendency to rain, but, on the whole, fine weather. Composing a Sermon as yesterday. Transcribing another, as yesterday. Read Mountville Castle, & the interesting biography of the Great Condé.

Thursday Feb. 4th.—

After a Frost a fine day. Composing a Sermon as yesterday. Transcribing a Sermon as yesterday. Rode to Wedhampton, & Rushall; called on Mr. Halliday's family, & on Mr. & Mrs. Peck. Heard from Mr. Travell. Wrote to Dowell. Read Essai sur la vie du Grand Condé & Mountville Castle, with which I am nearly surfeited.

Friday. Feb. 5th.—

A dull morning, with a forenoon of rain, the | afternoon fine. Composing a Sermon as yesterday. Transcribing as yesterday. Wrote to Mr. Travell. Rode to Devizes to the Bank

13. James Norris Brewer, *Mountville Castle, a Village Story.* (1808).

&c. Called on M[rs.] Tylee. Conversed with Charles Tylee, M[r.] Smith of W Lavington &c. Finished the interesting Biography of the Great Condé & began Lord Woodhouselee's (Fraser Tylter's) Memoirs of Henry Home, Lord Kames opus immensce neolis 2 Vols 4to; desultory, ascertaining Memoires pour servir a l'histoire of Scotch literature, science & manners in the 18th Century. Some Scotticisms, else the style agreeable, though rambling.[14] Read Mountville Castle, still bearable.—

Saturday Feb. 6th.—

A boisterous, stormy & rainy day. Completed a Sermon proving the Christian Religion to be a reasonable service. Read the Memoirs of Lord Kames, & Mountville Castle. Received a letter from Smith, my Vicar, from Chippenham, whither he seems to be come with a view of dislodging me; painful enough.[15] Read the first volume of a charming Novel Santo Sebastiano, or the Young Protector.[16] The author of the Romance of the Pyrenees wrote this.

Sunday Feb. 7th.—

A morning of very heavy rain, clearing after 11 o clock. | Being anxious to receive letters at the Post, rode to meet the mail at Devizes before morning Service at Stert, saw C. Tylee &c. Heard from Horne, Dodsworth, & Dowell. Preached at Stert, a Sermon upon the Faith of Abraham. Called upon M[rs.] Jaques. Afternoon Service at Erchfont; repeated the same Sermon, christened a child & churched two women. Wrote to Margaret, Dowell, & Collins of Salisbury respecting an advertised Curacy. Read Mountville Castle.—

Monday Feb. 8. White Hart Inn—Chippenham.

A very wet forenoon, thin mist & showers, about two o clock becoming fair. Read Mountville Castle, improving. Prevented till after mid-day pursuing my intended route to Chippenham to confer with Smith. Rode thither; both the weather & ways very bad. At Devizes conversed with M[r.] Gibbs &c. Repaired to the White Hart; whence to Smith's lodgings. Dined with him, & held a long conversation upon business, leading, I presume, to my finally leaving Erchfont at the expiration of my term.[17] —

Tuesday Feb. 9th.—Vicarage Erchfont.

A hard frost & very fine day. Walked over parts of the town of Chippenham before breakfast. Visited | & conferred with Smith. Mounted my horse at one o clock: reached home in two hours & a half. Finished Mountville Castle.—

---

14. Alexander Fraser Tytler (Lord Woodhouselee), *Memoirs of Henry Home, Lord Kames, 1696-1782).*
15. The relationship between Revd. G. Smith and Francis Witts was troubled from the outset. In the early days of the 'relationship' there has been a lighter time when Witts accompanied Smith on a short tour in Devon, but this seems to have been a temporary relaxing in a difference of opinions. What the problems were will probably never be known. Eighteen months previously on their first meeting, Frank had recorded 'an elegant young man of congenial taste . . .' An Agnes considered him 'an agreeable Gentlemanlike man. . . .'
16. Catherine Cuthbertson, *Santo Sebastiano.* (1806).
17. What the expiration of his term was has never been clear. Frank now begins a search for other curacies.

Wednesday Feb. 10$^{th.}$—
Very cold weather & wind, & a hard frost. Composing a Fast Sermon from Cowper's Expostulation. Transcribing a Sermon finished on Saturday. Rode to Devizes. Heard from my beloved Margaret. Called on M$^{rs.}$ Hillier & Harriet. Met Lediard with them. Rode with Jaques, & with Wood. Read the second Vol. of that fascinating Novel, Santo Sebastiano.

Thursday Feb. 11$^{th.}$—
A hard frost early, & shower of snow: afterwards thawed & was moist, misty, raw & windy, $^{\text{rain at night.}}$ Finished a Fast Sermon. Finished the 3$^{d.}$ Vol. of that most interesting Novel Santo Sebastiano. Read Lord Kames's Memoirs.

Friday Feb. 12$^{th.}$—
Very early in the morning, from 2 to 4, a terrible Hurricane with snow, hard frost; clear day, but extremely cold. Up during those two hours in apprehension of danger. Began to compile a Sermon upon the Duty of submission $^{\text{to GOD}}$ as enforced by the Imitation of Christ, from D$^{r.}$ Jones. Transcribing a Sermon as Wednesday. Read Lord Kames's Memoirs by Lord Woodhouselee, a mass of information unpleasantly jumbled together.

Saturday Feb. 13$^{th.}$—
A little more snow had fallen in the night; it froze hard; the | wind was cold, the sky chiefly clear, with a tendency to snow. Transcribing a Sermon as yesterday. Reading the life of Lord Kames.

Sunday Feb. 14$^{th.}$—
Some snow had fallen during the night, the frost was hard; the wind & air very cold. Morning Service at Erchfont, preached the Sermon, Christianity a reasonable Service. The same in the afternoon at Stert, where, as usual, I called upon M$^{rs.}$ Jaques. Read two Vol. of the Lady's Monthly Museum & Lord Kames's life by Lord Woodhouselee.

Monday. Feb. 15$^{th.}$—
An early frost, & snow had fallen in the night. The frost went, sleet & some rain fell occasionally, followed by a thick fog. Transcribing a Sermon for the Fast. Rode to Devizes. Called upon M$^{rs.}$ Hillier. Received letters from Hampshire respecting a Curacy, & a copy of verses as a Valentine, from some silly Girl. Called upon the Jaques's at Stert. Read the 4$^{th.}$Vol. nearly of the never flagging charming novel, Santo Sebastiano. Drank tea, played commerce, & supped at the Legg's, meeting the Butchers.—

Tuesday Feb. 16$^{th.}$—
A thaw & mild weather dissipating the snow. Transcribing a Fast Sermon. Finished the exquisite novel Santo Sebastiano. Received a favourable letter from the Bishop of Salisbury respecting my transactions with Smith. Wrote to M$^{r.}$ S$^{t.}$ John in Hants respecting the Curacy of Lockerly & East Dean, & to my own Margaret. |

Wednesday Feb. 17$^{th.}$—

Heavy rain in the morning gradually declining into a thick Mist. Being Fast Day, performed the prescribed Duty at Erchfont & Stert. Called on M$^{rs.}$ Jaques &c. Domestic disarrangements by the abrupt departure of the maid. Finished the exquisite Santo Sebastiano.—

Thursday Feb. 18$^{th.}$—

No actual rain, but mild misty weather. Rode to Devizes. Called upon Miss H. Tylee. Called at M$^{rs.}$ Hillier's, found her & Harriet, Susan Hughes & Mary Gibbs. Conversed with D$^{r.}$ Hill, M$^{r.}$ Jaques, &c. Heard from M$^{r.}$ Travell, Horne, Round, & Margaret. Wrote to Lady Lyttelton & Horne.

Friday Feb. 19$^{th.}$—

Something of a frost early the rest of the day very fine, anticipating spring. Preparing a Sermon for Sunday. M$^{rs.}$ Tinker, Miss Tinkers, & Miss Lawrence called. Visited Dame North & walked to the foot of Redhorn Hill.

Saturday Feb. 20$^{th.}$—

After rather an unpromising morning, a very fine day, anticipating spring. Visited poor John Sainsbury. Walked to the Foot of Redhorn Hill. Read supplementary pages to Hayley's life of Cooper. Wrote to my beloved Margaret. Preparing for my journey to Town.

Sunday Feb. 21$^{st.}$—

A hard frost, followed by a very fine day. Morning | service at Erchfont. M$^{r.}$ Halliday & family called & accompanied us thither. Preached upon the day of Judgment. Being disappointed of a place in the Post Coach, was compelled to drive my Gig to Kennet to meet the Chippenham Coacher. Took John to take back the Gig. Stopped at Stert & read the Evening service, but excused myself from the Sermon. Reached the White Hart by 5.

37. The Piccadilly Nuisance. A cartoon showing the front of Hatchett's Hotel, Piccadilly.

38. Berkeley Square.

o clock, the roads extremely heavy & bad. Proceeded in the double bodied White Lion Coach, an uneasy vehicle: roads worse & worse, as we advanced: my companions were Mr. Headley of Calne, Ned Poore, &c. Supped at Newbury.

Monday Feb. 22d.—17 Berkley Street, Portman Square.

After a hard frost, a very fine day. Arrived at 10 o clock in Piccadilly, & after breakfasting with Wm. Headley at Hatchett's, came to my Aunt Lady Lyttletons, whom I found economising but not comfortably. Miss Eycott & her neice, Mary Matthews, her inmates.—After dressing & refreshing myself, sallied forth; called at Hatchett's, walked to various parts of Town, walked with B. P. Witts, met various individuals of my acquaintance. Dined at five with my aunt: in the Evening to Drury Lane Theatre to see the new opera, Kais, or Love in the Deserts, a superb Egyptian & Arab Spectacle in which Braham sings transcendently songs of his own Composition.[18] The other best performers were my friend Storau, Mrs. Mountain, Bannister &c. The Mayor of | Garratt, followed part of which most amusing caricature I outstaid. Sat with Michael Wyatt. Wrote home.—

Tuesday Feb. 23.—

No frost, but raw & cold turning to rain at night. Called early on the Bp. of Sarum, by whom I was handsomely received, & conversed not unsatisfactorily on the subject of my engagement

18. *Kais, or, Love in the Deserts,* an opera in four acts with music by John Braman and William Reeve, libretto by I. Brandon based on the book *Mejnoun and Leila,* Isaac Disraeli. (1808).

39. British Institution, Pall Mall

with Smith. Visited the Miss Guydickens's very pleasantly. Passed an hour in the Gallery of the British Institution, surveying some of the rich collection of the oil paintings of modern artists there deposited. Many in every department are strikingly fine. Met several acquaintance, Hart Davis,[19] Jas. Brougham &c. Wrote to my Parents. Called on Horne & conversed with him for two hours on the Marriage Settlement business. Dined with him afterwards & even supped, meeting his Brother Mr. John Horne, & a Mr. Baines, a pleasant party.

Wednesday Feb. 24th.—

Unpleasant, cold, damp, weather. Sallied forth after breakfast. Visited the British Institution with great pleasure, inspecting more minutely the artists' performances. Visited the Panorama of Dublin in Leicester Square, giving an unprepossessing idea of that metropolis, probably, an unfavourable representation. Visited the Panorama | of Cader Idris in a Street adjoining the Strand; a bad representation of a very curious volcanic region; the Exhibition extending to Mr. Donovan's large collection in every branch of Natural History, very interesting. Wrote to my Parents; dined with Lady Lyttelton. Visited Covent Garden Theatre to see the new Comedy: Begone dull care; not a very interesting piece:[20] Fawcett's acting extremely good, the whole well supported; Miss Smith highly prepossessing. Followed by a silly Dance called Poor Jack, attractive to the Galleries. The whole concluded by the amusing musical entertainment, we fly by night:[21] in which Fawcett shone, as also the other performers. Sat near & conversed with Chad &c.—

19. Richard Hart Davis, (1762-1844). Hart Davis was involved in the Harford bank in Bristol and was M.P. 1812-31. In 1793 he was recorded as being Consul at Bristol for the United States of America.
20. Frederic Reynolds, *Begone Dull Care*, a comedy in five acts. (1808).
21. George Colman and Michael Kelly, *We Fly by Night*, a musical entertainment in two acts. (1805). This was performed at Covent Garden and the Haymarket over the next few years.

40. *Cross-section of Barker's Panorama at Leicester Square*

Thursday Feb. 25.—
Cold & raw weather, being a hard frost. Called upon the Bishop of Salisbury & made most satisfactory arrangements in my business with his Lordship. Rambled the whole morning with Chad &c. Visited the Panorama of Oxford, a most interesting effort of the Art, taken from the summit of the Radcliffe Library. Wrote to my beloved Margaret. Dined alone at the Oxford Coffee House. In the Evening to Covent Garden Theatre, where I was much amused by a very interesting Drama | a Swedish Fable, entitled the Wanderer, or the Rights of Hospitality.[22] Miss Smith very great, Charles Kemble excellent as the Hero. This was

41. *Covent Garden Theatre 1808, prior to the fire in September.*

22. Charles Kemble and August von Kotzebue, *The Wandered, or, the Rights of Hospitality.* A drama in three acts.

42. After the opera.

followed by a capital new Farce the Widow's Choice by Allingham, very humorous, much applauded, musical: Miss Decamp, Fawcett, Munden, excellent.[23]

Friday Feb. 26th—Saturday Feb. 27th Erchfont.

Entered my 26th year. The weather very fine. Paid Mrs. V. Snow a visit immediately after breakfast. The good ladies occupying Lady Middletons House in Portman Square. Transacted business with Horne. Wrote to Mr. Travell. Sat an hour with the Mrs. Snow's: Mrs. Anne deplorably altered & her maladies hopeless; met there Mr. & Miss Webb, & Mrs. Clitherow. After an early dinner at Lady Lyttelton's repaired to Hatchett's; took my place in the Bath (Pickwick's) Post Coach with three other Gents: an Irishman, a conversible Lawyer, & a Swiss, qui mores multorum &c.:[24] conversed a great deal, slept a little; took refreshment at Colebrooke, tea at Speenhamland, Beer &c. at Kennet: breakfasted at Devizes with the Bustons: reached home by 10. o clock; the day very fine: received letters from Margaret. |

A complete leaf is missing from the manuscript diary at this point. The leaf has clearly been roughly torn out without any care taken at all.

Monday March 7th.

Very dry, but very cold & windy. Dr. Hill & his son Captn. Hill called: rode with the latter to Conock; called upon Mr. Jones & Mrs. Warriner; rode with Jones & Hill to Devizes. Heard from Smith in Town; an embarrassing letter, which required a letter to the Bishop of Salisbury. Read the Novel, But Which?[25]—

---

23. This was the last time that Frank Witts enjoyed the old theatre, for it was burnt down on 30 September 1808 — just six months later.
24. Qui mores multorum — what are the manners of the majority?
25. Henry Whitfield? *But Which? Or, Domestic Grievances of the Wolmore Family.* (1807).

Tuesday March 8th.

Frosty, very cold, & windy; but dry & clear. Rode to Devizes with a letter. Compiling a Sermon, as on Saturday. Finished the Novel But Which? a moderate production. Read Southey's Madoc.[26] Wrote to Margaret.

Wednesday March 9th.

Similar weather. Finished the compilation of a Sermon as yesterday. Rode to Enford to make enquiries of the Revd. Jones respecting the Clergy Fund. Saw his Lady. Rode over the plain to Compton, Enford picturesque: the River, Bridge, Manor House & Church, a pleasant view from Hunts Cottage at Chisenbury. Returned through Upavon &c. Received a letter from Margaret, which I answered. Finished Southey's ponderous poem, but on the whole pleased. Continued the Memoirs of Lord Kames.

Thursday Mar. 10th.—

Very cold, severe, sterile, weather. Never left the House. Preparing & compose a Sermon upon | the Evangelical Character. Transcribing a Sermon finished yesterday. Read the life of Lord Kames. Wrote to Round.—

Friday March 11th.—

Similar severe weather. Rode to Devizes with my letter: returned by Crookwood. A fire destroyed thee cottages of four poor families in the forenoon. Began the Banks of the Wye or two summers in Clifton, a flimsy, new, novel.[27] Transcribing a Sermon, as yesterday.—

Saturday March 12.—

Equally cold & sterile weather. Transcribing a Sermon as yesterday. Read Memoirs of Lord Kames. Mrs. Freesler called. Read Sulpicii Severi Vita St. Martini, & King's Signs of the Times.

Sunday March. 13.—

Similar dreary weather.—The Morning Service at Stert. Called upon the Jaques's & Gale's. Catechized & preached upon the Endurance & improvement of afflictions. The same Sermon at Stert. Began an infamous Novel: The infidel Mother by a wretch styling himself C. Sedley Esqr. a misrepresentation of high life, as abounding in abundant crimes, a high drawn caricature of individuals well known, pampering vice under the pretext of decrying it.[28] — |

Monday March. 14th.—

No change in the weather. Rode to Devizes. Called upon Mrs. Tylee & the Hilliers. Wrote to the Revd. G. Smith. Finished the infidel Mother & the Banks of the Wye.—

---

26. Robert Southey, (1774-1843), *Madoc,* (1805).
27. Anonymous, *The Banks of the Wye, or, Two Summers in Clifton.* (1808). The was by the same author/ess as *The Winter in Bath.*
28. Charles Sedley, *The Infidel Mother.* (1807).

Tuesday March 15th.—

No material change in the weather. Rather milder. Composing a Sermon upon the Evangelical character. Mrs. Legg called. Churched a woman & christened her child. Read the Memoirs of Lord Kames. Received letters from Horne & Margt. Wrote to the latter.—

Wednesday March. 16th.—

Finer weather, but still very cold. Rode to Devizes. Received a very unpleasant letter from the Bishop of Sarum, subversive of his former promises. Replied to it. Read Memoirs of Lord Kames.

Thursday March. 17th.—

Finer weather; yet very cold. Rode to Little Cheverel & called on Mrs. Richards respecting the Clergy Funds. Called upon Mrs. Rogers at Eastertons. Composing a Sermon as Tuesday. Received a letter from Margaret. Began Dr. Gillies's History of the World from the age of Alexander to Augustus.[29] |

Friday March 18th.—

A very cold, raw, windy day with a tendency to snow. Dreadfully alarmed immediately after breakfast by a raging fire in the drawing room Chimney; but by timely assistance of many young & active villagers with our own exertions though the flame had risen to a great height over the thatch we quelled the furious Element in less than half an hour. This disorganised us for the remainder of the day. Mr. Harry Snook called. Read with attention Dr. Gillies's new History of old times.—

Saturday March. 19th.

Cold, cheerless weather. Composing a Sermon as Thursday. Studying Dr. Gillies's History. Did not leave the house.—In the morning a good deal of snow had fallen; in the Evening very heavy rain.

Sunday Mar. 20th.

Weather grown milder, much rain had fallen, & more came down besides a mist; Wind turned to the Southward. Morning Service at Erchfont, preached a Sermon entitled 'Contentment enforced by the consideration of GOD's general & particular providence.' Preached the same at Stert. Mrs. Legg & Mrs. Frusler called. Visited Mrs. Jaques as usual. Dined very agreeably at the Gales; meeting John Grant &c. Heard from Round. Began Mr. Geo. Moore's Tales of the | Passions: one vol. contains one novel illustrative of one Passions Vol. 1st. the only one published: contains the courtezan, illustrative of Revenge.[30]

Monday March 21st.—

Mild air & rain falling throughout the day more or less. Wrote to my beloved Margaret. Wrote to Dowell. Read Moore's Courtezan.—

---

29. John Gillies, (1747-1836), *History of the World from Alexander to Augustus.* (1807).

30. George Moore, *Tales of the Passions, in which is attempted an illustration of their effects on the human mind.* Volume 1. was *The Courtezan*, in which is attempted the passion of revenge. Volume 2. was *The Married Man* in which was attempted the passion of jealousy. (1808).

Tuesday March 22nd.—

Rain till midday. Afterwards fine. A frost at night. Composing a Sermon as on Saturday.—Finished Moore's Courtezan & began Mad. de Genlis Duc de Lauzun.[31] Received a letter from the Bp. of Sarum. Replied to it & wrote to Margaret. Studied Dr. Gillies's History.—

Wednesday March 23d.—

Cold, unpleasant weather, after a hard frost—Rode to Devizes. Called on Harriet Hillier & the Tylees. Finished Mad. de Genlis Duc de Lauzun.—

Thursday March 24th.—

A tendency to snow, which fell partially throughout the day. Composing a Sermon as on Tuesday. Studied Dr. Gillies's History. Began Clarkson's Portraiture of Quakerism.[32]

Friday March 25th.

A hard frost, & very cold air. Altering a Sermon on seriousness in religion from Dr. Paley. Rode to Devizes. Read Clarkson's Portraiture of Quakerism.— |

Saturday March 26th.—

Cold weather but finer than usual of late. Finished altering from Dr. Paley the Sermon on Seriousness in Religion. Studied Dr. Gillies's History. Wrote to my own Margaret & to Horne.

Sunday March 27.—

Bitterly cold weather. Morning service at Stert, before which I rode to the Post, & received letters from Dowell & Margaret; preached the 1st. of two Sermons upon Love of our Neighbour; called on Mrs. Jaques & the Gales. Evening Service and the same Sermon at Erchfont, churched two women, Christened two children. Began P. P. Pallet's Bath Characters, a Caricature Satien invidious, dirty, mock humour.[33]

Monday. March 28th.

Less bitter weather & more sun. Altering a Sermon for Good Friday from Mr. Newton. Finished the Bath Characters. Read a Sermon on toleration by Sydney Smith, very sensible, but homely; & written against a Party,—probably, for a Party.—Charles Giddings called in the afternoon.—Sent a remittance to Messrs. Allaway & Osmond.[34]

Tuesday March 29th.—Cote, near Bristol

A hard frost in the morning, a warm sunny noon, & cool Evening. Left home before six o clock A.M. to visit Dowell at Cote. Breakfasted at the Crown Inn, Melksham; drove my Gig. Called on Mrs. Poore, admitted to her Bedside for an instant her operation over about

---

31. Stéphanie Félicité de Genlis, (Comtesse de), *The Duke of Lauzun*. (1808).
32. Thomas Clarkson, *Portraiture of Quakerism, Taken from a view of the Education and Discipline, Social Manners, Civil and Political Economy,Religious Principles and Character of the Society of Friends*. (1806).
33. Revd. Richard Warner (pseudonym Peter Paul Pallet), *Bath Characters, or, Sketches from Life*. (1807).
34. Messrs. Allaway & Osmond are listed in Pigott's Director for Reading in 1830.

| a week. Next to Bath. Miss Powell. To the Elephant & Castle. Called on the Granvilles. Walked with them to Stoney the Coachmaker's &c.—To the Taylor's & Bootmakers. Set off between two & three for Bristol, the lower road, took up Holdship the Cheltenham Quaker Glover. Found my friend, very ill; Mr. & Mrs. Dowell, Mr. Hetling, Miss Webb & Mr. Jos. Hutchinson made the Evening's party, played Whist in the Evening.

Wednesday March 30th.—Elephant & Castle Bath—

Less sun than yesterday, still very cold.—Breakfasted with Mr. & Mrs. D. William forced to pass the forenoon in his Chamber. Rode to Clifton. Called upon Mrs. Carrick & Mr. Garden; walked with Marcus Maccausland.—Sat with Dowell an hour before an Early Dinner: after which by six o clock returned the upper road to Bath, to the Elephant & Castle, where I slept after supping with Mr. Russel, the Wine Merchant.

Thursday March 31st.—Erchfont Vicarage

Left Bath very early; the morning cold, showers of snow from time to time through the Day. Breakfasted at Atford. The 1st. Somerset Militia, commanded by Sir C. Bamfylde in two divisions upon their route to Bristol.[35] Called for an instant on the Hillier's at Devizes. Came home by 12 o clock; Dressed to attend the grand funeral of the late Jacob Giddings of Etchelhampton to Erchfont. Walked to Jaques's at Stert: where a Chariot of four took us to Etchelhampton. Many Farmers &c. Tiresome waiting, cold meat &c. Jaques, Brabant & myself in the Chariot, Gale & many others on horseback. The solemnity lasted from 2 to 7 o clock.— |

Friday April 1.

A finer day than the preceding, but still cold.—Rode to Devizes. Met W W Salmon upon a painful business. Wrote to Mr. Travell. Heard from Margaret. Called on the Hillier's, Newmans & Jaques's. Walked with the latter from Devizes to Stert. The remainder of the 1st. Som. Mil. upon the Route. Drank tea, played commerce & supped at the Butcher's.

Saturday April 2.—

Fine weather, but cold.—Walked about the premises. Mrs. Jaques, Miss A Gale, & Mary Gabriel drank tea with us.—

Sunday. April 3d.—

Windy, showery, damp weather—Morning Service at Erchfont. Preached upon our Duty to our Neighbour. 2d. Part. Rode to Stert. Called on the Jaques's. Wrote to Margaret.—~~Beg~~

Monday. April 4th.—

Very rainy, boisterous, but less cold weather. Finishing the alteration of a Sermon from Mr. Newton for Good Friday. Wrote to Horne.—Read a pretty French tale, in imitation of

---

35. Sir Charles Warwick Bampfylde, (1753-1823). Bampfylde was of Poltimore, Cornwall and Hardington Park, Somerset. He was M.P. for Exeter, 1774-90, and 1796-1812. He was a member of the 1st Somerset Militia from 1790, rising to Lieutenant-Colonel, 1807-9.

Florians Numa Pompilius. Phatime & Zoroe by by M. Alciator de Marseille.[36] Began Le Maistre, Travels on the Continent.[37] —

Tuesday April 5th.—

Almost incessant rain, till the Evening. Began the alteration of a Sermon for Easter day from Mr. Newton. Continued Le Maistre's Tour & Phatime | & Zoroe.—

Wednesday April 6th.—

A day of continued rain.—Composing a funeral Sermon upon Job.7.20.—Read Phatime & Zoroe & Lemaistre's Travels.—

Thursday April 7th.—

No cessation of rain. Composing a Sermon as yesterday. Heard from Margaret. Read the same books as yesterday. Wrote to Margaret & Hornes.

Friday April 8th.—

Weather not settled, but less wet, warmer, but cold showers at intervals. Rode to Devizes. Received a letter from Mr. Travell, to which I replied. Called upon W. W. Salmon & Mrs. Jaques.—Preparing Sermons for next week. Mrs. M. Giddings called. Read the Red Tyger.[38]

Saturday April 9th.—

Very fine weather, yet a little cold after an early frost. Drove my Mother to Rushall to visit Mrs. Peck; found her & her husband & fine family at home. They are pleasant people. Composing Sermon as yesterday—Read the Red Tyger & Phatime & Zoroe.—

Sunday April 10th.—

Very mild, fine weather. Morning service at Stert. Called on the Jaques's & Gales. Preached upon the indispensable disposition of seriousness in religion. | Catechized the children. Preached the same Sermon at Erchfont. Catechized & rewarded the children with cakes. Mrs. Halliday & her party called after church. Began Miss Gunning's Farmer's Boy.[39]

Monday April 11th.—

Very beautiful weather. Drove my Mother to Devizes. Called on Mrs. Hill & Mrs. Tylee. Met Misses Tylee, & Hillier. Transcribing a funeral Sermon. Began one of Beaumont & Fletcher's Plays. The Humorous Lieutenant.[40] Extremely interesting.

---

36. Bernard Alciator, *Phatime et Zaroé,* (1807).
37. John Gustavus Le Maistre, *Travels on the Continent after the Peace of Amiens, through parts of France, Switzerland, Italy and Germany.* (1806).
38. Anonymous, *The Red Tyger, or Truth Will Out.* (1808).
39. Elizabeth Gunning, *The Farmer's Boy.* (1802).
40. John Fletcher, (1579-1625). *The Humorous Lieutenant,* (1619). So popular were the Jacobean plays of Beaumont & Fletcher that they were usually considered to be joint authors. In fact this play was written by Fletcher himself without the assistance of Francis Beaumont (1584-1616).

Tuesday. April 13.[40]—

Cold & windy, but fine. Drove my Mother to Stert to call on Mrs. Jaques & the Gales.—Christened Mrs. Crook's infant. Churched a woman. Buried John Crook of Bromham after preaching a funeral Sermon. Passed two Hours ex officio at Robt. Crook's (the Son's) house previous to the funeral. Mr. Webster the Curate of Bromham there. Received a joint letter from Mr. Hartley of Settle, Mrs. Backhouse & Margaret. Read Beaumont & Fletcher's Ring & nothing.[42] Read the Farmer's Boy. |

Some good few leaves are cut from the manuscript diary here, but the only days missing are Wednesday and Thursday, the 13th and 14th of April. Nothing of significance is record in the diary of Agnes Witts. On the 12th Frank drove his mother to Devizes for some shopping to assist the poor people who had suffered from the fire. The following day he drove his mother on a visit to Mrs. Warriner. The leaves must have been taken out at that time. When the new recto page starts Francis Witts writes the year — an unusual circumstance.

Journal:

1808.

Friday Ap. 15th.—Vicarage, Erchfont.

Good Friday. Very fine warm weather. Morning service at Erchfont, preached a Sermon appropriate. Walked to Stert; officiated, and preached the same Sermon. Called upon the Jaques's & Gales. Buried a Corpse and christened a child. Read Miss Gunning's farmer's boy. Also Beaumont & Fletchers excellent Comedy, the Spanish Curate.[43]—Preparing a Sermon for Easter-day.

Saturday April 16th.

Easter Eve. Very fine weather; a cool wind. Prayers at Erchfont in the forenoon. Drove my Mother to Easterton & Littleton; called upon Mrs. Rogers & Mrs. Tinker. Administered the Sacrament to Saml. Plank—Read Beaumont & Fletcher's loose play, the Custom of the Country.[44] Prepared from Mr. Newton a Sermon for Easter-day.

Sunday April 17th.

Easter–day. Much colder weather, a sharp wind, & one or two showers of sleet or snow. Morning Service at | Erchfont: administered the Sacrament to a large number of communicants. Preached an appropriate Sermon. Walked to Stert to Evening Service. Preached the same Sermon. Called upon Mrs. Jaques & the Gales. Mrs. Legg & Mr. & Mrs. M. Giddings drank tea with us. Read Beaumont & Fletcher's good comedy, the Elder Brother.[45]

---

41. This was actually the 12th.
42. Of the fifty-two plays listed for Beaumont and Fletcher, singly or together, this play title does not appear.
43. John Fletcher, in collaboration with Philip Massinger, (1583-1640). *The Spanish Curate.* (1622).
44. Fletcher and Massinger, *The Custom of the Country.* (Printed 1647).
45. Fletcher and Massinger, *The Elder Brother.* (Printed 1637).

Monday April 18th.

Cold & cloudy weather. Dr. Dodsworth, the Canon of Windsor, my Vicar's Senile & Patron,[46] called early & conferred with us two hours, on his road from Devizes to Salisbury; apparently, a genteel, but crafty man. Rode to Devizes, by Wick, that I might find the Hillier's House. Dined at Mr. Peck's, at Rushall, whither we went in a Post Chaise. We met Mrs. Brereton, & dined pleasantly, returning in the Evening.

Tuesday April 19th—

Very unseasonable weather, being cold, with a heavy snow, & storms of sleet. Attending the annual Parish Vestry for passing accounts &c. Wrote to Round, Dowell, Margaret, Hoares. Administered the Sacrament to Dame North &c. Read Beaumont & Fletcher's fine but impassioned Maid's Tragedy.[47] — |

Wednesday. April 20th.

A cold, dull, forenoon, terminating in snow, sleet & rain, lasting till night. Married James Cooper, the Stert Clerk. Called on the Jaques's. Mr. J. accompanied me to Devizes. It was the Green Fair. Rode with Mark Giddings. Conversed with Tylees, R. Dean &c. Wrote to Horne.—Read Beaumont & Fletcher's entertaining comedy, the Scornful Lady.[48] —

Thursday April 21st.

Snow, rain, & sleet falling heavily in the forenoon & Evening. The middle of the day being dry overhead, I walked to Redhorn Hill &c.—Read Beaumont & Fletcher's excellent Drama Philaster,[49] & the strange production, the Mad Lover.[50] —

Friday. April 22nd.—

Heavy rain, hail & sleet great part of the day. Rode to Devizes. To the Bank. Administered the Sacrament to an old North. Read Beaumont & Fletcher's excellent comedy, Rule a Wife & have a Wife.[51] Began Xenophon's Κυρου Παιδεια [52] —

Saturday April 23d.

Glimpses of sun & fair weather at mid-day, otherwise heavy storms of hail & rain with short intermission. Received a letter from Margaret, which I answered: | Studied Pliny's letters. Read the Prefaces to Beaumont & Fletcher's Works also Le Maistre's Tour.—

Sunday April 24th.

Very stormy, wet, & windy. Morning Service at Erchfont. Preached upon the Duties of Parents. Received a Parcel of Deeds from Horne being the rough Draft of the proposed

---

46. Senile in this sense as a characteristic of old age rather than as lacking in mental faculties.
47. Fletcher and Beaumont, *The Maid's Tragedy.* (Written between 1610/11).
48. Fletcher and Beaumont, *The Scornful Lady.* (Performed 1610).
49. Fletcher and Beaumont, *Philaster.* (Written between 1608/09).
50. Fletcher (alone), *The Mad Lover.* (Performed 1616).
51. Fletcher (alone), *Rule a Wife and Have a Wife.* (Performed 1624).
52. Xenophon's Κυρου Παιδεια — *the Childhood of Cyrus*, a fictionalised account of the childhood and upbringing of the Persian kin Cyrus the Great. It was effectively a treatise on how princes should be brought up.

Marriage Settlement. Evening Service at Stert, whither I rode. Called on the Jaques's. Preached the same Sermon. Dined with M^r. Gale, to meet a M^r. & M^rs. Davis of Leytonstone, zealous & intelligent promotors of D^r. Bell's system of Education.[53] Made an agreeable visit, the family of the Gabriel's being also present. In the Evening, after I returned reading the Settlement. Also read Miss Gunnings Farmer's Boy.

Monday April 25th.—

Less rain, than yesterday, but much of that, with snow & hail fell. Examining the Deeds from Town, returned them, & wrote to Horne—Reading the Farmer's Boy & Lemaistre's Tour. Received a letter from the Bishop of Sarum, appointing me to meet him there to-morrow. Drank tea at the Legg's. Met M^rs. Butcher. |

Tuesday April 26th.—Antelope Inn, Salisbury.

A cold raw morning with sleet & snow: a dull forenoon, heavy rain before dinner. Left home between five & six o clock A.M. for Salisbury in the Gig, breakfasted at the Antelope, dressed & wrote to the Bishop, who did not arrive till Evening. Walked; met Gaisford, & two M^r. Baker's sons of D^r. Baker of Freshford. The younger George invited me to dinner. Read Tunle's Translation of a work of Abbé Winkelmann's on Grecian Sculpture, & Painting. A very pleasant dinner: the Party, the two M^r. B's, Gaisford, M^r. T. Davis, M^r. Bill of Oriel, M^r. Andrews of the 2^d. Somerset Militia. Went at nine to a grand rout at Canon Price's in the Close: a very numerous party, cards &c.—Conversed with our own set, Miss Tinney, Adjutant Bob Bassel, &c. Supped at Baker's, & got early (in the morning) back to the Antelope.—

Wednesday April 27th. Vicarage Erchfont.

A cold raw morning, an East wind, & heavy rain from 10 A.M. till sun set & after. Had an audience of the Bishop at 8 o clock & apparently I transacted my business well. Left Salisbury at 10 A.M. for Devizes, where I arrived in 4 hours wet through, in spite of all precautions. Stopped at the Hut, & Lideway. Attended the Clergy meeting, as Steward of the Pottern Deanry. Paid my arrears. The party at Dinner consisted of D^r. Welles, M^r. Francis, M^r. Mayo, M^r. Ledyard, M^r. Dodwell, Mr. Williams, Herbert Hawes, M^r. Seymour, & M^r. Goddard. A

53. Andrew Bell, (1753-1832). Bell was born at St. Andrew's and after graduating at the university there he spent some years as a tutor in Virginia, in America. On his return he took orders, and in 1787 sailed for India, where he held eight army chaplaincies at the same time. In 1789 he became superintendent of the male orphan asylum at Madras, and having been obliged from scarcity of teachers to introduce the system of mutual tuition by the pupils, found the scheme answer so well that he became convinced of its universal applicability. In 1797, after his return to London, he published a small pamphlet explaining his views on education. Little public attention was drawn towards the "monitorial" plan until Joseph Lancaster, the Quaker, opened a school in Southwark, conducting it in accordance with Bell's principles, and improving on his system. The success of the method, and the strong support given to Lancaster by the whole body of Nonconformists gave immense impetus to the movement. Similar schools were established in great numbers; and the members of the Church of England, becoming alarmed at the patronage of such schools resting entirely in the hands of dissenters, resolved to set up similar institutions in which their own principles should be inculcated. In 1807 Bell was called from his rectory of Swanage in Dorset to organize a system of schools in accordance with these views, and in 1811 became superintendent of the newly formed "National Society for Promoting the Education of the Poor in the Principles of the Established Church." He died at Cheltenham, and was buried in Westminster Abbey. His great fortune was bequeathed almost entirely for educational purposes.

very good dinner, & wine tolerable. Some quarreling ensued & much folly was uttered. Got home by nine in the Evening. Heard from my beloved Margaret & M$^{r.}$ Travell.

Thursday April 28$^{th.}$—

A dull day, cold & rather damp. Packing up for our journey to Bath. M$^{r.}$ C. Mayo called.—Wrote to the Bishop of Salisbury. Read Lemaistre's Tour, & Miss Gunnings Farmer's Boy. Wrote to M$^{r.}$ Goddard of Deverell Longbridge & M$^{r.}$ Richards.—

Friday. April 29$^{th.}$—

A dull day without rain. My Father & Mother set out for Bath, about half past nine in a Chaise. Accompanied them to Devizes. Called on | M$^{rs.}$ Tylee, sat with her & Harriet Hillier. Dined at John Gale's. Met a M$^{r.}$ Grant, the Gabriels, W. Wood, in the Evening, M$^{rs.}$ Jaques. Read Lemaistre's Travels.

Saturday April 30$^{th.}$

The wind changed, a return of fine weather, being mild & pleasant. Wrote to George to Miss Naish & M$^{r.}$ Jones of Enford. Sowing Flowerseeds. Walked in the fields, with Mesdames Butcher & Legg. Dined at home, drank tea & supped at the Legg's, meeting Butcher & his wife & M. Giddings & his wife.

Sunday May 1$^{st.}$—Bell Inn Gloucester.—

Very fine summer weather. Engaged in parish business & preparing for my departure to meet my beloved Margaret at Gloster. Left Erchfont at nine o clock, giving morning Service at Stert; to the Jaques's before, at the Gales after Church, no Sermon, but a Sacrament. Rode off before twelve with Will. Wood as far as Rowde, passed through Chippenham without stopping dined at Spencer's at Malmsbury. Pursued my way through Tetbury & ~~Bownham~~ Minchin-Hampton, by Bownham House to the Fleece Inn | at Rodborough. Left there my Horse & Dog & took a fast trotting Hack to Gloucester. Arrived at that place by nine, where I had the happiness to meet my friends, M$^{rs.}$ Backhouse, Miss Richardson & my beloved Margaret. Supped & retired.

43. Rodborough Manor
T. Way, Lith. London.
Sanders

44. *Huntsman and dogs at inn.*

~~Tuesday~~ Monday May 2d.—No. 3. Alfred Street Bath.
Similar beautiful weather, & very hot. Walked with my sweet Margaret before breakfast in the College Yard & down to the bridge over the Severn. After Breakfast with the Trio, minutely examined the Cathedral & Pin manufactory.—Left Gloucester between eleven & twelve to Bath. Rodborough the first stage 12 miles fine & beautiful road, particularly, the latter part, thro' the clothing Villages. Mounted my own Horse again at Rodborough, & proceeded to Petty France, 15 miles, the former part picturesque. Nailsworth Hill divides the precious from the vile. Dined at Petty France & baited the Grey; in the afternoon drove into Bath by half past seven o clock. My Father & Mother's charming | lodgings in Alfred Street received me first; thence I escorted my Ladies to No.1 Queen Square. Where my Father & Mother came to welcome them. Retired after Tea.—

~~Wednesday~~ Tuesday May 3d.

A beautiful summer's day; very hot: breakfasted in Queen Square, where my Father & Mother called. To Stone's the Coachmaker's, where I left Mrs. B's chaise to be repaired. Walking at times with the party, which was Shopping, with Rowden, Smith, Wilkins, &c.—The B's dined with us, Mrs. B. my Margaret, my Father & myself walked in the Crescent & fields.

~~Thursday~~ Wednesday May 4th.

Similar beautiful weather. In Queen Square after breakfast & nearly till dinner time. Wrote to the Clerk. To Barlow's the Wine Merchant's, Upham's library &c. Walked with my beloved Margaret in Sidney Gardens &c. After dinner we all drank tea with them: walked in the Crescent fields &c.—

45. Lansdown Crescent.

~~Friday~~ Thursday May 5th.—

Less sultry, therefore more pleasant. In Queen | Square most part of the morning, walking with Rowden &c. Afterwards with my Father & Mother called on the Reads, & on the Grocer Pierpoint in Argyle St. Wrote to Mr. Hartley. Dined & passed the rest of the day in Queen Square. Mr. & Mrs. Witherington called in the Evening. My Father & Mother drank tea with us. Walked a little with my beloved Margaret in the Square.—

Friday May 6th.—

Very fine summer weather, but less sultry. Shopping with the Backhouses &c. Mr. Travell, Dr. Baker, & Mrs. F. Baker, called on us. Called on Mr. Worthington in the Upper Crescent, & on Lady Riddell. Walked with Charles Parry &c.—Dined at home. Dressed for a party at Mr. Worthingtons in the Evening. Many assembled to Conversation & Music: Mr. Richards & his Daughter, professional performers, the young Miss Worthingtons &c.— |

Francis Witts appears to have stopped keeping a regular diary at this point, and does not recommence until January 1820. Through the diaries of Agnes Witts and the occasional letter or family document, the story can be pieced together. In between all of this there are a few journals which Francis did keep, mainly during travels.

First the diaries of Agnes Witts: 13 May 1808 '. . . Mr. Witts and I set out early to visit my Brother & Mrs. Ecles at their pretty little Villa near Weston . . .'

Mrs. Ecles appears to have been Ferdinand's sister-in-law, and was presumably a Rollinson before she married. Mrs. Ecles had previously held a house in London, and may well still have done, but they also spent much time at Bath with Ferdinand using curates for his livings at Upper Slaughter, Blunsdon and Walton.

46. The Comforts of Bath — Cards.

17 May 1808: '. . . My Brother Travell dined here and Mrs. Ecles came to tea . . .'

After that there is nothing much to record until 30 May 1808 when Francis married Margaret at Dowry Square Chapel. The service was conducted by William Burslem, a very old family friend. On 8 June 1808 Edward and Agnes left Bath for Cheltenham. After two days staying with her sister, Anne, they booked into Weavers Hotel, opposite to her sister, having seemingly failed to find suitable lodgings.

On 14 June 1808 Agnes mentioned the death of old Mrs. Guydickens, one of her Tracy aunts. On 17 June she recorded: '. . . visited . . . & old Mrs. Timbrells . . . ' The under-lining is by Agnes to emphasise the point. She and Edward were assiduous in cultivating the old ladies who had the power of presentation to the living at Upper Slaughter.

On 28 June 1808 Frank and Margaret arrived at Cheltenham from Wiltshire. Their honeymoon destination was not recorded, but it appears that after only a few days away they went to their new home at Urchfont. On 13 July 1808 they headed back to Urchfont, leaving Edward and Agnes at Cheltenham. Francis recorded the trip in a rather ebullient and literary fashion.

Witts Family Paper F383

Route from Cheltenham to Erchfont.

Wednesday July 13$^{th.}$ 1808.—

A few days in the middle of this month were more oppressively hot, than is generally experienced in England; many years are said to have passed since the temperature of the air had been so inflamed, so enervating. From the listless gait, & pallid features, of those, who sauntered abroad, from the exhausted efforts of labourers & animals one might have deemed the English Vallies to have been visited by an African Sirocco; so little elasticity remained in the atmosphere, that the objects of animated nature seemed stagnate & dull. In truth, upon this day, in the shade, Fahrenheit's Thermometer stood at 90°, & in other places a higher point was observed.—Some fell beneath the intense heat, most were languid, few so bold, as like us, to undertake | a stage in an open Carriage, at four o clock in the afternoon—But perseverance & punctuality are such golden qualities, especially, in young persons, that my beloved Wife & myself ~~a~~ braved the sultry, scorching, sky, $^{\&}$ intended to reach Cirencester in the afternoon, a distance of 16 miles, whence a longer journey upon the next day would bring us to a secluded, but peaceful, home. Our repast, before we set forth, was attended by my Father & Mother, who with us had been residents in Weaver's Hotel; one of the more eligible houses of public reception in the gay resort, we were about to quit. We had passed more than a fortnight at Cheltenham; where, if my Wife had parted for the first time for many years from an attached Mother, & myself, in the same person, from an excellent friend, we had also the satisfaction of enjoying the society of my rational, sincere & affectionate friend, John Round. He saw | us seated in our independent, but unobtrusive, Equipage, a simple gig, & we proceeded gaily from a Town, where, as usual, much vexation had been mingled with much pleasure, tho' perhaps we had been stung more sensibly by a proportionably small share of the former, than we had been soothed by an abundance of the latter. For a very inconsiderable distance we pursued the Oxford & London Road, the same, by which the public conveyances pass to Glocester, tho' indifferent, the best of the high roads in the vicinity of Cheltenham, round which place, the friable materials can ill resist the throng of Carriages, or the more rude grating of Waggons laden with stone & timber for the profusion of buildings, which yearly extend the boundaries of this seat of summer dissipation . The intense glare of the sun upon the white surface, which ascended before us & behind in clouds of | suffocating dust was exceedingly oppressive, & must be hardly less obnoxious to the Inhabitants of smart Lodging Houses to the left of the road, or even to those of the Cottage, the residence of M$^{r.}$ Gray, a little without the turnpike, embosomed in a pigmy wood. We may be excused this expression, for behind these dwellings of fashion, the Eye may range over fields of taste: may observe the rich harvest ripening in

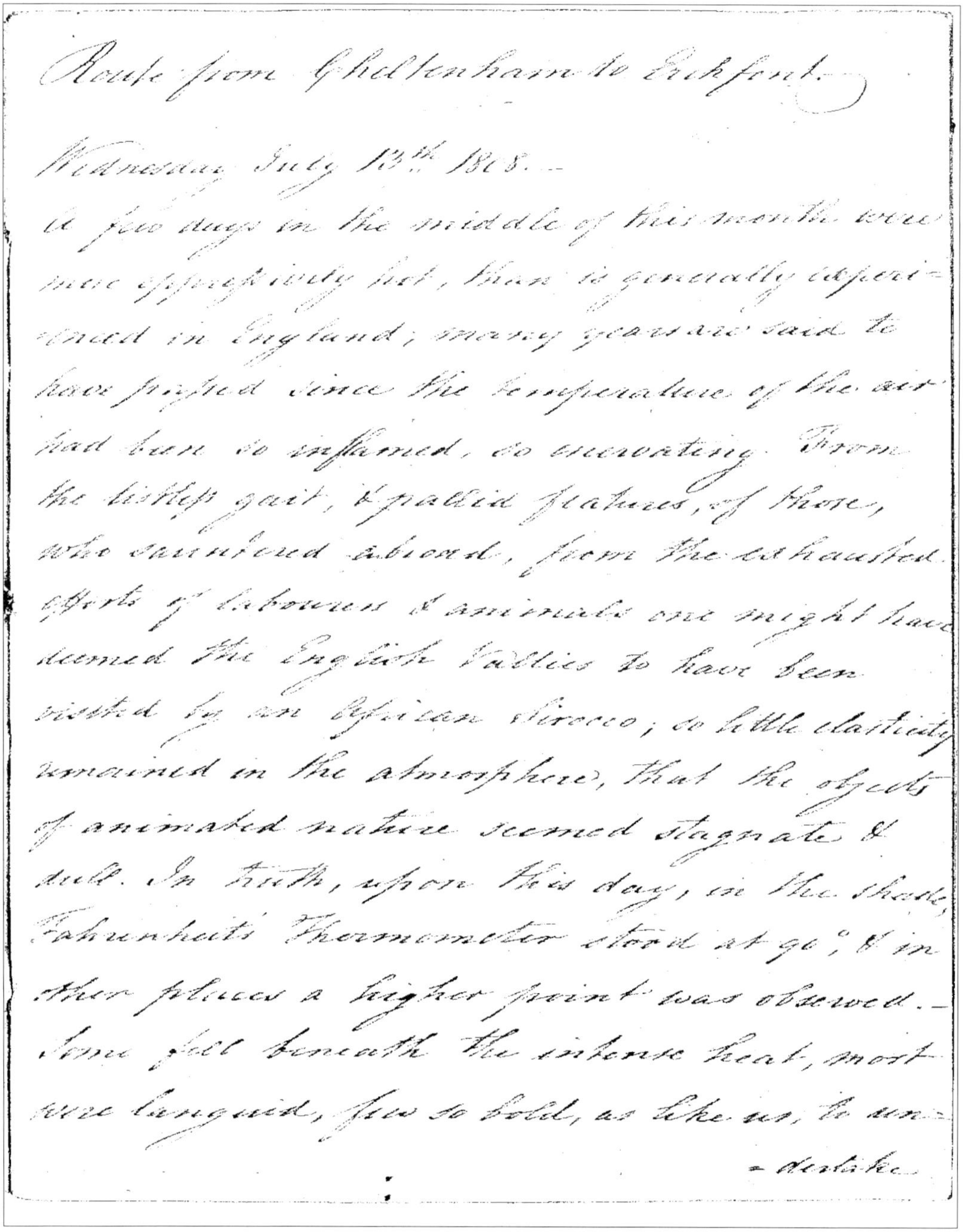

Route from Cheltenham to Erchfont.

Wednesday July 13th 1808.—

A few days in the middle of this month were more oppressively hot, than is generally experi-
-enced in England; many years are said to have passed since the temperature of the air had been so inflamed, so enervating. From the listless gait, & pallid features, of those, who sauntered abroad, from the exhausted efforts of labourers & animals one might have deemed the English Vallies to have been visited by an African Sirocco; so little elasticity remained in the atmosphere, that the objects of animated nature seemed stagnate & dull. In truth, upon this day, in the shade, Fahrenheit's Thermometer stood at 90°; & in other places a higher point was observed.— Some fell beneath the intense heat, most were languid, few so bold, as like us, to un-
-dertake

various shades, till the browner green melts into the woodland, & this yeilds to the turfy summit, which with broken surface forms a flowing horizon beneath an azure sky. But the road, which we were to pursue, diverging from the route to Oxford, caused us to turn our back for a time to this scenery, conducting us by a long lane, inclosed by rich hedges, the Village of Charlton being as yet invisible among the trees to the left, the hamlet of Sandford diversifying the foliage to the ~~lef~~ right. The fields upon either side teem with | rich morsels for the landscape painter, seldom do we meet with such groupes of trees, such exquisite foregrounds, so much of simple nature near so much of spurious art. Wise is the person, who prefers these rural & almost lonely walks to the tumult of the street, or the croud of the library, where fashionists consume the irksome morning of a day of lassitude. Sandford consists of a farm & two or three lodging houses, & belongs to the parish of Cheltenham. Charlton Kings, the Village to the left, lies partly on the London Road, partly in a beautiful, wooded, fertile, valley, rivalling any of those in Devonshire. It is resorted to as an agreeable residence by many respectable visitors, besides the old inhabitants of the place; many of the small retreats are picturesque & comfortable; the Church is handsome, & from many points of view a beautiful object: the Revd. Dr. Heming is the present Curate. We were now upon the road from Cheltenham to Bath, & a worse can hardly | be conceived; more rugged, more uneasy, or more trying to the strength of the horse or patience of the driver. As we slowly advanced, oppressed with heat, & retarded by the intricacies of holes & ruts, we had on our left Mr. Prinn's Park & grounds. The residence of this Gentleman is in Charlton, being an old family mansion, commodiously & handsomely modernised. The grounds & Park are agreeable & well wooded, & appear to great advantage, backed by hills & groves, extending towards Dowdswell, a beautiful Village upon the London Road. We had, during this Visit to Cheltenham, not enjoyed the hospitality, which Mr. Prinn so well understands shewing; as he & his Lady were during that time absent at Weymouth. To the right we had Sandford field; once deemed the Montpellier of the neighbourhood, & resorted to by invalids as a drive or ride within the power of moderate strength, & remarkable for a salubrious air. There | There also the mind was exhilarated by the rich Panorama of the Country, as this field commands a view of that Circle of Hills, which incloses the Valley of Cheltenham, & forms

47. Churchdown Hill (Chosen Hill).

48. *Horse and trap.*

the chief charm of the Scenery. This field adjoins the property which Mr. Thomson is now so judiciously converting into a Promenade for the multitudes, that resort to Cheltenham, & as it well is much frequented by riders, will probably soon become, as it well deserves to be, more ~~frequente~~ visited by the gay, than the abominable high roads, which are every forenoon so thronged with Equipages & Equestrians.—As we approached the ascent of Leckhampton Hill, the bare & level elevation, which closes the Valley to the South, we observed the labourers languidly working in the hayfields; indeed, the heat was so excessive, that our poor Horse was already more covered with sweat, than a fox chace would have effected in ordinary weather. The plain, turfy face of | Leckhampton Hill well contrasts with the other eminences in this vicinity, & although singly considered, it is far from picturesque, yet it adds much to the finishing of the picture, by the long naked line, precipitately ending in a Cliff, ~~which~~ rising over the cincture of foliage, which reaches half way to the Summit. This hill is composed of a coarse limestone, in which are found embedded a profusion of valuable fossil productions. To the Botanist it abounds also in interest; during a former visit to Cheltenham I had, in the Month of July, found upon its brow, the elegant Orchis Pyramidalis, the

49. *Leckhampton Court.*

50. Turnpike House on Leckhampton Hill.

Ophrys Monarchis, the Asperula Cynanchica, & in the woods & pastures beneath the beautiful Lathyrus Nassolia, the Campanula Glomerata, the ~~Nassolia~~ Lysimachia Nemorum &c. But this hill is still more interesting, if, as is the opinion of some, & particularly, of the eminent Chymist, Mr. Accum, the Saline & | Sulphureous subterraneous Streams, (for springs they can hardly be termed,) which have rendered Cheltenham so ~~salubrious~~ celebrated, are generated here, flowing downwards, & gradually contracting in their progress those Medicinal Qualities, which varying in their potency & character are applicable to a diversity of complaints. The Quarries upon this hill afford ~~also~~ stone, partly for building, but chiefly for repairing the roads, yet this is of so friable & soluble a nature, that one will hardly find in any part of the Island worse roads, or, their usual concomitant, more frequent & highly rated tolls. Ascending the summit the Village of Leckhampton lies amongst rich sloping pastures to the right. The Church is a romantic object; its form is regular, & a handsome steeple rises from its centre. Not far distant from it is a moderate House, the property of Mr. Fry.—Above, upon the brow of | of the Hill, the summit ends in an abrupt cliff of shelving rude rock, upon the face of which a fragment of firmer consistency remains prominent in the rude Giant form of a Chimney, which has been unanimously ascribed to the Residence of his Infernal Majesty. From the spot, which this promontory overhangs, the Valley of Cheltenham is surveyed to the greatest advantage; both the near & remote objects are happily combined, & highly interesting. The Eye surveys considerably more than three fourths of a grand circle: the first point to the right being the line of elevated forest scenery, which unites Leckhampton with Dowdeswell Hill; upon the declivity of the latter, embosomed in Wood; is discerned the picturesque Village of the same name with its rustic Church, whilst the confined valley extending from thence to Cheltenham exhibits a pleasing contrast of | wood, meadow, & Cornland, subtended below by the Romantic Village of Charlton, its handsome Tower, & the Demesne of Mr. Prinn. The latter is surmounted by the wooded summit of Batteldown Hill, above which the Horizon is formed by the higher eminence of Hewletts, beneath the turfy brow of which Mr. Agg's Seat & woods appear to great advantage. An undulating line of lofty ground, being the top of Cleeve Cloud, continues to form the boundary of the View; the fine foliage of Queen Wood contrasts well with the rugged quarries above, whilst it harmonizes admirably with the pasture grounds beneath, in the bosom of which is the Hamlet of Southam, with its venerable mansion, the Seat of the DelaBeres, & the beautiful village of Prestbury; the latter is separated only by two short miles ~~from Cheltenham~~ ~~by~~ through corn fields & meadows, from Cheltenham which thus becomes the centre of a circle of magic beauty. | A range of hills of various

51. Southam.

form & character unite Bredon Hill with that last described; here the Valley considerably widens, in the expanse of which the Villages of Bredon & Cleeve & the tower of Tewkesbury Church are prominent objects. As the horizon bends towards the north ~~East~~, we notice the Likky, the high elevation between Bromsgrove & Birmingham; which is united by other elevated ground to the gigantic, picturesque, Malvern Hills, which form the Western segment of the circumference of our View. Upon the side of these beautiful mountains, whose outline appears peculiarly fine ~~in~~ from this point, ~~of view~~ the Village of Great Malvern is discerned, & the site of Worcester is distinguished in the Valley beneath. A faint, & sometimes interrupted, wavy, silver line indicates the course of the Severn, while the city of Glocester, with its magnificent | Cathedral, at a distance of eight or ten miles, appears to great advantage between the two romantic Hills, Chosen, & Robin Wood, upon the biforked summit of the former of which the whitewashed Church makes a pleasing resting point for the Eye. The high ground in the Forest of Dean forms the background of this riante scenery,[1] which now rapidly contracts to to the foreground on the left, which is relieved by the wooded hills projecting from the level & bare summit of Leckhampton. Immediately beneath the feet of the Spectator, a valley of small & beautiful enclosures, the Villages of Badgeworth & Leckhampton, & the animated landscape of Haymaking afforded a delicious finish to an exquisite prospect. As we slowly wound up the remainder of the ascent, we were much pleased with the general character of the hill, rich & verdant in wood & pasture. | The summit presented a fine prospect of an abundant harvest, upon both sides of the road, the fields of corn being terminated to the right & in front by flourishing beech woods. Before we reached Birlip we crossed the direct road from Glocester to Frog-Mill, Oxford &c; before the former place it falls into the London & Glocester Road, which runs thro' Cheltenham; here it climbs the Hills by a steep & narrow ravine. Not far distant from the intersection of this road, & that, which we pursued, is the spot called Seven Wells, & generally assigned as

1. Riant — laughing, smiling, cheerful.

52. Miserden.

the primary fountain of the Thames. The situation of Birdlip is cold and cheerless, upon a very lofty promontory projecting into the Valley; the Village is ~~very~~ insignificant, except as it is ~~in~~ close to the celebrated Birdlip View, which does not come within my present scope, both as we passed on without diverging from our route, having lately enjoyed it, & as it | chiefly consists of those features, which have been so tediously described above. This View is best seen from a field upon the brow of the hill, which, being now arable land, has lost the stronger marks of antiquity, which belonged to it, as a Roman Camp or fort; a situation more commodious could not have been selected for the protection of a military Road, which it as essentially commands, as it amply surveys the wide & rich Valley of the Severn. The road, to which I allude, is that, which we were to pursue, leading up Birdlip Hill from Glocester, (Glevum) to Cirencester (Corinium or Durocornovium) nearly in a straight line

53. Cotswold House, North Cerney.

54. Cirencester.

over the Cotswold Hills; being very undulating, till it reaches the Valley which it traverses in a straight line of about five miles to Glocester. The shelving bank, which falls from the brow of the hill below the Camp is full of valuable fossils. Dr. Parry of Bath, who has a ~~valuable~~ rich mineralogical | collection from Gloucestershire, is much indebted to this part of the County. At Birlip we turned from the road, which we had hitherto pursued, & which leads to Bath, to follow the Roman Road described above. Some slight refreshment had invigorated both ourselves & our steed, painfully exhausted, as we were, by the ascent of Leckhampton, in exposure to a Sun so glaring, & an atmosphere so unusually heated. Our road to Cirencester continued over the Cotswold Hills; we were, therefore, much cooler comparatively, though the oppression was still very great. We had a ~~great~~ considerable advantage also in the improvement of the road; the firmer materials & more level surface facilitated the labour to the Horse. As we advanced, upon the right hand, from Birlip, two Villages present themselves romantically situated; the nearer, with a rustic white church upon a woody knoll, surmounts in a pleasing manner, retired Dells varied with Pasture & Beech Wood. Farther | and still to the right, a very extensive & flourishing verge of Plantation already improves the somewhat bleak district, which, in the course of years, it will highly adorn. This verge marks the Estate of Mr. Pitt,[2] a very opulent individual of Cirencester, whose industry and legal connections have enabled him to make very extensive acquisitions in this County. Thus, he has a ~~very~~ great interest in the Town of Cheltenham, & Brimpsfield, the Estate, which we now passed, is, probably, very valuable. Situated in a rich Valley to the right, but out of view from the Road,

2. Joseph Pitt, (1759?-1842). Born of humble origins, the son of a carpenter, Pitt grew to enjoy considerable wealth. Pitt grew in wealth slowly, practising in law and by degrees entered into speculation as a brewer, farmer, land-jobber and banker. In the latter he was very successful, in the Cheltenham firm of Pitt, Gardner, Croome, Bowley and Wood. Pitt became M.P. for Cricklade, 1812-1831. Pitt maintained extensive connections with Cirencester. He and his clerical son feature later in the diaries.

55. Cirencester.

is Miserden Park, the Seat of M$^{r.}$ Sandys, an agreeable man, whom, upon a former visit to Cheltenham, I had known by our mutual friend, M$^{r.}$ Usticke. Cotswold House, upon a knoll in a wooded Valley to the left, is the retreat of the eminent D$^{r.}$ Baillie, of London, whose medical skill, while it ensures him a magnificent income, hardly allows him leisure to enjoy himself in the Country Seat, | which he has purchased. As we advance towards Cirencester, Lord Bathurst's extensive line of superb woods forms the boundary of a flat country to the right, at the extremity of which is a Village & Church, at a considerable distance. Below, & in front, is the magnificent Gothic Tower of Cirencester Church, which forms from every direction so lofty & ~~very~~ elegant an object; to the right is the little Church of Stratton, & the residence of the Rev$^{d.}$ M$^{r.}$ Daubigny, its rector. No object of greater interest than those, which I have named, marked this stage of sixteen miles. We entered the Town & drove to the Ram a very good, old fashioned Inn, through a neat, ancient Street, in which some handsome houses intervene between those, which bear the marks of our antique domestic Architecture, Gabel Ends, & pointed Pediments. Cirencester was a Roman Station of considerable importance, as we judge from the numerous remains of Roman Antiquities, which have been found there, and | from the Roman Roads passing through, or originating in, it. Of the former the subterraneous remains, baths, mosaic pavements &c. similar to those lately discovered at Woodchester, Wellow &c. are the most remarkable, and have been well elucidated by the erudition of M$^{r.}$ Lysons,[3] to whom all lovers of antiquity are highly indebted; & who has ably illustrated the time-worn remains of this interesting County. Of the antient roads, the route to Glocester has been already mentioned; another led from Cirencester to Bath, nearly in the direction of the present turnpike road—; a third is thus traced in an old Itinerary:—a Durocornovio, (Cirencester) Stationem incognitam (probably Froxfield, where Roman Remains have been found;) XXIX—Spinas, (which was more

3. Samuel Lysons, (1763-1819). Lysons was an archaeologist and illustrator of great skill. In the 1790s he was responsible for excavating and illustrating, in fine detail, the mosaics at Woodchester Roman Villa. One of the illustrations from this work provides the illustration for the dust jacket of volume one of these diaries.

56. Samuel Lysons, 1763-1819; by Sir Thomas Lawrence.

probably Thatcham than Speen; although the name of the latter is evidently derived from the Roman Station, yet the distance better accords with the former;) XV—Calevam (which was almost undoubtedly Reading) XX miles. In the appropriation of the | Stations to modern sites I have followed the learned Dr. Becke, in his acute Paper in the 15th. Vol. of the Archaeologia upon the ancient inhabitants, Stations, &c. in Berkshire.—Of the road thus traced the first Station, supposed Froxfield, would be the spot, where the Route from Winchester (Vindomis) to Cirencester, & that from London to Bath, (~~of~~ to which the latter part traced above belongs,) would cross. Cirencester has never wholly lost its ancient consequence; it has always been one of the principal Towns in Glocestershire, its borough very respectable, the markets large, the inhabitants opulent. According to the returns to Parliament there are 885 houses, & 4130 Inhabitants. Michael Hicks Beech Esqr. a very opulent man, (brother of Sir Wm. Hicks Bart. of Gloucestershire,)[4] resident at Williamstrip in this County, or at Netheravon in Wilts, has long represented the Borough. J. Cripps Esqr., a native of the Town, has lately succeeded to the other seat.[5] The church of Cirencester merits minute | attention, not less from its beautiful architecture, ornaments, & remains of antiquity, ~~as~~ than for the pleasing spectacle, which a well pewed, clean & warm place of worship offers: it is one of the most handsome parochial churches, which I have visited. We did not view it at this time; but having shortly before minutely examined it, I shall here insert the result of our observations & enquiries.[6] The building is so entirely envelloped by dwelling houses, that the very handsome & rich Gothic Tower, & the grand porch, of the same architecture, in the Market place, are the only parts of the exterior visible, unless the Stranger should be conducted into the spacious Churchyard behind. The Porch above mentioned is a very massy building, of two ranges of Gothic bow-windows surmounting an arch, which forms the Entrance; the whole is finished by a range of battlements, and affords a very antique character to

4. William Hicks, (1754-1834). Hicks succeeded to the baronetcy on the death of his father Sir Howe Hicks in 1801. The family seat was at Williamstrip Park, Gloucestershire. He was succeeded by his brother, Michael Hicks-Beach.
5. Joseph Cripps, (1765-1847). Cripps inherited a cloth mill in Cirencester from his father and extended the family business by brewing and banking. Cripps became M.P. for Cirencester, 1806-12, 1818-41, He was a staunch friend of the slavery abolitionists. He was a director of the Van Diemen's Land Co. from 1825 until his death, ending up as Governor by 1842.
6. From this comment it is fair to assume that part of their honeymoon was a tour of the region in his gig drawn by Lidelexey.

57. Francis Edward Witts by Jagger of Cheltenham,1808.

the Space, in which it stands, which is heightened by the peculiar forms of the old dwelling houses around, & the economy observed in the planning of narrow | avenues, or paths; streets they can scarcely be termed. The Church consists of a nave, two side aisles, a chancel, & four chapels; transept there is none, since the Tower occupies the Western End. The nave is separated from the side Aisles by lofty, richly ornamented, slender, clustered Columns; above the pointed arches on either side are ranges of ligh~~ted~~ Gothic Windows, the whole finishing in a handsome timber roof. The Western Window consists of a profusion of specimens of fine painted glass, carefully collected from different parts of the church, & judiciously arranged by the taste & antiquarian knowledge of M^r. Lysons. The disposition of the pews in this part of the Church is very excellent, as a great part of the congregation are accommodated in a range of gradually rising seats, extending across the base of the nave, in front of the West Window, which, however, ^they^ do not obscure. An antient wooden carved screen separates the nave from the Chancel; the interval of the arch above | is occupied by an organ. The pulpit adjacent to the first column from the Chancel, upon the northern side, is of stone, very richly carved in the Gothic style. The floor of the nave presents some brasses of the 16th. Century. The Southern Aisle contains a handsome Gothic stone font, with Shields, well carved, sculptured, & formed. A wainscoat, in the same aisle, of oak, with Gothic carved niches, in a very good style, enriched by the letters IHS, gilt & sculptured, merits passing attention. The Northern Aisle contains a modern marble font of good form. It is separated from a Chapel, dedicated to the Holy Trinity, by a range of columns, & arches partly filled up with glass, & above by the backs of various excellent Seats, forming a Gallery, incongruous, indeed, to the original character of the Church, but necessary in consequence of increased population. Trinity Chapel is interesting to the Antiquarian upon more than one account, & I shall here be indebted | to M^r. Lysons's sagacity & research, who has incidentally illustrated this part of the Church. The floor is strewed with many rich fragments of monumental brasses of the 15th. Century, of which sufficient remains to affix certain dates, & to illustrate the refinement attained in this style of ornament. |

Although this narrative is headed 'Route from Cheltenham to Erchfont' it appears to have been left unfinished. The next narrative is a journal made during a visit to Craven in June the following year (1809). In the meantime, gaps can be filled from the diaries of Agnes Witts. The first entry of interest relates to a commission Agnes had given to Mr. Jagger, miniaturist of

Cheltenham: 19 July 1808: '. . . call'd at Jaggers the Painters to take a view of Franks Picture . . .' 15 August 1808: '. . . after luncheon walk'd with Mr. Crofts & to see Franks picture . . .'

This miniature of Francis Witts also appears in the colour section of Volume One. It shows a stout young man with fair hair, a fashionable cravat and pronounced features with a strong nose.

The next few entries relate to the decline and death of Ferdinand and the flurry of activity with the Timbrell sisters to ensure that Francis is not jostled out of his half-promised elevation to Upper Slaughter. The sisters owned the advowson and had the power of presentation: 27 August 1808: ' . . . bleak intelligence of my Brother . . .' 9 September 1808: '. . . wrote a long letter to Frank . . .' 12 September 1808: '. . . rec'd letters from Mrs. Granville & my Sistr. Travell with a sad account of my poor Brother . . .' 27 September 1808: '. . . on our return home rec'd the melancholy news of the Death of my poor Brother at 4 that afternoon in a letter from my Sister wch. letter I answered directly & wrote to Frank.' 28 September 1808: '. . . went out before breakfast to call on Mrs. Timkbrells relative to the living at Upper Slaughter met with a less favourable reception than we expected.'

On 4 October 1808 Francis and Margaret arrived at Cheltenham and the next few days are spent anxiously, following on from the less favourable reception of his mother a few days before. Then, suddenly, all is well: 8 October 1808: '. . . a visit from the older Mrs. Timbrell made it certain that our Dear Son was to be Rector of Slaughter great general joy. . .'

On Saturday 15 October 1808 Francis returned to Urchfont to do his Sunday duties, leaving Margaret with his mother. He returned to Cheltenham on the Monday. On the following day he rode off to Upper Slaughter on Lidelexey to do a reconnaissance. The business side of the arrangements with the Timbrells Francis left to his mother: 21 October 1808: '. . . Mr Witts & I visited Mrs. Timbrell & did some matters of Business . . .'

On Saturday 24 October 1808 Francis is recorded as being off to Upper Slaughter early: 'Frank set off early for Upper Slaughter & return'd before Dinner, Margaret & I puddled through the dirt to see Dr. Charles Parry's drawings . . .' 25 October 1808: 'Dry but lowering till after mid-day when it became extremely wet, and towards evening perfectly tremendous from wind as well as rain a miserable prospect for poor Frank & Margaret who set out early in their gig to return into Wilts. By way of Winchester.' Quite why they had to go to Winchester is unclear, but presumably it was connected with ecclesiastical arrangements.

Three days later Edward and Agnes moved into more permanent accommodation in Essex Place, Cheltenham, and on the following Monday, 31 October 1808 they arrived at Urchfont for what Agnes referred to as a 'talkative evening'. They remained with their son and daughter-in-law, not returning to Essex Place until 8 November by way of Cirencester where they had over-nighted — expensively: ' . . . left our <u>Dear</u> Inn the Ram at Cirencester at ½ past nine from the extreme badness of the roads towards Cheltenham we were 3 hours performing the stage.'

With many arrangements to make, Francis and Margaret were soon back at Cheltenham:

Wednesday 23 November 1808: '. . . our Dear Son & Daughter did not arrive until seven o'clock & then almost wet thro' happy to see them safe after such a perilous journey. . .'

This appears to have been their formal move from Urchfont, for nothing further is recorded relating to that curacy. On the Friday the young couple went to Upper Slaughter and remained there three days, surveying the rectory, village, and surroundings. Francis made a further visit of two days, the remainder of the time appears to have been spent in Cheltenham, but it appears that arrangements for Christmas were for Margaret to be back in Yorkshire with her mother: 19 December 1808: '. . . the preparations for the approaching departure of Frank & his wife made it an unpleasant busy day . . .' 20 December 1808: '. . . my Son & his Wife left us to commence their journey into the North, such a parting very trying . . .'

The visit in the north was to last more than three months, for Francis did not arrive back until 5 April 1809, and even then he was alone. Exactly why they were away so long in unknown, but one assumption may be that Margaret was pregnant and that she miscarried while in Yorkshire. Another possibility is that she was very homesick. While the young people were away, Agnes and Edward accepted an invitation from Lady Hereford, first cousin to Agnes, to stay at Stanway House. They arrived there on 2 February and remained for thirty-four days.

When back in the south, Francis went to Oxford for some purpose, possibly to receive his M.A., and he wrote to his mother on 16 April from there. On 17 April Agnes and Edward were back with Lady Hereford, and Francis arrived there on 7 May on his way back from Evesham where he had been staying with his friend, William Dowell. The following day, Monday 8 May 1809, Francis headed north to rejoin Margaret.

It is unclear who was taking the duty at Upper Slaughter at this period. There was presumably a curate appointed to act in the interim, but surprisingingly Agnes records little on this matter. From hints thrown out later in the Diaries it seems that it may have been William Dowell.

The next we read from the pen of Francis is dated almost four weeks later when the young couple made a trip to Craven on their way back to Gloucestershire.

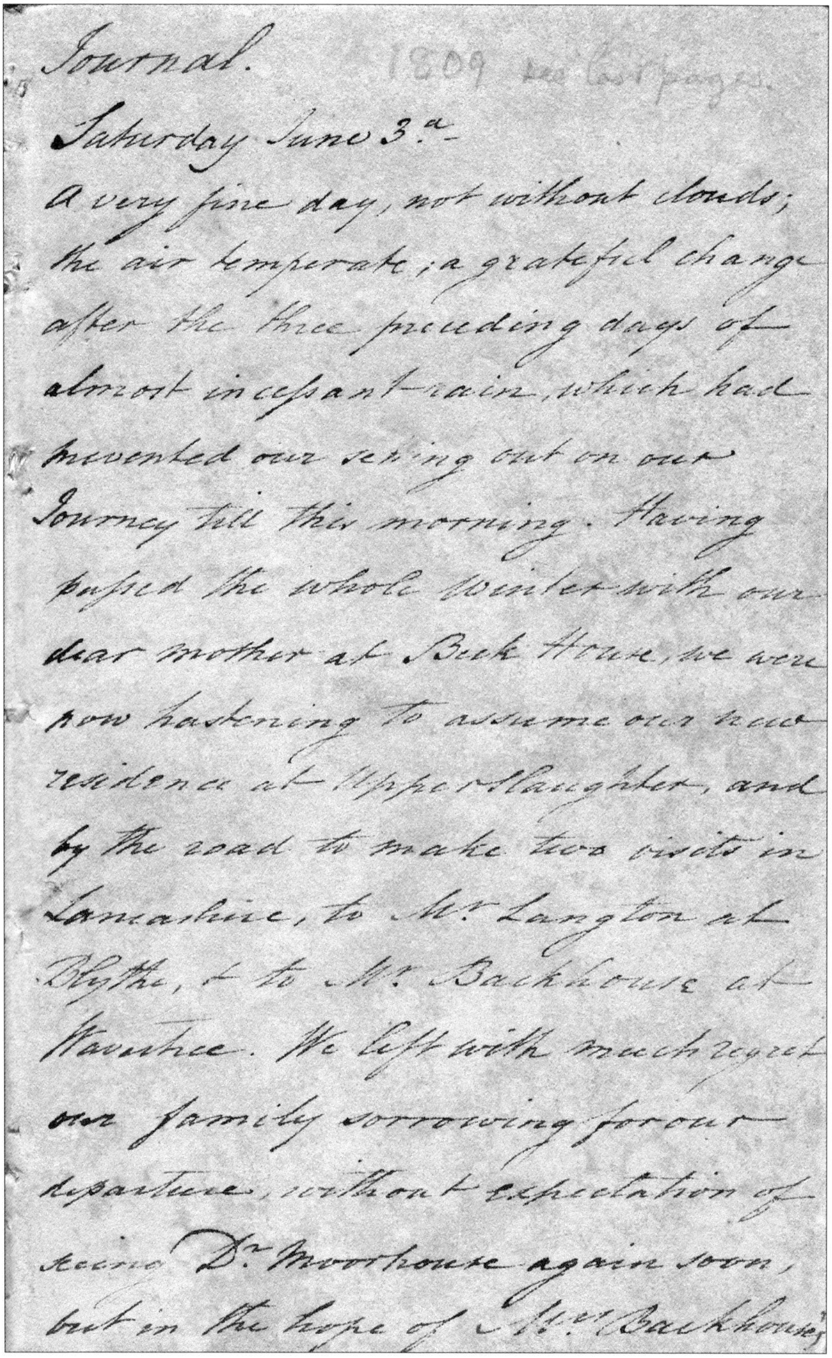
Journal. 1809 see last pages.

Saturday June 3d.

A very fine day, not without clouds; the air temperate; a grateful change after the three preceding days of almost incessant rain, which had prevented our setting out on our Journey till this morning. Having passed the whole Winter with our dear mother at Beck House, we were now hastening to assume our new residence at Upper Slaughter, and by the road to make two visits in Lancashire, to Mr Langton at Blythe, & to Mr Backhouse at Wavertree. We left with much regret our family sorrowing for our departure, without expectation of seeing Dr Moorhouse again soon, but in the hope of Mrs Backhouse's

Witts Family Papers F384

Journal.

Saturday June 3d.—

A very fine day, not without clouds; the air temperate; a grateful change after the three preceding days of almost incessant rain, which had prevented our setting out on our Journey till this morning. Having passed the whole Winter with our dear mother at Beck House, we were now hastening to assume our new residence at Upper Slaughter, and by the road to make two visits in Lancashire, to Mr. Langton at Blythe, & to Mr. Backhouse at Wavertree. We left with much regret our family sorrowing for our departure, without expectation of seeing Dr. Moorhouse again soon, but in the hope of Mrs. Backhouse's | & Miss Currer's overtaking us at Blythe, the former we anxiously wish in better health. Our first stage, to Whalley, was long and hilly; 21 miles. The valuable land, which skirts the Ribble was exchanged for poorer soil, beyond Rathmell, the first place we passed through, a township in the Parish of Giggleswick. We ascend to Rathmell, the view backwards towards Ingleborough & Penygent, Settle &c. very fine. The road is indifferent. At Rathmell is a Chalybeate Spring. Between Rathmell & Wigglesworth, a township in the Parish of Long–Preston, the Country is barren, the road hilly, & rough. At Wigglesworth is a free-school & a sulphurated spring, devoid of saline qualities. | As we approach Forest Becks the scenery improves, by the addition of hedges & woods; the road rough & hilly. Oak grows here in profusion. The Village of Bolton, to the left, is a picturesque: a little farther, is Bolton-Hall, the seat of a merchant in Liverpool, of the same name, newly purchased; it is old, stands well above the Ribble, & is finely flanked with wood. The country to the right is pleasing; a short distance brings is to Sawley, & crossing a bridge over the Ribble, having Mr. Peel's very pretty residence on the right, we stopped to take hay & water at a public-house. Sawley contains the inconsiderable remains of an Abbey, of which an interesting account is contained in Dr. | Whitaker's History of Craven: most of the houses have in them some remains of the ancient structure. This spot being extremely picturesque & fertile suited well the interested view of the monks: these have yeilded to a more active class of people, manufacturers in Peel's Cotton works established here.[1] Thus in

1. Sir Robert Peel, (1750-1830). Peel's father was referred to as the father of the Lancashire cotton trade, having established a calico printing works at Blackburn under the name of Haworth, Peel & Yates. Robert entered the firm at the age of 23 and adopted the methods of Arkwright as to the mechanical methods of saving labour. In 1790 he had purchased the Tamworth property of the 1st Marquess of Bath and by 1796 made good his title to most of the Drayton manor. Having established cotton mills in the district he took up residence there by 1799. He was the first 'cotton king' to sit in parliament being M.P. for Tamworth, 1790-1820. As early as 1803 he was being eulogized as a model of a self-made man, self-educated, well-informed and philanthropic. Peel was a supported of Pitt. In his maiden speech he pointed out that the wealth of the country depended on the industry, not the size or scope of its population. His first son, Robert, was Prime Minister, 1841-6.

these sequestered Vallies indolent monks have been succeeded by a depraved population of labourers. Sawley is extra-parochial.—The meadows adjoining to Sawley are very beautiful. We saw the Country to great advantage from the beautiful variety of light & shade this day: In a valley extending beneath Long~~b~~ridge Fell, a mountain stretching towards the Forest of Bolland, we perceived Grindleton Chapel. Not far from Sawley is Smithies-bridge | over a brook, which separates the Counties of York & Lancaster: the scenery here is very pretty. Chatburn, a little farther on, is a small village, in a pretty vale, under limestone rocks, which lie in an inclined stratum. Beyond Chatburn is Worston, a small hamlet at the foot of the Giant Pendle-Hill; which, with the two mountains, which I have named above, is esteemed among the highest mountains in England. It is a long ridge, rising from the West to the East, bare at its summit, wooded & cultivated on its lower slopes. Pendle-Hill is the genuine Habitat of the Lancashire witches. It is a fine object to the surrounding country in a circuit of many miles. To the right we had the Borough of Clitherow, rendered picturesque | by its Castle, and ruined Tower, & the Tower of its Church. The Castle & manor of Clithero are the property of the Duke of Buccleugh,[2] the Church is under the Rectory of Whalley, which included a district larger than some Counties. The history of this Country is well recorded by Dr. Whitaker, in his History of Whalley,[3] of which place, by a sort of poetic Justice, he has recently been instituted Rector. A rich and well wooded scenery surrounds Clitherow, & extends to Whalley. Standen Hall, the seat of Mr. Aspinall, is to the right of the road, near Whalley, a handsome house, with good plantations.[4] The situation of Whalley is eminently beautiful, & illustrative of the good taste of the monks, who long ruled in this fertile Valley. Seated on the banks of the Calder, it is surroun- | -ded by beautifully wooded heights, or rich valleys. The ruins of the monastery give an interest to the Village. While our horse baited, (we travelled in our Gig,) my Margaret & myself, visited the Church, & remains of the Abbey. The former is little remarkable, but in the Church Yard are three antique Crosses, which Dr Whitaker believes to be commemorative of the preaching of Paullinus in this then desert Country. One of the crosses, upon which are the letters I.H.S. appears to me to be a form less ancient than the other. Referring to the Historian of the Abbey, for the details of its interesting history, I will only add, that we found a handsome gateway, (probably, that which led to the Abbot's lodgings, & within a spacious Courtyard, part | of the Abbey converted into a dwelling house: this seemed to have been repaired since the dissolution of the House. Beyond, in an orchard, are more remains of cloisters, arches, &c very picturesque. The Abbey Mill, close adjoining, is still in use. Beyond, we observed an old Barn, wh. evidently had formed the outer Choir of the Conventual Church; the Gothic windows were blocked up: as were the retiring arched door-ways. A bold background of timber under this and the cottages beneath an interesting object, particularly, when viewed from a meadow by the river, where the woods of Clerk-Hill, the Seat of Lady Gardner, retire behind the bridge, & the steep Eminence, Whalley Nab, overhangs with its wooded brow the valley & river below.— | We inspected also the remains of a Gate way, which seems to have been one to the

---

2. Henry Scott, 3rd Duke of Buccleuch, (1746-1812). The Duke of Buccleuch's main estate was at Dalkeith.
3. Thomas Dunham Whitaker, *History of the Parish of Whalley.* (1806).
4. Standen Hall was built in 1757 by James Aspinall. The owner in 1807 was Richard Aspinall, presumably the son of James.

chief entrances to the monastic enclosure; it is a large square ivied Tower with an arch way beneath; the roof groined; the windows Gothic, and hung with ivy; yet the whole too solid to be very picturesque. The Vicarage, (not Rectory) of Whalley is in the gift of the Archb. of Canterbury; it is of small value, but some churches under its Jurisdiction, of moderate value, are in the Patronage of the Incumbent.—

From Whalley we proceeded to Blackburn, a short stage of six miles, of hilly & rough road. Crossing the river by a bridge of three arches, we ascended Whalley Nab, by a tedious pull of two | miles. Soon after passing the turnpike is a pleasing view of the Abbey Remains, across the Stream, which appear to advantage, intermixed with foliage. The view over the Valley is very fine, offering a most fertile Landscape. On the side of Long-ridge Fell is discernd Stonihurst, a seat belonging to Mr. Weld, of Dorsetshire, appropriated as a large Seminary for Roman Catholic Youth. On the summit of Whalley Nab, we bid adieu to the interesting Country, & passing through some barren enclosures, & over Billington Moor, now ascending, now descending, we shortly fall down towards the large manufacturing Town, Blackburn, which is situated | amid a circle of uninteresting Hills, devoid of timber, of unpleasant outlines. Near the Town is Little Harwood, a large, rather vulgar place, formerly the property of Col. Clayton. We found Blackburn crowded with the Blackburn Reg. of Local Militia, chiefly inhabitants of this neighbourhood, Burnley, Colne, Padiham, Clithero, &c We were accommodated at the New Inn. After tea we walked over the Town, which, in general, is dark, and ugly. King Street is the best. There are three Churches; two comparatively modern; one of them, probably of recent erection, is a handsome large building. The trade of the place is chiefly in Cotton.— |

Sunday June 4th—

After some early rain in the morning, the weather cleared up for an hour of two, but heavy showers of rain fell subsequently, till even. the intervals being dark. We proceeded from Blackburn between 7 & 8 o clock, with the intention to breakfast at Rose Whittles, a public house between Chorley & Preston, on the road to Blythe, 10 miles from Blackburn. We now were to exercise our ingenuity in discovering crossroads, but we went accurately, having received correct information. Leaving Blackburn by the Preston road, & King Street, the first object, which we remarked, was, about a mile from B. to the right; Witton — the seat of Mr. Fielding, one of an opulent family of manufacturers, beautifully situated on the side of a hill, em- | -braced by woods, and seeming to comprize every convenience. Beyond is the seat of Mr. Butler. Livesey is a straggling township, through which we passed. Moulding-water next attracted our attention, for the general face of the country was uninteresting, the Hills being of a heavy outline, & barren, the soil indifferent. But the spot, which I mentioned, is very romantic, a clear stream rushes through a narrow valley, under a Knole of red rock, clothed with Oak Trees & other timber; Mr. W. Fielding has recently erected a large mansion at the foot of this rock, where a Cottage would have been more in character; but the whole is pleasing. A steep hill raises us from this dell, & we soon left the turnpike road, which was very tolerable, for an extremely rough cross road on the left. Here | the face of the country was very dull. We passed through Brindle, a small village, where we were glad to exchange our vile road for a pavé: and in Lancashire a paved road is synonimous with a good one; though in the course of this day we often proved the reverse, when we passed over what was old & broken. Radburne & Clayton Green are the next places through which we passed: beyond the latter we crossed a pretty retired valley. At length we reached the main road from Manchester to Preston, near Cuerd~~ale~~en Hall, a Seat of Mr. Parker: & leaving the Tower of Leyland, a village, to the right, we reached Rose Whittle, a lone Inn of secondary rate, where we breakfasted & baited our horse.[5] The Country here is very flat, the hed- | -ges, meadows & timber luxuriant.

We were now 12 miles distant from Blythe; the road for five miles very tolerable, through shady lanes; we were much incommoded by heavy rain. The tower of Leyland still on the right; when we had it behind us, we were pleased with a small group, Shaw Hill, a retired well wooded spot. At Croston, a village, through which we passed, which lies very low, is a Seat of Mr. Trafford's, a Roman Catholic family; the Parsonage, Mr. Masters's, is a pretty spot, situated on the ground once occupied by a religious house. A vile mock-ruin gateway marred the place. Mr. Hill also resides here. Two miles farther is Rufford, where we came into the great pavè from Liverpool to Preston. The road from | ~~Marston~~ Croston to Rufford is vile, the land extremely low, bounded by deep & wide ditches, often overflowed. At Rufford is the modern seat & plantations of Sir Thomas Hesketh.[6] The Church and Village are neat. Between Rufford & Burscough Bridge, where we pass the Liverpool & Preston Canal, the face of the Country rather improves; not that it loses its characteristic lowness, but some distant elevations & finer timber. At Burcough, a long, not ugly, village, are the very inconsiderable remains of an Abbey. To the left we perceived the woods round Lathom House the Seat of W. Bootle Esqr. M.P. for Newcastle under Line.[7] At Burscough are diverged to Blythe Hall; Mr. Langton's house is seated in about 50 Acres of well planted ground; it is | old & of a Gothic form & character, elegantly furnished. After being introduced to our Host and Hostess, who received us with polite attention, we dressed and dined.[8] Mr. Langton is blessed with four fine children; three boys & a girl: his neice Miss M. Hornby of Kirkham

---

5. This stretch of road, from Wigan to Preston was known from the journals of early travellers to be one of the worst stretches of highway in the country. By the 1840s Rose Whittle's public house was replaced by New Inn Farm. This, in turn was demolished before the Second World War.
6. Sir Thomas Dalrymple Hesketh, (1777-1842). Hesketh, of Rufford Hall was born in New York and succeeded to the baronetcy in 1796.
7. Edward Wilbraham Bootle (afterwards Bootle Wilbraham), (1771-1853). Wilbraham Bootle had a long parliamentary career. At this time he was M.P. for Newcastle-under-Lyme, 1796-1812. He was a warm supporter of Pitt and his politics would have pleased Francis Witts. He was captain of the Loyal Ormskirk Volunteers and in 1809 was lieutenant colonel of the Leyland and Ormskirk regiment of the Lancashire Militia. By 1823 he was lieutenant colonel commandant. He was created Baron Skelmersdale in 1823.
8. The host and hostess were Thomas and Ellen Langton. They had moved to Blythe Hall in 1804. Their daughter, Anne (1804-1893) was to become famous as a painter who specialised in landscapes and miniature portraiture. In 1837 she settled in Upper Canada and she, together with the Currers feature later in the diaries. Anne, together with her older brother John and younger brother William were educated at home by their parents and private tutors. The family travelled extensively in Austria, Belgium, France, Italy, Germany and Switzerland. Following the Napoleonic Wars, Thomas Langton's business in England became unstable and in 1821 the family was forced to return to England from their travels and studies. On their return they were forced to sell their mansion, dismiss all but one servant, and move to a small town house in Liverpool. At age 16, Anne took on many of the housekeeping duties and the care of her aging parents while continuing her art work. Following further financial losses the family moved to Bootle. In 1833 John moved to Canada. By 1836 William had become a very successful Manchester businessman and he offered to pay his family's living expenses, but the next year the family including Miss Currer decided to join John Langton in Canada. They finally settled on John's farm on Sturgeon Lake, near Fenelon Falls, Ontario.

in Lancashire, and M$^{rs.}$ Langton's neice Miss F. Currer are at present inmates of Blythe Miss E. W. Bootle, Sister of the Senator, drank Tea with us. This Lady resides with her mother at the Almonry, a house appropriated for a Chaplain, within the boundary of Lathom Park.

Monday June 5th—

A succession of almost uninterrupted rain prevented our leaving the House, & even fire-side, except, that I walked in the grounds for a quarter of an hour, with M$^{r.}$ Langton before dinner, and alone in the Evening. We had no | company, but read and conversed:—The House is not very large: 20 years ago was a farm-house, altered & gothicized to its present state. The grounds arc pleasingly disposed; from some walks is a view of the remains of Burscough abbey, at other points the Spire & Tower of Ormskirk Church: in the Horizon Parbold Hill &c. A steward of the Derby family, the proprietors, a Vandal, some 50 years back demolished the respectable relics of Burscough Abbey, leaving only the inconsiderable fragments now subsisting unappropriated to the repairs of cow-houses & stables.

Tuesday June 6th—

A showery windy day, of threatening aspect. We went to Ormskirk through Burscough in M$^{r.}$ Langton's | Carriage, accompanied by our host & hostess. Ormskirk is two miles distant from Blyth. To the left of the Town is Cross-Hall, the seat of Col. Stanley, one of the members for Lancashire.[9] The town is built of brick, & seems to consist of four irregular streets. We drove to the Church, which is a singular edifice: there is a very heavy tower at the West end, in which are hung the bells brought from Burscough Abbey, on its dissolution; and a steeple crowns the porch, the summit of which rises above, & seems to jostle the Tower: Probably, this whimsical anomaly in architecture results from the caprice of the Architect. I understand, there exists no record on the subject; but rumour assigns the oddity to | the dissention of two sisters, old maids, founders of the Church, who could not agree, which of the two styles of building to adopt, that with a tower, or that with a spire. The view from the Churchyard towards the coast is extensive, level & wooded: the Spires of Meols, a small bathing place, & of Halsall, are visible. The interior of the Church offers a curious medley of ancient & modern pews; the structure of the nave and side-aisles is modern & incongruous, the galleries overlooking the Pulpit most unpleasantly. The Chancel is ancient. There are some old altar-tombs, probably removed from Burscough Abbey, most stripped of their brasses, one retaining its very handsome delineation of a Knight† in full

† an Ecclestone|

length. There is a Chapel of the Derby family, which is their principal place of interment; it is ~~deicated~~ decorated with ~~Ensigns~~ Banners & Escutcheons; two or three mutilated marble monumental statues represent Ancestors of the Derby family: on one of these I observed the three armed legs, the arms of the Isle of Man. The crest of the Derby family is also sculptured here; it is an eagle standing above an infant swathed: this crest is frequent as a Sign on Inns in

9. Thomas Stanley, (1749-1816). M.P. for Lancashire, 1780-1812. Colonel Stanley sat as M.P. in the interest of his third cousin once removed, the Whig 12th Earl of Derby. Stanley was a colonel in the 1st regiment of the Lancashire Militia.

Cheshire & Lancashire. The vault is neither spacious nor deep; it is indecorously & negligently closed, & made an object of curiosity. Many leaden coffins have probably been removed from Burscough Abbey, as also the monumen- | -tal statues above named: we remarked the mouldering coffin of the Earl of Derby beheaded at Bolton in this County by order of the parliament for his adherence to the cause of Charles the 1st—the coffin of a member of the family, who died at Venice; the coffin of an unusual form, not being shaped to the outline of the corpse:—the coffin containing the remains of a member of the family, who died abroad, & whose embalmed bowels are contained in a separate chest. The sister of the present Earl, who died lately, directed, that her remains should not be brought hither, as she scorned to lie in a vault, in which at some time she should be elbowed by the corpse of an Actress: the present Lady Derby was the inimitable Miss | Farren.[10] The Vicarage of Ormskirk is extensive: Lathom, Burscough, Scarisbrick &c. are townships within its compass. Its income is small in comparison with other valuable livings in the Patronage of the Derby family. Mr. Stanley, a distant relation of Lord Derby, is Vicar. On our return to Blythe, we walked in the Grounds. After dinner Mrs. Backhouse & Miss Currer arrived from Beck House.—

Wednesday June 7.—
Less rain than on the preceding days; the wind high, and the rain occasionally falling; the air cold. Occupied in the preparations for our departure for Mr. J. Backhouse's at Wavertree near Liverpool, my dear Margaret's Uncle. Mrs. Backhouse, still very much indisposed accompanied us. We | quitted Blyth about 3 o clock, after an early dinner, parting with regret from such amiable persons, as compose its family. I learnt with pleasure, that Mr. Langton, who wished to go to Liverpool, intended to avail himself of the opportunity of a seat in the Gig: Margaret accompanied her Mother. From Blythe to Liverpool the distance is 15 miles: through Ormskirk, and by the great road, which leads from Liverpool to Preston. We passed through Burscough & Ormskirk, as yesterday: Cross Hall near the latter is only a farm House. Col. Stanley, its owner, commands the Lancashire militia. This Country from Rufford to Liverpool produces a vast growth of potatoes of the best quality, which are much cultivated. |

The journal ends suddenly in a similar manner to the narrative from Cheltenham to Erchfont the previous year. There is now a gap of three years before the next surviving narrative of another trip to the north. As usual, the diaries of his mother fill in some of the gaps.

27 June 1809: ' . . . My Dear Frank & his wife came down from Slaughter . . .' Francis and Margaret stayed with Edward and Agnes for three days. In the middle of July Edward and Agnes visited Upper Slaughter, not without some painful memories for Agnes of the troublesome times visiting her brother back in 1793 — the last time she had been there: 18 July 1809: '. . . at six o'clock we set off for Upper Slaughter found the roads excellent, arrived there soon after nine & met with a delightful reception from our Dear Children;

10. Elizabeth Farran, (1763-1829). Elizabeth, an actress of note, first appeared on the stage in Bath in 1773 and in London in 1777 in *She Stoops to Conquer*. She was a favourite on the stage for twenty years before marrying Edward Smith-Stanley, 21st Earl of Derby, (1752-1834).

which made up to me for the natural agitation of returning to this Place. . . .'

Two weeks later George arrived, but Agnes was so intent on visiting Lady Grey, her first cousin once removed, (a daughter of Lady Elcho) who now, by coincidence, had bought Swerford Park, the old Oxfordshire home of Edward and Agnes, that Agnes hardly gives any time to her second-born son. Agnes was very self-centred, and Swerford had more attraction! 3 August 1809: '. . . at Breakfast came our long look'd for Son George stout & bonny, after a four years absence from us sorry he had managed it to come only an hour before we set out for Lady Greys at Swerford Park the country over which we pass'd appeared greatly improved during our long absence from it, by the abundant growth of the several plantations & our Dear Old Place perhaps more than any, our Dear Relative rec'd us with most marked kindness . . .'

Agnes is occasionally thoughtless and tactless. In her diaries perhaps it did not matter. She had been at Swerford for almost a week, ignoring George back at Upper Slaughter — even though he had been away for four years. When he followed her to Swerford, all she could note was her frustration that her wonder boy, Frank, had not accompanied him:

9 August 1809: '. . . my Son George came to Dinner, much vex'd his Brother could not accompany him . . .'

They returned from Swerford to Slaughter on 11 August and found Frank's friend William Dowell on a visit. George returned to his regiment at Canterbury on 28 August 1809. Three days later another old college friend arrived, and Agnes recorded the event approvingly: 1 September 1809: '. . . walk'd in the meadows before time to dress to receive Mr. Dowell & his friend Mr. Trevenen the former went to Stow to sleep, an agreeable change in our party . . .' Then on 15 September Edward and Agnes returned home to Cheltenham.

Edward and Agnes moved on to Calwich to stay with the Granvilles for two months, after which they called in at Hanbury as usual, on William Burslem, all part of their often repeated journey cycle. On 27 December they were back at Cheltenham, at which time Francis and Margaret joined them for a stay of several weeks. On 9 January, brother George arrived and on 31 January 1810, Frank and Margaret returned to Upper Slaughter.

Francis was always ambitious, and one exchange of letters shows that he may have asked his mother if her close relationship to Mrs. Brougham might lead towards patronage from Henry Brougham — perhaps surprising at this stage as Brougham had only been an M.P. for one month, but it may have been simply a letter of congratulation to Brougham at this stage — a case of oiling the wheels.

3 March 1810: '. . . rec'd a letter from Frank & answered it & wrote to Mr. Henry Brougham . . .' 7 March 1810: '. . . rec'd letters from Mr. Henry Brougham & Frank . . .'

One month later and Agnes was back at Slaughter: 1 April 1810: '. . . a summons for me to Upper Slaughter my Daughter being taken ill & fear entertained that she would miscarry this hurry prevented me going to Church & I set out to her about 4 o clock . . .' 4 April 1810: '. . . much concerned to feel myself under the necessity of returning to my poor invalid at

Upper Slaughter for which purpose a Stow chaise came for me & I arrived there at 3 o'clock much hurt to find Margaret not so well having suffered sadly from her breasts grew better in the evening & was carried into the Dressing Room . . .'

In between these trips to Upper Slaughter, Edward and Agnes had been spending much of their time with Lady Hereford at Stanway. This had a benefit on three fronts — it pleased Lady Hereford, it kept them close to Slaughter, and it enabled them to rent out their house in Cheltenham, eking out their funds. At the end of September, Agnes recorded a visit from Edward's brother John — the first time they had seen him in many years: 28 September 1810: '. . . the day was ushered in most agreeably by the early arrival of our good Brother John out of Shropshire who we had not seen for 19 years of course his appearance had undergone a great change . . .'

One of the few surviving letters from Francis to his wife Margaret is dated 17 November 1810 and provides some interesting domestic information:

Upper Slaughter
Nov. 17. 1810.
My beloved Margaret has, I hope, punctually received
the letter, I wrote her from Wilmslow the second day of
my Journey, and now, ever anxious to give her pleasure,
I hasten to tell her what farther befel me, premising, that
I arrived safe here to dinner to-day. When I left Wilmslow
it rained most violently, and thoroughly wet me through before
I got to Congleton, where I borrowed Breeches & Stockings,
while my own were dried, and where I slept. The next
morning I found said Breeches so tattered with their soaking
and drying, as hardly to hang on till I came to Newcastle,
where I fortunately met with a similar pair of leathers ready
made for a Guinea, and sold my ancient of days for two
shillings. Thus equipped I walked, while my horse baited
to call on my old acquaintance Carless, at Wolstanton,
a mile & half from the Town; he was absent from home, but
I saw his wife, whom I did not much admire. If you
stop at all in Newcastle beyond a bait, I advise it to be
at the Inn adjoining the Theatre. Proceeding, I dined at
Stone, where I heard so good an account of the Alehouse
at Cannock, that I pushed forward to make it my night
Quarters. The place is neat and the people very civil, &

58. Letter from Francis to Margaret, 17 November 1810.

Upper Slaughter
Nov. 17. 1810

My beloved Margaret has, I hope, punctually received the letter, I wrote from Wilmslow the second day of my Journey, and now, ever anxious to give her pleasures, I hasten to tell her what farther befell me, promising, that I arrived safe here to dinner to-day. When I left Wilmslow, it rained most violently, and thoroughly wet me through before I got to Congleton, where I borrowed Breeches & Stockings, while my own were dried, and where I slept. The next morning I found said Breeches so tattered with their soaking and drying, as hardly to hang on till I came to Newcastle, where I fortunately met with a similar pair of leathers ready made for a Guinea, and sold my ancient of days for two shillings. Thus equipped I walked, while my horse baited to call on my old acquaintance Carless, at Woolstanton, a mile & half from the Town; he was absent from home, but I saw his wife, whom I did not much admire. If you stop at all in Newcastle beyond a bait, I advise it to be at the Inn adjoining the Theatre. Proceeding, I dined at Stone, where I heard so good an account of the Alehouse at Cannock, that I pushed forward to make it my night quarters. The place is neat and the people very civil, & would suit you vastly well to sleep at, if it answered in point of distance, there being a nice bed room, where I slept, and a good double bedded Room, but you must not stop there Thursday night, as I did, for fear of being serenaded till eleven o clock by an admirable club of Singers & Musicians, by whom I was much amused. I there wrote to George, as from Newcastle I did to Mr. Bradstock. Friday my first Stage was from Cannock to Birming^m. from whence I have brought your Pearl Crescent, completely new strung, I am told, with a new frame, all of which was quite necessary, at the Expense of a Guinea. The box from Richards's, which I have just opened, & which has long been here, seems all right. After luncheon at the Swan, I made a long stage to Henley, where I found very good accommodations & slept at the Swan, which also would you, if necessary. This morning I breakfasted at Stafford, and wishing to explore, and at the same time save a mile or two riding, I made Campden my baiting place: the roads very bad & not passable for a carriage. At Campden I was much pleased with the old Church and monuments, while I staid, & I got here between three & four by Condicote &c. I found all tolerably well; the greatest change is the absence of the fine Elm at the footbridge, blown down with three or four of our trees in the shady walk, this day week. The water looks extremely well, and the mud as I expected. The Servants well, and the house neat, and all as it should be, except an explosion of bottled Ale in the Cellar. The fever in Upper Slaughter is less bad than in other places round. Two of Thomas's Children have it now, and some are recovering. Some adults have had it. One of Wilcox's & one of James's Girls have fallen victims to it. Farmer Cook is much as he was, Molly Blandford worse within these few days, Nancy Packer quite pure again. Our little Cow gives milk only from half her udder in consequence of her attack: we have, I hear, a fine fat Calf. Mr. Garland stays the Winter at Eyford not being able to sell his corn to advantage. The Stow ball, which was fixed for the 12th. Is put off on account of the Death of the Princess Amelia. Our Greenhouse looks very nice and full. The fireguards are come from Stanway and suit well. Mr. Hurd officiated last Sunday. The window Curtains in the dining room were put up before I came. Thomas and Parris did the water works with little additional Expense comparatively. The Brewing has been well managed. I do not think, the Grey has suffered essentially by his journey, though much pulled down. Thus my dearest Wife, I have prattled all I yet know or have seen and have scarce space to tell, with what anxiety I shall look for the letters daily till I receive an account from you. Pray GOD it may be in every respect favourable! I pray for you all, & think of you very frequently. Need I warn you, my beloved, for mine and another's sake, not to be in the slightest degree imprudent? I yearn for our happy meeting. This day fortnight I hope at latest. No letters met me. I feel quite well, excepting a little Cold in my head & scarce any fatigue. My Love to your Mother & Grandfather. I rely on Providence to bless us in the fulfilment of our anxious hopes, both in this Journey & hereafter. Kiss this part for the sake of your tenderly attached Husband

F. E. Witts

Mrs. F. Witts
Beck House
Settle
Yorkshire

Francis had left Margaret at her Mother's house, and quite clearly from the letter it shows that she was pregnant. If the assumption regarding the earlier miscarriage is correct, it appears that Margaret suffered twice. On the third attempt she did bear the child. The next reference of note is for 19 April 1811 when Agnes recorded that Margaret gave birth to the baby girl some weeks prematurely. To begin with all was well, but problems set in and the baby died on 10 May. At this time Mrs. Backhouse was staying at Slaughter and it appears that Agnes preferred to keep her distance, especially as the aged Dr. Moorhouse, Margaret's grandfather, was also part of the party at Slaughter.

Edward and Agnes had given up their house in Essex Place, and after returning from Stanway they lodged with her sister Anne, but after six weeks they were, perhaps, outstaying their welcome, and Backhouses or no Backhouses, they headed to Slaughter: 19 July 1811: '. . . a fine tru summer day without oppressive heat, well suited to our little journey to Upper Slaughter, left Cheltenham soon after twelve full of grateful sentiments to my Sister for her kindness during the six weeks we had spent with her had a tedious drive from rough roads, found the old Dr. & Mrs. Backhouse yet remaining . . .'

59. Swan Hotel, Birmingham.

Four days later there is the first reference to the Aston family — to feature to a very large extent in the diaries. Young Frederick was to become Frank's pupil, and after finishing his degree at Oxford became his curate at Stanway in a relationship that was to last for the remainder of the Diarist's life. Mr. Aston senior had taken up residence at the nearby Eyford Park. 23 July 1811: '. . . Mr. Aston & his son Frederick drank tea . . .'

For the next few days Agnes had to grit her teeth: 3 August 1811: '. . . before tea arrived Miss Currer out of Lancashire according to expectation having had a favourable Journey of 4 days in my Son's Gig drawn by Mrs. Backhouses Coach Horse & driven by her Coachman . . .' 5 August 1811: '. . . Miss Currer's lively conversation a great relief . . .' 12 August 1811: '. . . Mrs. Backhouse & Miss Currer, Frank & Margaret set out early for Cheltenham leaving us in care of the old Doctor . . .' 15 August 1811: '. . . walk'd towards L. Slaughter before dinner being the last day before the departure of Dr. Moorhouse & Mrs. Backhouse the cheerfulness of the party in general was rather forced . . .' Then after the Backhouse party had departed, John Witts comes on the scene again. Part of the reason for the families not being closer had been that Agnes had not got on with John's wife, but she was now an invalid at home and John had taken to travelling without her. 21 November 1811: '. . . Frank set off early in the morning in his Gig for Cheltenham to meet his Uncle John Witts, whom he brought home to Dinner, most happy to see him, a cheerful evening . . .'

For 1811, most of the year went by without much of note. Edward and Agnes had taken up their roaming habits once more in order to save money. On 8 October they arrived back at Cheltenham to stay with Anne for two weeks, then on 22 October 1811, they migrated to Calwich for their annual visit to the Granvilles. From there on 2 November they received a letter from George, on his route to Malta. By 17 December they had left Calwich and as part of the usual cycle were at Hanbury. There, a few days later, Agnes received letters from Frank: 21 December 1811: '. . . rec'd two Letters from my Son Frank the second subjoined to one of Anne Witts's containing an account of the sudden Death of her poor Mother, truly sorry for my Bror. John. Anne was one of the three children of John Witts. The others being Apphia and John. They feature later in the diaries.

On Boxing day Edward and Agnes arrived at Stanway to be the guests of Lady Hereford, and on New Year's Eve Agnes saw her favourite son again for the first time in a good few weeks: 31 December 1811: '. . . Frank looking fat & blooming. On 12 January 1812 Agnes proudly recorded Frank's first appearance at the Session as a magistrate. He is just 28 years old. In May, after a long while without news, she received a letter from her second born: 16 May 1812: '. . . letter from George from Messina — a great relief to my mind as he was well . . .'

In March 1812 Frank and Margaret were away from home, but the exact location is unknown and entries in Agnes's diary provide no clues. Wherever it was, Frank referred to it as 'a sweet spot' in a short verse dated 8 March 1812. Presumably the verse was initially scribbled and then written up in fair hand afterwards, for it exists on the back of a letter dated 2 November 1813.

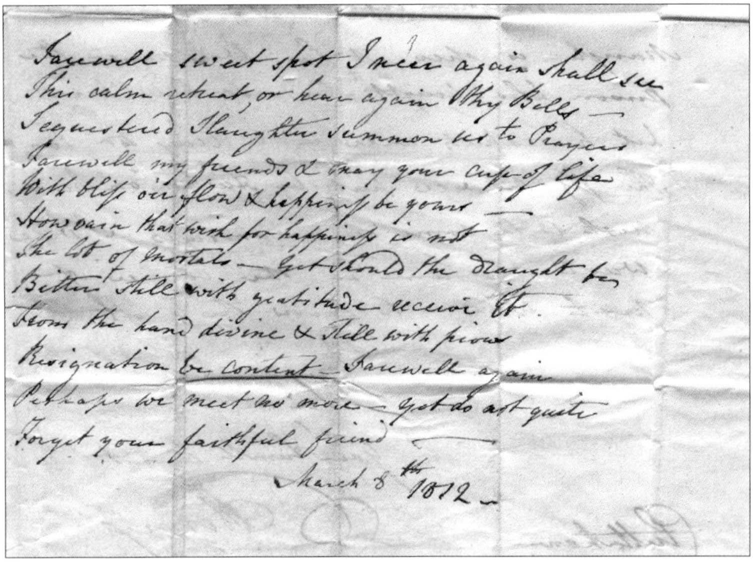
Farewell sweet spot I ne'er again shall see
This calm retreat, or hear again thy Bells —
Sequestered Slaughter summon us to Prayers
Farewell my friends & may your cup of life
With bliss o'er flow & happiness be yours —
How vain that wish for happiness is not
The lot of mortals — yet should the draught be
Bitter still with gratitude receive it.
From the hand divine & still with pious
Resignation be content — Farewell again
Perhaps we meet no more — yet do not quite
Forget your faithful friend —
March 8th 1812 —

60. Verse composed 8 March 1812.

On 4 June 1812 Edward and Agnes spent a few days at Cheltenham with Sister Anne and on the 19th they migrated to Upper Slaughter. From 27 until 7 July 1812 they stayed with the poor Lady Grey at Swerford.

Francis and Margaret had planned a long trip to the north, and on 3 August 1812 they departed, first to towards Calwich. They were to be away until November. It appears that Francis used the services of Mr. Hurd as a curate and for much of their time away, Edward and Agnes were house-sitting at Upper Slaughter.

3 August 1812: '. . . our beloved Children set out at seven, as soon as it ceased raining on their long journey intending to go as far as Warwick, a trying parting and we felt their absence greatly.'

61. The first Montpellier Spa.

Witts Family Papers F386

Tour into the North.
1812.— |

On Monday the 3d. of Aug. 1812, my wife and myself began a Northern Tour, leaving my Father & Mother at Upper Slaughter, who wished to remain some time longer there, and keep house in our absence. Mr. Hurd, of Naunton took charge of my Church. Our first point was Calwich, the Seat of our old and respected friend, the Revd. Mr. Granville. Our mode of conveyance was our Gig. The Stages this day were to Moreton 8 miles, to Halford Bridge 9 miles, to Warwick 12 miles. The night had been very wet with much thunder and lightning: we started at 7 o clock, with a gloomy and perturbed sky; but had little or no rain till we reached Warwick, the storm not having gone so far as Halford Bridge; but at Warwick we arrived on the approach of a very violent storm of thunder & rain, which in some measure impeded our pleasure in the grounds of the Castle. To Halford Bridge where we baited, the road was not new to us; at Moreton | we breakfasted. The road from Halford Bridge to Warwick is for the first six miles very moderate, for the last six admirably good, being a fine level of gravel between flourishing Elm trees. The whole Country is very picturesque, though not hilly; the foliage very fine, and the corn very luxuriant. Oaks thrive very well. On leaving Halford B. the Park of Evelyn Shirley Esqr. at Lower Eatington is on our left hand: further on to the right are the plantations of Sir C. Mordaunt, at Walton, the Member for the County.[1] Wellesburne is a very picturesque village, with several pretty residences, and the seat of Bernard Dewes Esqr. elder brother of our friend Mr. Granville, whom we expect to meet at Calwich. Here we came into the road from Banbury. Barford is the next place on the route; immediately on leaving which we crossed the Avon by a handsome bridge. Warwick, situated on an eminence and crowned with the majestic tower of St. Mary's Church is a very beautiful object. The entrance through the suburbs of the Town leads through an archway to the High Street under a Tower, which is a remain of the ancient fortifications | which once surrounded the Town. At the other end of this street is another gateway under a Chapel, also of old forming a part of the wall of the Town, and an elegant building. In this street is the Inn, at which we halted, the Warwick Arms. We hastened to the Castle, situate on the verge of the Town, on the banks of the Avon, near the road to Leamington. Much has been done during the present Lord's time to improve this magnificent residence, perhaps, too much for his Lordship's comfort, who is understood to be very poor, and unable to live at home,

1. Charles Mordaunt, (1771-1823) of Walton Warwickshire. Mordaunt was M.P. for Warwickshire, 1804-1820. He was captain of the Warwickshire Militia, 1794, and captain of the Warwickshire Yeomanry Cavalry, 1801. He succeeded his father as 8th baronet in 1806.

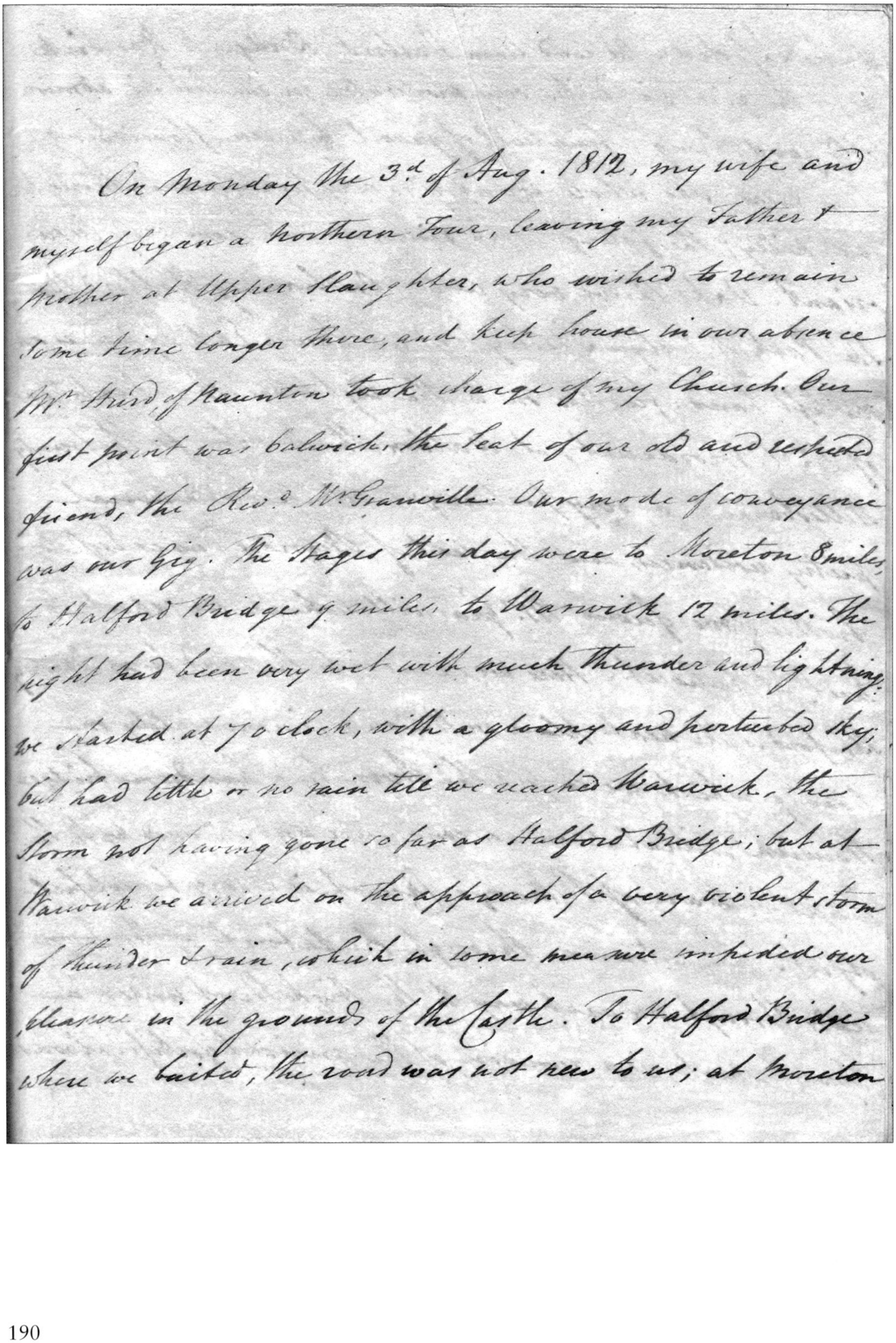
On Monday the 3d of Aug. 1812, my wife and myself began a northern Tour, leaving my Father & Mother at Upper Slaughter, who wished to remain some time longer there, and keep house in our absence. Mr. Hurd of Naunton took charge of my Church. Our first point was Calwich, the seat of our old and respected friend, the Revd. Mr. Granville. Our mode of conveyance was our Gig. The Stages this day were to Moreton 8 miles, to Halford Bridge 9 miles, to Warwick 12 miles. The night had been very wet with much thunder and lightning: we started at 7 o clock, with a gloomy and perturbed sky; but had little or no rain till we reached Warwick, the Storm not having gone so far as Halford Bridge; but at Warwick we arrived on the approach of a very violent storm of thunder & rain, which in some measure impeded our pleasure in the grounds of the Castle. To Halford Bridge where we baited, the road was not new to us; at Moreton

62. Pencil sketch at Halford Bridge by Francis Witts.

though the place is admirably kept. The recent alterations are much to be approved, and if, as I am informed, of his Lordship's taste, his Lordship is not so weak, as he is sometimes represented. The Porters lodge is an ugly, but we were told temporary mass of masonry. Here we were required to write our names and place of residence. Under the custody of the Porter are the marvellous remains of Guy Earl of Warwick, whom tradition marks above 8 feet high. His porridge pot, a fine brazen vessel of more than 100 gallons measure, in which punch is made on the heir apparent of the Earldom attaining his majority. | His flesh hook, out of all proportion to those used by the sons of old Eli, his sword, his shield, his stirrup irons, his horse's armour, his walking staff, his lance, the dun cow's rib and horns, an elephant's scull, and divers other matters of connoisseurship, which (in the style of propria quae maribus) it would be too tedious to relate. The approach to the Castle is a winding gradual ascent cut out of the solid rock; on each side are flourishing plantations crowning the wall of living masonry, down which festoons the beautiful Antirrhinum Cymbellaria, & the Privet luxuriates in bloom. Emerging from this rocky defile, a most happily projected heath extends to the Castle moat; the native grasses, diadelphious plants, and broom vie with the choicest culture in beauty and surpass all the gardener's art in appropriate effect. Beyond the moat, rise in grey majesty the Castle Towers & walls, their bases fringed with shrubs & trees, their summits with loop holes, battlements & machicolation in full perfection. To the left is a Tower; then between two lower towers, the Gateway into the | Court, then another giant tower, a face of massy rampart, and another Tower; foliage, tints, angles, windows, battlements, all harmonize and produce an effect, I never saw equalled. Within is a beautiful irregular Court; to the left are the grand apartments in their genuine state, in front, the ancient keep, crowned with the most luxuriant foliage, to the right, the Castle walls, and in them archways leading to the pleasure grounds. We were ushered into the great hall by the venerable old housekeeper M^rs. Home, a Scotchwoman, who is an excellent antique in modern dress, and who having acquired in long servitude the friendship of the noble family, will be some time their benefactress by bestowing on its representative that fortune, which she has acquired by shewing their baronial Seat. She soon resigned us to a deputy. The hall

63. View of part of Warwick.

is a noble apartment, commanding a noble view. The Avon washes the Castle walls, broad, fringed with wood, flowing between banks of dressed ground, embracing an island, issuing beneath an elegant single arch bridge, rippling round the | remaining pieces of an old bridge, rushing down a Cascade; and winding on through luxuriant meadows. The Castle Mill, forming part of the Offices, a true appendage of baronial Hospitality, now, alas! let to a baker, is not the least interesting object in the foreground. On the opposite side is the Park, and the more distant grounds and woods. In the hall are some good Portraits: most of the paintings in this Seat are Portraits. The first Room is the large Drawing Room, then the Cedar Drawing room, then the gilt room, then Queen Anne's State Bedroom, and dressing room &c. The Armoury, Dining Room, Chapel, and Breakfast room with the above are all the apartments shewn. We observed in our transient survey many very beautiful Cabinets, some very curious ancient china, some Etruscan Vases, much curious armour of various sorts, ages, and nations, some beautiful specimens of painted Glass, tapestry &c. Several paintings by Rubens, Vandyke, Titian, Holbein, Poussin, Salvator Rosa, | Rembrandt, Vanderveldt, Teniers, Gerard Douw, particularly interested us; but the rapidity, with which one surveys these apartments gives no opportunity for observing with judgement on individual pieces. The Chapel is well finished, and appropriately fitted up; the views from all the Apartments, chiefly portions of that seen from the Hall, are exquisitely beautiful. On leaving the Castle the head Gardener attended us round the dressed ground, which, altogether consists of 100 acres. Though so contiguous, the Town is quite secluded, except where the Tower of St. Mary's Church affords a beautiful object. The trees both ancient and those more lately planted are in high beauty, the turf delightfully kept, the Gravel walks wide and perfectly unis,[2] the grouping of Trees most tasteful, & the beauties of the Castle & more

2. The word 'unis' here is quite distinct. His intended sense may be guessed at, but the word is not in the Oxford English Dictionary.

64. Warwick Castle, Guy's Tower.

distant scenery well made use of. The Spacious greenhouse was built to receive a magnificent antique vase, the gift of Sir W$^{m.}$ Hamilton to the present Earl in 1774. It was | found in the ruins of Adrian's villa at Tivoli, is of white marble of vast size placed on a suitable pedestal and raised on three stone steps. I think, the Vase is circular, it is made of white marble, the handles are exquisite, the frieze round the margin beautiful, and before & behind are groups of masks in alto relievo. It is a most choice specimen of ancient sculpture. Some superb & gigantic Geraniums in full blossom occupy in Summer the remainder of this Spacious building, till the Collection of Plants is brought from the open air; these are too vast to be moved. We next pierced the intricacies of a beautiful and thick wilderness, till we emerged on the verdant bank of the Avon under the Castle walls. Nothing can exceed the beauty of some single trees, and groupes, Spanish Chesnuts, Cedars, Weeping Willow &c. The mass of foliage clothing the keep of the Castle is highly luxuriant. To look upwards to the vast buildings stretching along the | banks of the River is very fine; we did not fail to remark the luxuriance of the vegetation on the walls & rock, Lysimachia, Lavender, Ivy, in richest profusion. We next ascended by a winding gravel walk the ancient keep, which is fenced by a stupendous face of masonry, on the summit of which is the Watch Tower, the highest point of the Castle, commanding a very extensive view. The summit of the Mount, a level surface of turfs boasts in the centre a fine and very picturesque Italian pine. Warwick and its castle are of the remotest antiquity: it is the scite of the Roman Station Præsidium, and was a fortress in the Saxon ages, when the keep was a rude Castle for the protection of the possessions of the Earls. In the fabulous days of Arthur, Arthgal a Knight of his round table, & Earl of Warwick wore as his Crest a bear, significant of his name: he is fabled to have had an encounter with a Giant, who assailed him with a young tree | torn up by the roots, the boughs broken short off; hence the device of the Bear & Ragged Staff, worn by the

3. The earl was George Greville, Earl Brooke of Warwick Castle, (1746-1816).

subsequent Earls of Warwick. Guy, Earl of Warwick, in the days of Athelstane was still more renowned. When that Monarch was besieged in Winchester with his nobles & his dominions overrun by the Danes, it was agreed that the possession of the realm should be with him, who, of the two contending nations, should conquer in single combat. Colbrand was the Danish Champion, &, to make a long story short, Guy became his antagonist, conquered him, & saved his Country. After this Exploit, he retired to his native place, where devoting himself to religious solitude, he is reported to have ended his days in a Cavern of a Cliff, on the banks of the Avon, near Warwick. This beautiful spot, $^{\text{Guy's Cliff,}}$ where is now the seat of B. Greatheed Esq$^{r.}$ is on the road to Kenilworth. Some of the buildings of the Castle bear the name of the champion Guy: with the common absurdity of giving questionable antiquity | to what is so truly $^{\text{ancient;}}$ for those parts of the Castle were constructed in the 17th of Rich$^{d.}$ 2$^{d.}$ AD 1394 by Tho$^{s.}$ Beauchamp Earl of Warwick. The view of these towers & the whole groupe from the bridge over the Avon is remarkably striking.

After taking a hasty dinner we sallied forth to view the beautiful church of S$^{t.}$ Mary's, but the Even. was almost too far advanced to admit of a fair inspection of its architecture. An inscription round the Tower intimates, that this Church, which is collegiate, was originally built by Roger de Newburg in the R. of Stephen, afterwards entirely rebuilt by Thomas Beauchamp, Earl of Warwick, mentioned above, in the year 1393, destroyed by a dreadful conflagration 1694: erected in its present majestic and elegant style under the auspices of Queen Anne in the memorable year 1704. The tower, which is at the west end of the Church is erected on groin arches, supported by four piers. The extreme height | of the tower is 174 feet. The length of the Church, including the Choir is 186 feet. The breadth 66 feet. The cross aisle 106 feet. The height of the ^{roof} 42½ feet. The entrances to the Church are to the West, & in the same part is a handsome organ. The Church is well pewed, with Galleries & Stoves. The monuments are very interesting: one of Marble presents the Effigies in brass of Thomas Beauchamp, Earl of Warwick & his wife. This great peer was Governor of Guernsey, Alderney

65. Guy's Cliff.

66. Chapel at Guy's Cliff.

&c. in the R. of Edw. 3. Governor of Richard the 2^d. during his Minority, but afterwards falling into disgrace, was condemned for high Treason, and banished to the Isle of Man, but recalled by Hen. 4th. He died AD. 1401. He rebuilt this Church, which had been begun by his father, Thomas, Earl of Warwick, who with the Lady Katharine Mortimer his wife was interred in the Choir of this Church, where is a massy tomb of Composition with a marble Cornice to their memory, but now without Inscription. He died 43^d. Edw. 3. 1370. On the two sides & on the Ends of | the Tomb are 36 images of weepers, as they are styled, standing upon as many coats of arms. Dugdale, in his Warwickshire, as he is in all points, very interesting so in his account of contracts made for furnishing monuments in this Church. The Choir is built in an excellent taste, the ceiling, windows, niches &c. are all fine. The vestry Room contains an ancient collection of Books, founded by the celebrated antiquarian Historian Rous, commonly termed Rossus Varvicensis, of whom Dugdale speaks with so much pleasure. Beneath the Vestry is the Mausoleum of the Warwick family. In the former chapter House an elegant octagon Room is the remarkable monument of Fulk Lord Brook, erected during his life for himself and family. It is of black and white marble, but most notable for its striking inscription, so often noticed: "Fulke Grevil, Servant to Queen Elizabeth, Councellor to King James, and friend to Sir Philip Sydney." The Lady's Chapel is a building of extraor- | -dinary beauty, founded by Richard Beauchamp E. of Warwick, Son of the Earl Thomas, mentioned above, as having rebuilt the Church & Choir. This part of the structure was commenced 21. Hen. VI. AD. 1443 and finished 3. Ed. IV. 1464. Dugdale informs us, that it cost £2481. 4. 7. when wheat was at 3/4 per Quarter: taking wheat at 5/ per bushel, or twelve times the sum, the expense of this building was equal to £29.774: 15:— The Shrines, in which were formerly golden images, and the other Cabinet Sculpture are truly beautiful. In the windows is painted glass. Behind the Altar was the Library of John Rous now moved to the Vestry. Adjoining the Chapel is the very curious ancient confessional communicating by

67. Kenilworth Castle.

an oblique aperture in the wall, as well as by a Lattice window with the Choir. The middle of the Chapel is occupied by the marble tomb of the Founder Richard Beauchamp, on which is his effigy, in armour, made of fine latten brass, doubly guilt. At his head a swan, at his feet, a bear & griffin. A hearse, or frame, of brass, gilt, over the monument, | served to support a pall. Around the tomb are fourteen images of brass, gilt, called weepers, under the feet of each is a coat of arms. They represent different branches of the family. Eighteen lesser images representing Angels also surround the Tomb. An inscription in uncouth English gives the following account of this great nobleman. Richard Beauchamp, Earl of Warwick, Lord Despenser of Bergevenny &c. died at Rouen 1439. He was at that time Lieutenant General of the Realms of France and Duchy of Normandy by appointment of Hen. VI. The Executors of his will, by which he founded this Chapel, fulfilled his bequest, and translated his remains from France. A noble marble monument in the Chapel is adorned with ~~marble~~ Statues of Robt. Dudley, E. of Leicester & Lettice his wife, daughter of Francis Knolles, Knight of the Garter and Treasurer to Queen Elizabeth. This distinguished favourite was a fifth Son of John, Duke of Northumberland, Earl of Warwick, Visc^t. Lisle. He was E. of Leicester, B. Denbigh Knight of the Garter and of S^t. Michael, Master of the | Horse to Queen Elizabeth, then Steward of the Household, Privy Counsellor, Justice in Eyre on this side Trent, commander of the English army sent by Queen Elizabeth into the Netherlands: Lieutenant Governor of England against Philip the 2^d. of Spain in 1588, in which year he died. Some lines commemorative of the virtues of his Lady, are hung near the tomb, which were written by Gervas Clifton. I shall have occasion to revert to this distinguished favourite in writing of the ruins of Kenilworth Castle. The monument of Ambrose Dudley, Earl of Warwick, Brother of the E. of Leicester, presents his effigy in full armour. He was eventually heir of his Father the D. of Northumberland, Master of the Ordnance to Queen Elizabeth, Lieutenant General in Normandy, Knight of the Garter, & jointly with Edwd. Lord Clinton, Lord Admiral of England, Lieutenant General in the North. He died 1589. On the North side of the Tomb under their peculiar coats of arms, are inscriptions naming the degree of consanguinity and

68. Kenilworth Castle from the gate house.

intermarriages &c. of various connections of this noble family—the same on the South side. Another sprig of | the same tree, or as quaintly described on the tomb "the noble Impe" was here interred; Robert, Baron Denbigh, son of Robert Earl of Leicester, who died at a tender age in 1584.—Still more: there is a tablet inscribed to the memory of Catharine, widow of Sir Richard Levenson of Trentham, created Duchess Dudley by Ch. 1. This Lady was Daughter of Sir Robert Dudley, who was Son of the Earl of Leicester by Alicia Daughter of Sir Thomas Leigh of Stoneleigh, & widow of Lord Sheffield. This marriage was private, for fear of the displeasure of the jealous Queen, & was shamefully evaded by the Earl who falling in love with Lady Essex married her in Lady Sheffield's life-time. By Lady Sheffield he had Sir Rob$^{t.}$ Dudley, to whom he left his property after the decease of his brother Ambrose, Earl of Warwick. Sir Rob. endeavoured to substantiate his legitimacy, but by the intrigues of Lady Essex, a decree was issued from the Star Chamber, putting a stop to all proceedings in the matter. Naturally disgusted with these transactions, | Sir Robert withdrew to the Continent, where his learning and great qualities so recommended him to the favour of Ferdinand the 2$^{d.}$ Emperor of Germany, that the prince created him a Duke, in consequence of which Ch. 1. conferred the like dignity on his daughter. I shall have occasion to revert to this branch of the family under Kenilworth. A hospital founded by Rob$^{t.}$ E. of Leicester 1586 affords a commodious retreat to a master and twelve decayed brethren, who are commodiously lodged, & receive each an ample income; the appointment is with the Earl of Warwick. The brethren are required by Statute to wear blue cloaks, the bear and ragged Staff being emblazoned on the Sleeve, whenever they go out into the Town. We regretted, that the approach of night prevented our Examining with greater minuteness the exterior of this beautiful Church. There is another a modern Structure, dedicated to S: Nicholas, near the Castle. We walked thro' the principal streets of the Town, its high situation gives every advantage of cleanliness. | The streets have lately been paved, which adds much to the commodiousness of the town. The

Prison is a very large & fine building, and the Court House &c. is in the Exterior an ornamental Structure. The Priory, a seat of the ancient family of the Wise's is situated close to the town. The Borough is represented in Parliament by Lord Brook & M^r. Mills. Lemington Spa in this neighbourhood is rapidly rising in estimation; its water resembles that of Cheltenham. The Inn at Warwick in which we were, is spacious, but not very clean.

The following day we pursued our route. The earlier part of the morning was foggy, great heat ensued, and in the afternoon we had light showers, a very heavy thunderstorm falling at Lichfield just before we reached that place. We started for Kenilworth, a stage of five miles at a very early hour; the thickness of the atmosphere prevented our discerning all the beauties of this very rich and fertile drive. We passed much fine corn & | timber. A mile beyond Warwick is Guy's Cliff. To the road there is nothing particularly attractive in this place; doubtless, its interior is well worthy of attention, and to the antiquary, as the scene of the romantic tales of Guy, & as the residence of Rous it is highly interesting. Dugdale must be consulted on these points. We breakfasted at Kenilworth at a very comfortable Inn. The town is long and straggling with some good houses, commanding views of the Castle. The Church has an ordinary appearance. Near it are the very inconsiderable remains of a monastery founded by Geoffrey de Clinton in the 12th. Century, which after the Dissolution was annexed to the domains of the Castle.

The ruins of the Castle are at some distance from the Town, situated on an eminence projecting over some fine meadows, which in the days of baronial splendour were covered with water, forming a spacious and beautiful lake. The grey relics are admirably clothed with ivy, and a fine turf extends | between the different groupes of ruins. The original gateway was built by Robert Dudley Earl of Leicester, who greatly enlarged the Castle; the archway being now filled up forms with the remainder of the building a large farm house: it was a very handsome structure with four square corner towers. To the right on entering is a massive tower, of rude architecture & vast size, vulgarly called Cæsar's Tower; this is the most antient part of the Castle and was its citadel: three sides are entire, the fourth was dilapidated by order of Oliver Cromwell. It seems to have consisted of one vast room on a floor with a variety of closets formed in the ponderous walls. Beyond the Keep, we ascend over the fragments of extensive apartments to some turret staircases in good preservation, and to a range of arches above each other, by which it appears, that this part of the Castle was three Stories high, and must, when all around was wood & lake, have commanded a very pleasing view. Adjoining these remains we distinctly trace the great hall, 86 feet long, and 45 wide, with a lower | apartment of the same dimensions, in which the inferior guests were entertained, while the hospitality of the great Barons was displayed above. This hall must have been a very noble apartment, some remains of a frieze, the windows, oriel windows, and a recess for a sideboard, may all be accurately traced. A range of very much dilapidated building succeeds, where probably were the presence chamber & other apartments of state; of these little more remains than ivy clad fragments of arches and walls. The very extensive square building adjoining these was the addition of Robert Earl of Leicester, and is rapidly falling to decay. It consisted of many apartments for the accommodation of a large family. Other buildings, now quite removed, seem to have connected this part of the castle with the great Tower and to have formed an irregular inner Court. The antient Stables are still used for their original purpose by the farmer, who |

occupies the Castle. From some points the spire of the church forms a very pleasing object. Without the castle wall is a mound, formerly terminated at each end by a tower, the ruins of which are still considerable. This mound, while it served as a head to the great lake, which, washing the walls, must have added so essentially to the grandeur of the noble residence, served as a tiltyard, on which jousts and tournaments were displayed. It had been, previously to the erection of the other gateway, the approach to the Castle, and in times of feudal warfare must have been of difficult access to an invading enemy: but in the days of the splendid Leicester formed a most commodious stage for the display of that pageantry and flattering pomp, with which his ambition prompted him to welcome his Royal Mistress. From the tiltyard we had a beautiful near view of these most interesting remains: and returned to our Inn by a pleasant footpath through wooded | fields. The same Geoffrey de Clinton, who founded the monastery in Kenilworth, and who was Chamberlain and Treasurer to King Henry the $1^{st.}$ built the Castle about 1120. In the $11^{th.}$ of Hen. 2. the Castle and its domains were vested in the Crown; & in the $19^{th.}$ year of the same reign. AD. 1173. it was garrisoned by the King on his Son's rebellion. In the beginning of King John's reign, Henry de Clinton, grandson to the founder released to the King all his rights to the Castle, and it remained in the possession of the Crown, till granted by Hen $3^{d.}$ to the E. of Leicester. Hen. 3. in 1242 greatly repaired and beautified the Castle, but two years after granted if for his own and his wife's life to Simon de Montford, E. of Leicester, to whom he had given his own Sister in marriage. Leicester headed an association of Barons against his Sovereign, disgusted by the weakness of the King towards unworthy favorites. The associated Peers formed themselves into an oppressive and tyrannous | oligarchy: when Prince Edward, Henry's eldest Son, taking advantage of the discontent subsisting against them, raised an army to deprive the Barons of their newly acquired power. Being joined by the King, they met the Barons' army near Lewes, when the latter were victorious, and made the King, his brother & the Prince of Wales, prisoners. The latter, however, soon escaped, & encountering again the Barons' army near Evesham, under the command of Montford, totally routed them and he fell in the engagement. ~~He fled with~~ The remains of his troops fled to Kenilworth, and took refuge in the Castle. Prince Edward, having thus released his Father, proceeded with his victorious army, to besiege the castle. Henry de Hastings defended it for six months, during which time young Montford was privately dispatched ~~by his uncle~~ to solicit succour in France, which he could not procure, so that, at the expiration of that time, the garrison, worn out by famine & pestilence, were obliged to surrender. During the siege the | King gave here his niece in marriage to the D. of Brunswick, and the Queen and her ladies from Windsor honoured the camp with her company on that occasion. In this Camp was made the celebrated Dictum de Kenilworth, a decree signed by twelve persons, Bishops & Peers, chosen by the King. The object of it was to mitigate the severity of the Parliament holden at Winchester, by which the Estates of the rebels & their adherents were confiscated: but this decree sentenced them only to a pecuniary fine of not more than five years income of their estates, nor less than two. In 1267 the King granted the Castle with its domains to his youngest Son Edmund, whom two years afterwards he created E. of Lancaster. In 1279 a great festivity was held in this Castle, where an hundred knights and as many ladies sat round a round table, and a week was spent in martial tournaments and gallant sports. Roger Mortimer, E: of March was the chief | promoter of this entertainment. The Castle continued in the house of Lancaster till the reign of Edward the 2$^{d.}$ The weak & unlimited prodigality of this monarch excited universal discontent, and his subjects flew to arms under the guidance of the E. of Lancaster. Their resentment was chiefly directed against Piers Gaveston, the King's favourite. His retirement to Flanders suspended their indignation, which burst forth on his return, when, besieging him at Scarborough, they took him prisoner to Warwick and beheaded him near that Town. Spencer supplied Gaveston's place in the weak monarch's affection, and similar effects followed. The King was obliged to banish his minion, but soon afterwards, finding himself strong enough, turned his arms against the unprepared Barons. The E. of Lancaster retreated towards the North, where he was taken prisoner in a skirmish, & executed at Pontefract. The Spencers were now recalled and received in redoubled favour, so that the Queen & whole nation were exasperated against them. The Queen making a | pretence to take the young Prince her son to France to do homage for the duchy of Guienne, retired with many discontented Barons to that Country, from which she returned with an army, and was soon very numerously joined. The unfortunate Edward attempted to escape by Bristol for Ireland, but, being cast on the coasts of Wales, was taken prisoner, & confined in Kenilworth Castle. His end was truly distressing: he was deposed, & his Son Edw. 3$^{d.}$ declared King. From Kenilworth he was removed to Berkley Castle, & thence to Corfe Castle, & back again, after having visited other places of durance, to Berkley Castle, where he was cruelly murdered at the instigation of the Queen & her favourite, Mortimer. In 1327. Edw. 3$^{d.}$ restored Henry, brother to the late E. of Lancaster, to that dignity, the Earldom of Leicester, this Castle, and all his brother's Estates. His Son was afterwards in the same reign created D. of Lancaster; but dying without male issue, John of Gaunt, 4$^{th.}$ Son to Edw. 3. married one of his daughters, | and obtained this Castle as part of her dowry, his Father granting him the Dukedom of Lancaster. This prince considerably added to and beautified the castle. He died in 1399, & his Son Henry, sirnamed Bolingbroke, succeeding to the throne under the title of Hen. 4$^{th.}$, the castle again came into the hands of the sovereign, where it continued for several successive reigns. Hen. 7. united it to the Duchy of Cornwall, & Hen. VIII. considerably repaired and ornamented it. After his death it regularly descended to Edw. VI. Mary & Elizabeth, the latter of whom granted it to Robert E. of Leicester, already named, & whose monument we had visited at Warwick. He is said to have expended sixty thousand Pounds in improvements of the Castle. It was in July, 1575, that he received his Sovereign with all the magnificence and pageantry of the age at this Castle, of which visit some curious & entertaining relations remain. In enumerating the monuments in the Church at Warwick I discussed at some length | the family succession of this powerful peer. Suffice it here to say, that Prince Henry, eldest Son to Jas. 1. having bargained with Sir Rob$^{t.}$ Dudley, then resident abroad, for the purchase of this Castle, which purchase money was, however, never paid, & Prince Henry dying soon after, Prince Charles, his brother, took possession of it as his heir, & kept it till he came to the crown. He then granted it to Rob Carey. E. of Monmouth & his family. In their possession it remained during the reign of Charles, but during the usurpation Oliver Cromwell parcelled the manor among his ~~soldiers~~ officers, who greatly dilapidated it, but held it till the restoration. Ch. 2. renewed the lease, granted by his father to the Earl of Monmouth's daughters; but it being again almost expired, he granted the reversion to Lawrence Lord Hyde, second Son of Lord Chancellor Clarendon, whom he created Baron of Kenilworth Castle & E. of Rochester. Descending to the ramifications of that family, it now belongs to E. Clarendon. |

Our next stage was to Coleshill, 13 miles. Through Kenilworth, and on leaving it, are some beautiful views of the Castle. We left the road to Coventry on the right, distant little more than five miles, and advanced through shady lanes, and a well wooded Country, but the soil did not appear of the best quality, and the road was rather sandy in parts; sometimes stony and watery near the rivers, which intersect this district. After passing along Wooton Green, a common of considerable extent, we crossed the River Tame at Moulding Bridge, and a little farther passed by Stone Bridge over the same river, near which embosomed in fine woods is Packington Hall, the seat of the Earl of Aylesford.[4] Before we reached Coleshill, we observed to the left of the road, a very comfortable little residence, and not far from the town is a large pool or lake, one side of which is well ornamented with planting. The steeple of Coleshill Church, which is very lofty & beautiful, (once still more striking, as it has been | reduced in height,) is a very ~~striking~~ fine object. The Church stands on elevated ground, and the town, though not on the side, by which we approached it, is situated on a very considerable ascent. From the Churchyard is a very extensive view of a well wooded and fertile County; I understand since, that there are some curious monuments of the Digby Family in the Church. The Earls of that name have a park in a low situation adjoining the Town, but I was told, the house had been lately pulled down. We found an excellent Inn at Coleshill, where we partook of a cold dinner. Near this town is an old & regular castle, the Seat of Mrs. Dilke, Maxstoke Castle. In the Parsonage House at Colesill, which is a very good house, Mr. Palmer resides.—

From Coleshill to Lichfield is a stage of 15 miles. We descended the steep hill on which the Town is built, and after rising another eminence, through no very interesting Country, we again crossed the Tame at Curdworth Bridge. This river after passing by Bir- | -mingham, flows into the Trent. Near Curdworth Bridge on the right is Ham's Hall, C. B. Addersley Esqr. The village of Wishaw is about two miles farther; the Country still uninteresting: in its vicinity is a seat of Mr. Moxhull, & beyond, still more to the right, Middleton Hall, the seat of Lord Middleton.[5] At Bassett's Pole we were on a very considerable elevation, and descended for some distance near & through some fine woods, the property of Sir R. Lawley, and not far from his seat, Canwell Hall. The view in the direction of Lichfield is here improved. We passed without knowing it, at the time, a little way on our left, about this part of the road, an encampment, of, I think, three Regiments of Militia, and four troops of Cavalry, on Sutton Coldfield Heath; they are stationed there to secure the peace of the neighbourhood, which is so thickly peopled with manufacturers. Beyond Bassett's Pole is Weeford, &, nearer Lichfield, Swinfin, where is a dull seat of the Gentleman of that name, a bold Courser, & noted for his breed of Greyhounds. We were now within two miles of Lichfield, & the Spires of the | Cathedral appeared to great advantage. After a long drive we were glad to reach the Inn, in time to survey the Cathedral, which, to my wife, was a new object.

The Cathedral and close, in which it stands, surrounded by prebendal and collegiate houses, ~~stands~~ is situate on the declivity of an eminence, separated from the City of Lichfield, properly so called, by a fine pool, formed by the surplus of springs, which are conveyed from

4. Heneage Finch, 4th Earl of Aylesford, (1751-1812). The earl died two months after the Witts' passed by his estate.
5. Henry Willoughby, 6th Baron Middleton, (1761-1835).

some distance to supply the Town & Close with water. We approach it by a Street, formed on one side by a range of elegant modern buildings, containing ample accommodations for a certain number of widows and orphans of Clergymen. Each widow has a separate tenement, an allowance of, I believe, £40 per Ann. & is inadmissible if her income from other sources exceed £30 per ann. This admirable institution emanates from the charity of the late And. Newton Esq$^{r.}$ a native of Lichfield, and long a resident in India, but who passed the latter end of his life in this city. He bequeathed considerable sums to to the English free school here, and to various public | charities. But this proof of his munificence, which is yet hardly finished, (he died only in 1806,) will not be completed at a less expence, including the endowment, than £40,000. All monuments, whether with propriety or not, I will not say, having been levelled, the centre of the Close consists of a verdant and beautiful turf, close to the walls of the Cathedral. A walk runs round the whole, partly well sheltered by trees, but some were removed ~~a long time~~ a few years back, to the great indignation, and in spite of the Poetic remonstrances, of the well known Miss Seward, who passed a long life in this Close chiefly, principally residing in the Bishop's Palace, which, like the Deanery, is a dull building to the North of the Cathedral, rarely, if ever, occupied by the Bishop, who resides at his Episcopal Seat, Eccleshall, not far from Stafford. The diversity of the other houses surrounding the Close adds to its agreeable appearance: from the Eastern side the view extends towards S$^{t.}$ Chad's Church, and a kind of suburb, divided from the city of Lichfield by a fine luxuriant meadow. |

The Cathedral, being built of a stone of a red, unpleasant colour, and friable texture, has suffered much from the ravages of time and the devastation of fanaticism. The old Spire, at the intersection of the Cross aisles with the Nave and Choir was destroyed in the civil wars, and the present, though not strictly harmonizing with the architecture of the remainder of the Structure, was erected by Bish. Hacket, the first Bishop after the Restoration, according to a model by Sir Chr. Wren, and is a noble specimen of the skill of that distinguished architect. Two smaller Sister Spires, of original architecture, coeval with the rest of the building, surmount the extremities of the Western façade, & with the other Spire serve to render the Cathedral so conspicuous and beautiful an object for several miles round. The Western façade is peculiarly rich, more resembling the style of French Cathedral Architecture, than most in England. It was | formerly decorated with a great number of statues ranged in niches, which peculiarly

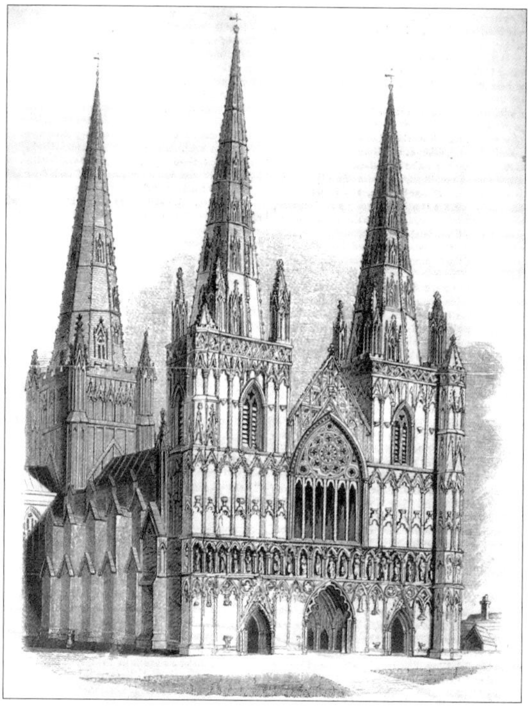

70. Lichfield Cathedral.

attracted the Vandalism of the Oliverians, and consequently very few remain uninjured, and many of those, which were not then cast down by fanatic prejudices, have since been removed. The spires in this part of the Cathedral, which appear to have been erected in the 13th. Century rise gracefully from the supporting Towers. What remains of the Statuary contrasts advantageously with a clumsy Statue of Ch. 2., which occupies a niche in the façade. The three western portals, and especially the centre one, are most beautifully enriched with sculptured ornaments, not uninjured, but worked in a more durable stone, than the generality of the building. The Northern Portal is deeply recessed after the Norman manner, though not with a circular arch: it is also much decorated with nearly obliterated Sculpture. The southern Portal is of the same character, but was | considerably altered towards the close of the 17th. Century. The window over the grand portal is very fine. Of the rest of the Exterior of this Cathedral it suffices to say, that it is in the style of the 13th. Century. The nave & its aisles afford a beautiful specimen of the interior architecture of this age, during the reign of Henry 3d. from 1216 to 1272. The rich clusted [FN] columns with foliated Capitals, the windowed galleries & fretted roof have a light, elegant and solemn effect. The celebrated Mr. Wyatt in his alterations of this Cathedral has here judged most judiciously in removing all the tablets, which disfigured the columns, and monumental Inscriptions are now placed in the niches of the aisles of the Nave. Among those, which occupy this part of the building is a monument to the memory of Lady Mary Wortley Montague, in the inscription on which is commemorated her introduction of the practice of Inoculation for the small pox into this Country. The design is a female figure leaning on | one arm, over a vase, on which is inscribed M.W.M. Opposite to this is the monument of Dean Addison, Father of the celebrated author, Dean of this Cathedral & Archdeacon of Coventry. The conclusion of the inscription is as follows: "Ab eo eximias naturiæ dotes, morum innocentiam, benevolentiam erga homines, in Deum pietatem, luculentiem, si quod alium, patrimonium, accepit filius natu maximus Josephus, sæculi sui decus: qui in optimi parentis consortium, dum hoc ipsi marmor adornaret, præpropeia" morte adscitus est AD. 1719." The internal length of the Nave is ~~18~~ 180 feet, the breadth of the nave and aisles 66. The height of the vaulted roof 60. The exterior length of the whole Edifice 400: the height of the Central spire 258, that of the western Spires 183 feet. The transept aisles are in similar taste with the nave. In the Dean's consistory court, adjoining the South Transept is the bust of the celebrated Samuel Johnson, with this Inscription: "The friends of Samuel Johnson, | LLD. a native of Lichfield, erected this monument as a tribute of respect to the memory of a man of extensive learning, a distinguished moral writer and a sincere Christian. He died the 13th. of Dec. 1784, aged 75 years." Another monument of this illustrious man is in St. Paul's Cathedral. Near this memorial to Johnson, and after a design of the same artists, James Wyatt, architect, & Rich. Westmacott, sculptor, is a similar bust of the celebrated David Garrick, with the following inscription. "Eva Maria, relict of David Garrick Esqr. caused this monument to be erected to the memory of her beloved husband, who died the 20th. January, 1779 aged 63 years. He had not only the amiable qualities of private life, but such astonishing dramatic talents, as too well verified the observation of his friend "His death eclipsed the gaiety of nations, and impoverished the public stock of harmless pleasure "Johnson". Not far from these | monuments is an exquisite piece of sculpture erected by Westmacott to the memory of Mr. Newton, whose munificence has been adverted to above. The design refers to his noble institutions, the female figures representing a widow and orphan of poor Clergymen, and the boys children of a Charity School. A Medallion gives his portrait, beneath which is an Inscription. On the opposite side of the aisle from these monuments is a tablet inscribed by Miss Seward to the memory of Savile, Vicar Choral of this Cathedral, a man who possessing fine taste in sacred music, and a fine voice was long eminent in this choir, and a secondary performer at different music meetings. Miss Seward had a romantic and womanish friendship and admiration for this person, which she proved by a copy of verses inscribed on this tablet, not less than by her frequent mention of him in those letters, which she left for posthumous publication. I believe, the monument to the Seward family, with the Inscription by Walter Scott, is not yet erected. The ~~of~~ internal length | of the Transept is 149 feet; the breadth 28 feet. Thus far all is well, but though the remainder is perfectly elegant & neat, I doubt whether the alterations designed by Mr. Wyatt are quite correct in taste. The Nave is separated from the Choir by a Screen and organ, and, to keep the whole interior perfectly warm, by a vast glass window, which seems to me an anomaly in such a place. The screen is a valuable discovery of Wyatt's; when he was preparing to throw together the Choir and Lady's Chapel, which has here, as at Salisbury, been much objected to by connoisseurs he discovered, behind a cumbrous and incongruous wooden altar piece, an original Gothic skreen, the same which had originally decorated the building, when completed by Bish. Langton, who at the beginning of the 14th. Century lengthened the edifice, over which he presided by ~~by~~ the addition of the Lady's Chapel, and who otherwise improved the structure by placing the vaulted roof over the Transept. This skreen then contained the Shrine of St. Chad. In the civil wars it was so mutilated as to discourage any attempt to restore it by Bishop Hackett, | whose zeal in the restoration of his Cathedral from the ravages of the civil war, was before alluded to, but was capable of being completely repaired by Wyatt, who selecting a part of it for this Skreen used the remainder for the altar piece, in both which dispositions he evinced great taste and skill. The length of the Antechoir or Skreen is 15 feet, that of the Choir 180; the breadth of the Choir with its recesses 37, the breadth of the Chancel 26. The ~~pre~~ stalls of the Dean, the Precentor, and two other Canons are in the Skreen, the remainder were erected during Bish. Hackett's alterations, and are well carved, and handsome. From the time of this prelate to 1788, very few alterations or repairs had been made in the structure, but at that period its dilapidation was so great, that it was put under a complete revision by Mr. Wyatt, and the plans of that distinguished Artist have been executed at a very great expense. An act of Parliament was necessary for the purpose; by mutual consent of the Parties concerned the number of Canons Residentiary, who ~~were~~ are appointed by the | Bishop, was reduced from six to four, and the emoluments of the two first, which fell vacant, were appropriated to the very heavy charge contracted by the Chapter for the repairs and alterations. I understand, the debt incurred has now been paid off, and a very sufficient fund is created for the occasional expences necessary to keep this beautiful structure in perfect order. The four residentiary Canons now are, I believe, Dr. Vyse, Dr. Buckeridge, Mr. Nares, & Dr. Outram. There are also seventeen Prebends, also in the gift of the Bishop. The superiors of this conventical body enjoy a very good income from their station; the prebends are of little value. Dr. Woodhouse, the Dean, has, I am told, a fine piece of preferment. The Bishop, of whom more hereafter, is Dr. Cornwallis, Brother to the late Marquis, and resides chiefly at Eccleshall Castle, a Seat belonging to the See, not far from

Stone: he is also Dean of Durham. His throne in the Choir is of Bishop Hacket's Erection. Between it and the Altar the space is occupied by a number of very elegant and commodious Seats, which are let, first to the Inhabitants of the Close, & then to | residents in the City, and the rents are applied to the fund for keeping the Cathedral in repair. These pews are highly finished, and convenient, but do not appear to me suitable to the Choir of a Cathedral. Under the floor of the Choir is a contrivance to introduce warm air into the building thro' apertures corresponding with flues underneath, according to a patent invention of Moser, which well answers the purpose designed. The altar restored by Wyatt is in very good taste, the ceiling of the Choir is singularly elegant, though not finished in the richest style of Gothic Tracery, which, indeed, prevailed at a later period than the erection of this structure. There are nine windows in that part of the Choir, which was the Lady's Chapel; and seven of them are filled with ancient painted Glass, which formerly decorated the dissolved abbey of Herckenrode in the Bishopric of Liege, from whence they were purchased by the assistance of Sir Brooke Boothby. This Abbey, one of the most magnificent & richest in the Low Countries, was founded in 1182—for twenty five Cistertian Nuns, who rebuilding their | Chapel in the sixteenth Century, had adorned it with some of the choicest specimens of the glass-staining art, precisely at the period, when that art was brought to the highest perfection. These admirable remains were brought into this Country during the short peace of Amiens, in very good preservation, and with the original purchase money £200, the Carriage, repairs, placing them in the windows, and every incidental expence, they were ~~placed~~ set up at length at a cost of about £1000. The designs of five of these windows are scriptural subjects, the other two are filled with portraits of eminent persons in the age, in which they were painted. They display great brilliancy of colouring, and in point of design are rather executed from the Italian than from the Dutch, Flemish or German Schools of Painting. The dates upon this glass are all between the years 1530 & 1540.—The two remaining windows have been filled with modern painted glass: one contains the arms of the Bishops of the Diocese from the æra of the reformation to the present time, with those of the see of Canterbury, the see of Lichfield, Langton the founder of this building, and Bp. Hackett, its restorer. Bp. Langton was Keeper of the Wardrobe, Treasurer & | afterwards Chancellor to King Edward 1st. Besides adding the Lady's Chapel &c. to the Cathedral, he greatly improved the Close & City. It was this prelate, who incurred the resentment of Edwd. 2d., when Prince of Wales, by reproving his extravagance, a freedom, which at the instance of his favourite, Piers Gaveston, that Prince revenged by severe persecutions on his succeeding to the throne. Yet Langton would not retaliate, when the King & his Minister were reduced to the greatest distress by the association of the Nobles and the Clergy against them. Nor was this magnanimous loyalty ungratefully received by Edwd. when he regained his power. Langton held this See from 1296 to 1321, and his monument is one of the few of ancient date remaining in the Cathedral. Hackett was Bishop from 1661 to 1670. His elaborate monument & its long inscription are placed under the arch of a window beautifully sculptured. Among the Bishops, whose arms are collected in this window, are three prelates, who were engaged in the translation of the Bible by Royal authority: Bishop Bentham by Q. Elizabeth; Abbot, afterwards Archb. of Canterbury, and Overall, who died Bishop of Norwich by King Jas. 1st.—Other eminent | persons, whose having held this See is thus commemorated are Hough, who died Bish. of Worcester in 1743, and Hurd who likewise filled that station at a late

Period. The remaining window contains the arms & names of the persons composing the Chapter of this Cathedral, whether Canons or Prebendaries, from 1806 to 1808 inclusive. Two other pieces of painted Glass, part of the remains from Herckenrode Abbey are to fill the windows at the Eastern end of the Aisles, but they are now under the hands of the proper artists. The great North Transept window is intended to be filled with modern painted glass, now under the hands of the artists, and to present the figures of the principal founders and Patrons of this Cathedral, chiefly copied from original representations. The first in the series will be Oswy, King of Northumberland, who, in 656, conquered the kingdom of Mercia, and founded in it the Cathedral Church of Lichfield. This spot is said to have been chosen by the King, as that where a large number of Christian Martyrs had suffered death under the Diocletian persecution. From this circumstance the City acquired its name, | as the field of corpses, (in modern German Leichname) and the armorial bearings of the City represent this legendary scene of slaughter. Cedda or Chad, the first Stationary Bishop of this See, will occupy a niche contiguous to Oswy. This distinguished Prelate adorned the seventh Century, was canonized, & considered the Patron of this and many other Churches.—The third worthy in this list will be Offa, King of Mercia, who obtained from the Pope the erection of Lichfield into an Archiepiscopal See in 786. This preeminence lasted only during the life of one Prelate. Stephen, Richard 1, and John, Kings of England, will be among the Benefactors collected in this window.—Three Bishops also, Roger de Clinton, Bishop from 1129 to 1152, (by whom the more antient parts of this Cathedral were begun, a munificent Prelate, who assuming the Cross, joined the Crusaders, and died at Antioch,) Bishops Langton & Hackett, whose merits have been noticed above, will fill the remaining niches in this window. The Bishop's Consistory Court adjoins the Southern aisle of the Choir. This with some of the adjacent columns, which could be only par- | -tially modelled to the pointed, ~~style~~ are evidently of the Norman style, and the oldest part of the structure, that part erected by Roger de Clinton in the 12th. Century. In this part of the building is the remainder of the Tomb of Dean Heywood, who deceased in 1492. It was not an unusual fashion then to pourtray two effigies on monuments, one representing the defunct in health and in robes of state, the other on a lower range representing him emaciated and lifeless. This latter figure alone subsists. On the North of the Inner Choir is the ancient Chapter House with the avenue to it from the Northern Aisle of the Choir. A number of niches on the face of the wall front the door of the Chapter House. I was informed, that these were ^ anciently appropriated to such members of the Chapter, as might be under any disgrace for misconduct, to whom it was enjoined as a penance to be stationed in these niches, when the Chapter went in solemn process into their house, & then to be admonished. This statement had been given to the Verger, shortly before we visited the Cathedral, by a Roman Catholic Priest | conversant with the ancient ceremonies of his Church, and well acquainted with the architecture of foreign Cathedrals. The Portal of the Chapter House is very elegant workmanship of the beginning of the 13th. Century. The building itself is octangular, 45 feet by 28, and the vaulted & richly embossed roof is supported by a clustered column, whose capital is beautifully and elaborately worked, and well deserves the attention of the antiquarian, being a plain Norman shaft, around which separate columns are filletted, and unite their Capitals, but are not united in themselves. Forty nine stalls surround this room. The canopies above them are in the very earliest stage of pointed architecture, the cornices or exterior arches being supported by finely sculptured heads. Arches of the same style occur in the Western Front & in the aisles. The Chapter House has suffered much from puritanical violence. Above the Chapter House is the Library, which we did not see; it contains a very ancient copy of the Gospels in Latin called Textus Sti Cedde. This Library was completely | ransacked in the civil war, but has been restored by subsequent donations. Lichfield was a great sufferer during that turbulent period, perhaps, as much by the lawless Royalists, as by their Puritanical adversaries. Early in the contest, the Close, being surrounded by a wall & fosse, was garrisoned for the King; and in March 1643 was compelled to surrender to the enemy. In the following months it was recovered by Prince Rupert, and continued in the possession of the Royalists till after the fatal battle at Naseby. The King in his retreat from that decisive conflict passed through Lichfield, and was lodged in the Close, as he was twice afterwards in the same year. In 1646 this garrison finally surrendered to the conquerors, when the Royal cause became quite hopeless. Both the Cathedral & City of Lichfield have been well described, & their History given with precision by the Revd. Thos. Harwood, in his History and antiquities of Lichfield.

Having minutely examined the Cathedral we directed our steps towards the market place about the centre of the City, to view the house once occupied ‸ by, (I believe the birth place of,) the great Doctor Johnson. It is a large | old building, at the corner of a street, now inhabited by a brazier. It was nearly dark, but, I imagine, in the best light Lichfield can only be reckoned a very secondary town.—It is a station for French Prisoners on Parole. We were disappointed of meeting here my Cousin John Witts, Capt. in the Marines, who commands a recruiting party at Lichfield, but ‸ he was with his friends at Lydleys Hays,[6] when we passed through. We retired early in order to rise with the dawn, & prosecute our Journey to Calwich. We did not find the Swan Inn particularly good. The present representatives in Parliament for the City of Lichfield, are Col. Anson, a brother of Lord Anson, & G. G. V. Vernon, Son, I believe, to the Archbishop of York.[7] The Population of Lichfield rather exceeds 4500 souls.

The next morning, Wednesday, Aug. 6th.[8] was cold and gloomy; the weather afterwards improved about the middle of the day, but some rain fell after we arrived at Calwich. We determined to divide our first intended stage to Uttoxeter into two, and breakfast at Abbots Bromley, ten miles distant from Lichfield. The road was familiar to me: passing thro' an enclosed country | of pasture, meadows & corn; but rather flat and dull. We left Lichfield by the same road, which leads to Rugeley, Stafford &c., and which winds through a rich and beautiful valley beneath some highly picturesque eminences on the left, in the bosom of which lies Beaudesert, the seat of the E. of Uxbridge, and which passing by Lord Curzon's at Hagley, terminate at Wolseley Bridge, where the Trent cuts short the line which ~~they~~ ‸ the heights were forming. About two or three miles from Lichfield the road to Sudbury diverts. Hansacre is the first village on the road, which we passed thro'; between it and Lichfield we passed near Seats of F. P. Elliot, & — Patton Esqrs. Between Hansacre and Hill Ridware we

---

6. John Witts was first cousin to Francis Witts, the son of his Uncle John, younger brother to his father, Edward Witts. John was a captain in the Royal Marines. He is mentioned frequently later in the diaries. His father was the rector of Lydleys Hays, Shropshire.
7. George Anson, (1769-1849). M.P. for Lichfield 1806-1849; George Granville Venables Vernon, (1785-1861). M.P. for Lichfield 1806-1831, Oxfordshire 1731-1861.
8. It was actually Wednesday the 5th, not the 6th of August.

71. Ashbourne, the home of Court Dewes.

crossed the Grand Trunk Canal, which by a navigation of 99 miles, including 6 miles the length of the D. of Bridgewater's Canal, which it joins, unites the rivers Trent and Mersey; ~~following~~ falling into the latter at Runcorn, and beginning its course from Wilden ferry on the Trent, from which place there is an uninterrupted navigation to Hull, as there is from Runcorn to Liverpool. | Many collateral cuts fall into or spring from this noble line of inland navigation in its progress across the island. In this part of its course the canal keeps very near its Parent River, which we also crossed in this earlier stage of its devious career: it rises in the high lands of Staffordshire & passing by Stone and Sandon, Rugeley & Burton, makes a northern sweep by Nottingham and Newark, till it joins the Humber at another Burton. Beyond Hill Ridware is Blithbury, another small village. Abbot's Bromley is a very poor town, not numbering 850 Inhabitants, and we found in it a very moderate ale-house, where we breakfasted as we could, civility making up for other defects. The Church at Abbots Bromley is a spacious building, but did not seem in any respect particular. A large brick House at the entrance of the Town is inhabited by Mr. Wolseley, a Son of Sir W. Wolseley: the seat of the latter is at Wolseley Bridge, not far distant.

After breakfasting and baiting our horse we pursued our route to Uttoxeter, seven miles. The country | is much more interesting; we passed through and near some fine woods over undulating ground: the verdure of the fields and luxuriance of the timber was very pleasing. The Hamlet of Bagot's Bromley almost adjoins Abbots Bromly, & not far distant is Lord Bagot's Seat at Blithfield.[9] It is not within view of the road; but we passed by part of the Park; the soil of which there appeared very unpromising but we soon plunged into fine dark woods. Near Wills Lock about five miles from Abbots Bromly is Loxley, the Seat of Mr. Kynnersley, but not seen from the road, and on an eminence above Uttoxeter is Highfield, a place belonging to M. Marston. The view on descending to the Town is very fine; the wide & fertile valley of the Dove is visible, bounded by the rising, fertile & well wooded border

9. William Bagot, Baron Bagot of Bagot's Bromley, (1773-1856).

72. *View of the Northern Entrance into Dovedale.*

of Derbyshire; Lord Waterpark's Mansion at Doveridge,[10] with the Church at the same place, & Lord Vernon's more ancient Seat at Sudbury, being prominent features | in the Landscape. ^ Both are in Derbyshire. In the beautiful meadows below Lord Waterpark's, which extend between the banks of the river & the foot of the eminence an annual coursing meeting, which I once attended, is held, at which a very numerous party of sportsmen meet, and some of the finest greyhounds in England are run. Uttoxeter is a place of considerable inland trade, having great facilities of canal communication for conveying the agricultural produce of this district, as well as the cottons manufactured in the numerous mills, which have been of late years erected in this neighbourhood. The town contains about 2800 inhabitants. The Inn, where we stopped, the White Hart, is not very well regulated; we were not long, however, detained in this place, where we only baited. During our stay, we walked into the Market place, which was very much crouded, it being market day, and I particularly observed large baskets of bilberries from the adjoining high lands offered for | sale. We looked into the Church, where the Curate was reading prayers to a thin congregation. It is an ancient building. The living is in the gift of the Canons of Windsor, and at present, I believe, is held by the President of Worcester College, D^r. Landon.

From Uttoxeter to Calwich the distance is 8 miles, through an unusually pleasing country, following the vale of the Dove, except where the road skirts an eminence to avoid a long detour made by the devious stream. We continued within the limits of Staffordshire, the opposite bank of the river being in Derbyshire. A Canal terminates at Uttoxeter, near the entrance of the Town, by which we left it. I believe, its course is through very fine scenery to Manchester, and from the extent of the warehouses, which we observed, & the bustle around them, I should judge the traffic along it to be considerable. This Canal is new, since I travelled this road in the close of 1807. It rather diminishes the beauty of the first four miles of the drive. Within one mile of Uttoxeter a road to the left leads to Cheadle; we pursued the right

10. Richard Cavendish, 2nd Baron Waterpark, (1765-1830).

73. View into Hope Dale from the Winnats.

hand road towards Ashborn. A mile farther is Crakemarsh situate in rich meadows | among lofty trees. A mansion house and ornamented Cottage here both belong to Cotton Shepherd Esqr., the former is at present tenanted by Trevor Wheler Esqr.[11] eldest Son of Sir Charles Wheler of Warwickshire, as Mr. Shepherd is eldest Son of Sir Thomas Shepherd of Bucks. Both these Gentlemen are remarkably pleasant hospitable men. About a mile beyond ~~Rocester~~ Crakemarsh on a rising ground to the left is Woodseat, the residence of Mr. Bainbrigge. A little farther a road goes to the left to Cheadle, pursuing which for a mile or two, a turn to the right conducts to the ruins of Craxall Abbey, interesting remains, which I visited some years ago on a former visit to Calwich. At this time we pursued the direct road to our friends over the little river Churnet, which flowing down a beautiful valley from the mountainous heights of Wever soon joins the Dove. Immediately on crossing this Stream we are in the village of Rocester, which is in no respect remarkable; Cotton mills & weaving employ the population of this place. Soon after we ascended Barrow Hill, near the summit of which Mr. Whyte's house & grounds | command a fine view down the fertile valley of the Dove. The road over Barrow Hill being recently diverted the ascent is considerably lessened. On the other side of this hill, as we descended, the view is still finer, to the left the mountain Wever, its base clothed with wood. Wooton Lodge hidden by the dark woods of its glen; Wooton Hall, once the temporary residence of Rousseau placed on a commanding height,[13] secluded from the valley, and embowered in trees; below it the village of Ellaston, & its neat Church, forming beautiful groups in every direction; at our feet a neat cottage, the residence of Mr. Riddlestone. Over this in the fine luxuriant Vale of the Dove, chrystal Calwich, reposing in the bosom of fine

11. George Venables-Vernon, 2nd Lord Vernon, (1735-1813).
12. Trevor Wheler, (1763-1830). He succeeded to the baronetcy in 1821.
13. Jean-Jacques Rousseau, (1712-1778). The Swiss born philosopher Rousseau lived at Wooton Hall from March 1766 to April 1767. He was a friend of the Granville family and frequently at Calwich.

scenery, the fair centre of the whole delicious picture. Following with the eye the course of the river we observed, each forming a pleasing feature, the villages of Mathfield[14] & Snelston, and the distant Spire of Ashbourn: while to the right & below us the silver Dove glides round the hill, on which we stand, after passing beneath the Gothic Church of Norbury, which with its pleasant adjacent | Rectory house crowns a well wooded knoll. Such beautiful and extensive views brought us to the sequestered lanes leading to Ellaston, a very pretty village, through which we passed, and soon arrived at the hospitable mansion of our friends.—

It is not my intention to delineate circumstantially a place so familiar to me, to which I was happy to introduce my ~~friends~~ wife, as also to its excellent master and mistress. We found Mr. & Mrs. Dewes of Wellesbourne with their Son, Mr. Granville's guests: he is Mr. G's elder Brother. Miss Louisa Port, Mr. G's great niece, resides with them. Two daughters of Mr. Wheler of Crakemarsh were also on a visit at Calwich. Mr. Cotton Shepherd & Mr. Wheler, both well known to me of old, were added to our dinner party. Miss Shepherd accompanied the former, as also the Revd. — Lownds, Brother to the Member for Bucks.

The following day I had the pleasure of shewing my wife the beauties of this charming vale, & rowed the ladies on the lake. The Revd. B. Port, Rector of Irlam, Mr. Granville's nephew, & an old acquaintance of mine, called on us.[15] We dined at Wooton Hall. This | pleasant and retired place, the property of Mr. Davenport of Cheshire is now rented by my old acquaintance A. J. Ram, Son of Col. Ram, Member for Wexford, who married Miss F. Port, Mr. Granville's niece.[16] He has a lovely young family. We found there, inmates of the House, Mrs. Port & her unmarried Daughter, Mrs. Ram's mother & Sister, with whom I had long ago been intimate, & Mr. Hake, the worthy and zealous Curate of Ellaston, who superintends the education of Mr. Ram's son. Mr. & Mrs. Whyte of Barrow Hill joined the party, & the day passed most pleasantly.

The next day we visited Mrs. Granville's School for poor female children at Ellaston, which is in every point under excellent management. The village is remarkably pretty, the Parish very extensive. Mr. Davenport's Son is the Rector; it is in his Father's Gift. The Parsonage House is tenanted by Mr. & Miss Manwarings, Son & Daughters of the late incumbent. We made a morning visit to Mr. & Mrs. Wilson at Wooton Lodge, about two miles beyond Ellaston. This singular place is beautifully situated on an abrupt rock overhanging a fine deep glen issuing | as it were, from the bosom of Wever, & ~~finely~~ richly clothed with wood. The accompaniments on all sides are extremely rich ~~& fine~~. The house itself was built by Inigo Jones in the castellated stile, & has a most strikingly romantic appearance, where it is situated. The interior has recently been fitted up with great taste & expense. The house contains a valuable collection of paintings. Mr. Wilson is only tenant, but for a long term to Major or Col. Unwin, whose brother, the Rector of a parish in Derby, I had met with at Flasby, the Seat of his Father-in-Law, Mr. Preston, in Craven. Mr. & Mrs. Whyte & a party of Gentlemen, met to bowl at Mr. Granville's before dinner & added to our party. Mr. G. & Mr. Dewes are very partial to this exercise and adepts in the game; without any very strong relish for it, it is impossible to be engaged in it with them without feeling an interest in

---

14. Mathfield. This must be Mayfield.
15. This is the Bernard Port who declined offering Frank the curacy of Ham back on 22 January 1806.
16. This is Fanny Ram, née Fanny Port who Frank fell in love with back in Cheltenham, in October/November 1801.

74. Pencil sketch of Chee Tor, Derbyshire, by Francis Witts dated 13 August.

the sport, nor on a bowling green commanding such a silver scene without acknowledging its luxuriance. Mr. & Mrs. Egerton Leigh, of Broadwell, our acquaintance & neighbours in Gloucestershire, arrived unexpectedly on a visit of a few days in the Evening. |

The next morning, Saturday Aug. the 9th.,[17] we continued our Journey, our next point being Buxton, where I had been advised to bathe, to repel a strong tendency to Rheumatic Gout. The day was overcast, and the afternoon cold & rainy. We parted with regret from our very kind and agreeable friends after breakfast, and on leaving Calwich were undecided whether to visit the beautiful valley of Dovedale, which to my wife would have been a novel place. To myself all this neighbourhood, and the road to Buxton is so familiar, that I shall not very fully describe this part of our Tour. Our irresolution was soon removed by a trifling accident, which occurred to our harness but which rendered it necessary to us to go through Ashbourn, in order to get it remedied. From Calwich to Ashbourn is a distance of four miles, the continuance of the same turnpike road, which we had travelled from Uttoxeter. Pursuing the valley of the Dove no scenery can be more rich or beautiful. Between Calwich & Hanging Bridge we pass Mathfield, where is on one side of the | road a good Gentleman's Seat, the Village Church is on the other. The opposite bank of the Dove, in Derbyshire still offers very pleasing views. At Hanging Bridge over the Dove, the Valley expands or rather branches towards Ashborn in one direction, Okeover, Irlam &c. in the other. The view in the latter quarter is very beautiful a fertile valley, which the traveller knows to terminate in such romantic scenery as that of Dovedale & Irlam, boasting also of Mr. Okeover's seat, where is so rich a treasure of paintings, fertilized by so beautiful a stream, and bounded by the curious sugar loaf eminence. Thorp Cloud with other picturesque hills, must attract attention and admiration. At Hanging Bridge we came into the great road leading from Ashbourn, I believe, to Leek. We staid at the former place near an hour, calling on Mrs. Court Dewes. Mr. C. Dewes,

17. Saturday 8 August 1812.

75. Pencil sketch of Chee Tor, Derbyshire, by Francis Witts.

is Son of Mr. Dewes of Wellesbourn, by his first wife, Mrs. Granville's Sister, and by the decease of poor John Granville,[18] heir to his Uncle's, as well as his Father's large Property. He was at home, & B. Port we found there also. While we remained at Ashbourn our broken harness | was repaired. Ashbourn is a populous Country Town & reckoned pretty and cheap. The Society is rather numerous and good. The Church at one ~~hi~~ end of the Town, is a fine ancient building, with a beautiful spire, and at the other Extremity is a seat of Sir B. Boothby,[19] tenanted by Mr. Arkwright. Numerous French prisoners are stationed here on parole.

Our next stage to Newhaven was very hilly the distance nine miles. The first part of the ride is rich and pretty, thro' woody lanes, by Sandy Brook and Bentley. From the latter village the road begins to rise, and passing on the right Tissington the Seat of Sir H. Fitzherbert,[20] and on the left the eminencies of the romantic Dovedale, we launch on the wild, mountain, woodless heights of the Peak of Derbyshire. Now rising, now descending, we at length arrived at the Group of Inns, which constitutes Newhaven. They principally belong to the Duke of Devonshire, and are in the vicinity of the village of Hartington, from which place that family derives its second title. The chief Inn at Newhaven is very spacious and well ma- | -naged. We dined comfortably at this place, & proceeded forwards to Buxton, where we arrived at dusk. The distance was eleven miles, & the country resembled what we had passed between Newhaven and Bentley, equally bleak and exposed but rather with a descent than ascent. I omit dwelling on the well known features of Buxton & its vicinity. We drove to the St. Ann's Hotel, which during the period of our stay we found a well regulated house, the accommodations & table good, the Stables well managed, and the charges reasonable.

---

18. John Granville, the only son of John and Harriet Granville died in 1801. See the Hoppner portrait of him in the first colour section volume 1.
19. Ashbourne Hall, the property of Sir Brooke Boothby, (1744-1824).
20. Henry Fitzherbert, (1783-1858).

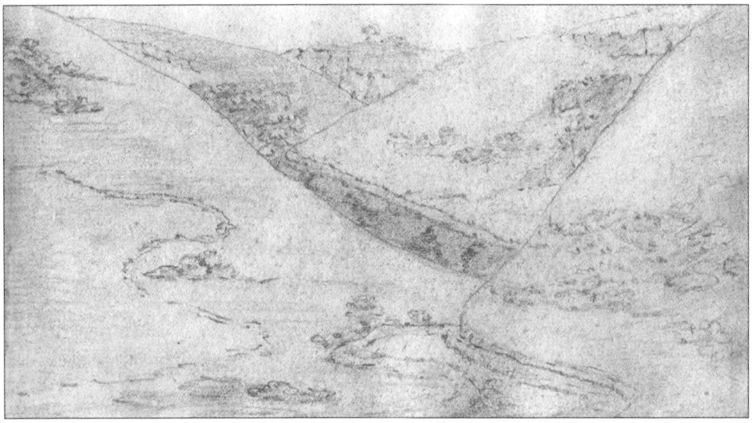

76. Pencil sketch of King Sterndale, Derbyshire, by Francis Witts.

The following morning was rendered interesting by being the day of the consecration of the New Church at Buxton. The weather was remarkably fine, & the inhabitants of the adjacent country flocked in in very considerable numbers, affording a very gay & numerous addition to the inhabitants & visitors of this place. The munificence of the late Duke of Devonshire has been amply displayed in the building the Church in question, at an expence, I am told, of £20,000.[21] The former Chapel of Buxton | was very small and incommodious: now by act of Parliament, the place is erected into a Parish independent of Bakewell, to which it was a Chapelry: and what is a little curious, the new Church is erected on a spot of ground out of the former limits of the Parish, and even in another diocese, but now by this new act the whole is placed in the jurisdiction of the Bishop of Litchfield & Coventry. The church is modelled after that of St. Paul's, Covent Garden, built of the beautiful stone of this Country.

We passed about ten days at Buxton, during which time I bathed & drank the Waters, & then proceeded by an often travelled road, which I do not therefore purpose to detail to Beck House. Our first day's Stage was to Manchester, our second to Clithero, & on the third day we reached Mrs. Backhouse's, where we remained till the ~~end~~ beginning of November.—

77. Pencil sketch of Clitherow, by Francis Witts dated 18 August.

21. William Cavendish, 5th Duke of Devonshire, (1748-1811).

There is now one of the largest gaps in the diaries, from 1812 to 1817. As usual some information on what was happening in the family can be obtained from the diaries of Agnes Witts.

On 12 November 1812 Francis and Margaret returned to Upper Slaughter. The next we hear is a month later when he has an accident: 7 December 1813: 'poor Dear Frank return'd to us at Noon found he had met with a sad accident on Saturday by a fall from his horse which dislocated his left shoulder but happily being instantly put in place . . .'

From 11 December to 21 December 1812 he was in Oxford. Then on 2 January he was back at Upper Slaughter having spent much time at Cheltenham with Margaret, now pregnant and have the utmost care taken of her following her several miscarriages. Back at Cheltenham later in the week they were entertaining friends that Francis and Margaret had made at Buxton: 9 January 1813: '. . . Miss Markham & Mrs. & Miss Hayes, at the Plough, Frank's Buxton friends who spent the evening with us & play'd vingt une, very good humor'd, pleasant people . . .'

On 30 January Francis and Margaret returned to Upper Slaughter and a few days later Edward and Agnes went for one of their long stays at Stanway. On 2 March 1813 Margaret gave birth to Edward, and there is joy that after such troubles she at last is successful in producing an heir. In this respect Margaret had similar troubles to Agnes, who suffered much with miscarriages and still births until Francis had been born. Mrs. Backhouse stayed at Upper Slaughter, so unusually for Agnes she does not rush to see her grandson, and waits for two months, eventually going over on 2 May 1813.

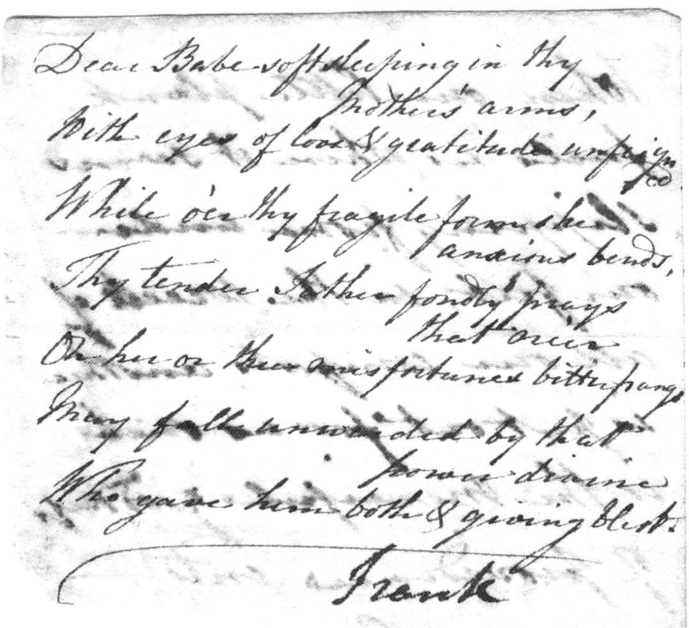
Dear Babe soft sleeping in thy mother's arms,
With eyes of love & gratitude unfeign'd
While o'er thy fragile form she anxious bends,
Thy tender Father fondly prays that ne'er
On her or thee misfortunes bitter pangs
May fall unwarded by that power divine
Who gave him both & giving blest.
Frank

78. Verse written by Francis Witts c.1813.

79. Thomas Hulley's Assembly Room, Cheltenham; opened 1810 and replaced in 1816.

On 24 June Edward and Agnes eventually returned to Cheltenham and then on the 30th Agnes recorded the death of old Dr. Moorhouse, Margaret's grandfather, at the age of 82.

A letter from George of 6 July announced that he was now on the island of Ponza. Then, after just a few days back at Cheltenham, Edward and Agnes were on the move again, this time for a stay at Malvern where they settled for lodgings on Roberts Row.

The following entries from Agnes Witts's diary are worthy of note for this period:
5 October 1813: '. . . much amused through the evening with reading Pride & Prejudice . . .'
10 October 1813: '. . . both services excellent sermons both from Dr. Graves & his son, between had several fussy calls from Lady Lyttelton & Miss Eycott . . .' 24 October 1813: '. . . Received a letter from Mrs. Granville fixing a day for our arrival. . .'

On 28 October 1813 Edward and Agnes left Malvern and the 'fussy' Lady Lyttelton and headed to Calwich their annual stay, this time lasting a month. On their return, they overnighted at the Kings Head, Gloucester, and on 3 December 1813 they passed by 'Rodboro Inn to Bath' and on their arrival at Bath settled on 17 Argyle Street for their lodgings. They remained for two months and then on 4 February 1814 passed through Gloucester once more on their way to Lady Hereford at Stanway, in this way they continued to eke out their meagre capital by staying with friends and family.

While at Stanway, Agnes recorded a few items of interest: 28 March 1814: '. . . the trio arrive from Upper Slaughter . . .' 31 March 1814: '. . . Frank went to the Justice Meeting at Stow but came back to Dinner as did Charles Keysall from Bredon, no events took place but tiresome disputatious conversation. Wrote to Lord Elcho. . . .' 19 April 1814: '. . . Lady Corkes usual rodomontade exceeding even itself. . .' 25 April 1814: '. . . Ldy. Corke and Orrey made her departure to the regret of no one. . .' 8 May 1814: 'Frank to London on business for himself and Lady Hereford . . .' 14 June 1814: 'Letter from George in Genoa . . . letter from Frank to notifie his being gone to Oxford to meet the Emperor & King . . .' This last entry is enigmatic. The visitor to Oxford was no less than the king emperor of Prussia, Frederick William III.[22] *A few days later Edward and Agnes were regaled with the great event by the curate of Stanway who had also been to Oxford. 18 June 1814: ' . . . Mr. Charles Keysall here the greater part of the day full of anecdotes from the Oxford celebrity from entertaining Emperor King & Prince Regent . . .'*

The following week another entry of importance shows that the living of Stanway, in the gift of Lady Hereford, was about to come the way of Frank: 24 June 1814: '. . . Mr. Eddy his two Daughters & a cousin walked over here and staid two hours, his visit open'd the resignation of Mr. Lightfoot to the Living of Stanway, which of course was very interesting to us, My Son having long had the promise of succeeding to it. . .' 12 July 1814: '. . . Frank to Stanway to consult Lady Hereford.' 16 July 1814: '. . . we had the comford of knowing our Dear Son George was landed on English ground by a letter to his Brother . . .'

George was to stay at Upper Slaughter, or at Cheltenham with his parents from 30 July 1814 until 31 January 1815. During this stay in Gloucestershire, he made a nine days visit in October to stay with his patroness, Lady Lyttelton at Malvern. It appears that Lady Lyttelton had a soft spot for George. He then returned to the Mediterranean and was never seen again, dying on board ship on his eventual attempt to return home in 1823.

On 24 August 1814 Francis and Margaret made another extensive trip to Yorkshire, not returning until the end of November. During his absence he took a curate, Mr. Wellford, the son of an acquaintance of his Uncle Broome.

At the end of November, Agnes at long last saw her beloved son after his long trip to Yorkshire: 30 November 1814: '. . . Frank arrived to Dinner in great good health and looks. . .'

On 9 January 1815 Francis was inducted to Stanway, and his income rose from the additional living. On 14 January the family learned of the death of Edward's brother Richard in London.

In March, Lady Hereford was anxious for company to relieve her loneliness at Stanway: 6 March 1815: '. . . rec'd a letter from Miss Hamilton full of kind expressions from Lady Hereford about our soon going to Stanway . . .' On the 14th Edward and Agnes went, this time for a stay of more than three months. While there Agnes recorded her concern on hearing the news that Napoleon had left Elba and was raising an army — her concern due to the fact that George was still in Genoa: 18 March 1815: '. . . wretched accounts from France made us all agitated . . .' In May, the family from Upper Slaughter visit Stanway: 4 May 1815: '. . . our Upper Slaughter friends arriving between three & four, Mrs. Backhouse with them . . .'

22. King Frederick William III, (1770-1840), king of Prussia 1797-1840. Frederick was an ineffectual king, leaning heavily on ministerial advisers such as Baron von Steim, Prince von Hardenburg and Count Gneisenau. The latter of these, August Wilhelm Antonius Graf Neidhart von Gniesenau, (1760-1831) was a secret envoy in England and Francis Witts met him in Buxton in 1812 when taking the waters there and enjoyed several evenings of confidential conversation. He records this in some detail in the diary entry for Friday 17 March 1826. Why Agnes should underline 'meet' would seem to indicate that he had been specifically invited to see the king in person, but why who by is not known, and why is this not referred to in the entry for 17 March 1826 when he mentions having seen the king in Weimar in 1799?

15 December 1815: '. . . letter from George Just on the move from Marseilles – to Genoa . . .' In January Francis went on an urgent trip to Malvern, to see his Uncle John staying with his elder sister, Lady Lyttelton, and on 4 January John died. This now left two brothers, Edward and Broome, and two sisters, Apphia and Sarah (Mrs. Stone).

On 11 October 1814 Agnes recorded that she was at an auction buying furniture, and it seemed that they had finally decided to settle in Cheltenham and to travel less, but nothing much came of it. By 1816 they were tiring and Edward was less well. To set up a home they borrowed £400 from Agnes's sister Anne, which Francis stood surety for, and which he eventually had to pay when his aunt died. In the middle of 1816 Agnes provided the evidence of their settling: 20 June 1816: '. . . went to Belle Vue Place to finally settle for taking Mrs. Macleans House there . . .'

The early part of the summer they spent at Upper Slaughter, and moved back to Cheltenham at the end of July: 3 August 1816: '. . . recruited servant Elizabeth Richards, much buying of furniture . . .'

Towards the end of the year it became clear that Edward's illness might be serious: 23 September 1816: '. . . Mr. Witts unwell in his stomach wrote to George at Malta. . . .' 2 October 1816: '. . . Mr. Witts so unwell in his stomach . . .'

27 October 1816: '. . . Mr. Witts not being so well again . . .'

By Christmas day the last hours came: 25 December1816: '. . . I was alone supported under such a trial by witnessing his pious resignation at the approach of Death his senses perfect & his power of joining in the sacred Duty of receiving the Sacrament from the hand of his Son truly edifying, my Sister, Anne, Margaret & myself forming the congregation round the sick Bed, poor Dear soul he lay perfectly at ease throughout the rest of the day giving to all around him a noble Pattern of the last hours of a true Christian.

Edward died the following day. There is then a gap in the Agnes's diary until 1 February 1817 when she recorded moving to Upper Slaughter for a while. It had been a year of deaths for the Witts family which must have come as a shock to Broome, Apphia and Sarah, for in the space of one year their three younger brothers had died, Richard, John and then Edward.

For additional income Francis took in pupils. His first pupil had been Frederick Aston from Eyford Park. This was to create a long lasting bond, for after Oxford Frederick became Francis Witts's curate at Stanway and the two men remained good friends until Francis died in 1854. In 1817 Francis took the son of a neighbour from Salperton under his tuition: 3

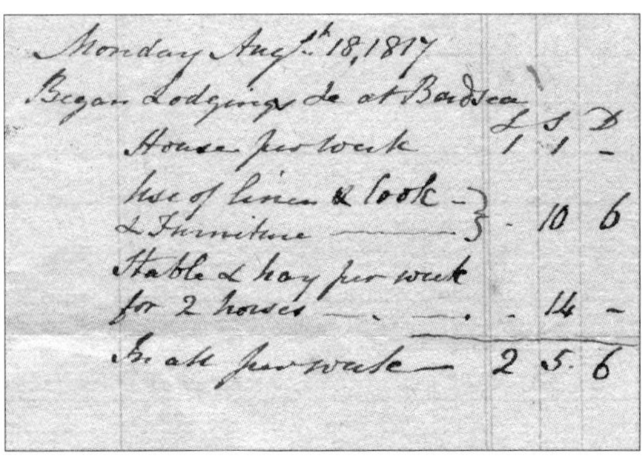
Monday Augt. 18, 1817
Began Lodgings &c at Bardsea

	£	s	d
House per week	1	1	–
Use of linen & cook & Furniture	-	10	6
Stable & hay per week for 2 horses	-	14	–
In all per week	2	5	6

80. A note on lodging costs, August 1817.

March 1817: '. . . Mr. John Brownes arrival to begin his studies under my Son . . . Mr. John Browne arrived before Dinner, a shy but gentlemanlike youth . . .'

In later life Francis Witts was critical of his son Edward enjoying the pastimes of fishing, cricket and other leisure activities. He seems to have forgotten his own younger years for all of these activities were enjoyed by himself: 16 June 1817: ' . . . Frank long out fishing . . .'

In June Lady Hereford died at Stanway, and now the property fell to Lord Elcho, the son of lady Elcho who was soon to regain the family title of Earl of Wemyss, a title which had been under attainder from the days of his great-uncle at Culloden. Agnes remained at Stanway after Lady Hereford's death and she was joined there on 18 July by Francis just returned from Birmingham. He appears to have been seeing Margaret off on her way to the North. By the end of August he joined Margaret and young Edward at the seaside and they then proceeded on a tour of the Lakes.

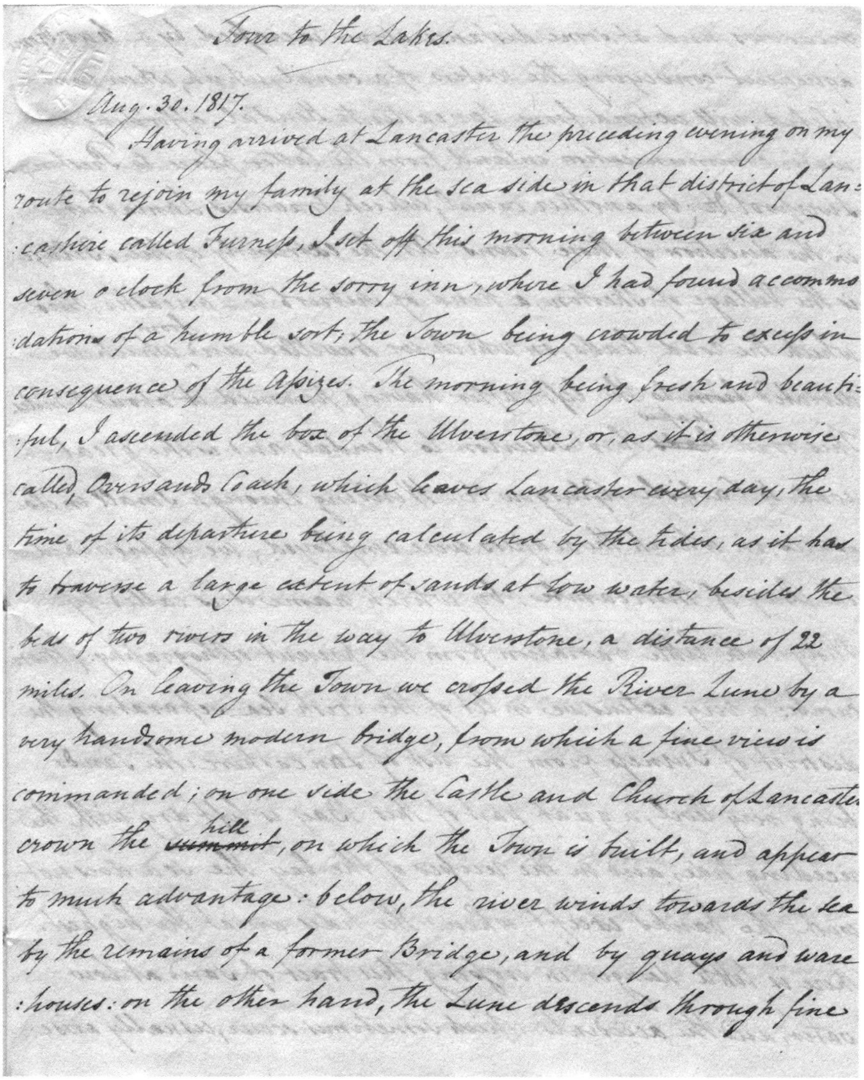

Tour to the Lakes.

Aug. 30. 1817.

Having arrived at Lancaster the preceding evening on my route to rejoin my family at the sea side in that district of Lan:cashire called Furness, I set off this morning between six and seven o clock from the sorry inn, where I had found accommo:dations of a humble sort, the Town being crowded to excess in consequence of the Assizes. The morning being fresh and beauti:ful, I ascended the box of the Ulverstone, or, as it is otherwise called, Oversands Coach, which leaves Lancaster every day, the time of its departure being calculated by the tides, as it has to traverse a large extent of sands at low water, besides the beds of two rivers in the way to Ulverstone, a distance of 22 miles. On leaving the Town we crossed the River Lune by a very handsome modern bridge, from which a fine view is commanded; on one side the Castle and Church of Lancaster crown the ~~summit~~ hill, on which the Town is built, and appear to much advantage: below, the river winds towards the sea by the remains of a former Bridge, and by quays and ware:houses: on the other hand, the Lune descends through fine

Witts Family Papers F387

Tour to the Lakes

Aug. 30. 1817

Having arrived at Lancaster the preceding evening on my route to rejoin my family at the sea side in that district of Lancashire called Furness, I set off this morning between six and seven o clock from the sorry inn, where I had found accommodations of a humble sort; the Town being crowded to excess in consequence of the Assizes. The morning being fresh and beautiful, I ascended the box of the Ulverstone, or, as it is otherwise called, Oversands Coach, which leaves Lancaster every day, the time of its departure being calculated by the tides, as it has to traverse a large extent of sands at low water, besides the beds of two rivers in the way to Ulverstone, a distance of 22 miles. On leaving the Town we crossed the River

81. Lancaster.

Lune by a very handsome modern bridge, from which a fine view is commanded; on one side the Castle and Church of Lancaster crown the ~~summit~~ hill, on which the Town is built, and appear to much advantage: below, the river winds towards the sea by the remains of a former Bridge, and by quays and warehouses: on the other hand, the Lune descends through fine | meadows, and at some distance above is crossed by a handsome aqueduct conveying the waters of a canal, which, when completed, will extend from Lancaster to Kendal, affording a water communication inland from the latter place to Preston, Liverpool &c: by another canal, which traverses Lancashire in the direction of those towns. At the extremity of the Bridge is the village of Skerton, a kind of suburb to Lancaster, thro' which the road leads, on which we travelled, and from which we deviated to the left, after having pursued it about 2 miles. This road ~~leads~~ passes thro' Burton to Kendal, and is the great road to Carlisle, Glasgow &c. Winding through small inclosures, in which the reapers were employed, we approached the Bay of Morecambe, by which name it is called by Pliny with little variation from the present orthography: (Moricambe:) a very extensive inlet of the Irish Sea separating the district of Furness from the rest of Lancashire: the sands being very level, a great part of this Bay is left dry with the receding tide, and in the recesses of the bay the sea does not wash the banks except when the tides are at the highest. There is little danger in crossing this tract of sand at low water, and the accidents, which sometimes occur, usually arise | from ignorance or presumption. We entered upon the sands at Hest bank, about three miles from Lancaster; this is a groupe of a few houses, the principal of which is an Inn affording accommodations for bathing; little dressing rooms of painted wood are placed here & there on the beach. From hence, according to the information of the Coachman, the distance to the point, where we again came upon dry land is 11 miles. The air on this wide expanse of sand was chill and sharp, and the drive novel and interesting. On the right is a bold shore, deeply indented in some places, and opening into bays in others, valleys, which stretch far into the country, bounded by hanging grounds, cut into inclosures, interspersed with groves and woods, adorned with cottages, farms and villages; mountains behind mountains, and others again just seen over them, close the forescene. At entering on the sands, to the left, Heysham point rises abruptly, and the village hangs beautifully on its side. On the opposite side of the bay, over a vast extent of sands, Piel Castle, the ancient bulwark of the coast, is observed. In front appears a fine sweep of country sloping to the South. To the right is seen Warton crag. Grounds bearing from the Eye for many miles, variegated in every pleasing form, by woods and rocks, | are terminated by the Cloud-topt Ingleborough. At the bottom of the bay is Arnside Point. The Cartmel coast now, as we advance; becomes more pleasing. Between that and the point just named is a great break in the coast, and through the opening the river Kent rolls its waters to join the tide. In the mouth of the estuary is a little conical Isle, cloathed with wood and verdure. At the same time a grand view opens of the Westmoreland mountains tumbled about in a most surprizing manner. At the head of this estuary is the village of Heversham, the little market Town of Millthorp,[1] & Dallam Tower, the seat of D. Wilson Esq$^{r.}$ To the North, Whitbarrow Scar, a huge arched & bent cliff of an immense height, shews its storm-beaten front. To the left of this is Castle Head, the seat of the late John Wilkinson Esq$^{r.}$ on a commanding point. Nearer to the eye the beautiful

1. Milnthorp.

village of Grange is observed, with many white houses dotted among trees. This village is frequented for sea bathing. Thos. Maude Esqr. , a banker in Kendal, has a seat here. At the side of the River of the Sands, the Kent, a guide on horseback is in waiting to conduct travellers over the Ford. The priory of Cartmel was anciently charged with this office, and had an endowment for its maintenance. The salary of the guide is now paid by the receiver general of the County, and he is also provided with a house rent-free. He levies contributions ~~also~~ too | on those, who pass; I heard him condole with the Coachman on the paucity of Lawsuits in the district of Cartmel and Furness, and that their harvest, the passage of suitors to the Assizes, was very bad this year: I thought it a proof of the goodsense & amity of the inhabitants. The route across the sands is certainly very striking and impressive. As the traveller pursues his way over a plain apparently immense in extent, continued in a dead level, and uniform in appearance, he recollects, that, probably, but a few hours before, the whole expanse was covered with some fathoms of water, and that certainly it will soon be so again. At the same time he sees, on his left hand, the retreated ocean ready to obey the mysterious laws of its irresistible movement, without any barrier to stay it a moment, where it is. These recollections rouse the attention, which is still more interested, when on the verge of the river he gently descends to a broad & rippling expanse of water, where a solitary being in horseback is descried, hovering on the brink, or encountering the stream, in order to conduct him through it. The several particulars peculiar to an arm of the sea, fishermen, ships, sea fowl, shells, weeds, all attract the traveller's notice. He watches the progress of the turf carts, conveying fuel in different directions from the mountain mosses across the sands, while horsemen, and pedestrians with naked legs, traverse the sands in all directions. |

On reaching the shore, we found ourselves in Cartmel, a small district belonging to Lancashire, but united to Westmorland a little below Bownesson Windermere Water, from whence it extends itself between the rivers Kent and Leven, & so intersects the great bay of Morecambe. From the public house, where we reached the shore, the distance is three miles, before we again entered on the sands. Ascending an eminence, through a lane, bordered by fine fields of grain, the road being good, you drop down on the Village of Flookburgh, in which, among other pretty residences, is a handsome house of W. Sunderland. Near Flookburgh is a Spa, frequented by those, who suffer from cutaneous disorders. This medical spring, added to the pleasant environs, good air and vicinity to the sea, attracts many summer visitors, who are chiefly accommodated in the Inns. Near Flookburgh, in a recess of the mountains, is Cartmel, where was anciently a priory, and still a fine old Church; this place was not in our route. Having passed thro' Cark, a township, in which are large buildings for carrying on the Cotton manufactory, and now untenanted, we approached Holker, near which is a fine place, belonging to Lord Geo. Cavendish, situated under ~~fine~~ grand wooded mountains, on the margin of the estuary of the Leven, in a park, which shewed fertility of soil, | and skill in agriculture, a mild climate, and a profusion of noble trees.

Here we again launched our vehicle on the Leven sands; three miles across. The coast is deeply indented, and the peninsulas are beautifully fringed with wood. On the right, a bold bending rock presents a noble arched fore head; and a fine slope of inclosed grounds mixed with wood, lead the Eye to Ulverstone, the port & mart of Furness. It lies in a valley bounded by lofty but bare hills stretching to the Northward, and uniting with the gigantic masses, which embosom Coniston Lake. In front Conishead shews its pyramidal summit, completely clothed in wood. At its feet is the Priory, the Seat of M^r. Braddyl, shielded by a wing of hanging wood, climbing the side of a steep hill. The Village of Bardsea, with its rocks and hanging woods, stands still farther to the left in a delightful point of view. In front, a sweet fall of inclosures, marked with clumps of trees and hedgerows, gives it a most picturesque effect. The coast beyond is of singular beauty, consisting of hanging woods, inclosed lands and pasture grounds, varied in every pleasing form. On the right you have a grand view of Alpine Scenery: the mountains seem increased in magnitude since they were first seen from Hest bank. You trace the outline of the retiring bay, into which the Leven pours its stream, flowing | from Windermere lake, as the Crake in the same quarter discharges the waters of Coniston Lake. At the ford of the Leven another guide attends to conduct passengers across. At the dissolution of Conishead priory, the Salary of this guide was continued by the Crown, and he also demands from travellers a compensation for his safe-conduct. The beds of both the Kent & Leven Rivers often are changed in situation, which makes the services of a guide indispensable. The channel is now near the Ulverstone side. Below the ford in the midst of the bay a small Island crowned with trees is a conspicuous object; amid the foliage a ruined chapel appears, where in ancient times service was performed by the Monks of Conishead Priory.

From the public House on the Shore, where we left the Sands, the distance to Ulverstone is more than a mile. A large manufactory stands about mid-way on the left hand: on the right, is seen a cut or canal communicating at one end with the Sea; at the other with a dock adjacent to the Town; this canal facilitates the commerce of the place. The aspect of the Town is very pleasing; clean, neat, well aired streets, of a plain stile of architecture; and the outskirts ~~chiefly~~ principally consist of neat modern residences, in gardens, chiefly on eminences, which command fine prospects of the bay. At the Sun Inn, after | a comfortable breakfast, I had the happiness of again embracing my wife & child, who came in M^rs. Backhouse's Carriage to convey me to their lodgings at Bardsea, three miles distant. Nothing can be prettier than this drive; which principally lies through M^r. Braddyl's park & grounds, amid corn fields, ripe for harvest, pastures, & woods. At Bardsea is an old Hall, the property of Maj. Braddyl, son of the owner of Conishead Priory: to which is annexed a deer park. The Cottage at Bardsea, which we occupied, was within three minutes walk

82. Pencil sketch of fresh herrings, by Francis Witts.

83. Pencil sketch of Cottage, by Francis Witts.

of the beach: from the sitting room a side view extended over the Sea to the S.W. where it was overhung by a fine and extensive wood, called Sea-wood: in front, a beautiful field of wheat under the sickle; backed by a wood, on the margin of which were two or three white Cottages delightfully situated. Our accommodations were very comfortable; not in the style, indeed, of the great marts of vanity and fashion on the Southern Coast, for Bardsea is but little known, beyond its immediate vicinity, and few persons resort thither. Two families came almost daily from Ulverstone to enjoy the sea breezes, and when the tide was high, to bathe, but there are no machines, a secluded bend in the shore is the dressing room. The beach is very stony, called here the shillow: beyond, the sands are very extensive and level, but curl & retain moisture, so as to preclude walking across with dry feet. Hardly | a day passes, but ships are seen passing and repassing to or from Ulverstone, or other inferior ports higher up in the bay. The walks along the beach are very agreeable, particularly at the high tide; you are, as it were, on the margin of a lake, noble mountains are its barrier, & its sides fringed with wood or cultivated fields.

My visits to Ulverstone during the week, which I passed at Bardsea, enable me to give the following account of that place. The weekly market for Low Furness has long been established here to the prejudice of Dalton, the ancient capital of the district. It is crowded with the productions of the fertile tract, of which it is the Imporium. The articles of export are iron-ore in great quantities, pig and bar iron, oats, barley, beans, potatoes, bark & limestone. The iron mines are in the vicinity, and are worked on a very large scale: the principal are at Whitrigs, Stainton and Adgarly. The ore is found in a limestone stratum, mixed with a variety of spars of a dirty colour. There is much quartz in some of the works, which admits of a high polish. Mess$^{rs.}$ Fell and Burton, to the latter of whom, a man of the greatest urbanity of manners, gifted with strong sense & judgment, and possessed of extensive information, we were under obligations for many and assiduous polite attentions, have a large manufactory, at Ulverstone & in its vicinity, of Linen & Checks, which are in high estimation: they import their flax from Ireland, with which country they keep up an active trade in vessels of their own. These gentlemen | are also in partnership as bankers. The Church of Ulverstone is about a quarter of a mile from the Town, finely situated at the foot of a hill, commanding glorious prospects. Its outward appearance is unpromising, being plain in structure, in architecture resembling most of those in the North Western parts of England, long buildings with low towers. But the public Spirit of the Inhabitants of Ulverstone has improved the interior to a most commodious & handsome place of worship. The organ is well toned, & played upon by a blind man, who received his instructions at the celebrated asylum for the blind at Liverpool, and does credit to that benevolent Institution. The altar is very handsome. The East window consists, in its upper part, of paintings in glass, representing our Saviour's resurrection; faith and devotion, two female figures copied from the celebrated window~~s~~ in the Antechapel of New College, Oxford, with the four Evangelists. The whole is well executed, if the colouring be not considered too gaudy. The lower part of the window, being closed, is occupied by an oil painting, representing the dead Christ, previous to his being entombed, with the two Marys, and the beloved Disciple, preparing for embalment. This painting is a good copy of an altar piece in the Chapel of the Portuguese Embassy in London, and was done by Major Braddyl, whose productions are highly creditable to his taste. The reading desk and pulpit, the latter of which I filled on the second Sunday of my stay in this neighbourhood, are in front of the Altar. Ulverstone | is well provided with charitable Institutions. A large national School for boys and girls, instructed both of the week days and on Sundays, is held in a commodious building adjoining the Town. A provident Bank is established on the same principles ~~of~~ as those in Edinburgh & other parts of Scotland, affording Interest on small sums at 4 pr. Ct. the Trustees, who are responsible for the money invested, lodge the ~~money~~ deposits in the hands of Messrs. Fell & Burton. This is doing good, but not going far enough, deposits in Provident Banks should rest finally on public securities; however responsible private security may be, one great object in the promoters of Provident Banks should always be to direct the Depositors to the advantages of investing in the public funded securities of the nation. A medical and Lying in Charity with others of much utility are warmly supported & well directed. It is proposed to erect a Chapel of ease to supply the want of room, which in the increasing population of a prosperous town is here, as in most other places, complained of, and Mr. Sunderland, a Gentleman, resident in Ulverstone, father to the Minister of the parish, and a proficient in architectural drawings, has furnished a plan for an elegant and commodious building. The Church of Ulverstone is, I believe, only a perpetual Curacy, or donative, and has not a revenue exceeding £300 per ann. yet | it is the Mother Church of several Chapels, chiefly to the North, & bordering on Coniston Lake, some of which will again demand our attention. The Revd. Mr. Sunderland is justly held in high esteem by his parishioners, among whom he discharges with zeal & affection the amiable and important duties of a parish priest. The population of Ulverstone exceeds 3000~: the patronage of the Church is in the Braddyl family.

Sep. 1.

We devoted this morning to an excursion to the ruins of Furness Abbey, about six miles distant from Bardsea: the road, generally speaking, being good. Ascend Birkrig, an eminence, overhanging the village of Bardsea; the lower parts of the Hill are clothed with wood and verdure; the summit is common, with fern and rock. From the highest point is seen a glorious and most extensive view, well meriting the slight fatigue of ascent. You have a perfect panoramic prospect of all Low Furness, with most of the giant mountains of the higher part of the district. On the Northern Horizon you particularly notice the lofty & romantic outlines of Coniston Fells, which stretch across the summit of the Lake of that name. Carrying the Eye to the West, a line of mountains connect the Fells above named with Black Comb, an enormous round hill in the County of Cumberland, and in the direction of Ravenglass, between the estuary called the Duddon sands, & the | Irish sea: the height of Black Comb is estimated in the Trigonometrical survey of Col. Mudge at 1919 feet.[2] In this direction the Isle of Man may be distinctly seen. Proceeding along the Horizon towards the South West, you observe a cluster of Islands, which lie at the extremity of Furness, all low, but of different shapes, Walney, Barrow, Pile of Foudrey, Foulney and others smaller than those now named. There the bay of Morecambe may be considered to commence, as at Heysham Point on the opposite coast, near Lancaster, and the whole bay lies, as it were, below your feet; with all the noble features, so frequently adverted to before. Lancaster Town & Castle are distinctly visible in a fine point of view, under a screen of high ground, over which the dark moors of Clougha rear their mighty top. Ingleborough, behind many other mountains, towers as the Monarch of the Hills: the height of this is estimated on the same authority, as is quoted above, at 2361 feet. Tracing the outline of the Coast, the Fells of Cartmel & Westmoreland Mountains form the rugged frame of this mighty landscape. As a foreground, Ulverstone & its port, the Park & grounds of Mr. Braddyl, the Village of Bardsea, the Groves round the Village of Urswick, and the undulating, low, cultivated, hills of the Maritime part of Furness, afford a pleasing relief to the Eye and imagination wearied with the survey of the remoter features of this ~~mighty~~ noble prospect. |

Descending the hill, you reach the Village of Urswick, an enchanting picture; the houses, all of the humbler sort, but neat & in good repair, are placed on the Margin of a large clear pool, almost deserving the name of Lake, certainly, the Northern appellation of Tarn. Groves and meadows encircle this water, on whose bosom floats a little schooner-rigged boat, belonging to an amateur of sailing, who resides here. In a meadow gently rising from the Water, stands the Church, a long, neat, whitewashed, unobtrusive building. Bardsea is a hamlet to this parish. From hence the road winds through woods & inclosures rich with corn, the hills, in the bosom of which the Iron ore is found, being on our right and left, to Dalton, once the capital of Furness, when the prosperity of the Monastic Establishment of Furness Abbey extended itself to its dependant and adjoining Town: it is now a long dull village, containing about 1200 inhabitants; the Street rises up a gentle Hill, precipitous on the other side, on the brow of which stands the Church, a neat whitewashed building. Not far from the Church is an ancient, much dilapidated, low, square, tour, where the Abbots of Furness anciently held their temporal courts, and in the lower parts of which offenders were imprisoned. It was also in troublous times, probably, a military post for the protection of the Monks, whose territories and privileges were wide and important. |

2. William Mudge, (1790-1854). Mudge published several works relating to the trigonometrical survey in association with Thomas Colby. See Biographical Index.

Not quite a mile beyond Dalton are the ruins of Furness Abbey: winding along a narrow valley commanded by the Church and Tower, through which a rapid brook directs its course towards the sea, from which Dalton is not more than two miles distant, you ascend a steep brow at the termination of the dell, again to drop into another narrow and wooded glen. Crossing the brook by a bridge, a lane diverging to the left quickly leads you, beneath fine foliage, and by mouldering walls presenting the remains of arches, where in ancient times was one of the gates to the Abbey inclosure, to a cluster of buildings, called the Manor, consisting of two farm houses, with their offices, one of which is the manorial residence of the proprietor, Lord Geo. Cavendish, though never occupied by him, except on occasional visits, & tenanted by the farmer. It is a rambling old Hall, but has a modern and vulgar look amidst the fine Gothic ruins, near which it stands. These are of a dark brown stone, very numerous, and lofty, covering nearly the whole breadth of the narrow valley, where it is at the widest. An ancient wall, in which is still a gateway entire, encircles the whole enclosure of the Abbey, and from various points of view the ruins present themselves most favourably, among fine old trees; the brook precipitates itself thro' the dell, in many places concealed beneath the foundation of the buildings, where it has been overarched. In one spot, where the vault had fallen in, leaving | a large chasm over the water, we observed a fisherman throw his line into the hole with repeated success for trouts. Furness Abbey was founded by Stephen, Earl of Mortagne & Boulogne, afterwards King of England, AD 1127, and was endowed with the Lordship of Furness and many royal privileges. It was peopled from the Monastery of Savigny, in Normandy, & dedicated to St. Mary. In ancient deeds it is styled St. Mayre's of Furness. The monks were of the order of Savigny, whose dress was of grey cloth; but on receiving the rule of St. Bernard, they assumed the white robe of the Cistercians, and such they remained till the dissolution of monasteries. It was in the neighbourhood of Furness Abbey, that the imposter Lambert Simnel landed from ~~Eng~~Ireland, to personate the young Earl of Warwick, Son of the Duke of Clarence, early in the reign of Hen. 7. after having been declared King in Ireland in an age fertile with deceptions of the sort. Near the Abbey, on an eminence commanding an extensive range of country, a beacon was erected to prevent surprise and call in assistance. The ruins cover a considerable space of ground. The round & pointed arches occur in the doors and windows. The fine clustered Gothic & the heavy plain Saxon pillars stand contrasted. The walls shew excellent masonry; are in many places counterarched, & the ruins discover a strong cement. The east window of the Chapel has been noble, and some of the painted glass, which once adorned it, is preserved in the East window of the church at | Bowness. On the outside of this window, forming the termination of an arched festoon, is the head of the founder, & opposite to it, is that of Maud his Queen, both crowned & well executed. Without the building, in the area, near the window, are more than one monumental slab with crosses engraved & inscriptions nearly illegible. Within, in the south wall of the eastern end of the Chapel, are four seats, adorned in the Gothic taste. In these the officiating priest, with his attendants, sat, at intervals, during the solemn service of high mass. In the middle space, where the first barons of Kendal are interred, lies, amid the weeds, which cover the floor, a procumbent stone figure of a man in armour, cross legged. The tower, in the centre of the Chapel, has been supported by four magnificent arches, of which only one remains entire. Of the outer choir little remains, except at the western Extremity, where seems to have been a tower of considerable dimensions, perhaps, the belfry. Of the Transept Aisles, a remarkable deformity appears to have existed in that to the North, without apparent reason or necessity, since the door, which is the principal entrance, is on one side of the window above it; the dimensions of which are very noble. The remains of the Chapter House are ~~very~~ fine: it has been a ~~noble~~ grand room of 60 feet by 45. The vaulted roof, of which, now, no part remains, was supported by six pillars in two rows, at thirteen feet distance | from each other. The entrance or porch to this part of the edifice is still standing; a fine circular arch, beautified with a deep cornice and a portico on each side. Contiguous to these remains are those of a noble apartment, (perhaps, of two, one over the other,) and meant for the refectory and dormitory, in which the Gothic windows & recesses, in great dilapidation, afford a fine subject for the pencil of the artist skilled in the portraiture of architectural antiquities. Other ruins, to which it would be difficult to affix a name indicative of the use, to which the apartments, of which they were a part, were applied, connect this quarter of the structure with that, which is in greatest preservation, but separated from the interior inclosure of the Abbey buildings by an ancient wall, in which is an arch for a gateway. This square structure of considerable size, finely clothed in ivy, & fringed with those plants, which love to grow on time worn walls, consists within of a spacious apartment, supposed to have been the school house of the abbot's tenants; the roof, (and it is the only roof remaining among the ruins,) is a single ribbed arch, which groins from the walls. Such are the ruins of Furness Abbey; they well repay a visit, and the traveller may pass an hour with pleasure in rambling within the venerable inclosure, tracing new groupes of picturesque beauty, as the aged remains cluster among the foliage around. |

Another excursion from Bardsea was to Holker, the seat of Lord Geo. Cavendish, mentioned in my route from Lancaster. Having crossed the first channel, we bent our course to the left, instead of directly across the sands, which brought us to the other side of the park from that, which I had before passed. Regaining the land, we followed an excellent road, across a level plain, once, doubtless, covered by the sea, now extending at the foot of the Cartmel fells, clothed with plantations, heath & fern, and uniting with wooded promontories faced with rock, as well as with the undulating grounds of the park and plantations. Part of this flat is turbary,[3] and the inhabitants of Ulverstone & its vicinity bring from hence their fuel; the rest seems to have been recently broken up for cultivation, & bore heavy crops of oats & other corn. We entered the park near the Village of Holker, and pursuing a gravel road through it, leading from the neat lodge, by which we had access to the grounds, we wound, thro' this lovely spot, under fine trees, to the House. It is an ancient building, doubtless, possessing many comforts, but, tho' spacious, contains no very handsome apartments, nor any costly furniture. To the left of a low Hall, is a small library: in the Hall are the arms of various families connected with the Estate, thro' whom it has descended to the present proprietor, Brother to the late Duke of Devonshire,[4] who with his family were absent from Holker. In the dining & drawing | room are a few fine pictures. A landscape, ascribed to Claude Lorrain, is a very fine production, exhibiting a view of the Tiber, with a temple of ~~the muses,~~ Apollo, the nine muses &c. Another, said to be by Claude, represents the departure out

3. Turbary – a tract of land where peat may be dug for fuel.
4. Lord George Cavendish, (1754-1834). He was the brother-in-law of the notorious Georgiana, Duchess of Devonshire. Lord George was M.P. for Derbyshire and also a strong Fox supporter.

of Egypt: two smaller views deserve notice. There is a fine portrait of St. Francis of Assisi, a very striking picture, in the attitude of prayer. By Rubens there is a large landscape: two fine Church pieces by B. Neess, (the figures by Elshamer; with others by Wouverman, Hobina, Teniers, Swanevelt, Zuccarelli, Ruysdail &c. In the drawing room is a fine bust of Charles Fox, & another of the late Duke of Devonshire. The apartments command very striking & beautiful views. Returning through another part of the Park, we passed the melancholy spot, where, not many years ago, the unfortunate Son of Ld. Geo. Cavendish, a fine and amiable young man, was precipitated in view of the house from his open carriage, and killed on the spot.[5] At a gate on the opposite side of the Park to that, by which we had entered, we regained the sands, and returned to Bardsea.

We spent one morning in a drive to Aldingham & Rampside. The route to the former is through Sea wood the beautiful grove, which overhangs the sea, a little beyond Bardsea, lower down the coast. We then passed thro' the Hamlet of Baycliff, and through rich inclosures wound to Aldingham, the situation of which is very striking. The groupe of buildings | embowered in trees, consists only of the Church, the Vicarage, & the residence of a Gentleman's family, all dressed ground, adorned with luxuriant shrubbery, & perched on the very margin of the beach. The Church, a plain ancient structure, with Saxon remains, rudely fitted up within, is embanked by a strong wall to resist the encroachment of the Sea, which at Spring tides clashes with fury against the Church Yard. Indeed, it is rumoured, that the sea has much gained on the land in this quarter, & that the Church anciently stood more inland. The living is valuable, & (I am told,) in the presentation of the Chancellor of the Exchequer: the present incumbent is the Revd. Mr. Stonard, formerly tutor to Col. Lowther,[6] second son of the Earl of Lonsdale. Various townships belong to this parish, thus singularly circumstanced as to the Church, posted at the Verge of the Sea, and with only one contiguous dwelling except that of the Vicar; the distance from Bardsea to Aldingham is about three miles. From thence to the point, on which Rampside is situate, is reckoned a distance of six miles along the sands, which way we followed. The coast gradually declines in height, loses the wooded dress of the part, we had left, and is truly uninteresting. As ~~you~~ we advanced, the ruins of Piel Castle, with one or two vessels lying at anchor beneath them were in view; behind them the long, flat island of Walney stretched from N.W. to S.E. & in front of it we observed the smaller isles, of | which the principal are Foulney and Barrow. Walney is a fertile district, the farmers having great advantages from using Seaweed as manure. In Barrow, is the seat of Mr. Michaelson. These islands forming an outpost as it were, protecting the southern shores of Furness from the waves of the Irish Sea, are accessible at low tide, excepting Foudry, on which Piel Castle is placed. As for Rampside, a more cheerless spot cannot be found. It consists of a row of Cottages facing the South East, without Timber to shelter them, ~~exce~~ or one interesting feature besides the Sea. Here, however, some few persons resort for sea bathing, being accommodated at a small public House; a larger is no longer kept open, probably, from lack of custom. One tenement is dignified by the name of Rampside Hall, its distinction is a row of 12 chimneys, side by side, on the ridge of the roof. We returned to Bardsea, well satisfied, that we had chosen ~~Bardsea~~ it in preference to Rampside.

5. William Cavendish, (1783-1812).
6. Henry Cecil Lowther, (1790-1867).

It remains only to close the narrative of our excursions in this part of Furness, by naming the delightful walks in Mr. Braddyl's park & grounds at Conishead Priory. Three principal objects attract attention, a modern ruin on a beautiful knowl above the house surrounded with wood, & commanding a fine view; a Hermitage in the woods, fitted up with painted glass; & a Monumental Edifice on an eminence in the park of Bardsea Hall, from which the bay is beheld to great advantage. The walks in the woods and grounds are | charming. The House is spacious & ancient, but in no respect remarkable; it contains some portraits, among others, of the Prince Regent & Duke of York, and some specimens of Major Braddyl's skill in painting.[7] To the library belongs a Manuscript of St. Augustine's Letters &c. formerly the property of the Monks of Conishead Priory, in excellent preservation, which I saw at the Stationer's at Ulverstone, Soulby's, whose skill in book binding deserves to be named.

At a little distance from Ulverstone on the road to Bardsea, one of the oldest and humblest cottages was pointed out to me as the birth place of Mr. Barrow, the Undersecretary of the Admiralty, whose publications recording the visit he made to China in the suite of Lord Macartney, to the Cape of Good Hope, to Cochinchina, & his life of Lord Macartney, have been very generally read and approved.[8] His aged mother resided here to the end of her life.

Not having any botanical work with me, I was unable to make any useful remarks on the Flora of Furness: one plant I noticed on the coast in flower, the Chelidonium glaucium, the sea green leaves of which beautifully contrast with its yellow petals. |

Monday Sep. 8.

A beautiful day; the atmosphere being rather dense was not particularly favourable for beholding distant and extensive views, yet by no means unsuitable for near groupes. We left Bardsea on our tour to the Lakes. Our first object was Coniston Lake in Lancashire, and in that district termed High Furness. The distance from Ulverstone to the foot of the Lake at Lowick Bridge is 8 miles, consequently from Bardsea 11. Passing thro' Ulverstone we ascended by the School House adjacent to the Town, where the National School is taught. To the left is a wooded valley among the hills. Through this the road to Broughton, a small market town in High Furness, passes. Broughton is situated at the head of Duddon sands, so called from a river of that name, which, dividing Lancashire from Cumberland, there flows into an arm of the sea. As we advanced, a huge hill rose above us to the right, recently planted with larch and Scotch firs, which clothed the steep beautifully, and among which the furze beamed in full blossom and rich fragrance. For some distance as we proceeded the ground was undulating, but on the whole we continued to ascend. On the right, between receding hills, we caught a view of the head of the bay of Ulverstone near Penny Bridge. The fields, through which we passed, were chiefly cultivated with oats, barley, and potatoes: but the grain far from ripe. | The vale to the left was divided by hanging inclosures and scattered farms, half way up the mountains sides, the various heads of which are covered with heath & brown vegetation. About three miles from Ulverstone, near a farm house on the left at

7. Wilson Braddyll, (1756-1818). Braddyll was a friend of the Prince of Wales, which goes some way to explain the portrait.
8. John Barrow, (1764-1848). *Travels in China.* (1804); *Travels into the Interior of South Africa.* (1806); *The Life of Lord Macartney.* (1807); *The Life of Lord Anson.* (1839) and *The Life of Lord Howe.* (1838). Barrow was created a baronet by Robert Peel in 1835.

the brow of the hill, we had the first distant view of the lake, finely intersected with high peninsulas. To the N.E. ~~the lake~~ it seems to wind round the feet of the mountains. The whole range of Coniston fells is now in sight, and under them a lower sweep of dark rocks frown over the chrystal surface of the Lake. About three miles beyond we passed to the left Lowick Hall, a retired & ancient mansion, once the residence of a family of the same name. Behind this a dismal scene of barrenness presents itself; clustered grey rocky mountains, variegated with some few stripes of heath. A little beyond, we passed Lowick Chapel, one of the humblest edifices for prayer, but commanding from the area, in which it stands, a magnificent view of Coniston Fells, & the mountains round the lake, though not the lake itself. Lowick is a Chapelry to Ulverstone, as are Blawith, Torver & Coniston, villages situate on the Western Bank of Coniston Water. Adjoining the Chapel yard is a School as humble as the Chapel itself; the business of instruction was going on within, some fine tall country boys were loitering round. When I asked if the <u>Clergyman</u> was Master, my question was not understood; when I varied my terms & enquired, if the <u>Parson</u> | taught School, I was directly answered in the affirmative, and that he lived in a contiguous house, a mean abode and divested of comforts, though placed in a beautiful country. A little beyond is Lowick Bridge, and a humble public House near it, from which the sounds of rude & boisterous merriment issued, and deterred us from entering. We strolled to the Chapel & enjoyed the prospects, it presented, while the Horses baited for an hour.

Close to Lowick we crossed the river Crake, which bears the waters of Coniston Lake into the Ulverstone Bay at Penny Bridge. It is a rapid, clear stream, falling in a cascade just above Lowick Bridge, and gliding down a beautiful valley, which branches off to the right, the Hills on the northern side being richly clothed with wood. Fine oak Coppices climb the mountain sides on the ~~Western~~ Eastern border of the lake, and are very valuable both for bark & charcoal. Hence the scenery often suffers a temporary injury, and the banks are periodically, though never all at the same time, denuded of the rich brush wood, which fringes the summits, overhanging the lake. Another article of export is constantly met with on the road side, or in carts descending to the sea coast, having been first brought in boats down the lake from quarries in the mountains at the farther extremity; this is slate, of an | excellent quality, and much sought for. As we advanced ~~along~~ towards the eastern border of the Lake, along which the road is formed, the Crake glided through meadows on our left hand, beyond which the Whitewashed Chapel and scattered cottages of Blawith appeared to advantage. Having passed an Iron forge, & ascended one of those undulating swells, over which the road leads, & which are so favourable for displaying the lovely features of the scene, we reached ~~at~~ the little hamlet of Nibthwaite, where, to use an expression of the Poet Gray in his tour to the Lakes, an expression applicable to all the Villages & most of the Towns in the district, the Houses seemed as if dancing the Hays. Convenience seemed as much disregarded as symmetry or regularity: the angles of the different cottages were combining in every possible direction; rocks, grey like the houses, & as large as most of them, intervened between next door neighbours, and gave a grotesque appearance to the whole. Lime seemed carefully avoided in the structure, and the side walls piled up of a ruder, greyer slate than the covering, which seldom served as roof to more than one story. At Nibthwaite we reached the Southern extremity of the Lake. Here it is narrowed by rocky prominences from both sides; forming between their curvatures a variety of pretty bays. The whole length of the lake is about six miles, and the greatest breadth about three quarters of a mile. The greatest depth, by report, exceeds | not forty fathoms. A little higher the broadest part commences, and stretches, with small curvatures, to Waterhead. The shores are frequently indented, and one picturesque bay opens after another in a variety of forms. A little beyond Nibthwaite is a grand prospect of the charming expanse. From the rock on the left of the road, you have a general prospect of the lake upwards. Two promontories project far into the water; the broadest is finely terminated by steep rocks; and both are insulated when the lake is high. Upwards, over a fine sheet of water, the lake is again intersected by a far-projecting promontory, which swells into two eminences; between them the lake is again caught, with some white houses at the foot of the mountains. More to the right, over a fourth headland, you catch another view of the lake, bending to the N.E. The noble scenery improves as you proceed along the banks. In some places bold rocks conceal the lake entirely: in other places abrupt openings shew the lake anew, and there, when calm, as when we passed, its limpid surface, shining like a crystal mirror, reflects the azure sky or its dappled clouds, in the finest mixture of nature's clair-obscure.[9] On the Western side the shore is more variegated with small inclosures, scattered cots, groves & meadows. The next point, where we left the Carriage to view more in detail the glorious prospects, which invited our admiration, was opposite to the second peninsula as we ascended the Eastern side of the Lake. The oak coppice on | this promontory had been lately felled, and a solitary workman, rude in attire and begrimed in his smoky occupation, was busy in collecting the small branches, and disposing them in a large circle to be burnt into charcoal. Several piles had already been arranged with much nicety for this purpose; others had been burnt out and left a black circle behind. A little farther we found the charcoal burner's hut: no American wigwam was ever more rude: a cone constructed of branches, covered with thick sods of earth, a large stone being placed at the summit to resist the wind, & a low aperture being left for entrance at one side, was all the habitation: a fire place in the centre, over which a kettle was suspended; on one side rude and scanty domestic utensils, on the other a couch of fern strewed with rugs & old garments; such was the interior of the abode occupied, perhaps, for many days in succession, by the rude tenant of the woods; yet he could not emerge from his den without a most ravishing display of the sublime & beautiful. The rocky eminence, which forms the promontory affords a general view of the lake both ways. To the South, a sweet bay is formed between the horns of two peninsulas, and beyond that a fine sheet of water appears, terminated by the promontories, which form the straits, through which the lake has its outlet. From thence the shores are beautifully diversified by a number | of green eminences crowned with wood; & sequestered cottages interspersed among them, half concealed by yew trees, and above them a wave of rocky spiral mountains, dressed in brown vegetation, form the most romantic scenes. Behind this & a wooded eminence, a green hill cut into inclosures to the very top, in some parts patched with rock & little groves, has a beautiful appearance. Behind this a barren bleak mountain frowns in sullen majesty, and down his furrowed side the Black Beck of Torver, one of the feeders of the lake, rolls its

9. Clair-obscure. A term used in the eighteenth century. It was the French equivalent of the Italian 'chiaroscuro', meaning a style of painting in which only light and shade are represented; black and white. It also was used as an expression for describing the disposition of light and shade, or brighter and darker masses in a picture; an effect or contrast of light and shade in a picture or in nature.

fretted torrent. The village of Torver lies at the foot of the mountain. Just at your feet lies the oblong rocky isle of Piel; near it the dark points of half immersed rocks just shew themselves by turns. This is, perhaps, the finest picture of the lake, and, where it is smooth, the whole is seen reflected in the shining surface of the watery mirror. On the western side steep rocks form the shore. The Eastern side is much embayed. The higher extremity of the lake is here in view, yet it seems to wind both ways behind the opposite promontories. The range of naked rocks, which cross the head of the Lake, now appear awful from their sable hue, & behind them an immense mass of mountains has a most stupendous appearance, &, as it seems, inaccessible height. Returning from this point to that spot, where we had left our carriage, a succession of pretty bays opened upon us, as we advanced: the banks | became more wooded, & more cultivation appeared. On the western margin stands the lady of the lake, Coniston Hall, concealed in a grove of tall trees, and, above it, the village of the same name. The hall has only changed masters twice since the conquest, and has belonged to the family of Fleming, to whom it now appertains, most of the time. Behind the village of Coniston, down the barren sides of the loftiest mountain, a cataract is precipitated, issuing from its inner recesses. On the bosom of the lake a skiff with sails was gliding along, forming an interesting addition to the view. Besides the pleasing groupes of white cottages among the fields on the opposite side of the lake, two very charming villas attracted our notice on the Eastern side. The first of these, the property of M. North, and on sale, is, however, not so enviable a spot, as the second, belonging to Col. Smith, whose lot it has been to reside in places remarkable for picturesque beauty, as Piercefield on the banks of the Wye was once his abode. His present residence is charming, & I have since been told, that the views from his grounds, to which strangers are admitted without interruption, are peculiarly grand and striking. I cannot omit to mention, that this Gentleman was Father, and this place the dwelling, of the late lamented Miss Smith, so well known by her amiable character, her accomplishments, and her learning. The remains of this regretted lady were interred at Hawkshead, in which parish her Father's residence is situate. More than one sympathetic traveller will make a pilgrimage to Miss Smith's grave, and involuntarily acknowledge, that the scenery in | the midst of which her mortal remains are deposited, harmonizes with her pure and elegant mind.

To fair Fidele's grassy tomb
~~Each~~ Soft maids and village hinds shall bring
Each opening flowret's earliest bloom,
And rifle all the sweets of spring.

Having ascended to a considerable height above the lake, before we reached Col. Smith's villa, where we descended again to the margin, at its head, we soon arrived at the Waterhead Inn, one of the neatest and most comfortable, which I know, and there halted for the rest of the Evening and the night. The distance from Lowick Bridge is about 9 miles. Our Inn is placed on the very edge of the Lake, in a little circle of meadows, surrounded with lofty mountains; on one side the summits are bare, the sides rocky & grey, on the other, fine young woods creep up the strong precipices, and soften the rugged features of the scene. In front of this grand amphitheatre of mountains, a beautiful knoll is surmounted by the elegant Villa of M. Knott Esqr. who has considerable property in this neighbourhood: his house must command

84. Windermere, Water Head.

a delightful prospect of the lake. Two fine trees overhang the little Inn, beneath the foliage of which, as from the cabin of a vessel, a superb water scene is displayed; boats are moored at a little distance; the boat house, however, is in a bad taste of mock Gothic: the road before the windows | winds round the extremity of the lake to Broughton by Coniston, another road to Hawkshead diverges at the Inn to climb the mountains behind M^r. Knott's house.

Immediately on our arrival the Host enquired of us, whether we wished any Char for dinner: a luxurious fish caught in this lake & Windermere. On our replying in the affirmative he conducted us to a trunk formed in a little rill in an adjacent meadow. Here mine host keeps his store under lock & key & with a rude net, soon brought to view a number of fine fish from half a pound to a pound in weight. It is a beautiful fish; its vivid colours, (a peculiar tinge of red bordering on purple,) glittered in the Sun. One shilling is charged for each fish added to the usual dinner; as the value of them for potting is considerable, they do not enter into the customary bill of fare. At Windermere, as also on Coniston Water formerly, these fish were only caught in the Winter Season by nets, but within two or three years the fishermen have learnt the art of trolling for them with very long lines baited with a minnow. This delicious fish, the flesh of which is of a deeper red than any Salmon, was well known to the Romans. The Scarus is recorded by Horace in his ~~Epistles~~ Epodes 2.50.—

After dinner we took a boat and rowed on the lake till dark. The wind was rising from the South, & as the Boatman & myself rowed against it, the waves rippled angrily against

85. Lakes View.

the | head of the skiff. There was, indeed, a considerable bottom swell, as it is called: the water rolling in vaster waves, than could have been expected on a fresh water lake. Virgil's description of the agitated Benacus occurred to my recollection, though the bosom of Coniston water was not so disturbed. A thin veil of mist, almost everywhere transparent, was driving impetuously forward among the cavities and along the barren sides of Coniston Fells: filling the glens to the North of the lake with rolling wreaths, each retiring wave of mist being propelled by another. Yet the summits remained generally visible, the mist hardly ever soared 2577 feet high, for such, on reference to Mudge's Survey, I find the height of the Old Man, as it is called, the highest peak of these fells. From their bosom copper and slate are extracted, down their sides roll Torver Beck & Coniston Beck to feed the lake, at their base lies the sequestered village of Coniston with hedgerows, white Cottages, & residences of a superior order. At the Waterhead amid the windings of a romantic defile of rocks, a dell winds to the interior recesses of the mountains, named Yewdale, which, I am told, in rude wild scenery, well repays the traveller for the fatigue of a ramble. Impelling our boat against the wind and waves as low as Coniston Hall, opposite to it, and in the Centre of the Lake is a delightful view, which we highly admired, in the tints of Evening, as the mist had now dispersed, but which in a | morning must be still more striking. I cannot well imagine any combination of scenery more enchanting than is here represented to the eye, nor do I wonder at those, who assign to Coniston Water the palm of beauty above the other English Lakes: at least, to those, who, like ourselves, visit it before the rest, it appears the most charming, because it first arrests the admiration. We landed near the remains of Coniston Hall on a little quay, formed for the deposit of the blue slate of the mountains, & embowered by ancient trees. Of the Mansion, all, that remains, is a humble dwelling for a tenant, the greater part being converted into barns, stables and outbuildings. The ivy clusters about the ancient circular chimneys, which are characteristic of the domestic architecture of this district, & the whole building presents an interesting groupe for the pencil of the artist. Beyond the Hall we strolled through two or three beautiful meadows towards the Village, which, however, we had not

86. Windermere from near Rigg's Hotel.

time to explore: the winding footpath conducted us thro' a hayfield, where the husbandman was busy in housing his crop, and though the season was late for these labours, his hay seemed abundant, and its fragrance was diffused thro' the dewy atmosphere. On returning to our boat, we found the surface of the lake more calm, the wind had shifted to the N. and we rowed back thro' a gentle ripple. Yet such is the mutability of the Elements, that after we | had regained our apartments in the Inn, we again heard the boisterous waves rolling to the pebbly beach under the influence of the South-wind, which the weather-wise of the Country told us indicated rain, but we were happy the next morning to find them false prophets.

Tuesday Sept. 9.

The morning was delightfully fresh at a little past six o clock, when we prepared for our day's excursion. The silver mist crept along the lake & meadows, in places aspiring to rise the summit, which, clothed in pure æther, appeared above with every outline distinctly marked. It was not as on the preceding evening, when the mist rolled impetuously along, but a silvery calmness now rested over the whole vale. We did not get into the Carriage till we had ascended the steep hill towards Hawkshead, which place is 4 miles distant from Waterhead. A few hundred yards of level road led us by a meadow in front of Mr. Knott's residence, to a groupe of ancient cottages overhung by fir trees, at the foot of the hill, & most strikingly picturesque. Behind, the plantations of the gentleman just named fill the hollow beneath the precipitous crags, which encircle this extremity of the valley, and through these plantations we slowly ascended for, I should suppose, a mile & half. The road has been recently much improved, and its track in some places diverted to render it less steep. As we approached the summit, & looked back on the valley at our feet, we had delightful | prospects over the lake. We surveyed the valley & expanse of water as far down as Coniston Hall on the one side & below Fent Lodge, Col. Smith's seat, on the other; the mist had now nearly deserted the lake, as the influence of the Sun grew stronger, & the limpid surface shewed the reflected landscape in the most accurate manner; each groupe on the Water's Edge had its real portrait, while the massy mountains protruded their bare & jagged summits into the centre of the lake. We had now passed the plantations; the heights, on which we were proceeding were beautifully tinted with the two common species of Erica, & the elegant Parnassia Palustris often peeped forth between the tufts of heath & fern. A little beyond, to the right, a road turns to Ulverstone, by which we should have come on the preceding day, had we not descended to Waterhead, & still a little farther to the left a road winds along the side of the mountains, descending to Ambleside at the head of Windermere. Here we had the first view of this grand lake, looking over the valley of Hawkshead, & the high range of hills, which separates it from Windermere; this sufficiently shews the height of the eminence, on which we were. From this point we rapidly descended towards Hawkshead, down steep hills, & narrow winding road: the hedges on either side just allowing us to remark a rich succession of meadow and corn land, interspersed with Coppices | and dotted with white washed farms & Cottages. The northern barrier is formed by gigantic rocky mountains, stretching from the head of Windermere ~~in each~~ East & West, and appearing to defy all passage. As we drew nearer to Hawkshead, we noticed successful plantations of larch & fir; when we had reached the foot of the hill we observed a small groupe of ancient cottages embowered in trees, amidst which we thought we discerned the remnant of a Chapel, at least a window, which seemed to belong to some such ecclesiastical Edifice. Near this another road turns northward to Ambleside. Hawkshead, which we now entered, is a neat little town, consisting of white washed houses, disposed in the most grotesque manner, regular only in irregularity. The white, long, Church stands on a knoll at one extremity of the Town, & ^{there} must be a fine view of the lake, which fills the valley, from the Church yard. The Grammar School at Hawkshead is said to be in good repute. The Inn, which we passed, appeared neat. The Town contains nearly 650 Inhabitants. Our road now laid across the valley, a little above the head of Esthwaite Water, to a small hamlet, called Colt-house on the opposite side of the valley from Hawkshead, and in our way we crossed the brook, which feeds the lake, hastening to the beautiful calm expanse about a quarter of a mile to our right. On the left at some distance, surrounded by a belt of plantation, we saw | Belmont, the Seat of — Townley Esq$^{\text{r.}}$ which, though not itself a picturesque object, must command a charming view of the lake & valley. These are accompanied by none of the grand features of Coniston Water; its characteristic is repose; calm, soft, beauty; the water seems to tarry with delight in the bosom of the vale, surrounded by gentle hills, clothed with verdure or cultivation, enriched with groves, & enlivened by neat residences & Villas on each bank. Some of these are of recent construction. The surface of the lake, as we passed along its eastern margin, was smooth as a mirror, & reflected every object, every tint: the Hills at the lower extremity are the boldest in the Environs, being diversified by rocks & wood. Esthwaite Water is 2 miles in length, and half a mile in breadth, intersected by a peninsula from each side jutting far into the lake. Perch, pike, eel, & trout are found in this lake, but no char, although it communicates with Windermere, into the Western side of which a brook bears its waters after a short course from the Southern extremity. Leaving the charming Valley, I have endeavoured to describe, by an eminence, from which we have a delightful view of the scene, we leave, and on which is situated the Hamlet of Sawrey, chiefly consisting of one or two neat residences, the road proceeds thro' lanes over undulating ground to another hamlet, called Farther Sawrey, where a very steep Hill brings | us to the summit of the Eminence, which runs along the Western Shore of Windermere. The view from hence is very striking; a long reach of the noble lake appears at our feet, the Eastern Shore, consisting of a low range of Mountains, stretches on the opposite side, towards the South the Lake winds round a promontory, & on its banks are discerned some beautiful villas with their accompanying dressed ground. But we hastened forwards, as this partial survey of the sublime piece of water, to which we were bending our course, only sharpened our desire of more entire familiarity with its outline, and adornments, than this spot, could afford. We, therefore, quickly descended a hill alarmingly steep by a winding road, through plantations formed by M^r. Curwen, a large proprietor on the banks of Windermere, about 25 years ago. When at the foot of the hill & on the Margin of the lake, a level road led us through a grove to the Ferry House, an Inn, situated on a little peninsula at the narrowest part of Windermere, but where its charming scenery may be seen to the highest advantage. The distance from Hawkshead is four miles.

Our first care at the Ferry House was to procure breakfast, as the morning air had sharpened all our appetites. The Inn seemed very comfortable: no post horses are kept there. Some fine Sycamore trees overhang the Lake in front of the parlours. The house and stables | occupy the point of a peninsula, which stretches into the Lake, backed by the wooded heights, which form its western boundary. Near it grows, I am informed, the yellow poppy, Papaver cambriscum. The views from every window and from the Ferry Point are delightful, but as they do not differ from those, which are beheld from what is called M^r. Curwen's Station, to which we afterwards ascended, I defer mentioning them till the description of that celebrated spot brings me more immediately to the details. The morning continued lovely, though not gaudy; the skiffs passing along and across the lake, the Ferry boat conveying travellers, on foot, horses and carriages to & fro, gave a delightful vivacity to the scene more immediately before us. We were soon ourselves to become passengers across the lake, as the arrangements, which we had made for our tour included the return of our little boy and female attendant from this place to Beck House by Kendal. Four years and a little more

87. Pencil sketch view near Ambleside, by Francis Witts.

do not give the disposition of mind suited for the contemplation of nature's charms, and the charge of a child is rather troublesome on such excursions, as that, which we were now making, however cherished on ordinary occasions. Yet parental solicitude led us not to quit our treasure till we had landed him safe on the point opposite to the Ferry House, from whence he continued his route to Kendal in his Grandmother's Carriage, which returned to meet us in the Evening at Ambleside. The passage is perfectly safe & easy; although | about the year 1634 forty seven persons, returning homewards from a fair at Hawkshead, were overtaken by a Storm, while they were crossing the ferry, and all drowned.

The walk from the Ferry House to M^r. Curwen's station is short & beautiful. Arriving at a gate, admittance was afforded us by an aged female issuing from a neat dwelling within, a porter's lodge, overhung with trees & shrubs, and decorated in front with flowers, especially carnations. Creeping plants, among which we particularly noticed a species of mountain rose, hung on the masses of solid rock, which formed in places the side wall, as it were of the gravel walk, by which we ascended to the Pavillion, & the Arbutus, with other tender shrubs, bore witness to the mildness of the Climate. An intelligent female conducted us to the Edifice situate at a proper height on the side of the Mountain to command a grand view of the lake: there is no architectural merit in this Structure, Gothic without, yet of no real taste. Within are two spacious apartments, saloons; the upper one with numerous windows in the several directions for the fine points of view. Several panes of glass variously stained throw peculiar tints rather curious than pleasing on the landscape: round the Walls are hung Engravings representing various scenes of sublime or picturesque natural beauty in England & foreign countries, but none | perhaps, more striking than the gorgeous prospect which this apartment commands.

The lake at the foot of the mountain is here studded with islands, forming a most picturesque archipelago. The largest, clothed with wood and distinguished by the Villa of M^r. Curwen presents itself in its full length. The ferry point, closing with a wooded island, forms a fine promontory. Just behind this, the mountain, retiring inward, makes a semicircular bay,

88. Rydal Water.

surrounded with a few acres of verdure, sloping upward from the water's edge. Above it the mountain rises abruptly, clothed with foliage. An extent of water of twelve miles in circumference spreads itself to the North, frequently intersected with promontories & spotted with islands: of these Mr. Curwen's comprises 30 acres, and traverses the lake in an oblique line. Another, of an oval form, was once marked out by an oratory, and bears the name of Lady's Holme. Beyond the cluster of islets the glorious sheet of water bears from the Eye towards the North in successive curves, bounded on the west by the continuation of the mountain, on which the building is situated. On the Eastern side the immediate shore is much cultivated: hanging grounds, woods, groves & enclosures all terminate in rocky uplands of various | forms. The lake in some places swells into spacious bays, fringed with trees, the bushy heads of which wave beautifully over the crystal waters. The parsonage house below Bowness is seen sweetly seated under a range of tall firs. Following the same line of shore, above the east ferry point and on the banks of the bay, the Village itself & its white church are seen. Various mountains, various in their outline, as in their names, Bannerig & Orresthead, Troutbeck Park, Hill-Bell, Fairfield and Rydal, form the barrier to the East. To the South of Bowness, and indeed, behind it, the hills are less ~~up~~ abrupt and towering, more tame and sloping. Villas, groves, and meadows vary the margin of the lake. To the South and from the Western shore, at three miles distance, Rawlinson's nab, a high crowned promontory, shoots far into the Lake, and from the opposite shore Storrs, another wooded promontory, stretches far into the Water: this peninsula boasts the fairest Villa on the shores of Windermere; opulence and taste have conspired to decorate a spot eminently favoured by nature: a charming mansion and grounds, with a large Estate here, belong to Col. Bolton, of Liverpool, a merchant well known for his extensive commercial concerns & wealth, who possesses also, a most beautiful Estate & ancient | mansion, yet acquired by purchase, in the West Riding of Yorkshire, Bolton Hall. Over Rawlinson Nab, the lake spreads out in a magnificent sheet of water; & following the winding shore far to the South, it seems lost behind a promontory on the Eastern side. Such is the view from this

89. Derwentwater.

delightful spot: but words can only afford a naked outline, and no description can at all equal the delicious combinations of wood and water, hill & vale, mountain and meadow. I know not whether it would be improved by greater bustle on the lake; probably, the two or three skiffs, and the ponderous ferry boat, traversing here and there the calm expanse, form more agreable accompaniments to the scenery than a fleet of boats with gay streamers, music & the show of busy mirth. Such a scene, however, is annually to be witnessed from this Pavillion, where the Company assemble to view the Regatta or Boat races, which were instituted some years ago by Mr. Curwen on Windermere, as they are not unusual on the other lakes, particularly on Derwent Water. There was a melancholy hour, when once wailing and shrieks must have resounded to the spot where the Pavillion now stands, instead of the buz of voices attuned by cheerfulness, which ascends thither on the | days, when the Regatta is kept. I allude to a fatal day in the year 1634, when forty seven persons, returning homewards from a fair at Hawkshead, were overtaken by a storm, while they were crossing the ferry, and all were drowned.

Returning to the Ferry house from the Station we took a boat to convey us up the lake to Ambleside, intending to deviate to picturesque or striking points as we pursued our little Voyage. An active waterman was our pilot, whom I assisted to ply the oar, and our first direction was towards Harrow, a little farm house opposite to the Ferry house, and situated on a green knoll sloping to the lake. Mr. Curwen's island from this stand appears with much variety of shore, indented and embayed; almost surrounded with islets; adorned with ancient oaks and scattered trees. The lake is caught over the Island; and the village and church of Bowness hang on its banks.

The large Island itself was next visited by us. A winding gravel walk goes entirely round it, and we made the entire circuit. The ground is laid out with taste, in lawn and shrubberies, & many fine trees grow upon it. On the centre of the Island is a mansion of singular form |

90. Windermere from Lowwood Hotel.

being circular, but said to contain numerous apartments and to be an excellent family house. It is at present occupied by one of the Sons of Mr. Curwen, the Proprietor, a married man with a large family. He was represented to us as a very studious person, and to such an one the residence must be peculiarly suitable. All conveniences of life come by boat, and all society must be sought over the waters: the boat House, therefore, which is well filled, is an essential appendage to this almost unique Seat: the Gardens, where Mr. Curwen keeps a horse, are on the Lancashire shore. The family repairs to the Church at Bowness for public worship.

From the South side of the Island you look over a noble extent of water, bounded in front by waves of distant mountains, which rise from the water's edge. The two ferry points form a picturesque Strait; & beyond, Storrs, on the one side & Rawlinson's nab on the other, shoot far into the lake; Berkshire & Crowholme Islands break the line in this noble expanse of water. |

The Journal catalogued as F387 finishes here and is clearly unfinished. Part of the common place book, or rough book that Francis Witts used has survived and is catalogued as F393. In fact, Francis Witts used the back of the sketch book for his notes, demonstrating that he had run out of other writing material. This further demonstrates his methods of working and also provided information for the few days following, 10-14 September 1817.

91. Windermere from near Storrs.

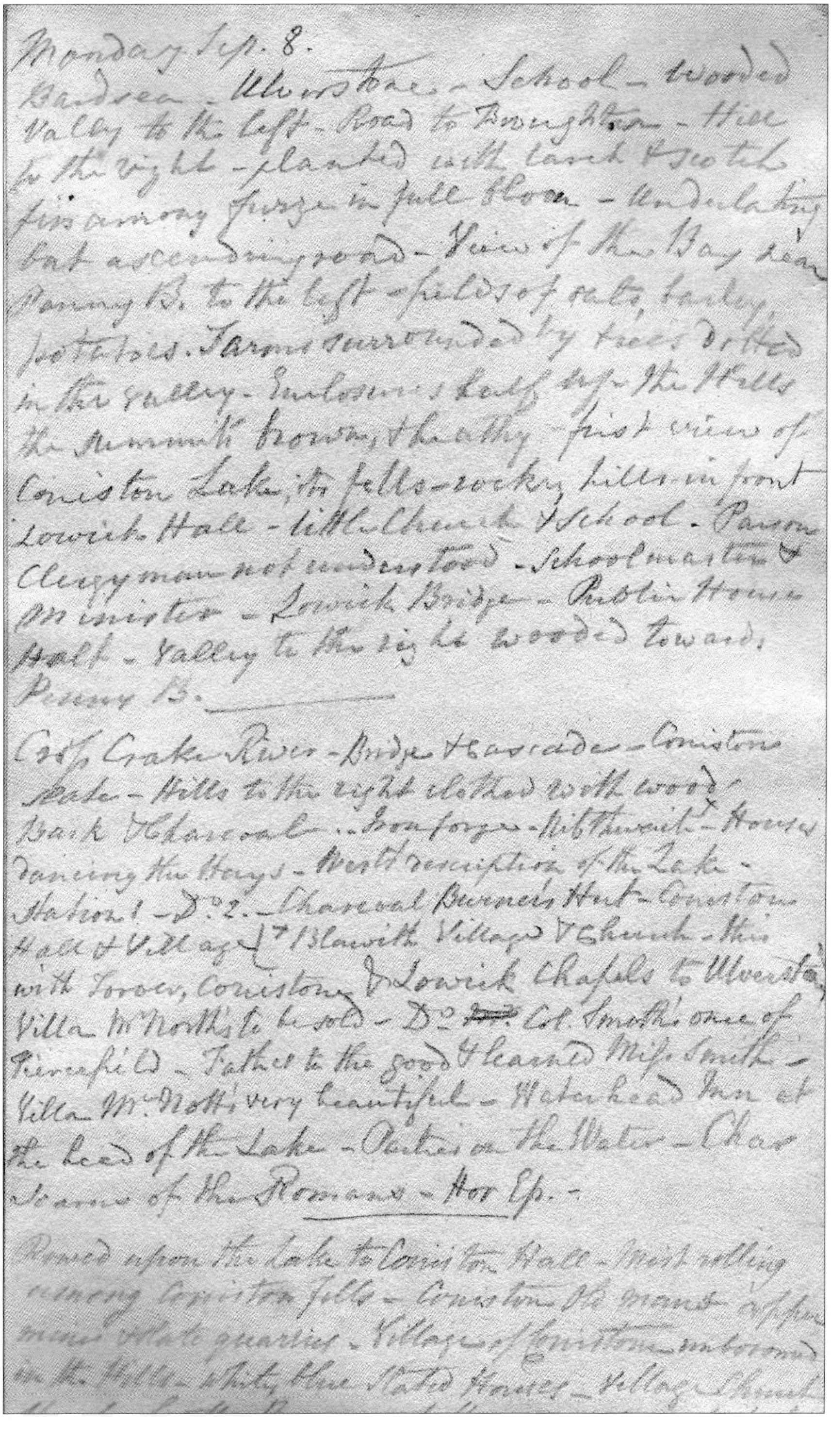
Monday Sep. 8.
Bardsea – Ulverstone – School – Wooded
Valley to the left – Road to Broughton – Hill
to the right – planted with larch & scotch
firs among furze in full bloom – Undulating
but ascending road – View of the Bay near
Penny B. to the left – fields of oats, barley
potatoes. Farms surrounded by trees dotted
in the valley – Enclosures half up the Hills
the summits brown & heathy – first view of
Coniston Lake, its fells – rocky hills in front
Lowick Hall – little Church & School – Parson
Clergyman not understood – Schoolmaster &
Minister – Lowick Bridge – Public House
Hall – Valley to the right wooded towards
Penny B.

Cross Crake River – Bridge & cascade – Coniston
Lake – Hills to the right clothed with wood
Bark & Charcoal – Iron forge – Nibthwaite – Houses
dancing the Hays – West's description of the Lake –
Station 1 – D° 2. – Charcoal Burner's Hut – Coniston
Hall & Village – 1st Blawith Village & Church – this
with Torver, Coniston & Lowick Chapels to Ulverston
Villa Mr North's to be sold – D° Col. Smith's once of
Piercefield – Father to the good & learned Miss Smith –
Villa Mr Knott's very beautiful – Waterhead Inn at
the head of the Lake – Parties on the Water – Char
Scarce of the Romans – Hor Ep. –

Rowed upon the Lake to Coniston Hall – Mist rolling
among Coniston fells – Coniston Old Man – copper
mines & slate quarries – Villages of Coniston embosomed
in the Hills – white, blue slated Houses – Village Church

Witts Family Papers F393.

Martin Lister of the R. Society—had the degree of Doctor of Physic conferred on him by the Univ. of Oxford 1683—(great nephew of Matt Lister Doctor of Phys. of Basil in Germany—born at Thornton in Craven. fellow of Oriel, Retainer to Mary Countess of Pembroke Physician to Q. Anne, Consort of Jas.1 Knighted 1636—President of the Coll. of Physicians in Lond. died at Burwell nr. Louth in Lincolnshire aged 92.—) Martin Lister was declared Doc. of Phys. by virtue of Chancellor's Letters—he was a Practitioner at York—then in Lond. was educated at S$^{t.}$ John's Coll. Camb was of the Royal Society & Fellow of the Coll. of Phys M Lister born of Yorkshire Parents settled in Co Bucks. about 1638. Fellow of S$^{t.}$ Jns. by Royal mandate 1660—by Ch. 2. being a Royalist. Ma. 1662—travelled into France 1668. Settled at York 1670. Lived there many years—Removed to Lond. 1683—AD 1698 attended E. of Portland in his Embassy fm. Wm. 3^{d} to France, 1709 Physician to Q. anne Died 1711–12

Monday Sep. 8.

Bardsea—Ulverstone—School—Wooded vally to the left—Road to Broughtown—Hill to the right—planted with larch & scotch firs among furze in full bloom—Undulating but ascending road—View of the Bay near Penny B. to the left—fields of oats, barley, potatoes. Farms surrounded by trees dotted in the valley—Enclosures half up the Hills the summits brown, & heathy—first view of Coniston Lake, its fells—rocky hills—in front Lowick Hall—little Church & school—Parson Clergyman not understood—Schoolmaster & Minister—Lowick Bridge—Public House Halt—Valley to the right wooded towards Penny B.

Cross Crake River—Bridge & cascade—Coniston slate—Hills to the right clothed with wood—Bark & Charcoal.—Ironforge—Ribthwaite*—Houses dancing the Hays—West's description of the Lake—Station 1—Do. 2.—Charcoal Burner's Hut—Coniston Hall & Village (*Blewith Village & Church—this with Tower, Coniston & Lowick Chapels to

92. Coniston from the wood above Bank Ground.

93. *Wastwater.*

Ulverston) Villa Mr. North's to be sold—Do. Col. Smith's once of Piercefield—Father to the good & learned Miss Smith—Villa Mr. Nott's very beautiful—Waterhead Inn at the head of the Lake—Parties on the Water—Char Scarus of the Romans—Hor Ep.—

Rowed upon the Lake to Coniston Hall—Mist rolling among Coniston fells—Coniston Old man & copper mines & slate quarries—Village of Coniston embosomed in the Hills—whity blue slated Houses—Village Church sharp South Breeze—bottom swell—Depot of slate—Coniston Hall—Seat of the Flemings—in ruins almost—a barn & farm house round chimneys,—ivy—getting in hay—Mist cleared away—wind shifted to a gentle breeze from the R. not able to hoist sail— comparatively calm hills behind Water head—background of grotesque romantic rocks—foreground of rich wooded hills with meadows to the head of the lake.

Coniston Fell. Height—according to Mudge's Trigonometrical Survey 2577 feet.—Black Comb 1919 feet. Ingleborough 2361 ft.—Yewdale

Tuesday Sep 9. Tent Villa

Misty morning—Vapours on the lake hills & fells summit above Waterhead— Groupe of houses—picturesque grey buildings—wooded eminences—backed with rocks tinged with Erica, of two species—Parnussia Palustis—In Knott's house & grounds—Back View of the Lake—Reflection in the Water—real portraiture—much improvemt of the road—Turn to Ulverstone—Do. to Ambleside*—Steep descent—Enclosures of meadow & corn ground—groves—little white farms dotted about—Giant rocky mountains form northern Barrier—successful plantations of Larch & fir—near Hawkshead *(Distant view of Windcomred, over the mountains) groupe of ancient cottages & seeming ruins of a Chapel one Window—Turn to Ambleside—Hawkshead pretty little Town—634 Inhabitants White

Houses—White Ch. Commanding situation of the Church—Houses in & out like a dog at a fair—neat looking Inn—said to be a good school there—Bell Mont Mr. Townley's at the Head of the Lake—fine view down the Valley—soft pastures—cultivated fields—groves & gentle hills—go round head of Esthwaite Lake still as glass—reflecting eving tint—Villas on its banks—background of rocks wooded hills at the foot of the Lake—keep along eastern Shore:—ascend to Catthouse—descend among picturesque enclosures to Sawrey—rises a very precipitous hill—again descend a hill as steep—between woods planted about 25 yr. since by M. Curwen (Ricardi Watson Episcopi Landavensis cineribus sacrum obiit Jul 4th. AD 1816. At. 79) Beautiful winding road to the Ferry House—trees before it—view under the trees to the S.—Berkshire Blared—Storr Hall (thus far in Journal*) Rawlinson's Nab—Breakfast ferry boat. parted from Edward—returned—to Mr. Curwen Pleasure House—approach thro' Gate—Winding road—garden flowers—trailing roses—rocks—arbutus—edifice—two rooms—spacious, three Windows—view from that to R. superb—see West Mr. Carwen Junr. with his Bro. in law in lower apartment—Ryatton—Harrow point—M. Carwen's heard—walked round it.—Islands To Bowness.—Church—Window—Mr. Grieve's House Mr. Bellonyse—Yellow House Mr. Pringle—White House Mr. Taylor.—View from rock above Village—West—M/c Watson's Tomb—Took

Card. Wolsey
Strype—
Herberts Life of H. 8—
Fiddes Proposal for a Life of Card. Wolsey —

94. Vale of Keswick.

95. Grasmere from Red Bank

Boat again—rowed up to head of lake Rayrig—Calgarth—John Wilsons *(lower down Fell Foot Eminence Summer House in memory of Captn. King—Bell Grange Mr. Curwens untenanted—Dove nest—Low Wood—Brathon Hall. Clappersgate—Turnpike Gate. Road to Ambleside—Town like all in Westmorland—old higgledy piggledy places—very sketchy—Salutation Inn—Dinner—Walk to Stockgill farm, one mile up Hill—amid an Oak grove—dashing over rocks down hill—above coming down in one stream, then dividing into two on each side a huge mass of rock crowned with trees—then reuniting in one, & fretting and fuming on thro' the dell*. Then to the Church on an eminence—a view of the lake down the Valley—new Church old Tower—(*View into the hollow valley formed near Rydal with the tinge of the setting sun on the summit of the mountains—Carriage returned from Kendal.

96. Grasmere from Loughrig Fell.

97. Derwentwater.

Wednesday Sept 10—

Gloomy morn—mist on the Mountain Tops—above & hot—Breakfast. Besk of the Company—Exhibition of Lake drawings &c by an artist of the name of Green. Descend to a Valley winding among rocky & wooded hills—By the river Rothay—Still on Turnpikes—Rydal Village—Seat of Sir D. Fleming on the right—on an eminence under Rydal Head embowered with trees—Out of repair & overgrown—Domestic funds—Mount—the abode of the Poet Wordsworh—Old domestic our guide to the Falls—Upper Fall in two descents—amid an oak Grove—walk formed but rude & neglected—two points of view—fine distant view of Windermere fine timber trees—miniature fall below—rude house—bridge &c—Smart visitors in Carriages—Rydal lake—Planed & clear as a mirror—wooded & land—sedge & reeds—reflection of the mountains trees &c Slate quarries or rather mines—Ascend Grasmere Hill—view of G. Valley, Church &c.—Mountains as named in West—drive along the Valley—ascend Dunmail Raise—View backward on the Valley, babbling brook dashing down rocks in pastures to the left—more heard than seen—(Waterfall above Vill. of Grasmere in a recess of the mountains—Height of Grasmere falls 2756 feet—most of these becks & Rydal among the rest form a continued rough Cataract—whom fringed with oak brush wood delicious—not so near Dunmail Raise Hill) Division of Counties—Rude Cairn—View from thence of Leatherwater The mountain streamlets rolling down the gullies—no trees—silvery lines of foam—descent towards Keswick—at the base of Hellvellyn—Wythburn*—public House—Church humble & rude—interior—situation of the Pulpit reading desk & altar—fringe of wood round head of lake—new plantations—Seat at the opposite side of the Lake—rise & lose the lake—previously narrowed so as to admit a bridge being thrown over—widens afterwards with two wooded Islands—in general the width of a fine river.—not a rush to be seen—the bottom rocky—shaving side of Hellvellyn—height 3055 feet—descend to Vale of S$^{t.}$ John's, Thulkeld fell behind—Smallthwaite Bridge—clear raped brook carrying off Leathers water—Fine pyramidal rock covered with wood at foot of the

Lake opposite to a grey silvery rock—Over a rude common—turfs for fuel see West. Ascend to Carth rigg, eminence above Keswick—descend to the Town—Magnificent Birds Eye View of the Valley—Enchanting Ground Skiddaw—Crorthwaite Church—Bassenthwaite Derwent Water Lakes—Royal Oak Inn full Queen's Head Inn—numerous parties—Museums—Exhibition of paintings—Town Hall Allens—Dinner—Walk to the Lake Lodgings Crow Park—Races—Greenwich Hosp. Estates—Lords Derwentwater—Cockshull Hill—Castle Hill—Row on the Lake—Vicar's Isle Gen Peachy See West's Tour-Guide & Boatman—Lord W. Gordon's two houses—Newlands—Buttermere Mary married again to a farmer—Cromack—Wast Water—Ennerdale—Sir Jo. Morehead—Mr. Pocklington—Walk beside the head of the Lake—reedy bugs—

Thursday Sept 12

Gloomy morn—mist on Skiddaw &c Mr. Southey's—Other Houses in same direction Crosthwaite Church & Parsonage. View—River Greta—Manufactures—spinning—Dying—Drive to the head of the Lake Road 13 miles round—in general very bad & hilly Views of the Lake—Mr. Pocklington's at Barrow—waterfall above the house Oak Groves—Barrowside—Lodore—little Water—Waterlath—Cupidity of the Guide—mountain bridge—resume the road—Derwent slowly falling into the lake—swampy fields—head of the lake marshy—hill to the left rock & wood—the bridge of Grange & Ford—ascend the defile of Borrowdale—Castle Crag—Worse road—Slate—Mounts & Mountains—heath—Drizzling rain—mist on the distant mountains—Bowderstone Dimensions—Derwent meandering at the foot of Castle Crag—Valley - Rosthwaite—fields & meadows—trad mines—mountains towards Ravensglass—Vale winds towards Hawkshead See Southey's Don Manuel de Espirella & West—return to Grange*—take the road other side of the Lake—steep narrow & rocky—often scooped out of the side of the Hill—commanding superb views of the Lake—precipitous Hills Lord W. Gordon's woods & place—Valley of Newlands—Mountains & road to Buttermere—Portinscale—Dark Groves—Sir F. Morshead Cottage—other Cottages—Crosthwaite* Church—Home called on the Allens—dined—drove to Bassenthwaite* Lake—under Skiddaw—height 3022—4 miles before we reach the lake—dull & uninteresting much planting—harvest going on—lake winding for four miles—On the West the wooded hills Wythop Brow Mr. Spedding's—mischouses—*loaping Sheep quere Scots or Yorkshire—larch answers well—Wet land near Derwent Water—draining much wanted but hardly practicable

98. Pencil sketch of waterfall, by Francis Witts.

99. *Skiddaw.*

Friday Sep. 12

Dull morn. occasional gleams of sun—mist on the mountains dust flying—Leave Keswick—Greta River Seat on its bank in a grove of oaks—Leting Hill—young Plantations—long ascent—view backward—wooded valley of this Beck to the left mountains enveloped in mist—mountains to the right when up the Hill—the same under which we travelled from Ambleside—Sun endeavouring to break out—Descend & again approach the Greta—cross a Mountain Stream flowing into it—omitted to notice the Druid's Temple mountg. to left begin to clear—cultivated half up—summit bare heath—Vale of St. John's to the right—very interesting—Cross the Greta—bridge narrow—glen beautifully wooded wide valley—Haymaking. To the r. Glendorumakin & Roell Fell further off detached—To the left Saddleback—Frelkeld Vill. & Church—Frelkild Fells. West p 107, 108.—Penrith Coach Gullies crossing the roads—detached neat farms & dwellings Go along a wide cultivated dull treeless vale—leaving Saddleback behind ascend a long slow hill—leaving Mill fell to the right much common ground—furze & reeds.—no heath

100. *Honister Crag.*

*(Mr. Speddings Shepherds reasons for seeing Borrowdale—what God had left unfinished).
*(near Grange very large holly bushes)
new Enclosures under Mill Fell—Oats very green—wide valley back towards Kesw. undulating Ground—desolate lumpy hill to the right—turn to the right between 10 & 11 milestone thro new inclosure—Mill fell still to the right Matterdale winding uninteresting vale enclosures without trees—corn backward leave Mill Fell behind—Village begged Corn or Hay at a little farm—Pretty farm near quoze King of Matterdale—better land—descend in face of grander mountains—Matterdale Ch. monument of a bonesetter's wife—
Posthumous fame SW—Church warden

1686

CS. Mason

flat single monument—good advice—bad rhymes
Remember to keep holy the Lord's day
On it refrain from drinking & from play
Then in Latin
Favoum tuum toto corde quaesivi
Igitur secundum verbum tuum
miserere mei—This is the Epitaph of the bonesetter who died 1727 aged 80 years—Hospitable inhabitants of a neat farm House—Prince of Matterdale Enter Gowbarrow Park by a wide gate—Sweep of Ullswater—Place full—new larch plantations in the park—View to Patterdale Island—Mountains in mist—By W. Scott Esqr.
I climbed the dark brow of the mighty Helvellyn
Lakes and mountains beneath me gleamed wide
Nought was heard but by turns as the Eagle was yelling
And starting around me the echoes replied
On the right sheding Edge the red tarn was bending
The Cachidecam the left verge was descending
One high nameless rock in front was ascending
Which marked the sad spot where the Wanderer died.
Dark green was this spot on the brown heather mountain
Where the pilgrim of nature lay stretched in decay
Like the corpse of an outcast abandoned to weather
Till the mountain wind wasted the tenantless clay
Yet not quite forsaken tho' lonely extended
For faithful in death his mute favourite attended
And chased the wild fox & the raven away.
How long didst thou think that his silence was slumber
When the wind waved his garments how oft didst thou start?
How many long days & long nights did thou number
As he faded before thee the friend of thy heart
And oh! was it meet that no requiem read oer him
No mother to weep & no friend to deplore him
And thou little guardian alone stretched before him
Unhonoured the Pilgrim from life should depart

101. Upper Reach of Ullswater.

When a Prince to the fate of a Peasant has yielded
The Tapestry waves dark in the dim lighted Hall
With Scutcheons of silver the coffin is shielded
And the Pages stand mute by the canoped pall
Thro the hall at dark midnight the torches are gleaming
In the proudly arched Chapel the banners are beaming
For adown the long aisle sacred music is streaming
Lamenting a Chief of the people should fall

Far meeter thy death gentle Lover of nature
To lay down thy life like the meek mountain Lamb
When wildered it drops from some rock high in stature
And draws its last breath by the side of its dam
Far meeter thy death mid the desart lakes lying
Thy obsequies sung by the grey plovers flying
With one faithful friend out to witness thee dying
In the arms of Helvellyn & Cachidecam

Un & une font deux
C'est le nombre heureux
Pour la galanterie
Mais quand une fois
Un & une font trois
C'est la diablerie.

102. Keswick.

(*Wassenthwaite also called Brand Water)
(*Crossthwaite Church has under it Borrowdale, St. John's, Newlands, Thornthwaite, & Wythbury in patronage of Bish. of Carlisle)
*Churches & Alehouse's often built adjoining in the north according to the adage
Wherever God erects a house of prayer
The Devil always builds a Chapel there

Camden calls Helvellyn Lanvellin—Part of Ambleside in Windermere Parish remainder in Grassmere StockGill divides—Ambleside the Ambogluna of the Romans—Chapel in par. of Grasmere Inhabitants nominate the Curate—nomination formerly in Rector of Grassmere often in the N. fallen to the Inhabitants on their augmenting Stipend before too small for candidates, so Rectors could not prevent Troutbeck Park birth place of Judge Wilson, Lady Holm in Windermere had a Chapel on it—Bowness Church patron Sir D Fleming—
Mist thickened to heavy rain—Storm on the Lake waves dashing & foaming—proceed by the Western shore, leaving Gowbarrow Park behind—road good—thro groves of various trees down to the water Edge—beautiful Birches—Alders—oak—Mountain Ash—rocks—retired dells—Place Fell Martindale Fell—Steep brows—bays of the lake View of Patterdale—Church & Meadows—road to Ambleside—Helvellyn—Mr. Askew's sweet place by the Water—another mansion—Patterdale Ch. several pretty little dwellings—Turns in the road—Inn—Bustle Carriages of all sorts & sizes—Postboys Boatmen Gents & Ladies Landlady & Kitchen—Smart Servt. all drenched in rain. no beds—dined in a bedroom—Rain went off—returned by Gowbarrow Park—probably 21 miles from Kesw. to Patterdale—10 to Pooley B. Lyulph's Tower—road along Lake See West—Mr. Marshalls handsom new House very dark 2 miles before we got to Pooley B.—bad road at last—low lumpish Hill—tea refreshing, books inn quiet & neat—Water millocke—fancy Force near Lyulph's Tower—Lyulph a traditionary Chief of Elder times—Tower a modern Erection Chapel at Martindale—

Saturday Sep 13

splendid morn—ascend yew brag—sublime view—Penrith—Carlisle—Lowther Castle—Scotch Hills Dacre Castle & Church—Barton Church Saddleback—Dulemarin—M Trazell's—Villas farms &c on Lake & sides of Hills Mill Fell—Matterdale Heved & Lake a Mirror—seen down to Gowbarrow Park Dunmallet & Roman York—Gradually ascend & wind round Hill—Askham—Hill Ch. & Vicarage—M^r. Leech and Family—Lowther River—Lowther Parsonage—Ch—Park & Castle—Visited the mansion—M^r. Smirke—The Courtyard—Porter's Lodge—Gothic Castle—Vestibule—Hall—Staircase—Hall too small—come too soon on the Staircase—Saloon—Dining Room—plate—Drawing Room not finished—Library—Breakfast room—Lady Lonsdale's Room & Boudoir—Cloisters—Conservatory—Stables—Yard Coach Houses—Marq. Exeter—E. of Westmoreland—Col. & Lady Eleanor Lowther—Terrace—view—fir trees—park—Drive thro' it to Clifton—To Brougham Hall—M^rs. B—Chapel—Castle Ruins—Old friendships—Road to Shap new Village—Plantations—dreary tract of new Enclosures or Common Village & Inn at Shap—

Sunday Sep 14.

Fine morn. Shap Fells for 12 miles—Granites & circle of Stones—fine view of Kent dale—

No further papers survive for 1817 or the beginning of 1818. The next record is a journal catalogued as F385 commencing 30 August 1818. As usual the diaries of Agnes Witts fill in a few of the gaps.

103. Brougham Hall

On 30 October 1817 Agnes left her friends at Calwich and on the following day reached Stanway where she stayed overnight. On 1 November 1817: she reached her sister's house, providing extra evidence that during her periods of absence she rented out her own premises: '. . . the new road through the vale 13 miles extremely good . . . my Sister's house our headquarters, mine being occupied, had converse with my Anne . . .'

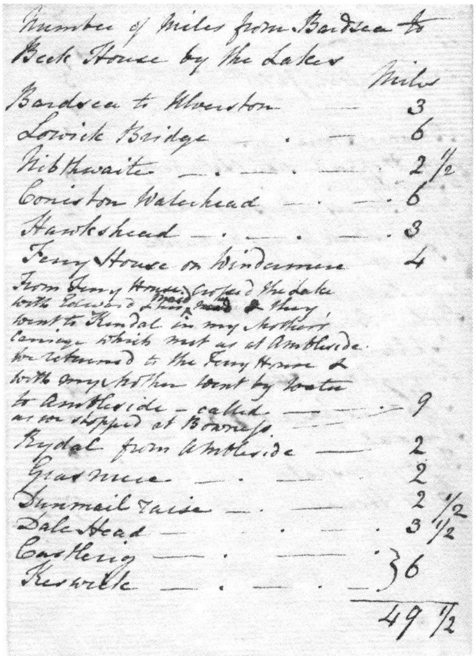
Number of Miles from Bardsea to
Beck House by the Lakes
Miles
Bardsea to Ulverston — 3
Lowick Bridge — 6
Nibthwaite — 2 1/2
Coniston Waterhead — 6
Hawkshead — 3
Ferry House on Windermere 4
From Ferry House crossed the Lake with Edward [illegible] & they went to Kendal in my Mother's Carriage which met us at Ambleside. We returned to the Ferry House & with my Mother went by water to Ambleside — called as we stopped at Bra[illegible] — 9
Rydal from Ambleside — 2
Grasmere — 2
Dunmail raise — 2 1/2
Dale Head — 3 1/2
Castlerig — 6
Keswick —
49 1/2

104. Distance travelled page 1 1817.

For all of December Agnes was extremely ill, the usual complaint of severe gout which left her bedridden and incapable of writing. For two days in April 1818 Lady Lyttelton stayed with her. Whether this was a pleasure or an intrusion is not mentioned in the diaries, but Agnes had mixed feelings about her eccentric sister-in-law. From 25 April until 20 May Agnes stayed with Anne while her house was being decorated and on 4 June she left Cheltenham for Upper Slaughter. In a rare celebration of George's birthday they have a syllabub: 10 June1818: '. . . had a syllabub under a Cow in honor of my Son George's birthday.'

On 26 June Agnes left Slaughter for Stanway where she was a guest with old Lady Elcho. On 1 September she was back at Slaughter, but only Margaret and Edward are there, for Francis had gone on a trip into Yorkshire on business.

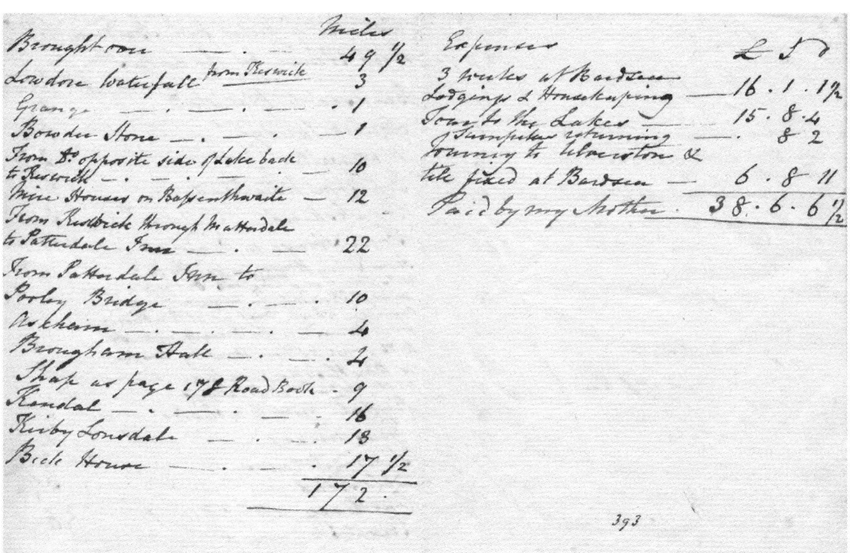
Miles
Brought over — 49 1/2
Lowdore Waterfall from Keswick 3
Grange — 1
Bowder Stone — 1
From D° opposite side of Lake back to Keswick — 10
Mine Houses on Bassenthwaite — 12
From Keswick through Matterdale to Patterdale Inn — 22
From Patterdale Inn to Pooley Bridge — 10
Askham — 4
Brougham Hall — 4
Shap as page 178 Road Book — 9
Kendal — 16
Kirby Lonsdale — 18
Beck House — 17 1/2
172

Expenses £ s d
3 weeks at Bardsea Lodgings & Housekeeping — 16 . 1 . 1 1/2
Tour to the Lakes — 15 . 8 . 4
Turnpikes returning — 8 2
Journey to Ulverston & till fixed at Bardsea — 6 . 8 . 11
Paid by my Mother 38 . 6 . 6 1/2

393

105. Distance travelled pages 2 & 3 1817.

Witts Family Papers F385

Journey into Craven—1818.—

Sunday Aug 30th—

After performing Evening Service at Lower Swell I mounted my horse, having before parted with regret from my dear wife & child. My first Stage was to Halford Bridge in Warwickshire; 16 miles from Upper Slaughter. No incident occurred on the road, to which I was not a stranger. The Spire of Toddenham, beyond Morton in Marsh, to the right is a pleasing object: the Rector, Mr. Malcolm, Brother of Sir John Malcolm, a General well know in India as a brave officer & skilful diplomatist, and able historian, & of Sir Pulteney Malcolm an Admiral recently stationed at St. Helena, is an excellent Clergyman, a man of much information, & pleasant in Society. The Parsonage House at Stretton on the Fosse is a neat abode; the Rector is Mr. Longford, & the Living is in the gift of his family. The Evening was fine, the tints of the setting sun soft & rich: in viewing the Western Horizon I thought on the placid & bright ending of the days of Warren Hastings,[1] who was buried at Daylesford this day, & at | whose funeral I should have attended, had I not been anxious to begin my Northern Journey I reached Halford Bridge Inn about seven o'clock: the well dressed Inhabitants of the village were, (many of them) walking in the Gardens, & on the bowling green of the Inn. Almost all the Corn is got in; I saw but one field of barley out.

Monday Aug 31.—

A delightful morning; bright sun & cool air: the only inconvenience was, that the flies were very busy in the lanes. To Southam; 16 miles of indirect road, but well suited to an Equestrian.

---

1. Warren Hastings (1732-1818). Warren Hastings had been appointed first British Governor General on India in 1773, controlled by a council of four. On relinquishing this position in 1785, he returned with his wife to England, together with a fortune of £80,000. In 1787 Hastings was impeached by the House of Commons for actions he had taken in India as Governor General. The impeachment action was led by Edmund Burke on rather malicious grounds. The case for impeachment was opened in the House of Lords in February 1788, with a hearing lasting thirty-five days. It was then adjourned and resumed in April 1789. The full and extremely complex case lasted 145 days over seven years and was not finally completed until 1795 when the Lords proceeded to debate on their judgment. During the trial numberless testimonials and addresses were made on Hastings' behalf, many by Indian princes. The Lords finally pronounced Hastings innocent of all charges brought against him on 23 April 1795. The cost of Hastings' defence was £70,000 and left him without means of subsistence, but the East India Company came generously to his aid. He received addresses of congratulation on his acquittal from various quarters and was even offered a £2,000 pension per annum by the nawáb of Oudh, which he declined. From his retirement at Daylesford he was occasionally a celebrated guest of the Prince Regent and attended dinners celebrating Wellington's victories, at which of one such dinner he was made the subject of the first toast. Warren Hastings died at Daylesford 22 August 1818 and was buried in Daylesford church. Francis Witts was well acquainted with Hastings and his wife. For fuller details see the Biographical Index.

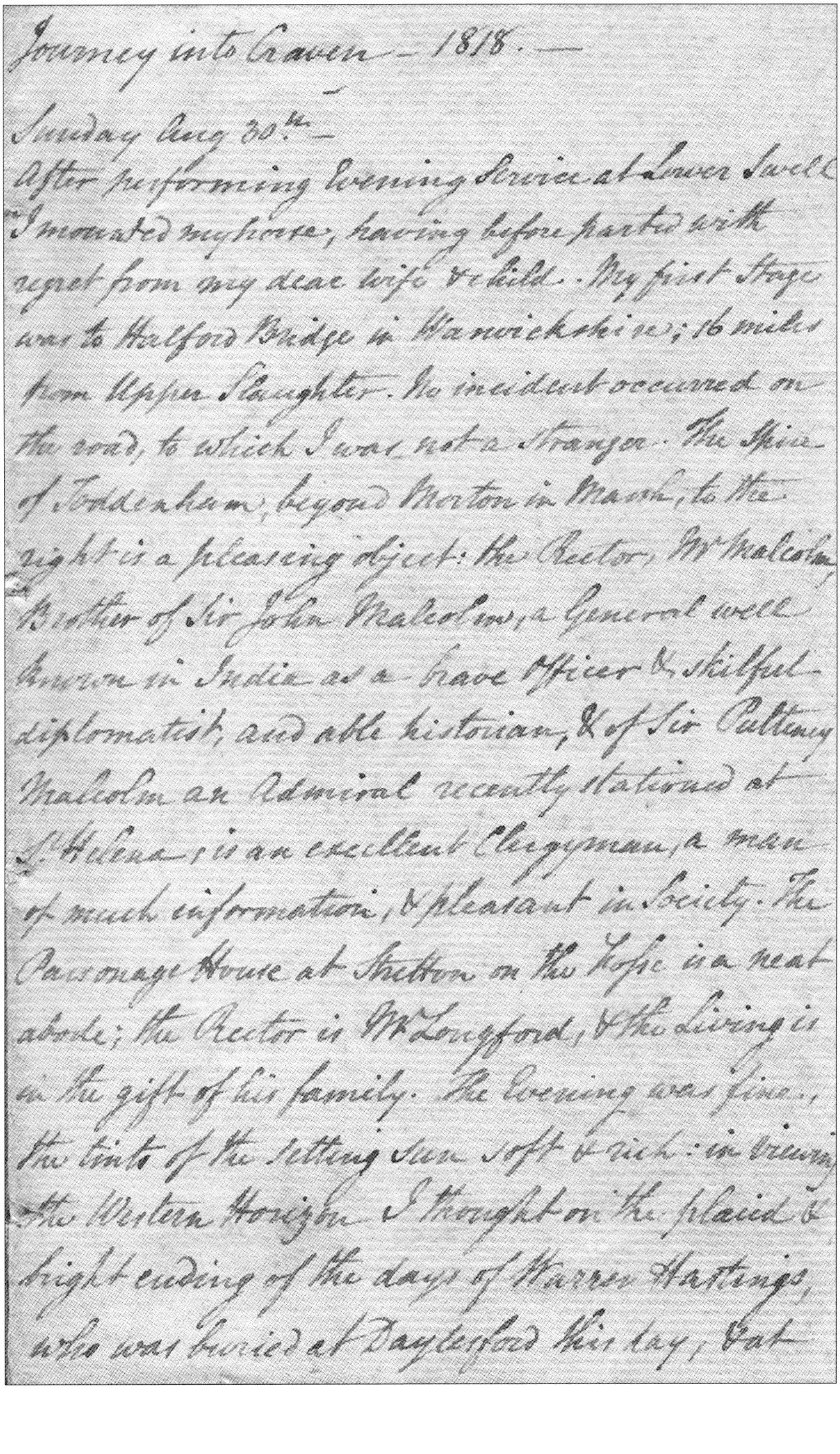
Journey into Craven – 1818. —

Sunday Aug 30th. —

After performing Evening Service at Lower Swell I mounted my horse, having before parted with regret from my dear wife & child. My first Stage was to Halford Bridge in Warwickshire; 16 miles from Upper Slaughter. No incident occurred on the road, to which I was not a stranger. The Spire of Toddenham, beyond Morton in Marsh, to the right is a pleasing object: the Rector, Mr Malcolm, Brother of Sir John Malcolm, a General well known in India as a brave Officer & skilful diplomatist, and able historian, & of Sir Pulteney Malcolm an Admiral recently stationed at St Helena, is an excellent Clergyman, a man of much information, & pleasant in Society. The Parsonage House at Stretton on the Fosse is a neat abode; the Rector is Mr Longford, & the Living is in the gift of his family. The Evening was fine, the tints of the setting sun soft & rich: in viewing the Western Horizon I thought on the placid & bright ending of the days of Warren Hastings, who was buried at Daylesford this day, & at

Soon left the Turnpike road leading to Warwick, & pursued for 10 miles the ancient foss road. It is chiefly a green lane; carried straight up & down hill across the country; sometimes keeping along the sides of the fields; often bordered with fine trees, oak, elm & ash. To the right is seen the long eminence of Edge Hill, at the foot of which is Kineton & the field of strife in the civil wars. Crossed a turnpike road leading from Kineton. To the | left Walton & its woods, the Seat of Sir Chas. Mordaunt, Member for the County. Pass by the plantations & park wall of Compton Verney, the Seat of Lord Willoughby. Here cross a turnpike road, leading from Banbury to Wellesburne & Strutford. No village or town on the line of the Fosse road, which I left, where it meets & crosses the Banbury & Warwick road at a farm house, formerly an inn, called Harwood's House. From thence by a village road to Harbury; a long straggling village; the Church is near the Centre of it, & opposite to it a neat modern house, probably the parsonage. Rather more than a mile from Harbury got into the road to Warwick from Daventry thro' Southam, & speeded to the latter place: the situation of which is advantageous. It is a pretty chearful country town, with a handsome Church, & some spacious houses adapted for Gentlemen's families. The Craven arms seems a good inn; where I breakfasted; having left Halford Bridge about six o'clock I reached Southam about nine |

The harvest was generally housed, except here & there a field of late barley. Lime is used for manure on the arable land. The Country is undulating, & well clothed with wood in coverts & hedgerows. The meadows & pastures much burnt up. Windmills frequent. One near Harwood's House is erected on a circular arcade. The distant tower of St. Mary's Church, Warwick, is a fine object from different points on the Fosse road. Near Southam is a pleasant looking old fashioned house & grounds, called Stoney Thorpe, the Seat of the Fouquiers. Most of the dwellings in this part of the Country are of brick.

From Southam to Rugby, 11 miles. Leaving the former place by the Coventry road, the route to Rugby soon diverges to the right & proceeds thro' a flat uninteresting Country, improving near Rugby. The fields were mostly ~~arab~~ pasture & meadow: more barley was left to cut than I had hitherto seen. The country studded with distant villages, chiefly with Spires. Cross the Warwick & Napton Canal, and near the Bridges a large Limestone Quarry. Pass to the left, very near the road, Lemington Hastings, where is the Seat of | my venerable Octagenarian acquaintance, the Revd. Sir Chas. Wheler. Through Kites Hardwick a little Village; here the road is made of coarse gravel, almost as heavy as sand. Ascend towards Dunchurch, a road village, with a Church & Tower, and large windmill. There cross the Coventry road: the Inn at Dunchurch is spacious. Between Dunchurch & Rugby saw to the left Bilton; the mansion enveloped in groves, not far from the Church on a Knoll. Bilton is classical ground, for here Addison resided after his marriage with Lady Warwick, & here lived his Daughter by her, in retirement and a single life, not unvisited by the affliction of a deranged mind, dying in 1797. An ascent leads to Rugby, & Rugby brought to my mind my two pupils & friends, F. Aston & J. Browne; both were at this great School. The School & large close diversified with lofty Elms, under the shade of which the young men were sauntering in groupes, or seated on benches is at the Entrance to the town on the right. The buildings are of a handsome Style of Architecture, suitable to the æra of the foundation, which was early in the | reign of Elizabeth. Lawrence Sheriff is the founder, who went to London, a poor boy from Rugby, or its vicinity, amassed a fortune & endowed this school. But what is so generally known, & to myself so familiar, it would be idle to detail. The Architect of the School buildings is

Hakewill and they do much credit to his taste & skill. The town is a poor little Country place; the large brick houses are mostly occupied ~~by~~ as boarding Houses for the boys; many of whom were passing in the Streets, when I arrived. The Inn is the Spread Eagle, not so nice as that at Southam. The Church is a spacious building, of which all except the tower seems to have been newly erected in 1814. Walked in the School Close; the Head Master's House forms a part of the buildings. Dr. Wooll has a high character as Superintendent of this great Scholastic Establishment. Baited my horse & ate Sandwiches.—

To Lutterworth, 7 miles. An excellent gravel road leading through a gently undulating Country, diversified with rich foliage. Crossed the sluggish, sedgy Avon: not long afterwards the Oxford & Coventry Canal, & passed through the little village of Brownsover, the Church of which seemed shorn of tower or spire. The road led by the plantations of | Coton, the seat of Mr. Grimes. Beyond, passed through the little village of Cotterbach, which is in Leicestershire. The neat Church with a new Tower stands opposite a comfortable & spacious dwelling, probably, the Parsonage. The Marriotts, I think, are from Cotterbach. The distant view of Lutterworth is pleasing: its venerable tower & church well crown the knoll, on which it stands. Just at its entrance a road diverges to Market Harborough. The town is small, neat, consisting of brick houses, with the appearance of little trade. The Church is an interesting edifice; interesting to the Protestant; for here died Wickliffe, Rector of the Parish, in 1387. He had been presented to the living by Edward 3. A portrait of him is preserved in the Church, which is spacious & well pewed. A portrait representing a person of different mien, but said to be a portrait of Wickliffe, is in the possession of my worthy friend, the Revd. Mr. Hippisley, Rector of Stow. He brought it from his Estate at Lambourn in Berks, & it may be genuine, for Lambourn belonged to John of Gaunt, Duke of Lancaster, the patron & protector of Wickliffe. The Rectory House adjoins the Church & seems a commodious residence, being situate in a pleasure ground. | The living is in the gift of the Crown. The present incumbent is the Revd. Mr. Johnson. He succeeded the Bishop of Gloucester, Dr. Ryder, an amiable & well meaning but injudicious man, whose biass towards a certain class of opinions is too decided. I found good accommodations at the Denbigh Arms.

Tuesday Sept. 1.—

A very heavy shower of rain fell about three o clock in the morning, & it continued raining more of less, sometimes heavily till nine o clock. To the Country the rain would be invaluable; to the sportsman on the first day of partridge shooting I suppose, inconvenient; as to myself I had no disposition to be wet through: & my great coat prevented that. It was an advantage, that the dust was laid ~~out~~. I set out for Leicester, 13 miles, about ½ past six o'clock. The country was level, fertile, well wooded, but uninteresting. Farms dotted about here & there, & Village Spires in all directions. The Church of Dunton to the left of the road seemed detached from the Village. Some Gentlemen's Seats | appeared at a distance. Passed thro' two Villages Blaby & Aylstow; the latter had near its extremity a neat house with grounds; probably, the Parsonage. Crossed a Canal; a bargeman told me, it was the Union, & named Lunnon as at one extremity of its course & Market Harborough at the other. A road from Bosworth came into that, which I was travelling. Stocking looms were at work in most of the Cottages on the side of the road, which was in general good, but unequal. The view of Leicester at about three miles distance was pleasing. It stands on elevated ground: four churches rise from among trees, two with spires, two with towers. At the entrance to the town are the Infirmary & the Lunatic Asylum. Got to the Three Crowns Inn by nine o clock to breakfast.

The rain ceased, & enabled me to walk in the town. The market place is spacious, with many good Shops, & a Town hall is in the centre. Of the two Churches with Spires, one is dedicated to S^t. Martin & the other to S^t. Mary. S^t. Martin's Church is a spacious & handsome building. Adjoining are ancient Almshouses appropriated to 20 old men. S^t. Mary's is of mixed architecture. | I observed much Saxon work round the Chancel windows. Adjoining to this Church is the site of the former castle of Leicester, & within its bounds a spacious room, appropriated to the purposes of the County assizes. Near the Castle remain two gateways in preservation, one larger than the other. Following an old & infirm clergyman, with a distorted foot, whose gown announced that he was about to perform Service, & a bell was tolling, I found him enter into the Chapel of the Hospital of the Holy Trinity, & followed him there. The scene was striking, & would be well pourtrayed by one of those ingenious artists, who so successfully paint the interior of a rustic place of worship. I gazed for a few minutes on the feeble Minister & his aged & infirm con:gation; men & women advanced in years & marked by infirmity, the men in black gowns with badges, ranged in seats in the Chapel & Antechapel, low, gloomy & humble in architecture. I went into the body of the Hospital & saw a nurse, who conducted me to some to the cells, (shall I call them) miserable tenements allotted to the Alms people. There are 90 in all; but all do not in habit the hospital; each pensioner has 2/8 a week & each nurse, whose office is | to wait on the Alms people, clean their apartments and attend them in sickness, had 3/4 ½ a week. The appointment rests, as I was told, with the Corporation. Of the Churches with towers, one is dedicated to All the Saints, the other to S^t. Margaret. I observed some Saxon work over the West door of the former. I entered the latter, which is a spacious & commodious place of worship. The tower is handsome: there is an organ, & ancient carved Stalls in the Chancel. I observed an ancient marble recumbent Statue on a Monument, said to be of a Bishop Penny. M^r. Burnaby is Vicar, as I was told. The County Gaol has a fine façade on which under a representation offasces, a cap of liberty, (why on a gaol?) fetters &c is the name of the Architect. Bars and bolts decorate the front of the House of Correction of the town. As I passed the Streets, I observed several useful charitable institutions of ancient & recent foundation, Schools, House of Industry &c. The streets are intricate & narrow, no flagged pavement, & good spacious houses are in bad situations. The façade of the Assembly rooms, modern building, attached to an Hotel is handsome. Stocking frames ticked in most houses, particularly in the outskirts of the town, | where the buildings are mean & the ways dirty. Indeed, I saw ducks & pigs in the best parts of the Town. The Rev^d. M^r. Robinson, author of Scripture Characters, a man of great odour among the Evangelical, was, I believe, Rector of S^t. Mary's, & there his Monument is placed by subscription, to which the Bish. Of Gloucester lent his countenance & aid. Leicester is the Ratae or Ragae of the Romans: a Roman Milliary found not far from hence was set up, with a railing round it; which, as I passed on horseback, I could not examine. At the Abbey of Leicester, Card. Wolsey breathed his last AD. 1530. Leicester has a population of nearly 16000 Inhabitants.

From Leicester to Loughborough 11 miles. The weather very close & hot, heavy clouds, threatning rain, but little fell. The road in general very good. A canal at the outskirts of

106. Leicester Abbey.

Leicester, but so many occur in this Country, that it is difficult to recollect the direction, in which they run, & information is often hard to be got at from the stupid persons, whom one accosts on the road side, & whose dialect is often unintelligible. I Pass thro' the Village of Belgrave; a neat little Church, & several good gentlemen's houses mark out this place. Beyond, ascend a hill, but the country in general is level & uninteresting. On the summit of this hill is a handsome Gentleman's Seat. Further on to the right is Wanlip, a Village & Seat of Sir Chas Hudson, whose daughter we know.[2] A tesselated pavement was found here. To the right the Country is a dead level; to the left at some distance rise a chain of hills, forming, as I was told, the district called Charnley Forest. In a hollow, near the road to the left, is Rothley a village, Church & Seat, I believe, of Mr. Babington, late Member for Leicester & now, if I mistake not, Member for the County.[3] Passed through Mount Sorrel a long town, or village, ill built, & ill paved, & poor looking. It is situate under the brow of a long, bare, insulated rock of granite of a reddish colour; one is surprized to see such a mass appear on the surface, & rise to a considerable height in a country so level. A little Chapel is in the middle of the Town, a Chapel of ease, I I apprehend, to an adjacent Village, mother Church. Beyond Mount Sorrel a range of knolls succeed, richly clothed with wood. At the foot of these is the Village of Quorndon, well known in the annals of foxhunting, as once the head quarters of the

2. Charles Thomas Hudson-Palmer, (1771-1827). Hudson adopted the name of Hudson-Palmer in 1805 on the death of his mother. He succeeded to the baronetcy in 1813. His son, George Joseph Palmer was later (1836) married Emily Elizabeth Holford, daughter of George Holford of Westonbirt. The daughter who the Witts' were acquainted with is not known.
3. Thomas Babington, (1758-1837) of Rothley Temple, near Leicester. M.P. for Leicester, 1800-1818.

Leicestershire hounds, & the residence of Hugo Meynell of sporting celebrity.[4] Loughborough is not far beyond Quorndon, where at the Anchor I took a cold dinner. The town is well built, the market place spacious, but the streets intricate & ill paved. I visited the Church, a very handsome structure with a tower at the West end, a nave, one Aisle to the North, two on the South side, very well pewed, with an Organ. In the Chancel on the Monument of a former Rector were the words μηδεις εν έκλληςία θαπιέσθω,[5] an excellent rule, which was followed in the case of this divine, but, though recorded on his tomb, the objectionable practice still continues in the Church. On another tablet I observed an Error in the Inscription, where a certain gentleman is said to have married | a daughter of a Pettiplace of Swinbrook Co. Oxon; it should have been Fettiplace. A communicative Sexton told me, the living was in the gift of the Bish. of Lincoln, & that the present Incumbent is a Dr. Hardy: whose spacious parsonage adjoins the Church Yard: the same informant stated the value at £1800 per Ann.

To Nottingham, 15 miles. The road unequal, in some places good, in others heavy & rough. A threatning Evening, & one hard shower fell, when I was near Nottingham. The Country is more pleasing near Loughborough, than beyond. It improves towards Nottingham. Passed through the Villages of Cotes & Hoton in Leicestershire, & of Rempstone in Notts. At some distance to the left of the latter place is Stanford Hall, a handsome seat. The next village is Corlingstock, or in the pronunciation of the Country Costock. Bunny, a large Village, with a Seat of Lord Rancliffe; in a bad situation, without neatness, or the appearance of good keeping.[6] Part of the | house is an ancient brick structure, harmonizing with an edifice near the road; a school house, no doubt; for over the door I read Disce aut discede. Nemo egrediatur, ignarus Arithmetices, with sundry other Latin notices. Was this school founded by that forefather of Lord Rancliffe, whose theory & practice of wrestling were cast in such high repute, that one of his poetical Encomiasts predicted, that the contests for strength and mastery at Bunny, would one day rival the Olympic games?[7] There is a good deal of wood near Bunny. Bradmore was the next village. Beyond it is Ruddington, near which the road passed, & where there seemed to be some good houses. From hence the road winds round an eminence towards Nottingham, the first view of which is very striking. The town is placed on an amphitheatre of hill at the foot of which flows the Trent, where the Lene unites with it. The bold rock, on which the Castle stands forms the boundary to the left. | The stately tower of St. Mary's church gives a grandeur & elevation to the central part of the mass of buildings. The Village Church of Sneinton on the summit of excavated rocks forms the boundary to the right. The bridge over the Trent has a great many arches, but the stream glides thro' a few only. Canals & all the apparatus of commerce mark the exterior of the

---

4. Hugo Meynell, (1735-1808). Meynell was generally seen as the father of modern fox hunting. He became Master of Fox Hounds for the prestigious Quorn Hunt in 1753 and continued in that role for another forty-seven years. The hunt is named after his home, Quorndon Hall. Meynell pioneered an extended chase at high speeds through open grassland. Borrowed the pioneering breeding techniques of his neighbour Robert Bakewell, Meynell bred a new form of hound with greater pace and stamina and with a better sense of scent.
5. μηδεις εν έκλληςία θαπιέσθω — nobody should be buried in church.
6. George Augustus Henry Anne Parkyns, 2nd Baron Rancliffe, (1785-1850).
7. Sir Thomas Parkyns, (1662-1741). The baronet published a book, entitled *The Inn Play, or the Cornish Hugg Wrestler*, giving full directions how to 'break all holds, and throw most falls mathematically.' The 3rd edition, published in 1727, was sold Humph. Wainwright at Bunny, in Nottinghamshire, and a very quaint and curious little volume in the opinion of Cornelius Brown an historian of Nottinghamshire in 1896.

107. Mrs Siddons

Town, the Streets towards the heart of the Town, are narrow & intricate, & many on a declivity. Through these crowded avenues I made my way just at dusk to the Blackamoor's head Inn, where I was well accommodated.

The sight of a placard announcing, that Miss O'Neille was about to perform the character of Belvidera in Venice Preserved, a treat, which I could not have expected on my Journey, hurried me to the Theatre, & I found the piece already commenced, but the enchantress had not yet trodden the stage.[8] With difficulty I obtained a seat, for the boxes were crowded: the house, more spacious than Country Theatres in general, was | but a poor structure, but genius and feeling atone for many deficiencies. Venice & her state are themes of interest in more ways than one; I can say with Lord Byron.

—Otway, Ratcliff, Schiller, Shakespear's art, Had stamped her image in me—

I believe, the only time, I had seen this interesting Drama represented, was when M[rs.] Siddons performed Belvidera: it was, when I was a boy, at Edinburgh, & though not recollecting to have [ever] read the play with any attention, I recognized the striking passages, as deeply engraved upon my memory. Jaffier was tolerably performed: Pierre still better, and though the meeting on the Rialto took place in an umbrageous grove Pierre declaimed not the less impressively against oligarchical tyranny. I thought, the Gods of the Nottingham theatre applied with a spirit not different from that ascribed to the general tone of their political opinions, the expressions used by the arch-conspirator against the constituted authorities of his city; but, perhaps, the Gallery in any populous place would have done the same. The vehemence & firmness of Pierre, | as contrasted with the indecision of Jaffier, alike actuated by revenge, ruined fortunes, uncontrollable love, and the exquisite fondness & delicacy and feeling of Belvidera, make this drama inexpressibly interesting, and when Miss ONeill personates the devoted wife, what scenic Exhibition can go beyond. The mellow measured tone of sadness in some passages, the bursts of affection in others, the scorn of insulted purity in another, the terrific reality of her delineations of madness terminating in dissolution, leave nothing to wish for. Such, at least, were my feelings, as I withdrew from the theatre, the moment the Tragedy had ceased, without the smallest inclination to see the farce.

Wednesday Sept. 2.—

A lovely morning: bright sun & cool air. Before breakfast I walked over part of the Town. The market place is spacious & the buildings, which surround it, in general, of a respectable

8. Eliza O'Neill, (1791-1872). The play was *Venice Preserved*, by Thomas Otway.

108. Taking Amusement.

order. It is of an irregular figure, nor is ~~le~~ it level: indeed, most of the Town is built on rising ground. A spacious modern Edifice, consisting of Town hall, Market Shambles, Police Office &c. forms one side of the | market place. I pursued my way thro' narrow steep streets, which led me towards the summit of the Castle Hill. The first public building, which I saw in that direction, was the Infirmary, which appeared spacious, and being on an eminence, detached from other buildings, the air must be pure. Not far from the Infirmary is an elegant new Church dedicated, as I was told, to St. James, of the Gothic Order. Still further, I observed an ancient gateway, the only remains, as I suppose, of the Norman Castle, which is said to have been founded by William the Conqueror. The Structure at present occupying the summit of this mighty rock, is a very large & palace like mansion of the Duke of Newcastle, now inhabited by two Gentlemen's families. The Castle recalled to mind Col. Hutchinson & his matchless wife.[9] The impression was stronger on learning, that the eminence directly above the Castle, & now crowned with modern houses, the residence of persons of opulence, was Standard Hill, being the place on which the unfortunate Charles raised the Royal Standard. Proceeding beyond the Castle, and to its foot, I found my- | -self in a spacious enclosure of short turf, forming a bason among sloping banks of sand rock, called the Parks. The view of the bold face of the Castle rock is very interesting; at its feet flows the Trent, and its base is clothed with gardens & plantations. The Park is traversed by various paths, on an eminence to the right I observed a range of barracks. Excavations in the Sand rock once used as dwellings, perhaps, as hermitages, are found in this Park. After breakfast I traversed the Town in other directions. The County Hall is a very handsome structure with a façade of simple architecture to the Street. It was erected, I think, full 30 years ago, the Architect being Monypenny. St. Mary's Church is a noble pile of building, standing boldly on a rock: its architecture of the most striking Gothic,

9. Francis Witts had read the book back in July and August 1807 when he was curate at Urchfont.

particularly as regards the disposition of the Windows. It is a Vicarage. Considerable repairs are now proceeding both within & without; those on the exterior seem now designed with just attention to the original style of the building | former alterations, perhaps, then called improvements, were of the most incongruous description. Witness the Western end, which has been entirely rebuilt in a bastard Grecian Style, and of the same sort, are the Screen separating the outer from the inner Choir, strangely contrasting with the old black oak pews & stalls, the patchwork of the Ceilings and other parts of the building. Galleries have been erected, which, as usual, greatly disfigure the structure, some hide ancient tombs, with sculptured Canopies & recesses, but there seemed little very interesting in sepulchral monuments, though there were many records against the pillars & walls. The noble tower rises from the Centre of the Church, which has a nave transept aisles & chancel. It occurred to me whether, in so populous a place, it would not be feasible, (to promote religion & virtue,) to appropriate the outer choir as a free Church for the lower Classes of the people, at hours distinct from the service in the inner choir. St. Peter's Church, in a low situation, is only | marked by its lofty steeple. It is an old Church. Nottingham is believed by some to have been the Causennis of the Romans. Antiquaries trace its present name to the unsavoury appellation Snottingham. Among its illustrious natives two of later years well demand mention, the learned and democratic Gilbert Wakefield, the amiable but short lived Henry Kirke White. Nottingham contains nearly 30000 inhabitants. The political principles of the Magistrates, and leading persons, who are chiefly dissenters, are much at variance with those of the Government, and such has been the spirit of the Town, that the County Magistrates have been invested with a conjoint authority within its limits with the Justices of the Corporation.

To Mansfield 14 Miles. Ascending the hill from Nottingham, the eye is struck with the humble tenements on each side scooped out of the Sand rock: chimneys are contrived through the roof or solid mass of rock above: and the roof itself covered with | with mold affords a garden to the inhabitant beneath. About a mile from Nottingham below a range of Windmills is the race course, with a large handsome brick stand. The road is broad, carried over undulating ground, the soil thin on a bottom of sand rock. I observed fields, in which the labourers were sowing Turnipseed, as I was told, for the third time this Season. Some Villas are to the right. Day brook is a small village at the foot of an eminence over which the road passes called Red Hill. Here roads branch off towards Newark & Southwell. I was now approaching the limits of Sherwood Forest, the scene of the exploits of Robin Hood & Little John, and the no less familiar encounter of Hen. 2. & the Miller of Mansfield: & I had persuaded myself, I was to pass through a Sylvan tract, rich in foliage if deficient in stately timber. But as I proceeded, the Country grew less fertile & trees less frequent; the enclosures were more recent, & the heath land common. | There are, indeed extensive new plantations, which in a course of years will replace the shorn honours of the district. Larch is lavishly planted & suits the thin sandy soil well. The first belts & masses of wood encircle a large brick house, called Sherwood Hall the seat of H. Cope Esqr. Further on to the left the eye catches some buildings, which are part of Newstead Abbey, the property of lord Byron.[10]

10. George Gordon, 6th Lord Byron, (1788-1824). Byron had sold the ancestral estate of Newstead the previous year, (November 1817) in an attempt to solve his financial difficulties, and so they were not now the property of young wayward literary lord. The estate was some 3,200 acres, and the price obtained from the purchase, Colonel Wildman was £95,000.

They are out of the line of the road; a great part of the Structure is, I believe, in ruins, as that part, of which I caught a peep, seemed to be. I met few persons or carriages on the road; at a distance I saw a groupe of mounted sportsmen, descendants of the lawless forester I will not suppose, but clad in Kendal Green. A hill of some length conducts the Traveller from the higher level of the forest to the valley, in which Mansfield is situate: it seemed a thriving place is in a fertile spot. The Town is very ancient and the Church respectable in appearance. The Cotton Trade appeared to flourish. I took cold meat in what seemed a very comfortable Inn; the Crown, was, I believe, the sign.

My next point was Rotheram, a distance of 22 miles, chiefly a cross road, not much | frequented, and rather sandy. The Afternoon & Evening were fine, till it was dark, when rain & wind came on, as I got near Rotheram, where I arrived at a later hour than I usually reached my Journey's end: before nine o clock. Indeed, I found my horse rather flag. The early part of the road and as far as Pebley Lane, where I gave my horse a feed of corn, was undulating country, through fields, pretty equally divided into arable & pasturage: a fertile, tranquil, but dull country. At Pleasley, a village, about three miles from Mansfield I entered Derbyshire, & crossed a corner of that County. The next village was called by my informer Stony Uffen; it turned out to Stony Houghton. Six miles further is Clown; to the left of the road about half way between these points is Bolsover with its Castle belonging to the Duke of Portland, but not in sight. The Castle was built in 1613, & the Duke of Newcastle, the Lord, entertained Charles 1. & his Queen there in 1633. A fine monument in the Church there of Sir Cavendish, the founder of the Castle, is, I believe, worthy of observation. After Clown comes the village of Knitacre, and beyond on the left is Barlborough Hall, the seat of C. H. | Rhodes Esqr. I was much pleased with this place: the mansion is ancient & castellated; the timber round it fine, & the land good. Separated from it by the Turnpike road is a large body of Water, almost deserving the name of lake, caller Pebley Pool: a very pleasing object. After a short bait at an Inn at Pebley lane, which is about 12 miles from Mansfield, I pursued my course to Rotheram, but as the dusk of Evening soon came on, I could see but little of the Country, except that it was much diversified by hill, & intersected by roads, in following one of which by error I had nearly deviated materially from the proper line. Entering into Yorkshire the road passes over the Chesterfield Canal, & between that & Rotheram goes through two Villages, Aughton & Whiston. I was glad to reach Rotheram, my horse & myself were tired: both found good accommodation & rest at the Crown Inn.—

Thursday Sept. 3.

A very fine day, till towards the close of evening, when very heavy rain fell, after I had reached the end of my day's Journey. Good roads and a fresh horse were wanting to make this day's travelling thoroughly agreeable: As to the former, there was heavy | sand great part of the way, or rough heavy materials, dross from iron works, potteries &c, were used in the repair. In some parts, however, the road was not to be complained of. As to my horse, he began to shew, that he felt the length of the journey, by disinclination to proceed out of a walk or jog trot. I set out before breakfast on a Stage of 12 miles to Barnsley. While my horse was preparing, I walked round the Church Yard: the sacred Edifice is ~~a~~ very spacious, surmounted by a lofty spire, and of the Gothic order, having been built in the Reign of Edward 4. The town consisting of dark coloured stone houses stands on a declivity on the banks of the River Don: the Streets are narrow & irregular. On the opposite side of the river the Village of Masborough, separated only by the bridge, on which I observed an ancient small Chapel of Gothic architecture, is larger than its neighbour, the Town; more populous also. Rotheram I understand to contain more than 3000 Souls. In Leland's times it was noted for its iron works. These are now principally followed in Masborough, were are very extensive forges, and most branches of the business are carried on, on a very large scale, by Messrs. Walker. A larger dissenting Academy is, or was, established at Rotheram. I had some difficulty in getting clear of the Town & its environs; for owing to the want of direction Posts, | I pursued for half a mile a wrong direction, which I was obliged to retrace, but at length found myself, in the high road & open fields. The Country round Rotheram appears fertile & much diversified with rising ground. I ascended a hill with a Villa on its summit, & on the opposite side had a fine view of Wentworth Park the Seat of Lord Fitzwilliam,[11] rising above the village of Greasborough, a populous place, situate close to the Coalpits; this useful mineral was busily conveyed along a rail road & inclined plane, the straight line of which by no means harmonized with the fine ground & foliage beyond. At the village of Greasborough, following the advice given me, I diverted from the turnpike road, & availed myself of the Peer's liberality, who does not object to travellers crossing his beautiful domain. Nor is it a circuitous route, but rather more direct than the main road, which follows the boundaries of the park. After riding through the village of Greasborough I descended into a little wooded valley by an excellent road which soon led me to an outer lodge of the Park. The view within the Gates is very striking, on the right, towering above wood, is seen a magnificent mausoleum, erected by the noble owner to the Memory of the distinguished relation, to whom he is indebted for the Estate, the Marquis of Rockingham.[12] On | the left rising from a mass of wood, which overhangs an extensive piece of water or lake is a Column erected in honour of Admiral Keppel.[13] Nearly in the Centre on very high ground from amidst a mass of foliage a lofty triangular tower shoots towards the sky, from which, as I was informed, most extensive prospects are beheld, the eye even catching York Minster. The whole park & grounds on a gentle elevation are richly clothed with wood. On a fine lawn, which I traversed I noticed some noble cattle, & among them two of East Indian breed, as I judged from the excrescences between their shoulders. A second lodge led me into that part of the park, which more immediately adjoins the mansion. It is a princely erection, with a very long front, well worthy to be the chief residence of an opulent British Peer. Approaching nearly to it, the road winds by one end of the house, through a lawn, crowded, at the time I passed, with deer towards the boundary of the Park, near some spacious stables, the space between which & the house seemed occupied with fine gardens | laid out in good taste. The back front of the Mansion, as seen through trees, appeared to be of red brick, the principal front, was cased, I suppose with stone or stucco. On leaving the precincts of the Park, I passed by a very large & apparently well disposed range of farm buildings, with a noble rick

---

11. William Wentworth Fitzwilliam, 2nd. Earl Fitzwilliam of Norborough, (1748-1833). Fitzwilliam was a strong Whig and a life-long friend of Charles James Fox.
12. Fitzwilliam succeeded to the vast estates of his maternal uncle, Charles Watson-Wentworth, Marquess of Rockingham (the Prime Minister at the time) on his death in July 1782.
13. Augustus Keppel, 1st Viscount Keppel, (1725-1786). Keppel held sea commands during the Seven Years' War and the American War of Independence. During his final years he served as First Lord of the Admiralty.

yard, in which the labourers were busy in thatching the corn ricks. This adjoins the village of Wentworth, which from its neatness & apparent comforts has all the marks of profiting by its vicinity to the mansion of its rich & powerful Lord. About a mile & half beyond the village the road joins that from Sheffield to Barnsley; near Lankersley Park, which is to the left. Still farther, & still to the left, is a prospect of Wentworth Castle & Park situate on a commanding eminence, well backed with wood, the Seat of F. J. Vernon Wentworth Esq$^{r.}$ Many views of this fine place occur along the road for three or four miles. Where a road diverges from the Turnpike road, leading to Wentworth Castle, is an obelisk in a clump of trees. Beyond is the Village of Worsborough, a pleasant rural place embowered in trees with a neat Church, situate on the Edge of a steep hill. | Descending this hill, I passed an old Mansion pleasantly seated, & its foot was deformed, (shall I say?) with a range of Ironworks, as they seemed, enveloped in all the horrors of heat, dirt & smoke. Vast masses of ore melting in huge heaps of ignited ~~cold~~ ^{coal}, exhaling sulphureous vapour, & dimly glaring in the full day light; furnaces vomiting forth lambent flame amid wreaths of black smoke; noise & bustle among the begrimed workmen; all was frightful enough by the broad day; by night it may answer our imagination of Pandemonium. From this point a very steep hill, & very long, leads to the summit called Bank Top, on which formerly stood a good Inn, now converted into a Gentleman's house, an exposed place of abode & in an unfinished state; at least, planting is wanted to give an air of comfort, which is not conveyed by the semblance of a castle, partly in repair, & partly in ruins, which has been studiously given to the house & garden walls. From hence a mile of sandy road on a gentle declivity leads to Barnsley, well termed black Barnsley, built on the side of a hill, apparently a thriving place, at least I judged so from the numerous new buildings in its outskirts. I went to the White Bear: such was | if I mistake not, the sign of the Inn, where I breakfasted, & baited my horse. I made as usual a little tour of the Town, in which I saw nothing attractive, on the contrary, the Church was ordinary in its structure, the streets narrow, ill paved & crooked, & the Houses black & comfortless in their general appearance.

From Barnsley to Wakefield 10 miles. The day continued very fine & warm, the country, diversified with hill & vale, with an abundance of wood was very pleasing, but the road in general very sandy & heavy, which with the sluggishness of my horse rendered the Stage very tedious. A long descent from Barnsley brought me to a small river & canal; the former, the Dearn, the latter the Dearn & Dove Canal. From hence the road ascends, & keeps on very high ground for a considerable distance. Some very useful alterations were in progress on the road, which, though they rather rendered it worse now, will amend it essentially. These alterations occur more particularly near Staincross, & in the vicinity of Woolley Park, the Seat of G. Wentworth Esq$^{r.}$ embosomed in groves, on the left of the | road. There is a considerable descent to New Miller Dam, before arriving at which you see on the right Chevet Hall the Seat of Sir Tho$^{s.}$ Pilkington.[14] The groupe of houses at New Miller Dam is very advantageously situate on the margin of a fine head of water, a pool, or small lake, the margin & banks around which are well planted. This I presume to be a reservoir for come canal. Beyond New Miller Dam & within two miles of Wakefield is the village of Sandall, & near it on a Mount

14. The reference Francis Witts was using was out of date, for Sir Thomas had died back in 1811. The current baronet and owner was Sir William Pilkington, (1775-1850).

the scanty ruins of a Castle. The village is rural & neat, & was the residence & living of the late Dr. Zouch, Prebendary of Durham. Near this place the Duke of York, Father of Edw. 4. was killed in battle, to commemorate which event, his royal Son caused to be erected on the bridge at Wakefield a chapel, still extant, and a very delicate morceau of Gothic architecture. The town of Wakefield appears to advantage as it is approached. The Church with a lofty spire stands in the midst on the highest part of | the Town, which extends upwards from the Calder River, on which it is situate & which is here navigable. I repaired to the White Hare Inn, where I found comfortable accommodations, & spent the night, having arrived too late & my horse being too tired to perform the stage to Bradford.

I took two surveys to the Town. The old Church is a very handsome edifice in the Gothic Style, and pewed in a most excellent manner: the painting above the Altar is a humble production and the monuments though numerous are not remarkable. Several are inscribed to the memory of different branches of the Pilkington Family. Besides this spacious ancient Church is a handsome modern building dedicated to St. John, situate in a remote part of the Town, and contiguous to some new & handsome buildings, the residences it maybe presumed, of the gentry of the place. One Row & three sides of a Square form this new Town, & the Church stands | in the centre of the square. It is a handsome edifice, well fitted up within, & calculated to hold a large congregation. The Altar pieces are indifferent paintings: a series of monuments to different members of one family are large, expensive & not remarkable for taste. The newly erected Sessions House, situate between the old and new part of the Town, is a very elegant modern stone structure after the model of a Grecian Temple. At a distance from the Town, I observed, but did not approach, the Bridewell appropriated to the West riding. Wakefield is also the place where the Register Office for the West Riding is kept. This Establishment is eminently useful, and has long existed to the credit of the District, for which it is the Depository of Deeds. Middlesex alone in England has a similar Office: in Scotland the Deeds for all the Kingdom are registered at Edinbro'. The Office of Registrar is elective; the qualification to vote being a freehold of £100 | per Ann. and at the last two vacancies has been warmly contested: the Emoluments are considerable, and the Office is held by a very respectable Magistrate. Wakefield is on the whole a neat & pleasant country town: some part of it is open and spacious. A company of actors were there, with a celebrated tight rope dancer, but he had not on me the attractive influence of Miss ONeill. Heavy rain coming in drove me to my Inn. I will add the following desultory notes on Wakefield and its vicinity. The Church was built in the R. of Hen. 3. The living is a Vicarage in the Gift of the Dean & Chapter of York. The Bridge over the Calder was built in the R. of Edw. 3. and the Chapel on it was built by Edw. 4. in memory of his Father Richd. D. of York & those of his party, who fell in the battle before the Walls of his Castle at Sandal, when aspiring to the throne in 1460. The river Calder is navigable above Wakefield to Elland near Halifax. The Cloth manufacture is carried on in the Town & neighbourhood, & | a Cloth Hall is appropriated to the Trade in this as in most of the adjoining Towns. The population of Wakefield exceeds 8000 Souls.

Sept. 4. Friday

The early part of the morning was very rainy; but it held up, and I reached Bradford to breakfast between 10 & 11 o clock, though the aspect of the clouds was very threatening. Occasional showers fell during the rest of the day; more rain descending as I advanced towards the Craven Mountains. The road to Bradford is 14 miles of most uninteresting Country; the way black, muddy & rough; collieries, colliers, their carts, engines, & rail roads, objects most adverse to the picturesque, offend the eye incessantly. The Country is populous, but the villages and rows of houses are unprepossessing in appearance, & the appearance of all, men, women & children, rude & forbidding. East & West Ardesley, Tingley, Bruntcliff, Adwalton, (in the dia- | -lect of the Country, Athelton) Wisket Hill & Dudley are the chief places on the road as they occur. There is a long descent into Bradford, which occupies the side of a steep hill, & the valley at its foot, a black mass of buildings, & a place of active commerce. My wearied horse was glad to rest and bait.

I strolled over the Town, which is gloomy with narrow Streets, yet not without good houses. I entered the ancient Church: it is spacious & seems calculated to accommodate a large congregation. The pews, galleries &c were of old black oak. The Exterior contrasted well with a new freestone church in the higher part of the Town, apparently but just finished. My next observation, (for I saw little in the town to note) is that Archb. Sharpe of York was born here in 1644; he died in 1713. A canal form the Leeds and Liverpool navigation comes to Bradford. Its population amounts to almost 8000 Souls. |

To Keighley 9 miles. Soon after leaving Bradford, the Traveller enters Craven; and after the brown & parched pastures of this dry summer my eye was most agreeably refreshed by the beautiful verdure of this favoured district. After ascending a steep & long hill, & descending on the opposite side, the road lies entirely thro' the valley, thro' Cottingley and Bingley, and there is not any where a more interesting & picturesque ride than that from Cottingley Bridge to ~~Skipton &~~ Keighley and thence to Skipton. But as these vallies are familiar to me, I shall here close my hasty journal by adding, that after a ride of 9 miles to Skipton where I slept, I reached Beck House on Saturday Sept. 5—a distance of 16 miles where Mrs. Backhouse received me with her usual affectionate Welcome. |

Route

Upper Slaughter to	Miles
Halford Bridge	17
Southam	16
Rugby	10
Lutterworth	08
Leicester	12
Loughborough	12
Nottingham	15
Mansfield	14
Rotheram	22
Barnsley	12
Wakefield	10
Bradford	14
Keighley	09
Skipton	09
Beck House	16
	196

The next gap in the diaries of Francis Witts lasts until January 1820. In the meantime Agnes provides information as usual.

After a few days with Margaret and Edward at Upper Slaughter, Agnes went on a visiting journey. First she was at Park Gate, Hertfordshire to stay with her friend Elizabeth Hatton, arriving on 10 September and staying there for four weeks. By 10 October she was at Sunbury visiting Mrs. V. Snow. She had been friendly with the Snow family for many years. After three-and-a-half weeks there she was back at Upper Slaughter.

In November Agnes was back in Cheltenham and on the 11th she recorded Margaret being there to 'consult on her health'. As a result of this, Francis took Margaret to Bath. Margaret continued in indifferent health for the remaining thirty-one years of her life.

Agnes was also unwell and beginning to feel frail. Her attacks of gout increased, the worst the following year being in May: 5 June 1819: '. . . incommoded by gout from 9 May until 5 June — attentive nursing of my two servants . . .' 15 June 1819: '. . . I had no visitors but Capn. Phillips to receive his rent . . .'

Most of the summer and autumn Agnes stayed at Upper Slaughter with an occasional visit to Stanway. In August she recorded the commencement of tuition of Frank's new pupil: 15 August 1819: ' . . . Mr. Thos. Saumarez second son of Admiral Sr. James Saumarez, who came to be placed under my Son's tuition . . .'

In January 1820, after a gap of twelve years, Francis Witts took up pen again with the intention to maintain a regular series of diaries.

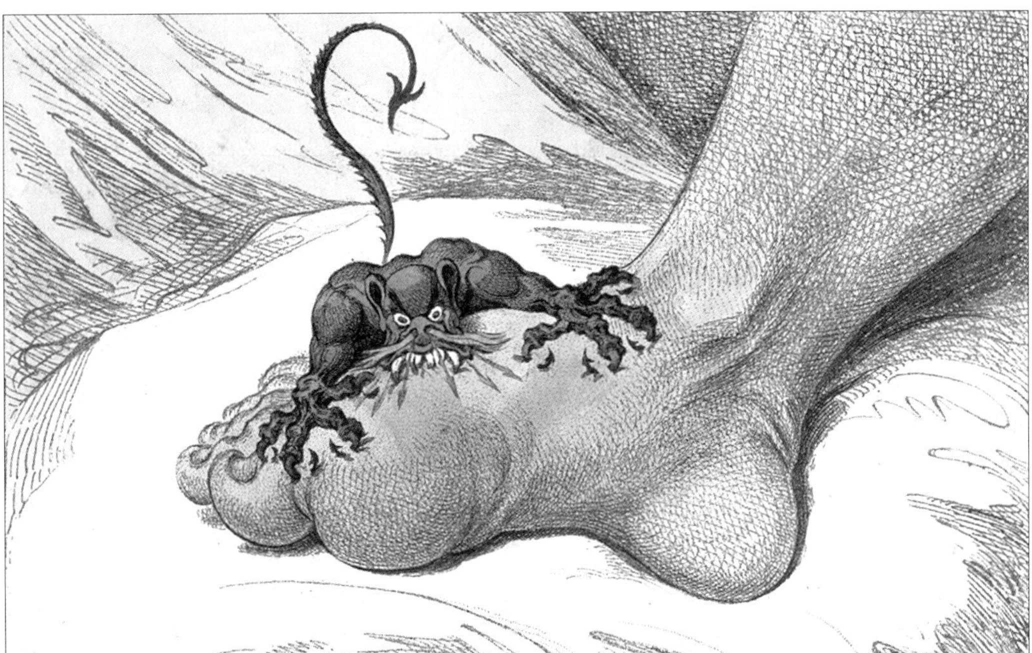

109. James Gillray cartoon on Gout.

Witts Family Papers F308

Diary—1820

Jan 3.

Left Upper Slaughter for Bath in the hope, that another course of the waters may essentially strengthen my dear wife's constitution. Having sent forward my man Servant and horse we travelled post with Edward and a maid. The weather very cold, frost & snow; more of the latter between home & Cirencester and between Petty France and Bath, than between Cirencester and Petty France. The roads very slippery, and though a horse fell in the chaise in the streets of Tetbury, we providentially escaped any accident. We were comfortably accommodated at the Elephant & Castle.

Jan. 4.

Fixed ourselves in our old lodgings, N°. 5 Union Street.

Jan. 5.

My wife put herself again under the medical charge of our old and skilful friend Col. Cooper, whose liberal and gratuitous attentions she had so largely shared last winter. Nearly twenty five years have passed since my first acquaintance with him: bred to physic, and attached to a science, which he thoroughly understands, prosperity, the love

110. The Bath Races.

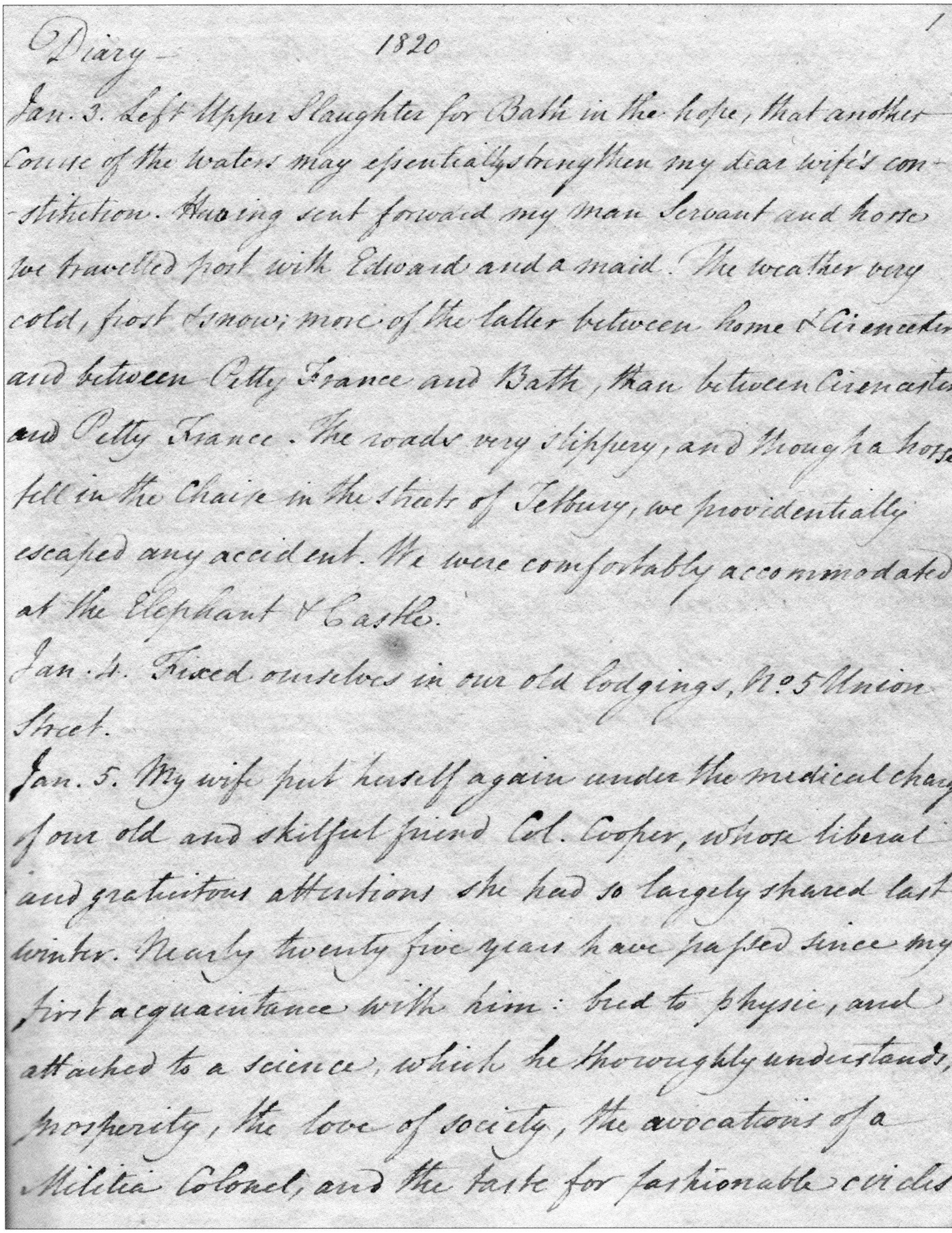

Diary — 1820 1

Jan. 3. Left Upper Slaughter for Bath in the hope, that another course of the waters may essentially strengthen my dear wife's con-stitution. Having sent forward my man servant and horse we travelled post with Edward and a maid. The weather very cold, frost & snow; more of the latter between home & Cirencester and between Petty France and Bath, than between Cirencester and Petty France. The roads very slippery, and though a horse fell in the Chaise in the streets of Tetbury, we providentially escaped any accident. We were comfortably accommodated at the Elephant & Castle.

Jan. 4. Fixed ourselves in our old lodgings, No. 5 Union Street.

Jan. 5. My wife put herself again under the medical charge of our old and skilful friend Col. Cooper, whose liberal and gratuitous attentions she had so largely shared last winter. Nearly twenty five years have passed since my first acquaintance with him: bred to physic, and attached to a science, which he thoroughly understands, prosperity, the love of society, the avocations of a Militia Colonel, and the taste for fashionable circles of society, the avocations of a Militia Colonel,[1] and the taste for fashionable circles |[2] have not diverted his active mind form the pursuit of the healing art, and the result is, that his friends and the poor are widely benefited by his advice.

We spent the Evening at Mrs. Aston's: my old pupil Frederic A. had been with us much in the morning. We had delicious music. Mr. Aston's daughter, Mrs. Watkins, is a most superior private singer: and indulged us with several delightful songs; Italian, Handel's & others. A Mr. Harrington, Grandson of the late learned & musical & good Dr. Harrington of Bath, played on the flute & sang with taste. Naldi, one of the first singers & teachers in England, Mrs. Watkins's old Master, was also there: his Physionomy Italian of the worst order, his skill & powers wonderful. A duet with his daughter, the subject a Music Master and his pupil, is a charming buffa. Madam. Naldi is an interesting girl, and lovely singer; unceasing tuition and practice have produced the perfection of the science, that simplicity & apparent ease, which is truly difficult. Another curious Buffa, mixing trick and mimicry with good music was sung by Naldi, being his own composition; the teaching a Parrot, the subject. |[3] Naldi in conversation spoke with Enthusiasm of the sacred music of his countryman Marcelli, and related this anecdote. Marcelli, a noble Venetian, and devoted to the Musical science, was a most dissipated character, without religion and devoted to pleasure: his friend Justiniani, a noble Venetian also, was remarkably pious, & cultivated poetry with great success. He earnestly endeavoured to instil serious views into his friend's mind, but in vain. When one day, as Marcelli was going to Mass, a stone in the pavement giving way he was engulphed with eminent danger of his life in a vault beneath; his preservation appeared to his warm imagination a signal & almost miraculous intervention of Providence, & his mind was opened to religious impressions. He consulted his friend Justiniani, how he should improve these; his friend suggested to him to employ his musical talent in the service of GOD by setting the Psalms to music, & engaged to adapt a practical translation. Thence originated the sacred strains of this admired master.

Among Mrs. Aston's guests were Mr. Stafford Smith, the friend of Bp's Warburton & Hurd, Rector of Fladbury. |[4] An amiable & cheerful Clergyman of the old School, residing much at Bath; strongly contrasted with Mr. Crook, Rector of the Abbey Church, in other respects said to be a steady useful man, but an insufferable coxcomb. This Gentleman was elected by the Corporation of Bath, with which he was connected by relationship to some of its members in opposition to Mr. Archd. Thomas: the votes were at first equal: on a second election one of Mr. Thomas's friends gave way and turned the scale in favour of Mr. Crook, less of a pillar, indeed, but except for his conceitedness, well esteemed.

Jan. 6.

Dined with our friends the Dolphins: a happy young twelfth day party in the Evening.

In our morning walks met with a groupe surrounding some itinerant musicians; who exhibited a hare trained to dance at the word of command, to fire a pistol, with other eccentricities.

---

1. It was this same Colonel Cooper that Frank dined with in Salisbury back on 14 December 1807. *See* 27 December 1828 and the accompanying footnote relating to Sir John Hutton Cooper (1765-1828).

Jan. 7.

I had my first interview with Adm. Sir James Saumarez,[2] Father of my pupil, who is now with his family at Bath lately arrived from their residence in Guernsey. I found him a man of polite manners, of |[5] a fine erect person, and intelligent countenance. One likes to rest upon the features of a hero: and the exploits of Sir James Saumarez at Aboukir, and elsewhere, in the late long war, entitled him to rank very high in the list of British naval Commanders.

111. Admiral Sir James Saumarez.

In the Evening we went to the Theatre to see Kean in the character of Shylock, and it was truly well performed.[3] The justness of expression without exaggerated effort, the quick alternations from the passion of avarice to that of revenge, so strongly yet naturally marked, the malignant cast of features so well adapted, all disclose the great artist. Yet here and there seemed misconception and a want of study, which I think, I have observed in other characters performed by this admired Actor.

Jan. 9.

At Christ Church in the morning a Son of Archdeacon Daubeny preached on Gal. 6. 15. expounding the Scriptural sense of the words new creature, and laying down the meaning of the terms according to the Church of England in opposition to the new doctrines of Enthusiasts on conversion and non conversion: with a practical application on the commencement of the new year.

At the Abbey Church in the Evening, Mr. Grinfield, Minister |[6] of Laura Chapel, preached on part of Heb. 6. 1. let us go on unto perfection: a new year's Sermon with particular reference to the times, and the infidelity now afloat. Mr. G. with a loud voice and vehement manner, is by some esteemed a good preacher.

Jan. 13.

Old Colonel Barry still retains his accustomed seat by the Pump room fire every morning. This acute old man, who, in times past, was much in the confidence and society of the great and

---

2. James Saumarez, 1st Baron de Saumarez, (1757-1836). James Saumarez had a distinguished career in the Royal Navy. He was Rear Admiral 1801, Vice Admiral 1806, Admiral of the Blue 1814; of the White 1819. He was knighted as a captain of the Royal Marines in 1793, was second in command at the Battle of the Nile (1790), was created a baronet 1801 and obtained a victory over the French and Spanish fleets at Algeciras, 1 July 1801. In 1831 he was created Baron de Saumarez in the island of Guernsey. Thomas was a younger son and does not seem to have been a very diligent pupil much to the frustration of Francis Witts.
3. Antinomians believed that Christians were freed from the moral law by virtue of grace as set forth in the gospel.

112. Bath Abbey Church.

113. Sir Richard Colt Hoare.

able men of the day, as Lord Lansdown & others, is still devoted to society, and lives in public. His shrewd wit, quaint manner of expressing himself on subjects the most interesting with keen discernment and without prolixity, his still powerful memory and rich store of anecdote, bringing forth from his treasure things old and new, make him a pleasing companion even to those, who disapprove his democratical principles, which he does not needlessly obtrude. Mr. Hoare the Banker of Lombard Street, a very intelligent and cheerful man is one of the little circle round Col. Barry's chair before breakfast.—I often enjoy mixing in the conversation.

Jan. 16.

Mr. Grinfield at Laura Chapel preached an excellent discourse on Matt. 21. 28–31, expounding the Parable. |7 He forcibly pointed out the Antinomian error of those Enthusiasts, who, perverting Scripture, represent, that the greatest sinner makes the best saint.[4] He depicted in lively colours the modern Pharisee, both him who uses hypocrisy as a cloak of sin; and him, who narrowing the field of religion within his own prejudices, speaks censoriously of those, who do not come within his arbitrary pale, nor profess the shibboleth of his party.

4. Edmund Kean, (1787-1833). Kean made his first stage performance at the age of 4. His supporters arranged for him to have basic education, but ran away to sea as a cabin boy. At the age of 14 he obtained a position in a travelling theatre and he obtained an engagement to play leading characters at the York Theatre, performing in Hamlet. While he was in a travelling theatre, rumours of his ability reached the ears of George III and he was commanded to appear at Windsor Castle for a private performance. His opening at Drury Lane as Shylock, 26 January 1814 roused the audience to almost uncontrollable enthusiasm. This was the part enjoyed at Bath by Francis Witts.

In the Evening, a M[r.] Fisher of Worcester College, a Deacon, preached on Rom. 14. 22, 23 & 15. 1. 2. recommending toleration and moderation in controversy. This Gentleman appeared to me deficient in not distinguishing between material & immaterial points; concession as to the latter is the rule of the Apostle, and it should have been shewn, that fundamental truths cannot be given up without sacrificing the Gospel.

Finished the perusal of Archb. Secker's charges: from which the Clerical duties may be learnt without a tincture of enthusiasm or false gloss: yet a truly apostolical comportment would adorn him, who conscientiously acts up to the venerable prelate's rules. |[8]

Jan. 19.

Attended the concert, when an unusual style of performance was presented, namely, a little comic opera, made up of selections, chiefly from Il Fanatico per la Musica, the Music by Mayer.[5] Naldi and his daughter performed admirably;[6] the other vocalists were two Miss Ashes, a Signor Vercellin, a M[r.] OCallaghan, and a M[r.] Cole. A little Stage was erected at one end of the superb Ball room, with Indian Screens, forming conlisses, behind which the performers retired. The Comic acting of Naldi is excellent, his daughter moves with grace & ease, and in the second act executed a beautiful air by Rossini. In the second act also, Mr. Kalkbrenner a masterly performer on the Pianoforte played a beautiful Fantasia.[7]

114. The Interior of the Concert Room.

5. Giovanni Simone Mayer, (1763-1845). The opera was *Che originali* (1798), and the sub title was *Il fanatico per musica*.
6. Guiseppe Naldi, (1770-1820). Italian singer, pianist and cellist.
7. Freidrich Wilhelm Kalkbrenner, (1784-1849). Friedrich Kalkbrenner was born in Kassel, Germany. He studied at the Paris Conservatoire and achieved his fame between 1814 and 1823 as a performer and teacher in London. He moved to Paris and died there in 1849.

Jan. 21.

We dined at Sir James Saumarez's. We met there among others his Brother, Mr. R. Saumarez, late an eminent Surgeon at Newington, but now retired from professional practice. This Gentleman is author of a Treatise on Physical Science. His mind has been much turned to such pursuits, and he is an original thinker. In speaking of the eminent characters of Edinburgh, where he has lately been, he ranked Dr. Brewster very high, spoke of Professor |[9] Jameson as less scientific in his various pursuits than is generally supposed of: of Professor Leshe's powers he speaks highly, but represents him as a gourmand, and lover of good living.

An anecdote of Kean, the actor, worth preserving, was mentioned by Lady Saumarez. While he was labouring in his vocation in an itinerant company of performers, he visited Guernsey, where, having engaged in the instruction of one or two young persons in reading and elocution, he had serious thoughts of setting up a school, if he could have been secure of a limited number of pupils, and so totally abandoning the stage. Disappointment in this scheme proved advantageous by throwing him eventually in the way of judges of his merit as an actor. It is said, that Dr. Drury of Harrow School first pointed him out to Mr. Arnold, when manager of Drury Lane, as worthy of an engagement.

Jan. 23.

Mr. Grinfield at Laura Chapel in the morning preached an excellent discourse, expounding the narrative given by St. Mark of the miracle of the healing of Jairus's daughter, taking his text from C. 5. 40, and they laughed him to scorn. He adverted forcibly and eloquently to the |[10] late abortive efforts of the advocates of infidelity, who sit in the chair of the scorner, relinquishing even the semblance of argument and learning, and descending to parodies & burlesque, which the good sense and principle of the country have indignantly repelled with contempt and disgust.

In the Evening, Mr. Marshall, Curate of the Abbey Church, preached on 1 John 3.1. shewing in what sense we may be called the Sons of GOD, and what are our duties as such.—

Jan. 25.

The severe frost being gone, although the weather by no means was encouraging, & heavy rain soon came on after my departure, which lasted with little intermission till I reached my Journey's end, I set off about half past nine o'clock on horseback to visit my old & intimate friend Mr. W. Dowell, Vicar of Locking, whom I had never before had an opportunity of visiting there, and now particularly wished to pass a day or two with, that I might be introduced to his wife, a daughter of Mr. Chancellor Yonge of Norwich Cathedral, to whom he had been united last summer. My route lay through an intricate part of Somersetshire by an indirect route. Following the line of the Bristol Upper Road, and crossing the Avon by the |[11] Bridge communicating with the Lower Road to Bristol. A little farther on at the public House called the Globe, in the Parish of Newton, I left the Bristol road to follow that leading to Wells by Marksbury. The valley is here narrow and interesting: on one side of the river, on a fine wooded knoll, Kelstone House, the seat of Sir J. Hawkins: close to my left hand was the park of Mr. Gore Langton,[8] the Uncle of my young friend John Brozone, one

---

8. William Gore-Langton, (1760-1860). M.P. for Somerset, 1795-1806; Tregony, 1808-1812; Somerset, 1812-1820, & 1831-1832; Somerset East, 1832-1847.

of the representatives for the County of Somerset. It seemed to be a well wooded park, the ground finely undulating: the village and Church are on the eminence to the left behind the House. Soon reached the Village of Coston with its small Church, near to which the road passes, and there are some desirable little residences of the Cottage order for persons of a middling rank. This, indeed, seems characteristic of all the Somersetshire villages, through which I passed, having an appearance of neatness—it is to be hoped too, affording content. From this village the road ascends for some distance, and, passing over high ground, affords a prospect of rich woody hills & valleys. Marksbury, on an eminence, was the next |[12] village through which the road passed. A little beyond this place I left the road leading to Wells, and pursued another and less beaten route, but still a turnpike road, diverging to the right. From this point the road became more & more undulating, passing between hedges on high banks, between richly stored orchards, the land being in a larger proportion meadow & pasture than arable. The tufted hills & narrow dells were highly picturesque, & in another season the landscapes would have been delightful. The road, I now travelled, leads by the Village of West Harptree and Cheddar & Cheddar Cliffs to Bridgwater. Soon after turning from the Wells road, I passed Houndstreet, a Seat of the Pophams; the House was not visible, but the Stables were, a handsome pile of building, and the park contained some fine rough ground with picturesque timber and plantations.—Now ascending, now descending, seldom for any considerable distance on level ground, I next rode through the pretty village of Chelwood; beyond that is |[13] Stanton Wick, where a cross road leads on the right to Bristol; indeed, I passed many tracks tending towards that great vortex, most of which must, I suppose, traverse Dundry Hill, which was a conspicuous object to my right, as the Chain of the Mendip Hills now began to be in my front: running in an Easterly and Westerly direction, but sadly obscured by the rain. At Stanton Wick I passed near a large Glass House, and soon after came upon a pretty retired old Court House, Sutton Court, the Seat of a Mr. Strachey, who is greatly improving the place. It is near Stowey, a village to the left of the road, on the side of which Stowey Mead, a pretty modern Cottage. Then through Sutton Wick, and leaving the lower Hills to my left, crossed the valley directly towards the Mendip hills, at the foot of which lies the Village of West Harptree, like all the rest pretty and rural. Here leaving to the left a road leading through East Harptree to Wells, distant eight miles I entered the Village, & closed a stage of sixteen miles. |[14] At the humble public house of the Village, I baited my horse & rested for an hour. The Churchyard boasts some magnificent clipped Yew trees: & opposite to it is a handsome old Court house. I now quite changed my direction of travelling, and followed the line of the Mendip Hills, traversing the roots of them towards the point, where, they terminate in the Bristol Channel. They remind me somewhat of the Malvern Hills; yet the valley, from which they rise is not so level as that of Worcestershire. Neither are they, generally, I think, so lofty: nor so denuded of wood; on the contrary, at intervals, clothed from the summits to the base with sweeping coppices & coverts; and while the top affords a delicious short turf, the sides are rich in pasture, meadow, orcharding and some arable. The whole way to Locking, about 13 miles, was a rich landscape, worthy of an artist's admiration in a genial season. The valley to the right wide & well diversified,—bounded by eminences stretching along in a parallel direction and interupting the prospect |[15] of the Valley of the Avon and Bristol. The first three Villages on the road were Compton Martin, Ubley, and Blagdon. The former two sweet retired places:

there is a peculiarly elegant character in all the Village Churches and Church Yards in this district, and the excessive neatness of their Thatch sets off the humblest Cottages. Blagdon is a large & straggling village: the tower of the Church lofty and conspicuous, in the fine stile of the Somersetshire Country Churches, which are built with a certain uniformity in a correct Gothic, supposed to have been so re edified, as a reward for loyalty, in the reign of Hen. 7.—The Ornaments & pinnacles of Blagdon tower seem, however, allowed to go out of repair. The place itself gives name to a now almost obsolete controversy, in which, as many think, Mrs. Hannah More did not appear to her credit.[9] Immediately beyond Blagdon passed through Rickford Combe, a delicious sequestered valley, sweetly wooded, watered by a fine, clear, rapid brook, which has not only attracted some paper manufacturers, perhaps, |[16] the least intrusive of manufacturers in sequestered hills, and least apt to disfigure a sweet spot, but also tasteful opulence: for a Mr. Howorth, an East Indian, has fixed himself here, & is making plantations & a residence. Some of his decorations, however, I did not admire, particularly a range of gates, posts, rails etc for a lodge, all of the grotesque limbs & knots of gnarled oaks fancifully arranged & fitted for the occasion. A little beyond, high on the side of one of the steepest and most wooded parts of the Mendip range is the seat of Dr. Whalley (still, I apprehend, alive, but in embarrassed circumstances,) which I had once visited from Clifton, many years ago.[10] This gentleman, possessing a taste for ornamental gardening, furnishing, & shewing off, had here created a little paradise in a most inaccessible spot: overlooking the superb valley below, the terraces winding among the coppice wood, communicating with each other by turf steps. Then the House, of plain exterior containing a series of rooms each a little cabinet of |[17] prettiness. Such I remember it; now it seems stripped of all attraction, but its romantic situation and magnificent prospect. The hamlet adjacent is called Lower Langford. I had now crossed more than one road heading towards Bristol: one of these, I presume, traverses the Mendip range by the celebrated and beautiful pass of Cheddar, alike celebrated for its beautiful scenery, and its cheese. Beyond Lower Langford, I soon came into the great road leading from Bristol to Bridgewater, near to where it mounts the Mendip to reach the valley on the other side, but did not follow it far, for at Churchill Turnpike I diverged to the right, by shady lanes to Banwell, still keeping at the base of the Mendip Hills now rapidly declining, but still diversified in form, clothing of wood, or turf, or meadow, and in direction towards the sea. Besides several insulated houses, pretty cottages & groupes, Banwell intirvened between Churchill turnpike & Locking: a large rambling village with a very handsome Church & Tower: Dr. Randolph, formerly of Laura Chapel, Bath, and |[18] a Prebendary of Bristol, author of a course of Advent Sermons, and an energetic preacher, is the present incumbent. Thence retired lanes led to Locking, where I arrived by half past three, and was most hospitably received by my friend, who soon made me feel quite at home in the society of himself & his amiable and unaffected wife & her two sisters.

---

9. Hannah More, (1745-1833). The controversy was between the curate of Blagdon, Revd. Thomas Bere who was also the rector of the nearby parish of Butcombe and the Revd. Sir Abraham Elton, (1755-1849) of Clevedon Court on the one side, supporting Hannah More. Pamphlets were written in 1801 by Bere railing against Hannah More's Methodist schools and the controversy raged for several months.

10. Monday 10 September 1804.

115. Ornamental cottage at Banwell.

Jan. 26.

The village of Locking stands on a low ridge rising out of the valley at the foot of the Mendip hills, & overlooks on each side a range of flat land, called the Moor, evidently once covered by the Bristol Channel, now fertile meadows of alluvial soil, and drained by deep & wide cuts, provincially called Reens, which are carefully examined by a Commission of Sewers, with a Jury, feast, fines etc: penalties being affixed if any occupier suffer the reen in his lands to become choked up. The village does not contain above twenty five houses, & the whole of the parish belongs to the Merchant's Company in Bristol as Trustees for Colston's charities, (I believe) & is let on lives. The Vicarage is in their gift, & was bought |[19] of them for the next presentation by M$^{r.}$ Dowell Sen$^{r.}$ The house, in which my friend lives, with a small farm adjacent, is likewise held on lives, there being no parsonage. It fronts the South West facing the Mendip Hills, where they are agreeably diversified in form, clothed with a coppice wood, or terminating in turfy slopes. A little hamlet in the vale, Elborough, in the parish of Hutton peeps forth amidst its orchards; the opposite eminence is surmounted by a Windmill, & the contiguous cottage of the Miller:—a peaceful scene; the House is small, but very comfortable, a lawn, garden & orchard environ it, & nothing can exceed the luxuriance of the Evergreens, the Arbutus, Phillyrea, Laurestenius, Cistus &c. even after the late severe frost. The Village seems embosomed in trees. The Rev$^{d.}$ M$^{r.}$ Jenkins has a neat place in it, but without the advantage of a prospect: the owner has shewn a grotesque taste in recent improvements, as he probably terms his alterations. It is to be regretted, that unavoidable circumstances prevent any intercourse between the families of M$^{r.}$ Dowell & M$^{r.}$ Jenkins. The Church & Church Yard are interesting objects: the tower of the latter is of the customary elegant Gothic of the Village Churches of the |[20] district, but somewhat dilapidated: the body of the Church has recently been rebuilt under my friend's superintendence in a very correct taste with Gothic windows. Within the pews are judiciously arranged so as to bring the Villagers immediately below the reading desk & pulpit on comfortable seats. The ancient stone pulpit remains, handsomely carved, of the Gothic style; & the ancient font, of Saxon or Norman taste, is a very curious relic: it is an immersion font, a square block lined with lead, resting on a low circular column: at each extremity of the sides a figure of truly rude sculpture with arms extended, so that the four figures clasp hands respectively in the middle of each face of the font: the rest of the architectural ornaments of each face made up of various wavy zigzag & other mouldings and devices.— |[21]

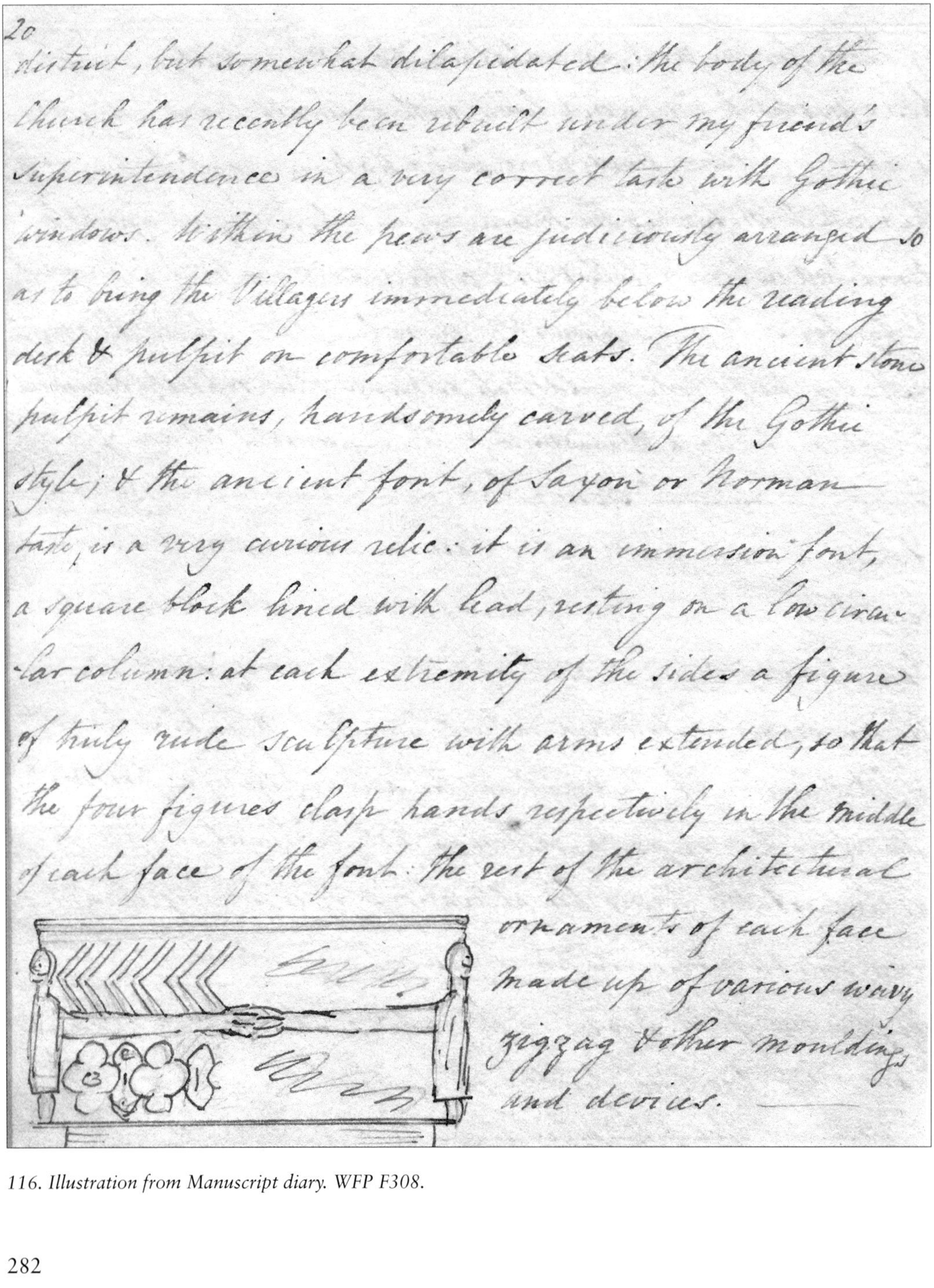
20
district, but somewhat dilapidated: the body of the
Church has recently been rebuilt under my friend's
superintendence in a very correct taste with Gothic
windows. Within the pews are judiciously arranged so
as to bring the Villagers immediately below the reading
desk & pulpit on comfortable seats. The ancient stone
pulpit remains, handsomely carved, of the Gothic
style; & the ancient font, of Saxon or Norman
taste, is a very curious relic: it is an immersion font,
a square block lined with lead, resting on a low circu-
-lar column: at each extremity of the sides a figure
of truly rude sculpture with arms extended, so that
the four figures clasp hands respectively in the middle
of each face of the font: the rest of the architectural
ornaments of each face
made up of various wavy
zigzag & other mouldings
and devices.

116. Illustration from Manuscript diary. WFP F308.

The wall of the Churchyard is kept in repair by no less than twenty seven persons according to their proportionate share in the Moor previous to its inclosure; each person's length is ascertained & his compartment marked on a stone in the wall with the initials of his name. I had never ~~mar~~ met with this custom before. We walked to the summit of that part of the Mendip chain, which fronts Locking, and the view is very striking, though the weather was rather hazy. The most attractive object is the Bristol Channel, of which the long reach is seen, intervening between Minehead & Clefden, the former on the Devonshire side, the latter on that of Bristol. In the first named direction are the Quantock Hills: nearer to us and terminating the line of the Mendip Hills, projecting into the Sea, is Brean down, an insulated eminence, nearly cut off from the land at high water: the Church belonging to it is one of the benefices of Mr. Stafford Smith, the next height in the line of Mendip is surmounted by the white washed Church of Uphill. In the midst of the Channel two small Islands are seen, the Steep & flat Holmes; |22 the former, somewhat resembling the Bass Rock, may be called the last of the Mendip range, & is not

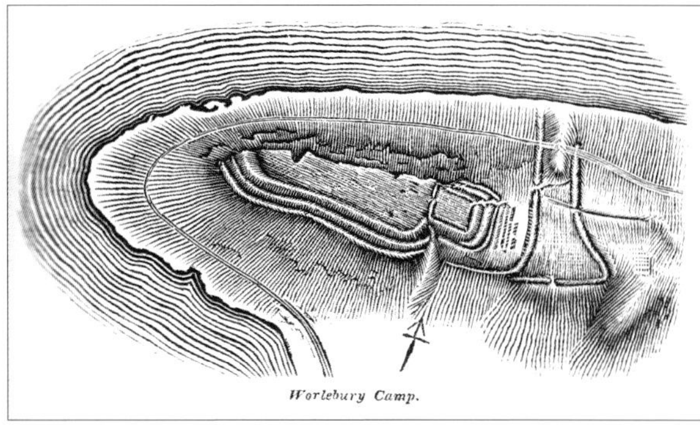

117. Worlebury Camp.

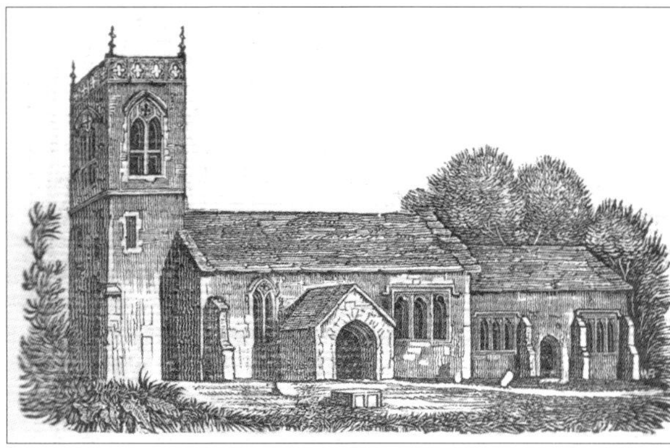

118. Weston old Church.

119. Weston-super-Mare.

120. *Congresbury Church.*

inhabited: a farmer tenants the other. Between Brean down and Worle Hill the Coast is quite flat & uninteresting, being the sea line of the large Valley intervening between the Mendip and its parallel range. On this shore, but close beneath the point of Worle Hill are the buildings of Weston Super Mare, a village, which has much increased of late years, since it has been the resort of strangers in the bathing season, and, though not in itself an attractive spot, its contiguity to Bristol makes it convenient to inhabitants of that great city. Worle Hill is a very marked feature of the prospect, being a noble terrace of turf which must command a superb sea view: its in land extremity is the scite of the Village of the same name, with several conspicuous residences, at least five miles distant from the spot where we stood. Beyond, on the horizon, are the heights of Clifdon (where is the Seat of Sir Abraham Elton) of Walton, in the vicinity of which Walton Castle, late the residence of Mr. Hart Davis, the Representative for Bristol, whose rise to wealth and |23 subsequent fall have of late excited so much remark.[11] The rich valley between us and these points contains numerous villages and much romantic scenery: Congresbury, (pronounced Coomsbury) Wrington, Brockley

121. *Congresbury Parsonage*

11. Richard Hart Davis (mentioned above) failed in his speculations, some of which were very dubiously linked to his position and influence in Parliament. In May 1819 he was forced to wind up his interests in Ball, Davis, Charles & Richard Vaughan & Co., and the Bristol Brass and Copper Company. He also retired from Harford's Bank. He continued to represent Bristol until 1831.

122. Monastic barn at Worle.

with its romantic combe or valley &c. The whole is a truly noble view, while the foreground is extremely pleasing. Close at our feet is the Village of Hutton reposing in the bosom of a fine sweep of Covert lying on the slope of a portion of the Mendip range: its neat Church, its ancient Court House with a low tower, now passed from the last of an ancient family to be divided among the low bred kindred of a menial, whom he had taken to his bed and made his heiress, yet interesting in its degradation, and looking like the old fashioned Seat of the Country Squire amid its yet unfelled Groves. The Hamlet of Elborow, the Village of Locking, the Orchards surrounding each of these, are pleasing features, which the freshness of the Turf, the stillness around, and the distant sound of the waves dashing on the Shore, gave a peculiar zest to the Spot, so that I do not wonder, that my friend, enthusiastically fond of the beauties of nature should make the Hill his almost daily resort in fine weather. |24 The spot, where we stood, must be three miles from the shore. The fine mountainous line of the Welch Coast was barely discernable from haze. Our intention was to have ascended still higher, so as to have reached the summit of the hill, and to have looked over into the Country on the opposite side of the range, but a heavy shower drove us home. Several pits are sunk by the country people in these hills, in search of veins of lead and calamine ore, probably with as little success as skill. Observing the turf on an elevated spot covered with chaff, I found, on enquiry, that the farmers in this country winnow their corn in a very primitive manner, dragging it in their waggons by a long team of oxen to these high and exposed points, and then winnowing with the fan in the current of air. Oxen are almost exclusively used here, yoked two abreast, with very heavy timber yokes, and little or no harness. Teazles are cultivated for the supply of the Clothiers & carried to great distances by jobbers, who travel through the Country: the plant is a biennial; so that the harvest is only every alternate year: they are cultivated with garden management in rows, & carefully hoed to keep down the weeds; at this Season they look like fields of lettuces; it is customary to be a joint concern between the owner |25 of the soil and the cultivator; the former receiving half the crop in lieu of rent. The returns are very uncertain: the harvest itself being not only variable in produce, but the price of the article liable to great vicissitudes.

Jan. 29.

It had been my design to stay two entire days only with the Dowells: but a very severe cold, which I had caught, brought on one of my old violent attacks in the head with fever, which compelled me to remain a third day. But finding myself now able to ride, I left Locking after breakfast, to return to Bath, having experienced much kindness from my friends, and greatly pleased with the females of the party. I only wish, my old friend had some society, for by some fatality there is hardly a soul, even among those of his own profession, with whom he can assort, and that his circumstances were somewhat better.

Finding, that the road to Bristol was but little further, and more level, I resolved to take it, and following the direction, in which I had travelled on my way to Locking as far as Churchill Turnpike, I there came into the road from Bristol to Bridgwater: the distance from Locking to Bristol about nineteen miles. At Churchill I struck across the |26 valley, for four or five miles, through a fine rich country, passing by Langford Inn & Village and several pretty residences. On the left is Wrington, with the handsome tower of its church, apparently the residence of several families in easy circumstances: Barley wood, the abode of Mrs. Hannah More is in this parish. To the right a church & low tower on the summit of a hill is an interesting object: adjacent to it a Gentleman's Seat: if I am not mistaken, Mr. H. Addington's. Ascended Red Hill: the name indicates the nature of the soil; a groupe of houses with large lime kilns on this hill; other hamlets and nests of cottages occur on the road side but no regular village. The view towards the Country, I had left, very fine. From hence for three or four miles the road passes over high ground, indifferent soil, and uninteresting: then the road descends by another long hill into the vale of Bristol. Here the view is very striking, whether in respect of the natural fertility of the tract surveyed, the grandness of some of its features, or the impression excited by the prospect of one of the first commercial cities of the empire. The view of the Village of Long Ashton amid its groves to the left, the long front of the princely |27 mansion of Sir Hugh Smith reposing beneath the slope of Leigh down & its plantations:[12] the strong features

123. Brean Down and Black Rock.

124. Uphill Church.

12. Sir Hugh Smyth, (1772-1824) of Long Ashton Court.

125. Bristol seen from Pill.

of S[t.] Vincent rock, gradually developing themselves as the eye approaches them more nearly, the long sweeping ranges of freestone buildings, some entire, some incomplete, crowning the Hill of Clifton & blending gradually with the buildings on the eminences ~~of~~ above Bristol, all gradually absorbed in the dim hazy mass of the mighty city—such are the general features of the prospect, which not seen by me for many years, now forcibly arrested my admiration under the most favourable gleam of winter Sun, and excited the recollections of years gone by, when we resided at Clifton. But fine as is this view, it is lost nearly two miles before reaching the city, on entering the village of Bedminster, & pursuing the track of its narrow street: this village forms one of the suburbs, and a gloomy tiresome approach. At length, the road crosses the new Course of the River Avon, one of the grand improvements made some years ago in connection with the Docks, by which such great service was rendered to the trade of the city, by opening readier access & safer riding |[28] for the shipping. Here I was glad to avoid the well known and intricate tracks of Redcliffe & Temple Street by pursuing the road, which runs along the side of the magnificent Canal, up which the tide now flows: and at length reached an inn at the end of Temple Street & consequently at the entrance of the city from Bath, where I obtained a bait for my horse. After an hour's delay I again set out for Bath, twelve miles of often travelled road, on which the only new object was the iron bridge over the Canal, close under Totterdown Hill, part of which had very recently been broken down, (yet not so as to interrupt the passage over) by a barge descending amid the sheets of ice during the late frost. I reached my dear wife & child to a late dinner, happy to find myself again with them & less fatigued than might have been expected by my ride.

On arriving at Bath I heard for the first time of the death of His Royal Highness the Duke of Kent, who departed this life on the 23d. at Sidmouth, being carried off rapidly by an inflammation on the lungs, the consequence |[29] of a neglected cold.[13] The best feature in this Prince's character was the warm patronage of charitable institutions; as a soldier he had excited enemies by rigid exactness in matters not essential and the abridgment of old privileges; in private life, he was expensive in the arrangements of his house & household with a most precise minuteness; he died in considerable embarrassments, as, indeed, he had long lived. His widowed Duchess, Dowager Princess of Leiningen, & Sister to Prince Leopold of Cobourg, has borne him one daughter, the Princess Alexandrina, who stands nearest in succession to the Crown of these realms on the Demise of the King & the elder Princes of the House: the Prince of Wales, Duke of York, Duke of Clarence, being at present without issue. The Duke was 53 years of age. His infant princess is about nine months old.

Jan. 30.

By the Mail Coach this morning arrived the mournful ~~all~~ intelligence of the decease of our venerable & good old King: it was at first not absolutely authenticated, but proved correct.[14] He departed at 35 min. past eight yesterday Evening at Windsor: nature being exhausted by an attack of diarrhoea; a late access of this disorder had been checked, the |[30] present baffled the remedies of the medical attendants. It was a blessing, that he had no return of reason, as often occurs before dissolution to persons afflicted with insanity, so that his last moments were not embittered by the contemplation of the pitiable state, in which he has past the last nine years of his eventful life, nor was awakened to the loss of his Queen & his Granddaughter. He rests in peace & his works do follow him! He is gone to receive his reward, & his memory will be embalmed in the grateful hearts of all good Englishmen. The public mind had been prepared for the event by the rumours of ten days past. He was 82 years old & had reigned more than 59 years.

At the Abbey Church, Mr. Crook, the Rector preached on Eccl. 9. 2. A declamatory sermon with reference to the anniversary of the Martyrdom of Ch. 1.—Neither good in matter, nor in manner. I think it a mistake to observe the anniversary on a Sunday; it seems to me a misconception of the words of the rubric; and that neither should the service be performed nor the fast kept, when it happens on a Sunday. Yet some divines hold a different opinion: in particular, Archd. Jefferson of Colchester, now here: |[31] on the other hand Arch. Thomas reads the rubric, as I do. Certainly, it was anomalous, that a Sermon on the occasion should be preached, and the service not read: M. Marshall, the Curate, going thro' the ordinary duty for Septuagesima Sunday.

---

13. Edward, Duke of Kent, (1767-1820). Edward, son of George III and Queen Charlotte was educated in Lüneberg and Hanover and took a strong interest in Freemasonry. He was a Colonel in the army and served at Gibraltar, 1790-91 and in 1791 he went with his regiment to Canada. He distinguished himself in the West Indies campaign against the French in 1794. He was created Duke of Kent in 1799. As part of the pending succession crisis, Edward married Maria Louisa Victoria, widow of Emich Charles, reigning Prince of Leiningen, (who died in 1814). She was the sister Leopold Saxe-Coburg, later the first king of the Belgians. The marriage was in 1818, and the following year Princess Victoria was born.
14. King George III, (1738-1820). George was the son of Frederick Prince of Wales and grandson of George II. He ascended the throne in 1760. He suffered repeated bouts of mental illness, thought to be porphyria and in 1811 his eldest son, George, became Prince Regent. The King was commonly known as 'Farmer George' from his interests in agricultural improvements.

Feb. 4—

Attended the consecration of Bathwick new Church by the name of St. Mary's; the duties of the Bishop of Bath and Wells being performed by Bishop Ryder, of Gloucester. The Bishop also preached on Hag. 2. 9. His style of preaching has the same fault as his charges, a sing song tone, meant for pathos and devotion. His discourse was orthodox, not deep, nor remarkable for eloquence: some remarks on the revival of religion in later times (a word savouring a little of Methodism) appeared to me carried too far. Something to the same purpose was in his last charge, & these justly reprehended by a critic in the Christian Remembrances. The Church is a beautiful Gothic Structure, highly creditable to the taste of skill of the Architect, Mr. Pinch. It is said to have cost £14000: the pulpit, front of the galleries, recess of the Altar, Organ &c. are of beautiful carved oak in very correct taste; the church consists of a centre aisle & |32 two side aisles, being calculated to hold 1400 persons:—a proportion of the seats being free. Mr. B. Barker has presented the Church with an altar piece, representing the Nativity; the Artist is new in Historical painting & succeeds far better in landscapes: the Virgin, child, & groupe of angels are superior to the shepherds.[15] Mr. Field, the Organist of the Abbey, played on the Organ, for this occasion, & a fine choir from the different churches performed some chants & an anthem in a very superior manner. Tickets, at five shillings each, were issued, the produce to be applied in aid of the Erection; a measure much censured by many: about six hundred persons were present.

The new King was this day proclaimed in Bath.[16] The procession was headed by a troop of Lancers now quartered here: then a band of music, then a volunteer rifle corps: then the children of the Blue Coat School: then the Mayor, (Mr. Allen) & Town Clerk, (Mr. George) the latter reading the Proclamation at certain Stations, elevated in a kind of chair with the Mayor, into which they ascended at the appointed Stations; then the Corporation, Alderman &c. in their robes; then the Generals, Admirals, Clergy, Medical Men & others followed by a band of music; the whole closed by |33 Volunteer Yeomanry. A feast in the Guildhall closed the day.

Feb. 5.

We returned home from Bath, without other inconvenience than a pair of weak horses from Cirencester to Northleach. We were glad to return to Upper Slaughter; I trust, the medical advice my wife has received during our stay at Bath, & the use of the waters, will essentially strengthen her constitution.—

Feb. 7.

My pupil, Mr. J. Saumarez, returned from Bath to resume his studies.—

126. Sergeant Lott, an officer at Cato Street.

15. Benjamin Barker, (1776-1838). Thomas and Benjamin Barker of Bath were notable painters, specialising in fine landscapes.
16. George IV, (1762-1830).

127. Front of premises at Cato Street.

Feb. 10.

The Under Sheriff for the County came to Stow to proclaim George the 4th. He was in his progress for that purpose through the principal Market Towns. The band of Music preceded us, and the Bells rung a merry peal. It being Market day, several Gentlemen were present and assisted: Mr. Chamberlayn, as Lord of the Manor, Mr. Hippisley, (Rector) Messrs. Ford, Leigh & myself, Magistrates; Sir H. Dryden, Mr. Jones, Mr. Croome &c.—

The new King is now recovering from his late severe indisposition, an inflammation on the lungs, which seized him immediately on his accession. He is believed to have been in imminent danger.— |34

Feb. 12.

The Duke of Kent's remains are interred at Windsor this Evening.

Feb. 13.

Preached a funeral sermon on the death of our good old King: on 2 Sam. 3. 36.

Feb. 15.

Returned from Cheltenham, whither I went yesterday to visit my poor Mother now again suffering by a very severe fit of the gout.

Feb. 18.

This day's newspaper contains the recital of the splendid ceremonial of the funeral of our late good King, at Windsor, on the night of the 16th. Inst.

The public mind has been much interested of late in the accuracy of rumours of an Insurrection in Spain. Thus much seems certain, that a most serious mutiny has arisen among the Spanish Troops assembled in the Environs of Cadiz with a view to an expedition for the recovery of the revolted provinces of Spanish South America; that the insurgents are in considerable force, & little or no progress has been made in subduing them; that Cadiz is threatened by them, & |[35] that a strong party within its walls favours the constitutional cause, as it is called. It cannot but be desired, that Spain should be delivered from the Tyranny & priestcraft, under which it now groans.—

It is reported, that the Duke of Berry, Son of Monsieur & nephew of the King of France, has been assassinated at Paris.[17] This event would reduce to a small compass the present reigning family: the present succession is Monsieur, the Duke d'Angouleme, the Duke of Berry: the Duke of Angouleme has no family, nor prospect of any: the Duke of Berry, by his wife, a Neapolitan Princess, no male heir, I believe the Orleans family are then nearest to the Crown.

Feb. 20.

The rumour of the Duke of Berry's assassination is confirmed: the murderer, Louvet, a person of the lower orders, is believed to have been actuated by political fanaticism: he is taken.

This day the Queen Caroline, Consort of his Majesty, was not prayed for by name, agreeably to a recent order of Council. The fact strongly marks the sense of her character entertained |[36] in the highest quarters. It is rumoured, that his Majesty strongly pressed his Ministers to commence measures for a Divorce; which they declined under the sanction of an opinion unfavourable to such a measure from the Law Officers of the Crown. It is believed, that the King gave way after a tender of their resignation by the Ministers.

An immediate dissolution of Parliament is announced. The arrangements of the Civil List, heretofore made by the expiring Parliament on the demise of the Crown, is deferred till the Meeting of the new Parliament, on the ground, that the present is a new case, both as to the period of the Year, when the Royal demise occurred, & as the present King was already virtually reigning before the decease of his Father.

Feb. 25.

The news came of the discovery and discomfiture of a most diabolical conspiracy against the lives of his Majesty's Ministers, whom it was resolved to assassinate, while met at a Cabinet dinner at Earl Bathurst's in Mansfield Street.[18] The villains were found in horrible conclave in a loft near |[37] the Edgeware road, near thirty in number, arming themselves for their dire enterprize. The Police had obtained late information of the plot, and twelve

---

17. Charles Ferdinand, Duc de Berry, (1778-1820) was the younger son of Charles X of France and Marie-Thérèse de Savoie.
18. The Cato Street conspiracy of 23 February 1820. The 'Condition of England' question was a much mooted topic in the years after Waterloo. A group of radicals calling themselves the 'Spencean Philanthropists' after Thomas Spence had been involved in such episodes as the Spa Fields Riots in 1816. Their beliefs were a mixture of radical socialism and violent republicanism. One of the main players at both Spa Fields and the Cato Street conspiracy was Arthur Thistlewood. Their plan was to overthrow the Government and set up a Committee of Public Safety which would supervise a radical revolution. After the death of George III a general election was called as usual on the death of a monarch. George Edwards, one of the Spenceans, suggested that the group should seize the opportunity to kill the entire cabinet during this time of crisis. An advertisement in the newspapers announced that a 'grand Cabinet dinner' was to be held at the home of the Lord President of the Council, Lord Harrowby, in Grosvenor Square. This provided an ideal location for the conspirators to do their work. Unfortunately for the conspirators, George Edwards, was a Government spy. Found guilty of high treason, Thistlewood and four others were hanged on 1 May 1820. Thistlewood was also decapitated, as prescribed for traitors.

128. Rear of premises at Cato Street.

Police Officers under the direction of M^r. Birnie, the Magistrate, undertook the desperate duty of apprehending the Conspirators. They fought with desperation; Arthur Thistlewood, the noted turbulent demagogue, & partner of D^r. Watson, as he is called, a partaker in the former Spa Fields riot, seemed a leader here, & murdered with a Sword one of the Officers. He escaped at the moment (the Evening of the 23^d.) but was arrested on the following day. Many on both sides were wounded, & daring acts of intrepidity were performed, while many providential escapes occurred. In the darkness & confusion of the horrible combat, many escaped, nine only being taken, exclusively of Thistlewood; all of the lowest orders: the only other person of notoriety in custody was Davidson, a man of colour,[19] & of late a furious orator among the Radicals in Finsbury Market &c. Large quantities of arms & ammunition were found on the spot, and depots have been seized elsewhere. Other suspected persons have been since apprehended, & |38 much intelligence appears to have been gained by Government & the Magistracy. Let us hope, that the infuriate plot is effectually baffled, and thank GOD for its discovery and overthrow. A party of the Guards assisted in the affray, but did not come up till some minutes after it began. Other accounts state, that the plan was to massacre Ministers at a Cabinet Dinner at Lord Harrowby's in Grosvenor Square.

Finished the perusal of by far the greater part of Evelyn's Memoirs; omitting the tracts republished, & only glancing at the antiquated correspondence of Ch. 1. & 2. with their Statesmen & Ambassadors, curious relics & pregnant with matter to the Historian of that age. The Journal & correspondence of M^r. Evelyn is most interesting, whether it be regarded as a faithful portraiture of the eventful times, in which he lived, or as exhibiting his own most amiable and Christian Character, or as replete with anecdotes of distinguished persons in every station, mixed with observations connected with a wide circuit of literature & science. |39

---

19. Davidson was coloured. The diarist in this sense means the word in its literal sense, and not as 'a colourful character'.

Feb. 26.

Completed my thirty sixth year. I give GOD thanks for his great mercies to me & mine, humbly praying for his aid to correct my many failings, and beseeching his protection in future.

129. Sergeant Legg, an officer at Cato Street.

Feb. 28.

Mr. Hurd mentioned a circumstance to me this day strongly illustrative of the facility, with which new doctrines are spread among dissenters ~~of~~ from the Church, & of the unsteadiness of opinions in congregations not restrained by creeds and articles. The Anabaptist meeting House at Naunton was erected by Subscription for the use of the Church, (as they term it) assembling there. Since the demise of its regular Minister some years since there has been no appointment of a permanent successor (ordained according to their tenets:) the worship has been uncertainly performed, & the Sacraments not administered. The adherents of the party now holding Antinomian doctrines & recently seceders from our church, who consider Mr. Snow as their leader & pastor, gained entrance some time ago into this meeting, and a majority of the Subscribers profess the new opinions: |40 now, say they, we are the Church: the Anabaptist church recently meeting here is dissolved, & the authority rests with the majority of subscribers; forming a church here: the Anabaptist minority shall therefore cease to have service in the Meeting house, & either join us or not come at all.

Feb. 29.

Parliament was dissolved.—

Mar. 2.—

My dear Son Edward's seventh birthday. May the Almighty give strength to the powers both of his mind & body, & may his Parents train him up in the ways of religion & in useful learning!

Mar. 3.

At dinner at Mr. Hippisley's I met among others Lord Northwick[20] and his brother, the Rector of Burford in Shropshire: also a very intelligent and travelled Man, Mr. Lechmere of the Rhydd, Worcestershire. The conversation turned much on foreign travel,—Italy, Switzerland & France. Lord N. has spent much time abroad.

20. George Rushout, 2nd Baron Northwick, (1770-1859).

Mar. 5.

This day read a form of prayer & thanksgiving for his Majesty's recovery from his late dan- |41 -gerous illness. It had not reached me earlier.

Mar. 12.

The news from Ireland has been for some time very alarming. A combination of misguided peasantry in the Counties of Galway & Roscommon & the adjoining districts, excited partly by religious differences, partly by want, partly by high rents, partly fomented by turbulent spirits, calling themselves Ribbon men, & swearing in adherents to illegal combination, sally forth in organised bands, strong enough to cope with large detachments of police & soldiery; many lives have been lost, & much damage caused. Some blame is imputed to the terror & apathy & want of energy of the Country Gentlemen & Magistrates: what, indeed, can be hoped for in a land of absentees?—[21]

The reports of the insurrection in Spain are very obscure and contradictory, but it is plain, that the royal party is not strong enough to crush the Constitutionalists, whose principles seem gaining ground, & fresh symptoms of revolt are noticed in various & detached parts of the kingdom.

Mar. 14.

I was told, that the dispute between the Anabaptists |42 and Antimonians at Naunton mentioned above (Feb. 28th.) was compromised by an agreement, that each party should use the Meeting house for worship on alternate Sundays.

130. Huntsmen & dogs.

21. The wearing of ribbons to denote the association with the orange party or the various Catholic associations was common in Ireland. The Catholics at this time were wearing green and white ribbons.

Mar. 15.

I have great reason to thank GOD this day for his preservation, having been thrown from my horse, when hunting, by his becoming entangled in a slough; for I was not at all hurt by the fall.

Mar. 16.

Finished the perusal of Latrobe's Journal of an Expedition to Southern Africa, in the course of which the Author traversed the colony of the Cape of Good Hope and resided for a considerable time both at Cape Town & the two Moravian Settlements in that Country. Mr. Latrobe is a Minister of that respectable Sect, and was sent with a commission to visit the Missions & fix on a station for forming another. It is impossible not to admire the Christian temper of these religionists, their unobtrusive assiduity and practical good sense, and one must join in rejoicing at the success waiting on their efforts to |[43] civilize and convert the barbarous natives. Mr. Latrobe's narrative, though defective as a composition, is highly interesting from its touching simplicity, cheerful ~~portraiture~~ piety, & lively portraiture both of nature & society. It is also remarkable for candour and generosity: no acrimony, no censoriousness.[22]

Mar. 23.

The information is arrived of the issue of the constitutional Insurrection in Spain; for so it may be called, as the object was the re-establishment of the constitution as settled by the Cortes in 1812: A revolution has been accomplished in a manner most creditable to the Spanish nation; though commenced by the Military, few, if any, enormities have occurred: the sense of the Country went along with the sentiments of the leaders, & all Spain declared herself with a consent the most remarkable, and, as light spreads with rapidity, so the principles swiftly pervaded every corner of the Peninsula. The Monarch in his Capital & his bad advisers were absolutely left alone; no blood was shed, but the expression of the public sentiment was so decisive and overwhelming, that he yeilded to necessity; engaged to take the oath prescribed by the Constitution, to call the Cortes, to abolish the Inquisition, to release | the multitude of State Prisoners; all this was forthwith done; and an absolute monarch one day, he was a limited one the next. The Constitution gives the Cortes a powerful control over the Sovereign in matters of legislation & in restraint of possible deviations: the Executive power resides with the Prince, and the principles of the national Constitution promise a wonderful regeneration of this important but fallen portion of Europe.

Mar. 24.

Sir James & Lady Saumarez with their two Daughters called here on their journey from Bath into Northamptonshire, where their eldest Son resides.

Mar. 25.

Learnt with satisfaction, that Sir Francis Burdett has been found guilty of publishing a libel against the Government and soldiery. This most important trial took place at the Leicester Assizes, being the County, in which Sir. F.B. wrote a letter commenting in the most violent

---

22. Christian Ignatius Latrobe. *Journal of an Expedition to South Africa in 1815 and 1816.*

terms on the Transactions at Manchester on the 16th. August last, and addressed to the Electors of Westminster.[23] Best was the Judge; Serj. Vaughan conducted the prosecution; Sir F. Burdett defended himself. |45

Mar. 30.

Learnt the issue of the important trial, which has lasted ~~eight~~ ten days at York before Mr. Justice Bayley: namely, of the notorious demagogue Hunt with several others for their conduct at Manchester on the memorable 16th. of August. The prosecution was conducted by Mr. Scarlett, the defendants pleaded their own cause, & Mr. Hunt shewed himself a most skilful advocate. A host of witnesses were examined on both sides, & the Judge shewed the strictest impartiality. The verdict against Hunt & others his Companions purports, that they were guilty of conspiring to hold and holding an unlawful assembly under unlawful banners with a view to excite contempt and dissatisfaction against his Majesty's Government and the Constitution. The result is most satisfactory, as it promises to check most effectually the recurrence of turbulent public meetings for objects professedly constitutional, but with unconstitutional array calculated to excite alarm, as to members & organization. The trial had been removed to York by the petition of the Defendants under the presumption, that they would not have met with an impartial Jury in Lancashire. Some of the Defendants were acquitted. |46

Apr. 2.

In the course of the past week the venerable Octagenarian, and eminent painter, Benjamin West, President of the Royal Academy, received the honours of a public funeral at St. Paul's.[24] Sir Joshua Reynolds had been interred with similar respect. Sir Thos. Lawrence is elected President in the room of Mr. West.

Apr. 5

The Sovereign has testified his high sense of the talents of the eminent Poet, (perhaps, the unrivalled Novellist) Walter Scott, by raising him to the dignity of Baronet.

Apr. 9.

The accounts from Spain announce a horrible massacre in Cadiz on the 10th. Ult. arising out of the recent revolution, but not occasioned by any bad feeling on the part of the adherents of the Constitution. It does not clearly appear how far the Officers of the Garrison attached to the cause, which the King has now disclaimed, are implicated,

---

23. Peterloo. The Peterloo massacre was the result of a cavalry charge into a crowd of people at St. Peter's Field, Manchester, 16 August 1819. The gathering had been peaceful and between 60,000 and 80,000 had come to hear Richard Carlile, John Cartwright and Henry Hunt speak. The local magistrates took alarm at the number gathered and William Hulton, the chief magistrate called in the Yeomanry, many of whom were drunk, and they charged at the cart bearing the speakers. When matters became confused the regular army were called in to rescue the Yeomanry and restore order. Eleven people were killed and more than 400 injured.

24. Benjamin West, (1738-1820). West was born in Springfield, Pennsylvania and he gained fame with many of his paintings of the American Revolution. He was a favourite painter of George III. His most famous painting is probably the death of Wolfe at the Heights of Abraham, 1770.

but the aggression, and that premeditated, arose from the brutal, bigotted & infuriate Soldiery, who falling furiously on the unarmed citizens, while assembled to engage in the ceremony of adhering to the constitution, butchered them without mercy for a considerable time, |[47] driving them for refuge to their houses, while a scene of plunder ensued. More than five hundred are said to be killed & twelve hundred wounded. It appears, that the King and his former advisers are not implicated.

Apr. 10.

Went to Cheltenham on my way to the Quarter Sessions at Gloucester, & dined & slept at my Mother's now quite recovered form her late severe fit of the gout.—

Apr. 11.

Attended the Quarter Sessions at Gloucester, & took the oaths of Allegiance & supremacy in consequence of the King's accession. Among other matters of considerable importance in the administration of the affairs of the County was one, in which I was greatly interested, viz. the introduction into the Bridewell at Northleach of a System of Prison Discipline for offenders committed or sentenced to hard labour, by the erection of a flour mill to be worked by such Prisoners. The subject had occupied much of my attention since my return ~~to~~ from Bath, having been brought forward at the Epiphany Sessions by Mr. Ford, & referred to the Visiting Justices, of whom I was the Senior, Mr. Price of Coln St. Dennis being my Colleague. After a varied correspondence, & frequent consultations with |[48] my brother Magistrates, and the Surveyor of the County, I had drawn up a report recommending the Measure, & pointing out the proper way of carrying it into effect, which I this day presented to the Court; enforcing its contents by reading extracts from the correspondence above referred to, & stating additional facts. On the motion of my friend the Hon. & Revd. Dr. Rice, seconded by Mr. B. Cooper M.P. for Gloucester, it was resolved without division, that the Visiting Magistrates with their neighbouring Brethren, should carry the measure into effect. We had expected considerable opposition, but the reason of the thing seemed to silence all captious objections, & the only views not in our favour were those of the Chairman, Dr. Cooke, & Mr. Cripps M.P. for Cirencester. The plan was warmly supported by Messrs. Pye, Ford, Dr. Timbrell, Pitt, Price, Hurd, Leigh & others.

The news from the manufacturing districts is again very alarming; though happily the promptitude & energy of the Magistracy supported by a strong military force & the loyalty of the better sort have succeeded in suppressing the most daring revolutionary attempts. The western part |[49] of Scotland in the Vicinity of Glasgow, Paisley, Greenock &c. is now highly convulsed, and insurrection had proceeded so far, that on the anonymous mandate of a party styling themselves a committee for forming a provisional Government, secretly and widely posted in all corners of the West of Scotland, the infatuated manufacturers struck, & crowded the streets and highways without work & with all the appearance of gloomy resolution to combine in revolutionary movements. Depots of pikes & other arms have been seized, & many conspirators are in custody: blood also has been shed; a party of deluded & armed radicals having engaged with some regular cavalry & yeomanry & been routed.

In the neighbourhood of Huddersfield also similar overt acts of rebellion have occurred

& have been put down by the spirit of the Magistrates with the aid of the soldiery, in short the manufacturing districts are surcharged with the most inflammable matter, & it may be said——incedis per ignes Suppositos cineri doloso.[25]

Apr. 13.

Among the numerous trials, which have ended in |[50] the condemnation of the ~~numerous~~ many low agitators of the misguided population of the manufacturing districts, that of Sir Charles Wolseley & one Harrison a dissenting Minister has been remarkable. They were tried at Chester for seditious language at a meeting held at Stockport, & very decisive evidence was brought against them; so that the Jury under the direction of Mr. Warren, the Chief Justice of Chester, found them guilty, and Harrison has had verdicts returned against him under two other indictments for exciting his auditors to subvert the Established government in Sermons. Nothing can be more remarkable than the gross infatuation of Sir C. Wolseley, a man of fortune & rank in the Country;[26] nothing more disgusting than the impious effrontery of his compeer, who not satisfied with turning the toleration granted to him as a religious dissenter into an opportunity of disseminating sedition, glories and exults in having done so.

Apr. 15.

Our domestic circle was increased by the arrival of my Mother in law Mrs. Backhouse from Yorkshire. She |[51] has not visited us for nearly five years, but is now about to stay a considerable time with us previous to the new residence, which she proposes fixing on at Gloucester, with a view to be nearer to us. She has accordingly let Beck House for a term of years, and undergone in the prosecution of her object a fatigue, to which her constitution is very unequal, & for which we should therefore be more sensible of her attachment in leaving her old neighbourhood for our sakes.

Apr. 20.

A special commission is now engaged in trying Thistlewood and the other Cato Street Conspirators. Thistlewood is found guilty of high treason on the clearest evidence. Wild and visionary as were their schemes, they surpassed in atrocity most of the nefarious plans of destruction recorded in history. It clearly appears, that a subversion of the Constitution & the dethronement of the King were in contemplation. Providence mercifully averted a scene of horrid massacre and confusion, & brought the catastrophe to revert on the wicked projectors.

Apr. 26.

The first meeting for this Season of the Stow Cleri- |[52] -cal Society was held this day. Nineteen Clergy dined together as usual, and I presided instead of Dr. Rice, now keeping Residence on his Prebend at Worcester.

---

25. incedis per ignes Suppositos cineri doloso — Simon, translation reqd. this slipped through the net
26. Sir Charles Wolseley, (1769-1846), 7th Baronet.

Apr. 27.

The King went this day to open the new Parliament in state. The proceedings of the legislature will be of the most important order, & the Country will look with impatience to the discussions arising on various most important points. It is not supposed, that Ministers have lost much strength by the late Elections. Ultra Whiggism prevails, indeed in Westminster and Middlesex, Mr. J. C. Hobhouse having been returned with Sir F. Burdett for the former, & a Son of the late Mr. Whitbread with Mr. Byng for the latter.—In the City the noted Ald. Waithman has been compelled to beat a retreat. The efforts of the radicals to get a footing have been frustrated, though Hunt tried at Preston, Cobbett at Coventry, & Wooler at Hull. In this part of the Country there has been neither contest nor material change.

May 1.

Five of the wretched conspirators found guilty ~~at~~ of High Treason were this day executed. Thistlewood, Davison, Brunt, Ings & Tidd. Those less prominent in the foul |[53] designs, and who were allowed to amend their plea of not guilty & throw themselves on the mercy of the crown, are transported for life. One only, probably entrapped into participation in the last bloody scene in Cato Street, seems reserved for a milder punishment. The wretched culprits died with all the daring effrontery, & hardened villany of their conduct since their apprehension, justifying and glorying in their offence: & renouncing all belief in Christianity

131. Cato Street Conspirators execution with the executioner showing the head of Arthur Thistlewood.

132. *Charles Cooper.*

133. *Arthur Thistlewood Cato Street Conspirator.*

134. *William Davidson.*

135. *James Ings.*

spurned the pious offices of the Ministers of religion. Davison the man of colour was the only exception, who seemed touched with a deep sense of his own guilt & the necessity of making his peace with GOD since his sentence.—

May 5.

Finished Ivanhoe a tale in three Vols. by the admirable author of Waverley &c: supposed to be Sir W. Scott.[27] This is the first prose work, the personages, events & scenery of which are exclusively English; the story is thrown very far back in History, to the reign of Richard Coeur de Lion. John his Brother with his plotting train of attendants, Robin Hood & his gallant band of outlaws, the Lionhearted Monarch himself, the Saxon Gentry as contrasted with |[54] the Norman Barons, the chivalric exercises of the age, the Knights Templars, the rich & cringing Jew are all ably delineated in this work, which with all the energy of a rich and fertile imagination owes much of its attractiveness to its author's deep researches into antiquarian lore. One female character, a Jewess, of every period & of no period, for she is a beau ideal, supernaturally beautiful in form, character, & mind, is the diamond of the casket. Nor let a Jester almost worthy to rank with those of Shakespeare ~~to~~ be omitted.

May 12.

At Stow Fair this day Mr. Large of Broadwell Oxfordshire, an eminent agriculturist, whose assistance I had called in as Land Surveyor here and at Stanway pointed my attention to a sheep bred by him & killed by a butcher of the place. Its size was indeed enormous: as it weighed 69 lbs to the quarter; the shoulder 35 lbs: and so in proportion; nothing could be more healthy than the whole appearance of the sheep; it was a three shear sheep; I believe, of the mixed Cotswold & Lincolnshire breed. Mr. Large is remarkable for the size & small bones, and fine wool of his sheep, & makes |[55] large sums by the letting and sale of his rams.

May 17.

At the archdeacon's visitation at Stow, the Sermon was preached by Mr. Archdeacon Rudge from Eccl. 1. 9. The preacher represented to his reverend auditors, how needful it is to examine the signs of the times, and reviewing the History of the Church, collect by analogical reasoning the probability of future events, in order to adopt measures for opposing the current of doctrines or measures [in] hostility to the welfare of the Church. He drew a sketch of the progress of the Church from the Apostolical age, struggling for existence under pagan & Jewish prejudices & persecutions till it became the Religion of the Roman Empire; traced it amidst the conflicts of contending heresies; glanced at the assumptions and usurpations and corruptions of the See of Rome: took a view of the Reformation in this country, the relapse to Popery, the reestablishment of Protestant ascendancy, the introduction of Calvinistic doctrines & consequent dissent. From this brief survey he collected the pregnant causes of apprehension as to the Security of the Church, whether the Pretensions of papists be considered, or the high notions of rigid Calvinism, or the dangerous doctrines of Antinomianism, or the spread of infidelity be contemplated. He adverted with disapprobation yet with charitable candour to the erroneous liberality of those, who unite in public charities |[56] with professed antagonists of the doctrines of the Church of England. On the whole he delivered a very sound & pertinent discourse.—

---

27. Sir Walter Scott, (1771-1832). *Ivanhoe*, 1819.

The newspapers this day communicated the judgments passed in some of the late important cases of trial for sedition; judgments highly gratifying to the friends of order and tranquillity—Mr. Hunt is sentenced to two years & a half imprisonment in Ilchester Gaol and at the expiration of that time to find sureties for his good behaviour himself in £1000 and two others in £500 each for five years. Three of his deluded followers, Johnston, Healy, Bamford, are sentenced to one years imprisonment in Lincoln Gaol, & to find sureties for their good behaviour, themselves in £200 & two others in £100 each for five years.—Sir C. Wolseley is sentenced to imprisonment in Abingdon Gaol for a year & half; sureties as in the case of Mr. Hunt: his colleague Harrison to a confinement in Chester Gaol for a year & half: sureties £200 & £100 for five years.[28]

May 19.

My young friend Frederick Aston arrived from his Brother-in-law's, Mr. Watkins's, Berkley near Frome, to pass ten days with us. His recent creditable examination for his Bachelor's degree has released him for the present |[57] from academical labours, and, while it makes him tread as on air, cannot but give me, as his former tutor, cause of sincere satisfaction.

May 27.

The fertile genius of the admirable author of Waverley and the other tales of olden time has led to a still later production than that of Ivanhoe, so lately ~~comm~~ [al]luded to. This new work, entitled the Monastery, like most of the former, is founded on Scottish Manners, history and superstitions.[29] The scene is placed in the Lowlands, in the period of the unfortunate Mary Queen of Scots, while the tottering basis of Papal power was yeilding to the rigorous onset of protestant assailants. The author has availed himself largely of local and romantic machinery, which destroys the probability of his fiction, & leaves the mind unsatisfied: yet with this defect, much remains, that is beautiful in the delineation of scenery, the contrast of character, of rude & warm feeling. The principal characters are the Monks of a rich Monastic Institution, particularly the zealous Sub-Prior set against the equally zealous reformer:—two Brothers, one energetic, headlong & warlike, the other mild, contemplative & affectionate: a lovely, but not very interesting heroine, with a rustic |[58] and artful, though simple, beauty, as a foil: a fine Gentleman & conceited Knight of Queen Elizabeth's court; border thieves & barons, Scottish intriguing nobles, pedlars, millers, et hoc genus omne, fill up the canvass.

May 31.

My young friend Frederick Aston left us for Oxford to take his Bachelor of Arts degree.

June 3.

Read in the newspaper the account of the death of Mr. Archdeacon Thomas. This learned & sound divine will be a great loss to the Church of England: his manly firmness leading him to stand with unbending fortitude in the gap to defend orthodox opinions. Perhaps, there was a

28. The imprisonments were more for show than anything, the Government not wishing to alienate the manufacturing areas. Hunt, in particular, never paid his sureties.
29. *The Monastery*, 1820.

roughness of manner in him, but it was redeemed by masculine sense, & a clear understanding. I had the honour of his acquaintance, & had partaken of his hospitality; he shone in the domestic circle of a most amiable family. His controversy with the Bishop of Gloucester is an epoch in the modern records of our Church. We need such defenders, & may they arise to replace him! In the Diocese of Bath & Wells such a character was highly valuable. |[59]

June 7.
The newspaper this day mentions the death of the celebrated Irish patriot, Mr. Grattan, in his 74th Year. This distinguished orator died in London, whither he had come to bear his testimony in his place in the House of Commons, as representative for Dublin, to the cause of religious freedom, as it is termed, which he had so long pleaded.[30] Mr. Grattan has been chiefly known in England by his energetic & eloquent support of the claims of the Roman Catholics.

June 11.
The country has been most painfully agitated this week past with the return of the Queen from the Continent, an event, which threatens to convulse the nation. Rumours had long prevailed, that her Majesty was on her return from Italy, to brave the insinuations of levity and worse than levity, even profligacy, brought against her, ~~to~~ the truth of which her exclusion from the liturgy seemed to confirm. Distant and cautious allusions to the subject had been hazarded in Parliament. She arrives at St. Omers: is there joined by Lady Anne Hamilton, Sister to the Duke, & one of the Ladies of her family; also by Alderman Wood, remarkable for having through popular favour held the mayor- |[60] -alty of London two years, and for his warm opposition to Government; a man of talent and activity of mind and body, a bold aspirer to popular applause.[31] Her Majesty appears to have thrown herself on this person for advice and to have followed his counsel with fortitude indicative of innocence, or daring, the accompaniment of abandoned principles. My old acquaintance, the eminent Henry Brougham, who has long been legal adviser to her Majesty, & has recently been recognized as her Attorney General, repaired also to St. Omers, to afford his professional counsel: & was accompanied thither by Lord Hutchinson, the gallant General, who was long ago distinguished in Egypt, & who on this occasion was bearer, as personal friend of the King, of certain propositions to her Majesty. From what has transpired, it appears, that these were, that a revenue of £50,000 per ann. should be allowed her, on condition of her living abroad, not assuming the title of Queen of England, nor any other appertaining to the Royal Family. It seems, that these propositions were received by her Majesty with high disdain, and that neither entering |[61] into farther negociation, nor acting with deliberation, as recommended by Mr. Brougham, she adopted the extreme resolution of instantly passing over to England, under an idea, that the Government of France might take measures to prevent her, though apprized, that on setting foot in England Ministers would bring down

---

30. Henry Grattan, (1746-1820). Grattan from Tinnehinch, County Wicklow, was M.P. for Malton, 1805-1806 and Dublin, 1806-1820. Grattan came from a distinguished legal family and in England developed a life-long friendship with Charles James Fox. Grattan was a champion for the Roman Catholic cause although a protestant himself. He was a leader for the cause of Ireland and prominent in the general spirit of Enlightenment.
31. Alderman Sir Matthew Wood, (1768-1843), 1st baronet. Wood was highly unusual as he was Lord Mayor for two consecutive years, 1815 and 1816.

136. Queen Caroline cartoon, June 1820.

to Parliament a message, the result of which would be an exposition of the misconduct laid to her charge. She set out for Calais, embarked on board a common packet boat, and accompanied by Alderman Wood & Lady A. Hamilton landed at Dover: Lord Hutchinson & Mr. Brougham being left behind. From Dover ~~to~~ her progress to London was triumphant; the roads lined with spectators, cavalcades joining her, the populace drawing her carriage, and her entrance into London marked by the clamorous applause of the mob, shouts of triumph in her favour, even in front of Carleton House, ushering her to the residence of Mr. Alderman Wood in South Audley Street, where she took up her abode. Ministers immediately brought down to Parliament a Message from the King expressive of his design to lay before both houses a series of |62 documents relating to her conduct abroad with a view to farther proceedings, & moved for a select committee in each house to examine & report, whether any and what proceedings should be instituted; whether in the nature of an impeachment or of a legislative measure. Warm debates ensue; in the course of which Mr. Brougham brings down a message of complaint from the Queen, who remonstrates against the appointment of secret Committees; but the measure is carried, in the Lords; in the lower House the moderate men & County Members propose adjournment of the debate in hopes to preclude the wretched disclosures anticipated, by negotiation for private adjustment of the differences. These milder counsels prevail; the Committee in the Upper House adjourn their day for entering on the investigation from time to time; & the Minister in the Commons in like manner postpones the debates; finally negociations are commenced, but with what probability of success remains to be proved. The tumultuous populace of the metropolis |63 are strongly excited by these events, and give way to disgraceful excess. Illuminations are called for, and the call is partially obeyed. The houses of those, who refuse, or who are thought to be inimical to the Queen's interest, are attacked, & doors and windows are broken. Order is with difficulty restored by military patroles. The Queen after some days, listening to better counsels, withdraws form the house of Alderman Wood, and betakes herself to one in Portman Street, belonging to Lady Anne Hamilton.

June 13.
My Mother arrived to-day on her customary summer visit, last from Cheltenham, where she had been spending a few days with my Aunt M^rs. Travell: as she had been before for a month with Lady Lyttelton near Malvern.

The papers contain an account of the Execution of Louvet the Assassin of the Duke de Berry at Paris: the investigations on his trial prove, that the nefarious deed was one proceeding from uncommunicated & ferocious political fanaticism, engendered in |64 abandoned and Deistical principles. The capital of France has not been without its riots; occasioned by a meditated alteration of the Election law, but suppressed without much effort by the police & military.

June 18th.—
This week the remains of the lamented M^r. Grattan, accompanied by some of the most illustrious characters in the Country were deposited after a solemn funeral, in Westminster Abbey, nigh to those of Pitt and Fox. High encomiums from eminent men of both parties were pronounced on the distinguished Patriot of Ireland, when a new writ for Dublin was moved by Sir James Mackintosh.

June 21.
The negociation with a view to settle the differences between their Majesties without public disclosures has failed. It was conducted by the Duke of Wellington and Lord Castlereagh on the part of the King; by M^r. Brougham & M^r. Denman on that of the Queen. It seems to have been conducted with much temper. On the side of Ministers, the Queen's privileges were recog- |65 -nized, accommodation for leaving the Kingdom in a royal yacht or ship of war was promised, an ample income, & public recognition as Queen at some one foreign Court to be named by herself were conceded: on the other hand her Majesty consented to reside abroad, in deference to the expressed wish of Parliament, but claimed entire & universal acknowledgement of her dignity on the Continent, & the restitution of her name to the Liturgy. The latter point being strenuously resisted by Ministers, the negociation ceased.

Among the deaths in this day's paper is that of the venerable Sir Joseph Banks, at a very advanced age.[32] This highly scientific Philosopher, & munificent patron of science & literature was President of the Royal Society. Blessed with a princely fortune, great zeal, & high talents, his life has been spent in fostering & promoting scientific researches for a long period of years. His admirable library is left to the British Museum: the title is extinct.— |66

June 25.
The same moderate party, which had recommended delay in the proceedings of Parliament as to the royal disagreements, in hopes of the final settlement by negociation without public disclosure, make another effort in the same spirit & views; & a resolution and address to the Queen proposed by M^r. Wilberforce & seconded by M^r. S. Wortley are acceded to by the House of Commons. The purport of these documents is, that the House and Country will not view farther concession on her Majesty's part as an indication of conscious guilt; but

32. Sir Joseph Banks, (1743-1820), 1st baronet. Banks was a noted naturalist and botanist and took part in Captain James Cook's first great voyage, (1768-1771).

137. *Joseph Banks.*

as a farther proof of her deference to Parliament, and her wish to prevent measures subversive of the best Interests of the Crown & Nation; that, therefore, she is solicited to waive her demand of specific introduction into the Liturgy, and general admission at foreign Courts;—in the hope, that an arrangement may yet be made of a private nature.

June 27.

The Queen rejects the proposal made to her by the House of Commons, wording her refusal in a complimentary style of respect to the source of the advice, |67 but decidedly declining to follow it. She petitions the House of Lords to be heard by her counsel at the Bar, which being unanimously granted, Messrs. Brougham & Denman claim on her behalf a delay of proceedings, in order, that she may have time to gain testimony from Italy to rebut the allegations to be brought against her. In the House of Commons Lord Castlereagh gives notice of a motion on the subject on a future day, from which it appears, that the proceedings against her Majesty, if any, are to emanate from the Lords, & that the secret charges are not to be laid before a secret committee of the Lower House.

June 29.

I joined a musical party at M^r. Hippisley: D^r. Hague & his Daughter (he the Professor of Music at Cambridge) are the principal performers; both excellent players on the Violin; M^r. Jeaffreson, Sir H. Dryden, also on the Violin; Miss Hippisley on the Violoncello; M^rs. & Miss Jeaffreson on the Pianoforte. The Music chiefly Haydn's, Mozart's, Handel's, Le Cluir's[33] & Tindal's; with vocal music intermingled, from the |68 works of Shield[34] & Cherubini. A rich treat.

June 30.

At length the Secret Committee of the Lords meets to open the documents containing the charges against the Queen; and from the language of Ministers, it appears, that if their report be unfavourable a bill of pains & penalties against her is likely to be brought in: in the mean time her Majesty seems to act incautiously and daringly: moving about in public and the

33. The Le Clairs were a noted French family of violinists and composers. The eldest was Jean-Marie Leclair, (1697-1764), considered the founder of the French violin school. The composer in question could also have been one of his three brothers, Jean-Marie (the second of the same name, (1703-1777); Pierre Leclair, (1709-1784) and Jean-Benoît Leclair, (1714-1759?).

34. William Shield, (1749-1829). Shield was a theatre composer of note. He published many of his song and violin compositions and his first opera *The Flitch of Bacon* (1778) was an amazing success. He became the opera composer for the Drury Lane theatre and for Covent Garden. The music from Shield's opera, *Poor Soldier* was very popular in America and said to be George Washington's favourite.

populace dragging her carriage: talks of going to Drury Lane, but changes her mind: goes to Guildhall soon after a turbulent meeting held to address her at that place: receives addresses from corporations & public bodies, her answers to which are cautiously worded.

The Bishopric of Bristol is now vacant by the death of Dr. Mansel, Head of Trinity College, Cambridge,[35] who obtained that See from the friendship of the late Mr. Perceval.—Dr. Kaye, Divinity Professor at Cambridge, and head of Christ's College, in that University, |[69] an able divine, and accomplished Scholar, is nominated to the vacant See.[36]

July 4.

We derived much satisfaction to-day in the receipt of a letter from my Brother. It appears, that the news of his promotion to the rank of Captain in the Royal Artillery, which places him on half pay, was brought to him at Malta, by his friend the Hon. Captn. Pellew, a son of Lord Exmouth, commanding the Revolutionnaire. That officer was conveying to Constantinople, Mr. Frere, the Diplomatist; to hold the situation of Minister Plenipotentiary to the Porte, in the Interval between the departure of Sir R Liston the actual Ambassador, & the arrival of his successor, Lord Strangford. Captn. Pellew having warmly pressed George to accompany him & Mrs. Pellew, who sails with her husband on the Voyage, two short hours sufficed him to prepare for his departure, obtain the General's leave, & bid farewell for a time to the Island, where he has so long been on active service. A fortnight brought them to the end |[70] of their cruize, and the Palace of the British Embassy. Nothing can be more animated & interesting than my Brother's sketch of the voyage, country & society: nor are many better calculated to appreciate & describe such scenes.

July 5.

We passed the Evening at Mr. Hippisley's retreat: as he calls a Summer House situate in his plantation at the foot of Stow Hill. No wonder, that the more than Octagenerian Owner delights in these groves of his own plantation & rearing, laid out with simple and judicious taste: while the hospitality of himself and his amiable daughter makes all their acquaintances happy to visit them. Music, such as I named a little above, added to the zest of the rural fete.

July 7.

The die is cast: the Secret Committee of the Lords having made their report on the miserable documents relating to the Queen's misconduct submitted to them. They state, that her Majesty appears to have been living in disgraceful, licentious & adulterous intercourse with one Bartolomo Bergami or Pergami, whom from a menial office (that of Courier) she |[71] raised to a situation of confidence in her suite; caused to be decorated with honourable orders, and the title of nobility, herself assuming the privilege of creating an order, with which she invested this minion. Bergami accompanied her Majesty to the shores of France, & there previously to her embarkation for England withdrew from her service, and returned

35. William Lort Mansel, (1753-1820), Mansel was Master of Trinity College, Cambridge from 1798, and Bishop of Bristol from 1808, holding both positions until his death.

36. Kaye Bishop of Bristol (17??-1853) Master of Christ's College, Cambridge and Bishop of Bristol from 1820 to 1827, after which he was translated to Lincoln. Kaye was a religious writer of note.

to Italy; a measure adopted by another male attendant to her Majesty, calling himself Count Vasali. Rumour has long fixed on this Bergami as the Paramour of the deluded Queen.

Lord Liverpool on the following day brought in a bill of pains and penalties against the Queen, the preamble of which recites the substance of the report, and the Enactments go to the Deposition of her Majesty from the rank, style & Title of Queen of England, and to the dissolution of her marriage. Strong emotion is necessarily excited by these measures: investigation on oath of the charges, and a defence of the conduct alledged against her Majesty, with attempts to prove the charges false, must precede the final discussion of the Bill. |[72]

July 13.

Proceedings against the Queen are stayed till August 17: in the mean time each party is active in procuring witnesses; foreigners daily arrive. The postponement is necessary, in order, that four Judges, at least, may be present at the Investigation, & the progress of the Assizes will not allow that number to attend on an earlier day.

I attended the Gloucester Sessions this week. The weight of business called for a division of the Court, and Mr. Cripps was appointed to preside at the trial of Prisoners. Dr. Cooke, as usual, presided in the other court.

July 15.

Another Bishop is just deceased. Dr. North, of Winchester;[37] having held the See nearly forty years. He was brother of Lord North, and seventy nine years of age. He is to be succeeded by the learned Dr. Tomline, Bishop of Lincoln,[38] the friend of Pitt, whose works have rendered him an object of high respect to all orthodox members of the Church.—

July 22.

My pupil, Thomas Saumarez, finally left me this day, and relieved me from a burdensome responsi- |[73] -bility and duty. Without any direct moral defect in character, he was a most unpleasant inmate; not only slow of apprehension, treacherous in memory, without application and observation, but sullen, unsocial, awkward.

The public papers mention another bloodless revolution to have taken place by the agency of the army; in Naples; the public sentiment rapidly prevailed; & the promise of a constitution resembling that of Spain as lately restored was extorted from the Sovereign. The march of public opinion in the overthrow of despotism is very remarkable at this time; it is only to be hoped, that rational liberty may be every where obtained without convulsions.

July 26th.—

The annual meeting of the Trustees & Managers of the Provident Bank Stow. As Chairman of the Committee of accounts, I laid before the meeting the Treasurer's report and other Documents relating to this useful Institution; some of the features of which are as follow:

---

37. Brownlow North, (1741-1820), Bishop of Winchester, 1781-1820.
38. George Pretyman-Tomline, (1750-1827). Pretyman cnahged his name to Pretyman-Tomline in 1803. He was Bishop of Norwich, 1787-1820, and Winchester, 1820-1827.

total number of Depositors on the books to July 1. 1820—372. (The Institution was formed in 1816.—Stock Depositors 67: amount of Rcd 3 pC$^{t.}$ Ann. 10512.6.1.—Government Debentures |74 £11850.—Deposited from June 30. 1819 to July 1. 1820.—340.—Withdrawn this year in Principal, Interest & Dividends £1261.13.9.—Interest & Dividends due this year £668.4.7.—Total Assets of the Institution over & above all demands—£166.0.8. The description of depositors as to their occupations is also very gratifying.

Deposited in the past year (not including Dividends & Interest unclaimed & added to Principal)

By	5 Journeymen	102. 6. 0
	38 Labourers	1197. 7. 4
	3 Benefit Societies	74. 4. 0
	28 Minors	294. 16. 2
	3 Single women	217. 0. 0
	7 Widows	600. 0. 0
	6 Farmers	370. 0. 0
	23 Male Servants	491. 18. 6
	34 Tradesmen	1360. 0. 3
	30 Female Servants	300. 13.10
	13 Not particularly described	125. 1. 9
	190	5133. 7. 10

M$^{r.}$ Hippisley in the chair.— |75

Aug. 9.

The news arrived of the decease of the Duchess of York.[39] This princess was in her 53$^{d.}$ Year, and has long been in very declining health. She departed at Oatlands on the 6$^{th.}$ Inst. She was of the Prussian family, never had any family, and is commended for her charitable disposition and affability.

The trial of Major Cartwright, the aged partizan of parliamentary Reform, Wooler, the Republican author and Editor of the Black Dwarf, with Edmonds & Lewis Radicals of Birmingham & Coventry, postponed from the last Assizes, is just concluded at Warwick. The defendants are all found guilty of the misdemeanour charged against them in the indictment, namely, unlawfully conspiring at a public meeting at Birmingham to alter the existing constitution of the Country, & throw discredit on the laws of the land, by assuming to themselves the right of Electing the notorious Sir Cha$^{s.}$ Wolsely Bart. to represent Birmingham in the House of Commons, by the title of legislatorial Attorney. Judgment to be pronounced next term.— |76

Aug. 14.

The accounts from Italy shew, that the Revolution at Naples has not been unattended with disastrous consequences. The information is yet very vague of what has passed in Sicily, but it appears, that Palermo has been the scene of violent convulsions and that much blood has

39. Frederica Charlotte Ulrica Catherine, Duchess of York (1767-1820). Frederica was the eldest daughter of Frederick William II, King of Prussia. She married Frederick, Duke of York in 1791.

been shed in resistance of the Neapolitan authorities. It may be gathered, that the Sicilians wish to be separated from the kingdom of Naples, or desire a constitution different from that proposed on the continental dominions of their Sovereign, and it is much to be lamented, that the cause of rational liberty should be impeded by rash & violent efforts rending the members of an ancient union & reducing both branches to a state of feebleness. It is strongly surmised, that the Austrian Government views with alarm & disapprobation the recent events in Southern Italy as portending revolutionary movements in their possessions in the North of Italy, & is even preparing to suppress the spreading principles by an armed force.

Aug. 15

My Mother left us to join her friend Lady Elcho lately arrived at Stanway. |[77]

Aug. 19.

The important Trial of the Queen has at length commenced. The House of Lords entered on the proceedings on the 17th. The attendance of all peers not above 70 Years of age, nor in bad health, nor out of England prior to a certain date, is enforced by heavy penalties. The Queen attends the House in person, veiled, as well she may be: her progress to the House from St. James's Square, where and at Brandenburgh House, Hammersmith, she has temporary residences, is in State: Lady Ann Hamilton, her female attendant. Ald. Wood & Lord Arch. Hamilton wait on her, besides her counsel. The Judges are in the House of Lords to resolve legal questions. The Queen's progress is every where attended by multitudes of favourers. Indeed, her party has used every exertion to court the multitude, & throw odium on the King his Ministers, & the High Court, which is to decide on her case. This seems to be the object of the high-drawn & exaggerated language of her Majesty's answers to the many indiscreet and factious addresses made to her from various parts of the Kingdom, emanating not only from corporate bodies, but from Mechanics and "thinking" artisans, even from |[78] wives & Mothers, prejudging the cause & determined to believe the Queen all purity, the King, Government, & Parliament all corruption. To the same effect also is a long, vehement, & personal letter to the King dated a few days since, really a manifesto to the people, much unlike Ann Boleyn's beautiful letter of remonstrance; for this is libellous in every paragraph.—

Monday Aug. 21.—

We left home on a Tour, with Mrs. Backhouse, who wished by the way to look after a house for her future residence at Gloucester. Her carriage & horses were our mode of conveyance & soon brought us to Frogmill, 10 miles distance, where we baited, & in two hours reached Gloucester, 12 miles farther. We went to the King's Head Inn: looked round the Town, the Spa & its new buildings, visited the County Hall, & Gaol. At the latter I had an interview with Jos. Palmer, a Sheep Stealer, whom I had committed & who had been tried, sentenced & left for execution: tho' found guilty on the clearest & most direct evidence, this hardened young man, persisted in denying his crime, & at the same time, that he had every reason to believe, that |[79] he would be hanged on the following ~~day~~ Saturday: nor did my admonitions appear to affect him more than other exhortations, which had been addressed to him.

The newspaper announced the promotion of the Bishop of Exeter, Dr. Pelham, brother of

Lord Chichester, to the vacant Bishopric of Lincoln.[40] This Prelate is not distinguished for talents or learning.

Tuesday Aug. 22.—

The morning was taken up in farther enquiries and arrangements with a view to Mrs. Backhouse's future residence. We looked into the Cathedral, where some alterations are going on under the auspices of Dr. Griffith, Prebendary & Master of University College, whose taste in architecture & painting is generally known: as also his admirable work on wood, called poker painting, by which he produces portraits almost rivalling colours in delicacy of light and shade, & truth of expression. After a luncheon we set off for Ross—sixteen miles, crossing the Severn by a very handsome new bridge of a single arch, in the construction of which great skill & science have been displayed.—This bridge unites the city of Gloucester with the Isle of Alney, which |80 is formed by the separation of the Severn into two channels, & consists of large meadows. It was the scene of the contest & duel, which, according to some annalists, occurred between Edmund Ironside, the Saxon, and Canute the Dane, in 1016: the issue of which was the division of England between those Kings: Edmund to reign in the South, Canute in the North. But the crafty Dane soon cut off the highspirited Saxon.—We left Alney Isle by Overbridge, with the hamlet of the same name, where a road to the right diverges to Upton & Ledbury. Having left the paved causeway we came on a delightful level road, & passed on the right Highnam, the seat of Sir B. W. Guise, one of the representatives of the County: but not his residence as he generally lives, when in the Country, at Rendcomb, near Cirencester. Highnam House is a structure of red brick with free stone or stucco decorations; and much after the style of Inigo Jones, who is said

138. Rendcombe.

40. George Pelham, (1766-1827). Pelham was the second son of Thomas, 2nd Earl of Chichester. After starting in a military career he turned to the Church and was Bishop of Bristol, 1803-1807, Exeter, 1807-1820 and Lincoln, 1820-1827.

to have given the plan; it resembles, indeed, Coleshill House near Faringdon, the Work of that Architect. Near Highnam, to the left a road diverges to Newnham. The Country is very fertile & rich, partly meadow & partly corn land: The view of Gloucester Cathedral, and the eminences skirting |[81] the Vale, & forming the ascent of the Cotswold country is very beautiful: to the right are seen the Malvern Hills rising from the Worcestershire Vale, & in front are May Hill, & other eminences in the forest of Dean. After passing the Villages of Churcham & Huntley we left the level country, & wound over undulating ground between the Hills; having on the right May hill, a conspicuous round topped eminence, distinguished by a plantation on the summit, and its base richly fringed with furze, alder, & brush wood: indeed, all this pass winding among wooded knolls is very picturesque, & the foliage relieved by the red ochreous soil and ricks. To the left, in the direction of Blaisdon & Michel dean are fine masses of wood, sweeping along the Hills, in the bosom of which is situate the pretty village of Longhope, with its spire: the preferment, I believe, belongs to Mr. Probyn, Archd. of Landaff. Spires, indeed, prevail in this district, as at Lea, the last village in Gloucestershire, through which we passed. We soon entered Herefordshire: the country is extremely fertile both in tillage & pasture; lime is used as manure for the arable land. On our left, as we advanced, was the long Hill richly clothed with wood of very great extent called Penyard chace, at the back of which, not within our view, are the trifling |[82] remains of Penyard Castle, a small fortress, dismantled in the civil wars. We passed also not far from Bury Hill, the undoubted scite of the ancient Roman Station Ariconium; being to the left of the road. The Village of Weston, little more than two miles from Ross has a church with a tower, & two or three very pleasantly situated Mansion Houses. The View of Ross is very pleasing: the Church embosomed in trees crowns the summit of the gentle eminence, on which the town is built; but its streets are narrow, intricate & steep. Driving by the ancient Market House we came to the Inn, the Swan & King's Arms, where we had comfortable accommodations. Our first object was to visit the Prospect field, Church & Churchyard: passing thro' the latter,

139. Highnam.

140. Ross-on-Wye.

beneath ~~of~~ a row of Elms planted by the well known Man of Ross, we entered the Prospect field, a square plot of ground, neglected now, but retaining the original wall & Gateways built by the benevolent Mr. Kyrle. It forms the summit of the hill, overlooking a wide extent of Country, towards Hereford, through, which the River Wye, in mazy windings, meanders through fine meadows, but yearly encroaches more and more on the bank towards Ross. The setting sun lighted up the horizon & |[83] distant hills, some of them in Brecknock & Radnorshires, others in Shropshire & Worcestershire; like all birds' eye views, this is rather tame than interesting or picturesque: tho' the horse-shoe curve of the river, which is here a noble, calm, tho' rapid stream, backed by the foliage, in which the ruins of Wilton Castle are buried on the margin of the river, and near which a bridge of several arches is thrown over the Wye, forms together with the road leading to Hereford, a pleasing landscape. The Prospect field is the site an ancient mansion of the Bishops of Hereford. A long walk planned & planted by the Man of Ross, leads from hence for nearly a mile to a plantation overlooking the River, which also owes its origin to the Theme of Pope's judicious praise. A pleasure house is at the extremity, but all now out of repair. The Church is a spacious edifice in good repair, but having been frequently altered, there is no great uniformity of style or architecture: the tapering spire, which is a very elegant object was partly rebuilt under the auspices of the good Mr. Kyrle; whose taste for architecture & planting was as beneficial to the Town, where he resided, as his benevolent and social habits were creditable to himself. The interior of the Church is very neat & clean: the Galleries & Organ loft are fitted up with incongruous taste; the front of the Organ is |[84] said to have been formerly in Salisbury Cathedral. There is a groupe of very interesting monuments of the Rudhall family, who were settled in this neighbourhood on a manor of the same name. One altar tomb with superincumbent figures records the death~~s~~ of one of the family, a Serjeant at law, in the reign of Hen VII. His wife lies by his side. Another similar tomb is to the memory of a descendent, who died in 1637, & his figure with that of his wife, a Pitt, is recumbent, in white marble, in the elaborate dresses of the time. The sculptor is said to have been Corelli, a foreigner employed in this Country; children in various attitudes & dresses are sculptured round the base, designating the various issue of the deceased. The tomb mentioned before is decorated with sculpture in the same manner. A marble Statue in Roman Costume, as large as the life is erected to the Memory of the loyal General William Rudhall, who defended Hereford against the Parliamentarians in the civil wars. The Clerk, who shewed us the Church pointed to a simple machine used in those times for laming cavalry horses; being pieces of iron, with three points, thrown in the roads, by which the enemy was likely to pass. They were called Cats. Among these |85 ancient tombs is a modern pedestal & bust, admirably executed by Theed, the Sculptor, being the tribute of his friends & neighbours to the late Mr. Westfaling, who died possessed of the Rudhall property, which had devolved to an heiress of the name of Westfaling, whose name on his marriage he assumed: his paternal name was Brereton, the Son of a Gloucestershire Clergyman: he was an active & useful Magistrate & Country Gentleman: Mrs. Westfaling survives him. An inscription on the Pedestal in English & Latin, the former a Translation of the latter, was written by Dr. Luxmore, formerly Bishop of Hereford, now of St. Asaph. The Westfalings are descended from a Bishop of Hereford of that name, who died in 1601. The window behind this cluster of monuments is filled with modern painted Glass, containing the arms and crests of the Brereton & Westfaling families. The Chancel is in many respects interesting: the Eastern Window~~s~~ contains some remains of painted glass, ancient: among other figures is one of the pious Bishop Thomas Cantilupe, of Hereford, who died in 1282, was buried in Hereford Cathedral, & was canonized in 1310. Such was this prelate's sanctity, that pilgrimages were performed to his tomb, even from distant countries. The Bishops of Hereford assumed his paternal coat of arms, which they now use. |85 He is said to have been the last Englishman, who was canonized; & Matthew of Westminster records 163 miracles as performed in a short space of time at his tomb; which still remains. Another figure represents a Mercian Queen. The burial place of the Man of Ross is marked by a flat stone in the Chancel, but the inscription on it was not placed till long after his death; as also the Monument to his Memory, with his bust in relief, was erected long after his decease. The excellent Mr. Kyrle, a pattern to Country Gentlemen, was born at White House in the Parish of Dymock in Gloucestershire in 1637. He died in 1724. His residence, now a private House in the Market place, was nearly opposite the Market House, on the steps of which he was used to make the weekly dole of bread to the poor, from the proceeds of the tolls of the cornmarket. He was a warm loyalist & staunch Churchman: (the great bell of the Church was his gift;) and his benevolent spirit rejoiced in administering to the general good, and exciting others to deeds of charity. The altar piece is a richly ornamented tablet of gilt leather, appropriately adorned, & was the gift of one Scott, who was a manufacturer of such articles. He & his brother, Walter Scott,—though neither a poet nor a |87 novelist, a man of ten thousand—left this town to try their fortune in the Metropolis, poor blue coat boys, having been bred up in a charity School here. Walter was a plaisterer, & having made a handsome fortune, left by his will £200 per ann. from his monies in the fund to restore the decayed

Institution, to which he had been indebted for his Education, & which is now, in consequence, carried on with spirit, affording cloaths and instruction to 60 children, 30 of each sex. What heart does not approve & bless this "grateful restorer"? for such are the words, by which he is designated on the tomb in the Church Yard, erected to his memory. The Chancel contains other Monuments with some elegant inscriptions, chiefly to deceased Rectors, their wives & branches of their families. In the East window of the North Aisle, two young Elm trees spring from an old root without, & are carefully trained, as being offcuts from one of the original trees planted by the Man of Ross, but now cut down. The Benefice is a Rectory of considerable value; I was told £1000 per ann: in the gift of the Bishop or Chapter of Hereford; & Mr. Underwood, a Canon of that Cathedral, is the present Incumbent. The parsonage house, with a large garden, apparently an excellent mansion, adjoins the Church Yard.— |88 Having returned to our Inn, to tea, the Newspapers of the day claimed our attention; being the first of the series of horrible developments of the imputed adulteries and gross indecencies of the Queen. The Examination of Witnesses in support of the bill of pains & penalties is likely to last a considerable time, and satiate the Country with the narrative of profligate amours, & abandoned favourites. The advocates in the cause arrayed on the side of the Prosecution are the Attorney General (Gifford) and Solr. General (Copley) with Dr. Adams as a Civilian on the side of the defence, the Queen's Atty. & Solr. Generals (Brougham & Denman) Mr. Williams & Dr. Lushington. Most of the Witnesses are expected to be former domestics & persons employed in the Queens service as labourers, tradesmen &c: Servants at Inns, where she stopped during her travels; & persons who sailed with her during her Levantine Voyage. And, indeed, such persons were the probable witnesses of such degrading transactions, which drove all persons of character or rank in life from the Society of the Queen. Most of these Witnesses are lodged in Cotton Garden,[41] where accommodations have |89 been provided for them. They are thus in constant readiness to be called into the House of Lords, are closely guarded,

141. Pencil sketch view on the Wye between Monmouth and Ross, by Francis Witts.

41. There was a Cotton Garden in Lambeth, and as the reference is to 'both sides of the river, perhaps this was the place.

both on the side of the River, & in the Avenues leading to Cotton Garden, as the popular prejudice against foreign witnesses, the clamour of the Mob in favour of the Queen, and the manifest indications of riot, make such precautions necessary for the security of the persons of the Witnesses.

Wednesday Aug. 23.—

A lovely day in every respect, & admirably suited for our day's excursion by water to Monmouth. Having given orders to the Coachman to meet us at that place with the carriage, the distance being about eleven miles, we took boat about nine o clock, after breakfast. The Innkeeper supplied us with the boat: the expence of which inconsiderable; 2 Guineas to Monmouth: 4 to Chepstow: we engaged the boat for the two days; & were rowed by three very civil intelligent men, one of whom paddled in the Stern; they were little tradesmen, to whom these Summer gains & the excursion are desirable; the owner of the boat provides them with provisions, but they expect a present from the party at the conclusion of their voyage, when they tow the boat back against the stream to Ross. The boat is provided |[90] with an awning, which may be occasionally used to shelter from sun, or cold or rain. For the first few miles the banks of the river are rather tame & uninteresting; the beauty of the scenery hardly developes itself till beyond Goodrich Castle: the water is a rapid, smooth, dark coloured stream, & remarkable everywhere for the extraordinary sinuosities of its course. The river rises near the summit of Plinlimmon Hills in Montgomeryshire, & dividing the counties of Radnor & Brecon, passes thro' the middle of Herefordshire; then becomes a second boundary between Monmouthshire & Gloucestershire, & falls into the Severn a little below Chepstow. The distance from Ross to Chepstow is about 40 miles. The river is navigable to Hereford by barges of from 18 to 40 Tons; but these are unable to ascend unless the quantity of water be of moderate height; shallows often impede them in summer, & floods in winter. It is owing to the occasional rapidity of the stream, that it is crossed by so few bridges. Beneath one of these, Wilton Bridge, built in 1597, a heavy structure of several arches, we passed a little way below Ross; here the horse shoe curve of the stream round a large meadow terminates. The causeway from Ross leads over this bridge towards Hereford, 14 miles; and the road to Monmouth |[91] diverged to the left beyond the Bridge. The arch next the village of Wilton was broken down by the orders of Gen. Rudhall, in the wars of Ch. 1. to impede the rebel troops in their march to Hereford. The Village of Wilton on the opposite side of the river to Ross is adorned by the ivied remains of an ancient Castle near the Water's Edge, embosomed in trees, and but little distance from the bridge. This castle in feudal times belonged to the Longchamps, & descended from them to the Greys, ancestors of the Lords Grey de Wilton, it was demolished by the Royalist Governors of Hereford in the civil wars. The property is now vested, as I understand, in Guy's Hospital. Gliding onwards through meadows, we passed beneath the sloping banks, which owe their foliage to the Man of Ross: his spire rising from a tufted knoll forms an occasional interesting object; and the more distant & richly clothed Hills of Penyard & the chace are rich features in the scene. The banks on the right side of the river gradually rise, & one promontory or knoll, fringed with wood to the edge of the river which encircles it, ~~leads~~ is surmounted by a Gentleman's Seat, called Pencraig; the House commands a lovely reach of the river, the meadows beyond, & the Town & Church of Ross, in the mellowed distance. Here & in many of the |[92] meanders

142. Pen and wash near Abergavenny, by Francis Wittts.

of the river we met with rapids in the stream, down which the boat bounded, while the rowers rested on their oars: and during all this day's excursion the oars broke up the delicate landscape of nature reflected on the glassy surface with inimitable truth & chasteness of colouring. Nothing is more beautiful than this watery landscape;

Along the downward sky the white clouds sail
And now the radiant orb disclose, now veil;
Embossed with waving woods, the fair serene
Beflects each tint, that gilds the varied scene.
But soon the fisherman in thoughtless mood
Steers his light bark across the tranquil flood;
Chased by the bark the ~~mimic~~ trembling mountains fly,
Each mimic tint escapes the searching eye,
And rippling waves the liquid landscape pour
In circling eddies to the winding shore.†

†In beautiful taste are the lines of Statius, describing a villa on the Bay of Naples.
"Quum jam fessa dies, et in ce quora montiiopaci
Umbra cadit, vitreoque natant prætoria ponto.—

Of all light barks the lightest is the coracle of the Wye, the rude British canoe, still in use on this & other Welch rivers: it consists of a skin, canvass or other material caulked over & made impervious to the water, stretched over a frame work of light wood, much in the shape

143. Pen and wash view of Llanfoist near Abergavenny, by Francis Witts.

of a tortoise shell, & calculated to hold only one navigator. We saw two or three lying on the banks, they being still in customary use; but |93 it being harvest time the labours of the field engrossed all the fishermen, who might otherwise have been venturing in these cockleshell boats, which seem little able to stem the current, or meet the agitated surface of the stream: they are so light, that the owner can easily carry them on his back from place to place. After passing the promontory of Pencraig, the ivied & rent Towers of Goodrich Castle opened on our view: being on a finely wooded knoll on the right bank of the river, round which the Wye courses in a semicircular sweep. The left bank consists of meadows, & a champaign tract bounded by distant hills and the Town & Church Spire of Ross, distant about four miles. There is here a ferry across the River, communicating with a road leading to Ross; the boat is guided by a rope, stretched across the stream, a custom certainly in use in the 14th. Cent. Near the ferry house we landed, & the Boatmen rowed round the hill, on which the Castle Ruins stand to the opposite side of the Peninsula, where they waited for us. Under the guidance of an old dame, ever watchful for the arrival of a party, in this touring season, we crossed a field or two, till we ascended the Hill & entered into the thick grove, which clothes the declivity. Here our conductress left us, not without a claim on our purse, to clamber up a very |94 steep & winding footpath to the crown of the hill & precincts of the Castle. Here another guide awaited us, an inhabitant of the neighbouring village, well skilled in the Cicerone's Art, knowing a little of taste, a little of antiquity, a little of landscape painting. Our first view of the ruins had presented us with a confused groupe of ivied, ruined Towers; now, standing on the edge of the Castle ditch, partly choked with rubbish, & fringed with ample foliage of forest trees, we took a minute survey of the remains. The Castle in its perfect state formed a parallelogram; one side, overhanging the river, rises abruptly from a precipice of rock richly clothed with brush wood, springing from the clefts & fissures: at the lower extremity of this side, according to the course of the Wye is the tower, (12) which flanks the main entrance on one side, corresponding to another tower on the other side of the gateway. The upper extremity of this side of the parallelogram terminates in what is called the Ladies Tower, (7) & doubtless contained the apartments of the females of the family; in this Tower is a huge rent or breach, occasioned by the ~~alt~~ artillery of the Parliamentary forces during the Siege of the Castle, in 1646. (The accompanying rude |95

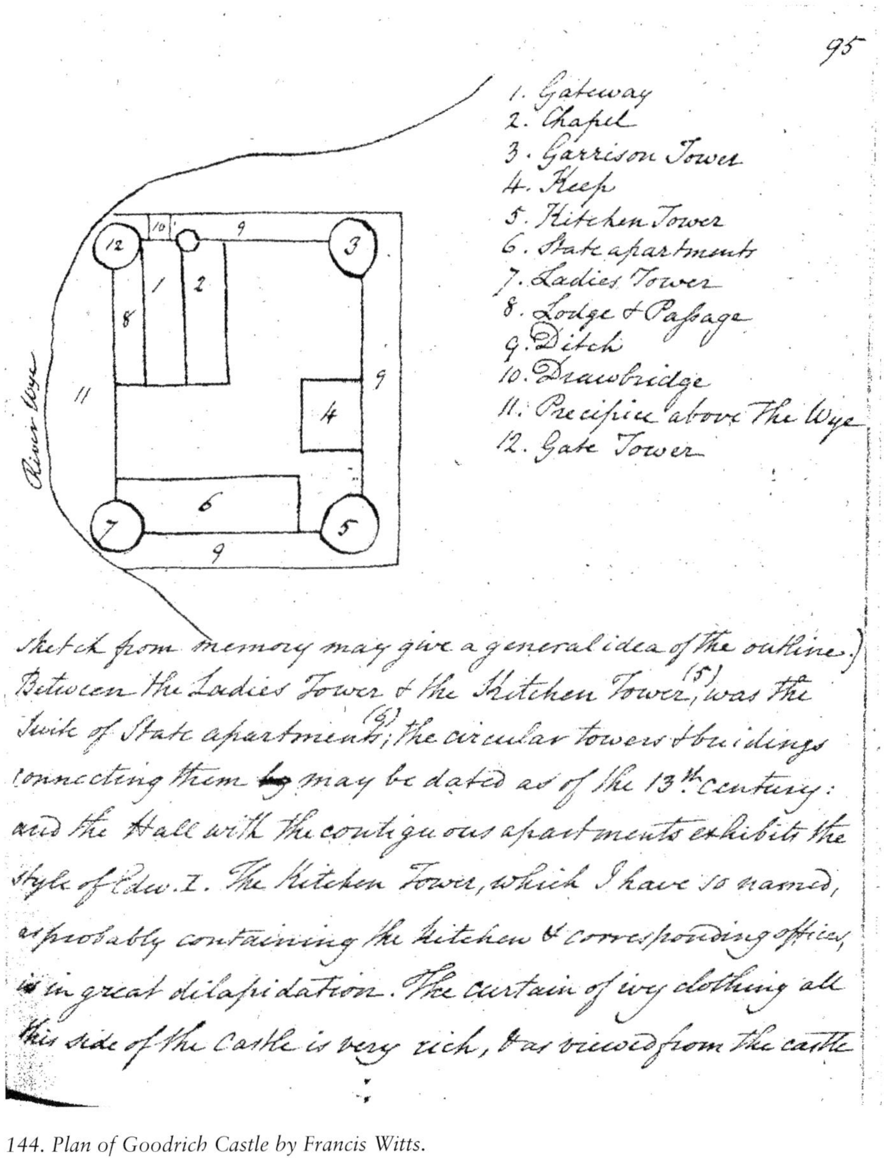
95

1. Gateway
2. Chapel
3. Garrison Tower
4. Keep
5. Kitchen Tower
6. State apartments
7. Ladies Tower
8. Lodge & Passage
9. Ditch
10. Drawbridge
11. Precipice above the Wye
12. Gate Tower

sketch from memory may give a general idea of the outline.) Between the Ladies Tower & the Kitchen Tower, (5) was the Suite of State apartments; (6) the circular towers & buildings connecting them ~~by~~ may be dated as of the 13th Century: and the Hall with the contiguous apartments exhibits the style of Edw. I. The Kitchen Tower, which I have so named, as probably containing the kitchen & corresponding offices, is in great dilapidation. The curtain of ivy clothing all this side of the Castle is very rich, & as viewed from the castle

144. Plan of Goodrich Castle by Francis Witts.

1. Gateway
2. Chapel
3. Garrison Tower
4. Keep
5. Kitchen Tower
6. State apartments
7. Ladies Tower
8. Lodge & Passage
9. Ditch
10. Drawbridge
11. Precipice above The Wye
12. Gate Tower

sketch from memory may give a general idea of the outline.) Between the Ladies Tower & the Kitchen Tower, (5) was the Suite of State apartments; (6) the circular towers & buildings connecting them ~~by~~ may be dated as of the 13th. Century: and the Hall with the contiguous apartments exhibits the style of Edw. I. The Kitchen Tower, which I have so named, as probably containing the kitchen & corresponding offices, is in great dilapidation. The curtain of ivy clothing all this side of the castle is very rich, & as viewed from the castle |96 ditch beautifully picturesque. The architectural remains of the State apartments are also very beautiful: Especially two pointed arches separated by a slender shaft. The views from the ruins on the side overhanging the River are equally beautiful & extensive: on the opposite side of the Wye in the valley is the village of Walford, sweetly situate beneath a wooded hill & embosomed in orchards: still more interest would have accompanied the groupe, had the Church retained its tapering spire, which was not long ago destroyed by lightning. Beyond the Kitchen Tower is the ancient Saxon keep, (4) close to the wall, which unites the

145. West Tower of Goodrich Castle.

146. Goodrich Castle.

Kitchen Tower with the Garison Tower, (3) but nearer to the former than to the latter. It is quadrangular, & unquestionably the first fortress erected on the spot, round which the other works & buildings have been formed, as the principles and plans of defensive warfare were developed in succeeding ages. In fact, the Saxon Castle was a massy square tower with a few adjoining offices: divided into stories, of which, the lowest, the donjon, was entered on a level with the ~~foundation~~ court; the upper apartments, which were appropriated to the family & garrison, were entered by a stack or flight of stone steps, now destroyed rising to |97 a door on the first story. In this tower a winding stone staircase leads from the first story to the apartments above, & the top of the Tower; and our guide was very solicitous with us to ascend it. This we did, but on nearly reaching the summit, when we were pressed to climb an unparapeted fragment, which, no doubt, commanded a most magnificent panoramic view, we declined the hazard of tumbling over ~~the~~ into the Court below, nor coveted the fame of martyrdom in the cause of the Picturesque. However, a party, which followed us, was more bold than we were, & perhaps, the danger was less than it appeared. From the height, which we had reached, the view into the undulating ground, adjacent to the Castle & village of the same name, was very interesting: on this side the fortress was most open to attack, & therefore it was judicious to strengthen this side the most by making the circular towers at the corners range with the ancient keep in line. The windows are all toward the interior of the Castle; none looking out on the Country over the ditch: (9) where they have not been altered in later times their style is pure Saxon: the three apartments of the Tower are only fourteen feet square each: the Tower itself is a square of twenty nine feet. The Garri- |98 -son Tower and the adjoining portions of the building towards the Gateway on one side & the Keep on the other are in a state of great dilapidation, though highly picturesque: ranges of stabling and other offices seem to have been in this quarter. No part of the edifice is more striking than the buttresses of the Towers, rooted, as it were in the ditch; so that the quadrangular form of the base, gradually receding as the building arose in height, is exchanged towards the summit for the circular. In fact, as sapping & undermining were most relied on in the attack of fortresses, every art was exerted to strengthen the foundations. The gateway (1) is a fine sample of the ancient contrivances for safety and defence, being constructed with remarkable strength and artifice. Flanked by towers, one circular of larger dimensions on the brink of the precipice overhanging the Wye, the other octangular, the entrance is long, narrow, & low, & the drawbridge (10) originally thrown over the ditch fitted exactly, when raised, to the arch of the gateway, and so formed an additional barrier. Various contrivances were adapted for resisting the progress of assailants in the length of the passage; |99 portcullises, (an invention not unknown to the Romans,) machicolations, projections in the side walls adapted for the insertion of massy beams across the passage, which would serve as a frame work for masonry, should the approaching of the enemy require the garrison to blockade themselves by an interior wall thrown up with haste. |

The diary comes to an end here — not unusual for the narratives of the various family tours, which start off with detailed descriptions and then peter out. Nothing survives for the period 24 August 1820 to 4 September 1822 — a gap of two years. The diaries then commence once more with a change in style. With occasional gaps in between, this is generally the style Francis Witts stays with for the reminder of his life.

As for the two year gap, the diaries of Agnes Witts continue to throw some light on family events. From August until the end of October, Agnes stayed at Stanway with Lady Elcho and her companion (or friend it is uncertain which) Miss Greenwood. That Miss Greenwood was also of 'a certain age' can be gleaned from the comments such as 'our trio of old Ladies cheerful . . . much talk among the <u>three</u> elderly ladies . . .

The Upper Slaughter family, including Mrs. Backhouse were back in Circulation as Agnes records a visit: 13 November 1820: My Son Daughter Grandson & Mrs. Backhouse came to Dinner & to stay the night . . .

Agnes spent December back at Stanway with Lady Elcho and for almost all of January and the first ten days she was back at Cheltenham, completely incapacitated by an illness and unable to keep up her usual daily record. Francis was in attendance at the

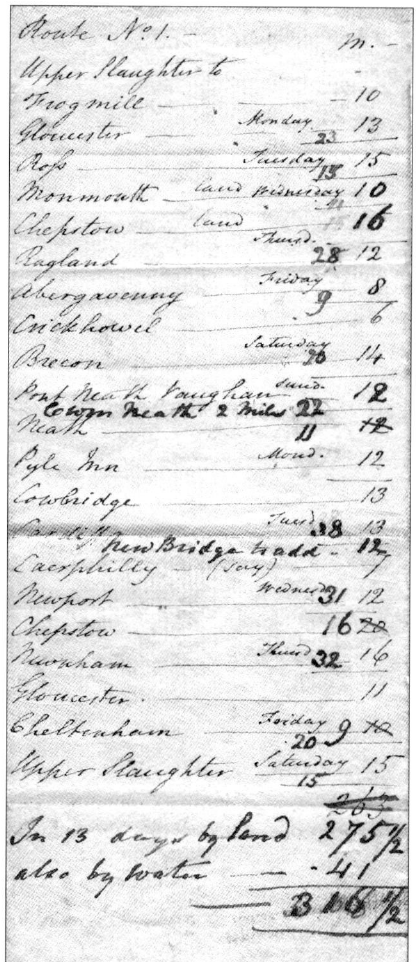
Route No. 1. — m. —
Upper Slaughter to
Frogmill — 10
Gloucester — Monday 23 — 13
Ross — Tuesday 15 — 15
Monmouth — land Wednesday — 10
Chepstow — land — 16
Ragland — Thursd. 28 — 12
Abergavenny — Friday 9 — 8
Crickhowel — 6
Brecon — Saturday 26 — 14
Pont Neath Vaughan — Sund. — 12
Cwm Neath 2 miles 22
Neath — 11 — 12
Pyle Inn — Mond. — 12
Cowbridge — 13
Cardiff — Tues. 28 — 13
New Bridge to add — 12
Caerphilly (say) — 7
Newport — Wednes. 31 — 12
Chepstow — 16
Newnham — Thurs. 32 — 16
Gloucester — 11
Cheltenham — Friday 20 — 9
Upper Slaughter — Saturday 15 — 15
263
In 13 days by land 275½
also by water — 41
316½

147. *Journey to South Wales.*

end of the illness and then went to rejoin Margaret and Edward at Bath. It seems that once more Margaret was trying the waters for a cure to her general malaise and also seeking the usual Bath medical advice. They returned to Upper Slaughter in March: 29 March 1821: . . . soon after one arrived My Son & Daughter their Dear Boy & Mrs. Backhouse in their way from Bath . . .

As usual, Agnes spent the early part of the summer at Upper Slaughter, and on 21 July 1821 left for a six week trip to Calwich. In October she was back at Stanway, and introduced to Lady Elcho's new companion, Miss Church.

One of the favourite visitors at Stanway House for dinner and cards in the evening had been young Charles Keysall, the curate. For more than ten years he had been a welcome addition to the old ladies who had enjoyed his spirited company. The time had now come for him to move on, and his replacement was Frank's old pupil, Frederick Aston. Agnes records the events: 19 November 1821: . . . Charles Keysall took his final departure . . . 24 November 1821: . . . Mr. F. Aston <u>the new curate</u> from Wood Stanway . . . 25 November 1821: . . . Much pleased with Mr. Aston's manner of performing . . . 26 November 1821: . . . I then left Ldy. Elcho and poor Dear old Stanway, with strong feelings of regret & in two hours got to my own little dwelling . . .

One of the fascinating social facts about the Witts family — parents and Son — is their lack of celebration of Christmas. For them Christmas appears to be no more than the church service, and apart from that, in almost all diary entries it appears if the day, and indeed all of the Christmas, New Year and Twelth Night period are little more than the usual routine. In 1821 for the first time Agnes records something special for Christmas Eve: 24 December 1821: . . . dined en famille with Mrs. Cooke on a Kentish roast turkey & Minced pies . . .

Life at Upper Slaughter went on as normal and Agnes records little other than the weekly receiving and sending of letters to her dear son. Occasionally she enjoyed a visit as Frank went on his way to the Sessions: 14 January 1822: . . . My Dear Son came to me at noon to take up his abode on his way to Gloucester Sessions, a fine chatty evening . . . 17 January 1822: . . . My Dear Son pass'd an hour with me in his way home . . .

By this time Mrs. Backhouse was now a resident at Gloucester, having moved south to be nearer her only family. She was a frequent visitor at Upper Slaughter. Young Edward was now at school in Bath: 26 January 1822: . . . to meet Mrs. Backhouse & my Grandson from Slaughter on their road to Gloucester & for him to go to school the next day to Bath . . .

Little more is to record other than the usual daily events.

Witts Family Papers F309

Diary

1822—Sept. 5.—

My cousins Ann & Apphia Witts came on a visit to us. They had left Cookham Grove, where they had been spending some time with their Uncle & Aunt Witts.

Sept. 9.

The Stanway party came to dine with us, consisting of Lady Elcho, my Mother, my cousins the Miss Guydickens's, & the companion of Lady Elcho, Miss Church.

Sept. 13.

Received a letter from my friend & Cousin Mr. John Backhouse, announcing that he & his wife had advanced on their road from Wavertree near Liverpool, as far as Birmingham, on their way to Gloucester & this place, with an intention to visit Mrs. Backhouse & ourselves: when he received a letter from his Patron, Mr. Canning, summoning him to London. It seems, that negotiations are on foot to secure to Mr. Canning a seat in the Cabinet at home instead of his going as Governor General to India, whither John Backhouse was to have accompanied him on a large salary as private Secretary.[1] The members of Administration cannot, it appears, fill up their ranks, thinned by the lamentable death of the Marquis of Londonderry, without recurring to Mr. Canning. John Backhouse will, doubtless, be placed

1. John Backhouse, (1784-1845). John Backhouse was first cousin to Margaret Witts and he had a distinguished career in the Civil Service. It cannot have been beyond the ambition of Francis Witts that his wife's cousin, a close friend of George Canning, might somehow oil the path to patronage in some appropriate Church office. John Backhouse was originally private Secretary to George Canning, and on Canning's elevation to Government became the Permanent Under-Secretary of State at the Foreign Office. It was largely through his influence and ability that the office became a permanent Civil Service position form that time onwards. The Backhouse Family Papers survive in Duke University Library Special Collection Holdings: Caribbean Islands and reveal information on business and personal correspondence of the Backhouse family, (principally of John Backhouse). Material for the 18th and early 19th centuries reflects the family's mercantile operations, including efforts to collect pre-Revolutionary debts in America. Other papers relate to Backhouse's career as Commissioner and Receiver General of the Excise Office and Under Secretary of State for Foreign Affairs, his service as private secretary to George Canning, his service with the diplomatic corps, his art collection, and his mercantile associates in Amsterdam and Hamburg. Other subjects include the Board of Control under Canning, and the British consulates at Canton and Amoy. Family correspondence contains numerous references to the Foreign Office and to relations with Circassia, France, Greece, Russia, Turkey, and the United States. Letters and diaries of Backhouse's son, George, and his wife include references to the slave trade and describe their life in Havana while he was commissary judge there. This son was named in honour of John's patron as George Canning Backhouse, and he was prominent in the anti-slavery campaigns in the West Indies. See Biographical Index for more information.

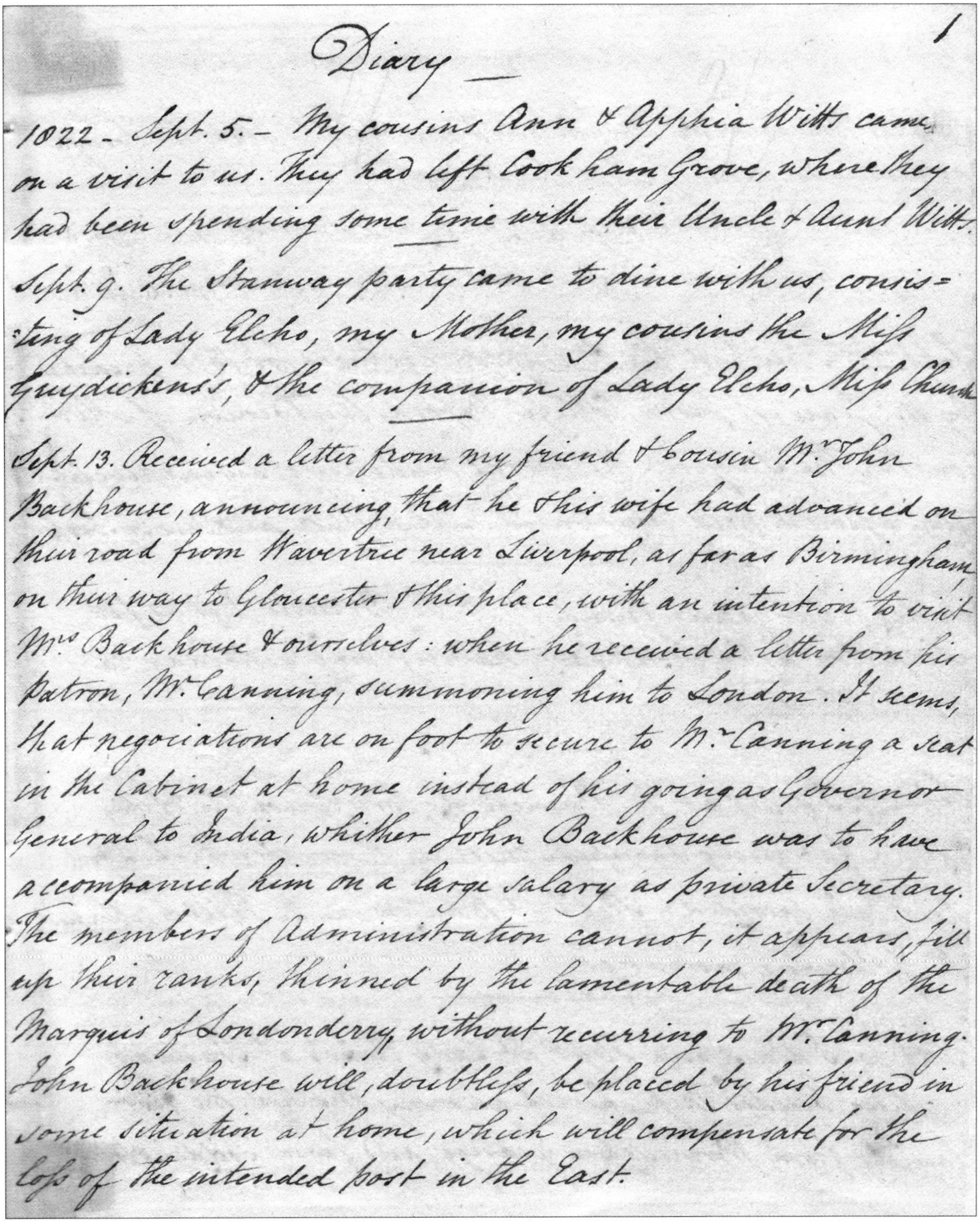

Diary — 1

1822 – Sept. 5. – My cousins Ann & Apphia Witts came on a visit to us. They had left Cookham Grove, where they had been spending some time with their Uncle & Aunt Witts.

Sept. 9. The Stanway party came to dine with us, consisting of Lady Elcho, my Mother, my cousins the Miss Guydickens's, & the companion of Lady Elcho, Miss Church

Sept. 13. Received a letter from my friend & Cousin Mr John Backhouse, announcing, that he & his wife had advanced on their road from Wavertree near Liverpool, as far as Birmingham on their way to Gloucester & this place, with an intention to visit Mrs Backhouse & ourselves: when he received a letter from his patron, Mr Canning, summoning him to London. It seems, that negociations are on foot to secure to Mr Canning a seat in the Cabinet at home instead of his going as Governor General to India, whither John Backhouse was to have accompanied him on a large salary as private Secretary. The members of Administration cannot, it appears, fill up their ranks, thinned by the lamentable death of the Marquis of Londonderry without recurring to Mr Canning. John Backhouse will, doubtless, be placed by his friend in some situation at home, which will compensate for the loss of the intended post in the East.

by his friend in some situation at home, which will compensate for the loss of the intended post in the East. |2

Sept. 16.
I dined at Mr. Bowen's, at Temple Guiting.

Sept. 18.
Mr. Canning is appointed Secretary of State for Foreign Affairs in the room of Lord Londonderry.—

Finished Dr. D'Oyly's Life of Archbishop Sancroft in 2 Vols. 8vo.[2] A very interesting memoir of that excellent, pious, firm prelate.

Sept. 25.
Finished the Bampton Lectures for 1821, preached by Mr. Jones, of Jesus College, Oxford, Archdeacon of Merioneth. The subject—the moral tendency of divine revelation assorted and illustrated.—A diffuse and heavy book.

Sept. 26.
Our young friend Mr. J. B. Browne left us for Salperton after breakfast, having come yesterday to spend the day.

Sept. 27.
I dined at Dr. Warneford's,[3] Bourton on the Hill, after a fatiguing turnpike meeting there, at which Lord Redesdale presided. Slept at Bourton on the Hill & returned the following morning.

Sept. 30.
I dined and slept at Lady Elcho's at Stanway, meeting, besides Miss Church and my Mother, the Gist family from Wormington Grange, and from Toddington |3 Mr. Eddy & his son, and Mr. David Hughes.

Oct. 1.
Attended the annual meeting of the Stow District Committee of the Society for promoting Christian Knowledge. Lord Redesdale presided. It appeared from the report of the Secretary, Mr. Ford, that there had been circulated in the course of the last year from the Depository of books at Stow—

109 Bibles
165 Testaments
334 Common Prayer books & Psalters
1272 Tracts.—

2. G. Doyly, *Life of Archbishop Sancroft*. (1821). William Sancroft, (1617-1693) was Archbishop of Canterbury, 1678-1690.
3. Samuel Warneford, (1763-1855). Warneford was rector of Bourton-on-the-Hill and a man of very great inherited wealth. He and his wife Philadelphia were childless and great philanthropists. For a fuller detail see the Biographical Index.

The annual meeting and dinner of the Stow Book Society was afterwards held, which I attended, and at which I was chosen Secretary, in the room of Sir Henry Dryden, who resigned. Mr. Pole, of Wick Hill, presided.—

Oct. 3.

We dined at Dr. & Mrs. Rice's at Oddington. I had, as usual, on Thursdays, passed the forenoon in transacting business at the Justice Room & Provident Bank at Stow.

Oct. 4.

My Mother arrived from Stanway on a visit: Lady Elcho having left that place for London & Ramsgate.

Oct. 8.

Miss Witts's left us for Gloucester, where they propose passing a little time in lodgings till Lady Lyttelton can |[4] receive them at Pickham Grove.

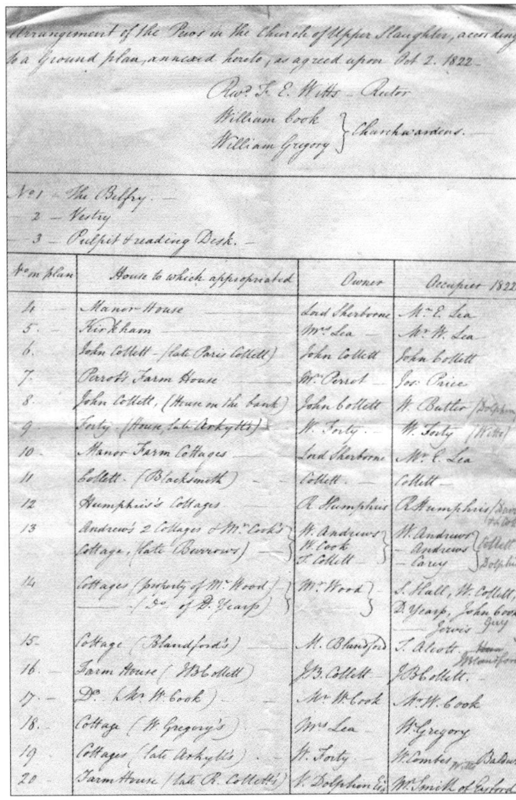

Arrangement of the Pews in the Church of Upper Slaughter, according to a Ground plan, annexed hereto, as agreed upon Oct. 2. 1822.

Revd. F. E. Witts – Rector
William Cook }
William Gregory } Churchwardens.

No. 1 – The Belfry. –
2 – Vestry
3 – Pulpit & reading Desk. –

No. in plan	House to which appropriated	Owner	Occupier 1822
4	Manor House	Lord Sherborne	Mr. E. Lea
5	Kirkham	Mrs. Lea	Mr. W. Lea
6	John Collett – (late Paris Collett)	John Collett	John Collett
7	Parrot's Farm House	Mr. Perrot	Jos. Price
8	John Collett, (House on the bank)	John Collett	W. Butler (Dolphin)
9	Forty (House, late Arkyll's)	W. Forty	W. Forty (Witts)
10	Manor Farm Cottages	Lord Sherborne	Mr. E. Lea
11	Collett (Blacksmith)	Collett	Collett
12	Humphris's Cottages	R. Humphris	R. Humphris (Davis & Collett)
13	Andrews's 2 Cottages & Mr. Cook's Cottage, (late Burrows)	W. Andrews, W. Cook, T. Collett	W. Andrews – Andrews – Carey (Collett, Dolphin)
14	Cottages (property of Mr. Wood) (Do. of D. Yearp)	Mr. Wood	S. Hall, W. Collett, D. Yearp, John Cook, Jervis, Guy
15	Cottage (Blandford's)	M. Blandford	T. Alcott. ~~Hum~~ W. Blandford
16	Farm House (J. B. Collett)	J. B. Collett	J. B. Collett.
17	Do. (Mr. W. Cook)	Mr. W. Cook	Mr. W. Cook
18	Cottage (W. Gregory's)	Mrs. Lea	W. Gregory
19	Cottages (late Arkyll's)	W. Forty	W. Combes, Widow Baldwin
20	Farm House (late R. Collett)	V. Dolphin Esq.	Mr. Smith of Eyford

148. *Upper Slaughter Pews. WFP R13 2 October 1822.*

Oct. 9.

The Newspapers state, that Mr. Canning has nominated our friend & relation John Backhouse, one of the Under Secretaries of State in the foreign department. I hope, we shall soon hear this confirmed by himself. His familiarity with public business, his assiduity, his acquirements and his talents calculate him to hold such an office with credit to himself and advantage to the public. His amiable and excellent character as a Son, a father, a husband, and in other relations of life, makes him well deserving of more prosperity than has yet fallen to his share. Finished a publication, entitled "Cromwell & his terms." By Thomas Cromwell 8vo. 1822. Written by a descendant, who has more than a family feeling for his hero. He is often his unqualified apologist: the principles of a modern reformer & whig often peep out. The book is written in a confused, conceited & bad style; but it is impossible to read without interest memoirs of the Transactions of those times.

|[5]

Oct. 14.

John Browne left us to-day having spent Saturday and yesterday at Upper Slaughter.— After an early dinner I accompanied Mrs. Backhouse to Gloucester, who had delayed her return home till the beginning of the Sessions week, that she might convey me thither.

Oct. 15.

Dr. Cooke, of Tortworth, as usual, was Chairman; Mr. Cripps, the member for Cirencester, presided in the second court, trying Prisoners. Among the leading Magistrates were the Duke of Beaufort, Mr. Holford, M.P. for Queenborough, a great authority on all matters relating to Prisons, Mr. R. B. Cooper, M.P. for the city of Gloucester, Sir W. Guise, member for the County, Messrs. Baker, father & son, Goodrich, Dr. Timbrell, Mr. Byles, Mr. Keysall, Mr. Phelps, lately one of the Commissioners in the investigation of Ilchester gaol & the alledged improprieties practised there, Mr. Goldney, Mr. Ludlow Walker &c.

The most important business before us was a charge of misconduct & cruelty brought by Mr. Jones, Chaplain of the County Gaol, against Mr. Cunningham, the Governor. The Chaplain, who had held the Station more than thirty years, and had been a Magistrate of the County for many years, |6 alledged several serious charges against the Governor, who for a very long time had been held an invaluable Servant of the County, equally humane, judicious & intelligent. The visiting Justices, Messrs. T. J. L. Baker, & Byles, had investigated the business, & brought forward a large body of evidence, collected by them, totally exculpating the Governor, and proving the chaplain to have been actuated by malicious motives, guilty of falsehood, and to have abused not only his situation as ~~Mag~~ Chaplain, but also as Magistrate, to compass his object, the degradation of the Governor. The Chaplain and Governor being confronted, the charges of the former being held frivolous & vexatious, & the defence of the latter quite satisfactory, in a very crowded room, the Magistrates unanimously voted Mr. Jones's dismissal from the Office of Chaplain. He is believed to be in very embarrassed circumstances.

Oct. 16.

A still stronger and more painful measure ~~still~~ remained, which was adopted at a meeting of the Magistrates; when 25 out of 27 decided upon addressing the Duke of |7 Beaufort as Custos Rotalorum to take the proper measures for the erasure of the name of Mr. Jones from the Commission of the Peace: on the ground, that he had in the late transactions perverted his situation of magistrate to follow up his own malicious & clandestine purposes. The two Gentlemen, who dissented, did so on the ground, that they had not heard the evidence read yesterday: others similarly circumstanced signed the resolutions, from a conviction of the propriety of the measure stated as it was with serious caution by the Magistrates, who spoke on the occasion.

The Revd. R. Cooper, Son of the Member for Gloucester was put in nomination for the vacant place of chaplain, appointed ad interim, and the Magistrates present pledged themselves to concur in his election at the Epiphany Sessions.

Oct. 17.

During my stay at Gloucester I frequently saw my cousins Anne & Apphia Witts, who were in comfortable lodgings.

Oct. 18.

I returned home: met my horses at Cheltenham, where I called on my Aunt Mrs. Travell, whom I had not |8 seen for a long time; she appeared to me much broken. The Miss Guydickens' were her guests.

Oct. 19.

Was the only Commissioner of the Evesham second district of roads, who adhered to an engagement to meet Mr. Stokes, the Surveyor, at Broadway hill, to view a proposed new line of road, which would materially diminish the steepness of the ascent. In the little ale house, "the fish," at the summit of the hill, are copies of verses in Latin and English, lauding the amenity of the vale of Evesham, descried from thence &c; these lines were written by the ingenious Mr. Greaves, the Author of the Spiritual Quixote.[4]

Oct. 26.

The newspapers announce, that Lord Amherst is appointed Governor General of India. This accomplished Nobleman was a few years since dispatched as Ambassador to China, and shipwrecked in the Alceste Frigate on his return.

Oct. 27.

Read Bishop Mant's second charge to his Diocese of Killaloe, delivered in 1821.[5] It is a judicious address on l9 points of discipline, ~~referring~~ exhorting the clergy to a strict adherence to the Rubric & Canons, requiring conscientious caution in signing testimonials, impressing the duty of erecting new churches and Glebe houses, where wanted &c.—

Oct. 30.

The newspapers announce the degradation and deprivation of the wretched Dr. Percy Jocelyn, Bishop of Clogher.[6] This prelate, nearly connected with the estimable family of Earl Roden, was peculiar for the assumed sanctity of his deportment, the hypocritical veil thrown over the grossest & most disgusting vice. Detected in London in the most revolting excesses of unnatural lust, which he indulged with a fatuity almost incomprehensible, & seized by the civil power, he & the object of his vice alike fled from their bail, while an Ecclesiastical court, composed of the Primate of Ireland, with four of his Brethren, have been engaged in recording the miserable evidence, which has justly led to his sentence of deprivation.

Oct. 31.

We dined at Mr. Croome's at Bourton on the Water.

4. Richard Graves, *The Spiritual Quixote, or The Summer's Ramble of Mr. Geoffrey Wildgoose.* (1792).
5. Richard Mant, (1776-1848), Bishop of Killaloe, 1820-1823, and Down and Connor, 1823-1848.
6. Percy Jocelyn, (1764-1843). Jocelyn was Bishop of Clogher from 1820 to 1822. Third son of Robert, 1st. Earl of Roden, he graduated with a B.A. from Trinity College Dublin. In July 1822, he was caught in a compromising position with a Grenadier Guardsman, John Moverley, in the back room of The White Lion public house, off The Haymarket, Westminster. He and Moverley were released on bail, provided by the Earl of Roden and others. Jocelyn broke bail and moved to Scotland where he worked as a butler under an assumed name. He was declared deposed in his absence by the Metropolitan Court of Armagh in October 1822 for "the crimes of immorality, incontinence, Sodomitical practices, habits, and propensities, and neglect of his spiritual, judicial, and ministerial duties". Jocelyn was the most senior churchman to be involved in a public homosexual scandal in the nineteenth century. It became a subject of satire and popular ribaldry, resulting in more than a dozen illustrated satirical cartoons and numerous pamphlets and limericks. The scandal was so great, that in the days following 'it was not safe for a bishop to shew himself in the streets of London' according to the then Archbishop of Canterbury.

Nov. 5.

Finished the Rev$^{d.}$ J. W. Middleton's "Ecclesiastical Memoir of the first four decades of the Reign of George the third, or an account of the state of religion in the Church of England |[10] during that period: with characteristic sketches of distinguished divines, authors, and benefactors." 8$^{vo.}$ 1822. Who M$^{r.}$ Middleton is I have yet to learn; his book may ^{be} briefly described an Eulogium of the Evangelical Clergy & their irregular ministrations. A Frontispiece representing Abp. Secker, Bishops Horne, Horsley & Portius would lead to an expectation of an interesting & useful memoir of the Church, but amidst much falsely fine writing, hasty narratives of matters interesting to the Church, faint praise of the Orthodox Clergy, and severe censure of what he calls the secular (worldly minded) Clergy, you find the real intention of the work to be the recording and lauding the overstrained labours of many fanatical adherents of Calvinistic doctrines and so called Evangelical Preachers.

Nov. 9.

The public papers announce the death of my acquaintance, Colonel Barry, at Bath, aged 73: whose society there and at Malvern has been to me a source of much gratification. Infirm in body, but vigorous in mind, his conversational talents were great; replete with anecdote, original in his thoughts, with a strong tendency to satire, but withal |[11] a very goodnatured and polite man, he was very generally versed in literature, had lived in the best circles, and acquired much esteem. The intimate friend of the first Marquis of Lansdown, his politics were decidedly Whig, but he was not violent in the expression of them, and men of Tory principles eagerly sought his society. He was a steady and orthodox Churchman, regular in his attendance on public worship.

Nov. 20.

My young Friend, and Curate at Stanway, Frederick Aston, accompanied by his college friend, M Walter Calverley Trevelyan,[7] left us after passing two days with us. The latter is eldest Son of the eldest Son of Sir John Trevelyan, who has large Estates in Somersetshire & Northumberland, in the latter of which Counties M$^{r.}$ W. Trevelyan's Father resides, at Wallington Hall. He is a young man of much research in science, particularly in Geology, & fond of antiquarian pursuits. He has recently visited the Orkney, Shetland & Ferro Isles, Jutland, Denmark & Copenhagen.

Nov. 22.

Finished the Bampton Lectures for 1820 by the Rev$^{d.}$ G. Fausset, late Fellow of Magdalen College. He was formerly of University. The Subject: the claims of the Established Church to exclusive attachment & support, |[12] and the dangers, which menace her from Schism & Indifference considered. The matter is forcibly and well digested and expressed: the tone of a zealous & orthodox Churchman every where prevails; in the discussion of Unity, Schism, Episcopacy, the Christian Priesthood, Forms of Liturgies, alliance between Church & State, toleration and test laws.*Nov. 26.*

---

7. Walter Calverley Trevelyan, (1797-1879). Walter became 6th Baronet Trevelyan in 1846.

Finished "the Rev[d.] H. H. Norris's respectful letter to the Earl of Liverpool &c. occasioned by the speech imputed to his Lordship at the Isle of Thanet Bible Society meeting Oct. 17. 1821. London 1822." M[r.] Norris, who is a Perpetual Curate of S[t.] John's Chapel, Hackney, & a Prebendary of Landaff, is an old combatant in the ranks against the Bible Society. His former work is of larger extent, and excited much attention, while it begat conviction in the minds of many, who had not been as inquisitive as M[r.] Norris, nor had access to so much of the secret history of the gigantic society in question. In his present work he addresses the Prime Minister himself on the contents of a portion of a speech delivered by him at an Anniversary [Meeting,] & quickly put into the most general circulation, as an undeniable testimony in favour of the society. M[r.] N. respectfully |[13] aims at developing to his Lordship the arcane, & systematic manoeuvring of the real leaders of the Bible Society; & truly, he adduces such extracts from their own reports, public harangues, regulations, financial tables and other sources, as must stagger the noble Lord, if he reads them with attention. The evidence produced by M[r.] Norris unquestionably shews the tendency of the Society to favour dissent and degrade the Church, to foster fanaticism and empiricism in religion by a most artful, intricate, & though~~ly~~ closely connected, yet widely ramified, organisation. It certainly appears, that the advantages accruing to the poor of this country are inconsiderable, for there is little gratuitous distribution of the Scriptures, & the Bibles are sold much dearer than they are afforded by our Bartlett's Buildings Society. The exaggerations & bombast & speechifying & ostentation of Bible Society meetings are any thing but pure Christianity, and [they] give occasion for much avowed and more private asperity & censoriousness on the motives & spiritual state of those, who have not been carried along in the torrent of Bible Society enthusiasm. Various instances are adduced, in which the Society has shewn precipitance, partiality, |[14] indiscretion & ignorance in their selection of Translators of the Bible into different languages, & persons to superintend the press in editing the scriptures in other tongues than our own. This is instanced in the Welsh, Irish, French, Icelandic, German, & Spanish Bibles. The Indian Translations are shewn to be got up in the most precipitate and inaccurate manner: and as to the foreign agents of the Society, it appears, that they are undisguised abettors of Sectarianism; too many proofs, indeed, exist at home, that patronage of dissent, and degradation of the Establishment are the leading objects of many active members of the Bible Society.

Nov. 27.

"Memoirs of the last ten years of the Reign of George the Second. By Horace Walpole, Earl of Orford. From the original MSS. 2 Vols. 4[to] Lond. 1822."—A very voluminous and in many respects important publication. The period, of which it treats, the cabals and secret history of the statesmen and parties, are little known to us by authentic memorials. Lord Orford was an eye witness, an intriguing, bustling, yet unambitious politician, replete with curiosity & from his various connexions with the political world in which he moved, able to acquire much curious information. |[15] His style is generally easy and epigrammatic; sometimes obscure; levity on matters relating to religion and morals a most reprehensible feature in his character; scarcely less so his bitter & sarcastic antipathy to various individuals, & some of high eminence, who figure in the scene. He gives us the only extant sketch of the parliamentary debates & style of oratory then in vogue, and we trace the early progress of the great Lord Chatham in his narrative, rising in the author's esteem, against his will, as it were, as the book proceeds. Copious on domestic policy & intrigues, Lord Orford is brief on foreign politics & war, but all his sketches are spirited. The anecdotes & character of George 2^{d}. the Princess Dowager, the Duke of Cumberland & others keep up a constant interest, the Trials of Adm. Byng & Lord Geo. Sackville, and Lord Ferrers are among the more interesting passages.—

Nov. 30.

"The Fortunes of Nigel. By the Author of Waverley. 1822 3. Vols. 8vo". Again the "great unknown" has put forth his strength in a tale of olden times.[8] The scene is laid in the Reign of James the First, who acts a principal part in the busy scenes of intrigue & villainy, which are represented. Charles I. as Prince, the favourite | Duke of Buckingham, and George Heriot, the King's Goldsmith, the same, who founded & endowed Heriot's Hospital in Edinburgh, are principal characters. The hero Nigel Olifaunt, Lord Glenvarlock, is the youthful head of a decayed Scottish Family prosecuting at Court his claim to the repayment of certain pecuniary advances made by his Father to the Scottish Monarch; and the customs & manners of court, town, & city, from the highest to the lowest ranks, is portrayed with a spirit, and a research, and an ease quite peculiar to the author.—I had nearly said, to Sir Walter Scott.

Dec. 1.

We were gratified by receiving a letter from my Brother Capt$^{n.}$ Witts, of the Royal Artillery, from Malta; his last communication received towards the end of August, represented him to be in very indifferent health, and that he intended, if he could meet with an agreeable opportunity by sea, before winter set in, to return to England to recruit his health, which is impaired by many years residence in the Mediterranean. Now, indeed, being on half pay, he is his own master, but partiality to the countries, in which he has so long resided, res angustel, the love of travelling, and seeing |[17] the world, have kept him in the Mediterranean: but not always at Malta; he has resided much at or visited Naples, the Ionion Isles, Corfu &c. the Greek Archipelago, Smyrna, the Troad, Constantinople, the Coasts of Syria & Egypt. He now talks of coming to England next Spring. We had been very uneasy at the unusually long time, which had elapsed since he last wrote, and dreaded worse accounts of his health, which, it seems, is recruited.

The newspapers mention the death of the Bishop of Calcutta in July last. The loss of D$^{r.}$ Middleton is very severe to the interests of Christianity and the Church in India. He was the first Bishop of his Diocese, and seemed to be eminently adapted for the novel, peculiar & arduous charge. His loss will be severely felt by the Ecclesiastical Institutions, which he either founded or fostered: most of which, especially, the Missionary College at Calcutta, were in their Infancy. He was a high Churchman, of very orthodox principles, indefatigable in his episcopal labours; the visitations of his Diocese, which extends over all our Eastern dependencies, were of themselves painful and remote voyages or travels: good

8. The author was Sir Walter Scott, a matter assumed in literary circles, but not to be confirmed for a little while yet.

sense, earnest piety, and sound discretion pervade all his charges & other published Tracts, which he has committed |[18] to the press ~~be~~ since he has been in India. His work on the Greek article stamped his character as a profound scholar, while it tended most ably to elucidate many disputed passages in the sacred text. Before leaving England he was Archdeacon of Huntingdon and Rector of St. Pancras.[9]

Dec. 3.

My Mother left us for her residence at Cheltenham.

Dec. 7.

"The Bishop of Gloucester's Charge to his Clergy at his third Visitation in 1822."—This charge, to which I listened in Summer with much attention, does credit to the sincere piety of the Bishop. The subject is one of much importance: the secular employments and the allowable recreations of the Clergy. The admonitions of the Bishop on these points are very important, cautiously addressed, and earnestly enforced.

Dec. 14.

Yesterday I went to Stanway, dined and slept at the Vicarage House, with my friend Frederick Aston, & returned home to-day. The object of my visit to Stanway was to distribute among the poor of the Parish £36 in clothing and coal, and money, which had been entrusted |[19] by Lady Echo to my award. The above sum is the proportion at the rate of eight shillings in the Pound, of a bequest of the late Viscss. Hereford, who in her will directed One Hundred Pounds to be given at her Funeral to the poor of Stanway. All the Legacies in her will have from failure of assets been paid in the same proportion. We gave away 454 Yards of Linen, 10 Tons of Coal, & £2. 10. 6 in money to the oldest persons, in the several hamlets of Church Stanway, Wood Stanway, Taddington & Hornsleasow.—

Dec. 17.

We dined at Mr. C. Pole's at Wick Hill.

Dec. 20.

I went yesterday to Cheltenham to meet our dear Edward on his return from School for the Christmas holidays. He arrived in a Bath Coach in perfect health and spirits, the same affectionate engaging child as ever. His Master, Mr. Hale, of Lyde House, Sion Hill, Bath, who is also Curate of Lansdown Chapel, Bath, gave me by letter a very good account of the whole of our dear boy's conduct & progress.

We dined and slept at my Mother's in Belle Vue Place. Frederick Aston was also at Cheltenham on his ~~pow~~ way to Gloucester, to be examined for ordination; on Sunday he |[20] expects to be ordained priest.

We called this morning on my Aunt, Mrs. Travell, whom we found in good health, considering

---

9. Thomas Fanshawe Middleton, (1769-1822).

149. Belle Vue Hotel.

her very advanced age. Her present Guest is my amiable and agreeable Cousin, Miss Buxton, ~~niece~~ Grand-daughter to ~~her~~ my Uncle & Predecessor in this living, Mr. F. T. Travell. With her is a nephew of hers, a sweet child, youngest Son of her late sister Mrs. F. Whalley. Miss Buxton together with her Brother-in-law, Mr. F. Whalley, who is Secretary to the Comptroller's Office, & her Cousin Mr. Naper, has lately discharged an act of duty and affection to the memory of their deceased Grandfather by causing to be erected in the Chancel of my Church a very elegant monument, designed by Mr. Naper himself, and executed by Mr. C. Rossi, the Sculptor, at an expence exceeding, I believe, £150.—In order to represent the character of a pious parish Priest, Mr. Naper has combined in his design the emblems of the beginning & finishing Sacrament, with the Liturgy. On a back ground of black marble is | sculptured in Statuary marble in high relief, a Gothic font, resting on a ponderous marble tablet, on the font rests in marble the book of Common Prayer, and on the book the patin and chalice, equally of white marble. The tablet is thus inscribed.

Sacred to the Memory of
The Revd. F. T. Travell—M A.
Who died on the 27th. day of September 1808
In the 69th. Year of his age
Having been 45 Years Rector of this parish.
May it often enjoy the blessing of such a Pastor!

The work is very beautifully finished by Rossi, who has done much of the fine national work in the monuments to illustrious naval & military characters in St. Paul's Cathedral. He had before executed in this neighbourhood, in the Church at Stow, a beautiful monument to the Memory of Mrs. Hippisley, wife of my worthy old friend, the late Rector of that parish.—

Miss Buxton gave me her wonted liberal donation for |22 the poor of this parish, in which her earliest years were spent: with this and an annual donation from the Dowager Lady Sherborne, lately received, my charitable fund is opportunely recruited.

We returned home to dinner to the delight of an affectionately tender & expecting Mother.

Dec. 24.

"Report of the Society for Promoting Christian Knowledge from Apr. 1821 to Apr. 1822. with the Sermon preached at the Anniversary Meeting of the Charity Schools in 1821". A very satisfactory report. The number of Subscribing members now amounts to 14650. The Society is printing an Irish Bible and Common Prayer Book, in the native language, for distribution in the remote parts of the Island. The whole number of Books and Tracts distributed during the year has been 1,222,382. The labours of the Society in the East Indies under the guidance of the lamented Bishop of Calcutta are proceeding prosperously, particularly as regards Schools, and the exertions of the district Committees. The Society has voted funds for the erection of a new Church at Vepery, one of its ancient Missionary |23 Stations. District committees are in progress of formation in some of the West India Islands. The balance sheet accounts for a sum of £56021. 5. 3. The Sermon was preached by the Bishop of Gloucester, and is written in his usual strain of impressive persuasion, more hortatory than argumentative, if not deep, earnest & pious.—

Dec. 29.

"Bracebridge Hall. 2 Vols. 8vo. 1822. By the Author of the Sketch Book". A singularly elegant work of the imagination and of taste: and by an American Author. His name is said to be Washington Irvine, and that he also wrote a vigorous Pamphlet several years ago in the height of the Struggle against France, in which the relations of the different European powers were examined with an earnest & eloquent bias in favour of Great Britain and her cause. I well remember the Pamphlet and the impression which it made. He must have resided in England for a considerable time, at least, must have studied us closely, and is distinguished from most of his countrymen, by a warm admiration & attachment to his "Father land", as he styles this country, not inconsistent, however, with an ardent love of the land of his nativity. He strives to |23 cultivate and impress on both people a respect & mutual regard for each other. Bracebridge Hall, like its twin brother, the Sketch Book, consists of a series of Sketches, Essays, narratives, chiefly illustrative of English society, scenery, manners, habits, feelings & customs; a certain connexion is given in the later production to the different papers by representing them as written during a visit to an ancient family seat in the North of England, the head of which, Mr. Bracebridge, is somewhat enamoured of ancient times, old fashions & antiquated customs. Amid the numerous inmates of the hall and the contiguous village the Author collects his dramatis personæ, his events, and topics; proceeding from one picture to another with uncommon spirit, chaste humour, eloquent description of nature, richness of fancy, tenderness, and invention. In one page we have the excellencies of Addison in his delineation of Sir Roger de Coverley, in another the tenderness of Mackenzie, in a third the sentiment of Sterne. This is, indeed, an elegant book, and has entitled its American author to repose in the collection on the same shelf with the Classics of England.[10]

——— |25

---

10. Washington Irving, (1783-1859). Irving was born in Manhattan and trained as a lawyer. He was a member of the American diplomatic staff in Britain. His best know works were *Rip Van Winkle* and *The Legend of Sleepy Hollow* both of which appeared in his *Sketchbook of Geoffrey Crayon*.

Dec. 30.

Yesterday we received the news of the death of an Aunt of my wife, Mrs. Wilson, formerly Miss Backhouse, relict of the Revd. Mr. Wilson, a Berkshire Clergyman. Of late years she had resided at Headington, near Oxford, to be near her son, the Revd. John Wilson, Fellow of Trinity College. No intercourse was kept up between the Wilsons and the Backhouse family, consequently we had no acquaintance with her: family feuds of old date brought about this estrangement. The information was communicated to us by John Backhouse, who, it seems, is about to resign the post of Under Secretary of State for foreign affairs, which he has held provisionally since the beginning of October, to Lord Francis Conyngham, second Son of the Marquis of Conyngham, who is Lord High Steward. This family ranks very high in royal favour, and rumour has long marked out the Marchioness distinguished by the Royal widower ~~in~~ with a very particular degree of attachment.

Dec. 31.

At the close of the year I have to mention the enlargement of the Church of Upper Slaughter, which has been to me a source of much anxiety, & the completion, |26 as in the case in all sublunary concerns, has in some measure disappointed the hopes, with which I engaged in the work. The increased population of the Parish, & still more, of the appendant extraparochial place, Eyford, required additional Church accommodation, & the proprietor of Eyford, Mr. V. Dolphin, had for some time voluntarily offered to be at the expence, when he should come of age. Towards the close of last year he expressed his desire, that the work should be begun, said, that he destined £300 to ~~his~~ its completion and pointed out his ideas on the mode of doing the work, namely, by taking down the ancient diminutive North aisle & erecting in its stead an aisle as large as the nave. The parish met him by engaging to erect a gallery across the new erection, and determined on building a Vestry, the expences of their proportion to be defrayed out of the funds accruing from the Church land, an Estate acquired in the reign of Elizabeth of 54 acres, & man^a^ged by a Committee, of whom I am one. The Estimate furnished by the Village workmen amounted to £230, but was understood to be a rough calculation, & by no means as the utmost limit of Mr. Dolphin's outlay. |27 It was expressly his wish, that the work should be performed in a correspondent manner to the appearance of the old part of the Church, which had been repaired, & fitted up under the superintendence of my predecessor & uncle, Mr. Travell, in an expensive & elegant manner many years ago, out of the Church Land funds. The work under my direction was executed in the course of the summer, increased room, for more than 70 persons, was gained, Mr. Dolphin was accommodated in the body of the Church with excellent pews for himself & domestics, ~~as~~ having before been only by sufferance admitted into pews in the Chancel, and every exertion was made to combine economy with convenience & the requisite neatness and finish of the work. When finished, every body seemed thoroughly satisfied with the arrangements and execution of the work, but an increase of expenditure had been incurred, from various circumstances, above the Estimate, both in the part allotted to Mr. Dolphin, and that allotted to the Parish: the whole expence exceeding £400, & Mr. Dolphin's share amounting to £319. That Gentleman had never once expressed an intention of limiting himself to the Estimate at £230, & indeed, frequently repeated |28 his design of appropriating £300 to the work. When I waited on him with the valuation he promised a draft for £300 within a week, & I reported his liberality with, as I thought, just ~~a~~commendations to the leading parishioners;—but within a few days instead of £300, £230 only was brought to me on his behalf;—it was pleaded for him, that he had overdrawn his banker, that the donation was liberal &c; but I could not but feel myself the victim of his versatility, & breach of promise, & the conclusion is, for many weeks have elapsed, during which Mr. Dolphin has not repaired his error, that he throws the £70 in dispute on the parish, while the Church land funds are very ill able to provide for this excess above the expence proposed to be defrayed out of them. To Mr. Bowen, who condescended to be Mr. Dolphin's Messenger to me, I wrote a warm but correct statement of the transaction, drawing the necessary inferences; these, as truth is unpleasant to those, who are told of their misconduct, greatly irritated: and from Nov. 1 to |[29] this date neither Mr. Dolphin nor myself have interchanged a word. My uneasiness arising out of these disputes has been very great; what can be more painful to the Pastor than variance with a leading parishioner? On a repeated examination of my own conduct I can only charge myself with too implicit reliance on the word of a young, versatile, extravagant man: my letter to Mr. Bowen was a mere detail of facts without intemperate expressions of resentment. It only remains for me to hope, that Mr. D. will sooner or later acknowledge to himself, that he acted illiberally towards the parish, and unhandsomely towards me, that he will therefore seek reconciliation; & most of all is it to be hoped, that a strong principle of duty may lead him habitually within those sacred walls, which both before & since these differences he has too ~~much~~ neglected to visit.

1823

Jan. 4.

Our friend Frederick Aston left us after a stay of two days. Always amiable, his character is daily maturing & developing itself: as a Clergyman, he is anxious, earnest, diligent to gain professional knowledge; in all relations kind hearted & cheerful.

--- |[30]

Jan. 6.

The Society for promoting Christian Knowledge in union with the incorporated Society for the Propagation of the Gospel in foreign parts, anxious to bear testimony to the learning, piety and great judgment & zeal of the late lamented Bishop Middleton, has recommended a Monument to his Memory in St. Paul's, the expences to be defrayed by subscriptions from the individual Members of those Societies. The Bartlett Buildings Society have also voted £6000 from their funds to the endowment of five Scholarships in the Missionary College at Calcutta, to be called Bp. Middleton's Scholarships. This admirable man is said to have saved nothing in India, having devoted his whole episcopal income to the cause of Christianity in the East. He leaves a widow, but no children.

Jan. 7.

"Three Dialogues on the Amusements of Clergymen". 12mo. Ascribed in the title page to Stillingfleet Bp. of Worcester, but I suspect not really written by him, rather the work of a later anonymous writer. Whoever be the author, it is a delightful little book, & well deserves

150. Oddington House.

the encomium passed on it by the Bishop of Gloucester in his late charge. The Dialogues are represented as having occurred between Dean Stillingfleet & a young Curate, and with much terse humour, |31 sound principle, and good humoured argument in a lively manner display the unsuitableness of many worldly amusements, of which Clergymen are apt to partake. The first dialogue treats of riotous & cruel diversions, hunting, shooting &c. the second of trifling & seducing, dancing, cards, assemblies &c. the third of innocent & instructive. Of course, and of right, for the arguments are unanswerable, the Curate, who loved hunting, shooting, dancing &c. but was really an ingenuous, well principled young man, and a competent scholar becomes a convert to the worthy dean, and ceases to join in unclerical amusements. This book was really the production of the ready & pleasing pen of the Rev^d. W. Gilpin.[11]

Jan. 8.

Dined at Oddington with Lady Reade and Sir John.[12] The usual showy display, & well lighted cheer. A large party as of old, Sir H. & Lady Dryden,[13] Sir C. & Lady Imhoff,[14] M^r.

11. William Gilpin, *Three Dialogues on the Amusements of Clergymen.* (1796).

12. Sir John Chandos Reade, (1785-1868). 7th Baronet of Shipton Court and Oddington. Lady Reade was Louisa, née Murray, (17??-1821). Sir John and Lady Reade had five children, four of whom died before Sir John made his will in 1856, the surviving daughter, Emily was mentally ill and incapable of looking after herself. The Lady Reade referred to is Sir John's mother, Jane, (1755-1846), second daughter of Sir Chandos Hoskyns, 5th Baronet.

13. Sir Henry Dryden, (1787-1837). 3rd Baronet of Canons Ashby. Dryden matriculated at Trinity College, Oxford in 1805 at the age of eighteen, and was presumably an acquaintance and contemporary of Witts. He succeeded to the baronetcy in 1818 on the death of his brother, John. He was in Holy Orders and was first curate at Adlestrop and then vicar of Ambrosden, Oxfordshire from 1821 to 1824, Leeke Wootton, Warwickshire from 1824 until his death in 1837.

14. Sir Charles Imhoff, (17??-1853). Sir Charles was the son of Lady Hastings, (1747-1837). She had been Baroness Anna Maria Appolonia von Imhoff (née Chapuset). She had met Warren Hastings on board a ship heading to Madras in 1768, and after divorcing the Baron eventually married Hastings, and he adopted her children. Sir Charles eventually inherited the estate. See the Biographical Index for full details.

& Mrs. Lechmere,[15] the Penystones &c.[16] How foolish it is to set out for a dinner party in the Country after dark, and drive seven miles.

Jan. 10.

Attended the quarterly Petty Sessions at Northleach Bridewell, after which I went to dine and sleep at Mr. Price's, the Rector of Coln St. Dennis. Met there among others a Mr. Lee, a Roman Catholic Priest, residing at Hatherop in this County, where he has a chapel. Sir John Webb, formerly |[32] possessor of the Hatherop Estate, was a Roman Catholic, which accounts for a chapel there. The present owner of Hatherop is Mr. Ponsonby, wife of Lady Barbara Ashley, Granddaughter & heiress of Sir John Webb & daughter of the late Earl of Shaftesbury.[17]

Acquired information respecting Schools in Gloucestershire endowed with Exhibitions to Pembroke College Oxford. It appears that the Rents of Aston Farm, in this immediate neighbourhood are appropriated to the maintenance of four youths elected from the Schools of Gloucester (Crypt) & Cheltenham & Northleach & Campden, one from each. The present rental is £300 per Ann. As to the School at Northleach it is endowed with ~~the~~ a portion of the Tithes of the living at Chedworth & the appointment of the masters is in Queen's College Oxford. The candidate for the Exhibition must be nominally at least a pupil of the School~~s~~. The Vicar of Northleach, the Head Master & the Bailiff of the Town nominate. At present the School is in utter decay: there is no head Master: the Revd. Mr. Tordiffe, chaplain to the Bridewell, is under Master, & teaches a few children the rudiments of Grammar, having an allowance to officiate as head Master should any pupils be found. The College has not for some years appointed a head master, being desirous by |[33] accumulation of the income set apart for him to erect a suitable School House & buildings, with the design of reviving the school and making it a provision for a Junior fellow.

Besides these exhibitions from Gloucestershire Schools to Pembroke College, the Sons of Gloucestershire Clergymen educated at that college are eligible to certain livings in Middlesex and Bucks; (Uxbridge & Colnbrook & two others situate in that neighbourhood;) the Patrons being found to present from a list of sons of Gloucestershire clergymen nominated by Pembroke College.

Jan. 11.

Attended a meeting at Northleach convened to support a projected bridge over the Severn at Haw Passage between Gloucester & Tewksbury, intended to shorten the communication between Hereford & London, through Cheltenham. Lord Sherborne presided, & it was reported, that nearly as much money was subscribed as was required: the Estimate being £24000 or £25000: & £21000 subscribed. Objections are started, grounded on the flat country on each side of the Severn at the spot proposed, the necessity of forming a causeway

15. The Lechmere family were probably related to the Worcester banking firm Berwick Lechmere & Company.
16. The Penyston family were related to Warren Hastings. Warren was his mother's surname. If this family tradition held true, then Penyston must have been his grandmother's surname as his father had been Christened Penyston Hastings.
17. Francis Witts clearly intended to write 'husband' and not 'wife'. This was just a slip that went uncorrected. The owner of Hatherop was William Francis Spencer Ponsonby, (1787-1855), 1st Baron de Mauley, a creation of 1838. He married Lady Barbara Ashley-Cooper in 1814.

4½ miles long, and the risk of inundating the country above the proposed Bridge and causeway, floods being already a frequent occurrence. |[34] A rival company of projectors also advocate a bridge at the Mythe near Tewksbury, to cross the Severn above its junction with the Avon, & consequently with less risk of obstructing the waters in wet seasons. A better line of road to Ledbury is alledged to be in favour of this scheme, which is evidently very advantageous to the interests of the Borough of Tewksbury, and it is affirmed, that the Route to the Metropolis through Stow would be shorter and preferable. Ample funds are subscribed for this project, and appearances lead to the belief, that each party will apply to Parliament to carry their views into effect.

Jan. 13.

We left home on a Visit to Mrs. Backhouse at Gloucester, this being the Sessions week. Our dear boy accompanied us. We staid an hour or two at Cheltenham to call on my Mother, who has been suffering severely by an inflammatory attack on the chest, which has left her very low both in strength & spirits.

Jan. 14.

The Sessions commenced. The bench was very much crowded. The Lord Lieutenant, Lord Apsley MP. for Cirencester,[18] Mr. Pitt, MP. for Cricklade, Messrs. Pye, |[35] Browne, Archdeacon Sandiford (Wells) Archdeacon Onslow, (Worcester) Archdeacon Probyn (Landaff) Dr. Timbrell &c.—

Mr. R. Cooper was confirmed in his situation of Chaplain of the Gaol. Letters addressed to the Chairman, Dr. Cooke & Mr. Cripps, and to Dr. Timbrell, by Mr. Jones, the late Chaplain, written in angry & intemperate terms, threatening to lay his case before parliament, and alledging other charges against the Governor, but charges, which might have been brought forward at the last Sessions, were laid before the Magistrates, who decided, that no farther steps should be taken on this most unpleasant subject, & that the writer, whose weakness & malice appear more & more strongly, should be left to his own remedy. At the same time it was agreed, that the proposed application to the Lord Lieutenant, to take the proper steps for Mr. Jones's dismissal from the Magistracy, should be for the present suspended: the Chairman having on the advice of some Magistrates delayed presenting it to his Grace officially, under a doubt entertained, that the Chancellor might decline to comply with the proposed measure. And, indeed, all purposes will be answered, if Mr. Jones, aware of the |[36] existence of such a document & the likelihood of its being presented in the proper quarter, shall abstain from exercising the Magisterial duties.—

Inspected the County Gaol, which since the last Sessions has been provided with a tread-mill for the employment of prisoners confined in the Penitentiary, in grinding corn, bruising malt, & raising water for the use of the Prison. The machinery appeared very well constructed, and the labour very irksome, but I doubt its being so hard as the Winch Mill, which is in use in some Gaols, and which has answered so well ~~since the~~ in Northleach Bridewell, where it was first erected & brought into operation under my superintendence

18. Henry George Bathurst, (1790-1866), Lord Apsley. M.P. for Cirencester, 1812-1834. Bathurst was the 1st son of Henry,

as Visiting Magistrate: neither does the Motion seem so suitable; for the Winch Mill brings into Action all the leading Muscles of the frame, particularly those of the upper part of the body, which are most applied in the usual occupations of labouring men, expanding the chest, & so directly contributing to the preservation of health, while the muscles of the legs, thighs & loins are chiefly exercised in the Stepping Mill. A smaller Tread |37 Mill has also been lately introduced into the Bridewell at Horsley. The cleanliness, order, discipline & silence of the County Gaol are above praise.

151. Joseph Pitt.

Jan. 18.

The Sessions will close this day. I returned home by Cheltenham to be ready for the duties of my churches.

Jan. 20.

I returned to Gloucester by Cheltenham on horseback.

Jan. 21.

Looked into the new Church at the Spa, now nearly finished. It is intended for the accommodation of the inhabitants of that new town, which within these few years has arisen round the Saline springs, and forms a genteel suburb to the city. It is extraparochial, and the Church under the auspices of the Bishop is erected by subscription. The Rev^d.^ Mr. Maitland is, I believe, to be the Minister. The edifice is slight, and erected, I should presume, at no very great expence; the interior will be commodious and well lighted; the recess for the Altar, the Pulpit & reading desk are strangely huddled together.

Spent the Evening at Mrs. M. Hunt's, an old resident in Gloucester, and a distant relation on my Father's side.[19]

Jan. 22.

Rode on the Tewkesbury road as far as the Village of Leigh. My acquaintance Mr. Pierce is Incumbent |38 of this Church, which is situate half a mile from the road to the left, about five miles from Gloucester.

Mrs. Backhouse had two or three acquaintances to tea.

19. Mrs. Hunt was in fact a maiden lady, Miss Mary Hunt, (1755-1835). She was the niece by marriage of Francis Witts' great-aunt Sarah Hunt, née Witts, the sister of his grandfather Broome Witts. For a detailed analysis of the Hunt family with pedigrees, see the introduction in volume 1.

Jan. 24.

Rode through the villages of Tuffley, Whaddon & Brockthorp. This is a new but very bad turnpike road to Stroud, winding round the foot of Robin wood Hill amid rich enclosures, which in summer would afford pleasing landscapes; the view from the eminence beyond Brockthorp, about 5 miles from Gloucester, is very commanding; you survey the magnificent vale of the Severn, from the Malvern Hills to below Newnham; the former eminences towered from the vale tipped with Snow and showing their waving outline to advantage against the leaden coloured sky: May hill & the other Eminences in the forest of Dean contrast well with the long silvery reaches of the Severn; the village towers afford resting points to the eye in the flat part of the landscape, & Robin wood Hill with the heights close in its rear are the prominent objects in the near distance. Gloucester with its Cathedral & towers appeared to much advantage as I returned.

——— |[39]

Jan. 25.

I returned home by Cheltenham. Seldom have I experienced such bitter weather. Snow came on as I left Cheltenham, with a keen east wind, as I rode, meeting me: it was with difficulty I could see my way, and the front of my horse as well as my own face were coated with ice, when I reached Upper Slaughter. For the last six ~~weath~~ weeks the weather has been very severe.—

The newspapers announce, that Mr. Vansittart retires from the Post of Chancellor of the Exchequer—He has been considered an able financier, but his health is said not to be equal to the fatigues of a Parliamentary campaign. In early life I met him at Copenhagen, when in the Winter of 1801–2 I was Secretary to Mr. Drummond (now Sir W. Drummond) Chargé des Affaires at that Court. Immediately before the rupture with the Northern powers and the first attack by a British fleet on Copenhagen, Mr. Vansittart was dispatched under Lord Sidmouth's administration, then just appointed, to co-operate with Mr. Drummond in the important negociations of the time. He was accompanied by Dr. Beeke, now Dean of Bristol. On the failure of the negociations and advance of the fleet we all returned to Britain on board of a sloop of war detached |[40] for that purpose. Since that time I have not had any personal acquaintance with Mr. Vansittart. He has the character of being a very pious man: he never shone as a debater in parliament.[20]

———

Jan. 26.

"The fourth Report of the Committee of the Society for the improvement of prison discipline &c. 1822" contains much valuable matter. A great spirit of amendment in the constitution and arrangement of prisons is afloat, and though some active members of this useful society are in more than one point theorists or enthusiasts, great good will probably arise from their researches and communications both as to British and foreign places of confinement. The introduction of hard & irksome labour, principally by the Tread mill, improved systems of classification, more zealous efforts for the moral cultivation of prisoner's minds, and for reclaiming juvenile offenders, are the leading objects of the Society's labours. The prisons

20. This statement was not quite true. Vansittart has called on Frank Witts at Cheltenham on Wednesday 31 July 1805 and sat some time with him. In fact Frank had also called on him in London on several occasions back in the summer of 1801.

of minor & local jurisdictions in this country are still very defective. The picture of Spanish and Portuguese imprisonment is frightful, but in those kingdoms amelioration dawns. Strong efforts are making in Russia. As a Magistrate I can testify to the increased information and interest prevalent on the subject: Felonies |[41] seem to be on the decline, in great measure, perhaps owing to the abundance & cheapness of food. It is confidently expected, that the extension of the system of discipline mills will operate to the diminution of minor offences. Gloucester Gaol is very justly and handsomely praised in this report.

Jan. 28.

The severity of the weather having prevented my return to Gloucester yesterday, I returned thither to day. A thaw has come on, but I found riding difficult, from the remains of snow on the hills, & flood between Cheltenham & Gloucester.

Learnt the news of the sudden death of the eminent Dr. Jenner, the discoverer of vaccination, which happened at Berkley on the 26th. Apoplexy was the malady, which quickly terminated his useful life at the age of 74. He was a man of distinguished talents, an original thinker, some times rather eccentric, but always kind hearted. I had known him for more than twenty years, and had frequently benefited by his intelligent and instructive conversation. He lived to see the test of experience applied to his great discovery, and though, perhaps, the high expectations originally entertained, that vaccination would prove an invariable protection against variolous infection, may have been disappointed, yet the wonderful controlling power |[42] of vaccination over that part of the human species has been most clearly ascertained. I have vaccinated many individuals of all ages, and never yet heard of one, who has been vaccinated by me, (all of them my parishioners) who afterwards caught the small pox. Dr. Jenner's fame was, perhaps, more extensively established in all quarters of the world, than in his native country. But here parliament justly rewarded in an ample manner the distinguished discernment and perseverance of this ~~able~~ eminent physician.

Jan. 31.

An Evening party at the Deanery. The venerable Dean, Dr. Plumptre, suffering under an attack of his inveterate malady, the Stone, could not meet his friends.

Feb. 1.

I returned home by Cheltenham, & had almost as bitter a ride, from the inclemency of the weather, as on this day sennight. I left my dear wife & boy at Mrs Backhouse's. The latter goes in a day or two to School. GOD bless him! he is a delight to his Parents. Endowed with very good natural talents, and competently advanced in school learning, I cannot be too grateful to Providence for bestowing on us a child so rich in every affectionate & amiable quality of the heart. |[43]

152. Edward Jenner,

The aspect of public affairs abroad is very threatening. There seems little doubt, that France will proceed to hostilities against Spain. A most dangerous crisis for the Bourbon Dynasty! France barely reviving from the agitations of the Revolution arrayed against revolutionary Spain! Great Britain does not sanction this interference by arms with the domestic concerns of a foreign state, but rather seems disposed to keep aloof from the contest, which it is believed, that our representative at the Congress of Verona, the great Duke of Wellington, dissuaded. Russia, Austria & Prussia abet the measures of France. Spain is represented as united and firm in resisting foreign dictation; and it ~~is~~ does not appear, that our Government in the present stage of the contest will take any measures hostile to our ~~ancient~~ late Ally.

Feb. 5.

"Proofs of Inspiration, or the grounds of distinction between the New Testament and the Apocryphal Volume; occasioned by the recent publication of the Apocryphal New Testament by Hone, By the Revd. Thos. Rennel, B.D. F.R.S. Vicar of Kensington. 1822". Mr. Rennel the acute, learned and zealous advocate of religion, who had already distinguished himself by his admirable Remarks on Scepticism, in answer to the ill placed Insinuations of the celebrated Surgeon, Mr. Lawrence, who in Lectures |43 to his medical pupils, had intruded his doctrines of Deism and Materialism, and whose work has since received the most signal stigma from the Chancellor, in an action brought before him, has again buckled on his armour against the Pestilent Unbeliever and daring publisher of blasphemy, Hone. This man having published in the most insidious form a collection of the Apocryphal writings claiming to be scripture, which have survived the wreck of the early ages of the Church, and having so arranged his work as to convey to the ignorant a notion, that they were generally received as Scripture in the times, when they were written, subdividing them into chapter & verses, in such manner, as to imitate the ordinary mode of printing the genuine Scriptures, Mr. Rennel meets his crafty design in a popular and most useful piece of reasoning & criticism. He begins by discussing and proving the extent, nature and claims of inspiration of the genuine Scriptures of the New Testament, from the testimony of the Apostles themselves & from that of their companions & successors. He applies the same test to the writings collected by Hone under the threefold division of authentic, doubtful & spurious productions; abundantly proving, that they |45 are not entitled to take their station in the Canon of Scripture as inspired, but that the Canon of the New Testament, as we admit it, is established on undeniable evidence, while it forms an integral system, no part of which has been lost.

Feb. 6

"A letter to the Right Revd. John (Kaye) Lord Bishop of Bristol, respecting an additional Examination of Students in the University of Cambridge and the different plans proposed for that purpose. By Philograntus. Lond. 1822".—Is not this pamphlet the production of Dr. Monk the Greek Professor at Cambridge, and Dean of Peterborough? It is a sensible recommendation of a material improvement much wanted in Cambridge. The Author advocates public classical examinations with gradations of honours, not omitting examination in~~to~~ the Elementary parts of Theology. Much difference of opinion seems to have existed at the Sister University, as to any deviation from the established routine, & if any, to what extent. Since the publication of this Pamphlet, a change has been determined upon, but coming far short of the recommendation of Philograntus. If I understand it right, undergraduates of two years standing are to be examined in the following books—The Gospel according to St. Luke: Paley's Evidences: 2 Books of Xenophon's Anabasis; & Cicero pro |46 Milone. This is fixing a Minimum, rather than exciting Emulation. The books are to be varied in different years: but surely, classical literature must not be so degraded on the banks of Cam, & the wise men of Cambridge will go much farther, as prejudices wear out.

Feb. 7.

Parliament met on the 4th. Inst. The King's Speech was received with general approbation. It announces the probability of war between France & Spain, laying down the principle, that interference in the domestic concerns of independent nations is inadmissible, unless in the case of manifest hazard and meditated aggression on the state, by whose government the question of interference is entertained. It appears, that Ministers still hope, that negociation and mediation may avert the threatened war. Neutrality in the first instance is manifestly our duty; but it is difficult to foresee, that, in case of war breaking out, we can long remain passive spectators. In the course of the debate, my old acquaintance, Brougham, poured forth a brilliant and vehement philippic against the principles of the confederated Monarchs. The occasion suited admirably the splendid talents of the violent Statesman and orator: defiance, |47 scorn, sarcasm, enthusiasm for liberal institutions, seem to have electrified the house. The speech holds out a prospect of diminution of burdens, and it seems, that a great reduction of the assessed taxes is contemplated. The agricultural distress is adverted to in the Speech, with the hope, that this grand evil will be gradually removed by the effects of the vast increase of prosperity and activity among the manufacturing & commercial branches of the community.

The Gazette announces, that the Hon. Fred. Robinson,[21] brother to Lord Grantham is appointed Chancellor of the Exchequer in the room of Mr. Vansittart. This young Statesman has shewed considerable Talent, in his late post of President of the Board of Trade, which he held with the Treasurership of the Navy. The latter office is given to Mr. Huskisson, long known as an able financier and man of business; who is the intimate friend of Canning. He had held the situation of First Commissioner of the Land Revenue. It appears that Mr. Huskisson is also appointed President of the Board of Trade.—

Feb. 8.

"Peveril of the Peak—By the Author of Waverley &c. 4 Vols 1823." The wonderful stories of legend, history, and anecdote of the olden times, are here again combined with the no less wonderful powers of imagination, spirit and raciness of the great novelist of the age. A very Junius in his peculiar line! |48 though it is less easy to imagine, why he preserves an incognito, which all the world believe, they have penetrated. Be it as it may, all classes should be grateful for amusement conferred, and not a few will gather from his pages snatches of

21. Frederick John Robinson, (1782-1859). Robinson was M.P. for Carlow, 1806-1807, and Ripon 1807-1827. He had a long public career, commencing as secretary to Lord Pembroke on his mission to Vienna in 1807. He was Under-Secretary of State for War and Colonies, May-Nov. 1809; Lord of the Admiralty 1810-1812; and had already been Vice-President of the Board of Trade from 1812 to 1818. See Biographical Index.

history, which they would not have the patience to collect from less mercurial sources. Here we have the dissolute court of Charles 2. contrasted with his father's gallant Cavaliers, and Sectaries and Roundheads of every calibre from the conscientious presbyterian to the wild Fifth Monarchy man. The gallant Countess of Derby (defunct, by the bye, long before the period, at which she is introduced;) the Merry Monarch himself, the profligate & versatile Villiers, Duke of Buckingham, the wits and sages of the motley court, a Villain—hypocrite of most diabolical Stamp, but inimitably traced, a gallant youth and lovely fair one to love & to be crossed in love and wed at last, treasons & plots, Oates & Col. Blood, even Geoffry Hudson the Queen's dwarf, cum multis aliis quos nune perscibere longum est[22]—and four volumes full of life & interest and stirring matter. Truly the talent of the man is admirable.

Feb. 11.

"Murray's Historical account of discoveries and travels in Asia from the earliest ages to the present time" 3. |49 Vols 8vo. 1820. A very interesting and instructive abridgement of the many voluminous, and, as to former times, scarce, works which relate to Asia; travels, voyages, history, statistical writings &c. The same author has published a similar compilation ~~of~~ from works relating to Africa in two Vols. embodying the collections of D. Leyden, now deceased, who had commenced a work on the same subject.—

Feb. 12.

It is announced that Mr. Vansittart is appointed Chancellor of the Duchy of Lancaster, in the room of C. B. Bathurst Esqr. of Lidney Park in this County, formerly a Chairman of our Quarter Sessions.[23]

Feb. 13.

"Matthews's Diary of an Invalid 2 Vols 12mo. 1822." A very interesting book. The author, a layman, an Etonian, and a fellow of King's College, Cambridge, records his observations in a tour made in pursuit of health to Lisbon, thence into Italy, where he visits all the principal cities in the ordinary circuit, Switzerland, which he traverses by the customary route, the South of France and home by Paris. Neither Ultra Tory nor Ultra Whig, neither a warm Religioniest, nor an indifferent Sceptic, disposed to think for himself on subjects of politics, manners, customs & taste, with enough of the details of impaired health to excite interest, he puts down the first impressions of the day on the different objects, which excited his observations or curiosity. |50 His mind is evidently richly stored with the treasures of classical and elegant literature; he does not pretend to be a guide or describe, in detail, buildings, paintings, statues &c: but perhaps gives a truer and more spirited book, though a sketch, than if he had amplified his materials into more eleborate description, & more studied encomium. One would like to keep

---

22. cum multis aliis quos nune perscibere longum est —
23. Charles Bragge Bathurst, 1754-1831). Bathurst was M.P. for Monmouth, 1790-1796, Bristol, 1796-1812, Bodmin, 1812-1818 and Harwich, 1818-1823. Bragge Bathurst had a long parliamentary career and was a contemporary and close friend of Henry Addington, Viscount Sidmouth who married his youngest sister. He was the father of Charles Bathurst, who was to continue the family tradition of being Chairman of the Quarter Sessions and who was a long-standing friend of Francis Witts.

his volumes in the pocket of the travelling chariot, or walk thro' Rome & Naples with them in one's hand. I do not wonder at the general partiality for this Diary.

Feb. 15.

I went yesterday to dine & sleep at Stanway Vicarage. M$^{rs.}$ Watkins, Frederick Aston's youngest Sister, was his guest: her husband is the Rev$^{d.}$ Nowell Watkins; as usual, her exquisite singing enchanted me; though certainly her voice is not what it once was: but her taste & expression remain the same.—"The Confessions of an English Opium Eater. 12$^{mo.}$ 1822." A very extraordinary little book. Eloquent, mystic, moitié narrative, (& thrilling narrative,) moitié metaphysical, what did the author really propose to himself? Doubtless excessive indulgence in opium, (if as it is intimated by the writer, it prevails to a great extent in this country,) |[51] must produce for a time visionary and dreamy extravagances of the imagination, wałking and sleeping exstacies, not worth realizing in this matter of fact country, and entail as exquisite pains ~~here~~ afterwards, as the author professes to have undergone. It is after all the production of a man of genius and a scholar;—perhaps of a Lake Poet.[24]

Feb. 16.

There seems to be no doubt, that a successor is found for the lamented Bishop Middleton in the person of D$^{r.}$ Reginald Heber; (for the University of Oxford has lately conferred on him by diploma the degree of Doctor of Divinity.) He was a little my Senior at the University, but I was never personally acquainted with him. He was originally of Brazennose College, where he gained three prizes, the Latin verse, the Latin Essay, and the English prize Poem, Palestine, which was a very elegant & spirited production. A mock heroic entitled the Whippiad, arising out of an academical feud between M$^{r.}$ Halliwell, a tutor of Brazennose and my old acquaintance, Bernard Port, now Incumbent of Ilam in Derbyshire, and circulated in MS., was much admired by his contemporaries, and was really a witty and sarcastic jeu d'esprit. Great hopes & expectations were justly formed of him; nor has he belied them, being certainly a |[52] very superior scholar, and able writer. He was elected Fellow of All Souls, but married early a daughter of D$^{r.}$ Shipley, Dean of S$^{t.}$ Asaph. He was ordained Deacon by the Bishop of Exeter, (Fisher, now of Salisbury) when I was ordained Priest and soon became the Rector of Hodnet in Shrophsire, a preferment in the gift of his half brother, Richard Heber Esq$^{r.}$ of Hodnet & Marton Hall in Craven, the distinguished Book collector, whose library is considered one of the finest & rarest in the Kingdom, and who, last year, was elected M.P. for the University of Oxford, in opposition to Sir John Nicholl, on which occasion I gave M. Heber my suffrage. Reginald Heber in process of time preached an able set of Bampton Lectures, selecting for his Subject the Operations of the Holy Spirit, and still more recently he has superintended an Edition of the complete works of Bp. Jer. Taylor, in 15 Vols 8$^{vo.}$, to which he has prefixed an interesting Memoir of the excellent Bishop, with a critical Examination & analysis of his writings. It is not very long since he was elected Preacher at Lincoln's Inn, on the appointment of D$^{r.}$ Lloyd to the Regius Professorship of Divinity at Oxford. He has enjoyed a large circle of acquaintance among literary and

---

24. Thomas de Quincey, (1785-1859), *Confessions of an English Opium Eater.* (1822).

eminent characters, and by that means |53 has doubtless acquired a knowledge of the world, which will be of great service to him in the Eastern hemisphere; there he is called to a most arduous duty, not only from the peculiar duties required in that vast diocese among bigotted Heathens, & lukewarm Christians, but also as successor to a prelate, whose piety, learning & judgment can hardly be equalled, surely not excelled.—His friends will feel great anxiety for his success in his hazardous vocation; but he will carry with him the prayers and earnest good wishes of every sincere Christian and hearty well wisher of our admirable Church.[25]

Monday Feb. 17.

I went to Cheltenham to pass a day or two with my Mother, who, I rejoice to say, is very much recovered, and now considering her age and inability of taking much exercise, in very good health and spirits.

Mrs. Cooke, an intimate friend of my Mother, spent the Evening with us. She is a widow of the brave Capt. Cooke of the Bellerophon, who was killed in the battle of Trafalgar.

Mr. Vansittart is raised to the peerage by the title of Baron Bexley.

Wednesday Feb. 19.

I rejoined my wife at Mrs. Backhouse's at Gloucester. A party in the Evening.

--- |54

Thursday Feb. 20.

A party and music at Col. Mason's.

Friday Feb. 21.

"Remonstrance addressed to the supporters of the Bible Society on the System of Visitation introduced by their district committees, and an appeal to those members, who are professedly attached to the Church of England. Lond. 1823." "An appeal to Scripture; the Church; and Facts; (sic) in reply to Remonstrance &c. By the Revd. B. S. Claxson Late fellow commoner (!) of Worcester College Oxford, & President of the St. Michael and St. Mary de Grace Bible Association, Gloucester. Gloucester 1823".[26] The former of these Pamphlets urges the usual arguments in a respectable manner, but, perhaps, without making the best of the cause. The latter is dull, laboured, and weak; arraying the common pretensions of the evangelical party with an attempt at argument, and a sprinkling of what the writer mistook for ~~cust~~ onction. This fellow Commoner is the Son of a retired and opulent Gloucester shopkeeper, Curate of St. Michael's Church in this city, and one among the servile imitators of Bish. Ryder in tone of voice and ~~imitators~~ manner, not less than they think themselves to resemble him in doctrine & in spirit. See Diary 2. 130.—

--- |55

25. Reginald Heber, (1783-1826), Heber was made Prebendary of St Asaph in 1812 and was Bampton Lecturer in 1815, Bishop of Calcutta, 1823. His fame survives from the numerous hymns he wrote. *The Whippiad*, recorded as an heroic comic poem remains in several manuscript collections and is also in print from collections of Reginal Heber's own writings and available to this day.

26. The 'sic' and exclamation mark in brackets are in the original manuscript diary.

Saturday Feb. 22.

We returned home from Gloucester.

Wednesday Feb. 26.

My fortieth birthday. May I [be] blessed with grace and strength to keep the good resolutions, I form: and may the work of self examination & circumspection be followed by blessed results through the mediation of the sole redeemer!

Friday Feb. 28.

The Right Hon. C. Arbuthnot, late one of the Secretaries of the Treasury is appointed First Commissioner of the Land revenue in the room of Mr. Huskisson.

Sunday Mar. 2.

Our dear Edward's 10th. birthday. GOD grant that he may continue in health, and increase in religious and useful learning!

Tuesday Mar. 4.

"Narrative of a tour taken in the year 1667 to La Grande Chartreuse and Alet by Dom Claude Lancelot, author of the Post Royal Grammars; including some account of Dom Armand Jean le Bouthillier de Rancé, Reverend Father Abbé, and Reformer of the Monastery of Notre Dame de la Trappe; with notes; and an Appendix containing some particulars respecting M. du Verger de Hauranne, Abbé de St. Cyran; Cornelius Jansenius, Bishop of Ypres; & also a brief sketch of the celebrated institution of Port Royal. Lond. 1813." A very singular and interesting book. Not a translation of |[56] the Tour to La grande Chartreuse & Alet, but the original is abridged & recast, as it were. A lively and somewhat mystical tone of piety runs through the whole. The description of the sequestered Monastery erected among rocks in the vicinity of the Alps is well drawn; equally so that of the retired Diocese & Town of Alet at the foot of the Pyrenees. There is a copious account of its Bishop M. de Pavillon, Uncle of the Poet, who seems to have been a prelate of primitive simplicity, piety & zeal, a man of considerable learning, but under discredit at court on account of his inclination to Jansenism, which was, indeed, evinced by his hospitality to the writer, who being one of the Port Royal recluses was at this time suffering persecution on account of their connection with the Jansenists. Dom Claude Lancelot was one of the first scholars & teachers of the age in the Seminaries of Port Royal, compiler of the celebrated Grammars of that institution & penetrated with a fervent piety. His narrative is addressed to Mother Angelica (Arnauld) a celebrated Sister and Abbess of the Nuns of Port Royal, who was, indeed, with the aid of many learned & pious personages of that day the reformer of the monastery, over which she presided. The tour contains many curious & interesting details of the Abbé de Rancé, reformer of the Monastery of la Trappe, a |[57] most singular enthusiast and possessed of singular influence. That gloomy monastery & its silent self tormenting inmates are described by Lancelot. An abstract is given of the lives & persecutions of the Abbé de St. Cyran & Jansenius, Bishop of Ypres: they may be styled the joint authors of the religious system named after the latter; for it was the result of the studies of the two friends, who extracted their doctrine of divine love and indefectible grace from the works of St. Augustin. From the same source Calvin's kindred principles were drawn, and the Jansenists in doctrine may be classed with the Calvinists, while in discipline they may be ranked with the Methodists. It was, indeed, to use a term familiar to the last mentioned sect, a time of great revival of religion in France, & the influence especially of the Abbé de St. Cyran was very great, spreading widely among the higher classes. In particular the Society of Port Royal, both the male & female religious, was deeply imbued with Jansenism That the doctrines did not proceed to the length of a separation from the Church of Rome, must probably be imputed to the strength of early and monastic prepossessions. The Jansenists and the Institution of Port Royal found very active enemies of persecution in the Jesuits, who spared neither exertion nor intrigue to suppress the doctrine & drive out its professors. Succeeding |58 with the Courts of Rome & Versailles, they at length accomplished their purpose; the leading Jansenists were imprisoned or driven into exile: and to the incalculable injury of the cause of education Port Royal was levelled with the ground, & the institutions attached to it entirely abolished. This Volume is from the pen of Mary Anne Schimmelpenninck.

Friday Mar. 7.

About midnight died Robert Bateman, who had lived with us for several years as Gardener & farming man: aged 43 years; a truly honest, industrious & upright Christian; a good husband, father, son, servant & neighbour; leaving an afflicted widow and four little children. He officiated as parish Clerk for his father in law, who survives him in decrepit old age. He had been gradually failing, though he had ceased from working only ten days: his decline was very rapid at last; his case appears to have been ulcerated lungs, joined to Angina pectoris.

Saturday Mar. 8.

This day Frederick Aston left us, having been on a visit since Wednesday.

Thursday Mar. 13.

I dined and slept at Dr. Warneford's at Bourton on the Hill: a large party.

Friday Mar. 14.

I accompanied Dr. Warneford to Evesham, |59 to attend a meeting of delegates from the Trustees of the three districts of the Evesham Turnpike road. My colleague and myself had been chosen by the 2d. District, the line of which extends from Bourton on the Hill to Evesham. We were to meet three Gentlemen from the Evesham Branch, & three from the Pershore Branch. The business proposed was to examine the Attorneys Bills for soliciting the Act in Parliament last Sessions, which on a first view appeared exorbitant. The three Solicitors had been desired to produce their bill; one of them, Mr. Hodson of Pershore, refused to sign the bill produced by the two others, Mr. Phelps of Evesham, and Mr. Griffiths of Broadway, stating, that he considered some of the charges unreasonable, the lawyers not being able to come to an understanding as to the amount to be preferred, the meeting was adjourned till a future day, when they should have agreed on the bill to be tendered. We met in the Council Chamber of the Corporation under the roof of the old Town Hall: a full length portrait of Sir Charles Cockerell, of

Sesincot, decorates this room.[27] He is returned by the Corporation on his brother in law, Lord Northwick's interest, but not without strong opposition, and great expence. The other member is Sir |60 W. Rouse Boughton.[28] The town of Evesham is a very pretty object, by whichever road it is approached, but the interior dirty & mean. The Gentlemen, whom we met, were Messrs. Hudsons (Brothers) & Hanford from the Pershore Trust: Mr. Hanford is a Roman Catholic of an old Worcestershire family: Messrs. Beale Cooper, & Perrot, of Cracomb, for the Evesham trust. Broadway Hill is wonderfully improved under the scientific management of our Surveyor, Mr. Stokes; and the whole line in excellent order.

I returned to dinner at Stanway Vicarage, where I slept, having business to transact with my Tenant.

Saturday March 15.—

I returned home, & found a letter from my friend Mr. J. Backhouse apprising me, that his final destination is fixed, & that he is on the point of receiving the Office of Commissioner of the Excise, worth £1300 per ann. He deserves it well: and for the sake of his family will soon reconcile himself to the change from the higher & more agitating occupations of politics to the Official routine & dullness of the Excise.

--- |61

Sunday March 16.

The Rt. Hon. C. Grant is appointed Vice president of the board of Trade in the room of the Rt. Hon. Thos. Wallace.

The aspect of affairs abroad is very threatning. Spain has declared war against France; Portugal has intimated a design of adhering to the fortunes of her peninsular neighbour. There seem to exist in France the seeds of discontent and insurrection, and the French army cannot, it is said, be depended upon. The Spanish court and Ministry are to remove from Madrid, an exposed capital, to the fortress of Badajos.

We have during the past fortnight more than once enjoyed the society of our old friends Mr. & Mrs. Dolphin, who have been visiting their ~~neig~~ nephew at Eyford: but the unpleasant coolness subsisting between M. Dolphin and myself has of course curtailed those opportunities of meeting, which would have occurred under other circumstances. The Uncle deplores the difference, which has arisen, but is without influence to procure a change of sentiment in his Nephew, whose conduct to me he does not attempt to justify: but I find, that by dint of misrepresentation |62 Mr. Dolphin has in some instances succeeded in creating an impression unfavourable to me in the minds of those, to whom he has spoken on the subject. Valuing, as we do, the John Dolphins, and regretting, as we ever have, their removal from Lower Slaughter, we cannot but rejoice, that new preferment, at least to be held for 16 years, has fallen to the lot of J.D., Lord Verulam having given him the Living of Pebmarsh in Essex, tenable with that of Wakes Colne, which he has now held for some years, & near which he resides at Copford Brook.[29]

---

27. Sir Charles Cockerell, (1755-1837), M.P. for Tregony, 1802-1806; Lostwithiel, 1807; Bletchingly, 1809-1812; Seaford, 1816-1818 and Evesham, 1819-1830, and 1831-1837. Cockerell was married to Harriet Rushout, daughter of John Rushout, 1st Baron Northwick. Cockerell was created baronet in 1809.
28. Sir William Edward Rouse Boughton, (1788-1856), M.P. for Evesham, 1818-1819 and 1820-1826.
29. John Dolphin had been the vicar at Lower Slaughter and a good friend of the Travell and Witts families. His wife had been a Miss Rollinson, and sister to the wife of Ferdinand Travell. The circumstances behind his loss of the living at Lower Slaughter are not known.

Monday Mar. 17.

"Letters from Horace Earl of Orford to George Montague Esqr. from 1736 to 1770. Lond. 1818. 4to." This series exhibits a faithful though not flattering picture of the times, and is written with singular spirit and vivacity. Matters of taste, the politics of the day, fashionable intrigue, the engagements, dress & pursuits of the higher ranks of society, no small share of egotism, warm attachment to one or two individuals, satirical strictures on the greater majority, abundance of bon mots and scandal make up these entertaining volumes. The writer develops |63 his character in his letters; in early life an active but not ambitious politician, vain, captious, witty, selfish: Literary in the lighter departments, critic of painting, architecture, bijoux & china, antiquary and herald, founder and admirer of Strawberry hill. The book, however, is both amusing and instructive; yet it contains few traces ~~of~~ of Christian confidence or Christian principle.

Friday Mar. 21.

We dined at Mr. Jeaffreson's at Longborough, meeting Sir C. & Lady Cockerell, Mr. & Mrs. E. Leigh, their brother & sister, Mr. & Mrs. Dumbleton, Mr. & Mrs. Hall, of Batsford, with his pupil, Mr. Tuffnell.

Saturday Mar. 22.

We dined at Mr. E. Leigh's at Broadwell, meeting the Jeaffresons, the Dumbletons & Mr. Vavasour.

Sunday Mar. 30. Easter-day.

"The Bishop of London's charge to the Clergy of his diocese 1822." A temperate, wise, and elegant address by a judicious, moderate, pious & learned Prelate. The law of residence and of curates is adverted to; and the necessity of high acquirements in knowledge & high correctness and prudence in character is enforced on the Clergy, by consideration drawn from the peculiar circumstances of the times. One would have thought, that |64 envy and malice would have been unable to find matter for censure in these pages. Yet has this charge of Bish. Howley been made the subject of a bitter article in the last number of the Edinburgh Review, which has been more violent & abusive than ordinary against the Church of England. Three articles are devoted to misrepresentation, bad arguing & vituperation of the Anglican Church at large, of the Bish. of Peterborough (Dr. Marsh) the Bishop of Durham (Dr. Barrington) and his Clergy, & the Bishop of London. But the fallacies, slanders, ignorance & malice of the party have been ably detected: Dr. Philpotts, Mr. Rennel, & Dr. Blomfield, (Archdeacon of Colchester) have taken the field against them in able refutations, besides other champions of less note, and the conductors of the Christian remembrancer.

Thursday Ap. 3.

I dined at Mr. Vavasour's, the Rector's of Stow,[30] meeting his brother in law, Mr. M.

30. Richard Frederick Vavasour, (17??-1853).

Vavasour,[31] Sir Henry & Lady Dryden, and Mr. H. Hippisley,[32] of Lamborne Berks, the Son of my deceased venerable friend the late aged Rector of Stow.—

——— |65

Monday April 7.

I left home on horseback in very heavy rain for Cheltenham, where I passed the remainder of the day & slept at my Mother's. My Aunt Travell, & her inmate Miss Louisa Whalley,[33] came to tea.

———

Tuesday April 8.

I proceeded to Gloucester to attend the quarter Sessions, &, as usual, took up my abode at Mrs. Backhouse's. The Assizes were not yet finished, but closed this day. Mr. Justice Best & Mr. Justice Richardson were appointed to the circuit, but the latter having been very much indisposed, his duties have been performed by Mr. Serjeant Bosanquet. Mr. Smith of Stapleton, near Bristol, brother to Sir H. Smith of Ashton in Somersetshire is the present high Sheriff.—In consequence of the Assizes & Sessions falling so nearly together, there were fewer Magistrates than usually attend. Dr. Cooke, in the Chair, Messrs. R. B. Cooper, Baker, Byles, Dr. Timbrell, Mr. Keysall, Newman, Purnell, Dr. Davies &c. were present. The Gaol having been cleared by the Judges, there was only one prisoner for felony, but the usual proportion of appeals, traverses &c.

Much interest was occasioned by the reading of various important letters on the same subject, which has now for six |66 months agitated the county, namely, the charges brought by Mr. Jones, the late Chaplain, against the Governor of the Gaol, and the consequent dismissal of Mr. Jones from his office. With a perseverance worthy of a better cause, Mr. Jones having failed in all his attempts to obtain a revision of his case & a hearing of farther alledged charges, by the Magistrates, has ventured on a long highly criminatory letter to Mr. Secretary Peel, containing the crambe recocta[34] of his former insinuations and charges, a tissue of the grossest falsifications & contradictions, & begging Government to send a commission of enquiry into the abuses of the gaol, as they did into ~~that~~ those at Ilchester. This was met by a very able, temperate statement of evidence, & exposition of fallacies, drawn up by Dr. Cooke, with the aid of written recollections furnished by Messrs. Baker & Byles, recapitulating all the proceedings, evidence adduced & votes of the Michaelmas & Epiphany Sessions. The Secretary for the Home department, having weighed all these documents, put an end to the correspondence |67 with Mr. Jones, by informing him, that not only did he not see the propriety of sending a commission of enquiry, but that the attentive consideration of the evidence convinced him that Mr. Jones' application did not arise form a sense of justice or love of truth, but was dictated by personal pique and malice. It is hoped & expected, that the matter will rest here. In the meantime, Mr. R. Cooper, Mr. Jones's

31. Marmaduke Vavasour, brother of Richard Frederick Vavasour. Marmaduke became curate of Broadwell in 1828 and then accepted the living of Ashby-de-la-Zouch in 1833. Marmaduke and Francis got on well and Francis later accepted the role of godfather to one of Marmaduke's children. See the Biographical Index.
32. Henry Hippisley, (1776-1838).
33. Louisa Whalley was the daughter of Frank's first cousin, Martha Whalley, daughter of his maternal uncle, Ferdinand.
34. crambe recocta — This seems to imply 'as tasty as leftover cabbage.'

successor, performs his duty in the most exemplary & able manner, so as to have called forth from the court a strong expression of their approbation & thanks.

I dined at the Kings Head with the Magistrates as usual.

Wednesday April 9.—

I omitted to mention yesterday the consecration of the New Church at the Spa by the Bishop of Gloucester, who preached a Sermon on the occasion. It is called Christ Church. The congregation, except the clergy in canonicals, whose attendance was numerous, was admitted by tickets, three shillings & sixpence each, and not very many tickets, in proportion to the number expected, were issued. I was not present.

I paid my respects this morning at Mrs. M. Hunt's to a hitherto unknown cousin, Mrs. Baring Goold,[35] who with her daughter |[68] was on a visit to Mrs. Hunt, & about to leave Gloucester to-day on a visit of a short duration to my Aunt Lady Lyttelton at Pickham Grove. Mrs. B. Goold is daughter of the late Mr. & Mrs. Sabine. Mrs. S. was Sister to Mrs. Hunt, of Boreatton in Shropshire & consequently cousin to my Father; the late Mr. Hunt's Mother having been a Witts, Sister to my Grandfather. The Baring Goold's reside at Teignmouth in Devon. Her brother Jos: Sabine was employed in the Tax Department; perhaps, is now; & is in many respects a scientific character. He is Secretary to the horticultural Society, and a distinguished Ornithologist. Another brother, Edward, is Captn. in the Royal Artillery, & a person of eminent attainments in the philosophical Sciences. He accompanied the Navigators, Captn. Ross[36] & Captn. Parry, on their Expeditions to the North Pole, or, more correctly, in search of a Northwest passage, as Astronomer to the expedition; but did not sail with the adventurous & able Captn. Parry in his third Voyage. Much anxiety begins to be felt for news of the Arctic navigators; I saw Captn. Parry at Bath, shortly before his last departure, & was introduced to him by his excellent & highly talented brother, |[69] my valued acquaintance, Dr. C. W. Parry, of Bath.[37] It was a most pleasing spectacle, when Captn. P. received the freedom of the Corporation of his native city, Bath, accompanied with an ~~gold~~ oaken box made of a fragment of the Vessel, in which he explored the icy seas, & ornamented with a medallion in gold, representing one of the Icebergs of the frozen ocean, and the discovery ships, as pourtrayed on one of the plates engraved for the narrative of the Voyage. It is impossible to see & know Captn. Parry without admiring him as a model of the intrepid, cool, collected, intelligent, cheerful, friendly British Sailor; to these qualities science & courage & judgment of the highest order are united. Nor do I here introduce him merely in a parenthesis; as he is likely, should Providence bring him home from his hazardous enterprize, to unite himself with Miss Browne, another of my Sabine connexions; Mrs. Browne, Sister of the above named, being the wife to a gentleman of large fortune acquired in China in the East India Company's Service, whose country seat & estate are at North Mims in Herts. To return to Captn. Sabine; he has been again, &, I believe, still is engaged in taking, under the sanction

---

35. Diana Amelia Baring-Gould, née Sabine, (*c*1775-1858). Diana's mother, Sarah had been first cousin to Frank's father, Edward. Diana was therefore his second cousin. Her grandson, Sabine Baring-Gould, (1834-1924) was the famous writer, with over 500 works to his name. He is perhaps best known as the writer of *Onward Christian Soldiers*.
36. Sir John Ross, (1777-1856). Ross was a Scottish rear-admiral and Arctic explorer.
37. Sir William Edward Parry, (1790-1855). The marriage was not to come about as it turned out that Miss Browne had had a youthful escapade eloping with a boy gardener. See the introduction and Biographical Index for details.

& direction of the government, astronomical observations, which have for their object the |70 elucidation of many highly important points of Geography, Geometry, & Navigation. These researches have carried him on the coast of Africa, &, I believe, will require a voyage to the extremity of Northern Europe, & another visit to the regions of the icy Sea. An unmarried Sister, an amiable woman, resident at Bath, completes, I think, the Sabine family.

Thursday April 10.—
Mrs. Backhouse had a small party.

Friday April 11.
I left Gloucester, the Sessions being closed. Called on my Mother at Cheltenham. Instead of taking the usual road to Cheltenham, I went by Barnwood &c. as far as Brockworth, & from thence took the new Turnpike road from Painswick to Cheltenham. The part, over which I rode, is level, across the vale, passing through the Village of Shurdington, & at some distance from Mr. Lawrence's Seat there. The Estate belongs to the Infant Son of the late M.L. who died a few years since. Badgworth is seen to the left under Churchdown (or Chosen) Hill. The view of Birdlip Lackington & Cleeve Hills, with the other Gloucestershire eminences, Malvern &c.—in the distance is striking. In the Village of Shurdington is a cottage & garden, not very antique |71 yet far from modern, which must have belonged to some worthy Hollander, the plaister on the front being so laid on as to leave the words "Niets zonder Arbyt"—nothing without labour—very prominent to the view. The farther part of this Turnpike road, towards Painswick, creeps up the side of the Hills, above Prinknash Park, through a most picturesque line & commands a splendid view of the Vale of Gloucester.

The Bishop of Gloucester this day consecrated the new church dedicated to the Holy Trinity, at Cheltenham: it is in the Gothic Style; the funds for its erection have been, I am told,

153. Badgeworth.

chiefly supplied by Lord Sherborne; the duty will be performed by Mr. Jervis, the Vicar of Cheltenham, & his curates. Tickets of admission at five shillings; many object to this arrangement on principle: has any one a right to close the doors of the church to those, who do not chuse to pay, but do chuse to enter? Neither was I present on this occasion; hastening to return home, where I arrived to dinner.

Saturday April 12.

The Papers assert, that the French army has crossed the Bidassoa under the command of the duke D'Angouleme, professing to advance into Spain as friends to combat with revolutionary leaders, and to deliver from thraldom |72 the King and royal family. It was erroneously stated above, (p 61) that Spain had declared war against France, & that the Court had withdrawn to Badajos. The fact is, that the Court & Ministry & Members composing the Cortes have retired to Seville. Little effectual preparation for war has been made by the Spaniards; their finances are in the utmost disorder: and faction dominates with blind vehemence. Perhaps, France, however unprincipled her interference may be, will traverse the country without much opposition, while the revolutionary spirit may be quashed, & the old regime under certain modifications may be restored. It is understood to be the policy of our Ministers, now that all attempts at mediation have failed, to observe neutrality as to the belligerents.—

Monday Ap. 14.—

"A candid appeal to the Religious Public in a letter addressed to the inhabitants of the Forest of Dean, occasioned by the dismissal of the Revd. Isaac Bridgman A.B. of St. Edmund's Hall, Oxford, from the Curacy of Trinity Church, in the said Forest. Ross. 1823. With a preface by the Revd. Rowland Hill A.M." "A reply to the above by Henry Berkin, A.M. Perpetual Curate of the church of the Holy Trinity, Forest of Dean, Glo'stershire. |73 Gloucester 1823". Mr. Berkin, Incumbent and Projector of one of those new Churches in the Forest of Dean, (an extraparochial district), which were so much at the heart of Bishop Ryder to erect, and of which he has now consecrated three, is an Evangelist divine, and high in the Esteem of his diocesan. He engages an advertising candidate for orders, gives him a title, the Bishop ordains him; he turns out a man of fiery zeal, with an unbounded appetite for preaching, coarse & familiar in his extempore Sermons, skilled in procuring the sympathy of the lower orders in his alledged wrongs, eager to assort with dissenting teachers (& admitting Rowland Hill into his pulpit) insolent to his Bishop and rector, and when ousted by the revocation of his licence, sets up forthwith as a Dissenting Minister, in the same district, in which he was Curate, thus introducing dissent into the Forest, as if the natural consequence of new churches provided with Evangelical Ministers were the establishment of meeting houses. Bishop Ryder appears to the greatest advantage of the three performers in this drama; for he exhibits unusual firmness without abandoning his mild & pastoral manner, and less of puritanical bias, than might be expected has found its way into his letters, many of which are recorded |74 in the two pamphlets. But both his Lordship, and his friend Mr. Berkin & the Clergy at large may learn this lesson; that the Scale of Enthusiasm is graduated up to ~~by~~ boiling heat; and that encouragement given to exaggerated feelings & principles, to zeal without judgment, & earnestness without sound learning, is more likely to foster Schism & dissent, than promote the glory of GOD and the spiritual welfare of mankind. Independent of their local Interest, the Pamphlets well deserve attentive perusal. The Bishop & Mr. Berkin must have been much harrassed by the contumacious Curate: for Mr. Bridgman, he is a violent, disingenuous, rancorous man, with a vulgar mind: & the old Patriarch of Surry chapel, Rowland Hill, laughs in his sleeve, for he has gained an ardent proselyte A.B. a hot convert from the Church, and a prospect of rearing a plentiful crop of dissent from the seed sown by the Evangelical Clergy of the Bishop of Gloucester's new Churches in the Forest of Dean.

Tuesday April 22.

"Memoirs of the Court of James the 1st. By Lucy Aikin. 2 Vols 8vo. Lond. 1822" A very valuable, instructive & entertaining work by the authoress of similar memoirs of the court of Queen Elizabeth. It is to be hoped, that |75 Miss Aikin will continue her interesting illustrations of the history of the Stuart family. Miss Aikin is daughter of Dr. Aikin, a literary veteran in many departments, lately deceased, & sister of Mrs. Barbauld. There is little or no trace in these volumes of dissenting prejudices.

Wednesday April 23.—

The first meeting of the Stow Clerical Society for this year: 13 gentlemen dined together. Sir Henry Dryden, Curate of Adlestrop, in the chair; Hon & Revd. E. Rice, Prebendary of Worcester & Rector of Oddington & Great Risington, (Brother to Lord Dynevor) Mr. Ford, Rural Dean, Rector of Little Risington & South Cerney, Mr. Malcolm, Rector of Todenham, (Brother to Sir John Malcolm eminent for his Military & diplomatic transactions in the East, & author of some valuable works on Oriental subjects, also to Sir Pultney Malcolm, a distinguished Admiral, who served at St. Helena during the early part of Bonaparte's imprisonment,) Mr. Eyre, Curate of Blockley, Worcestershire, Mr. Jones, the Secretary, Curate of Upper Swell & Broadwell, Mr. Pierce Incumbent of the Leigh, & perpetual curate of Sevenhampton, Mr. Morgan, curate of Fairford, Mr. Jeaffreson, Vicar of Longborough, Mr. Vavasour, Rector of Stow, Mr. Western, |76 Rector of Kingham, Oxfordshire, and myself: also Mr. Winter, Curate of Condicote & Daylesford.

154. Bourton-on-the-Hill.

Thursday April 24.

After the ordinary business of the day at Stow, I proceeded to Bourton on the Hill, where I dined & slept at Dr. Warneford's, meeting only Mr. Large of Broadwell, Oxfordshire, an eminent land surveyor, who is engaged in laying out Dr. Warneford's rectorial allotments under the new inclosure of the Parish of Bourton on the Hill, having been employed by Dr. W. to protect his interests during the progress of the Act.

Friday April 25.

Accompanied Dr. Warneford to Evesham, to bring to a conclusion, if possible, the business, which had been left unfinished on Mar. 14. On our way we were met by Mr. Stokes, the District road Surveyor, who prevailed on us to deviate from the high road about two miles before we reached Bengeworth in order to view a line of road constructed by him, & extending from Bengeworth to three farms, the property of a gentleman of the name of Porter. Nothing can exceed the solidity and level surface of this road formed of large gravel blended with a blue lime- |77 -stone; the greatest skill is shewn by Stokes in taking his line; he trusts nothing to the eye, but measures all his work by a level, in this & other points of his practice he follows Mr. Telford, rather than MacAdam. There is every reason to expect, that in a few years the turnpike roads from Chipping Norton to Worcester, and the whole Worcester district, all which are under his management, will bear ample testimony to his zeal & science. He submitted to our inspection a broadwheeled (9 inch) waggon with flat soles and nails wholly countersunk, as far superior to the ordinary conical construction. In fact these wheels roll with an entirely equal pressure, insomuch, that you may place a sheet of writing paper under one of the wheels, as the waggon is proceeding on the road with a load of five tons, and not perceive any crease or irregularity of pressure on any part of the paper.

We were engaged for five hours in examining the accounts submitted to our judgment, and were obliged after all to adjourn the business to the following day. The same gentlemen met, as on the former occasion, with the addition of Mr. Blayney, a Solicitor of Evesham, and Clerk of the Peace for Worcestershire. |78

155. A carrier's wagon .

Dr. Warneford and myself dined and slept at Cracomb four miles beyond Evesham, in the parish of Fladbury, on the upper road to Worcester, the seat of Mr. Perrot. We left Evesham by the Alcester road, from which the Worcester road diverges to the left. Close to Evesham are rich garden grounds, producing very early crops, and let at high rents; much of this land belongs to a Gentleman of the name of Rudge, who by letting his property in these small lots, retains a great influence in the Elections for the Borough, which he exercises in favour of Sir W. Rouse Boughton. We passed M. Rudge's new built mansion, in a very bad mock Gothic style, & unsheltered by timber, but the house must command a fine view of Evesham, the Avon, Bredon Hill & other surrounding eminences. A ridge of low hills, and the soil on them very moderate, runs nearly parallel to the river, and the meadows on its banks shew every mark of fertility. The Avon is navigable, with locks contructed on it: the property of the navigation, I believe, from Tewksbury to Evesham, belongs to Mr. Perrot. The situation of Cracomb is commanding, on a wooded knoll at the extremity of the line of high land above mentioned, rising above the river at some distance from it, & commanding |79 very fine views of the Avon, to Evesham, of the distant range of hills, Broadway, Stanway, Cleeve Hills &c. In front, about a mile distant is Fladbury on a steep bank of the river, with its church, rectory &c. On the opposite bank of the Avon is Cropthorn, situate on a gentle swell. Fladbury is a rectory in the gift of the Bishop of Worcester, but is now understood to be an option belonging to the Family of the late Archbishop of Canterbury. The Incumbent is the Revd. Martin Stafford Smith, the friend of Bishops Warburton & Hurd, the widow of the former of whom he married, but is now united to a second wife. He is in advanced age, though stout in health, & resides for the greater part of the year in his house in Queen Square, Bath, where we have visited him, and enjoyed his private concerts. The living of Fladbury is very valuable. Bredon Hill rising beyond it is a fine feature from Cracomb. The house at Cracomb, without exhibiting a spacious front, is a large & roomy family mansion, apparently built within 30 or 40 years. We were very hospitably received by Mr. & Mrs. Perrot, & met Dr. Cooper, of Bengeworth, Mr. Hudson, of Pershore, two of the Gentlemen, with whom we had been transacting business in the morning. Mr. & Mrs. W. Pruen, & a young Clergyman of the name of Garratt, residing at Dumbleton |80 who attends Mr. Perrot's boys in the capacity of private tutor. Dr. Beale Cooper, who has resided many years at Bengeworth, which is a large village on the opposite side of the river from Evesham & forming a suburb to the borough, has only lately assumed the title, with a view to practice as a Physician, having in earlier life been in the medical profession. Lord Beauchamp, whom he has attended in a very lingering & alarming illness, and who has benefited much under his care, has advised him to bring into active service the diploma, which he had long in his possession; he is a quick man, of considerable attainments, but not a finished scholar, and has been long actively engaged as a Magistrate for the Counties of Worcester & Gloucester, & in the transaction of the public business of the neighbourhood, as well as of the borough of Evesham, in which he supports the Northwick interest. Mr. W. Pruen, Curate to Mr. Stafford Smith, has long had an academy at Fladbury, in some repute: he is originally from Cheltenham and brother to the Revd. T. Pruen, Curate of Dursley, who had not the advantage of an University Education, & entered the church after trying more than one line |81 in life. He is an old acquaintance of mine, & a diligent compiler, having published by subscription a work on the liturgy & being now engaged in a work on Episcopacy. He is disappointed, that

Dr. Jenner's Executors have not entrusted him with the papers & documents necessary for writing the learned doctor's life; and alledges not only that his long habits of intimacy with Dr. Jenner, but the express understanding between Jenner & himself on the subject, pointed him out as the proper person. Of course he feels indignant, that the materials are placed in the hands of Dr. Baron, an eminent physician at Gloucester, who will, most probably, produce a very interesting work. The medical profession & others have been raising subscriptions for a monument to Jenner, to be erected, most likely, in Gloucester Cathedral.—I should have mentioned Mrs. Perrot sooner: she appears to be a person of very considerable talent & extensive acquirements; she is now busy in preparing a work on the Ornithology of Worcestershire to be published in parts with an expensive series of portraits of the different birds illustrated by a scientific |82 and interesting account of their habits &c. The drawings, (we saw above 50 of them), are remarkably well executed. Mrs. Perrot is a proficient in Music, appears to have a great talent for conversation & activity of mind, devoting herself to the education of her family of four boys & a girl, & competent to superintend the classical studies of the former.

Saturday April 26.

Constant rain from morning till night.—We left Cracomb at 11 o clock, & accompanied by Mr. Perrot repaired to Dr. Cooper's, at Bengeworth, where we met Mr. Hanford, of Woolershill, one of the Committee entrusted with the examination of the litigated accounts, & brought to a conclusion our tedious labours. After a welcome hot luncheon between four & five o clock, I set off home, where I arrived to tea thoroughly wet. Dr. Cooper shewed me several curiosities, which deserved more attention than the time would permit me to give them, among the rest some very old printed books, an original picture of Charles 1. a pair of sea unicorn horns of remarkable length, a pearl of large size in its shell, and the whole inner surface of the shell converted into a similar substance with the pearl.

Monday April 28.—

"Essays, moral, philosophical and itomachical on the important science of good living. By Lancelot Sturgeon Esq.—1822." An entertaining jeu d'esprit.

Tuesday April 29.

Mr. Large, of Broadwell, arrived, by appointment, to look over, with a view to reletting, my farms here and at Stanway. W. Gregory having given me notice to quit the former, & the Courts' term in the latter being out at Michâs. Mr. Large is a very considerable farmer & sheep breeder:—his stock has long been in the highest repute, & the size, to which he brings his fat sheep & rams, is surprizing: I have seen a prize sheep of his slaughtered, & weighing about 70 lbs per quarter. His prices for letting rams for the season are from seven to ten & fifteen guineas; the bone remarkably small, & the wool of the finest quality. He is very largely employed, in this & the neighbouring counties, as land surveyor, steward, & arbitrator; is skilful & intelligent in his profession; a very cool headed and well conducted man. I had before employed him here & at Stanway. We rode over the rectorial farm.

Wednesday April 30.

We rode to Stanway & over the vicarage farm there. F. Aston is absent on a visit to his friends at Ealing.

——— |84

Thursday May 1.

Mr. Large left us.

———

Friday May 2.

Mrs. Backhouse arrived from Gloucester to pass the time with Margaret of my approaching Journey to Yorkshire.

———

Monday May 5.

I set out on my Journey into Yorkshire, proceeding by Birmingham. I went post to Shipston, 18 miles. Immediately after passing Moreton in Marsh, we came on the works for the railroad from Stratford to Moreton, the road forming, & excavations with a bridge are going on. I am holder of two £50 shares in this concern, but do not expect, it will be profitable. To the Country it must be advantageous, as affording a communication between the Cotswold hills & the Stratford Canal, whereby the Grain of the former will be cheaply conveyed towards Birmingham, & coals, manure, iron & general goods brought up in return. Lord Redesdale has engaged largely in the concern.

While waiting for a coach at Shipston I walked about the town, & its immediate environs, it seems to be a poor place, & no stir in it. The Stour is a very small river.

From Shipston to Birmingham 33 miles: by the Oxford day-coach. About a mile from Shipston Mr. Townsend's |85 at Honington a little further, Mr. Shirley's at Eatington; Mr. Fellowes lives at Torlton. Excavations for the new rail road. The Coffee room at the Hen & Chickens warm & full of blundering Hibernians.

———

Tuesday May 6.

Very fine weather. Left Birmingham at 7 o clock on the outside of the Sheffield mail; to Sheffield 76 miles, by Lichfield, Burton upon Trent, Derby & Chesterfield. Between Birmingham and Sutton Coldfield, at Erdington, they are building a new church in free stone, Gothic & very neat. On the extremity of Birmingham on the Oxford side I observed also a very elegant & elaborate church just erected in the florid Gothic style, which, I understand, had been opened for service a few weeks since. It is very gratifying to observe the spirit at present abroad of increasing Church accommodation in all populous districts. Near Sutton Coldfield is Sir Hartopp's handsome seat.[38] Between Lichfield & Burton Mr. Levett's at Wichenor Park, & near the latter Town Sir R. Gresley's place at Drakelow.[39] Between Burton & Derby Sir — Everitt's at Egginton.[40] From Derby we

38. Sir Edmund Cradock-Hartopp, (1749-1833). Born as Edmund Bunny, Sir Edmund inherited the Cradock estate from his maternal uncle, Joseph Cradock and the Hartopp estate through the maternal line of his wife. By Act of Parliament at Michaelmas 1777 he took the name Cradock-Hartopp. He was M.P. for Leicestershire, 1798-1806.

39. Sir Roger Gresley, (1799-1837), 8th Baronet of Drakelow. Sir Roger succeeded to the baronetcy in 1808. He was M.P. for the City of Durham, 1830-1831; Romney Marsh, 1831-1832 and for South Derbyshire, 1832-1837.

40. Sir Henry Every, (1777-1855), 9th Baronet of Egginton, Sheriff of Derbyshire 1804-1805. Francis Witts was mistaken in his name, referring to his as 'Everett'.

took the road to Chesterfield through Alfreton, provincially called Offerton, |86 an inconsiderable place. The road from Derby to Chesterfield this way is through pleasing, undulating country: I had never travelled it before; another line avoids Alfreton & passes by the Peacock Inn & Belper: both unite between Alfreton & Chesterfield. Before reaching the ~~former~~ latter place we passed Sir — Hunloke's at Wingeworth; the Baronet is a minor.[41] Between Chesterfield and Sheffield the country improves in beauty, & is, indeed, very rich & varied, in wood and hill. But the volumes of smoke from steam engines & furnaces disfigure the fair face of nature, & the unpastoral appearance of the lower classes is more in harmony with the manufacturing pursuits of the district than its natural beauties. The Seats of the opulent manufacturers in the environs of Sheffield are neat villas pleasingly situated on the sides of the hills or summit of the knolls, and at sunrise, before the Vulcanian operations commence, the country must appear to much advantage. At Sheffield also we observed a new Gothic church forward in progress. The mail from Birmingham arrives at Sheffield at the same hour as the mail from London to Leeds, and the passengers by the former have a preference to such seats as may be unoccupied in the latter. I was |87 fortunate enough to be able to avail myself of this facility for pursuing my journey, and after a hasty dinner proceeded onwards to Leeds by Barnsley & Wakefield 33 miles. The first stage, which is only 7 miles, &, indeed, the whole of the road to Barnsley is very hilly, and, making allowance for the fire & smoke in all directions, through a fine country. Soon after ascending the hill from Sheffield you see Rotherham at four miles distance in the valley,

156. Pickford's Wagon and the Leeds Coach.

41. Sir Henry John Joseph Hunloke, (1812-1856), 6th Baronet of Wingerworth. Hunloke died unmarried at Grafton Street in London and the baronetcy became extinct. Francis Witts had known the young baronet's grandmother, Margaret, Lady Hunloke at Clifton. He had called on her on Wednesday 12 September 1804.

& much of the drest ground of Earl Fitzwilliam's fine seat. I had passed thro' the park on my last Journey into Yorkshire in 1818, when I rode down, taking the line of Rugby, Lutterworth, Leicester, Nottingham, Mansfield & Rotherham, and joining the road from Sheffield half way between that town & Barnsley. Chapel town & Worsborough, each situate in woody dells, are distinguished by enormous iron forges; at the former the pipes for the London gas company are cast. In a field near Barnsley, I observed a multitude of men of the lower class assembled apparently in consultation, and on enquiry learnt, that the Linen weavers of this town has struck; the sort of linen manufactured here is of a coarse heavy description, common sheeting, shirting & table linen: it has been a custom |[88] of the trade to allow the weavers a perquisite what are called fents; the fag end of the piece to the extent of a yard; but this being found to lead to great roguery and pillage, whole pieces being sometimes cut up into fents, the masters have determined to discontinue this practice, and give them a shilling on each piece in lieu of the fents; to this the turbulent workmen will not agree, & this is the second time, that they have struck. Their conduct on this occasion has been very violent; breaking looms, smashing windows, & rescuing prisoners, who were in custody by the civil power. The Yeomanry are in readiness to interpose, if the Magistrates fail to crush the combination. Such tumults are readily accounted for in a neighbourhood where Luddism and disaffection have recently prevailed to so alarming an extent. The Stage between Barnsley & Wakefield, which used to be very sandy, is now greatly improved by forming a road of better materials. We passed Woolley Park the Seat of Mr. Wentworth.[42] It was become quite dark, when we arrived at Wakefield, and shortly after leaving the town I put myself into the inside of the Coach, as there was a threatning of rain. We arrived at Leeds at 10 o clock, and were driven to the Hotel, where I found comfortable accommodations.

——— |[89]

Wednesday May 7.—

The Kendal & Leeds coach leaving the latter place at 10 o clock in the forenoon, I had time to take a hasty walk through the streets before breakfast; the main street, the Briggate is wide & handsome. I passed two or three churches, not remarkable in their exterior. Here, as at Wakefield one side of the town can boast some pleasant rows & streets of spacious and handsome residences for the Merchants. The distance to Settle by Bradford, Keighley, Skipton & Gargrave is 46 miles: all the country was well known to me except the first stage. The valley of the Aire, through which we passed from Leeds is very fine, & the ruins of Kirkstall Abbey very striking. Great improvements are making in the line of road from Bradford to Keighley, and, indeed, generally, all the way to Settle. The coach stopped for half an hour at Skipton, which enabled me to pay a short visit to Mrs. & Miss Lonsdale, relations of my wife, and by 5 o clock, I arrived at the Golden Lion Inn, Settle, where I found good accommodations. My Journey amounted, altogether, I believe, to 206 miles. I passed the Evening with our Solicitor, Mr. Hartley.

———

Thursday May 8.

Mr. Hartley having mounted me, I rode |[90] over great part of our Estates at Stainforth Hall, Sherwood House, & Helwith Bridge. The country is backward in vegetation, but the rains

42. Godfrey Wentworth, (1773-1834), of Woolley Park, nr. Wakefield, M.P. for Tregony, 1806-1808. Wentworth was Sheriff of Yorkshire, 1796-7, York 1814 and Captain of the Stainscross Yeomanry, 1798.

now beginning to fall, will soon produce the verdant carpeting, which distinguishes the Upper part of the Vale of the Ribble. The plantation, by the riverside, above & below the waterfall, are now become consequential, and clothe this mountain stream with that, which it most wanted: they flourish greatly; tho' none are above 13 years growth, they shew themselves very handsomely from many points. The plantations in the higher parts of the farm of course grow more slowly, than on the rich meadows, which border on the river. The tenant complains heavily; and I doubt not, the Graziers have had a very bad year; but the reduction, which we have made, is considerable.

I transacted various business, for Mrs. Backhouse & myself, & made some calls on our old acquaintance, finishing the day by dining at Mr. Hartley's.

Friday May 9.

Very heavy rain, part of the day. Engaged in the forenoon in the transaction of various business. Rode in the afternoon by Long Preston to Wiglesworth to meet some parties on an affair of importance relating to Mrs. Back- |91 -house's concerns. Returned to Cappleside with Mr. Geldard: a landed proprietor and large farmer, whose judgment & integrity are greatly valued in this district, & of whose advice Mrs. Backhouse and myself are accustomed to avail ourselves in transactions relating to this neighbourhood.

Saturday May 10.

Mr. Woods, Mrs. Backhouse's Tenant at Beck House, being returned from London, I called on him this day, and was much pleased with the alterations and improvements made at the House, which is now an excellent family mansion on a moderate scale. Mr. Woods is engaged in the manufacture of Paper in a very extensive way at a mill on the Ribble in the ~~parish~~ township of Langcliff. Called on different acquaintances at Giggleswick & Settle, & dined at the former place with Mrs. Bolland, meeting the Pearts, Robinsons & Geldards, and Mr. Rycroft, eldest Son of a baronet of that name, who has estates in this neighbourhood, at Little Stainforth, Calton Hall, and Coniston, but resides on his estates in Kent near Farnham. Sir Nelson Rycroft's younger Brother, Sir Henry Rycroft, Knight Harbinger to the King married Mrs. Naper, the widow of the Hon. James Naper, brother to the late Lord Sherborne, & daughter of my Uncle |92 Mr. F.J. Travell, Rector of Upper Slaughter. A sister of Mr. Rycroft's (for he was not then knighted) was married to Dr. Pelham, Bishop of Exeter, and now of Lincoln, and Brother to the Earl of Chichester. By this chain of connexion, I was in 1801 promised the appointment of private Secretary to Lord Chichester, then Lord Pelham, and recently appointed Secretary of State for the Home department; after some weeks expectation of an immediate introduction into that post, his Lordship caused to be intimated to me, that he should not require such services, because, I believe, his own appointment as Secretary for the Home department was only temporary, and I was disappointed of my promised place. Shortly after, I entered the University, and my views were decidedly turned to the Clerical profession.

Sunday May 11.

Attended divine service twice at Giggleswick Church. Mr. Clapham, the Vicar, read prayers, and Mr. Ingram, the Curate, and Head Master of the Grammar School at Giggleswick, preached. The school is in high repute, and frequented from all parts of the North, as well as by the young people of the immediately surrounding neighbourhood. After church I called on Mr. Ingram and his family, as well as on other old |[93] acquaintances, and dined at Mr. Hartley's, meeting Mr. Woods.—

Monday May 12.—

Very much engaged in business, with Messrs. Hartley, Geldard, Moorhouse, Slingsby & others till twelve o clock, then rode to Stainforth Hall, and accompanied by our tenant & his Father to the higher parts of our Estate there: found my plantation in Kearsden flourishing better than I could have expected on such high ground.

Dined at Mr. Peart's, a Banker in Settle, & formerly practising as a Solicitor, meeting a large party, and others came in the evening: among the guests were Mr. Wiglesworth, Rector of Slaidburn, and his second wife, Mrs. Clapham & Miss Gurnall, the Robinsons; the Ingrams, Mr. Rycroft, Mr. & Mrs. C. Ingleby &c.—

Tuesday May 13.—

Having been engaged in business up till the hour, when the Coach from Kendal to Leeds passed through Settle, and having got through the chief of my affairs, I left this hospitable neighbourhood for Skipton, 16 miles, where I arrived to an early dinner with Mrs. & Miss Lonsdale. In spite of boisterous wind, I walked in the Evening to Bow Bridge, about a mile out of the Town, to look at a house, |[94] into which she & her Mother are about to remove. It is at the extremity of the Village of Embsay, in a direction behind Skipton Castle and church.—

Wednesday May 14.

I borrowed a horse of Mr. Cooper, brother in law of Miss Lonsdale, & rode to look over Mrs. Backhouse's farm at Scale House, about four miles from Skipton, on the road to Kettlewell; it is situate in a valley between high fells, in the township of Rilston & parish of Burnsal, a part of the Estate being in the parish of Gargrave. The house is an ancient mansion, formerly belonging to the Fairfaxes, whose arms are to be seen in one of the principal rooms. The present tenant, Mr. R. Ayrton, is considered a very intelligent man in his line of life, and much employed, as a valuer of land, commissioner & arbitrator. Walked with him all over the estate before dinner. The plantations are coming on well, and the farm looked in very good order. I returned again to the hospitable roof of Mrs. & Miss Lonsdale, with the latter of whom I transacted business, it being my intention to travel homeward on the following day.

Thursday May 15.

I left Skipton on the coach for Leeds at ½ past five o clock in the morning; this is not the same coach, by which I had travelled from the South, but one, which passes daily between Skipton & Leeds as extreme points. At Keighley we took up a large cargo of manufacturers and others bound for |[95] Bradford market, it being the custom of this country to transact much business in trade on the market days, at Manchester, Halifax, Leeds, Wakefield, Bradford &c. By the time we had reached Bingley a spring of the coach was broken, & required a clip to secure it, and I walked forward to Cottingley bridge, where I again mounted the box, but was thankful to reach Bradford & discharge the load without farther accident: I believe, with four inside passengers we numbered 15 outside of the coach. At Bradford a coach from Halifax meets that from Skipton & one vehicle conveys the passengers from both places to Leeds: where we arrived about 11 o clock, and were driven to the Rose & Crown Inn. I had an opportunity to taking a walk in that quarter of the Town, where the best dwelling houses are found, and noticed two or three public buildings of modern erection & handsome architecture. After an early dinner, I left Leeds at 2 o clock on the top of the coach for Sheffield, 33 miles, where we arrived at the Tontine hotel at 7 o clock. I travelled this day 53 miles. I walked in the town along the principal streets till near dark. There are many shewy shops, particularly, of cutlery. The old church at Sheffield is a very handsome building. I met with good accommodations at the Tontine.

——— |[96]

Friday May 16.

The morning was very wet, but the afternoon proved remarkably fine. Though a passenger outside of the Mail to Birmingham, I travelled within all the way: by the same road as I had gone over on my way into Yorkshire. At Chesterfield we took up a Mr. Dixon, of Oxford, an eminent land surveyor, commissioner of inclosures &c., a person of very good manners, & cultivated mind, whose conversation proved very agreeable. We arrived at the Hen & Chickens hotel, Birmingham, at ½ past four o clock, where we dined, & Mr. Dixon & myself not meeting with a convenient opportunity of prosecuting our Journey by coach, agreed to join in a chaise, which brought us to Stratford on Avon by 9 o clock, where we parted; & where I found myself very comfortably lodged at the Red Horse Inn having travelled 98 miles this day.—

———

Saturday May 17.—

After an early breakfast I pursued my journey post to Upper Slaughter, 24 miles, where I arrived about 12 o clock, rejoicing to find myself again in my domestic retreat, and having much to relate to my dear wife & her mother of the business, which I had transacted while absent, & the observations, which I had made, & infor- |[97] -mation, which I had collected in their old neighbourhood.

———

Wednesday May 21.—

Frederick Aston spent a long morning and dined here.

———

Wednesday May 27.

We drove over to Stanway Vicarage to spend a day there, and meet our old friends Mr. & Mrs. Aston, Frederick's father & mother, who are visiting him.

———

Saturday May 31.

"A letter to Francis Jeffrey Esqr. the reputed Editor of the Edinburgh Review, on an article entitled "Durham Case—Clerical Abuses.—By Rev. H. Phillpotts D.D. Rector of Stanhope. Durham 1823". I have remarked before on the virulent attack recently made in the Edinburgh Review on the Church of England. One of the aggressions was against the Durham Clergy in a critique on Mr. Brougham's speech in defence of Mr. John Ambrose Williams, the Editor of a radical newspaper, published in Durham, against whom, by the orders of the venerable Bishop Barrington, an action had been brought for a libel contained in a paragraph of his paper, in which he commented on the fact, that the bells of the Cathedral & parish churches at Durham had not been tolled on the death of the late Queen, which he imputed to directions emana- |98 -ting from the Clergy of the place and originating in their political animosity to the Queen. The libel was sufficiently gross and comprehensive, full of abuse not only of the local clergy, but also of the whole body of the English Clergy. In spite of Mr. Brougham's terrible oratory, as the Edinburgh Reviewers call it, Mr. Williams was found guilty, & a sort of second Battery opened by the politicians of the great Northern Journal. Dr. Phillpotts buckles on his armour against them, irritated by a personal allusion to himself, and knowing himself to have excited by previous publications of a local interest, and of a political tendency, which had been roughly handled by the reviewers, ~~to have excited~~ the animosity not only of them but of their powerful friends and patrons in the North. While he fully shews the grossness of the libel in ~~the~~ question, and fully vindicates the Durham Clergy, he deals about controversial blows with considerable force & acrimony. In a word, one would not like to be an Edinburgh Reviewer & receive such a flogging, nor chuse to be the keen & roused flagellant. Dr. Phillpotts is a man of very considerable talent, Son of ~~the~~ a former Innkeeper at the Bell Inn in Gloucester, where his Mother, a respectable aged person, still |99 resides. He distinguished himself at Oxford, where he was of Magdalen College, by his public exercises, particularly by a panegyrical Latin Oration in praise of Sir W. Jones. He was patronized by Bishop Barrington, in whose diocese he has since resided. At one time he was Prebendary of Durham, but resigned that dignity on taking the very valuable living, which he now holds. He has always been a prominent loyalist, and in that respect strongly contrasted with his brother, who resides in Gloucester, and is a lawyer of great talents and experience. He has practised as an Attorney till within this twelvemonth, and is Chapter Clerk of the Cathedral; of late he has been called to the bar, & pleads at the Assizes & Sessions. His predilections in politics are wholly antiministerial.—

Tuesday June 3.

Mr. Rudge, the Archdeacon of Gloucester, held his Visitation at Stow, where a small proportion of the clergy of the Deanery attended. The Archdeacon preached, but was from indisposition ill able to discharge the duties of the day. He is much broken. He is Chancellor of the Diocese of Hereford, Rector of St. Michael's Church, Gloucester, & of Haresfield, near that city.

--- |100

Friday June 6.

I officiated at Bourton on the Water for Mr. Croome, preaching before the two Benefit societies, and a crouded congregation, though ill able to discharge the duty having been much indisposed for two days past.

Mrs. Backhouse returned to her residence at Gloucester.

"Quentin Durward. By the Author of Waverley &c. 3 Vols. 12mo. 1823"—The astonishing fecundity of this mysterious writer is again displayed in a new historical novel. In an entertaining introduction, it is very roundly asserted, whether sincerely is another question, that Sir W. Scott is not the author of the series of romances so generally ascribed to him; & towards the close of the work it is intimated, that the writer is a Scotchman. The present

157. Bourton-on-the-Water.

is a stirring, bustling tale. The hero, a young Scottish adventurer, bold, aspiring and quick of discernment, falls into the Service of Lewis 11. the politic, treacherous, superstitious, bold, but crafty & cruel monarch of France, who employs him as an agent in his intrigues, and schemes to circumvent his impetuous, powerful & passionate rival Charles Duke of Burgundy. Good conduct, firmness, good sense, warm attachment to the heroine, a Burgundian Countess, |[101] and good luck, carry young Quentin through unexampled risks, snares and trials of valour & military skill: affording to the author an opportunity of developing the manners of the 15th Century, pourtraying the chivalry, the arts of war, the diplomacy, the summary justice, the superstition, and many other features of the time. The subordinate characters, admirably sketched, are a Bohemian, or in modern phraseology, a Gipsey, one of the base agents of the crafty Lewis, his Provost Marshal with the attendant executioners, a court Jester, the rude Scottish archer, or body Guard, rich & mutinous burghers of Liege, the royal astrologer—&c.—

Tuesday June 10.

"Journal of a voyage for the discovery of a Northwest Passage from the Atlantic to the Pacific, performed in the years 1819–20 in his Majesty's ships Hecla and Griper, under the orders of Willm. Edwd. Parry. R.N. F.R.S. and Commander of the Expedition. Lond. 1821. 4to." The mention, which I have before made of the gallant Capt. Parry, makes me the more brief in the notice of this interesting work; interesting, not so much from its variety of incident, as from the proofs, it gives, of the blessedness of possessing cool fortitude, patient endurance, practical good sense, cheerful activity, qualities |[102] eminently displayed by Captn. Parry and his associates.

Friday June 13.

My Mother arrived from Cheltenham on a visit in good health and spirits.—

Saturday June 14.—

"A Sermon, preached at St. Paul's, on July 1. 1822—at the Visitation of the Bishop of London (Howley) By Ch. Goddard D.D. Rector of St. James's Garlick Hythe—London 1822." The text is 1 Tim. 6. 20,21.—The character of the heresy which sprung up in the days of the Apostles, and gradually spread with the propagation of Christianity, is delineated; as being an attempt to unite into one system oriental, grecian, & Jewish false philosophy &metaphysics: compounding a set of principles, calculated to conciliate the prejudices of the various classes of converts. The subject is too extensive & intricate for the compass of a visitation sermon, and no notes are given. It is, however, a sketch of a curious and important subject for theological research, evincing learning & reflection: ζωνανια δυνειοιδιν,[43] but not generally edifying.

Wednesday June 18.

The second dinner for the Season of the Stow Clerical Society. Eighteen clergymen met. Sir H. Dryden in the Chair.

--- |103

Friday June 20.

Our dear Edward returned home for the Midsummer holidays. GOD be blessed, that he is in good health. Mr. Hale writes to me in the most satisfactory manner of his conduct at school, as well as of his improvement.

Friday July 4.

We were afflicted with receiving most painful accounts of my brother from Malta, whose arrival from the Mediterranean we had been anxiously expecting for some time. In his last letters he had spoken of his shaken nerves & impaired health, but anticipated with satisfaction a return to England and removal from a hot climate, which he expected would recruit his strength. The letter, which arrived to-day, is written by a Gentleman signing himself C. Godfrey, but not giving any clue as to his situation in life, or even how he is to be addressed: it states, that George had determined on returning by the packet, by which this letter came; that he had accordingly come to La Valette from the country, where he had been residing at Zuricco, a village in the interior, during the winter months. That he reached Mr. Godfrey's, who had invited him to stay with him till the return of the packet from Corfú on the 1st. of May; and appeared in as good health as he had been for some time past. Mr. Godfrey soon observed an alarming flightiness about him, and on the 8th. May, his medical attendant took some blood from him, which relieved him. But he had several relapses, and on the 21st. May, when the letter was closed, was in |104 Mr. Godfrey's opinion entirely deranged. The first design was to send him home in that state by the packet, & arrangements had been made for the purpose, but his increasing violence prevented this being done, and an arrangement was made for his being received into the General Military hospital, yet with a view to his removal home by the next packet, if his state should admit of it. These overwhelming tidings, unaccompanied by any distinct medical report, and so vaguely communicated, that we cannot even answer the

---

43. φωναντα συνετοισιν — speaking to those who will understand him, from Pindar, Olympian Odes, II.152. He compares his own serious works to what he regards as the futile babblings of two others, thought to be Simonides and his nephew Bachylides.

letter of the writer, from ignorance of his address, were likely to fall with the bitterest force on his Mother, myself & Margaret; but something should be done to prepare for contingencies & for the worst; and so unfortunately vague is Mr. Godfrey's letter, that I do not see how I can take proper steps without going to London to consult his agents Messrs. Greenwood & Cox[44] & other persons capable of advising me what steps are proper to be taken either in case of his return to England in the melancholy state, in which he is represented to be, or in case of his continuing or dying in the same wretched condition at Malta. To a merciful Father in heaven alone can we look up for support under this affliction, praying to him to relieve & heal the suffe- |105 -rer in his good time & manner, and to strengthen his grieving Parent & brother and sister under the heavy stroke. As yet we know nothing definite either as to his bodily or mental complaints: of the former we had reason to believe they consisted of great debility, derangement of the organs of the stomach, & highly irritated nerves. As to the mind, his family, on both the Father's & Mother's side, is wholly free from hereditary derangement. His own constitution, originally strong, has been most imprudently tried by irregularity of living in his early career, & great trials of bodily strength in walking, riding &c. add to which the wear & tear of a military life, & long residence in the Mediterranean & Levant, and there is more room for grief than wonder, that his constitution is wrecked.—[45]

Saturday July 5.

Received an account of the death of Mr. George Daniell, a subaltern Officer in the East India Company's service, which took place at Vellore, from an attack of cholera morbus.[46] This estimable youth was the only surviving son of my cousin, Mrs. Daniell, daughter of my deceased Uncle, Mr. Richd. Witts. Mrs. D. has been unfortunate in her marriage, her husband, a Solicitor in town, with good connexions and prospects, having so misconducted himself, at the same time, that his affairs were deranged, |106 that he is forced to fly the country to avoid the penalties, which his misconduct has exposed him to. Mrs. D. resides at Lyme in Dorsetshire, & her family now consists of two daughters. The Son had been sent into India within a year or two, as a Cadet, the different branches of his family having interested themselves to procure him the appointment and to fit him out. Mrs. Daniell's mother was daughter and heiress of a Mr. Steere of Jays near Leatherhead in Surry, who died within three weeks of her husband in 1815. By M. Steere's will the eldest Son of the Marriage took the name of Steere with the estate on coming of age. Variances between him and his father, on attaining his majority, have alienated this gentleman from his Father's family.[47] His daughter

44. The business still survives to this day as travel agents Cox & King. The business was founded by Richard Cox, (1718-1803). Cox took in Greenwood as a partner in 1783. In the early years of the Revolutionary war with France Cox & Greenwood served 14 regiments of cavalry, 64 infanrry regiments and 17 militia regiments. At that time they were on Craig's Court, Charing Cross.

45. It had been George's intention to return to England for some time. In 1822 George had told Frank that he had moved to Zurrico where he hoped the mountain air would recoup his strength. As recently as 5 May he said in another letter that his doctor had recommended a course of Cheltenham waters, a plan he intended to adopt. Frank and his mother had known George was ill, but the severity came as a shock.

46. It is doubtful if Frank ever met his first cousin once removed. The relationship with Richard Witts' family was quite remote.

47. Lee Steere Steere, (1774-1842). Whether or not Frank ever met this first cousin is not recorded, but Lee Steere fell out with his father, Richard, over the management of his estate when he was a minor. The estate was considerable. In the mid-nineteenth century the Lee Steere family emigrated to Australia where they still flourish with substantial business interests.

is recently married to M. Ridley, a Prebendary of Bristol and a widower, a Son of Dr. Ridley, Prebendary of Gloucester, & a near connexion of Lord Chancellor Eldon.[48] Another brother of Mrs. Daniell, Mr. Richd. Witts, who like herself inherited a handsome competence from her maternal grandfather, is living in obscurity, at least little if at all noticed by his Father's family, having disgraced himself by low propensities, & forming mean & vulgar connexions. I have ever known little of this branch of my Family. Mrs. Daniell |107 I believe to be a very respectable and amiable person.

Sunday July 6.

I received another letter relating to my poor brother's melancholy state from a gentleman signing himself E. F. Phillips, and dating from Worlington Parsonage near Mildenhall, Suffolk. This gentleman is recently arrived from Malta, where he saw George early in May in very indifferent health but in a sane state of mind: of the melancholy change in that respect, he had been informed by a letter overland from Malta, and describes the seizure much in the same terms as Mr. Godfrey, adding it as his decided opinion that the alienation of mind originates in the use of strong medicines, which his impaired bodily health required.

---|

48. Sir John Scott, (1751-1838), 1st Earl of Eldon, Lord High Chancellor, 1801-1827. Sir John's son, also John Scott, (1805-1854), 2nd Earl of Eldon married Henrietta Elizabeth Ridley, daughter of Sir Matthew White Ridley, (1745-1813).

Witts Family Papers F310

Diary.

1823.

July 7. Monday.

In pursuance of my intention to endeavour to make some arrangements in consequence of the melancholy account of my poor brother's state I left home this morning for London, riding to Northleach, where I took a place on the Regulator, ~~for~~ and arrived at Hatchett's Hotel, Piccadilly, before seven o clock, being about 11 hours on the road. After dinner I walked down St. James's street and Pall Mall, and into Piccadilly again by Waterloo Place, which, however it may be open to criticism in its details, is, on the whole, a magnificent pile of building. A range of shops between Piccadilly and Burlington Street, roofed over, with sky lights, so as to afford a long covered promenade, was new to me, & struck me very much: it is called Burlington Arcade.[1]

July 8. Tuesday.—

I first directed my steps to the office of Messrs. Greenwood & Cox, the Army Agents, in Craig's Court, Charing Cross, as being my brother's agents, where I found an immense establishment, & having found out the Artillery department, consulted & advised with the superintendent of that part of the office on such steps as were advisable to be taken under certain foreseen contingencies, and ascertained the state of George's accounts. I was afterwards so fortunate as to find in Town my brother's intimate friends Captain & Mrs. Fleetwood Pellew.[2] |[2] They were residing in Grafton Street with Mrs. T. Chaplin, aunt of Mrs. Pellew, who educated her. Captn. Pellew is one of the sons of the gallant Admiral Lord Exmouth, and himself in the Navy: of late years he has commanded a Frigate in the Mediterranean, the Revolutionnaire, where his intimacy with my brother commenced. Mrs Pellew, who was a daughter of the late Sir Godfrey Webster,[3] by his wife, now Lady Holland, and born shortly before the adulterous connexion,

---

1. Burlington Arcade was built by Lord George Cavendish in 1817.
2. Admiral Hon. Fleetwood Broughton Reynolds Pellew, (1789-1861). Fleetwood Pellew married Harriet Webster, daughter of Sir Godfrey Webster (see below) in 1816. They had two children, the first, Harriet Bettina Frances Pellew was born in 1818 in Florence and lived a full life. The second, a boy, Thomas Chaplin Honorablis Fleetwood Pellew died at the age of nine months on board the Frigate Revolutionaire in 1819. It appears that Pellew was a hard man and in later life he provoked a mutiny on his ship. For more detailed information on George's close friend Fleetwood Pellew, see the Biographical Index.
3. Sir Godfrey Webster, (1747-1800), 4th Baronet of Battle Abbey, M.P. for Seaford, 1786-1790 and Wareham, 1796-

which commenced in Italy,[4] and united Lord & Lady H. sailed with her husband in the Mediterranean, & poor George was their frequent companion on their voyages. It was in their society and on board the Revolutionnaire, that he visited the Archipelago, Constantinople, the Troad, the bay of Smyrna, the Ionian Islands, Naples, Leghorn &c.—And would to GOD, that he had accepted their invitation & returned with them last year from the Mediterranean! From Captain Pellew I learnt, that the Gentlemen, who had written to me respecting George, were both employed in the civil department in Malta. He trusted confidently, that the alienation of mind would only be temporary, arising from his impaired health, & the effects of the climate, probably also from the use of strong medi- |[3] -cines: and quoted many instances of a similar nature in his own experience. GOD grant, that this hope may be realized, and that his ~~bodily strength~~ constitution may not sink beneath the united vehemence of bodily & mental disease? Captain Pellew kindly promised to write to his Uncle Saml. Pellew Esqr., Comptroller of the Customs at Falmouth, to ascertain in what state of body & mind my brother might be on his arrival by the Mediterranean Packet, supposing him to be so removed to this country: to communicate with me on the subject, to see that he had medical aid if it were required, & coercion, if necessary; in short, the object is to prevent his coming on us unexpectedly in an untranquil state, and to secure to him friendly attentions on his first arrival in England, with delicate consideration & the exercise of just discretion as circumstances may suggest. After leaving the Pellews, I passed the rest of the morning in writing duplicate letters to Mr. Godfrey, addressing him viâ Naples and Marseilles, a measure, to which I had been recommended to recur, as the July packet had already sailed.—

After dinner I walked to look at the new streets & squares in the West end of the town beyond Portman Square, particularly Bryanstone Square, where Lady Elcho's house is; |[4] her Ladyship, however, is now at Stanway. This and Montague Square may rather be called oblongs: they consist however, as also the adjacent streets of very handsome family houses; in the Vicinity of Bryanstone Square a very spacious church of Grecian Architecture is now erecting; the portico & spire will be very striking objects, if not in the best style. Berkley Square, through which I passed on my walk, is much improved, the mean houses on the Northern side being replaced by a very handsome row of gentlemens houses.

Wednesday July 9.

I breakfasted with my old friend, Mr. Round, late Member for Ipswich, at his house in Albemarle Street: Mrs. Round with her four children were in Hertfordshire at her Father's, Mr. Caswall's, of Sacombe Park.

I afterwards again called at the office of Messrs. Greenwood & Cox.

Called at the Comptrollers of Army Account's Office in Whitehall, to see my relation Miss Buxton, who resides in the Official residence of her brother-in-law, Mr. Fred. Whalley, Secretary of that department. Found both Mr. F. W. & Miss Buxton at home. |[5]

1800. Webster married Elizabeth Vassell in 1786 and divorced in 1797. Elizabeth had started a relationship with Henry Richard Fox (see below) in 1795 and bore his son in November the following year. Webster exacted severe terms for the divorce; £6,000 damages and her inheritance for life minus an allowance to her of £800 per year. Webster sank into oblivion and committed suicide in 1800.

4. Henry Richard Fox, (1773-1840), 3rd Baron Holland. Fox married Elizabeth in 1797 very soon after her divorce from Sir Godfrey Webster.

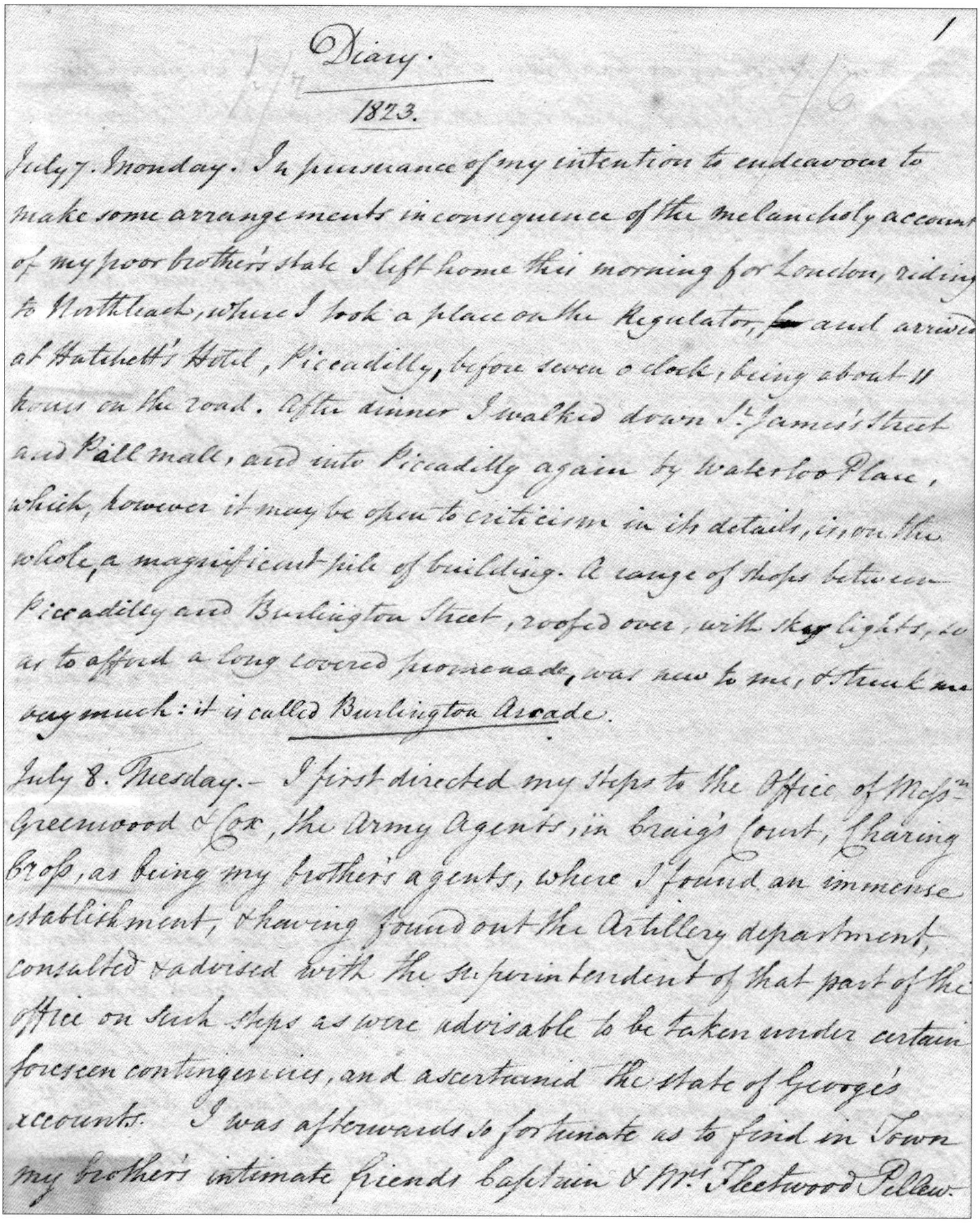

1

Diary.

1823.

July 7. Monday. In pursuance of my intention to endeavour to make some arrangements in consequence of the melancholy account of my poor brother's state I left home this morning for London, riding to Northleach, where I took a place on the Regulator, and arrived at Hatchett's Hotel, Piccadilly, before seven o clock, being about 11 hours on the road. After dinner I walked down St. James's Street and Pall mall, and into Piccadilly again by Waterloo Place, which, however it may be open to criticism in its details, is, on the whole, a magnificent pile of building. A range of shops between Piccadilly and Burlington Street, roofed over, with sky lights, so as to afford a long covered promenade, was new to me, & struck me very much: it is called Burlington Arcade.

July 8. Tuesday. – I first directed my steps to the Office of Messrs Greenwood & Cox, the Army Agents, in Craig's Court, Charing Cross, as being my brother's agents, where I found an immense establishment, & having found out the Artillery department, consulted & advised with the superintendent of that part of the office on such steps as were advisable to be taken under certain foreseen contingencies, and ascertained the state of George's accounts. I was afterwards so fortunate as to find in Town my brother's intimate friends Captain & Mrs Fleetwood Pellew.

158. Fleetwood Pellew.

On my return to Albemarle Street I passed through another part of the new buildings, a very magnificent street built in the form of a curve, and called Regent Quadrant, occupying the site of some of the old narrow streets in the quarter of Swallow Street. There is a spacious piazza on each side with very handsome shops, and when fully inhabited it will be a very handsome range of buildings. At present many houses are untenanted, and many not finished. The range of new streets continued much farther than it was convenient for me to follow it.

I afterwards walked with my friend Round to Whitehall Stairs, where we took a boat for the city, landing at the Swan Stairs. The day was delightful, and as I began to be much fatigued with walking, this mode of moving about was very acceptable, particularly, as it gave me an opportunity of enjoying the conversation of my old friend, without the interruptions of the crowded street. A short range of handsome new houses now erecting on the site of Richmond house, Privy Gardens, will be delightful residences with a superb view of the Thames. In the vicinity of Somerset House a fine range of new building is erecting for the Duchy of Lancaster Office. Between Blackfriars & London Bridge we passed beneath an enormous and, as I thought, heavy looking & ugly iron bridge, built |6 to facilitate to the communication between the city and Southwark, but not, I believe, much used. In fact, the avenues to it on the city side are very bad. In the city, I looked into Mr. Pole's counting house in Nicholas Lane, where I had five minutes chat with his son: then proceeded with Round to the Bank of England, where he was going to receive Dividends, in the New 4. per cent. Office. The celerity, self possession & punctuality, with which this is effected by the Clerks amid the hum and buzz of claimants is truly astonishing. I made an unsuccessful endeavour to pay my respects to two cousins of my wife's resident in Broadstreet, Mrs. Birkbeck & Miss F. Gardner, daughters of her Aunt, Mrs. Gardner, of Liverpool, wife of F. Gardner Esqr. & sister of the late Mr. Backhouse. Mrs. Birkbeck is married to a Physician in great practice in the city; brother to Mr. W. Birkbeck, Banker at Settle, and cousin to the Mr. Birkbeck of American notoriety, who having injured his circumstances by unfortunate speculations in trade, chose to lay the blame on the state of agriculture, though his farm was a profitable concern, on government, on taxation, in short, on everything, but his own improvident speculation. Under this impression he |7 emigrated to America, and possessing himself of a tract of wilderness on the banks of the Ohio, far to the Westwood, in the Illinois country, published a flourishing account in letters of the new colony, with a view to attract fresh adventurers into his prairie. His book being cleverly and spiritedly written attracted much attention, but the misrepresentation has been abundantly proved by other discontented emigrants, who found to their cost, that all was not pure comfort, nor disinterested brotherly love, or unceasing abundance in the back settlements. We took boat again at the Iron bridge and landed at Hungerford Stairs, and after some pleasant hours of his Society, I parted at the bottom of Albemarle Street, from my old & valued friend.

Having an hour's leisure, before I went to dress for dinner, I employed it in visiting Mr. Hayter's exhibition of his very elaborate picture of the Queen's Trial. The size of this historical painting is very large, and it represents the house of Lords as it was fitted up on that memorable occasion. The artist had to struggle with great disadvantages; the straight lines & right angles of the benches, & temporary galleries, the light entering from opposite windows in the building represented, the low situation of the Chancellor and the dignified personages |[8] around him, the uniformity of the blue and black of modern dress, the grey wigs and black gowns of the lawyers, were all unfavourable to the artist, who has nevertheless produced a most striking picture, filled with portraits of characters eminent for rank and talent. The moment selected is the examination of Theodore Majochi by the Lords, of whom Lord Grey is checking the prolixity of interpretation, in which Spinetti, the interpreter indulged. Lord Holland is on his legs behind Lord Grey. Mr. Brougham, Mr. Denman, Dr. Lushington & the other counsel for the Queen are prominent figures; not less so the Attorney and Solicitor General, with their Colleagues. The Queen is also a leading figure; in the foreground we have Lord Castlereagh, Lord Grenville, Marquis Lansdowne, Mr. Tierney &c. The resemblance of those Peers & others, whose countenances are familiar to me, I considered in general excellent; if any thing, they are represented as younger than they are. This striking picture is painted for Mr. Agar Ellis, M.P., and of the Portraits introduced a large proportion of the noble personages sat to the Artist: the likeness of others is borrowed from engravings &c.

I dined at Whitehall with Miss Buxton and Mrs. Fred. Whalley, meeting M. W. Whalley, a young man, who has been |[9] educated at Westminster School & Christ Church and is intended for the church. He is second son of my cousin, Mrs. Whalley, the Mother of Miss Buxton, by her second husband, the Revd. W. M. Whalley, incumbent of Waltham Abbey, but resident on his wife's estate, at Swerford, Oxfordshire, the old family property of the Travells, which she inherited on the decease of my Uncle & predecessor in the living of Upper Slaughter, F. T. Travell, my Mother's brother. A Henry Whalley was also of the party: he is son of the late Mr. C. Whalley, a solicitor, formerly of Stow, and afterwards in India, where he died, who was brother to Mr. W. Whalley, Fred. Whalley &c. This young man is a Clerk in the Comptroller's Office, & acts as secretary to his uncle Frankland Lewis M.P.[5] who is a member of a Commission for the investigation of certain departments of government in Scotland & Ireland.

Thursday July 10.

I returned home, travelling by the Regulator coach, which brought me to Northleach before four o'clock, where I met my horses. The Wycombe road is very much improved, being under

5. Thomas Frankland Lewis, (1780-1855), M.P. for Beaumaris, 1812-1826; Ennis, 1826-1828; Radnorshire, 1828-1834 and New Radnor Boroughs, 1847-1855. It would seem that Charles Whalley married a sister of Thomas Frankland Lewis.

159. London to Windsor stage coaches early nineteenth century.

Mr. Macadam's superintendance. For many miles out of London pumps are erected by the road side, and water carts belonging to the Commissioners |[10] are employed in conveying water from them to be sprinkled over the roads in dry weather to keep up that degree of moisture which is thought advantageous to the wearing of the road, as it certainly is comfortable to the traveller, otherwise exposed to the dust. That suburb of Oxford, which reaches from the bottom of Headington Hill to Magdalen Bridge is very much extended of late years.—

Monday July 14.

My mother left us on a visit to Lady Elcho at Stanway.—

I left home to attend the Quarter Sessions at Gloucester, to which place I proceeded on horseback, baiting at Cheltenham, where I called on my aunt Mrs. Travell. I found with her my cousin Mrs. Whalley, Mr. Whalley's unmarried sister, and Miss Louisa Whalley, daughter of the late Mr. C. Whalley. On reaching Gloucester I had the pleasure of finding Mrs. Backhouse well.—

Tuesday July 15.

The Quarter Sessions commenced. Dr. Cooke and Mr. Cripps, as usual, officiated as Chairmen in the respective Courts; the Right Hon. C. Bragge Bathurst, lately a member of the Administration, in which he held the Chancellorship |[11] of the Duchy of Lancaster, and was for a time president of the India Board, resumed his Seat on the bench. He formerly sat as chairman; his Seat in Gloucestershire is at Lidney in the Forest of Dean. Mr. Bathurst has probably finally quitted public life, as he is now no longer a member of Parliament. He was

160. Samuel Seyer.

bred to the law, was a hard-working politician, but not a man of great parts, prolix in parliament, a frequent speaker, but no orator. His connexion with Lord Sidmouth, which was by marriage, principally contributed to bring him forward. Other magistrates present at the Sessions were, Col. Kingscote, Dr. Timbrell, Mr. Keysall, Dr. Rice, Mr. Baker, Mr. Purnell, Mr. Campbell, Mr. Talbot, Mr. Hicks, Mr. Byles, Mr. Phelps, Mr. Ford, Mr. Price, Mr. Sayer, Mr. C. Crawley, Mr. Agg, Sir W. Hicks, Dr. Davies &c. &c. The principal subject of county interest under discussion was the Lunatic Asylum, lately erected in the immediate vicinity of Gloucester, and now sufficiently completed for the reception of 60 lunatic paupers, and a limited number of patients of a superior description. The establishment is not, however, yet finished to the full extent projected, owing to the insufficiency of funds. These have been supplied from three sources; |12 the county rates, the proportionate share to be borne by the City of Gloucester, and voluntary subscriptions. Of course the county purse has been largely drawn upon. The institution, certainly planned on too extensive and liberal a scale, had been languishing for some years, but has lately revived under the superintendence of the present visiting committee, the chairman of which is Mr. Talbot of Guiting. Dr. Shute, a physician of Gloucester, is at the head of the medical department.

Friday July 18.

I returned from Gloucester, riding home by Crickley hill in company with my neighbour, Mr. Ford, Rector of Little Risington. We had some heavy rain, more injurious to the gay vestments of the ladies attending Cheltenham races than to us. Indeed, the weather is very unpropitious not only for festive out-of-door operations, but for the more important concerns of agriculture; much hay is bleaching in the wet, & fears are entertained for the wheat.

Monday July 21.

Parliament was prorogued on Saturday last by commission. It had been understood, that the King would |13 attend, but the state of his health did not permit it. It seems, that the frequent attacks of gout and erysipelas, to which the Monarch has been subject during the winter, the natural consequence of free living in middle life, &, perhaps, to a late period, render it hazardous to the King to stand long or walk any considerable distance. To the same cause are imputed the privacy and caution observed in respect of our Sovereign's health, and it has been deemed advisable, that no drawing room should be held during the London season.

Public business has been very heavy on the members of the Legislature; as to foreign relations we still keep neutral in the contest, which agitates the Peninsula: the French army under the Duke d'Angouleme has advanced into the heart of Spain with little effectual opposition. Some fortresses hold out, and a guerilla warfare is maintained in the intricate and mountainous districts; but the invaders are in possession of the capital, where, under their sanction, a regency in the name of the King of Spain has been established. The constitutional faction, & the Cortes, holding the weak & unfortunate Ferdinand & the Royal Family in a sort of durance, have thought it expedient to withdraw from Seville to |[14] Cadiz, where they are now shut up, and on which place the French are advancing. Meanwhile the Constitutional Generals appear to be disunited, and their forces ineffective, the revolutionary faction seems to be crumbling, while some of the leaders are, perhaps, negociating for their personal safety, and others in a state of fanatical desperation. In Portugal, a counter-revolution has taken place, which restores the royal family nearly to their former power. Ireland has occupied a very unusual share in the deliberations of both houses: misrule is charged against the administration; an indisposition to conform to law is alledged on the other: the strong powers, with which government is armed, have enabled the Lord Lieutenant to keep under the rebellious turbulence, of which the South of Ireland was the theatre: but enough remains to beget the deepest apprehension. Circumstances occurring early in the Winter in Dublin, on occasion of a riot in the Playhouse, when Marquis Wellesley was insulted, and which it was foolishly attempted to exaggerate far beyond their real importance, have led to a most violent & fruitless recrimination in and out of |[15] Parliament, little to the credit of the sense, temper or judgment of Mr. Plunkett, the Irish Attorney General.[6] The result has been much increased bitterness between the Roman Catholic factious leaders, and the Orange Party: nor did the Lord Lieutenant display coolness or magnanimity. In short great irritation exists, and among other consequences the cause of Roman Catholic emancipation has essentially retrograded. Measures have been proposed & enacted to remedy certain evils attached to the tithe system of Ireland, & much breath & argument have been wasted, if Parliament be not more instructed as to Irish grievances & their causes than when they assembled. In this Sessions great reduction of Taxes has been effected; one half of most of the assessed taxes having been repealed, and some entirely given up. Mr. Robinson, as Finance ~~of~~ Minister, has shewn great talent, candour, and good humour. The prosperity of the commercial & manufacturing interests is admitted to be on the increase; & it is hoped, that a gradual improvement in our agricultural prospects has dawned. Mr. Canning has shewn more temper than was expected; one furious sally between him & Brougham excepted; |[16] and he has exhibited powerful talent as leader of the debates for Ministers; in his own department he has displayed his acknowledged pre-eminence. Much warm debate has taken place on parliamentary reform, but leading to nothing definite. On points relating to the public expenditure, ministers have shewn themselves active in promoting its curtailment, while the unwearied Mr. Hume sometimes right, more generally misinformed & vexatious, has, as usual, practically prolonged the Sessions by his motions for papers. The country is little aware of the expence incurred by these motions.

6. William Conyngham Plunket, (1764-1854), M.P. for Midhurst, 1807; Dublin University, 1812-1827.

Tuesday July 22d.

We left home on a short visit to Lady Elcho at Stanway. We found my mother & Miss Church her inmates, and Miss Langton arrived from Cheltenham soon after us. This Lady is daughter of the late Mr. Bennet Langton & the Countess of Rothes: her father was the intimate of Dr. Johnson. Lady Elcho looked better than we expected, considering the risks, which she has undergone of late; having had an alarming fall down stairs in her house in Town, & since that time a serious attack of indisposition. Mr. Eddy & Mr. F. Aston |17 joined our party at dinner; the former is Clergyman of Toddington in this neighbourhood, where he resides: he is also Incumbent of Hailes, Didbrook & Gretton.

"A letter to H. Brougham Esqr. M.P. upon his Durham speech, and the three articles in the last Edinburgh review, upon the subject of the clergy. Lond. 1823." This very able pamphlet, written not only in vindication of the clergy of the Diocese of Durham, but containing an able ~~vindication~~ defence of the Church of England at large, against the weak arguments popularly alledged against us, exposing also many of the gross current misrepresentations, is, perhaps, to be attributed to the able pen of Mr. Rennel, Vicar of Kensington. Dr. Blomfield, Archdeacon of Colchester, is said to have written another able answer to the virulent attack of Mr. Brougham & the Edinburgh Reviewers. Such champions prove that vigour, energy, and skill have not yet deserted the venerable fortress of the Episcopal church.—

Wednesday July 23d.

The dinner party consisted, in addition to the family in the house, of Mr. Wynniatt, of Staunton, and the younger branches of the Gist family. They reside at Wormington Grange in this neighbourhood.

——— |18

Friday July 25th.—

Mrs. Cross & Mrs. Ashmore, two worthy gentlewomen, sisters & widows resident at Didbrook, and Mr. C. Marshall of Snowshill, a respectable farmer of the higher class, and Steward of Lord Wemyss, dined with us.

Saturday July 26.

We returned home.

Tuesday July 29.

I let my Vicarage farm at Stanway to Mr. George Cook, a farmer there of considerable property & credit: 156 acres at a rent of 25/- per acre. At one period, viz. in 1814, this land was let for £300.—per ann. now it only amounts to £195: the present tenants would not give so much, &, indeed, I wished to part with them, as they are unpunctual in payment of rent, not sufficiently substantial, and unwilling to make improvement except wholly at my expense. Mr. G. Cook's brother is an artist in London in the line of historical painting; my uncle, Mr. F. Travell, put him forward in early life; two of his pictures, representing scenes from Sir Walter Scott's Lady of the Lake, which are very creditable productions of his pencil, I saw lately at Mr. F. Whalley's; they are the property of Mr. Naper.

——— |19

Wednesday July 30.

I attended the annual general meeting of the Stow Provident Bank. Dr. Rice presided, who is one of the ~~Vice Presidents~~ Trustees. We had only a small attendance of Managers. Mr. Pole, our able & indefatigable Treasurer, to whom the Institution is under the greatest obligations, was absent, although expected, as he is with his family at Wick Hill. In his absence it devolved upon me, as Chairman of the Committee of Accounts, or acting Managers, a situation, which I have held since the establishment of the bank in 1816, to read the annual report as drawn up ~~M~~ by Mr. Pole. It exhibits a prosperity, most satisfactory to those connected with the Institution, as well as to all, who highly and duly appreciate the value of that great engine for the improvement of the condition of the lower ranks of society, the system of saving banks: it far exceeds what I or other sanguine founders of this particular establishment ever anticipated.

The funds in the hands of the Society exclusive of 3 per cent Red annuities are as follow:

Government Receipts	£26,838. 6. 6
In Treasurer's hands	17. 2. 3
In Clerk's hands	287.10. 9
	£27,142. 19. 6

Red. 3. per Cent annuities—£3430. 19. 8.— |[20]
The profit made by the transactions, over & above all claims of Depositors, & available for contingent & unforeseen occurrences, and eventually disposable by the Trustees & Managers, now amounts to £494. 13. 1.
The total number of Depositors on the books is 591.
The total of interest & dividends due to Depositors up to July 1. is £1001. 17. 1.
Deposits made from 30 June 1822 to 30 June 1823 £9279. 1. 7.
Withdrawn in the same period—£3945. 5. 3.

The newspapers announce the death of Dr. Bathurst, Bishop of Norwich.[7] This prelate died in advanced age at Leamington. He has been remarkable for advocating the Roman Catholic Claims, and even very lately pleaded for them in the house of Lords. This bias made him very popular in Ireland, which he visited, and among the Whigs, but as a great majority of the clergy differ from him in this opinion, it proportionably lowered that estimation of him, which his respectable character would otherwise have caused. His son, the Archdeacon of Norwich, was a contemporary and acquaintance of mine at Oxford, where he was Fellow of New College, a very eccentric person, as he |[21] proved lately in pushing himself indecorously forward in favour of the wretched Queen, whose cause he warmly espoused. Another brother, also a contemporary of mine & a fellow of New College, having been sent on a diplomatic mission into Germany of a secret & ambiguous character during the domination of Bonaparte, was mysteriously cut off, and murdered, not without strong suspicion, that his destruction was owing to the machinations of emissaries of the French Government.

By a letter from Miss Backhouse it appears, that her Brother has not yet formally been appointed Commissioner of Excise, but that the patent is now making out.

7. Bathurst Bishop of Norwich

Friday Aug. 1.

It now appears from the same authority as announced the Bishop of Norwich's death, that he is alive & well. It is not a new thing to be misled by newspapers, but of late they seem determined to kill off bishops before their time. Dr. O'Beirne, Bishop of Meath was announced to be dead, two or three times before he actually paid the debt of nature.

Tuesday Aug. 5.

We parted from our beloved Edward, who returned to School by Gloucester, where he would arrive at Mrs. Backhouse's in the Evening, & proceed to Lyde House to-morrow.—

--- |22

Friday Aug. 8.

We dined at Mr. Ford's, the Rector of Little Risington, meeting Mr. & Mrs. E. Leigh, Mr. & Mrs. R. Wynniatt, Dr. Warneford & Mr. R. Phillimore, Rector of Shipton, Oxon, brother to Dr. Phillimore, a civilian, Professor of Civil law at Oxford, and one of the Commissioners of the Board of Controul. He is also M.P. and was the original father of the late marriage act, which was so over-nursed in both houses, that it soon died a natural death. Another brother is Captain of a Frigate, a brave & skilful seaman, who distinguished himself in the late American struggle by the capture of a Frigate. He now commands the Thetis.

Sunday Aug. 10.

"Bishop Horne's Considerations on the life & death of Abel: on the life & translation of Enoch: on the life of Noah: and on the life & death of St. John the Baptist. Lond. 1819." An admirably pious and eloquent collection of tracts by one of the brightest ornaments of British Episcopacy: the Considerations on the life & death of John the Baptist extend to a greater length than the others: this little volume issues from the depository of the Society for promoting Christian Knowledge. I have been reading it to the family on Sunday evenings.[8]

--- |23

Wednesday Aug. 13.—

The suspence, in which we have been plunged for so long a time respecting my unhappy brother, is now closed in a most painful manner by the receipt of letters from Falmouth, giving intelligence of his decease on the 8th. inst. GOD rest his soul! The information comes from Mr. Pellew, Collector of the Customs at Falmouth, agreeably to the arrangement, which I made in Town with his nephew, Captain F. Pellew, and from a Capt. Heathcote,[9] of the Ionian Service, an old acquaintance of my poor brother's, who was a passenger with him on board the Packet, and had taken a particular charge of him. A letter was also received by me from my former correspondent Mr. Godfrey, from Malta, apprizing me of the arrangements made for the passage. The Revd. Mr. Curtois ~~also~~, a Chaplain to the Forces, and also a passenger by the Camden Packet, sent me a certificate of having buried the sad remains at

8. The family in this sense is the household, including servants.
9. Henry Heathcote, (1777-1851). The identification is not certain, but this is probably the same man. He served in the Mediterranean and in 1812 took command of the *Scipione*, a 74 gun ship captured at Trafalgar. This was later decommissioned. Heathcote rose to the rank of Admiral.

sea on the 9th. It was on the Evening of that day, that the packet reached Falmouth, but so rapid was the decay of the body, and the uncertainty, when the vessel might reach the port was such, that this early interment was considered necessary. It seems, that he died on the morning of the 8th. about 8 o clock, of extreme debility, |24 but he expired without pain, & appeared sensible of the sympathy and attention, which he experienced from all on board, & particularly from the Surgeon of the Packet. From the expressions in the letters I conclude, that his mental alienation subsisted to the last, but that he was more tranquil & composed, before he left the Island, and indeed, at all times was perfectly manageable. What a wreck was there of fine talents, an ardent mind, diversified acquirements, and manly disposition! I await more precise medical details from the surgeon of the Packet.

161. George Anthony Witts.

Soon after the receipt of this mournful information, I mounted my horse for Stanway to impart it to my poor Mother, to tell her, I was her only surviving child. The stroke was heavy, but borne with resignation, & not without acknowledgment of the wisdom & mercy of Providence. I passed the rest of the day at Stanway, & slept there. We retired into a private sitting room, that we might be at a distance from those guests of Lady Elcho's, with whom we were less intimate. The kindness of her Ladyship was sisterly & feeling: the deceased was, indeed, justly esteemed |25 by her, and attended her late Lord in his dying hour in Scotland.[10]

Thursday Aug. 14.

I returned home to breakfast, & my Mother followed me some hours afterwards, preferring to pass the first days of grief in the society of Margaret and myself.—

Saturday Aug. 16.

Mr. Large dined here. The future & the actual tenants of the Vicarage farm at Stanway met him in the morning to settle the conditions of leaving and entering on the land. We also made unsuccessful efforts to let my rectorial farm here to two applicants.—

Monday Aug. 18.

My wife and Mother went to Cheltenham, to my Aunt Travell's in order to procure mourning.

"The History of the destruction of Jerusalem, as connected with the Scripture Prophecies. By the Revd. George Wilkins, Vicar of St. Mary's Nottingham, and of Lowdham in that county. 3d. Edit. Lond. 1822." A very well compiled and detailed view of the most extraordinary siege recorded in history, marked by the most striking interventions of Providence, in the accomplishment of the numerous sacred Prophecies, both antecedent to our blessed Saviour

10. Wild and exuberant as George was, he was much appreciated by Lady Elcho and Lady Lyttelton, and the latter appears to have put George under her patronage to a certain extent.

& uttered by him. The narrative must impress the Student ~~by~~ ^{with} the truth of a mission, confirmed by |[26] the most irrefragable and precise testimony of the divine prescience of its sacred promulgator: in these days of scepticism the reproduction in a popular form of this insulated proof must be highly serviceable. This valuable work was first pointed out to my notice in a letter of my lamented brother.

Wednesday Aug. 20.

My wife and mother returned from Cheltenham.—

Thursday Aug. 21.

Received a letter from Capt$^{n.}$ Heathcote containing some particulars of my poor brother, parts of which I shall transcribe. "We were most intimate in Sicily and in Genoa, but since the year 1815, though frequently making attempts to see each other, we never succeeded. Upon my arrival in Malta in the latter end of June, I learnt, upon enquiring for my old friend, that he was in the hospital, where I went to see him. The moment I approached he appeared in raptures, called me by my name & conversed occasionally upon old scenes; but he frequently became bewildered. The chain of memory appeared broken. I was spoken to by Gen$^{l.}$ Sir Manly Power[11] & the Adjutant Gen$^{l.}$ for his passage to England. |[27] He embarked on the 28$^{th.}$ of June. He was very much emaciated, but his appetite was always good. He read, but frequently told me, he did not find that pleasure in reading, that he had formerly experienced. In the state of his mind no change took place to the moment of his death. He was never violent: always passive and contented as an infant. x x x [12] On Sunday the 3$^{rd.}$ of August he came into the dining room of the Packet, where service was performed by M$^{r.}$ Curtois to the passengers, and crew, and nothing could be more impressive than his manner & pronunciation of the responses. I think, on the night of the 5$^{th.}$ he was seized with convulsions, which continued with intervals until the hour of his death; viz. about 8 in the morning of the 8$^{th.}$ from the time he was first seized with convulsions to the hour of his death he never spoke. I shall ever retain the desire of shewing the high estimation, in which I held the character of your Brother." &c. Comfort may be derived from the account thus transmitted by a kind friend; his joining devoutly in divine worship is a soothing reflection; amid all the fervour of youth & strength & all the force of temptation |[28] it is my persuasion, that my poor brother never lost his confidence in GOD, or let go his belief of Xtianity: many incidental remarks in his correspondence confirm this; and his studies were not unfrequently turned this way, more than might be expected from the ardent mind of a soldier long resident abroad.

Friday Aug. 22.

I received this day a letter from M$^{r.}$ H. Lye, Surgeon of the Camden Packet, giving a long & minute report of my poor brother's case. The opinion formed by D$^{r.}$ Tully, Staff Surgeon at the Military Hospital, at Malta, in which M$^{r.}$ Lye fully concurred, was, that there was a morbid accumulation of lymph in the ventricles of the brain, producing mild derangement, with great bodily weakness & emaciation & torpor of the digestive organs; "the case,"

11. General Sir Manly Power
12. The three x's are reproduced here as an exact transcription – presumably intended as an ellipsis.

observes Mr. Lye, "was hopeless, if the pressure on the brain could not be removed, if the more perfect digestion and assimilation of the food taken into the stomach & if nutrition, adequate to the wants of nature, could not be re-established: there was not delirium so violent as to require coercive measures of restraint to be adopted: |29 only abberration & imbecillity of mind impairing his memory and judgment." Mr. Lye then proceeds to relate the remedies, which he applied in the hope of correcting the malady, under which his patient laboured; their want of success; that he suffered very little pain, and expired in the manner stated by Captain Heathcote.

I cannot resist the temptation to transcribe a few lines from a letter, I received to-day from my worthy cousin Ann Witts: they are beautifully written, & flow from a clear head & feeling heart.—"It is, indeed, given to us to know, that "the sea shall give up her dead," that the depths of the vast ocean, any more than a few feet of earth, cannot retain the immortal spirit, and that the poor body of disease and corruption shall hereafter be exchanged for a glorified body, when parents and children and brethren and friends shall again be united to part no more. To my feelings it appears a mitigation, that the intellect remained clouded to the period of dissolution: to me it appears, that he was in mercy spared one bitter ingredient in his cup of suffering, the conscious- |30 -ness of dying just within reach of the promised land; and we may humbly trust from many passages of his letters to you, that his was a greatly corrected character, and from the attentive reading of the Scriptures, he mentioned, that he had been engaged in, we may hope, that much serious reflection had passed through his mind, previous to the fatal disorder, that unhinged his faculties."—

My Mother returned this day to Stanway in as good spirits as we can expect.

Sunday Aug. 24.

My dear wife's birth-day. She was born in 1786. GOD be thanked, that of late her delicate health seems rather re-established. I can never be sufficiently grateful for her constant affection, warm participation in my pleasures and griefs, anxiety to make me comfortable. She is a pattern to wives in her judicious care of her family, kind heartedness to her poor neighbours, and prudence in her own expences. I have to thank GOD for an union with a woman of virtuous & religious principles, good sense, and amiable temper. These qualities adorn the wife & the mother.

--- |31

Sunday Aug. 31.

Finished the perusal of Mant & D'Oyly's Edition of the Bible in 3 Vols. 4to. published under the sanction and at the expence of the Society for promoting Christian Knowledge. Few compilations have been so judiciously made, or are likely so materially to conduce to the diffusion of sound religious principles in the community. The plan is the elucidation of the sacred text, by a sort of variorum commentary: the notes being selected from the best divines of the church of England; critical, expository, didactic, hortative, as the occasion requires. I have gone through the whole very carefully and trust, that the perusal has been attended with a blessing. The Editors were Chaplains to the Archbishop of Canterbury. Dr. Mant is now Bishop of Down & Connor, having been recently translated to that See from that of Killaloe. He was bred up at Winchester College; it is singular, that he should have been among the number of the boys expelled from thence on occasion of a rebellion, & that the same lot should have fallen on another most amiable and pious divine, Mr. Bishop late Fellow of Oriel College, & now Rector of Ufton Nervet, Berks, the author of a series of excellent sermons for domestic |[32] use. Dr. Mant was also Fellow of Oriel, and preacher of the Bampton Lectures: his comments on Regeneration & the loose sense of the Baptismal Sacrament held by the Evangelical Clergy gave rise to what has been termed the Regeneration controversy, which has called forth much sound reasoning & diligent research among the Orthodox Clergy. Dr. Mant also published two volumes of sermons, much esteemed. His colleague, Dr. D'Oyly, a Cambridge man, is now Rector of Lambeth: as chaplain to the Archbishop of Canterbury, he examined me, when I took out a dispensation to hold the Vicarage of Stanway in 1814. He was at one time Christian Advocate, & published an able tract on the doctrine of Assurance. He is also Author of the valuable life of Archb. Sancroft.

I preached sermons to-day at Upper Slaughter, & at my curacy at Lower Swell,[13] in behalf of a collection now making by the authority of a King's letter, in aid of the funds of that excellent institution, the National Society for the Education of the Poor in the Principles |[33] of the established church. This society has been at work ever since the year 1811, and has accomplished a great deal in the dissemination of the Madras, or Dr. Bell's system of teaching, aiding in the purchase of sites for the erection of schoolrooms, assisting the various districts in the expences of building &c. Above all by the excellent management of its central school in Baldwin's Gardens, shewing the system in its perfection, and there educating & training schoolmasters and mistresses for situations throughout the country: so that now 350000 children are reported to be taught in the schools in connexion with the National Society, while yet much remains to be done both in Great Britain & her dependencies. The funds are nearly exhausted; the annual Subscriptions being only adequate for current expences & the support of the central School. From all steady churchmen the cause will receive warm support; the Clergy will doubtless discern the efficacy and value of the system pursued in the increase of their congregations; while the Magistracy will find it, it is to be hoped, in the diminution of crime. |[34] At Upper Slaughter I collected £2. 18. 9: at Lower Swell £1. 11. 5.—

———

The newspapers announce the death of the Pope Pius VII—at the age of 82. This amiable & upright Prelate was an Italian, by name Chiaramonti, a native of Cesena in the Romagna, and was elected Cardinal by the influence, as it is believed, of Napoleon Bonaparte, as also by the same interest he was raised to the purple at Venice in 1800. He was always considered a very estimable person, and suffered much by the arts, intrigues, false friendship & persecutions of Bonaparte, in whose power he always was till the downfal of that Usurper, when he resumed the papal rights & dignities at Rome after a wearisome captivity in France; for the Emperor Napoleon, having used him for his own ambitious purposes, finished by stripping him of his possessions & liberty. It is supposed, that Cardinal Rodolph of Austria, Brother of the Emperor of Germany, a young Prince, will be elected to fill the Papal chair, a measure, which will above all others serve to strengthen the Austrian power in Italy.

——— |[35]

13. Little is know of the circumstances surrounding the curacy at Lower Swell.

Tuesday Sept. 2.

Mr. & Mrs. Aston with their son Frederick from Stanway passed the day with us.—

Saturday Sept. 6.

I went to Stanway, to preach for the National Society, F. Aston exchanging duties with me. I found a large party of ladies at Stanway house: besides Lady Elcho, my mother & Miss Church, were there the excellent Sisters my cousins Guydickens; also the old, witty, intrusive Countess of Cork & Orrery: she was by birth a Monckton, and sister of the Earl of Galway.[14] This dowager without mercy quarters herself on her country friends during the Summer, returning the civilities received by invitations to eccentric fetes, and odd parties at her house in town during the London Season. Miss Vernon, more than a septuagenarian, was another guest: formerly a maid of honour to Queen Charlotte & sister to the notorious Lady Grosvenor;[15] a corrected character, it is said, ladylike in manner, but a bitter foe of old Cork & O: animosity not unfrequently exploding between them. Lastly on the preceding evening had arrived my fair & fat cousin Lady Rossmore, Lady Elcho's youngest daughter, from Ireland, where |[36] she had left her Lord, but attended by her stepdaughter Miss Westenra, a round insipid girl of twenty. Lady R. retains her wit, volubility, warmth of colouring in narrative, good opinion of her-self, & strong prejudices & partialities; does she repent in her secret soul of an union with a Peer of doubtful character & ruined fortune? and do the style & title of Irish Baroness compensate for Irish embarrassments, law suits & shifts? I doubt it. Mr. Eddy joined the party at dinner.—

Sunday Sept. 7.

I performed the duty at Stanway & Cutsdean, a chapelry in the parish of Bredon in Worcestershire, two miles distant from Stanway, of which F. Aston is the Curate. At the former place the collection for the National Society amounted to £5. 3. 3. at the latter 13/1.—

Monday Sept. 8.

I returned home.

---

14. Mary, Countess of Cork and Orrery, (1748-1840). Mary was the daughter John Monckton, 1st Viscount Galway and his second wife, Jane, daughter of Henry Westenra. Fanny Burney rather wickedly wrote of her: '*very short, very fat, but handsome, splendidly and fantastically dressed, rouged not unbecomingly, &c. . . . her rage of seeing anything* curious *may be satisfied, if she please, by looking in a mirror*'. She was noted for her eccentricities, and as a leader of fashion. Lord Broughton, writing in his diary in 1824 recorded: ' . . . *a very singular person. She is 76 years of age and has all the vivacity of 16. Her memory seems very accurate*'. Lady Cork had been a friend of Lady Hereford in London, but everyone dreaded her appearances at Stanway. Agnes Witts made two very telling diary entries: 19 April 1814: '. . . *Lady Corkes usual rodomontade exceeding even itself.*' 25 April 1814: '. . . *Ldy. Corke and Orrey made her departure to the regret of no one. . . .*' It was probably through the connection of Lady Cork that Lady Augusta Charteris Wemyss, (a daughter of Lady Elcho) married Warner William Westenra, (1765-1842), 1st Baron Rossmore, for she seems to have been Warner William Westenra's first cousin.

15. Henrietta, Lady Grosvenor, née Vernon, (17??-1828). On 1 March 1770 the Earl of Grosvenor exhibited a libel for adultery with H.R.H. the Duke of Cumberland, and obtained a separation accordingly. The connection with all of these 'friends' appears to have been the Court. Lady Hereford (who had died back in 1817) had been a Maid of Honour to Queen Caroline, as was Miss Vernon. Lady Hereford's now surviving sister had been a Maid of Honour to the Queen's mother-in-law, the Dowager Princess of Wales.

Wednesday Sept. 10.

We left home on a visit of a few days to my Aunt Mrs. Travell at Cheltenham, where we found |37 staying with her Mrs. Whalley & Miss Marianne Whalley, a daughter of the late Mr. C. Whalley.

Thursday Sept. 11.

Our evening circle was increased by the addition of Mr. & Mrs. Rosenhagen, & their guest M. Costantini. Mr. R. a very agreeable and respectable gentleman, labouring under a sad defect of vision, is just relinquishing his post as Comptroller of Army Accounts,[16] in which he is to be succeeded by the Hon. James Stuart, Brother of Lord Galloway, & of Edward Stuart, first Commissioner of the Audit Office, who married Lady Elcho's third daughter, Lady Catherine Charteris. Mr. James Stuart is as deaf as Mr. Rosenhagen is blind; and Col. Drinkwater of the Comptrollers Office threatens to provide himself with a speaking trumpet, his other colleague, Mr. J. King, labouring under the same infirmity.[17] Mrs. Rosenhagen is of the Packhurst family of Ripple, in Worcestershire, a branch of that settled at Catesby in Northampton-shire, of which stock was the learned author of the valuable Hebrew & Greek Lexicons adapted to the old & new testaments. M. Costantini, a |38 learned Italian, has been a traveller in most parts of Europe, and I boldly collected all my French to converse with him: nor was I unrewarded, for I found in him much eloquence, right sentiments, & extended information on literary subjects; both as to the Literature of his own country and that of France & Germany; nor is he illversed in that of England, though he does not attempt to converse in our language. His fortunes have, I apprehend, been impaired in the revolution, &, if I mistake not, he has been engaged in tuition. The friend of Alfieri, Monti, and other eminent Italian literati, his details on the literature of Italy were copious & interesting: he characterises Alfieri's Auto-biography as une folie: and quoted Alfieri as thus enumerating the authors calculated to form a high poetical taste; the Bible, Homer, Dante, Shakespeare, Milton, et voila tout. M. Costantini resided at one period at Berlin, & the charms of the lovely & virtuous Queen of Prussia seem to have impressed |39 him in the same manner as all those, who have moved within the sphere of her attractions. Never vision more beauteous walked this earth than this hapless Queen, when I saw her in the Court of Weimar in the summer of 1800, where with her respectable consort, her sister, the handsome & clever Princess of Tour & Taxis, & a brilliant suite, the little metropolis of the Duchy was graced with these illustrious visitors. Nor should I fail to mention the good and prudent, the simple minded, wise & virtuous Duchess of Weimar, whose sober dignity & calmness subdued even the ferocious insolence of Buonaparte in the hour of arrogance. M. Costantini spoke of her with the respect, which her character ever excites, of the Literary ornaments of Weimar, the old Wieland, composing in his cabinet amid wreaths of smoke, issuing from his Pipe, the highly gifted Goethe, vain of the little

---

16. The office of Comptroller of Army Accounts existed between the years 1703 and 1835. After 1806 there were three comptrollers, the first and senior on an annual salary of £2,000 the other two being on £1,500. Anthony Rosenhagen had been appointed in 1815; the Hon. James Henry Keith Stewart in 1823, both had been in the junior positions.
17. Colonel John Drinkwater had been appointed in 1815 becoming the senior on 1831. John King had been a junior in 1811 rising to senior in 1823.

162. Duntesbourne Abbots, the home of Dr. Baillie.

splendour of his post of Secretaire d'Etat pour les affairs etrangeres—of the important duchy of Weimar, and respond- |*40* -ing to the observations naturally addressed to him on subjects of literature by apothegms of diplomacy. M. Constantini intimated to me, that he had been an author, but not what were his writings. His is evidently a very cultivated talent, and being a willing listener, and most of the party disinclined or unable to converse in French, I had the advantage of hearing a volume of interesting anecdote & much just criticism. M. Costantini has published two Vol. of elegant Extracts in Italian Prose & Verse.—

Friday Sept. 12.

Mrs. Travell's tea table in the Evening was surrounded by a small party. Among them was Mrs. Maltby, the maiden Sister of Dr. Maltby, recently appointed Preacher at Lincoln's Inn, on the resignation of Bp. Heber. Dr. Maltby is a literary man, & excellent Grecian; his Sermons recently published exhibit a deficiency in the inculcation of the peculiar doctrines of Christianity almost enough to induce a suspicion, that they are not deeply imprinted on the heart of the Preacher. A~~nother~~ Sister of Dr. Maltby is married to Bp. Tomline; whose Chaplain, as well as Brother in law, Dr. Maltby is, or has been. It appears, by |*41* the statement of Mrs. Maltby, that a Mrs. Burgess, of Devonshire is the authoress of that valuable little work, "the Pilgrim Good-intent." I did not know before, that Joanna Baillie, the poetess, authoress of Metrical Legends, Plays on the Passions &c., is sister of Dr. Baillie, the celebrated London Physician: he is said to be at the last stage of life at his country seat near Cirencester, worn out by exertion in his great practice at the age of 62.—Another of Mrs. Travell's guests, was a Miss Beaufort, sister of Captain Beaufort of the Royal Navy, who has been engaged in surveying and laying down on the charts the coast of Southern Anatolia.[18]

Saturday Sept. 13.—

I rode home to attend the duties of my churches on the following day.—

Monday Sept. 15.

I was prevented from returning to Cheltenham to rejoin my wife, as I intended, by the necessity of staying at home to receive M^r. Large, who had fixed this day by letter, which met me yesterday, for endeavouring to treat with B. Wood of Nethercote. He accordingly arrived to dine & sleep, and a long evening was passed in vain discussion |*42* with Wood, who evidently will only engage on terms so low as to be inadmissible. The bad coming on, owing to Gregory being entitled to take all the manure off and carry away all the hay and straw without consuming it on the farm, a privilege arising from the manner, in which my late Uncle's Executors claimed to leave the land at his decease, and in addition an off growing crop of wheat make me almost despair of finding a tenant.

I omitted to mention on Saturday "Milman's Belshazzar" which I concluded on that day. The Rev^d. author is now Professor of Poetry at Oxford, where he is a member of Brazennose College. The work in question is dramatic, & the subject the fall of Babylon, the Bible, Herodotus &c. being the Authorities. There is much gorgeous poetry, much that is touching and simple, great elegance & taste. One loves to see a Clerical Poet woo the sacred muse, & M^r. Milman is capable of producing poetry of great beauty. Witness his Fall of Jerusalem, Samor Lord of the bright city, (Gloucester) the Martyr of Antioch; the two latter I have not yet read. M^r. Milman has preferment at Reading.

--- |*43*

Tuesday Sept. 16.—

I rode down to Gloucester, where my dear wife had arrived the evening before on a visit to M^rs. Backhouse. The Town was all alive with the approaching festivity of the Triennial Music Meeting.—

Wednesday Sept. 17.

At an early hour we repaired to the Cathedral, where service was to be performed, with sacred Music, & a sermon preached before a collection for the Widows & Orphans of the

18. Captain Francis Beaufort (1774-1857). Sir Francis Beaufort was a British naval officer and hydrographer. Beaufort was the creator of the Beaufort scale for indicating wind force. From the circle representing a weather station, a stave (as in musical notation) extends, with one or more half or whole barbs. For example, a stave with 3½ barbs represents Beaufort seven on the scale, decoded as 32-38 mph, or a "Fresh Gale". Beginning on a merchant ship of the British East India Company, Beaufort rose during the Napoleonic Wars to midshipman, lieutenant, commander and captain in the Royal Navy. Whereas other wartime officers sought leisurely pursuits at each opportunity, Beaufort spent his leisure time taking soundings and bearings, making astronomical observations to determine longitude and latitude, and measuring shorelines. His results were compiled in new charts. In 1811-1812, Beaufort charted and explored southern Anatolia, locating many classical ruins. His work was interrupted (at Ayas, near Adana) by an attack by Turks on the crew of his boat, during which he received a serious bullet wound in the hip. He returned to England, and drew up the charts himself, also publishing in 1817 his book Karamania; or a brief description of the South Coast of Asia Minor, and of the Remains of Antiquity.

distressed Clergy of the three Dioceses of Gloucester, Worcester & Hereford. This is the hundredth Anniversary of this excellent charity; the lay stewards on the present occasion were Mr. Estcourt M.P. for Devizes, of Estcourt House near Tetbury and of New Park near Devizes; Chandos Leigh, of Adlestrop, only son of Mr. Leigh of Stoneleigh Park, Warwickshire; & Mr. Goodrich, resident of Wooton in the immediate vicinity of Gloucester. Mr. Estcourt is a most useful member of the Lower House of Parliament, and Chairman of the Quarter Sessions for Wilts: his property near Devizes and his seat for that Borough he owes to his marriage with Miss Sutton, the eldest daughter & heiress of a gentleman of that name, |[44] whose wife was sister of Lord Sidmouth. From Mrs. Sutton and Mr. & Mrs. Estcourt, I had formerly met with great civility, when residing as Curate of Erchfont & Stert in Wilts for more than two years, from 1806, when I went into Orders, till the autumn of 1808, when I succeeded to the living of Upper Slaughter.[19] Chandos Leigh is an eccentric mortal, possessed of talent, & studious in an odd way. He has been a warm admirer of theatrical performances, & performers male & female; a poet in a small way; one of his earlier productions, "the Pleasures of Love," was by the prudence of his friends suppressed; another little volume has been lauded by the Edinburgh Reviewers; perhaps, not so much for the poetry as the politics of the poet, who with pretensions to hereditary toryism has on more than one occasion betrayed a strong bias to whiggism. He is married to a daughter of the late Mr. Willes of Alstrop, & resides much at Adlestrop, but without taking a share in the public business of the County or neighbourhood. The Clerical Stewards were Dr. Timbrill, Rector of Beckford, a strong headed, intelligent, active man; a leading magistrate of this county & of Worcestershire, & Treasurer of the Clergy Charity: Mr. Selwyn, a Prebendary of Gloucester, |[45] but precluded, as I understand, by mental infirmity from attending; so that Dr. Hall, another Prebendary, Vice Chancellor of Oxford, & Master of Pembroke College, officiated in his stead; & the Revd. Wadham Huntley, Rector of Eastington & Aston Blank, also absent & represented by the Revd. T. Pettat of Southrop, brother to Mrs. Browne of Salperton. We obtained very good seats in the choir, and the whole of the Cathedral within the Orchestra was extremely crouded: the Orchestra is erected in front of the Organ facing the Altar: the area between the Pulpit & Altar filled with Benches; the space occupied by the Altar is covered by raised sittings, one behind another in ranges, up to the top of the Screen, and to day, there were arranged here various schools, the young Ladies of each being dressed uniformly, which was a very pretty sight. On each side of the inner choir the large arches above the Stalls, opening into the Transepts, were filled with temporary galleries, that on the right being appropriated to the friends of the lay stewards, that on the left to those of the Clerical Stewards. These galleries being almost wholly filled with ladies in elegant morning dresses present a most beautiful parterre to the eye. Indeed, the spectacle, especially on those mornings, the second & third, when the admission is not free, |[46] is peculiarly brilliant. Not any other ecclesiastical building in the Kingdom, I believe, is better adapted for sacred music on a grand scale, and the united charms of solemn strains & exquisite architecture impress the mind in the most striking manner. The Dettingen Te Deum, the Overture to Esther, Dr. Boyce's Anthem (Charity) and

19. Mrs. Sutton's sister, Charlotte was married to Bragge Bathurst, the father of Francis Witts' close friend Charles Bathurst.

W. Knyvett's new Coronation Anthem were the Musical treats for the morning. Of the vocalists, Miss Travis, Messrs. Vaughan, Bellamy, Hawes & W. Knyvett appeared; among the instrumental performers, Mr. Cramer led the band, Marshall of Oxford was second Violin, the Lindleys on the Violoncello, Harper on the Trumpet, Willman on the Clarionet &c. &c. acquitted themselves admirably.—The service was read by Mr. Webb, one of the Minor Canons, and the sermon preached by Dr. Timbrill. The Preacher, taking his text from Rev. 14. 2, 3., expatiated on the use of music as expressive of religious praise, quoting the leading texts in the Bible, in which the employment of music in worship is mentioned; from hence he made a transition to the case of the inferior clergy, the expences incurred in an education at the Universities, the inadequacy in numerous instances of the provision made for the church, the costs of educating and placing out children, |47 the claims on the Clergyman's charity, and the necessity of maintaining a certain appearance in the world. The sermon was on the whole judicious, impressive and well written, but formally and monotonously delivered.—I had not been long in the Cathedral, before I was given to understand by Mr. Pettat, as representing Mr. Huntley, that it was wished, that I should undertake the office of clerical Steward at the next Music meeting. I had anticipated such an application, & from the uncertainty always attendant on such celebrities, whether the company ~~attendance~~ will be sufficiently numerous to pay the expences, or whether in the case of a dearth of company a heavy surplus would not be left for the Stewards to pay, I had almost determined to decline the office. But it was strongly pressed upon me, and I was so unwilling, that it should appear, that I was ~~unwilling~~ averse to act with Mr. Dolphin, who is appointed one of the Lay Stewards, that after some deliberation I promised to act as Clerical Steward at the next Triennial anniversary. My colleagues will be the Hon. Mr. Moreton, eldest son of Lord Ducie,[20] the Hon. James Dutton,[21] eldest son of Lord Sherborne, Vernon Dolphin; Mr. Bankes |48 Prebendary of Gloucester and Son-in-law of the Lord Chancellor, & Mr. Bowles, of Bremhill, Wilts, & Rector of Dumbleton in this Diocese; the Sonneteer, & Author of various poems, essays, occasional sermons &c. Three years will add, perhaps, a little steadiness to the very juvenile lay stewards, but their connections, at least as to two of them, will certainly insure a numerous attendance of opulent & fashionable visitors: the same will be the case as to my clerical colleagues, and I have reason to expect, that in Mr. Bankes I shall find an able co adjutor in the arrangements for the Music &c. I was introduced to Mr. Bowles by Mr. Lysons, the eminent antiquary, Rector of Rodmarton in this Diocese, an old acquaintance of mine on the Magisterial bench:[22] in the transient interview I had with him, I saw nothing very striking or prepossessing, nor anything indicative of genius; on the contrary his appearance was unfavourable, and his dress negligent: he is bald, and advanced in years. Mr. Bankes is a young man, |49 Prebendary of Norwich, as well as of Gloucester, son of the member for Corfe Castle, and Brother of

20. Henry George Francis Reynolds-Moreton, (1802-1853), 2nd Earl, 5th Baron Ducie, (1840). M.P. for Gloucestershire, 1831-1832 and East Gloucestershire, (1832-35). Reynolds-Moreton was styled Lord Moreton, 1837-1840. He married, 1826, Elizabeth Dutton, eldest daughter of John Dutton, 2nd Baron Sherborne.

21. James Henry Legge Dutton, (1804-1883), 3rd Baron Sherborne, (1862). Dutton married, 1826, Elizabeth, eldest daughter of Thomas Howard, 16th Earl of Suffolk. She died in childbirth, 1845.

22. Daniel Lyson, (1762-1834), vicar of Rodmarton and topographer. Daniel worked closely with his brother Samuel on antiquarian and topographical subjects.

one of the Members for the University of Cambridge.[23]—Before leaving the Cathedral we met F. Aston, who had arrived from Stanway to join our party: he breakfasted and dined at Mrs. Backhouse's, & slept at the adjacent inn. The Ordinary for Gentlemen is held alternately at the two principal Inns; this day it was at the King's Head. I dined there; Mr. C. Leigh in the chair. I sat agreeably, between Dr. Cooke, the Chairman of the Quarter Sessions, and Mr. Baker of Hardwick Court.[24] The party was very numerous, I should think more than 70 sat down, and among them the leading persons of the county. I may here as well enumerate some of the principal persons and families, who attended the music meeting on this and the following days. The Duke & Duchess of Beaufort[25] and the Ladies Somerset, the Duke of Buckingham on one morning from Cheltenham,[26] the Earl of Bathurst & Ladies Bathurst, Lord Apsley & Hon. Messrs. Bathurst, Lord Sherborne & family, parts of Lord Ducie's family, Lord Lilford,[27] Lord Calthorpe,[28] the Bishop of Gloucester & his family, the Dow. Lady Rossmore,[29] Mr. R. B. Cooper, M.P.,[30] Mr. Cripps M.P. & family, Sir W. Guise, |50 M.P., Col. Webb M.P.[31] Mr. Peirse M.P., Mr. & Mrs. Browne & family, Hon. Mrs. Tracy & family, J. Delafield Phelps, Col. Kingscote, Col. Berkley, Mr. & Mrs. Dolphin, Revd. J. Dolphin, Mr. C. Hanford, Mrs. Baker & family, Lord Redesdale,[32] Mr. & Miss Mitford &c. &c. I joined my wife & Frederick Aston in the noble room in the Shire Hall, which serves for county meetings, the nomination & Election of Representatives in Parliament &c. and on this occasion for concerts & balls. We obtained very good seats; there were more than 400 present, and the Selection of music was very judicious and tasteful. Both the instrumental & vocal

---

23. Edward Bankes, (1794-1867). Bankes was fortunate from a career aspect in the choice of his first wife, Lady Frances Jane Scott, who he married in April 1820, for Frances was the daughter of John, Earl of Eldon, Lord Chancellor. Bankes was educated at Westminster School and Trinity College, Cambridge. He was ordained in 1818 and fell into two family livings in Dorset, one as Rector of Corfe Castle, 1818-54. His home appears to have been Loughton Hall, Flintshire, and in his secular duties he was Magistrate and D.L. for Flintshire. In his Clerical appointments he was vicar of Stoke Bliss, Herefordshire, 1820-1823, Canon Residentiary of Gloucester, 1821-1867, vicar of East Farleigh, Kent, 1823-1832. Chaplain-in-ordinary to King William IV and to Queen Victoria, Canon of Bristol, 1832-1867. His first wife died in 1838 after giving him three sons and one daughter. In the following year he married Marian, daughter of Edward Rice, D.D., Dean of Gloucester. Bankes had more than the usual share of favours extended to the Great Lawyer's connections. Although he became enormously rich upon the death of his father-in-law, Bankes continued to hold his preferments for some years after he was incapable of performing the duties attached to them. For further information see the Biographical Index.
24. Thomas Barwick Lloyd-Baker, (1807-1886).
25. Henry Charles Somerset, (1766-1835), 6th Duke of Beaufort. The Duke was Lord Lieutenant of Gloucestershire from 1810 until his death. At the coronation of William IV he bore the crown of the Queen Consort. He married, 1791, Charlotte Sophia, (1771-1854), daughter of Granville Leveson-Gower, 1st Marquess of Stafford.
26. Richard Temple-Nugent-Brydges-Chandos-Grenville, (1776-1839), 1st Duke of Buckingham. Richard Temple was the only duke create by George IV, conferred as a mark of personal friendship.
27. Thomas Powys, (1775-1825), 2nd Baron Lilford. Lilford's son who succeeded him as 3rd Baron Lilford in 1825 married Mary Elizabeth, daughter of Lord Holland and Elizabeth Vassall mentioned above. She was therefore, half-sister to Harriet Pellew.
28. George Gough-Calthorpe, (1787-1851), 3rd Baron Calthorpe.
29. Elizabeth Lady Rossmore, (1732-1824). Lady Rossmore was for many years a leading member of Dublin society and would, in all likelihood, have seen Handel performing the Messiah there. She was the aunt of Lord Rossmore, the new husband of Francis Witts' cousin, Augusta. At the time of the Three Choirs she would have been 91 years old.
30. Robert Bransby Cooper, (1762-1845), M.P. for Gloucester, 1818-1830. Mentioned in volume 1.
31. Edward Webb, (1779-1839), of Stoke Bishop, near Bristol, M.P. for Gloucester, 1816-1832.
32. John Mitford, (1748-1830), 1st Baron Redesdale. Lord Redesdale was Attorney-General, 1799-1801 and Speaker of the House of Commons 1801-1802, Lord Chancellor, 1802-1806.

departments were admirably supported. The exquisite Vaughan, the powerful & scientific notes of Mrs. Salmon, the liquid & thrilling tones of Miss Stephens, the spirit and execution of Caradori, Mr. Sapio's fine tenor, the taste & simplicity of Miss Travis,[33] the deep rolling tones of Bellamy, tho' far inferior to the exquisite judgment science & refinement of Bartleman, afforded a rich treat. Nor was the Instrumental treat less rich: with such compositions as Haydn's, Rossini's, Mozart's, Cherubini's, Bach, Paer's, Clarke Whitfields's |[51] Bishop's, Calcott's & Attwood's, & such masters in execution as Cramer,[34] Lindley,[35] Marshall,[36] Nicholson on the Flute,[37] Willman on the Clarionet,[38] Bochsa on the harp,[39] it was impossible not to be delighted. Tea & a ball follow the concert, for neither of which we remained, being anxious to husband Margaret's strength for the ensuing days.

---

33. The references to Caradori are confusing, as in two places the name appears and it seems as if it is a male referred to rather than a female, and yet after a considerable search no male opera/oratorio singer of the name Caradori has appeared. It may be left to assume that Caradori was Maria Caterina Rosalbina Caradori-Allan (née Munck), (1800-1865). She was an Alsatian soprano of Italian birth. She had made her début in January the previous year at the King's Theatre, London, where she appeared as Cherubino in *Le nozze di Figaro*. In later life she was to achieve considerable fame, and she even appears (or gets a mention) in Thackeray's *Vanity Fair.* Mr. Sapio has not left much history, bit it is know that he sang at an opening concert at Stroud's new Subscription Rooms in 1834 when he was billed with Mr. Machin as 'Principal Singers at the Royal Festival, Westminster Abbey'. Miss Travis is elusive with few references to her. She is found performing in Birmingham, 5 to 7 October 1814. This was a performance under the Presidency of the Earl of Plymouth, Miss Stephens (afterwards Countess of Essex), Miss Travis, Vincent Novello (the publisher of after years), and Griesbach (oboeist), were among the "first appearances." Other references have her singing with the famous tenors of the time, one of which was in a glee, *There is a Lady sweet & kind, Madrigal for Four Voices* as sung by Miss Travis, Messrs. W. Knyvett, Vaughan & Bartleman, at the Hanover Square Concerts in 1817.
34. Franz (François) Cramer, 1772-1848. Cramer was a professional violinist and played at many of the provincial festivals. He succeeded his father Wilhelm as leader of the Antient concerts, and it is related that George III used to give him the right tempo whenever any of Handel's compositions were performed.
35. Robert Lindley, (1776-1855). Mentioned in volume 1. *See* the Biographical Index.
36. William Marshall was an Oxford music and musical instrument seller. He was obviously a gifted performer also.
37. Charles Nicholson, (1795-1837). Nicholson was one of the most celebrated flautists of the early nineteenth century in England, renowned for his big sound and bravura style. He played and endorsed flutes with big sounds made possible by large tone holes and large embouchure holes, and the head pieces were lined with metal. He marketed his design of instrument through other producers, such as Clementi & Co., Astor, and Potter, who inscribed them 'C. Nicholson's Improved' It was Charles Nicholson who broke away from the "German Flute" as made in London by the likes of Potter, Astor, Monzani et al, and introduced the "Improved Flute", and with it, a new era - the golden days of the cone flute that stretched from around 1816 to 1850 and beyond.
38. "The clarinet has long been considered by the whole musical profession as the most beautiful of wind instruments." So began Thomas Willman's Instruction Book for the Clarinet, published in 1825. Thomas Willman, German by birth, was probably one of the most famous clarinettists of his time. His career was varied and he even spent seven years with the Coldstream Regiment as bandmaster, (1818-25). As author of an early clarinet tutor, Willman wrote in 1824 "It is impossible for the upper notes of the clarinet to be of the right quality unless the reed and lip are sufficiently flexible in the chalumeau tones. This part of the clarinet scale, the chalumeau, is to commonly neglected by Practitioners.
39. Robert Nicholas Charles Bochsa, (1789-1856). Celebrated harpist and dramatic composer. He was born in France, where his father, Karl Bochsa, a Bohemian musician, was a flute and clarinet player. His musical talent developed very early, so that at the age of seven he played a piano concerto in public. In 1806, having already become very proficient on the harp, piano, the violin and flute, Bochsa entered the Conservatory of Paris where he took up composition and harmony under Catel and Méhul. Later he studied the harp under Nadermann and Marin, but formed an entirely new style of his own and completely revolutionized harp-playing. In 1813, he became first harpist to the Emperor Napoleon and, in 1816, was appointed to the same position for Louis XVIII. In 1817, being detected in large forgeries, he fled to London and never returned to France. In 1822, when the Academy of Music was established, he was made professor of the harp, but charges of misconduct were brought against him and in 1827, he was dismissed. See the Biographical Index.

Thursday Sept. 18.

Frederick Aston and myself repaired to the Oratorio in the Cathedral, my wife reserving herself for the evening performances at the Shire Hall. The music was the Redemption, a selection from the works of Handel, the airs being adapted to sacred words. The arrangement was originally made by Dr. Arnold: and concentrates some of the finest and least hacknied morceaux of the admirable composer. The Occasional Overture preceded the whole. The choruses were got up in the steadiest manner and with the finest effect. The fine reverberations produced by the long aisles, the music rolling along the lofty space, all peculiarly striking. All the vocal performers distinguished themselves greatly. Mrs. Salmon,[40] Miss Stephens, Miss Travis, Messrs. Vaughan,[41] Bellamy[42] & Hawes.[43] The quartett, "Their bodies are buried in peace", followed by the Dead March in |[52] Saul, was one of the most magnificent triumphs of music, which I recollect to have heard. There were, perhaps, from 1200 to 1500 persons present; the ladies all elegantly dressed, and the sight was truly beautiful. Very numerous & large parties resorted from Cheltenham. After dinnėr at Mrs. Backhouse's, we repaired to the concert: my wife, Mrs. B., F. Aston & myself, and tho' a little too late, contrived to get very good places not far from the Orchestra, in the front row. Mrs. Tracy and her family & Mr. Eddy & their family sat near us. The Room was extremely crouded: nearly 950 persons were present; without exaggeration, I might say, in the Newspaper diction, "all the rank & fashion of the County"—The selection of music was very beautiful, & the execution equally fine. Mr. Sapio, & Sign. Caradori were added to those mentioned in the morning. We retired before the ball.—

Friday Sept. 19.

Fred. Aston left us this morning. We went to the Oratorio at the Cathedral, the Messiah, which was equally well attended as the Redemption yesterday. I had obtained tickets for the Clerical Stewards Gallery, where the ladies were accommodated in the best places |[53] in the front row. Nothing could be more magnificent or a finer treat in Music than the performances this day. The eye was equally delighted, & to me the assembling of so many acquaintance as I now number in the County, was an additional relish. I dined at the Ordinary at the King's Head Inn, Mr. Estcourt in the Chair, sitting between Mr.

40. Eliza Salmon, née Munday, (1787-1849). Eliza was born in Oxford and made her Covent Garden début in the Lenten Oratorios on 4 March 1803. She was gifted with a beautiful voice, a charming manner and a face 'of dazzling fairness'. She married James Salmon, and in this year (1823) he joined the army to overcome financial difficulties and was posted to the West Indies where he died. Eliza continued to sing in London and at the Three Choirs. In 1823 her income was said to have been £5,000. In 1825 her voice suddenly collapsed and she never resumed public appearances.

41. Thomas Vaughan, (1782-1846). Vaughan was a popular and powerful tenor. He was considered by a contemporary to be more articulate, more natural, more simple, more dignified and therefore far more forceful than his colleague John Braham.

42. Thomas Ludford Bellamy, (1770-1843). Bellamy was a bass. He was educated in the choir of Westminster Abbey and sang in the Handel Commemoration of 1784. After a varied career and following the death of Bartleman he was engaged as principal bass singer at the Concert of Antient Music.

43. William Hawes, (1785-1846). Hawes was a Chapel Royal chorister from 1795 to 1801 and then a violinist in the Covent Garden orchestra. In later life he was far more involved in music publishing and in the production of adaptations of continental operas. His presence at the 1823 Three Choirs is quite surprising. In 1824 he was appointed musical director of the English Opera House (the Lyceum) where many of the opera adaptations were performed.

Hanford, a very agreeable Worcestershire Roman Catholic Squire, & Mr. T. Pettat. The President announced the collections at the doors of the Cathedral on the three days to have amounted to £759.14. 5 a sum much exceeding the collection made at the last Gloucester Music Meeting, & nearly as large as the largest collection ever made on a similar occasion. The health of the retiring Stewards was drank with enthusiasm, and that of the succeeding Stewards, now publicly announced, with encouraging greetings. We were all too tired to go to the third & last evening concert & ball.—

Saturday Sept. 20.

I attended a meeting of the Subscribers to a monument in memory of Sir. G. O. Paul.[44] This languishing testimony of gratitude for public services is now at last likely to be carried into effect. Mr. Cripps M.P. the chairman, produced sketches by Flaxman for the |54 consideration of the meeting, which consisted of a few leading Magistrates. It was unanimously agreed not to erect a statue on the great staircase in the Shire Hall: because the limited sum to be disposed of, £500, would only purchase a statue of what is called Haddersfield Stone; a Stone, indeed, very closely resembling marble; nor is there any prospect of a good likeness of Sir G. Paul being met with. A monument of statuary marble 4 feet 7½ In. high & 9 feet in length, to be erected in the Cathedral, was most approved, including two figures, on each side of the tablet, in height 3 feet 4 in., of wisdom & justice: on the whole an elegant design.

I afterwards repaired to a meeting of Magistrates at the Lunatic Asylum, the Bishop of Gloucester in the chair. Every interior arrangement of the institution appeared to be judicious. There are 17 Pauper Patients.

I rode home for my Sunday's duty, in the afternoon.

Monday Sept. 22.

In the afternoon I rode to Northleach to meet the Regulator coach on its return to Gloucester from London by which I rejoined my friends in Wellington Parade.—In the coach I met with a conversible old Baronet, Sir Mark Wood,[45] |55 who gave me his address in town No. 66 Pall Mall, with a cordial invitation. I believe him to have been formerly in Service in India. He has estates in Surrey, Monmouthshire & Glamorganshire.

Wednesday Sept. 24.

Called at Mr. Turner's house at Wotton half a mile from Gloucester to look at his collection of paintings. This gentleman, who is a banker at Gloucester, has several very interesting paintings, but as he was not at home nor was there a catalogue, the pleasure to be derived from inspecting them was much diminished. The choicest morceau is a Madonna, said to be by Corregio, very rich in colouring; a most melancholy, livid, downcast countenance,

44. Sir George Onesiphorus Paul, (1746-1820), 2nd Baronet, of Hill House, Rodborough. Sir George was a leading prison reformer with a national reputation for his pioneering work. He was well known to Agnes Witts as a neighbour when they lived at Bownham House, Rodborough. He was also closely related to the Snow family, very old friends to Agnes and Edward Witts.

45. Sir Mark Wood, (1750-1829), of Pall Mall, and of Gatton Park, Surrey, M.P. for Milborne Port, 1794-1796; Newark, 1796-1802 and Gatton, 1802-1818. Wood was Colonel in the East India Company's service and chief engineer of Bengal.

163. Hillfield, Gloucester.

enveloped in a dark blue mantle, a picture expressive of great mental woe and bodily exhaustion. A copy of Rembrandt; some good cattle pieces; two fine bold landscapes in the style of Salvator Rosa, rocks & waterfalls; an architectural piece representing a canal & street in the Low Countries, some Flemish paintings; an old portrait said to be of Mary Queen of Scots, and some landscapes form the principal part of the collection. The view from the windows of the Cathedral, Malvern Hills &c. is very striking.—

——— |56

Friday Sept. 26.

Mrs. Backhouse had a small card party.

———

Saturday Sept. 27.

I returned to Upper Slaughter, leaving Margaret with her Mother. I passed an hour or two on my way with Mrs. Travell, at Cheltenham.

———

Tuesday Sept. 30.

I omitted to mention a little Volume, which fell in my way at Gloucester; "May you like it? By a Country Curate." I read only the 2d. Vol., but as the first may not fall in my way, I will speak of it. It contained seven tales, all illustrating the same serious truth, the necessity of an abiding and prevailing sense of Christian obligation. The Stories are on the whole well selected & well written; the author combines something of Washington Irving's style, something of Crabbe. He has a fine feeling for country scenery & habits, & describes well tranquil domestic life. His religion is cheerful, & some of his situations pathetic.

———

Wednesday Oct. 1

The Gazette at last mentions the appointment of John Backhouse to the board of excise.

Dr. Baillie's death, whose illness was mentioned before occurred a week ago.

——— |57

Friday Oct. 3.

I went to dine and sleep at Lady Elcho's at Stanway. The party was reduced, since I was last there. Lady Rossmore, (now indisposed,) my mother, & Miss Church are still at Stanway, as also Mr. R. Stuart, a very fine lad, son of a Gentleman of fortune in East Lothian, and pupil of the Revd. Mr. Bland at Kenilworth. This young man is nephew of Sir W. Drummond, with whom I was for some months employed as his Secretary, when he was Chargé des Affaires for our court at Copenhagen (Journal 1. 39)[46] Sir W.D. now resides,[47] I believe, in the South of France: his religious principles do not accord with those entertained in Britain. In fact, he may be called a Deist, and, I fear, his moral conduct is not without a grievous stain. Thank GOD, that my principles did not suffer in youth by my intercourse with him. Sir W. Drummond is a Scotsman, his seat being at Logie Almond in Perthshire. He married a Miss Boone, a lady of large fortune, but the connexion was not productive of happiness. Educated at Oxford, (at Christ Church) he was high in the good opinion of Mr. Pitt, & represented Lostwithiel in Parliament. As a diplomatist, he represented the British Court at Naples, & at Constantinople, but has long retired from the Political |[58] world. He is an excellent Scholar, and of a very subtle mind: I use the word in a favourable sense, for acuteness: yet deeply sensible, that his reasoning powers have been lamentably misapplied. His "Academical Questions" must be denounced as a dangerous work, unsettling the mind on topics of faith, and eminently deistical. As a Poet he translated Persius, elegantly but diffusely, with an apparatus of notes. He published a poem founded on the Northern Mythology, which engaged him while I was an inmate of his family at Copenhagen. I was introduced to him by my friend Lord Elcho, & repaired to Denmark from Dresden, where during our sejour in Germany the appointment reached me. My excellent Parents had taken my brother & myself to Germany in 1798: we resided two Winters at Weimar, during part of which time Mr. Dukinfield, eldest son to Sir Nath. Dukinfield, an old friend of my Father, was placed under his care. Poor S. Dukinfield afterwards went into the Dragoons, and having made the unpropitious campaign with Sir J. Moore in Spain, was wrecked & drowned on the Coast of Cornwall, as he returned to England. From Weimar |[59] we repaired to Dresden, in which beautiful & interesting city we passed several weeks. My appointment as secretary to Sir W.D. made a change in our projected tour towards Vienna &c.: and the whole of our party bent their course with me to Copenhagen, remaining there till the following spring, when on the rupture with the Danes, we repaired to Britain, on board the Kite Sloop of War, dispatched from the fleet for that purpose. On our way to Copenhagen we passed thro' Berlin & Stettin, embarking on board a Swedish Vessel, at Schwinemunde, at the mouth of the Oder. To return to Sir W. Drummond; he is the author of several minor productions, chiefly on

---

46. This is a fascinating reference, for it does seem to imply that other journals existed. If this was Journal 1, what did he consider is earlier diaries, or were they somewhat dismissed as his own juvenilia? No diary for the period in Copenhagen is now in the Witts Family Papers.

47. Sir William Drummond, (1770?-1828), M.P. for St. Mawes, 1795-1796; Lostwithiel, 1796-1802. Drummond of Logie Almond, Perth, was orphaned at eleven. After studying at St. Andrews his delights in life were as an author and he became a profound and elegant scholar. He was an undistinguished diplomat, and served in Denmark, Sicily and Constantinople. He wrote several articles for the *Edinburgh Review* causing Sydney Smith to remark to the editor 'beware of Drummond your auxiliary: he is dull, wrongheaded, malignant and indiscreet'. He retired from public life in 1809 after failing to win government positions, and devoted his time to Edinburgh literary life. He died at Rome, reportedly 'a martyr to gout'. For further details see the Biographical Index.

Classical subjects and antiquities. I cannot but consider it as a blessing of Providence, that I did not accompany this able but dangerous man on any subsequent occasion.—Indeed, the exclusion of the English from the Continent, and the consequent interruption for many years of diplomatic intercourse, effectually barred any prospect of success in pursuing that line to which, by this appointment as Secretary, I had been introduced.

Saturday Oct. 4.

I returned home.

——— |[60]

Sunday Oct. 5.

"Bp. Gibson's Sacrament of the Lord's supper explained". An excellent tract circulated by the Society for promoting Christian Knowledge.

Tuesday Oct. 7.

Attended the annual meeting of the Stow district committee of the Society for promoting Christian Knowledge. Lord Redesdale in the Chair. The distribution of Books in this circuit is diminished this year; it is to be hoped, more because the wants of the neighbourhood have been diminished, than that the zeal of the Subscribers has lessened. The report this year notices the distribution of 85 Bibles
51 Testaments
250 Common Prayer Books & Psalters
400 Tracts.

The annual meeting and dinner of the Stow book Society succeeded: the Hon. & Revd. E. Rice D.D. in the chair.

Wednesday Oct. 8.

I dined and slept at Batsford Park, the seat of Lord Redesdale. The party consisted of the Hon. & Revd. E. Rice, D.D. Rector of Great Risington and Oddington, at the latter of which places he resides. He is also Prebendary of Worcester & Precentor of York. He is a most estimable man, with whom I have long been on terms of intimacy, acting |[61] as his colleague in the various public business of the neighbourhood, as magistrate and otherwise. His wife, formerly Miss Lascelles, daughter of the late Genl. Lascelles, of the Harewood family; her mother was Miss Catley, formerly a celebrated singer and public performer: with them were their two eldest daughters. Mrs. Pole, of Wick-hill, her son William, and her eldest daughter. Mr. Jeaffreson, Vicar of Longborough, and Mr. Ford. These made up the party with Lord Redesdale's Son & daughter, both pleasing young persons. Mr. Mitford has lately left Eton, and is about to become a member of the University of Oxford, and of New College. The venerable Peer at the age of 75 retains great activity of mind and body, and is now making considerable improvements on a large scale. He has been enabled by the late inclosure at Bourton on the Hill to make new approaches to his place, which before was inconvenient of access. The house itself is an excellent Mansion, situate in a well wooded park. The suite of apartments appropriated for company is very handsome, and furnished with some very good paintings, his Lordship being not only a connoisseur, but himself an artist. The library contains busts of W. Pitt & Spencer Perceval, |[62] the latter of whom was brother of the late

Lady Redesdale; who so much resembled him, that she sat to the artist after his assassination to enable him to put the finishing strokes to his work. The same apartment contains pictures of Lords Eldon & Redesdale, both habited in their robes as Lords Chancellor, the one of England, the other of Ireland: Lord Redesdale having held that high post in the legal profession several years ago. His legal career was extremely successful, and he is esteemed a very sound lawyer. He has held the several situations of Welch Judge, Solicitor General, Speaker of the House of Commons, besides that of Chancellor of Ireland. In the House of Lords he is a most useful member and well earns the pension, which he receives for his past services. Besides an active participation in all the legislative duties of the house, in which he is a frequent speaker, he is unremitting in his attendance on the Committees, and his services are invaluable in the Appeal business of the house, where his intimate knowledge of the law of Scotland, makes him a most use- |*63* -ful assessor to the Chancellor. His politics are those of the school of Mr. Pitt; on Irish affairs he is considered as great authority, and, I am sorry to say, entertains great alarm on the subject of the unhappy divisions, distresses and barbarities of that ill fated country. In private life, Lord Redesdale is a most attentive father, hospitable, obliging, ready to assist and advise in the public business of the neighbourhood. I have before partaken of the hospitalities of Batsford, and no family can be better regulated; his table and wines are excellent. As a companion few men are more gifted than his Lordship. He is very communicative, and possessing an extraordinary memory, is full of anecdote, illustration &c. His observations on history & past politics sometimes amount to almost dissertation, full of antiquarian lore: I have frequently been edified by his comments on constitutional points. Sometimes, indeed, he is a little prolix, and he has the usual defect of advancing years, that he sometimes repeats his anecdotes. His Lordship succeeded to the property at Batsford under the will of the late John Freeman Esqr., his aunt's husband, |*64* and who made him his heir on the demise of his only child, a daughter married to Mr. Heathcote, now Sir

164. Batsford.

John Freeman Heathcote, of Hants. by whom she had no children. Col. Mitford of Hants. is Lord Redesdale's brother, and a highly gifted man; he is the author of the best history of Greece in our language. He has adopted a singular theory as to orthography, which, with other opinions on the theory of language, he has developed in a distinct treatise.—The maiden sisters of Lord R. one of whom now survives, possessed very cultivated minds, & great readiness and taste in drawing.

The News are arrived of the election of a new Pope in the room of the late Pius VII. The suffrages of the Cardinals have fallen upon the Cardinal della Genga, an Italian prelate born in 1760, who has assumed the title of Leo XII.

Thursday Oct. 9.

I returned home after a fatiguing day at Stow, where among other business the accounts of the Foss & Cross District of Turnpike roads were audited, agreeably to the new regulations of the complicated general Turnpike acts passed in the last & preceding Sessions of Parliament.

--- |65

Friday Oct. 10.

I left home for Stanway, where I dined and slept at Frederick Aston's. A tremendous storm of rain during the night had the effect of laying under water the low country in various parts of the vale of Evesham.

Saturday Oct. 11.

After calling at Stanway House, where I remained till after luncheon, I rode to Bredon in Worcestershire to dine & sleep at the Revd. John Keysall's, Rector of that parish. Passed near Toddington, where the magnificent Gothic Mansion of Mr. Hanbury Tracy, the exterior of which is now completed, presents a very handsome object from the road. Mr. Tracy has combined in this structure, with much judgment & taste, & at very great expence, some of the most interesting morceaux of ancient Gothic Architecture from Oxford & other places. A tower rises in the centre copied from that of Magdalen College, and the cloisters & grand entrance of the same college are imitated in the principal front of the Mansion; the West window of Tintern Abbey appears in miniature in what is called a chapel return; but in fact is not a chapel, the interior being laid out in |66 domestic apartments. The remains of the old mansion of the Lords Tracy, not far distant from the new house, still afford a residence to the family, while the more splendid edifice is in progress towards completion. Mr. Tracy had some years since expended large sums in the improvement of the respectable seat of his wife's ancestors, which was itself a mansion house of the age of James I. Unfortunately the park is at a distance from the house, & on the other side of the turnpike road leading from Stow to Tewkesbury; but afforded no suitable scite for building upon. Mr. H. Tracy has for some years ceased to represent the borough of Tewkesbury. His politics are in opposition to Ministry, indeed, he is attached to the opinions of Sir F. Burdett, Dr. Parr, &c. The Tracy's of Toddington are the elder branch of the Tracy's of Stanway; few families can trace their origin higher, as they ascend to a period anterior to William the Conqueror, by an authentic pedigree. Of course, as connected with the Stanway Branch by my Mother's side, I claim kindred with the Tracy's of Toddington. Mr. H. Tracy was a cadet of |67 the Hanbury's of Monmouthshire, and assumed the name of Tracy, when he married the heiress of the last ~~Viscount~~ Baron of that name; the title is now extinct. Mr. & Mrs. H. Tracy have a large family, amply provided for by estates in Gloucestershire, Montgomeryshire and Somersetshire. The road to Bredon lies through the fertile valley at the foot of Bredon Hill, passing thro' Alderton, Great Washbourn & Beckford in Gloucestershire, Overbury in Worcestershire, Kemerton in Gloucestershire; the outline of the two counties being here much indented. At Beckford is an ancient seat of the Wakemans, a Roman Catholic Family of opulence: the old Squire & his sisters occupy the family mansion. At Overbury is the Seat of the Martins. Bredon is a large parish of very fertile land situate three miles from Tewkesbury on the banks of the Avon, which passes by it on its way to join the Severn at Tewkesbury. The opposite banks of the river afford a fine range of meadows in the parish of Twining in Gloucestershire. The Church is a large & handsome Structure with a lofty spire. The patronage of the Rectory was anciently in the Bishops of Worcester, |68 but has long been in private hands, and Mr. Keysall has now the advowson. The benefice is very valuable. Norton is a hamlet with a chapel: and Cutsdean is a chapelry belonging to Bredon, nearly insulated and surrounded by Gloucestershire, but itself in Worcestershire, on the hills, two miles above Stanway. The parsonage house at Bredon is a very old, long, rambling house, which has been greatly improved into a most comfortable residence by Mr. Keysall; the grounds attached are however of small extent. The Rectory is exempt from Archidiaconal Visitations, and the Rector holds his own visitation with the authority of Archdeacon. Land is allotted in lieu of tithes. Mr. Keysall is one of the King's Chaplains, & an acting Magistrate for Worcestershire & Gloucestershire. I have known him for many years, his Son the Revd. C. Keysall having been curate of Stanway for several years both previous to & since my incumbency. On his resignation of the Curacy I appointed F. Aston, who is also Curate of Mr. Keysall at Cutsdean.[48] With C. Keysall we have long been on very intimate terms. I had now |69 great regret on finding him in ~~great~~ deep affliction watching the death bed of his young wife, to whom he has been married about 15 months. She was a daughter of Dr. Woodgate, a Physician in considerable practice at Worcester, & having given birth to a daughter about 4 months since, has been rapidly declining ever since. The poor young woman was at Bredon, whither she had been removed some weeks ago from Ambroseden, near Bicester, where C. Keysall was curate to Sir H. Dryden. Circumstances arising from our mutual engagements had prevented our ever being introduced to Mrs. C. Keysall, although a visit to Upper Slaughter had been more than once contemplated and nearly accomplished. I fear, there is no hope of her life. Under this painful suspence C.K. has resigned the Curacy at Ambroseden. The other members of the family assembled at Bredon were Mrs. Keysall, second wife to Mr. K., & her Mother Mrs. Colton, who resides with them, & is widow of the late Canon Colton of Salisbury, a son of hers, a clergyman, is author of two works exhibiting talent; the former a satirical poem entitled Hypocrisy; the latter a prose publication, sketches of |70 character, with the Title "Lacon" or things as they are; containing, as I have been told, many shrewd and pertinent observations in morality. Mrs. Keysall Senr. is a very agreeable person in very indifferent health. Two daughters of Dr. Woodgate were also at Bredon in anxious attendance on their poor sister. I could have enjoyed a more close

48. This entry clarifies the matter of the curacy at Stanway, Charles Keysall did resign. Keysall was a favourite of Agnes Witts, the late Lady Hereford and of Lady Elcho.

inspection of Mr. Keysall's library, than the time & circumstances would allow: though not large it ~~fo~~ is select and curious.

Sunday Oct. 12.

After breakfast I left Bredon, lamenting the painful anxiety, in which all the members of the family were plunged, and which precluded my extending my stay with them. Mr. Keysall took me in his carriage to Tewkesbury. I had sent my horses home the preceding evening. I had been appointed on the suggestion of Mr. Keysall to preach the Anniversary Sermon for the Tewkesbury dispensary in the venerable Abbey Church. At some future time I shall hope to examine this ancient and grand monument of the piety of our forefathers in more detail. The massive Norman columns, the fine Western round headed window, the solid massive |*71* Tower, the interesting ancient monuments, covering the remains of many princes, nobles & warriors famed in the annals of olden time, all deserve to be examined at leisure. The inner choir has been fitted up for divine service several years ago at a considerable expence, and with judgment, except as to the pulpit, where the attempt to produce Gothic symmetry and lightness has ended in a very gingerbread sort of rostrum, in inferior taste, and it is to the preacher a most uncomfortable and, as it strikes one at first view, insecure pulpit. The congregation was not large, but very respectable. The Corporation in their robes occupied the seat appropriated to them. At their head was Mr. Dowdeswell, of Pull Court in this vicinity, Recorder of the Borough & one of its representatives.[49] He is a Master in Chancery, and from the short interview I had with him I should judge him to be a very intelligent man. Mr. Martin of Overbury is the other representative.[50] He calls himself a Whig, Mr. Dowdeswell votes with Ministers. Mr. Keysall read prayers: the Organ was well played, & several hymns adapted to the occasion were well sung. From all the Gentlemen connected |*72* with the Dispensary I met with great politeness, & the collection exceeded my expectations, amounting to nearly £24. The Gentlemen, who held the plates, met me after the congregation had quitted the Church, in the Vestry, a handsome Gothic apartment, perhaps, the ancient chapter house or library. As I passed thro' the Transept I saw the Monument (an inscription on the pavement) of Sir Paul Tracy, and in the Church an old mural Monument to the Memory of the wife of one of the Slaughters; an old family, now, I believe, extinct, who long held the Manor of Upper Slaughter, and resided in the ancient Mansion house of my village, at present occupied by a Tenant of Lord Sherborne, who is the present Lord of the Manor of Upper Slaughter. Mr. White is Vicar of Tewkesbury, and was at this time absent. He has held the living of Mickleton in this County. The Vicarage of Tewkesbury is not very valuable.—

Service being concluded, I went in a chaise to Gloucester to rejoin my dear wife at her mother's: arriving before I was expected, as I had not been looked for till the following day.

——— |*73*

Tuesday Oct. 14.

The Quarter Sessions began. Two chairmen were appointed, Dr. Cooke and Mr. Cripps. The business was not so great as usual. It is gratifying to find a diminution of crime everywhere

49. John Edmund Dowdeswell, (1772-1851), M.P. for Tewkesbury, 1812-1832. Dowdeswell had been offered an East India Company writership by the 3rd Duke of Portland, a friend of his father while he was still at Oxford, but declined it in preference for a legal career. Dowdeswell had a distinguished career in Chancery.

50. John Martin, (1774-1832), of Overbury, Worcestershire. M.P. for Tewkesbury, 1812-1832.

both as to the number and heinousness of offences. The Duke of Beaufort attended. Other Magistrates present were Messrs. Baker, father & son, Mr. Cooper, M.P. Sir W Guise M.P. Genl. Guise, Mr. Byles, Dr. Timbrell, Dr. Davies, Mr. Goldney, Mr. Newman, Mr. Browne, Mr. Talbot, Mr. Goodrich, Mr. Phelps &c. The number of magistrates dining together on the first three days of the Session at ~~Gloucester~~ the Kings Head, was rather less than is common. This custom of dining together & passing the evening in each others society tends much to maintain that friendly harmony & mutual good intelligence, which distinguishes the Gloucestershire Sessions, while it contributes to the dissemination of useful hints & information on many subjects, particularly as to the magisterial duties. The new Act of Parliament passed last Sessions for the regulation of Gaols & Houses of Correction, which will require a considerable change in our prison discipline and structures, was referred |74 to a committee of Magistrates, who are to meet in the interval between this & the next Sessions & then make a report. I am appointed a member of this committee; my colleagues are Dr. Cooke, Mr. Cripps, Mr. Holford M.P. Mr. Byles, Mr. T. Baker, Mr. Cheston, Mr. Goldney, Mr. C. Crawley.

Wednesday Oct. 15.

"The Spiritual Quixote". (By the Revd. Rd. Graves, Rector of Claverton) This comic romance, as it is called in the title page, is a clever production & had great praise assigned to it on its first ~~production,~~ appearance when the eccentricities and wild enthusiasm of the Methodists, both under Wesley & Whitfield, first attracted the notice of the public in their Tabernacles, field preaching, pangs of the new birth, and their Journals recording their tribulations & their triumphs. It is even now interesting as containing lively narrative, just views of enthusiasm, and glimpses of society & manners as they then were. The Spiritual Quixote is a Gloucestershire Gentleman of moderate estate, & his Sancho Panza the cobbler of his village. The scene is laid in that & the adjoining Counties. Episodes are not unsparingly introduced, & a love plot runs through the whole, ending happily in the |75 marriage of Mr. Wildgoose, and his return to sound and rational views of religion. There is a coarseness of expression and allusion in many parts, which would not now be tolerated. Mr. Graves, the author, was of the Mickleton family, & a man of considerable talent. He died Rector of Claverton a few years ago. He published some other minor works, and among ~~others~~ them a book called "Senilities": which truly betrayed the old age of the author: he lived to a very advanced period. (till his 90th. year) Lord Harrowby once told me, that he had accidently met with and purchased at Bath a copy of the Spiritual Quixote, provided with a key, mentioning the different persons, whose characters are poutrayed in the course of the Novel.

Friday Oct. 17.

The Quarter Sessions closed.

We passed the evening at Mrs. M. Hunt's in palace yard. We met her guests, two Miss Hunts, daughters of the late Revd. Edwd. Hunt, a Northamptonshire Clergyman & Mr. T. Hunt, High Sheriff of the same County, nephew to Mrs. M. Hunt, an intelligent young man educated at Christ Church Oxford, and who has travelled abroad.[51] I am related to all these Hunts, as also to those of Boreatton in Shropshire. |76 As thus;

---

51. Thomas Hunt was to be murdered the following year while on honeymoon in Italy. See the introduction in volume 1 for the full information on the Hunt family and the Biographical Index.

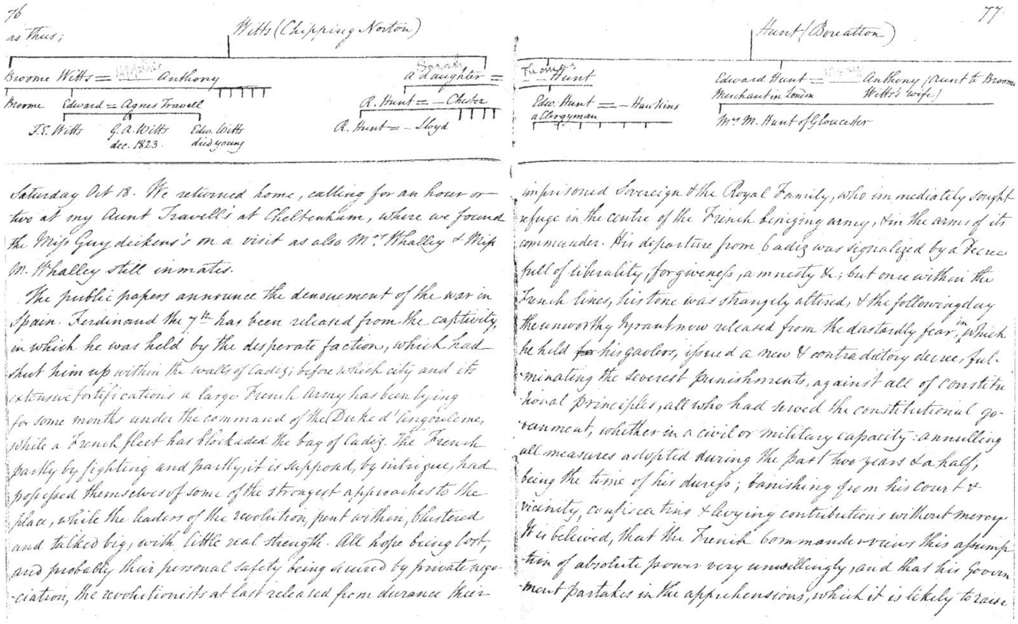

165. Family pedigree from Diary

Saturday Oct. 18.

We returned home, calling for an hour or two at my Aunt Travell's at Cheltenham, where we found the Miss Guydickens's on a visit as also Mrs. Whalley & Miss M. Whalley still inmates.

The public papers announce the denouement of the war in Spain. Ferdinand the 7th has been released from the captivity, in which he was held by the desperate faction, which had shut him up within the walls of Cadiz; before which city and its extensive fortifications a large French Army has been lying for some months under the command of the Duke d'Angouleme, while a French fleet has blockaded the bay of Cadiz. The French partly by fighting and partly, it is supposed, by intrigue, had possessed themselves of some of the strongest approaches to the place, while the leaders of the revolution, pent within, blustered and talked big, with little real strength. All hope being lost, and probably their personal safety being secured by private negociation, the revolutionists at last released from durance their |77 imprisoned Sovereign & the Royal Family, who immediately sought refuge in the centre of the French besieging army, & in the arms of its commander. His departure from Cadiz was signalized by a Decree full of liberality, forgiveness, amnesty &c; but once within the French lines, his tone was strangely altered, & the following day the unworthy tyrant now released from the dastardly fear, ^in^ which he held ~~for~~ his gaolers, issued a new & contradictory decree, fulminating the severest punishments, against all of constitutional principles, all who had served the constitutional government, whether in a civil or military capacity: annulling all measures adopted during the past two years & a half, being the time of his duress; banishing from his court & vicinity, confiscating & levying contributions without mercy. It is believed, that the French Commander views this assumption of absolute power very unwillingly, and that his Government partakes in the apprehensions, which it is likely to raise. |78 The Spanish monarch and his protector are returning to Madrid, and a French Army of occupation will, doubtless, be left in Spain to curb the revolutionary temper, which such bitter decrees are likely to foster. It does not appear that the Constitutional force in Catalonia is yet reduced, and like principles seem ready to burst out in other quarters.

Sunday Oct. 19.

The papers announce the unexpected return of Captains Parry & Lyon with their crews from the Northern Seas, bringing home their vessels in safety: and having lost four or five men from accident, and organic complaints. They have not accomplished their object, the discovery of a North West Passage from the Atlantic to the Pacific, which in this expedition they endeavoured to find in a lower latitude, than in their former voyages: in the course of the three summers & two winters of Captn. Parry's absence they have explored the perilous regions of Hudson's bay & the adjacent frozen seas, & were stopped in their progress westward by a barrier of eternal ice; so that in all probability, the impracticability |[79] of obtaining a passage this way to the Pacific ocean will be considered as satisfactorily proved. The ships have been, it is said, in much danger, but the excellent discipline, abundant and well selected provisions, nautical skill and intrepidity of the officers & crew, have surmounted all difficulties. Frequent & long intercourse was kept up with some Esquimaux tribes, and much detail of the manners & habits of these ignorant natives will be furnished to the public; it is doubted, whether the collections in natural history; mineralogy, botany &c. are very extensive or important. The expedition of course returned from the Northward. Public curiosity has been much excited by the return of these adventurous mariners, & general gratulation in the public prints and otherwise has attended them. Captn. Parry has been an object of much observation, & even his private concerns have been obtruded into the newspapers. It is said, that on enquiring for the lady, with whom he had formed a matrimonial engagement, Miss Browne, my distant relative, he learnt, that her affections had wavered during his absence, and his hopes of happiness |[80] in an union with her were frustrated. It is added, that the disappointment weighed so heavily on him as to bring on a most alarming & for sometime dangerous attack of illness. Of the correctness of these reports I cannot speak; time will develop their truth: certainly, rumour had anticipated poor Parry's disappointment. The Browne family were not at their house in Town, when Captn. Parry arrived: they were or had been staying at Malvern.—

A melancholy occupation awaited me this evening in looking over some boxes, forwarded from Falmouth, containing my poor brother's effects, papers &c. There is nothing of much value or importance. A few letters from private friends in the army, & a great many of mine & my Mother's addressed to him for some years past:[52] About 50 volumes of Latin & Italian Classics with some French books, but no good editions; brief marginal notes shew how diligently he had studied some of these Authors. But the most valuable proof of his studious habits and cultivated talents is a collection of Common Place books, 14 Vols. closely written

52. Few letters to George Witts survive in the Witts Family Papers, and none of those from Frank or his mother addressed to George. It may be presumed that Frank destroyed them. They would, in all likelihood have been rather embarrassing to the family and Frank would not have wanted to see critical letters from him and his mother to his now deceased sibling. The letters from George merit publication and will provide retirement enjoyment for this poor editor.

with an index, containing extracts of the |[81] most striking passages, which occurred in his very various course of reading in various languages, chiefly Latin, English, French and Italian. One Vol. of these is unfortunately missing; other volumes of printed works are not to be found: and we suspect, from the absence of many articles, which one must suppose him to have been possessed of, that various things have been abstracted in some way or other during his last melancholy illness, the hurry of his departure from Malta, or on the Voyage & arrival of the Packet in England.—[53]

Tuesday Oct. 21.—

I attended a meeting of the Trustees of the Gloucestershire District of the Crickley Hill Turnpike road: the district extends from Barrington to Crickley Hill in the direction of Gloucester, and towards the top of Dowdeswell Hill in the line of Cheltenham. It is now in agitation to avoid the latter steep & dangerous declivity by a deviation on the left of the road at the foot of the Dowdeswell Hill, winding ~~up~~ gently [up] the valley behind the Parsonage House, passing between Sandywell Park and the Village of ~~Wit~~ Whittington, crossing the Stow road at Andoversford, & rejoining the old London |[82] road just above Frogmill Inn: these alterations will be within the district of the Cheltenham Commissioners. After our business was concluded the Trustees dined together at the King's Head Inn; Lord Sherborne presided. Mess[rs.] Pole, Browne, Rice, Greenaway, Ford, Price, Hicks &c. were present.

Thursday Oct. 23.

We dined at M[r.] Pole's at Wick Hill, meeting Miss Mitford, (Lord Redesdale's daughter) M[r.] Buller, (M[r.] C. Pole's clerical Brother) the Jeaffresons & the Croomes, besides the different Members of M[r.] Pole's family.

Friday Oct. 24.

Stow Fair. M[r.] Large came to dine & sleep here. Renewed hopes of letting my rectorial farm.

Saturday Oct. 25.

Agreed with M[r.] John Davis, now tenant to M[r.] James Commeline, the Rector of Cowley in this County; for the occupation of my rectorial farm at the low rent of £140 per ann. about 13/ per acre, on an average of green land & arable. I am moreover to find him a house, or build one by midsummer next. There is a prospect of procuring |[83] that belonging to M[r.] Dolphin's farm in this parish, and tenanted by M[r.] R. Collett, of Bourton Mill. M[r.] Davis was formerly tenant to Lord Sherborne at Hinchwick & is considered a good farmer. He has been imprudent, but it is to be hoped, he has sown his wild oats. I was on the point of embarking in agriculture myself, had not this opportunity of letting the farm presented itself: other applicants had not offered more than 10/ or 11/ per acre. M[r.] J. Davis is to hold the farm for 7 years with the same privileges on his lease terminating as Gregory enjoyed. For

53. This is very puzzling for these Common Place books do not survive in the Witts Family Papers, and yet the comment that: '. . . *one of these is unfortunately missing*.' Seems to indicate that Frank held them in some value and it is unlikely he would have destroyed them. In fact, so much survives in the family papers that their disappearance is surprising as well as disappointing. It may well be that they are there and misattributed. A further search is called for.

the first 12 years of my incumbency my farm was let at £250 per annum. Mr. Large having assisted me in my arrangements with Davis, as also in settling other matters in dispute with W. Gregory, left us this day.

Tuesday Oct. 28.

Received the news of the decease of poor Mrs. C. Keysall, who died at Bredon on Thursday last.

Thursday Oct. 30.

My mother arrived from Stanway. The party there is broken up. Lady Rossmore, who had been joined by her Lord a few days before, has set out for Ireland. Lady Elcho goes in two or three days to London, where she |*84* is anxious to be near her son, Lord Wemyss, who is at his house in Stratford Place, in very bad health.[54] His Countess and unmarried daughters are with him; it was expected, that they would have come to Stanway in the beginning of this month; but Lord Wemyss's internal complaints grew so much more alarming on his arrival in London from Scotland, that his Physicians would not recommend him to leave Town. Though still very ill, it appears, that he has benefited by the attendance of Sir H. Halford & Dr. Luke.

After a day of severe rain, with a cold wind, the evening and night were very tempestuous, with sleet snow & rain.

Friday Oct. 31.

On rising this morning we were informed of the devastations of the storm last night. In our pleasure ground we have lost a very fine stately elm, the pride of the lawn, blown down without committing any injury. In the shady walk four or five fine elms have been uprooted. In the orchard a very handsome & productive spreading apple tree, besides smaller trees and limbs scattered in all directions over the grounds.

|*85*

Saturday Nov. 1.

"Bishop Jebb's (Limerick) Primary charge to his clergy 1823" A very pious, and judicious exhortation to the clergy, peculiarly applicable to the circumstances of the Irish church, but in most respects conveying valuable lessons to the Ministers of the Church of England. Many important points are ably touched, clerical studies and amusements, the proper modes of catechizing, preaching & reading the church service, attention to the temporal as well as spiritual interests of the poor: &c. The difficulties and peculiar duties of the clergy in the South of Ireland are discussed: residence, & parochial schools are especially noticed. The

54. Francis Charteris, (1772-1853), Baron Wemyss, 1821; Earl of Wemyss, 1826. Francis was the son of Lord and Lady Elcho. The earldom had been held under attainder after Francis' great-uncle, David Wemyss, had fought on the wrong side at Culloden. He was educated at Eton and then became A.D.C. to his maternal great-uncle, Lord Adam Gordon, commander of forces in Scotland, 1793-97. On his father's death he styled himself Lord Elcho and a few months later on the death of his grandfather, styled himself Earl of Wemyss notwithstanding the attainder. In 1810, on the death of his distant cousin, William Douglas, 4th Duke of Queensbury he inherited large estates in Peeblesshire including the castle and Barony of Neidpath. In 1826 he managed to attain the reversal of the attainder, and formally became 6th Earl of Wemyss. He married, in 1794, Margaret, 4th daughter of Walter Campbell. She died at Gosford in 1850. See the introduction in volume 1 and the Biographical Index for fuller detail of the family.

Irish Bench has reason to rejoice in the accession of a Prelate, so pious, earnest, and diligent, possessed also of valuable learning of a professional nature.[55] D$^{r.}$ Jebb has been author of a Vol. of Sermons, & of a work entitled Sacred Literature, comprising a review of the principles of composition laid down by Bp. Lowth, & an application of those principles to the illustration of the New Testament; an ingenious work.

The development of the unfortunate rupture between |[86] Cap$^{tn.}$ Parry & Miss Emily Browne has arrived sooner than I expected, in a copy of a letter on the subject from Miss Sabine, (Aunt to the young Lady,) to M$^{rs.}$ M. Hunt, and by her transmitted to us. It seems, that this Miss Browne is the same, who in early days was guilty of a juvenile indiscretion & elopement with a boy gardener at North Mims; of this I had heard before, and of the speedy separation of the silly fugitives on being pursued. When Cap$^{tn.}$ Parry paid his addresses, M$^{r.}$ Browne honourably told him her whole history: and then surely he should have retracted his offer, if he considered the past misconduct a bar to his prospect of happiness: nor could he then have been blamed. But during his late absence Parry's family has come to the knowledge of this transaction, which has so set them against the connection, that on Cap$^{tn.}$ Parry's return to England, & subsequent to his waiting on M$^{r.}$ Browne who was in Town, & writing very affectionately to Miss Browne in Worcestershire, they imparted to him the information they had collected coupled with the dying request of his |[87] Father, the late D$^{r.}$ Parry of Bath, whom on departing for his last voyage he had left in the last stage of paralysis, that this union should not be carried into effect. Contending emotions very readily understood threw him in^{to} a state of fever & delirium; Miss Browne, by her Father's advice, relinquished her claims to his hand on the ground of the prejudices existing in the minds of his family; & Capt. Parry, probably, under the advice & influence of his family expressed his resolution not to fulfil his engagements, a resolution of not marrying the lady, which he had timed better on the first hearing of her youthful faux pas. Such is the statement proceeding from the Brownes: and if true Capt. Parry though placed in a most painful dilemma is not in my view free from blame: but audi alteram partem.[56]

Sunday Nov. 9.

"A discourse concerning Baptismal & Spiritual Regeneration. By Sam$^{l.}$ Bradford D.D. then Rector of S$^{t.}$ Mary le Bow, London: afterward Lord Bish. of Rochester."[57] A very valuable, plain & orthodox discourse on the delicate subject of Regeneration & Renovation; republished for circulation by |[88] the Society for Promoting Christian Knowledge.—

Tuesday Nov. 11—

"Travels in various countries of Europe, Asia, & Africa by Edward Daniel Clarke. L.L.D. Part the third. Scandinavia Section the second 1823". This is the last of the six quarto

55. John Jebb, (1775-1833), Bishop of Limerick, Ardfert and Aghadoe. Jebb was well known as an author of sacred literature and had the reputation of a revivalist.
56. audi alteram partem — hear the other side.
57. Samuel Bradford had been chaplain to William III and then to Queen Anne. He became rector of St. Mary-le-bow in 1693, was later Bishop of Carlisle and finally, Bishop of Rochester. He was Dean of Westminster, 1723-31.

volumes containing this eminent traveller's account of some of those countries, which he has traversed; for we have no mention of France, Italy or Germany, which he visited. Denmark, Norway, Sweden, Lapland, Russia, Turkey, Greece, the Troad, the Archipelago, Egypt, Palestine &c. have afforded to his cultivated mind, active research, and acute powers of observation, a fine field. His volumes have been published at distant intervals; the first commenced with the tour thro' Russia, & its southern Provinces, both European & Asiatic, to Turkey: the portion last published narrates events preceding in order of time the journey thro' Russia, & refers to the years 1800 & 1801. The present volume is posthumous; but the larger portion was prepared by the author for the Press, and the concluding chapters have been compiled by his friends from his Journals. The style & matter is very interesting; Dr. Clarke seems to have been as partial |89 to the Norwegian & Swedish character, as he was disgusted with the Russian. The mines & minerals of Norway and Sweden are well suited ~~for~~ to the bent of the author's scientific researches; he is quite at home in all that relates to mineralogy & geology. He was professor of the former at Cambridge: the Library and Museum of which University he has much enriched by his collections made abroad. He was also an excellent classical scholar: an accurate enquirer into points of history and traits of character. It is no wonder, that he ranks so high among our writers of Travels. In this vol. we are conducted from Christiania thro' the Mines of Norway & Sweden to Upsala & Stockholm. Thence by a most dangerous winter journey and voyage he crossed the Gulph of Bothnia, visited the Aland Isles, the University of Abo, and other places in Finland, thro' which his route lay to Petersburg. The friends of Dr. Clarke are preparing a quarto Vol. to be published by Subscription, containing a Memoir of his life, copious extracts from his Journals, Letters &c. & some discourses prepared for public occasions.

——— |90

Wednesday Nov. 12.

Frederick Aston came from Stanway on a short visit.

———

Saturday Nov. 15.

Our friend Frederick returned home to-day.

———

Tuesday Nov. 18.

We had a dinner party. Mr. Ford, Mr. Croome, Mr. Hurd, Mr. Jones, Mr. F. Aston were our guests. F. Aston slept here.

———

Wednesday Nov. 19.

Mr. F. Aston left us.

———

Tuesday Nov. 25.

My Mother left us for Cheltenham. Her birthday was on the 23d. she was then 75 years old. Since she has been with us this time, she has never breathed the outward air, and so has avoided the cough often so troublesome to her. Her breathing is at times very bad, and her general health very fluctuating. Her great size makes all motion unpleasant to her, and her want of exercise causes a tendency to sleep in her chair. Her hearing & memory are both impaired, and her spirits droop much in the want of cheerful and varied society.[58] These symptoms of decline cause us much anxiety.

"Five letters addressed to the Rev[d.] G. Wilkins, Vicar of |[91] S[t.] Mary's, Nottingham; containing strictures on some parts of the first volume of a work entitled Body and Soul. By the Rev[d.] J. H. Browne A.M. Archdeacon of Ely, Rector of Colgrave, & late fellow of S[t.] John's College, Cambridge. Lond. 1823." Some months ago the first volume of "Body and Soul" fell in my way, when I perused the greater part of it; a second volume has since been published, which I have not seen. Though disinclined towards books professing to inculcate religious doctrines & principles in the progress of a tale, I was much attracted by what I read. The scene is supposed to be a large country town, and the leading characters the Rector & Curate of the parish, orthodox clergymen, active in their duties, learned, pious, cheerful, and far removed from the peculiar features, which mark the Evangelical clergy. Different sketches are then given of sentiments, habits and conduct in various circumstances ~~if~~ such as may be supposed to have occurred in the different circles and families of a provincial town. D[r.] Freeman & M[r.] Deacon or both ~~form~~ are leading characters in these narratives, which touch |[92] on many very important and interesting points of moral and religious and professional obligation, and particularly lead to a view and criticism of the mode of thinking & line of conduct of the Evangelical Clergy. It appears, that M[r.] Wilkins, whose useful work on the Fall of Jerusalem I noticed above, p 25. is well understood to be one of the anonymous authors of this publication, which was very extensively circulated and read. The Archdeacon of Ely, who, from other publications, was known strongly to favour the Evangelical clergy & their peculiar opinions, here arrays himself against the Authors of what he considers a very dangerous book containing gross and insidious misrepresentation of important doctrines, and certainly it must be allowed, that the writers of Body and Soul merit the charge of having expressed themselves on many points too vaguely and without due precision. The bias of the Archdeacon's mind is very discernible, but it is manifest also, that he is conscientious, and on some points, which he touches, in particular as to clerical amusements, it cannot be denied, |[93] that greater caution as to society and diversions is called for, as to many clergymen, who do not adhere to those views, which are styled Evangelical. M[r.] Wilkins, however warmly opposed by the Archdeacon, (and it seems that much controversial writing has followed, and no small stir ensued among the Nottingham Clergy,) may plead the sanction and patronage of ~~the Metropolitan~~ his Diocesan the Archb. of ~~Canterbury having~~ York, who has lately presented him with a prebend in the Collegiate Church of Southwell.

Thursday Nov. 25.

I dined and slept at D[r.] Warneford's, meeting Lords Redesdale and Northwick, Mr. Pole M[r.] Jeaffreson, M[r.] Ford, M[r.] Saumarez and M[r.] Eyre. Of the former ~~ap~~ peer I have spoken above: Lord Northwick's residence is at Northwick Park, Worcestershire, in the parish of Blockley;

---

58. Agnes Witts, (1748-1825), maintained her own diary from 1788 until 1825, and these provide much important family information. What was not known apart this entry by her son, was that she was a large lady! We did know that cheerful and varied society were important for her, for she bored quickly and had a vital and vibrant mind with a desire for intellectual and stimulating company.

he is advancing in years, still unmarried, a man of very polite manners, rather of the old school; has travelled a great deal, and converses very agreeably on many topics of history & research, which have at different times engaged his attention. He is a connoisseur in coins.

——— |94

Friday Nov. 28.

I returned home.

———

Saturday Nov. 29.

I dined at Mr. Croome's at Bourton on the Water, meeting Mr. Ford.—

———

Wednesday Dec. 3.

"A circumstantial narrative of the campaign in Saxony in 1813. By Baron von Odeleben, Lieut. Col. of Saxon cavalry &c. To which are subjoined the notes of M. Aubert de Vitry Editor of the French Edition. Transl. by Alfred John Kempe. 2 Vols. 8vo. 1820". A very valuable work; and particularly interesting to me, as leading me through scenes, which viewed in early life have strongly impressed themselves on my imagination. Taking up Buonaparte on his advance into Germany to combat the Allies in the spring subsequent to his retreat from Russia, the author, who was attached to his suite, accompanies him from Erfurt to Dresden, describing the actions on the route, particularly that great contest at Lutzen. From Dresden the farther progress of Bonaparte into Lusatia & Silesia is narrated, with the Battles of Bautzen &c. The interval of the Armistice, which Napoleon passed at Dresden, affords the writer an opportunity of describing the arrangements and habits of the extraordinary chief of the French nation and his satellites, in a period of repose from war, but of diplomatic activity |95 and preparation for a renewed contest. This picture of the manners, modes of living, conversation, etiquette, amusements, is to me more valuable than the portraitures of the fallen hero at St. Helena. The author well describes the restlessness and impetuo~~u~~sity of his nature, his extraordinary talents for military operations on a large scale, the subserviency of his dependents, their attachment to his person, the gradual decay of strength & relaxation of discipline in the French armies. At the close of the Armistice we again accompany Napoleon in his advance towards Silesia, in his rapid retreat, in his masterly defence of Dresden; we see the hunters drawing their nets round the hated monster, whose destruction is their object; Austrians, Russians, Prussians, Swedes hemming in the French on every side, till forced to abandon the fine position on the Elbe, the rout towards the plain of Leipzig ensues; on those plains we again witness the frightful agonies of the French armies reduced to the utmost distress, and participate in the triumphs of the Allies, & the horrors of the Saxons. Lastly we accompany the broken & routed legions, following their baffled and moody leader, in an |96 almost total relaxation of discipline; amid hostile attacks on every side, to Erfurt, the point, from which the narrative set out. A second part of the work contains a detailed relation by another hand of all that passed at Dresden, during the campaign of 1813, exhibiting the calamities, to which the inhabitants of a beautiful city & district were subjected during the period, that they were in the centre of military operations on the largest scale. This section of the work fills up the canvas, where Baron Odeleben left it vacant, as he only professes to narrate scenes, of which he was eye witness. The book concludes with a similar narrative of the events at Leipzig before & during the great engagement there, and an Appendix of documents including the official reports of the military operations & the dispatches of the British Diplomatists and Military officers attached to the Allied armies.

Friday Dec. 5.

"The Martyr of Antioch. By the Revd. H. H. Milman, Professor of Poetry in the University of Oxford, Lond. 1822. 8vo." A very beautiful poem, founded on the legend of St. Margaret. The scene is laid at Antioch in the Reign of the Emperor Probus, towards the close of the third century. Much splendid description of |97 the ancient worship of Apollo, the celebrated grove of Daphne, & the rites there performed, with a profusion of mythological lore brought forward in a very poetic form, serves as a contrast to the speeches, sentiments & conduct of the Christian Martyrs, resigned to death, ardent in faith & hope; chief of whom is the Heroine, St. Margaret, daughter of the aged Priest of Apollo, and beloved by Olybius, Prefect of Asia, who strives to win from the newly adopted faith the bride of his choice, but strives in vain, and is the unwilling author of the fierce persecution, in which the Martyrs of Antioch seal their faith with their blood.—

Sunday Dec. 7.

"A Treatise on the nature and constitution of the Christian Church, wherein are set forth the form of its government, the extent of its powers, and the limits of our obedience. By Will. Stevens Esqr." This useful and plain little tract is chiefly abridged from Archbishop Potter's excellent discourse concerning church government, and is circulated by the society for promoting Christian Knowledge. The worthy author is now deceased: he was Treasurer to Queen Anne's Bounty; a pious and zealous Member of our church, among the many able and serious laymen, who not less in the present age than formerly, conscientiously stand forward to approve & support the venerable fabric.

--- |*98*

Tuesday Dec. 9.

We dined at Mr. & Mrs. Rice's, at Oddington Parsonage, meeting Mr. Penystone of Cornwell in Oxfordshire, his son and daughter & Mr. B. F. Twisleton, the new Curate of Adlestrop, in room of Sir H. Dryden. Mr. T. is nephew of Mrs. Leigh Senr. and ~~cousin~~ of Lord Say & Sele;[59] Son of the Hon. & Revd. Mr. Twisleton, Archdeacon of Ceylon, who, by a singular latitude consented to by the Bp. of Gloucester, is Incumbent of the united parishes of Adlestrop and Broadwell, though living in another hemisphere at the time of his institution & induction by proxy. Mr. B. Twisleton is a Fellow of New College, and chaplain to the Bp. of Hereford. The only other guest besides ourselves was Miss Chabuzet, a German relative of Mrs. Hastings, widow of the late distinguished Governor General of India, who continues in advanced life

59. Gregory William Twisleton, (1769-1844), 14th Lord Saye and Sele. The new curate of Adlestrop was Frederick Benjamin Twisleton, (1799-1887). This young curate was destined to become 16th Lord Saye and Sele (1847-87) after the deaths of both his uncle and cousin. He was curate of Adlestrop, 1823-5, then rector of Adlestrop and Broadwell, 1825-52. He became Prebendary of Hereford, 1825 and Canon Residentiary, 1840; Archdeacon of Hereford, 1863-87. His wife was Emily, 2nd daughter of Richard Wingfield, 4th Viscount Powerscourt. She died in 1837, and he married secondly, 1857, Caroline, 3rd daughter of Chandos Leigh, 1st Baron Leigh of Stoneleigh. Twisleton features extensively in the diaries from this point onwards.

to reside at Dalesford. Mrs. Hastings's German extraction & early history is well known. The drawing room was filled with the Rice's numerous rising family. The eldest son is a great invalid, and at present unable to reside at Oxford; the second is deficient in intellect.

——— |99

Monday Dec. 15.

Mr. Newmarch, the Solicitor of Burford, dined and slept here; transacted some business with him.

———

Tuesday Dec. 16.

Mr. Newmarch left us after breakfast.

———

Wednesday Dec. 17.

The arrival of our dear Edward from school for the Holidays was a source of unfeigned delight to us. His grandmother Backhouse accompanied him from Gloucester, to spend the Christmas with us. Our joy was not a little heightened by the excellent report, which Mr. Hale gives us of general good conduct, and proficiency in learning. The latter, indeed, is fully attested by his bringing home a very handsome ~~and~~ silver medal, which was presented to him at the public examination of the school on Saturday last. Three of these Medals are distributed, being the annual gift of the Marquis of Salisbury; the custom having originated with the present Marquis's father. The other two are gilt. Edward is, I believe, the youngest boy in his class; he was examined in the first book of Virgil's Æneid.

——— |100

Thursday Dec. 18.

The annual meeting of the Trustees of the Cope Charity, who dined together at Stow. I attended as one of the official trustees: viz. as Rector of Upper Slaughter. Several of the surrounding beneficed clergy are trustees; there are few lay trustees, it being expensive to renew the trust as relates to them from such limited resources. The charity is limited to the parishes of Icomb and Stow, agreeably to the provisions of the will of the donor, a Col. Cope, who in 1690 left a rent charge of £33— per ann. on his estates at Icomb. Ten pounds go to the resident Minister of Icomb, where a day school is also maintained. The remainder of the fund, exclusive of a Pound left to meet the expences of the trustees at their annual dinner, is appropriated in charity at Stow, and in aid of the parochial schools there. Mr. Pole, Mr. Ford, Mr. Vavasour, Mr. Hurd & myself were the party. Mr. Pole is not a Trustee: Mr. Vavasour presided, as Rector of Stow. We adjourned to the Rectory to tea and coffee. The morning, as usual on Thursdays, had been devoted to public business in the justice room and Provident Bank Office.

——— |101

Monday Dec. 22.

I dined and slept at Stanway Vicarage with Fred. Aston, meeting a very intelligent and well informed man, apparently of sound principles, the Revd. Mr. Plumptre, Senior Tutor and fellow of University College. He is a nephew of the Dean of Gloucester. I also met Mr. Wynniatt of Stanton.

———

Tuesday Dec. 23.

Very early in the morning, before I rose, I received a letter from my wife, inclosing a card of invitation to attend the funeral of Mrs. Judith Lightbourne.[60] She had rightly judged, that I should consider this mark of respect indispensable; and after breakfast I left Stanway in a post chaise, for which I had sent from Broadway, and reached Cheltenham by half past one o clock. The road to Winchcomb is better than it used to be, and a great alteration has been made between that town & Southam, by which the road is carried round the tremendous hill, which it formerly ascended only to sink again into the vale by a precipitous descent. By thus skirting Cleeve Cloud there is no very heavy draught, but in many places the road, which was opened last |*102* summer, is in a very founderous state.

On arriving at my mother's, I had the grief to find her extremely ill; she had been attacked with one of those violent inflammations on the chest, to which she is so subject, and had been in considerable danger on the preceding day. Mr. Wood, the Apothecary, who has long attended her, was on the alert, and by copious bleeding and a blister the inflammation was now considerably abated, though she continued to labour much in breathing, and great stillness and quiet were absolutely necessary. A letter had been written by Mr. Wood to apprize us at Upper Slaughter of this dangerous seizure. My arrival at this juncture was very fortunate, and as the day advanced, the favourable symptoms continuing, there seemed not to be any necessity to change the arrangements, which I had already made for the next day. I called on Mrs. Travell & Mrs. Whalley, and drank tea with my mother's intimate friend, Mrs. Cooke, & her daughter, Mrs. Devonsher.

——— |*103*

Wednesday Dec. 24.

Finding, that my mother had passed a good night under the influence of opiate, and that no unfavourable symptom had shewed itself, I resorted at the early hour of ½ past eight in a mourning coach to the residence of the late Mrs. Lightbourne in a small street near the bottom of the town, where with her sisters, now deceased, she had resided since first their claim to the estates and fortune of the late Mrs. ~~Travell~~ Tracy of Sandy well Park was made. Mrs. Tracy was the heiress of a Sir William Dodwell, some time a Lord Mayor of London, originally from Sevenhampton, a village on the Hills, who dying, when his only child, this daughter, was an infant, left her a ward of Mrs. Tracy of Stanway. With her considerable property, amounting to £70000, the estate, mansion & park at Sandywell, Estates in Whittington and Sevenhampton, the Manor and principal estate at Upper Slaughter, and the advowsons of Whittington, Upper Slaughter and Badgworth were purchased. In due course of time one of Mr. Tracy's sons, an uncle of my Mother, became the husband of Miss Dodwell, and |*104* residing at Sandywell park was representative of Gloucestershire in Parliament. Their only son, Dodwell, dying before he arrived at man's estate, and Mrs. Tracy surviving her husband many years, the full disposal of the property rested with her. Of her father's family she had little knowledge, nor seemed solicitous to seek them out: chiefly living with the various branches of her husband's family. She survived till the close of the last century, and from a dislike of making a will, perhaps, also from not being quite aware or properly informed of the near approach of her latter end, she died intestate. An heir to her

60. Judith Lightbourne was the last survivor of the three Timbrell sisters. They had inherited much of the Tracy estate including the advowson of Upper Slaughter and through their patronage Francis Witts had been presented with the living in 1808.

personal property, which was extensive, was soon found in Lady Farnaby Radcliffe; but it was more difficult to ascertain, who were entitled to her real estates. Many claimants, all in very humble stations of life, started up, and among them three sisters of the name of Timbrell, descendants of a goldsmith in London, the younger of whom was the wife of one Lightbourne. The Attorneys, Welles, Gwynnett & Newmarch, who succeeded to the office in Cheltenham of Mrs. Tracy's Steward, Mr. Mark- |[105] -ham, took up and prosecuted at their own expence and hazard the cause of these sisters, and after much research, many difficulties, and great anxiety, established their claim in such a manner, as to leave little doubt of their ultimate success. At this juncture, in 1805, it occurred to my Father and Mother to make themselves known to the three sisters, and to solicit their patronage for me on the decease of my uncle Ferdinand Travell, the Rector of Upper Slaughter. The three sisters were pleased with the attention paid to them by a branch of the Tracy family, none of whom had before in any way recognised them, and on a subsequent interview, when I was introduced to them, gave me the promise of the living of Upper Slaughter, when it should be vacant, if my character and conduct in the interval should be such as to merit their patronage. They said, they should have satisfaction in doing what Mrs. Tracy had left undone, and as I was her godson, they considered my claim to patronage from her as strong. The humble station, in which these persons had moved, accounted for their want of education, manners, & neatness; their prejudices also |[106] were proportionally stronger; the elder was a woman of strong sense, but with a mixture of craft and violence of temper, which pervaded the others. In the interval between 1805 and 1808 a decree of court put them in possession of the Estates in litigation, with the exception of the Manor and land at Upper Slaughter, which they were advised to give up to two claimants Williams & Lea, whose pretensions were plausible, and their supporters active. As a continuance of litigation was much to be deprecated by the Timbrells, now advancing in years, an arrangement was adopted for terminating the cause by relinquishing in favour of Lea & Williams the Slaughter property, but when the Advowson of the Rectory was also demanded, the sisters said nay; they had promised the next presentation, and they would keep their word. This honourable adherence to their promise cannot in their circumstances be too highly appretiated; and to it I owe my institution. It has been my rule ever since to shew these Ladies every respect |[107] by occasional calls, and testimonies of my gratitude; but I was always anxious to avoid the imputation of hunting for a legacy, and unwilling to subject myself to the vexations attendant not only on their caprice, but on their low and vulgar habits. At times, indeed, I might from their language have fancied myself in high favour: earnest injunctions have been laid upon me not to do such & such things, when I should succeed to the Sandywell Property; with not ambiguous hints, that I was the fortunate object of selection; at other times I have been called on to vindicate their rights against supposed aggression; and Mrs. Lightbourne at one time decidedly promised to execute a deed conveying the advowson of Upper Slaughter to me and my heirs for ever; a measure which she chose afterwards to decline; nor have I seen her since, though I have frequently called on her. She was aware, probably, that she was not now free from the charge of flying from her word.—Rumour has long been busy about the disposal of Mrs. Lightbourne's property |[108] after her death; her elder sisters, dying according to their seniority, had left her sole proprietor. It had been for some time pretty well known, that the bulk of the fortune would centre in the family of Mr. W. Morris, brother of the late banker at & member for Gloucester, who by his marriage with the heiress of the Lawrence's, a yeoman's family at Sevenhampton, possessed a good estate in that parish, and whose son has assumed the name of Lawrence, with the immediate enjoyment of some of his grandfather's property, since coming of age. The young man has been well educated, & was gentleman-commoner of Magdalen Coll. Oxford, but is said to be of expensive habits. He was some time since engaged to the eldest Miss Browne of Salperton; but a little display of temper on the part of the Gentleman, some difficulties as to a settlement, & a want of gentility on the side of the Lover—brought the affair to a close, which had not been anticipated. It might have been otherwise, could the possession of the Sandywell property at so early a time, and Mr. Lawrence's emancipation from Mrs. Lightbourne's controul & caprice, have been certainly anticipated. In a word, Walter Lawrence |*108* is now the heir, to the exclusion even of a life interest to his father & mother, which was secured to them in a former will; and he owes his good fortune to the unwearied assiduity of his parents in their attention to all the wayward caprice, & to their bold indifference to all the low suspicions & vulgar surmises, and not less vulgar habits of the old lady, cujus hæreditatem captabant. It is singular also, that there was no affinity in the case, nor do I think the Timbrells had any surviving relatives; there was not even old intimacy or regard; on the contrary at times the Morris's & Lawrence's were objects of bitter sarcasm and vituperation. But in a lucky moment Mr. W. Morris contrived to lend the old ladies a large sum of money to enable them to pay off the bill of their then legal adviser, a Mr. Thompson of London, & so connected himself with them as that they were unable afterwards to disengage themselves. Mr. Thompson had at one period the good fortune of being the intended heir; but on some offence given the will made in his favour was rescinded. Dr. Christie, a skilful and worthy physician of Cheltenham, a native of Scotland, and formerly |*110* a practitioner in the Island of Ceylon has been lucky enough to secure to himself the advowson of the living of Badgworth, which he intends for his eldest son, and it is now held by a Mr. Hill. Mr. Gwynnett, an Attorney at Cheltenham, & who laboured hard to establish the claim of the Timbrells, a speculating man, much immersed in various business, and anything but prosperous, has after ~~various~~ many vicissitudes in the estimation of the three sisters, continued to secure to himself a noble legacy; some accounts raise it to £24000. This is a person, whom I have heard them belabour in no measured terms: how he regained the good opinion of Mrs. Lightbourne, himself & Mr. W. Morris but know. People of the name of Clifford are said to be handsomely provided for in the will, and as they were the humble & useful domestic friends of the deceased and her sisters, ministering to their comforts & contributing to their ease by bearing their wayward humours, and affording them a society suitable to their habits, it is well, that they have been properly considered. Mr. Fowler, the Apothecary of Cheltenham, is also reported to have been left a legacy. Such |*111* are the rumours current as to the disposal of Mrs. Lightbourne's property, and they are probably true in the main. She, poor old soul, was to be deposited with no little pomp, as her two sisters had been before her, in a vault, which they have retained during the fallen fortunes of their family, that they might tenant it at the close of a life probably not rendered happier or more virtuous by the unexpected succession to a considerable estate. This vault is in a burial ground in the Eastern part of London, & thither Mr. Hicks of Whittington was to proceed to enter the remains of the last survivor of his Patronesses. The funeral procession, which set out with due ceremony from Cheltenham, was to be broken up at Kilkenny, on the extremity of the Sandywell Estate, and the chief mourners, (in garb, if not in spirit) Lawrence, Morris, Gwynnett &c., were to rejoin the undertaker with his charge on Saturday in London. A breakfast awaited us, while Mr. Nicholson was marshalling his sable bands. The funeral party consisted of Mr. Jervis & Mr. Davis, as officiating Clergy of the parish of Cheltenham, Mr. Hicks, Mr. Hill, & myself, as incumbents of the |112 three livings of which Mrs. L. was Patroness; Mr. Gwynnett, Dr. Christie, & two Messrs. Fowlers. In an adjoining room were the chief mourners and their friends: Mr. W. Morris, Mr. R. Morris of the Gloucester bank, now resident at Cheltenham to superintend the branch of the establishment there, his cousin Walter Lawrence, and a friend of his Mr. Trye, of Leckhampton, a young man, recently come to his estate, whom I occasionally meet on the bench at the Quarter Sessions. It was midday before we reached the verge of the Sandywell property at Kilkenny, when the mourning coaches & attendant carriages with their company, after some delay, retraced their way to Cheltenham, & I, having sent for a Post-chaise to Frogmill, returned to Upper Slaughter.

Friday Dec. 26.

"Reliquiæ diluvianæ, or observations on the organic remains contained in caves, fissures and diluvial Gravel, and on other Geological Phenomena attesting the action of an universal deluge. By the Revd. W. Buckland B.D. &c.—Lond. 1823. 4to" A very important work, and interesting not |113 only to the professed man of science (a title, to which, I am sure, I have no pretensions) but to the divine on account of its confirmation of a general deluge at no very remote period of the earth, and such a deluge too as Moses has described, to the general reader, on account of the novelty and curiosity of the facts brought forward, and to the lover of logical reasoning by the close inductions, which the author draws in the fairest, and most unpretending manner from the facts adduced. Dr. Copleston, President of Oriel, high authority on such points, speaks of the work in the most flattering terms as an admirably supported argument. Mr. Buckland is Fellow of Corpus Xti Coll. Oxford, and Professor of Geology.[61] I remember him as an undergraduate, much esteemed by his acquaintance, but by no means expected to strike out new lights in science. He is enthusiastically devoted to that, to which he has applied all the strength of his mind, and a large fund of good sense, activity of body, and health. The ingenious manner, in which in his lectures he unfolds his system, demonstrates, & solves difficulties suggested, is much praised. Of British Geologists he must doubtless be called facile princeps; and is in constant |114 communication with the other scientific men, who follow the same pursuit in England, enriching the Geological Society's transactions with most valuable contributions. He is also in correspondence with the eminent Geologists of the Continent, particularly with the celebrated Cuvier, and his researches not having been confined to Great Britain, he has had the opportunity of visiting the collections & conferring with the Collectors and Virtuosi of France, Germany &c. In Mr. Buckland's inaugural Lecture, he mentioned the notion, which he, in common with other men of science, held respecting the creation, & which they conceive reconcileable with the Mosaic account, viz. to understand by the six days of creation, six periods of definite but long duration. The present work is intended to shew, that the structure of the earth, & the

61. William Buckland, (1784-1856), Professor of Geology and Minerology at Oxford.

organic remains contained in it bear testimony to an universal deluge, totally covering the earth, & producing most essential changes at a period comparatively speaking not very remote; thus bearing the torch before the sacred historian. The recently discovered caves in this Country & those in Germany long known, & accurately examined, and of late explored by Mr. Buckland himself |115 afford most important data for his reasoning; and much as everyone was tempted to smile, when they first heard, that a den of antediluvian hyænas had been discovered in Yorkshire, near Kirby Moorside, 20 miles to the N. of York, strewed with the bones of themselves & their prey, including all sorts of animals from an elephant & rhinoceros to a water rat & field mouse, yet it is impossible to read Mr. Buckland's reasoning without becoming a convert to his inferences. The work is illustrated with engravings of views, maps, plans, fossile remains &c.—and consists of very minute descriptions of, and reasonings on the celebrated Yorkshire cave, and its contents, the caves near Plymouth, others in Derbyshire, & Glamorganshire, those in the Mendip Hills, the celebrated caves of Germany, the osseous breccia of Gibraltar & other coasts of the Mediterranean; most valuable remarks are to be found in this work on diluvial & alluvial soil, the denudation of vallies, the effects of the deluge in transporting huge masses of rock and gravel &c. In this part of the work is a most interesting statement of the course of the vast bed of gravel, which may be traced from the primitive rock of the Lickey, down |116 the valley of the Stour into the great bason of Moreton in Marsh, thence by the valley of the Evenlode into that of the Isis, where meeting at Oxford with a similar bed deriving its origin from Lincolnshire & rolled down the valley of the Cherwell, the united stream proceeds along the Thames everywhere capable of being traced & often found in large quantities till it is lost as it were in Hyde Park. There are some very interesting remarks on the structure of the Cotswold hills, particularly as indicative of diluvial action, and an especial reference to the appearances of this neighbourhood, viz: on the line of road from Stow to Cirencester. On the whole, the public is greatly indebted to Mr. Buckland for having so thoroughly combined himself with his science, and the University of Oxford has great reason to be proud and grateful to her Geologist; for so thoroughly has he united himself with his Professorship, that he has recently presented the University with his very valuable collections, which will be deposited in the Ashmolean Museum, where he lectures.

——— |117

Thursday Dec. 30th.

I again repaired to Cheltenham to visit my poor mother, whom I found still in a very precarious state. Her breathing having become worse recourse had again been had to bleeding, which succeeded in abating the inflammation. She was still quite confined to her bed.—

———

1824

Thursday Jan 1.

I returned from Cheltenham, leaving my mother very weak and ill, but, as we trusted, not in immediate danger.

Friday Jan 2.

"Body and Soul. 2 Vols. 12mo 1823". Of this publication I made some mention above at the time when I read Archdeacon Browne's strictures on the first volume. I have now attentively read both volumes the latter having been published subsequently to M$^{r.}$ Browne's pamphlet, and contains a long article on Evangelism, stoutly & ingeniously defending the sentiments & opinions of the former volume. The authors pursue their design of enforcing under the agreeable form of narratives now lively |[118] and now serious or pathetic, the leading doctrines and duties of religion, inculcating sound views of rational Piety and discountenancing the affectation of moroseness or the assumption of exclusive righteousness. Some of the chapters are very good, in some there is too much levity, in others it is to be feared some personality of allusion. I understand, that D$^{r.}$ Wilkins is not the author of the principal part of the work, but that it is chiefly to be attributed to his curate in the parish of S$^{t.}$ Mary's Nottingham. The poetry, of which a good deal is inserted, is uniformly below mediocrity. On the whole the work fell short of my expectations.

Wednesday Jan 7.

Information, which we had received that my Aunt Travell had been taken ill, and was in danger, induced me to go over to Cheltenham this day. I found my mother still very weak & confined to her chamber, and my aunt relieved from the alarming |[119] attack, which had endangered her life. Her disorder was an obstruction of the bowels; but though she has obtained present ease, I cannot help anticipating a decay at no distant time. The constitution cannot stand many shocks at 85 years of age, and the digestive organs seem to perform their office very insufficiently. I found the poor old lady grateful for my attention, devout, and placid.

Thursday Jan. 8.

I returned home.

Monday Jan. 12.

I left Upper Slaughter to attend the Quarter Sessions. At Northleach I took a place in the Regulator, & reached Wellington Parade by 7 o clock P.M. In passing thro' Cheltenham I had made hasty enquiries and found that both my mother and aunt were going on tolerably well.

Tuesday Jan. 13.

The Quarter Sessions commenced. D$^{r.}$ Cooke presided as Senior Chairman & M$^{r.}$ Cripps as assistant. There was a large meeting of Magistrates; among them were the Duke of Beaufort, Lords Sherborne & Ducie, Sir. W. Hicks, M$^{r.}$ H. Beach & his Son, M$^{r.}$ Holford M.P. |[120] M$^{r.}$ Cooper, M.P. M$^{r.}$ Purnell, D$^{r.}$ Timbrell, M$^{r.}$ R. Bathurst, M$^{r.}$ Byles, M$^{r.}$ Talbot, M$^{r.}$ Goodrich, M$^{r.}$ Baker & his Son, M$^{r.}$ Clifford, M$^{r.}$ Ford, M$^{r.}$ Niblett, M$^{r.}$ Newman, M$^{r.}$ Goldney &c. D$^{r.}$ Cooke apologized for not having summoned the members of the Prison regulation committee appointed at the last sessions, alledging it to be his opinion, that delay was desirable on the subject, as tending to mature deliberations on so important a point, and promised to collect the committee between this & the Easter Sessions. Another Committee, of which I was nominated a member, was formed to ~~cull~~ consider the inequality of the County rates & report to the Court on the propriety of proceeding to a new assessment. The fact of the inequality is well known & admitted; Cheltenham for instance pays no more than many small villages of 250 or 300 inhabitants; and the same is the case as relates to Stroud, Wotton-under-edge & other places, which have vastly increased with the increase of the clothing manufacture. But to produce an equal rate will be next to impossible. The Committee of the Lunatic Asylum was |*121* obliged to apply to the Court for funds to carry on their current expenditure, as well as to pay some outstanding bills for the structure, furniture &c. After much discussion £2500 were voted from the County Purse. The Members of the Committee complain of the tardiness of Parish Officers and Magistrates of the county in sending pauper lunatics, known to be in the county, in consequence of which the Pauper ward continues scantily tenanted; it is answered, that the Committee began their arrangements on too large a scale; but I believe, it is universally admitted, that the institution is admirably conducted and very likely to accomplish its objects in the restoration of many serious cases to sanity.

Friday Jan. 16.

I left Gloucester, and passed the day and slept at Cheltenham. The Sessions were not concluded.—Finding my Mother less well, I delayed my return home till to-morrow. My Aunt Travell continues in a declining and precarious state. Miss Buxton is arrived from London and her attentions will be very valuable to her.

——— |122

Saturday Jan. 17.

I returned home, leaving both my Mother and Aunt better. My dear wife has been suffering during this & the past cold weeks from bilious spasms.

Monday Jan. 19.

"The rights of the English Clergy asserted and the probable amount of their incomes estimated in a letter to the author of Remarks on the consumption of public wealth by the clergy of every nation. By Augustus Campbell, Rector of Wallasey, Cheshire. Liverpool 1823". A valuable pamphlet written in a popular style, correcting the gross exaggerations and misrepresentations current on the subjects treated of: and doubtless a most useful reply to the enemies of the Church, whether serving in the ranks of the Edinburgh Review, or skirmishing in the pages of the Morning Chronicle, or venturing forth to single combat as detached pamphleteers. In this instance the Philistine has been levelled to the ground by ~~shewing~~ the force of a stone hurled from David's sling.

Saturday Jan. 24.

The newspapers announce the death of the Bishop of Lichfield and Coventry in the 81st. year of his age.[62] This prelate, Brother of the great Marquis Cornwallis, succeeded last year to the titles of his nephew, who died in middle life. The Bishop was also Dean of Durham; he was not |*123* remarkable for learning, or the high qualities of mind, but a kind and indulgent man in the various relations of life.

---

62. James Cornwallis, (1742-1823), Bishop of Lichfield and Coventry, 1781-1823. James Cornwallis was the 3rd son of Charles, 1st Earl Cornwallis. His uncle was Frederick Cornwallis, Archbishop of Coventry. He was the author of five sermons.

Tuesday Jan. 27.

Frederick Aston arrived from Stanway to pass two or three days with us.

Saturday Jan. 31.

F. Aston returned to Stanway.

Tuesday Feb. 3.

Mrs. Backhouse left us for Gloucester; carrying our dear boy with her; who will pursue his journey to Lyde House school to-morrow.

Thursday Feb. 5.

Parliament met on Tuesday: the Session was opened by commission, the King having been seized at Brighton with a fit of the gout, which prevented his alledged intention of delivering his speech in person. The Houses are therein congratulated on the prosperity of the Kingdom as evinced by the growing increase of the Revenue, the flourishing state of commerce & manufacturers, the improving condition of agriculture, & the universal tranquillity. Assurances are given, that the external relations of the kingdom afford no reason to apprehend an interruption of peace. The state of Ireland is represented to be ameliorated, but still demanding the cautious & vigilant attention of parliament. Prospects of |[124] a reduction of taxation are held out; although the necessity of a small increase of our forces both naval & military is intimated. This measure is called for by the disturbed state of the West Indian Colonies, which are now greatly agitated and irritated. The well meant, but injudicious and rather fanatical urgency of Messrs. Wilberforce, Buxton & others, forming a strong party in & out of the House of Commons, to advance from the abolition of slave trading to an emancipation of the slaves, and the resolutions of parliament in the last session, that an amendment of their state & improvement in education, religion and morals should be cautiously enterprized, with a view to their emancipation at a distant period, when their advancement in civilization shall entitle them to enjoy the privileges of freedom without danger to themselves or others, have been so artfully misrepresented to the Negroes, partly, as it would seem, thro' the Methodist Missionaries settled in the islands, as to lead them to conclude, that their emancipation was decided on in the Mother country, but withheld wrongfully from them by their Masters & the public authorities in the colonies. This error has led to a spirit of insurrection & an alarming rising of the slaves at Demarara, which was, however, |[125] soon suppressed, & recent symptoms of insubordination have displayed themselves in Jamaica. On the other hand a warm feeling of suspicion and resentment has been excited among the West Indian Resident Proprietors by the measures of Government & the same party at home. They are angry with administration & Parliament for legislating for them, contrary, as they alledge, to their rights, as having Colonial Houses of Assembly, with the members of whom resides the right of initiating Colonial laws. They complain, that the treatment of Slaves has been grossly misrepresented in the speeches and pamphlets of Messrs. Wilberforce &c., and that, on the contrary, the Slaves are generally treated with kindness, so much as to place them in the scale of comforts on a par with, or even above the English labourer. Undoubtedly, there has been great misrepresentation; still there is room for much improvement; & that should be imparted, not, as Messrs. Wilberforce & Co. would wish, by missionaries, representatives of sectarian Interests both in & out of the Church, but by a systematic introduction of a visible church Establishment under one or more Bishops, presiding over a more numerous body of Clergy, who shall devote their talents & zeal |*126* to the inculcation of sound principles of religion & morals, educating the lower orders both black & of mixed colour, according to a sounder system than at present prevails; in short, gradually and effectually, tho' perhaps slowly, leavening the whole lump, and spreading valuable principles thro' every class of the colonial communities.

Saturday Feb. 7.

"A charge delivered at the Visitation in July 1823 By Herbert (Marsh) Lord Bishop of Peterborough". The learned and orthodox prelate addresses his Clergy in temperate and plain language, glancing at the obloquy, with which he has been hunted down, on account of his strenuous endeavours by close examination of Candidates for Orders, & Clergymen nominated to Curacies in his diocese, to exclude from its precincts erroneous & strange & exaggerated tenets. He assures the Clergy, that the satisfaction he has derived in the support & confidence of his brethren of the Diocese & in their co operation in his views, far exceeds the vexations, to which he has been subjected. He speaks with gratulation on the increased number of ~~evening~~ second services established since his arrival in the Diocese, and on the valuable services of the Rural Deans, whom he has revived, as he had before done in the Diocese of Llandaff.

--- |*127*

Sunday Feb. 8.

The ecclesiastical arrangements consequent on the decease of the Earl of Cornwallis are now nearly concluded. Bishop Ryder has accepted the See of Lichfield and Coventry,[63] and his retirement from this Diocese, while it will be deplored by some, will be looked upon with indifference and even satisfaction by others. Every class in the church readily concedes to him the character of piety, gentleness & affability: but his strong bias in favour of persons and establishments & principles of evangelic character renders him an object of suspicion to sound and orthodox churchmen. His partialities are all in favour of the evangelical party, however he may be disinclined to the ultracism of some among them. The Bible Society & the Church Missionary Society, & the Society for the conversion of the Jews, enjoy his warmest support. His house & hospitality are open to the pupils of the leaders of Evangelism, his chaplains are selected from her ranks, and therefore it is not to be wondered at, that the Orthodox beneficed Clergy of the diocese have rarely been seen at the Palace, except, when business called them there. The city of Gloucester is crowded with enthusiasts male & female, lay & clerical, nestling under the shadow of his wing, whose wailings at his departure with be loud. His successor is a Divine of very opposite sentiments, D^r.^ |*128* Bethell,

---

63. Henry Ryder, (1777-1836). Ryder was the third son of Lord Harrowby. He was educated at Eton and St. John's Coolege Cambridge. In 1800 he was appointed to the family living of Sandon in Staffordshire and the following year became Rector of Lutterworth in Leicestershire. Ryder was appointed Canon of Windsor in 1808, Dean of Wells in 1812, Bishop of Gloucester in 1815 and Bishop of Lichfield in 1824. Ryder became an evangelical, and was thus disliked by the centre group of Tory traditionalist clergy, including Francis Witts.

Dean of Chichester, and author of an able treatise on the Question of Regeneration.[64] Dr. Bethell enjoys the patronage of the Duke of Northumberland. The Deanery of Durham vacant by the Decease of the late Bishop of Lichfield & Coventry, is conferred upon Dr. Hall, who has been Dean of Christ Church, since the retirement of Dr. Cyril Jackson. Ampler revenues recommend this removal to Dr. Hall, whose habits of expense have exposed him to difficulties, which mitigated considerably against his respectability and usefulness as Head of Christ Church. Tho' a learned and well intentioned man, his administration of that College has been in some cases very injudicious, particularly as compared with the government of his predecessor. Dr. Samuel Smith, a Canon of Christ Church succeeds to that Deanery, and Mr. Slade to the Deanery of Chichester.—

Tuesday Feb. 10.

"Letters from Spain By Don Leucadio Doblado London 1822. 8vo." This is in many respects a curious & interesting volume. If a writer in Blackwood's Edinburgh Magazine is not incorrect, the author is a Revd. Blanco White,[65] born of British or Irish Roman Catholic Parents settled in Spain, at Seville, and educated among the Dominicans & afterwards at the University for the Roman Catholic Priesthood, into |*129* which he was admitted, and from which in course of time, as new light in literature & a bolder spirit of inquiry than is common in the Romish priesthood gave him sounder ideas, he withdrew, & settling in England, where his studies received a right direction, & a bias to free thinking imbibed from the perusal of French writers was checked, he is become a Minister of our Established church. Such early habits and associations, and such a rending of the veil, calculate the author, under a fictitious name, & throwing his matter into an epistolary form, to furnish a map of curious information on the state of society, religion, education, manners, politics, & intrigues in Spain. He writes with considerable force & spirit. His picture of the prevalent superstition is quite enough to account for the degradation of that land, where enlightened priests are forced to be hypocrites or exposed to persecution, where corruption and dissoluteness debased the first circles of the court and the highest personages of the royal family, and where education is at the lowest ebb. The supposed correspondence extends from 1798 to 1808, and consequently includes that revolution, which led to the Spanish contest by the dethronement of Charles 4 & the accession |*130* of Ferdinand VII: a relation also is given of the first aggressions of the French under Murat, & the simultaneous rising of the Spanish people. There is an excellent

64. Christopher Bethell, (1773-1859). Bethell was educated at Eton and King's College, Cambridge. He became Bishop of Gloucester in 1824 and was promoted to Exeter in 1830 and with months to Bangor.

65. Joseph Blanco White, (1775-1841). Witts refers to White later during the Oxford University Parliamentary contest as 'the celebrated Blanco White'. He was born in Seville and christened José Maria. Of Irish-Spanish descent and in a strong catholic family, he at first was destined for the family mercantile business, but through the influence of his Spanish mother he was channelled towards the church. After six years of study he developed doubts about Christianity, and when the French invaded Spain he fled to Cadiz, and escaped to England in 1810. In London he was helped by Lord Holland and Lord John Russell who had both travelled in Spain and knew the country well. Through the influence of Richard Wellesley was employed by Juigné, a French refugee priest who had become a printer in London to produce a monthly periodical called *Español*. In England he turned once more to Christianity thinking that the Church of England had cast off all of the reasons for his rebellion against religion. After finishing with his magazine work, he signed the 39 articles on 10 August 1814 to qualify himself for acting as an English clergyman. In 1825 he published his *Evidences Against Catholicism* and in 1826 the university of Oxford conferred the M.A. degree on him in recognition of his services to the Church. For more information see the Biographical Index.

chapter on bull fights, others on the Monastic Institutions, the state of society in country towns, the ceremonies observed on the leading fasts & festivals &c.

Saturday Feb. 14.

"Remonstrance addressed to the supporters of the British & Foreign Bible Society on the System of Visitation as introduced by their district Committees, and an earnest appeal to those members, who are professedly attached to the Church of England "Lond. 1823". This pamphlet is by the Rev^d. R. J. Cooper of Gloucester, son of the member for that city, and chaplain to the County Gaol. I have the pleasure of his acquaintance, & do not know a young clergyman of more sound principles, piety, diligence in his professional duties, or rational zeal.[66] The usual strong arguments are drawn forth on this occasion, perhaps, with a little affectation in style, not to be wondered at in a young writer. The restless activity of the Evangelical party at Gloucester, developing itself in their urgent exertions for the Bible, Missionary & kindred Societies was likely to rouse the pen of M^r. R. Cooper, who stands almost alone among the Clergy of the place not connected with the Cathedral, uninfected with the prevalent delusions. See Diary 1. 54.

--- |131

Sunday Feb. 15.

"The Country Clergyman's advice to his Parishioners, explaining what they are to believe and do in order to be saved. Addressed chiefly to those, who are of the younger sort. Lond. 1812". An excellent little tract, from the stores of the Society for promoting Christian Knowledge. I have been reading it to the servants on Sunday Evenings.

Tuesday Feb. 17.

The alienation between M^r. Dolphin and myself had subsisted unaltered up to this time. We rarely met by accident, never in private society, and in public only at the Music meeting, where no recognition of each other occurred. On Friday last, however, an effort was made by two neighbours, men of honourable & benevolent principles, to effect a renewal of the interrupted intercourse between us. This interference on the part of M^r. Egerton Leigh, & M^r. Vavasour was unsolicited on either side, & arose out of a right feeling, that such a difference between two neighbours, one the Pastor, the other the Parishioner, was a matter to be regretted, and which it would be right to make an effort to conciliate. Accordingly, these Gentlemen first waited on M^r. Dolphin at Eyford, who, on learning their views, cordially agreed to terminate the difference by offering me his hand, and making no reference to past points in dispute. The same proposition was then |132 made to me, with an understanding, that the Mediators abstained from entering into the merits of the dispute. They said, the variance between us was generally regretted in the neighbourhood, and urged the usual topics on me. I replied, that I highly appreciated the benevolent feeling, which dictated the interference, & the gentlemanlike manner, in which they had come forward; that as a Christian, and still more as a Christian Minister, I was bound to seek peace & ensue it; that, therefore, I should receive the proposition made to me in the most cordial manner, with this proviso, that it

---

66. Cooper was the brother of Purnell Bransby Purnell who features extensively in the later diaries. The two brothers fell out and Francis Witts was to see the chaplain in a less favourable light.

should not be construed into concession on my part. That they, probably, were very right in restricting themselves & the parties from any discussion of the merits, but that I could not but repeat my full persuasion, that the Parishioners of Upper Slaughter & myself were the injured parties. After assuring me, that no concession was in their contemplation, and that their object was simply the renewal of social intercourse between Mr. D. & myself, the hour for meeting was fixed for one o clock this day, & at Mr. Vavasour's at Stow. We met accordingly: Mr. Dolphin & myself shook hands, nothing was said with reference to the cause of our meeting, and general conversation ensued. Mr. |*133* E. Leigh, Mr. Vavasour, and Mr. Bragge, a relation of Mr. Dolphin's were present. In the course of the half hour, during which we remained together at Mr. V's, Mr. Dolphin invited my wife & myself to dinner on Thursday. It is to be hoped, that good effects will arise from this day's interview: particularly, that the Dolphins may resume their almost forsaken pews in the Church, and so afford to their dependents & poor neighbours a better example than they have done, while their own hearts and principles are meliorated by the exercises of devotion. The past has been a lesson to me for caution in my intercourse with a young man devoid of judgment and deficient in strong principle: we must adopt a steady, natural line of conduct towards the family of Eyford, equally avoiding intimacy as coolness and improper reserve.

Thursday Feb. 19.

I had the gratification to-day of receiving a letter from my old acquaintance, Mr. Stevens, Fellow and Tutor of Wadham College, announcing the termination in his favour of the contest, which has been proceeding for some time for the Vicarage of South Petherwyn, near Launceston, in the gift of the University of Oxford, and vacant by the death of Dr. Shaw of Magdalen College. Three Gentlemen were candidates at first; Mr. Stevens, Mr. Williams, Fellow of Exeter, & |*134* Mr. Moore of Worcester College. The latter soon resigned: but a very warm canvass has been made by the friends of the remaining competitors, in which I have taken an active part, not unattended with success, Mr. Stevens being highly esteemed by me for exemplary character, and sound scholarship, and agreeable manners. I have known him intimately from my first entrance into the University. His claims on the Members of Convocation were strong: for many years engaged as Tutor of his College in the business of the place, and with very slender private means, he was likely to retire from his post without preferment: for his superannuation was at hand, which by the statutes of his College would bar him from any preferment in its gift, and terminate his fellowship, with the poor substitute of an inconsiderable annuity. This superannuation, which is peculiar to Wadham College, takes place, when a fellow has held his post eighteen years from the time of ~~their~~ his taking his Master's degree. The late Warden, Dr. Wills, who left the bulk of a considerable fortune, acquired within its walls, to the College, has, indeed, in some respects, mitigated the injurious effects of this Statute, by assigning annuities to the unfortunate superannuated fellows, & by assigning |*135* exhibitions, in increase of the Scholarships & Fellowships, to those, who adopt the legal or medical professions, thereby giving a quicker succession to the College livings to those, who follow the clerical profession. To return to Mr. Stevens: the friends of Mr. Williams spoke of the success of their canvass with such confidence as to give reason to think, that the strength was nearly balanced, and I expected a summons to the poll of the 26th. Inst. but a comparison of votes commenced on Monday & was concluded

166. Eyford Park.

yesterday, which shewed Stevens to be so far ahead of his competitor, that the latter immediately resigned. The number of pledged votes for the winner being 308, for the loser 247.—The living of South Petherwyn is worth, as I am told, £400 per ann.—

We dined to-day with Mr. & Mrs. Dolphin at Eyford.—A very sumptuous & fashionable entertainment, but far too splendid for his fortune. Nothing could be more easy or polite, or behave more properly under the peculiar circumstances than Mr. D. & his beautiful wife. Miss Browne of Salperton, Mr. G. Hutchinson, half brother to Mrs. Dolphin, a well informed conversible travelled man, Mr. Willan & the Revd. Mr. Bragge, Cousin to Mr. Dolphin, (the two latter of the |136 sporting genus) and Mr. Bowen, were inmates at Eyford. Sir Charles & Lady Imhoff, and Miss Chabuzet, with ourselves, formed the party. Sir C. Imhoff, a Major Genl. in our Service, is of German Origin, being son of Mrs. Hastings, the wife of the Governor General of India, by her first husband Baron d'Imhoff, whose second wife & family by the Second Couche I knew intimately in my early days at Weimar.

Feb. 26

I entered my forty second year. If it please GOD to permit me to live till its close may I be able to look back with satisfaction on the past! May he grant me grace to work out my salvation with fear and trembling!

Tuesday Mar. 2.

My dear Edward's birthday. He is eleven years old. May the Almighty preserve him to be a blessing to us, and a comfort in advancing years!

Friday Mar. 5.

"Memoirs of the private life of Marie Antoinette Queen of France and Navarre, to which are added recollections, sketches and anecdotes, illustrative of the reigns of Louis XIV, Louis XV

& Louis XVI. By Madame Campan, first lady of the Bedchamber to the Queen. 2 Vols 8vo. Lond. 1823". This is a very important & interesting book. The authoress was attached to the person of the |[137] unfortunate Marie Antoinette, and possessed her confidence from the time of her arrival in France to the day of her incarceration in the temple. Mad. Campan, in a most difficult situation & arduous times, displayed a discretion, a warmth of attachment, a strength of judgment, a moderation, and a power of making herself useful to her employers truly valuable. Escaping the horrors of the revolution with a ruined fortune, she applied her talents to the education of young females, for which task she had a singular taste & aptitude, & having for some time presided over the best & largest & most approved boarding school in France, she attracted the notice of Bonaparte, by whom she was deservedly placed at the head of a large establishment for the education of the daughters of the members of the legion of honour. Having lost her husband, and towards the close of her own life, her beloved son, she herself survived the return of the Bourbon family, but does not appear to have obtained their esteem, which she justly deserved by her devotion to her royal Mistress, whose life, character & virtues she describes in these posthumous memoirs. Good sense is the strong characteristic of the work: Madame Campan relates nothing but what she either witnessed or heard from persons engaged in the transactions, and on whose veracity she could rely. Consequently the work is not a history of the French |[138] revolution, its causes, intrigues, secret springs & progress, but a faithful picture of the interior of the Palace at Versailles, of the amusements, chagrins, modes of thinking and acting, customs, etiquette, private life, affections, antipathies, amusements, griefs, struggles, & horrors of the royal family & their immediate connexions & attendants. We see the King good, capable of applying himself to business & study, fond of geography and mechanics, but irresolute, awkward, cold; in the first years of his marriage strangely indifferent to his beautiful consort, in the latter period warmly attached. The Queen we behold young, beautiful, flattered, earnest to secure the affections of her husband & the love of France, devoted to her children, attaching herself in the bonds of friendship with almost a romantic fondness, fond of pleasure, impatient of the restraints of court ~~equ~~ etiquette; adored in her own circle, always the object of the hatred of the Anti Austrian party: in affliction resigned, in the transaction of public affairs active and intelligent, sensitive under the incessant obloquies, to which she was exposed: her character assailed by the grossest calumny, & made the object of the most intricate intrigues. In youth fond of amusement and dress, but always modest, though sometimes indiscreet: |[139] never for a moment engaged in any improper liaison de coeur, nor in any political party hostile to the interests of France. But monarchy in France was to fall, & drag in its ruin the amiable Sovereigns of the land: in the Court there wanted the energy, the science, the virtue, which might have ruled the storm, & brought the vessel of state into the safe haven of temperate monarchy. Altogether, this will be a most valuable aid to the future historian, who with high powers and extensive information shall hereafter trace with a vigorous intellect the annals of the French revolution.

Tuesday Mar. 9.

I left home in the afternoon for Gloucester, whither I was summoned to attend a meeting of the committee of magistrates appointed to consider the state of the county rate. I rode to Northleach, proceeded on the Regulator to Gloucester, and arrived at Mrs. Backhouse's to tea. Had the satisfaction of finding her pretty well.

Wednesday Mar. 10.

The following members of the committee to consider the inequality of the county rate attended: Dr. Cooke, Dr. Timbrell, Mr. T. L. Baker (the new High Sheriff), Mr. Byles, Mr. Cheston, Mr. Hyett and myself. Dr. |*140* Cooke presided and submitted a number of documents & calculations bearing on the subject, and illustrative of the point in question, the gross inequalities alledged to exist. These are found not only in comparing populous towns with country villages, but also in comparing places similarly circumstanced as to quantity & quality of land, inhabitants &c. Much discussion arose as to the expediency of resorting to the Property Tax assessments of 1812 for a guide in the forming a new rate, & the measure was advocated by the chairman. That part of the question was, however, adjourned, & we concluded to report to the Sessions, that the existing rate is palpably unequal, & that a new rate should be made.

I visited the Gaol, where the arrangements for the tread-mill are fully completed, by the paving the Court in which it is erected, building sheds to shelter the Turnkeys superintending the work, & the prisoners when off the wheel, particularly by the erection of separation boards between each prisoner at work, which totally precludes conversation at the work, but requires also that ~~one~~ each prisoner should tread on the same spot during the whole of the period allotted to him on the wheel. This, perhaps, as |*141* rendering the work more irksome, is desirable; unless the boards be found in warm weather to exclude air too much, or limit too much the vibration of the prisoner's body when at work.

Thursday Mar. 11.

I returned home, leaving Mrs. Backhouse after breakfast, and spending the morning with my mother at Cheltenham, who is quite well. Mrs. Travell also is greatly recovered. The day, as the preceding one had been, was extremely wet, and I travelled by coach to Northleach, & thence took a post chaise home. Found my dear wife suffering severely, as she has done for many weeks, from bilious spasms.

Saturday Mar. 13.

The newspapers announce the appointment of the Revd. Christopher Lipscombe, Fellow of New College, Oxford, to be Bishop of Jamaica. Mr. Sumner had been named, but it is said declined the office. Mr. Lipscombe was a cotemporary of mine at the University, where I occasionally met him, when I visited at the Common room of his college. He is a man of considerable talent, and distinguished himself by the prizes, which he gained, running, both at Winchester & Oxford, a race of competition with another able man of his time, Dr. Shuttleworth, now |*142* Warden of New College. Another Episcopal see, it is understood, is to be erected in our West Indian Colonies, the residence of the second Bishop being alternately at Barbados and St. Vincent's. The best results for the extension of Christianity & morality are to be expected from this measure of establishing episcopacy in these dependencies. Insurrection among the slaves has been put down, & the newspapers do not contain so many virulent speeches of members of Colonial assemblies as lately were to be found there. In the House of Commons it seems a tacit agreement to treat the momentous questions of West Indian policy with much delicacy and reserve, so as to prevent the utterance of anything calculated to irritate on the one hand, or to excite false hope on the other. The Chancellor of the Exchequer in his financial arrangements has given the planters a boon by a reduction of the duties on rum, & it appears, that the increased demand for sugar is such that the supply is now not much greater than the demand. Consequently, the West Indian Planters have a prospect of recovering from their depression.—

Wednesday March 17.

"Report of the Society for promoting Christian Knowledge. 1823." This admirable Society now reckons more than 15000 members, and is steadily prosecuting |*143* its important labours both at home and abroad. The total number of Bibles, Common Prayer Books & Tracts issued between the audit April 1822 & April 1823 is 1,400,711.—The total sum of money accounted for in the balance sheet is £57714. 19. 11. The decease of Bishop Middleton & the elevation of Bp. Heber to the See of Calcutta are prominent points in the report. The valedictory address in the name of the Society by the Bishop of Bristol, (Dr. Kay) and the answer by Bishop Heber, are beautiful compositions; the former simple & elegant; the latter impressive and a little florid. The same characteristics distinguish the two excellent sermons by the same eminent divines prefixed to this Report. By a new arrangement the anniversary Sermons for 1822 & 1823 are printed together, that the Society may be enabled in future to present the Members with the Sermon of the year soon after its being preached. The venerable Dr. Gaskin has resigned the Senior Secretaryship of the Society: two Joint Secretaries of equal rank, Messrs. Parker & Coleridge, now ~~bear~~ discharge those duties, which of late years devolved on Dr. Gaskin & Mr. Parker, as his Under Secretary.

——— |

Witts Family Papers F311

Diary.

1824

March 30. Tuesday.

I left home for Cheltenham on horseback, and at my Mother's met Mr. F. Newell, who acted as Commissioner to administer to my Mother an oath, as to the amount of my late poor brother's effects, it being necessary, that she, as nearest of kin, should administer. With the arrears of pay remaining in his agents hands the whole is under £100 and will only suffice to pay his debts and expences of administration.

My Mother is now in very tolerable health; I also found my Aunt Travell much recovered; Miss Buxton is on a visit to her. I dined and slept at my Mother's.

"Statement of facts and copies of and extracts from letters in reference to the refusal of the Hon. and Right Revd. H. Ryder D.D., late Lord Bishop of Gloucester, and now Bp. of Lichfield and Coventry to licence the Revd. Geo. Bonner L.L.B. as assistant Minister of Trinity Church, Cheltenham. In a letter to a member of the congregation. Cheltenham. 1824." Such is the title of a pamphlet, which has excited much attention in the populous & fashionable town of Cheltenham, where elegant critics of all ages and both sexes are keenly |[2] engaged in canvassing the merits of the dispute between Mr. Bonner, Mr. Jervis the Incumbent of the Church, & their late Diocesan. Mr. Bonner's eloquence in the pulpit has raised him a host of patrons & patronesses during the eight months of his ministerial engagement in this town. But the Bishop required, that the assistant Minister of the New Church should not only read and preach well, but take an active proportionable share of the parochial duties of the populous parish; and as Mr. Bonner shewed much disinclination to share these laborious duties, and at last only tardily consented to undertake them, his Lordship used the discretion vested in him of refusing him a licence, at the same time not insisting on his hurried removal from his post. To me it appears, that his Lordship was right in principle, but had better have expressed himself at first in more distinct and positive terms; that the Incumbent is not free from the charge of disingenuousness in his correspondence with Mr. Bonner; that Mr. Bonner, halting between two opinions, neither decidedly Evangelical, as it is called, nor decidedly of high church principles, aimed at mere pulpit popularity, |[3] and however correct his statement of facts may be, erred most seriously, in publishing to the world the divisions and feuds, which unfortunately have existed. It must be a very strong case, indeed, which can justify a clergyman in an appeal to his parishioners against his Bishop and his Vicar, much more justify him in alluding to the disputes in existence publicly from the pulpit, which Mr. Bonner did on the day, when he preached his farewell discourse. But Mr. B. relied on his popularity,

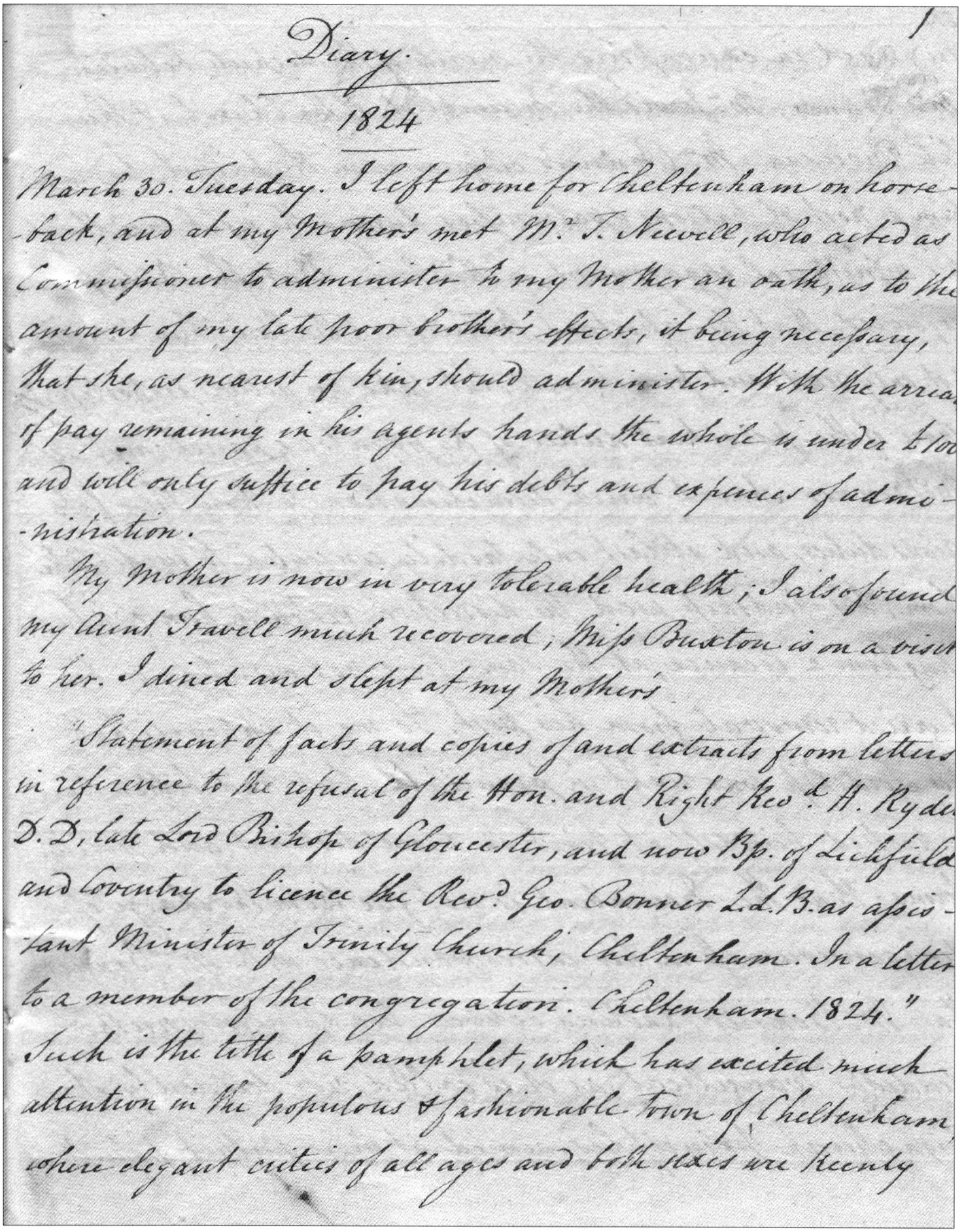

1

Diary.

1824

March 30. Tuesday. I left home for Cheltenham on horse-back, and at my Mother's met Mr. T. Newell, who acted as Commissioner to administer to my Mother an oath, as to the amount of my late poor brother's effects, it being necessary, that she, as nearest of kin, should administer. With the arrears of pay remaining in his agents hands the whole is under £100 and will only suffice to pay his debts and expences of administration.

My Mother is now in very tolerable health; I also found my Aunt Travell much recovered, Miss Buxton is on a visit to her. I dined and slept at my Mother's.

"Statement of facts and copies of and extracts from letters in reference to the refusal of the Hon. and Right Revd. H. Ryder D.D, late Lord Bishop of Gloucester, and now Bp. of Lichfield and Coventry to licence the Revd. Geo. Bonner L.L.B. as assistant Minister of Trinity Church, Cheltenham. In a letter to a member of the congregation. Cheltenham. 1824." Such is the title of a pamphlet, which has excited much attention in the populous & fashionable town of Cheltenham, where elegant critics of all ages and both sexes are keenly

167. Eastington House.

which is evinced by the readiness, with which subscriptions were raised to purchase for him, and present him with a piece of plate, a silver cup; and this to a man known only in the parish for eight months: truly, if all Clergymen, who do their duty well, are to be presented with addresses & cups, it will be a fine age for the Silver-smiths. But such is the fashion of the times; witness the projected address to Bp. Ryder, proceeding from a party, in which laymen were to combine with clergy, and ladies, no doubt, mingle with both, to compliment and laud the departing prelate, at the expense virtually of his predecessors & successors in the see, while a copious selection of works on divinity |[4] was to be purchased by subscription and be forwarded to Eccleshall Castle to grace the shelves of his Lordship's library: but this notable scheme was abandoned: the Bishop being advised to discountenance the measure. Nor must I omit to mention two other subscriptions of a like sort at Cheltenham, recently made: one for the Curate, Mr. Davies, lately presented by Bp. Ryder to a small living in the diocese, after six years arduous duty in the populous town of Cheltenham. The hard labour, he had undergone, his confined circumstances, delicate health, little family, & respectable character quite apologize for this measure, by which, I am told, fully £300 have been raised. As the bathos, however, of this rage of subscribing, comes a scheme for a knot of ladies, who witnessing, with emulation, the exertions made, as above stated, in favour of the regular clergy, resolve to array in gown and cassock of the best their pet preacher of the Tabernacle, a certain Mr. Brown, whose robes had waxed old and thread bare in the service; but now, with a purse of eighteen Guineas, he may not only rustle in dignified silk, but, peradventure, retain enough to equip |5 anew the lower extremities of his person.

March 31. Wednesday.

I proceeded to Gloucester to Mrs. Backhouse's, whom I found suffering from a bilious attack. The forenoon was chiefly taken up by me in seeing servants of different descriptions enquiring for places in our family, a quarrel in our kitchen having caused us to dismiss most of our domestics.

The commission of Assize for the County was opened this afternoon by Sir James Allan Park,[1] whose colleague, Sir W. Garrow,[2] follow~~ing~~ ed him from Monmouth. The new High Sheriff is my friend Thomas John Lloyd Baker, of Hardwick Court, a very worthy, intelligent country Gentleman & Magistrate, whose deserved popularity was sufficiently evinced by the very numerous party, upwards of seventy gentlemen, including the first names in the County, who dined with him. All the leading Magistrates &c were present. The hilarity of the evening was, however, exchanged for a strong feeling of gloom by a melancholy accident, which befel Mr. W. H. Hicks, son of H. Hicks of Eastington, an eminent clothier, and esteemed Magistrate, |6 as he was setting out to ride home about nine o clock. Though he appeared quite sober, when he left the party, the outward air had the effect on a disordered stomach of making him very unsteady, & bewildered him, insomuch, that he was found on the Bristol road, a little beyond the Spa, fallen from his horse & almost dead. It appears, that he fell on his head, that a sharp stone in the road cut his temporal artery, & that he bled to death. On the rumour reaching the King's head, that a Gentleman unknown, who had dined with the Sheriff, was lying a corpse at the Infirmary, Col. Webb, the Member for Gloucester, Genl. Guise & myself hastened thither to recognize the person, & arrange how best to communicate the calamity to the sufferer's family. This painful duty was undertaken by Webb, attended by Dr. Baron, the Physician attending Mr. Hicks's family, & Mr. Shrapnell, the Surgeon, who first saw the deceased, and a melancholy task it was. Winchcomb Hicks was unmarried, a young man of considerable expertness in commercial pursuits, & much beloved in his family. From sudden death, Good Lord, deliver us!

——— |7

April. 1. Thursday.

Attended the Cathedral Service. The Sermon was preached by Mr. R. Cooper, who officiates as Chaplain to the High Sheriff. As far as I could hear of it, for I was at a distance from the pulpit, and a great noise prevailed in the Cathedral, it was a very good discourse, but delivered with too great rapidity.

I attended at different hours both in the Crown Court and at Nisi Prius; Sir J. A. Park presided in the latter; Sir W. Garrow in the former; I did not hear any interesting cause in either

---

1. Sir James Alan Park, (1763-1838). Park was appointed vice chancellor of the Duchy of Lancaster in 1791 and became king's counsel in 1799. In 1816 he was promoted to the bench of common pleas, and knighted. He had a reputation as being sound, fair and sensible. His bad temper was legendary, and Witts touches upon this at the Gloucester Assizes on 1 April 1829.
2. Sir William Garrow, (1760-1840), M.P. for Gatton, 1805-1806; Callington, 1806-1807 and Eye, 1812-1817. Garrow was Attorney-General, 1806-12, Solicitor-General, 1813-1817; puisne baron of Exchequer, 1817-1832.

court. I dined in my magisterial capacity with the Judges; the party was numerous, exceeding thirty; among them the Duke of Beaufort, Lord E. Somerset, Hon. H. Morton &c.

I found my Cousins, the Miss Witts's, at Gloucester: they propose to pitch their tent there for some length of time, & are now on a visit to Mrs. M. Hunt.

Friday Apr. 2.

I returned home, calling on my way, at Cheltenham, on my Mother and my Aunt. I found my dear wife pretty well.

Tuesday April 6.

Our friend, Mr. C. Keysall, arrived from Bredon, on a short visit. |[8]

We had a dinner party; Lady & Miss Reade, Mr. & Mrs. Egerton Leigh, Mr. R. Wynniatt, Mr. Bowen, & Mr. Winter, besides ourselves & C. Keysall.

Wednesday April 7.

The first dinner this season of the Stow Clerical Society. Mr. Malcolm was in the chair. Ten Clergymen met.

Thursday April 8.

Mrs. Hurd dined with us.

Sunday April 11.

A letter this morning from my afflicted friend, Mr. Browne of Salperton, announced to us the sad tidings of his poor son's decease at Bristol Hotwells on Friday evening. For a long time my fears had anticipated an early conclusion to his life; but now, the blow is struck, it distresses me exceedingly. We had known him from a boy: on his leaving Rugby School, he was placed under my tuition, & was an inmate here at different times since his entrance at Oriel College, sometimes for the purposes of study, at others a cherished friend & guest. As a pupil, it was very rarely, that I had occasion to be dissatisfied with him; he had good sense, was a very fair scholar, and a truly moral youth. He was cheerful, attached, fond of the country, without affectation, sincere & open-hearted. All these |[9] good qualities developed themselves more & more, as he became older, & gave the fairest promise, that in after life he would be a most estimable country gentleman. After quitting me he remained for the usual time at Oxford, but did not take a degree; particularly fond of country amusements & field sports, he has chiefly resided at Salperton since; twice he made short excursions to Paris; and his character was rising in estimation throughout the country, and among all classes. Unfortunately the constitution of the Browne family is very weak; fond of active pursuits, & convivial, without proceeding to excess, he always taxed his strength too much; the result has been the cutting short a valuable life at the early age of twenty five. His friends had observed & lamented, that he grew thinner, & had the appearance of decline during the past autumn; but his rapid journey to the grave must be dated from the middle of January, when he burst a blood vessel. Since then he has been quickly wasting away; ten days before his death he was removed, (vain hope!) to Bristol Hotwells, & now the curtain is closed over one, of whom, I may truly |[10] quote the words of his poor Father, in the affecting letter, I have just received, "a more dutiful son, a more sincere friend, or a kinder gentleman, I am confident, never lived. Our poor friends, Mr. & Mrs. Browne, demand the deepest commiseration: child after child has dropped off, as each was rising to maturity; and at this moment the second daughter, a lovely girl of seventeen, is wasting away, as it is believed, in hopeless decline. Even the eldest daughter, a beautiful young woman, who with great difficulty a few years since recovered from a long nervous debility, gives room for serious alarm; having accompanied her poor Mother and brother to Bristol Hotwells, she has there been seized with measles, and was confined to her bed, when her brother resigned his breath. This is beyond the ordinary sum of human woe! This calls for all the sympathy & all the prayers of the friends of the family. A more upright, kind hearted, friendly man does not breathe than my afflicted friend; & how must he tremble, when he looks at his remaining children; besides those, I have named, a son & daughter about 13 and 14 years of age, delicate, hot house plants, apparently too slight to struggle with the least inclemency |[11] of season, or fatigue.

168. The Duke of Wellington, political cartoon.

Monday April 12.

Our friend, C. Keysall, left us for Bredon.

Tuesday April 13.

Mr. F. Aston dined here.

Thursday April 15.

My worthy old friend, Mr. Stevens, the new Rector of South Petherwyn, arrived from Oxford to pass a day with us; in cheerful spirits from the late success, which attended his election, & most grateful to those, who contributed to the attainment of his object.

Saturday April 17.

Stevens left us for London.

Monday April 19.

I this morning signed the deed of conveyance, by which eight acres and a little more of meadow land, in the parish of Bourton on the Water, are made over to the Governors of Queen Anne's Bounty for the augmentation of my Vicarage of Stanway. The price, £335, being the full amount of Bounty money, to which I am entitled; which has hitherto paid me only 2 per cent per ann: this purchase will realize 5 per Cent. the lands being now let at £17– per ann. & are well worth nearly that sum.—

——— |12

We left home about mid-day for Cheltenham to pay a short visit to my Mother; whom we found very well.—

———

Tuesday April 20.

The Duke of Wellington is now here for the benefit of his health. I saw him to-day for the first time. He was walking with my acquaintance, Lord Apsley, eldest son of the Earl of Bathurst. The great Captain of the age is much attached to this agreeable young nobleman. The Duke's countenance is very striking, but carries with it the appearance of a great wear and tear of constitution.

———

Wednesday April 21.

We dined at my Aunt Travell's.

———

Thursday April 22.

Walked to the Village of Charlton Kings. Since I have been in the interior of this pretty village several nice Villas and genteel cottages have been added to it. The Church is undergoing a complete repair; enlarged accommodation and galleries being provided, with new pews: the whole will be very neat. The Curate, the Rev[d.] Williams, of Jesus College, is very justly liked & respected; being a well informed, sensible and accomplished man.

Lady Elcho and Miss Church drank tea with my mother |13 on their way from Clifton to Stanway: poor Lady Elcho looked ill, and seemed in bad spirits.

———

Friday April 23.

We dined at M[r.] & M[rs.] Rosenhagen's.

———

Saturday April 24.

Leaving my wife at Cheltenham, I returned home to perform my duty. On my way to Upper Slaughter I explored the new line of road marked out, to avoid Dowdeswell Hill, which, diverging to the left at the foot of the hill, winds up the valley towards the village of Whittington; where it approaches Sandywell Park, there will be a cutting of thirty feet; running between Whittington Court & Sandywell Park, it crosses the Stow road at Andoversford, & comes into the original road to Northleach a little above Frogmill Inn. It will be a great relief to travelling, lead thro' a pleasing line of country, &, I believe, not be circuitous. It will shorten the distance from Cheltenham to Stow. But I am afraid, the moist and springy nature of the soil will make the road difficult & expensive to construct and maintain.

M[r.] Lawrence, M[rs.] Lightbourne's heir, has not been idle since the old lady's decease: he is about to make |14 Sandywell Park his residence, and is employing many people there in altering & modernizing the house, in enlarging the Park as far as the new line of road, & in planting. It is said, that he is about to marry some rich heiress.

April. 25. Sunday.

The newspapers announce the death of Dr. Beadon[3], Bishop of Bath of Wells at the age of 86. This Prelate was at one time head of a College in Cambridge and Tutor to the present Duke of Gloucester: also Bishop of Gloucester, in which see he was succeeded by Dr. Huntingford, now Bishop of Hereford. I am not aware, that he ever appeared before the public as an author. His very advanced age and his infirmities had caused him long to retire from the public discharge of his official duties. In the year 1806 I was ordained Deacon by letters dimissory from Bishop Beadon to Bp. Porteus, then holding the See of London, my nomination being given by the Revd. Mr. Merewether, Rector of Combhay and Foscote, in Somersetshire. I was to reside in the Parsonage at the former place, near Bath: but the death of the incumbent, which took place between my ordination at London, |15 and my arrival at Bath a very few days after, put an end to the engagement after I had once or twice officiated: new incumbents, by whom my services were not required, being quickly appointed to both parishes. In the course of the summer of the same year, I was appointed Curate of the united Vicarage of Erchfont & Stert, near Devizes, where I resided in the former till I removed into Gloucestershire, on being presented to the living of Upper Slaughter in the autumn of 1808. The Revd. G. Smith was Vicar of Erchfont, & ceased to reside on my taking charge of his parishes.

Monday April 26.

"Memoirs of Benvenuto Cellini, a Florentine Artist, written by himself: containing a variety of information respecting the arts and the history of the 16th. Century. Third Edition, corrected and enlarged from the last Milan edition, with the notes and observations of G. P. Carpani, now first translated by Thos. Roscoe Esqr. 2 Vols. 8vo 1823." This singular and interesting piece of auto-biography had been already presented to the British public many years ago in the Translation of a Dr. Nugent, and then excited much curiosity. The present Translator must not be confounded with the author of the life of Lorenzo de Medici. Horace |16 Walpole pronounced the life of Benvenuto Cellini to be more amusing than any novel. That species of writing has, indeed, been greately improved since his days, but the narrative of the Italian Artist is certainly most amusing. He seems to have been a man of fiery temper, and ungoverned passions, full of genius, daring, vain, proud, capable of warm attachments, quick of observation; commencing business as a goldsmith, he executed the most beautiful works both small and great in the precious metals, jewellery, stamping of medals, and sculpture, both in bronze & marble; the elegance and classic purity of his admirable designs was only surpassed by the execution; living in a country and age of artists, the cotemporary of Michel Angelo, Vasari & many others of great repute, he was in constant intercourse with persons of the highest rank and talents. Whether in contact with rival artists, or with Popes, Cardinals, Bishops and Courtiers, with Francis the 1st. of France, or the Emperor

3. Richard Beadon, (1737-1824). Beadon had been Bishop of Gloucester, 1789-1802, when he was then translated to Bath and Wells.

169. Bowden Hall.

Charles the 5th., whether defending the Castle of St. Angelo at Rome as a Bombardier, or imprisoned in the same fortress and escaping thence at the |[17] great hazard of his life, whether travelling in France and Italy, or engaged in passionate quarrels in the streets, which ended not unfrequently in homicide, in all occurrences of his life we see the same fearless and often insolent character, the same acuteness, jealousy, testiness; a mixture of superstition and libertinism congenial to the times; and on the whole a most curious portraiture of a most turbulent age, but one marked as the age of men of eminent talents in every department, as politicians, warriors, scholars or artists. He was born in 1500, and died in 1570: his great works were chiefly executed in Rome, Paris and Florence.—

I rejoined my wife at my mother's at Cheltenham.

Tuesday April 27.

We left Cheltenham after breakfast for Gloucester, to visit Mrs. Backhouse.

This is also the first day of the Sessions, which I attended as usual: and dined with the other Magistrates. Dr. Cooke presided as Chairman, with the assistance of Mr. Cripps to try Prisoners & Traverses. Other Magistrates present were Mr. Bathurst, Sir B. W. Guise, Genl. Guise, |[18] Mr. Phelps, Dr. Timbrill, Dr. Davies, Mr. Byles, Mr. Jenner, Mr. Hyett, Mr. Newman, Mr. Pye, Mr. Sayer, Mr. Wilbraham &c. The Powers of the Prison Regulations Committee were renewed with a reiterated assurance from the Chairman, that he would call the members of it to deliberate before the next Sessions. This has not unaptly been called the Tortoise committee. The County rate Committee reported, that the rate now existing was unequal, and recommended the making a new rate; the body of Magistrates present adopted their report and renewed the powers of the Committee, in order, that they might report to the next Sessions, what appeared to them the most advisable mode of proceeding in this business.

Friday April 30.

The business of the Sessions ceased this day.

I visited the Lunatic asylum, going over every part of the institution with the resident Medical man, Mr. Poyner, & attended thro' the female ward by the matron, Mrs. Chambers. Both these persons seem to be remarkably well suited to their station, intelligent, active, tranquil, cheerful. There |[19] is now one patient of the first class or opulent, two or three of the second, where a part of the expence is borne by the charitable fund, and more then forty pauper lunatics. The wards, sleeping cells, day rooms &c. were all very clean, considering the afflicted state of the inmates, and the arrangements for security seem extremely judicious. Fetters are not seen; the worst patients are secured to strong chairs, their hands fastened in leathern gloves or muffs, so contrived as effectually to hinder them from doing mischief to themselves or others; the legs were secured by a strap only in one case to prevent the poor wretch from kicking; in the worst patients the hair is kept close ~~and~~ cut, and a canvass dress is worn; others wear their ordinary attire; in the day room some females were at work, others reading the Common Prayer book. There are some very bad cases on the female side, most of these, when I visited them, were in the spacious yard attached to their ward. The men appeared all tranquil, sitting together in their day rooms, except five or six, who were busy working in the Garden. |[20] Divine Service is performed on Sunday, & occasionally on weekdays. Mr. Poyner said, he had not had sufficient experience to ascertain, whether the joining in religious worship were generally beneficial or the contrary to the unhappy inmates of the asylum; at present he did not notice any particular influence, which it had, except, that the desire to attend, arising from its being a change in the monotonous habits of the place, produced in some cases a self controul, from the fear of being excluded, if noisy. The institution is under the direction of a committee of Visiting Magistrates and subscribers, of whom my acquaintance, the intelligent and assiduous Mr. Byles, of Bowden Hall, near Gloucester, a very active and able magistrate, is the main stay.

Saturday May 1.

Leaving my wife with her Mother, in the hope that with change of air, and more genial weather, her health will be recruited, I set off for Upper Slaughter, summoned, as usual, by the duties of my profession, and purposing to remain, as a bachelor, there, for a fortnight.

Monday May 3.

"A charge delivered to the Clergy of the peculiar jurisdiction of the dean of Chichester at the Visitation in 1816. By Chr. Bethell M.A. Dean of Chichester, 2d. Edit. 1816. 8vo" This charge by the Bishop of Gloucester temperately |[21] treats of the prevalence of dissent from the church, which it traces to the pride and vanity of human nature. Prevalent errors are briefly adverted to more especially misapprehensions and misrepresentations of the doctrine of regeneration, which the author afterwards made the subject of a larger treatise.

Wednesday May. 5.

Mr. Rudge, the Archdeacon of the Diocese, met the Clergy of the Deanery of Stow to-day, at his visitation. The Sermon was preached in the Church of Stow by Mr. Davies, Vicar of Little Barrington, and Curate of Sherborne and Windrush. It was an excellent plain and earnest discourse on ministerial duties. A party of about 12 or 15 dined together with the Archdeacon, of whom I was one.

Thursday May 6.

At a meeting of the Commissioners of the Foss and Cross Turnpike roads to-day, at which I presided, a proposition was made by Mr. James, Engineer of the Stratford & Moreton Railway, for diverting a portion of the Turnpike road, near Moreton, as a mutual accommodation. At the same time this gentleman communicated much information on the subject of rail roads, with which he is connected, either in progress or in agitation. |22 The Stratford rail road, as he assured us, will be completed in the month of December next; and it is meditated to extend the communication by this mode of conveyance quite across the kingdom in this direction. £146,000 have recently been subscribed to form a railway between Liverpool and Birmingham; this will unite with the Stratford and Birmingham canal; at Stratford the rail road system is again in action to Moreton in Marsh. Thence a rail road is projected by the valley of the Evenload, thro' Wichwood Forest & by Cassington to Oxford, where it meets the Thames Navigation: and another rail way diverging at Oddington and proceeding by Idbury is meant to cross the country to Latton near Cricklade, there to join the North Wilts Canal & so extend a line to Bristol. These are sanguine schemes, but in the present redundance of capital, funds for the execution may be found, and they are more deserving of support than Columbian or Peruvian or Mexican loans, or than many other bubbles of this stock-jobbing age. Besides, the power of steam, and the new discoveries in science and mechanics, render easy and cheap schemes, which even a few years since would have been considered hopeless. The tram waggons now may be made to travel without horses by steam, and are so worked both in Yorkshire & Northumberland. |23 Mr. James gave me a sketch of such an engine, followed by and connected with a travelling supply of water for the boiler; steam is generated, the chimney of the moveable engine puffs out smoke, and away they go with a whole string of waggons laden with coal or other commodities towed at their rear: mens agitat molem;[4] they even now dispense with the chimney, and consume their smoke. Another project likely to be accomplished are stationary engines at intervals, say of four miles, on the sides of rail roads, with long chains, working the waggons backwards & forwards, two miles in each direction; by the aid of these engines they propose to ascend inclined planes, so that a dead level is no longer a sine quâ non.[5] In this way it is proposed to cross Talk on the Hill between Liverpool & Birmingham & to rise to Idbury from the Vale of Moreton. Another rail way now in agitation is from Manchester to Liverpool. The shares in the Stratford and Moreton rail way are rising in value, tho' probably still far from being at par.

Friday May 7.—

Another Bishop has paid the debt of nature. The aged, amiable and pious Bishop Buckner of Chichester is no more.[6] |24

4. mens agitat molem — the mind moves the matter.
5. sine quâ non — a condition 'without which it could not be.'
6. John Buckner, (17??-1824), Prebendary, Firle, Chichester, 1768-71; Prebendary, Eartham, Chichester, 1771-97; Residentiary Canon, 1785-97; Bishop of Chichester, 1797-1824.

I rode to Stanway, and dined with my friend F. Aston, meeting M. Wynniatt & Mr. Mackechnie. The latter Gentleman is a native of the Island of St. Christopher's, who at the mature age of 40 is desirous of preparing himself for holy orders, with a view of exercising his ministry in some of the West Indian Colonies; for this purpose he has placed himself for some months under the tuition of my Curate; he seems a well disposed intelligent man, but, I fear, Greek, after forty, will be a difficult enterprize both to Tutor and pupil.

Saturday May 8.

I returned home.

Tuesday May 10.

"St Ronan's well. By the author of Waverley, Quintin Durward &c. 3 Vols. 1824. 12mo" A man, who is always talking, cannot always talk well; and a writer, who is perpetually before the public, will sometimes write carelessly, languidly, and irrationally. Not that the celebrated novelist has not in this production many passages of great force & pathos; many admirable sketches of character, and happy delineations of vanity, folly, meanness and peculiarities of various kinds: but there is a more than romantic improbability in the tale; causes and their consequences fall in so strangely, |[25] there is on the one hand such unredeemed wickedness, on the other such a pitiable alienation of intellect, that the interest is greatly diminished. Thus, in the higher personages of the story, there is little to attach the reader, some dreadful wild catastrophe is foreseen from the first: and as to the figures, which fill up the canvass, the motley party of would be fashionables, men & women of taste and ton, at a petty watering place in Scotland, though at first amusing, becomes tiresome. The absent Minister, the jealous, cross, purseproud, yet feeling hostess at the old fashioned country inn, and the busy, bustling, intriguing sexagenarian, who materially accelerates by his blundering officiousness the denouement and tragic conclusion of the tale, are excellent sketches in the author's peculiar manner.

Friday May 14.

The two sees of Bath and Wells and Chichester are again filled, the former by the Translation of Bishop Law,[7] from Chester, the latter is given to Dr. Carr, Dean of Hereford.[8] Dr. Law stands very high in the esteem of the Orthodox members of the Church, and is a man of very sound talent and extensive theological learning. In judgment, |[26] activity and earnestness he is equally distinguished; and very valuable reforms and beneficial arrangements have been accomplished by his Lordship in the Diocese of Chester. He is an excellent and impressive preacher, his sermons as well as his speeches in Parliament on ecclesiastical points are full of close argument in the style of Paley, the old friend of his family. He is brother of the late Lord Ellenborough, and of an eccentric, but clever Mr. Law, who has for many years resided in America, where he has invested a large fortune

---

7. George Henry Law, (1761-1845). Law came from a distinguished family, his brother John was Bishop of Elphin and another brother, Edward was 1st Baron Ellenborough (1750-1818). Law was Bishop of Chester, 1812-24, and Bath and Wells, 1824-45.
8. Robert James Carr, (1774-1841), Bishop of Chichester, 1824-31, and Worcester, 1831-41.

acquired in India in land, which pays him very ill, & where he grumbles against the land of his nativity and that of his adoption, wondering that the former has not sunk to ruin as he had predicted, & that the latter has not answered his sanguine expectations Bp. Law's father was Bishop of Carlisle, and his Uncle Bp. of Elphin. It is generally understood, that Bp Ryder had set his heart on the Diocese of Bath & Wells, but accepted Lichfield and Coventry on finding, that Dr. Law had received the promise of the former, on Dr. Beadon's decease. |27 Dr. Carr, Dean of Hereford, owes his elevation to the See of Chichester to the personal favour of the King, as also he was indebted to his interest with the Sovereign for his former dignity. He is the Son of the late Rector of Ealing, and brother of a deceased gallant officer, who married the widow of the excellent Spencer Perceval. Dr. Carr, as Rector of Brighton, had a claim on the favourable countenance of his royal Parishioner, and, indeed, I believe, bears a very estimable character. He is much liked at Hereford.—

Sunday May 16th

"The life of the Rev. John William de la Flechere, compiled from the narratives of the Revd. Mr. Wesley: the Biographical notes of the Revd. Mr. Gilpin, from his own letters, and other authentic documents. By Joseph Benson. Lond. 1812. 8vo" This book comes from the press of the Wesleyan Methodists, and was lent me by an old female devotee and class leader of that sect, mother of my deceased honest gardner Robt. Bateman. It is a very prolix biography of one of the most guileless, amiable, pious and able among those Clergy of the Establishment, who enlisted under the banner of John Wesley. John William de la Flechere was |28 born at Nyon in Switzerland in 1729: he came to England after the age of 20, having had the advantage of a good education, & when he had acquired enough of our language became tutor in a Shropshire family. He remained in that situation some years, during which he became an attendant on the preaching of the Methodists, and an ardent enthusiast in religion. After a length of time passed in hesitation he resolved to embrace the clerical profession, was ordained, and at no long distance of time instituted to the living of Madeley in Shropshire, among the colliers, & iron manufacturers. Coalbrookdale is in that parish. He found his people ignorant and vicious; he attempted to reform them by the most unwearied exertions & enthusiastic efforts. Self denying, humble, charitable, instant in season and out of season, abundantly irregular in his ministry, and ready to avail himself of any assistance from men of like religious bias, whether they preached from the pulpit or the horse block, he effected a great change in the morals of his people, organized schools, prayer meetings &c impairing his own heath materially |29 by his exertions. He was best known by the name of Fletcher, & in advanced years married Miss Bosanquet, as imbued with the principles of methodism, if not more so, than himself. His tendency to consumption reduced him more than once to death's door, & required an interruption of his spiritual exertions. On occasions of these retreats he visited the South of France & his native Country, there also, as far as his strength allowed, doing the work of a missionary. He was held in high estimation by the Wesleys and other leaders of the Methodists, male & female, among whom his self denial, boundless charity, simplicity and enthusiastic devotional spirit acquired many sincere friends. The Countess of Huntingdon selected him as superintendant of her Methodist Seminary for educating pious youths for the Ministry at Trevecka in Wales, but he withdrew on conscientious principles from that institution, the foundress of which, having embraced the Calvinistic doctrines of

Whitefield, required them to be taught there. Mr. Fletcher was engaged in controversy with the maintainers of these principles, & wrote several books, which are in very high esteem among the Wesleyans. He died Vicar of Madeley in 1785, at the age of 56 years. His biographers consider many providential deliverances, which |[30] he experienced, chiefly in early life, of a miraculous nature and amplify them as ~~special~~ proofs of a special interference of the Almighty to protect a chosen vessel. His qualifications both of heart and intellect were, indeed, in many points, of the highest order, but his enthusiastic temper led him into irregularities of doctrine and discipline, which cannot be too severely blamed. To the same temper must be ascribed much puerility in his correspondence & recorded conversations.

Monday May 17.

I rejoined my dear wife at Gloucester, and had the comfort to find her health considerably amended.—

Tuesday May 18.

In our evening walk we called at a house in Wotton, a hamlet near Gloucester, where a Roman Monument had recently been found in digging foundations for a building about two yards below the surface. The situation is adjacent to the road, near where the road is decidedly Roman, leading from Glevum (Gloucester) to Corinium (Cirencester) The stone, which is an oblong of considerable size, represents in relief a |[31] Roman Knight on horseback, armed with his spear, and his sword girt on his right thigh: beneath his galloping steed an enemy lies prostrate, whom he is preparing to pierce, and who holds a short sword. The sculpture of the horse is particularly good. The face of the knight is mutilated. Beneath is the following inscription. Rufus Sita Eques Coh. VI. Tracum. Ann. XL. Slip XXII. Hæredes Exs. Test. F. curav. H. S. F. the frame work of the Bas relief is surmounted by three sculptures of the Heads of animals: a lion's head on each side, and a sphinx in the middle between them. A cinerary Urn nearly entire was found near the same spot. It is on the side of the same road about four miles farther, at Whitcomb, on the property of Sir W. Hicks, that the remains of an extensive Roman Villa were found some years ago: and recently an elaborate tesselated pavement has been discovered in Lord Bathurst's grounds near Cirencester. At some distance to the left of the same road in the parish of Withington, the remains of a Roman Villa with tesselated Pavement, Bath, Hypocaust &c. were found, which I visited, a few years back.—

--- |[32]

Wednesday May 19.

Mrs. Backhouse had an evening party.

Thursday May 20.

My cousins Anne & Apphia Witts, who still continue at Gloucester, with another lady, drank tea at ~~Miss W~~ Mrs. Backhouse's.

~~Friday~~ Saturday May 22.

We returned home through Cheltenham, calling on my mother. My wife's health, thank GOD, seems considerably improved.—

Sunday May 23.

"A letter to a Clergyman, on the peculiar tenets of the present day. By R. Bransby Cooper Esqr. MP. London 1824." A very valuable pamphlet by the conscientious and judicious Member for Gloucester. Such a publication by a layman is highly beneficial to the cause of orthodoxy. The delineation of the errors in doctrine held by the Evangelical Clergy and their followers is correct, calm, temperate and earnest. There is no obtrusion of deep and recondite learning, but an earnest and forcible view of scriptural, i.e. Church of England principles: the argument is stated without presumption in a clear manner; no forced inferences; no uncharitable insinuations. It was known to a few of Mr. Cooper's friends, that he was the |[33] anonymous author of two sound political pamphlets: they will hope to see his pen again employed in defence of the Church, which he conscientiously reveres. I have had the pleasure of his acquaintance for many years, and frequently acted with him most cordially in the administration of County affairs; he possesses sound & cool judgment, with liberal and gentlemanlike feelings on all points. He is brother of the celebrated Surgeon, Sir Astley Cooper; his fortunes have been considerably impaired by unsuccessful speculations in trade: his eldest Son, Mr. Purnell, enjoys his Mother's landed property in this County, and is an intelligent and firm magistrate, who has within these few years taken his seat on the bench; his second Son, Mr. R. Cooper, is the worthy & orthodox Chaplain of our County Gaol, a young Clergyman of considerable promise.

Wednesday May 26.

We dined at Mr. E. Leigh's at Broadwell, meeting Mr. Ford, Mrs. Hall of Batsford, her sister, a Mrs. Davenport, with her husband, Mr. Vavasour, & Mrs. Shakespeare Phillips and her daughter, from Cheshire.

Tuesday June 1.

"An itinerary of Provence and the Rhone, made during the year 1819. By John Hughes AM. Oriel College Oxford. Lond 1822. |[34] 8vo" This is a very spirited account of the author's tour from Paris to Lyons; thence by Vienne, Valence, Orange to Avignon, along the course of the Rhone; to Montpellier & Nismes on the one side; to Marseilles, Toulon, Frejus, Antibes, Nice on the other, ending with his entrance into Italy by the Col di Tende. There is much lively description of manners and modes of thinking & conversation; the scenery is sketched with much taste and in an intelligible manner; such I mean are his descriptions, for the etchings are vile scratchings; but a series of views engraved by the Messieurs Cooke ~~are~~ is published, illustrative of this Volume, which I have no doubt are executed in a superior manner. Mr. Hughes has the elements of a poet and frequently alludes to the classics of old, and the bards of modern times; if I mistake not, there are some prolusions of his own in that way; I identify him with one of the name, who has been among the recent ornaments of Ovid. The lively cheerful style of the book is very attractive, and while it is quite full enough to gratify the stay-at-home traveller, it is well adapted both as to size and matter to serve as an excellent itinerary to those, who have leisure to pursue their travels beyond the limits of their own country.

--- |[35]

Friday June 4.

"Narrative of an Expedition from Tripoli in Barbary to the Western frontier of Egypt in 1817, by the bey of Tripoli: in letters to Dr. Viviani of Genoa by Paolo della Cella M.D. Physician attendant on the bey: with an appendix, containing instructions for navigating the Great Syrtis. Translated from the Italian by Anthony Aufrere Esqr. Lond. 1822. 8vo." The eldest son of the Pacha of Tripoli, a barbarian of the most cruel, ungovernable propensities, and of the most infamous principles, having been by his greatly offended Father sent into honourable exile as Governor of that extreme part of his dominions, which occupies the site of the ancient Cyrenaica, and having there joined some rebellious tribes, at whose head he continued in a state of revolt, the younger brother was dispatched from Tripoli with a considerable force to subdue the insurrection and restore his Father's authority. The author accompanied him on this occasion as Physician, & kept a journal of the route, making such observations as the extent of his acquirements and the opportunity afforded him on the march allowed. And though a more learned traveller, with less constraint and more leisure, would, doubtless, have been able to furnish more valuable information on the almost untravelled tract, which the Tripoline army followed, a Tract |[36] also in many respects very interesting both as to its natural history and geography, its remains of antiquity and the manners and customs of the inhabitants, yet Dr. della Cella has accumulated many interesting facts, collected many instructive hints of character & the state of society, & reasoned plausibly on the various geographical & antiquarian questions, which arise in traversing the shores of the greater Syrtis, & the Cyrenaica. The latter affords a rich harvest of ruins, Ægyptian, Grecian & Roman: with fruits worthy of the Garden of the Hesperides; nomade tribes in a low state of civilization inhabiting a rich, hilly and well watered country, naturally producing the finest ~~products of~~ vegetable stores, dates, almonds, vines &c. and every ~~way~~ where a government barbarous, corrupt, tyrannical and debasing. Curious sketches of the character of the Bey and his Ministers, his army and his fanatical Marabouts, his want of discipline, his crafty manoeuvres, absence of true courage, & redundant treachery,

170. Washbourne.

occur in the book. Though the Author seems to have greatly enjoyed the fine scenery of the Cyrenaica, the fountain of Apollo at Cyrene, the ruins of temples aqueducts & towers, yet I suspect, he was not sorry, when the Expedition returned, and his alarms subsided.

——— |37

Tuesday June 8.

My Mother came to us from Cheltenham for her usual summer visit, and, thank GOD, considering her age and infirmities, she now enjoys good health.

———

Wednesday June 9.

Second dinner this year of the Stow Clerical Society. A very fine day favoured the meeting of a large party. More than twenty met—Mr. Malcolm presided.

———

Friday June 11.

The Gazette contains the appointment of the new bishop of Chester. It was well understood, that the choice of Government had fallen upon one of the first scholars of the age, particularly in the department of Greek literature, Dr. C. J. Blomefield, Archdeacon of Colchester & Rector of St. Botolph Bishopsgate.[9] He is a Cambridge man & in the prime of life; was reckoned an excellent preacher at the University, and is a most sound and orthodox divine. His pamphlet against the aspersions of the Edinburgh Reviewers & their partizans was greatly approved, & his familiar and perspicuous lectures on St. John's Gospel, his Sermon on family prayer &c., intended for the edification of his parishioners, were well calculated |38 to increase a spirit of rational piety & sound principles. The selection of such a man does great credit to our rulers.

———

Charles Baring Goold, a pupil of Mr. Price of Coln St. Dennis, arrived to-day on a short visit to us. He is a nice gentlemanlike lad, son of Mr. & Mrs. Baring Goold of Teignmouth, Devonshire. Mrs. G. is my cousin, having been a Miss Sabine.

———

Thursday June 17.

Our dear Edward came home for the midsummer holidays; he seems in excellent health & spirits, and Mr. Hale writes a most satisfactory account of his progress in his learning and good behaviour.

———

Charles Gould, who is a well behaved, modest, pleasing lad of fifteen, returned to Coln St. Dennis.

———

Saturday June 19.

I have omitted hitherto to mention the nomination of the Revd. Mr. Coleridge to be Bishop of Barbadoes. This gentleman, whose character stands very high, is a Student of Christ Church, and one of the joint secretaries of the Society for promoting Christian Knowledge. The ministerial arrangements consequent on the formation of the new sees not being concluded,

9. Charles James Blomfield, (1786-1857). Blomfield held numerous livings before becoming Archdeacon of Colchester, 1822-4, Bishop of Chester, 1824-8 and Bishop of London, 1829-56. Blomfield was an influential man within the Church and set about much reform including the reduction of pluralism and non-residence.

Bp. Lipscomb and Bp. Coleridge have not yet |[39] sailed for those colonies, where, it is to be hoped, they will be able gradually to effect much good by concentrating the interests, zeal & intelligence of the Episcopal Clergy, by spreading abroad a spirit of rational piety, by fostering, improving & giving a right direction to education, by ameliorating the tone of morality, and watching over the progress of true religion.

Tuesday June 22.

Our neighbour, Mr. Hurd, the Rector of Naunton, calling about dinner time, gave us his company for the rest of the day.

Saturday June 26.

I rode with my tenant, Mr. George Cook of Stanway, to look over a small estate advertised for sale in the parish of Great Washbourn, five or six miles from thence, between Alderton & Beckford. Some money, the interest of which is Mrs. Backhouse's for her life, and which then devolves to us, being included in our marriage settlement, has been for some years out on Mortgage, and at present is lent on the security of an estate at Ilmer in Bucks, the property of a gentleman of the name of Greenwood, who has given us notice of his intention to pay it in after Michaelmas, as he is about to sell his Ilmer property. We are, therefore, looking out for an investment |[40] in land or an eligible mortgage. The Great Washbourn Estate is about 108 acres, and is offered at £4500: probably, it would be dear at £4000. The land is good, but out of condition, the buildings very dilapidated. The vendors are the representatives of the late Mr. Fowke of Tewkesbury.

On my return I dined with Frederick Aston; his brother W. Aston & his wife are now on a visit to him. Mr. W.A. is a West India Merchant & broker, residing in the city.

Sunday June 27.

Parliament was prorogued on Friday by the King in person. His Majesty enjoys tolerable health, and passes his time chiefly between Carlton Palace & Windsor castle and lodge. His Palace at Brighton does not appear to be as much in favour as formerly. The State of Ireland has, as is usual, occupied a great share of the attention of Parliament: several new enactments & former acts amended testify the desire to introduce a better system into every department social & civil in that ill fated Country. Severe attacks upon the Episcopal establishment there have been made by the Opposition members, and repelled by statements of facts |[40] and the production of authentic documents. The disturbances prevalent in the South of Ireland give great reason for fear; but the renewal of the insurrection act arms the executive with a strong weapon for defence as well as correction. The so-called Catholic Association does all in its power to injure its own cause, by turbulent debating, violent petitions, aggravation, exaggeration, and assumption. The Orange Society recommends moderation, abstinence from processions &c.—but their existence, as a body bound by secret engagements in support of Protestant interests, is calculated to irritate, while the Government is probably rather hampered than aided by their operations. The affairs of the West Indies have also been canvassed at great length, and generally speaking, with much temper in parliament. An experiment is to be made in some of the conquered islands towards the introduction of a better system among the slaves, with a view to raising them in the scale of society, and giving them the privilege of leaving their property by will, and appearing as witnesses ~~of er~~ in courts of justice. A very long discussion lately took place on the case of a Missionary of the name of Smith, stationed at Demerara, who |[41] was brought to trial before a Court Martial, charged with being aware of the rebellion, that was breaking out among the slaves in that colony, but not communicating the information. Certain it is, that the principal leaders of the revolt were members of his congregation, and in habitual intercourse with him, & that he must have had a suspicion at least of what was going on. His style of preaching also had been incautious. He was condemned to death, but recommended to mercy: a sufficiently contradictory conclusion—Execution was staid by the Government in the Island: and matters were referred to Ministers at home, who sent out orders for sparing his life, but banishing him from the islands. The man was dead of a disease, which had long afflicted him, before the decision of Government reached Demerara. This case has been taken up by the dissenters with wonderful zeal, petitions were forwarded from every town & congregation for a review of the conduct of the local government, court-martial &c.—and in the speeches of Mr. Brougham, Mr. Wilberforce &c., Smith was held forth as a martyr, and all possible obloquy thrown on the Governor of the Island, the Members of the Court Martial &c. Undoubtedly, there was |[42] much to blame in the manner, in which the man had been tried, both as to the constitution of the court, and the nature of the evidence admitted, but it is difficult to believe, that Smith was ignorant of the intended revolt, and much allowance must be made for the agitated state of the island, the apprehensions and the irritability of the government & proprietors. Our relations with the States of Europe promise a continuance of peace; and the policy of government at once liberal, open, and manly, seems to command respect and deference from the cabinets of other nations. In Portugal an attempt to suppress all liberal institutions and establish pure despotic rule has been made by the Queen consort, and her son Don Miguel. They had already possessed themselves of the person of the King, and commenced with the support of the Military, (the prince being commander in chief,) a series of proscriptions against their opponents in principle. But the energetic measures of the members of the Diplomatic body at Lisbon rescued the king from his thraldom: he took refuge on board a British man of war in the Tagus, and placing himself in the hands of persons of liberal sentiments & talent, pur- |[43] -sued an energetic course, which has ended in the banishment of the Prince, who has gone on his travels into France, while his royal Mother is to live in retirement at a lone palace or convent. The public opinion has been loudly expressed in petitions to parliament and the speeches of popular orators respecting the recognition of those states in South America, which have thrown off the yoke of Spain, & established their independence. It is argued, that vast commercial benefits will be secured to the nation by a liberal and early acknowledgment. To this Ministers respond by the appointment of Consuls, to protect British Trade in those regions, & Commissioners, to ascertain & report the real state of affairs as to the alledged independence of the republics in question, and their probable durability. Indeed, a full recognition seems only delayed by diplomatic etiquette, & a negociation with the parent State, Spain, that she may, if she chuse, take that precedence in the recognition of these states, which should be conceded to her by other powers. An expectation was entertained, that the assessed taxes would have been taken off either wholly or in |[44] part: but the Chancellor of the Exchequer preferred reducing the duties on certain commodities, and so affording relief indirectly; the system of government at present is one of great liberality in respect of trade, and if their theoretical views of political economy be correct, great practical benefits will accrue to the country in a short time. One great financial operation has been most successfully accomplished, the reduction of the 4 per cents. which have been converted into a stock bearing interest at 3½ per cent. The customary activity has been shewn this Sessions both by the advocates of Roman Catholic emancipation & the friends of the Dissenters. Well aware, that the time would not suit for the attainment of the full prayer of the Roman Catholics, the exertions of their friends have been limited to obtain for those professing that religion in England an equality of privileges with those enjoyed by the Roman Catholics of Ireland: particularly, that they might be introduced into the Magistracy, and allowed to hold ~~the~~ offices in the revenue department without being called on to take the oath of supremacy. There appeared a strong inclination on the part of some members of the administration to grant this boon; even a Bishop, |[45] Dr. Ryder, professed, that he saw no harm in granting the petition, but other opinions happily prevailed, and the unshaken firmness of the admirable Lord Chancellor Eldon, [with] the able arguments of Bishops Law & Burgess, carried a large majority with them against the motion in the House of Lords. Towards the close of the Session, however, a bill was introduced & passed into a law with little opposition, by which the Hereditary Earl Marshal, the Duke of Norfolk, who is a Roman Catholic, is empowered to discharge the functions of his office in person without taking the oaths. His former deputy was his Protestant Brother, Lord Henry Howard Molyneux, who is recently deceased; and though it is difficult to avoid being jealous of any concession, on which may be founded an imaginary claim for farther relaxation of principle, yet this seems the least objectionable indulgence, inasmuch as, whatever might have been of old the political influence and power of the Earl Marshal, it is now reduced to a mere shadow. Nor were the Unitarians successful in their application to Parliament for leave to intermarry by their own forms in their own meeting houses, and so avoid |[46] what they represent as a most grievous burden on their consciences; listening to, and partaking in a ceremony, in the course of ~~the~~ which the doctrine of the Trinity is more than once solemnly adverted to. But here again the excellent friends of the Church in the Upper house of Parliament rescued her from becoming, as the Chancellor expressed himself, the handmaid of dissent. The sophistry & false reasoning of the Unitarians were most ably exposed by Bishop ~~in~~ Law in a speech worthy of his own Dr. Paley; and it would have been gratifying to the orthodox members of the church, if an equal firmness and equally sound reasoning had been displayed by the respected Premier, and the Metropolitan. The church has, however, reason to be gratified with the appropriation of the sum of five hundred thousand pounds for the erection of additional churches in populous places: and it is a measure, which will greatly conduce in the end to the cause of religion, morals, & loyalty. In certain quarters it was of course unpopular, as was also another grant of three hundred thousand pounds for the repair of Windsor castle. Ministers found the means for this liberality in the unexpected |[47] arrangement with the Government of Austria, by which they recovered two millions and a half, in composition with our Imperial creditor for loans to a far greater amount supplied during the wars with France.

———

Monday June 28.

I dined at Mr. Hurd's, the Rector of Naunton, meeting Mr. Wynniatt, Mr. R. Wynniatt, Mr. C. Keysall, Mr. Bowen, & Mr. Hawkins.—

Tuesday June 29.

Mrs. Croome died this day, after a very lingering decline. She leaves her husband, the Rector of Bourton on the Water, with a family of six children; the eldest about sixteen. Her loss will be severely felt by her family: to her children she was ever an attentive mother Mrs. Croome was daughter of Mr. Daubeny, a former rector of Stratton, near Cirencester, and niece of the learned divine and author, Dr. Daubeny, Archdeacon of Sarum. Her brother Dr. E. Daubeny, a fellow of Magdalen College, Oxford, and M.D. is an able chymist and mineralogist.

Friday July 2.

We dined at Mr. R Wynniatt's at Guiting Grange, meeting Mrs. Wynniatt, (Mr. R.W's mother,) Mrs. |48 Scoope, (Mrs. R.W's mother,) Mr. & Mrs. Woodyatt, Mr. Bowen & Mrs. Wynniatt of Staunton. Mr. Woodyatt is brother of the late Mrs. C. Keysall, is in the navy, and resides at Malvern.—

Saturday July 3.

Mr. C. Keysall came to us from Bredon. He has for some weeks past assisted Dr. Rice in the duty at Oddington, during the absence of the latter with his family in town. Mr. Hurd met him at dinner.—

Monday July 5.

Mr. C. Keysall returned to Bredon.—

Wednesday July 7.—

I notice in the papers with great regret the death of Mr. Rennel, the Vicar of Kensington, and Son of the able Dean of Winchester. The loss of Mr. R. is very serious to the church; his works in defence of true religion and national piety, and his able refutation of the assertions and arguments of the gainsayers of Christianity & our excellent church rank among the best and most convincing publications in Theology in modern days. He was amiable as well as learned, clever & judicious.

Friday July 9th.

We dined at Mr. Price's, the Rector |49 of Coln St. Dennis. I had previously attended at the Petty Sessions at Northleach Bridewell. We met Mr. Hicks Beach of Williamstrip, formerly member of Parliament for Cirencester, Mr. & Mrs. C. Pitt; (he is just instituted to the living of Haulton, void by the death of M. Waller of Hall Barn & Farmington); Miss Horrocks, daughter of the Member for Preston, & niece to Mrs. C. Pitt, Mr. Whitehead of the East Indian Company's naval Service, nephew to Mrs. C. Pitt, Mr. E. Hughes, a fellow of Jesus Coll. Oxford, Mrs. Price, Senr. & Miss Davis, Mrs. W. Price's Sister.

Saturday July 10.

My Aunt Lady Lyttelton arrived from Cookham to stay a day or two here. At the age of eighty one, she had been making a long and fatiguing tour, particularly, after a severe illness in the winter & spring, by which she been greatly debilitated. Among other places, she had formed one of the many guests at Stowe, the Seat of the Duke of Buckingham, on occasion of the Christening of the Marquis of Chandos's eldest Son, the heir of the Dukedom, which was celebrated with great and expensive festivities.[10] The ancient |*50* alliance between the Grenvilles & Lytteltons entitled my Aunt to appear, as on a former occasion, among the family friends of the Temples & Chandos's. She is now on her return to her house near Malvern, and is certainly considerably broken by her late severe indisposition, being both feeble & deaf: while on subjects, which interest her, her former earnestness & an enthusiasm approaching to romance, with a very comprehensive mind and considerable range of information, continue unimpaired.

Monday July 12.

Mrs. Backhouse having been led to expect my arrival at Gloucester this evening, previous to the Quarter Sessions, and there not being an opportunity of letting her know, that in consequence of Lady Lyttelton's arrival my Journey to Gloucester must be deferred till the following morning, I was under the necessity of leaving my Aunt for Gloucester, where I arrived by the Regulator in the evening, and found my Mother-in-law very well.

Tuesday July 13.

The Quarter Sessions commenced. Dr. Cooke and Mr. Cripps presided in the two Courts. Among the |*51* Magistrates present were Messrs. Pye, Goodrich, Keysall, Dr. Timbrill, Dr. Davis, Archdeacon Sandiford, Sir W. Guise, Genl. Guise, Crawley, Phelps, Newman, Price, Ford &c.

171. Westgate Street, Gloucester.

10. Richard Plantagenet Campbell, (1823-1889), 3rd Duke of Buckingham, (1861-89). Richard Plantagenet Campbell was born on 10 September 1823 and baptised 15 June 1824 at Stowe.

The committees appointed to consider the Gaol Regulations, and the alteration of the County rate had met on the 5th., at which time I had found it inconvenient to obey the summons sent to me. As to the Prison regulations little progress was made, and the Committee was desired to sit again & report to the next Sessions. The amount of salary to be given to the Chaplain under the new act was referred to them, and the worthy Mr. R. Cooper was at their suggestion allowed £200 per ann. the old Salary being doubled.

The report of the Committee as to the county rate was also adopted. It recommended the formation of a new rate on the basis of the Shire Hall rate, which itself was grounded on the Property Tax assessments. This committee is also to continue in operation.

The lingering affair of the monument to Sir G. O. Paul was again brought forward. It is now proposed to employ |52 a rising young artist, by name Sevier, who is to execute the monument in memory of Dr. Jenner, now in progress, and also to be erected by subscription. Mr. Sevier has produced an excellent bust of the Lord Chancellor. The difficulty of making a good resemblance of Sir G. Paul is great: the only guide, which Mr. Sevier had to follow in a bust exhibited this day was a small medallion in wax, the production of Lady Denbigh, Lord Ducie's daughter, many years ago, & though Mr. S.'s bust was very creditable to his talents, and represented a fine, stern, prominent featured, intelligent man, it was not a likeness of Sir G.P. This will, however, it is to be hoped, be remedied in another attempt, my old Schoolfellow & brother magistrate, the Revd. G. Crawley, having great skill in drawing likenesses, has furnished from memory a sketch of the departed Baronet, which in the principal features is a great resemblance, and which he has given to Mr. Sevier as an aid for the modelling his bust. The rest of the monument is proposed to consist of a tablet with an emblematical figure & drapery: to be erected in the Cathedral. |53 Lady Lyttelton, having left Upper Slaughter this morning after breakfast arrived at Gloucester to day to visit my cousins, the Miss Witts's, who still remain here, in lodgings at the Spa, where Mrs. Backhouse & myself past part of the evening.

Wednesday July 14.

After dining at the King's Head Inn with my brother Magistrates, as usual, I spent an hour at ~~the~~ Mrs. M. Hunt's in the evening to meet Lady Lyttelton, Mrs. Backhouse, & Miss Witts's.—

Thursday July 15.

After an early cold dinner, I returned home, the business of the Sessions being nearly concluded. My horses met me at Frogmill Inn, whither I came by the Coach.

Saturday July 24.

My two cousins Maria & Fanny Whalley, the younger daughters of Mrs. Whalley, two very pleasing and amiable young women of twenty and twenty two years of age, came on a visit to us from Cheltenham, where they had been staying some weeks with my Aunt Travell.

--- |54

Tuesday July 27.

Frederick Aston dined here.

Wednesday July 28.

The annual General meeting of the Stow Provident Bank was held. Lord Redesdale was in the Chair, and the Report was read by our indefatigable Treasurer, Mr. Pole. Eighteen Trustees and Managers attended. The following is a summary of the Treasurer's report & balance Sheet.

June 30. 1824	
Government receipts & Cash in hands of Treasurer & Clerk	£32,785.3.9
Cash due to Depositors	£32,280.8.8
Profit on the transactions from the commencement of the Institution over and above all claims from the depositors, and after all demands paid	£670.5.1
3 per Cent Annuities	£2201.19.2
Total number of Depositors 660	
Total of Interest due to 1 July 1824	£1141.1.2
Deposited from 30 June 1823 to 30 June 1824	£9203.7.2
Withdrawn in the same period	£4601.19.11 |[55]

A new act of Parliament has lately been passed, which considerably limits the operations of the Banks for savings and enjoins a regular and uniform system of management: the Act is to come into force on Nov. 20. and the Committee of accounts of our Institution, with Mr. Pole's assistance, has been occupied some time in revising our regulations and making them conformable to the provisions of the act, so that we might be prepared to commence a new æra on the 20th. of November agreeably to the views of the legislature. The principle and practical details came this day under discussion, but there existing some doubts as to the interpretation of some important clauses in the Act, the farther consideration of the proposed new regulations was referred to an adjourned meeting, to be summoned by the Committee of accounts, when those doubts should be removed by application to the Commissioners for the reduction of the national debt, to whose account the payments |[56] of all Banks for savings are paid. Mr. Pole will communicate with this body. General satisfaction was expressed at the prosperity of the Institution and compliments were paid, not undeserved, I trust, I may say, to the Treasurer and acting Managers. The Trustees, Managers, Treasurer and Committee of Accounts were reelected with some additions.

Thursday July 29.

Our agreeable cousins, the Misses M. & F. Whalley left us for Swerford.

Frederick Aston very unexpectedly came to dinner. He had been induced to ride over to communicate a very distressing event, which had happened at Stanway this morning, the suicide of one of the parishioners, a married woman, of the name of Kendrick, about sixty years of age, who drowned herself in the canal, a piece of water in the pleasure grounds of Stanway House. Kendrick, the husband, has resided at Stanway for some years, since he became bankrupt as an Innkeeper at Toddington; he is now committed to gaol, for refusing to answer questions put to him by the Commissioners |[57] of his second bankruptcy, his affairs being again involved. Kendrick &, I fear, his sons, are most unprincipled persons: the want of sound religious principle, uncontrolled passionateness of feeling, and dread of poverty and accumulated distress, have no doubt brought on the temporary insanity, under the influence of which the wretched woman has sought a watery grave.

Tuesday Aug. 3.

We dined at Mrs. Rice's, Bourton on the Water, who spends some summer months at her house there every year; at other times she resides with her protegé Mr. Morrison and his wife, also a former protegée, at Stoneleigh, in Warwickshire, where he is Curate, & takes pupils. The Morrisons are now with Mrs. Rice. We met Mr. & Mrs. Adams of Chastleton, with their Son & daughter. He is a worthy divine & magistrate for Oxon & Gloucestershire. Mr. & Mrs. George of Bourton on the Water, with her sister, Miss Whitehead, Mr. & Miss Croome of Cirencester, Mr. John Croome, the Rector of Bourton, and Miss Margt. Croome, his daughter, made up the party.

--- |58

Wednesday Aug. 4.

Third meeting of the Stow clerical Society Thirteen members dined together. Mr. Malcolm presided. Mr. Bowen was elected Chairman for the next year.

Friday Aug. 6.

Our beloved boy left us this day to return to school, in good health. May the Almighty watch over him! His warm affection, simplicity of heart, and quickness of apprehension endear him to all, who know him. Mrs. Rice of Bourton on the Water was kind enough to take him in her carriage to Bath, whither she was going, accompanied by Mrs. Morrison.

We dined at Mr. Ford's at Little Risington, meeting several of the Pole family, Mr. E. Leigh, & Dr. Warneford.

Wednesday Aug. 11.

We had the pleasure of a visit for some hours from our friends Mr. & Mrs. J. Round, who are on their way with three of their children to Tenby and other parts of Wales. They came to us from Mr. Barter's at Sarsden, where they had been passing a day, and after an early dinner proceeded in the evening to Cheltenham.

--- |59

Thursday Aug. 12.

Our friend Charles Keysall unexpectedly gave us the pleasure of his company to-day, dining and sleeping here.—

Friday Aug. 13.

Mr. C. Keysall returned to Bredon. He has taken the Curacies of Bretforton and Somerville's Aston; the former in Worcestershire, the latter in Gloucestershire: both places are near Evesham.

Saturday Aug. 14.

Frederick Aston came to dinner, and to spend a few days with us.

Sunday Aug. 15.

I exchanged duties with Frederick Aston, & dined and slept at Wood Stanway. Recent irregularities in the parish of Stanway, ending in the birth of three illegitimate children, the offspring of two young women of decent situation in life, and a married woman, whose husband has left her, seemed, particularly, in my good Curate's opinion, to require animadversion from the pulpit, which they according received from the Vicar.

Monday Aug. 16.

I returned home from Stanway.

--- |60

Wednesday Aug: 18.

Mr. F. Aston returned to Stanway.

Tuesday Aug. 24.

My dearest wife's birth-day: she is this day 38 years old. May GOD long preserve her to be a blessing to her son and myself! May her very delicate health be improved!

We dined at Mrs. Dolphin's at Eyford, meeting Mr. & Mrs. R. Wynniatt, & Mr. & Mrs. J. Eeles, a relation of Mr. D's, whom I have long slightly known, a very estimable person, formerly in the Victualling Office, and now residing in Herts. Mrs. Eeles appears a very pleasing person. Mr. Bowen was of the party, as also a professional performer from town, a Mr. Rovedino, son of a celebrated singer of that name and himself a beautiful singer, exhibiting on the stage of the Opera house, but with a voice better suited to a drawing room. Of course we had a good deal of beautiful music.

Friday Aug. 27.

I attended a meeting at Halford Bridge Inn in Warwickshire of the proprietors of the Stratford & Moreton Rail road. The day was beautiful & the long ride taken leisurely very agreeable: harvest and gleaning on every |61 side. A mile or two beyond Moreton I overtook Lord Redesdale, whom I joined, and we soon fell into very interesting & instructive conversation on various points. At Halford Bridge we met Mr. Langstone, of Sarsden ~~Park~~, Oxon, M.P. for Woodstock, Mr. Penystone, Mr. Atty, the High Sherriff for Warwickshire, Mr. Raine, Mr. Rice, Messrs. Bellamy & Barister, the Clerks, Solicitors at Shipstone, Mr. James the Clerk and agent of the Company, besides several other proprietors, but unfortunately there were not a sufficient number of shares represented by the gentlemen present or the proxies, which they held, to constitute a general meeting of the Company, 200 shares being the number required by the Act of Parliament. Probably, pique and ill humour kept some away. Nothing final or effectual could, therefore, be done, but another meeting was called for the 20th. September, the affairs of the company loudly demanding some judicious and energetic measure. It seems, that all the subscriptions received have been expended; in addition to which £10,000 have been borrowed, and more than £7000 |62 is owing, and yet such is the backwardness of the work, that, perhaps, £30000 more will be necessary to complete the road, that is, both the lines, that to Moreton, and the branch to Shipstone. Of this it is expected, that the Commissioners for the issuing exchequer bills on loan to the Managers of public works will advance £10000, and there is a claim on a large list of shareholders, who have not paid in their subscriptions, but of these several are insolvent, and legal measures will be necessary to enforce the payment of the greater part. So utterly empty was the purse, that those present, who were most interested, as holding the greatest number of shares, found it requisite to subscribe £800 to keep the workmen together, and enable the Clerk to meet the most necessary demands on the next pay day. The fact is, a great deal of money has been thrown away by want of due consideration in the outset, by employing incompetent surveyors, making improvident contracts, varying the line and system, and generally by want of experience on the part of those, who undertook to superintend the progress of the concern. |63 The present clerk and manager, Mr. James, seems a very intelligent man, & thoroughly conversant with such business, but he has only been employed of late. It is proposed, as far as possible, to use locomotive steam engines instead of horse labour on the road. Much of the work is in great forwardness, and the line to Moreton, if funds can be supplied, might be finished by Christmas, that to Shipstone also by Lady day next; but the means of raising money seems to me very difficult, and the disunion among the shareholders ominous. Could the work by any magic operation be immediately concluded, even should the expences of the work amount to £60000, I have no doubt, that it would from the first pay very reasonable interest to those, who have embarked their money, and that the trade would increase: but the question is, where are funds to be procured?

When the meeting broke up Mr. Rice and myself rode back by engagement with Lord Redesdale to Batsford, where we dined and slept. Besides Mr. John Mitford, and his Sister, we met a nephew of Lord R's. |64 Mr. Bertram Mitford, with his wife and daughter, all very pleasant persons, on a visit at Batsford. Mr. B. Mitford has a place under the Irish Government, & resides near Dublin. Of course this was procured for him by his Uncle, when Chancellor. The evening passed agreeably in conversation with interludes of music, looking over drawings and engravings &c. It was very pleasing to see the venerable peer in the bosom of his family, cheerful, easy, kindhearted, sincere, communicative: and it is impossible to pass some hours with him without carrying away a good deal of anecdote & information.—

Saturday Aug. 28.

I returned home.

Tuesday Sept. 7.

We had a dinner party: the Hon. Mr. & Mrs. Rice, and two daughters, from Oddington, Mrs. Rice, from Bourton on the Water, Mr. & Mrs. Price & Mr. C. Goold from Coln St. Dennis, & Mr. Vavasour formed the circle.

--- |65

Friday Sept. 10.

Our old friend Mr. Wellford came on a visit to us. I must retrace a little his history. He is the son of some very old and intimate friends of my Uncle Broome Witts, & as such was introduced to me by him in 1814, when Mr. Wellford, at a more advanced age than is usual, was about to enter into the Church. His views had in earlier life been directed to trade, which he had quitted from a desire to enter into the Church, although his family were dissenters. He had consequently gone to Exeter College. I was able to forward his wishes,

& oblige my Uncle, by giving him a title for orders on this living, and he resided here in the Rectory house, as Curate, during a visit of three months, which we made in Yorkshire. His next Curacy was Moreton in Marsh, Dr. Warneford having engaged him, as soon as he left us: and a most painstaking and conscientious Pastor he proved himself, acquiring the love and esteem of a large portion of his parishioners, & being generally regarded and valued by the neighbouring Clergy. But with very delicate health, and a mind not |66 greatly attuned to cheerfulness, accustomed also not to look on the bright side of things, he had imbibed and encouraged in himself many of those religious views, which mark the class known by the name of Evangelical; being devoid, however, of many of the weak characters of that party, ostentation, cant, or uncharitableness. In fact his understanding is excellent, and his benevolence warm. This cast, however, as it developed itself, proved very disagreeable to Dr. Warneford, who plumed himself on his high church principles, & a separation between the Rector & Curate ensued, which at the time required some delicacy of management, and at which I was present. Shortly after Mr. Wellford became Curate of Bray, near Maidenhead, where his sentiments & opinions were all congenial: the Vicar, Mr. Townsend, an excellent man, was like himself serious; and similar religious views prevailed in the parish & neighbourhood: there M. Wellford has now for several years resided, much respected & beloved; but is likely to be removed ere long, as the former Vicar being |67 dead, the living is now held for a short term by a non-resident, who will resign it to a nephew of the Bishop of Oxford, as soon as he shall be of age to take Priest's orders. Mr. Legge, however, is not yet Deacon. Mr. Wellford arrived here from Henley, where his Mother & Sisters reside; he has been at Eastbourn, enjoying a little holiday from the labours of his parochial charge, which are very heavy.

Monday Sept. 13.

Mr. Wellford left us to pass a day in & near Moreton in Marsh, that he might visit his old parishioners & neighbours.

Mr. G. Newmarch, the Attorney, dined here, having come on business relating to the money, which under our marriage settlement is on mortgage of an estate at Ilmer in Bucks. Mr. N. is about to leave Burford for Cirencester, where he is ~~about~~ to go into partnership with Mr. Lawrence.

Tuesday Sept. 14.

Our friend Wellford returned from his little excursion. I omitted to mention, that he is the author of a pamphlet on the controverted points about baptism; |68 in which he steers a middle course between the low tenets of the one party, and the ultra-doctrines of the other. He also printed an address to his parishioners at Moreton on leaving them, and a funeral sermon on the death of Mr. Townsend, the respected Vicar of Bray.

Wednesday Sept. 15.

The adjourned general meeting of the Stow Provident Bank was held this day. Very few Managers attended; Lord Redesdale took the chair, & in Mr. Pole's absence I laid the business reserved at the last meeting for consideration before the Managers present, who fortunately constituted a quorum. The regulations were passed, as altered conformably to the new Act of Parliament, and a hand bill directed to be immediately published and circulated, explanatory of the new system. Deposits are now limited to Fifty Pounds in the first year, and Thirty in very subsequent year, nor is any depositor allowed to hold more than £200 in any Savings Bank. Declarations are required from depositors, that they are |69 not possessed of funds in any other Saving's Bank, & a forfeiture of the funds so deposited ensues on a discovery, that the declaration is false. Benefit Societies are allowed still to make unlimited deposits. Depositors, whose account already exceeds £200, are not liable to have the surplus above that amount returned to them, but cannot make any farther deposit. There is no limit to the accumulation of interest not drawn. We continue to afford to depositors the accommodation of investing for them in the funds any sum, which they may wish to put out, and which exceeds in any case the limits imposed by the act, but, as in our former transactions, we are then answerable only for the value of the Stock at the market price, when sold, and we pay over to the owner of such Stock all dividends due to him, minus one per cent; & the expences of postage, brokerage &c. are charged to the individual.

Mr. Baillie, Curate to Mr. Rice at Great Risington, & private Tutor, to one of his younger sons, Henry, with his |70 pupil, dined with us to-day. Mr. Baillie was Wellford's predecessor in the Curacy of Bray.

Friday Sept. 17.

It appears from the newspapers, that the King of France, Louis 18. has paid the debt of nature. His dissolution has been for some time anticipated, as likely soon to occur. After a very chequered life of troubles, dangers, and disappointments, and the accomplishment of hopes so long deferred, that they were well-nigh abandoned, this aged head of the Bourbon family, oppressed with a load of fleshly infirmity, so that protracted life must have been burdensome, transmits his crown to his brother Monsieur, the former Count d'Artois, with every prospect of his wearing it in tranquillity, and continuing it in his sons and their representatives. No political struggle or alteration of men and measures is likely to ensue; the utter feebleness of health of the late king had occasioned a sort of transfer of power & interest to his brother, while yet alive; and Charles the 10th. will only have to manage the reins of government on his own |71 account. The late King was considered an estimable private character: not devoid of talent, or rather tact; and retained a grateful sense of the hospitality and protection, which he had experienced in this country, during the eclipse of the fortunes of his family.

We had a large dinner party. The Squire of Eyford & his wife; for the first time since the renewal of intercourse between us; his Uncle, our old friend John Dolphin, miserably altered in appearance from ill health, with his amiable wife, whose countenance also betrays great ravages made on her constitution by disease; their eldest daughter, a very lovely girl, just come out: Mr. & Mrs. Egerton Leigh, Mr. & Mrs. R. Wynniatt, Mr. & Mrs. Ford with ourselves making fifteen.

Saturday Sept. 18.

Our friend Mr. Wellford left us for Bray.

Tuesday Sept. 21.

My Mother left us for Stanway, where she is going to pass some time with Lady Elcho. Her visit |72 to us has been much longer than usual this summer, owing to Lady E's protracted stay in Town and on the sea coast. She has been arrived at Stanway about a fortnight. My Mother's state of health has varied much during the summer, and her spirits have depended greatly on her health: at all times her inability of moving & difficulty of respiration have been very painful.

Monday Sept 27.—

I dined and slept at Lady Elcho's; meeting, besides my mother and Miss Church, Genl. & Mrs. Fuller, Mr. C. Keysall, Mr. F. Aston & Mr. Marshall, Lord Wemyss's Steward Genl. Fuller has the 94th. Reg. and served in Spain: his wife a very pleasing woman, was a daughter of Genl. Floyd & sister to Mr. Secretary Peel's wife.

Tuesday Sept. 28.

I returned home.

Mrs. Backhouse arrived from Gloucester on a visit to us; she was accompanied by our distant connections, Mrs. M. Hunt, of Gloucester, and Misses Sophia & Caroline Hunt, daughters of the late Revd. Edward Hunt.

Monday Oct. 4.

The Hunts left us, returning to Gloucester; |73 the older lady is agreeable, well informed and conversible; the younger ladies amiable & pleasing.

"Redgauntlet. By the author of Waverley &c. 1824. 3 Vols." This is a very spirited, interesting book. The first volume, unlike any of the former productions of the great known unknown, is cast in the epistolary form, the latter volumes in the narrative & journal style. The scene is laid in Scotland, (Edinburgh & Dumfriesshire) and in Cumberland about twenty years after 1745, and Jacobite intriguers & intrigues are the leading features. Charles Stuart, the Pretender, of whom it is on record in the pages of history, that he visited England in disguise about that time, is introduced, and pourtrayed with great skill; his obstinacy, his illjudged partiality for a treacherous mistress, who domineered over him, the princely dignity of his address, and the attachment, which he excited, are ably drawn. The catastrophe is an abortive attempt at insurrection in his favour, foiled by the treachery of a partizan of the meaner order, and ending in a display of the forbearance and indulgence of the late king & his ministers. The hero is a spirited enthusiastic stripling, of Tory parentage on the father's side, but a Whig |74 on the side of his Mother, bred up in ignorance of his real name and future fortunes in the Scottish metropolis, under charge of an old fashioned Whig writer to the signet, to whose son, an excellent & acute young Advocate, he is warmly attached. The regard is mutual, and both the friends are involved in a series of dangers & difficulties among Smugglers, and other wild gentry on the Solway firth, where the grand Jacobite intriguer, Hugh Redgauntlet, Uncle, as it turns out, to the romantic hero, Darsie Latimer, possesses a mysterious & extensive influence. Lilias Redgauntlet, first the object of a castle-building admiration, and afterwards of sincere affection, when she turns out to be the hero's Sister, and so in no capacity of being his Dulcinea, is a well sketched character;

and of a love story there is no more than Darsie's delusion Of subordinate characters there are enow, & many excellent portraits. The Villain, Cristal Nixon, the insane Scottish Litigant, Poor Peter Peebles, the blind fiddler, Wandering Willie, the drunken captain of the Jumping Jenny, Nanty Ewart, the selfsubdued Quaker, Joshua Geddes, & his Sister Rachel, the hateful hypocrite Tom Turnpenny & others are excellently depicted.

——— |75

Tuesday Oct. 5.

Was held the annual meeting of the Stow District of the Society for promoting Christian Knowledge, at which the Hon. & Rev. E. Rice presided. The report made by the Secretary, Mr. Ford, was very satisfactory, in as far as it announced increased activity in the circulation of books & tracts: of which there have been issued from the depository
95 Bibles
108 Testaments
244 Common Prayer books
86 Psalters
1465 Tracts.

By the removal of Bishop Ryder to Lichfield, the place of Patron of our district Committee has devolved upon his successor, Bishop Bethel, who signified his acceptance of the Office in a very obliging manner. The Office of the Parent Society is removed from Bartlett's Buildings to Lincoln's Inn Fields, to larger & more commodious premises.

The annual meeting and dinner of the Stow Book Society followed; at which three new members were balloted into the Club. Dr. Rice presided.

——— |76

Monday Oct 11.

The annual meeting of the Trustees of the Crickley Hill Turnpike road, holden at Northleach, & followed by a dinner, at which Lord Sherborne presided; Messrs. Greenaway, Pettat, Broome, Ford, Hurd, Price &c. formed the party. I rode home dry, but the weather in the morning was extremely stormy, as it has been for the last few days, great quantities of rain having fallen.

———

Monday Oct. 18.

I left home for Gloucester to attend the quarter Sessions. I accompanied my neighbour. Mr. Jeaffreson, Rector of Longborough, who, having been recently put on the Commission of the peace for this county, was about to qualify. In passing through Cheltenham, I called at my Aunt Travell's, and was glad to find her in better health than I had expected, having received information two or three days ago, that she had experienced rather an alarming attack of illness. She had, however, rallied surprisingly. Mr. Jeaffreson and myself spent a pleasant evening together at Wellington Parade.

———

Tuesday Oct 19.

The Quarter Sessions commenced. Dr. |77 Cooke and Mr. Cripps presided as usual in the respective Courts. Among the Magistrates present were, Lords Dynevor, Ducie, Sherborne & Apsley: the Hon. H. Morton, Sir W. Guise, Mr. R. B. Cooper, Mr. Goodrich, Mr. Byles, Dr. Timbrill, Mr. Keysall, Mr. Ford, Mr. Goldney, Mr. Phelps, Mr. Newman, Archd Sandiford, &c.

Lord Dynevor & his son, the Hon. G. Rice Rice, MP. for Carmarthenshire,[11] qualified as Magistrates, and are likely to act in the same division as myself, their occasional residence being at Barrington Park, in which & the adjoining parishes of Great Risington and Taynton in Oxfordshire his Lordship has considerable property. Lord Dynevor is a very pleasant and affable man, and well versed in public business. His principal Seat is at Dynevor Park in Wales; he has only one son and several daughters. Mr. Rice is on the eve of marriage with a daughter of Lord H. Fitzroy. He is also about to assume the name of Trevor; having recently succeeded by the death of Visct. Hampden to a very considerable estate in Bedfordshire, subject to a large jointure to |78 Lady Hampden, formerly Miss Brown, eldest daughter of Mr. Commissioner Brown, (of the Excise) resident in Edinburgh, where, in my boyhood, I was very intimate in the Brown family. The Lord Hampden in question was succeeded in his title by his brother, the Honble. Mr. Trevor, who died after enjoying the title about three weeks, & he also left Mr. Rice a large property in money. The Rice's were connected with Lord Hampden's family by intermarriages. But for a mistake in the wording of a will, which made its operation different from the design of the testator, this Bedfordshire property would have devolved to my friend & neighbour at Oddington, Lord Dynevor's brother. Mr. Jeaffreson was prevented from qualifying, owing to an error in the spelling of his name, which will require correction by the Chancellor. The same circumstance occurred to myself, when I was about to qualify; my Christian name of Edward being omitted in the Dedimus potestatem. Mr. Croome, the |79 Rector of Bourton on the Water, and C. Greenaway Esqr. of Little Barrington both qualified at this Sessions to act in the Hundred of Slaughter. We shall have a numerous bench, but I doubt, whether its effective strength will be augmented.

Various ordinary and routine business was transacted. The Prison Regulation & County rate committees were continued, in the understanding, that they would bring forward definitive measures on their respective questions at the next Sessions.—

Different busts of Sir G. O. Paul for the approbation of the Magistrates & Subscribers to the proposed monument to his memory were produced, when the general opinion ran in favour of the bust exhibited at the last Sessions, provided some small alterations could be made, the new model grounded on a sketch by Mr. C. Crawley, not having in any respect succeeded.

In the course of the forenoon I called with Messrs. Croome and Jeaffreson to pay my respects to our new Diocesan, |80 by whom we were very politely received. Dr. Bethell is a hale man, not prepossessing in appearance, courteous in manner but without that air of affability & elegance, which distinguished his predecessor; his countenance indicates a very studious mind, & his general appearance induces the persuasion that his scholastic acquirements are solid & extensive.—

After dining as usual with my brother Magistrates, I spent the evening with my worthy Cousins the Miss Witts's.

---

11. George Talbot Rice, (1765-1852), 3rd Baron Dynevor, M.P. for Carmarthenshire, 1790-1793. Rice married, 1794, Frances, (1772-1854), 3rd daughter of Thomas Townsend, 1st Viscount Sydney. The son was George Rice, (1795-1869, 4th Baron Dynevor, M.P. for Carmarthen, 1820-31 and 1832-52. He married, (27 November 1824), Frances, (1803-1878), eldest daughter General Lord Charles Fitzroy.

172. Mr. Thompson's Montpellier Pump-Room.

Wednesday Oct. 20.—

I called on Mrs. M. Hunt. She had kindly copied for me a pedigree in her possession illustrative of the connection of the families of Arnold, Anthony, Skynner, Hunt, Witts &c. which throws considerable light on the family descent, of which before as relates to my Grandmother Witts & her connexions, I had but vague ideas.

Thursday Oct 21.

I was, as yesterday, chiefly engaged in Court till dinner, excepting short visits to Miss Witts & ~~Miss~~rs. Hunt [81] and at the infirmary, where the weekly board of Governors was sitting. It is, I find, determined on to enlarge the accommodation by the addition of a new ward.

The party of Magistrates dining together to day, was considerably reduced, and Dr. Cooke anticipated the termination of the Sessions to-morrow.

Friday Oct 22.

I left Gloucester on my return home. On my way through Cheltenham I passed some hours with my Aunt Travell; her voice, I think is more broken then it was; and altogether she is very feeble; but her faculties remain unimpaired. I reached home in the evening.—

Tuesday Oct. 26.

"Narrative of a Journey to the Shores of the Polar Sea in the years 1819–20–21–22. By John Franklin Capt. RN. F.RS &c. Commander of the Expedition. 2d. Edit. 2 Vols. 8vo London.

1824"[12] The Expedition in question was sent out by Government, in order, that while discoveries were attempted by sea in search of a North West Passage, the frozen regions of the Continent of North America might be explored. The Expeditions might meet and either might be essentially |[82] serviceable to the other by the communication of intelligence. The instructions to Capt. Franklin, who seems to have been equally well calculated for the task imposed on him, as his friend Capt. Parry for the duties, which he undertook, were to push his way to the mouth of the Copper Mine River, which had been visited by Hearne, & which flows into the Arctic Sea. He was then to trace the Northern coast of the continent of America as far as the season and other circumstances would admit. The Expedition consisted of Capt. Franklin, Dr. Richardson, a Navy Surgeon, whose acquirements enabled him to act as naturalist, Messrs. Back & Hood, Midshipmen, and Hepburn, an English Sailor. Messrs. B. & H. were well skilled in the scientific pursuits of their profession, and could assist their Commander in taking observations, drawing charts &c. they were also, particularly the latter, good draughtsmen, and possessed great energy of mind, patience, forbearance, judgment and other qualities, which eminently fitted them for the discharge of their arduous duties. Hepburn was a pattern for the British Sailor; attached to his Officers, cool, brave, obedient, active, intelligent. The Hudsons Bay & |[83] and North West Companies, now united, but then rivals in trade, were under engagements to promote the objects of the Expedition in every possible way, & generally speaking fulfilled their pledge, though the great tardiness and difficulty of inland communication by lakes & rivers, the inclemency of the climate, and the want, under which the settlements in the interior often laboured, frequently prevented the arrival & supply of many articles most essential to the necessities of the Expedition. The party set out from York Factory in Hudson's bay in canoes, accompanied by boatmen from the Orkney Islands, & Canadian Voyagers, & slowly worked their way up the rivers & lakes over portages & rapids, with many hair breadth escapes. Our travellers were ever eager to get forward, spared no fatigues, acquired information wherever they halted, & by availing themselves of the earliest season for setting out & the latest for travelling, reached Great Slave Lake, the utmost limits in that direction of European traffic. Beyond this point all was comparatively unknown, save to the Indian hunters. |[84] With a tribe of natives, Copper-Mine Indians, & their leaders, the party formed an intimate connection, engaging

---

12. Sir John Franklin, (1786-1847). Despite his father's opposition, Franklin was determined on a career in the navy and was on HMS Bellepheron at Trafalgar. Franklin first travelled to the Arctic in 1818, as a lieutenant under the command of John Ross, and became fascinated by it. On a disastrous overland expedition into the Northwest Territories of Canada along the Coppermine River in 1819-1822, Franklin lost 11 of the 20 men in his party. Most died of starvation, but there was also at least one murder and suggestions of cannibalism. In 1825 a second expedition set sail. This was a trip down the Mackenzie River to explore the shores of the Beaufort Sea, and was better supplied and more successful than his last. In 1828, he was knighted by George IV and in 1836 appointed Governor of Tasmania, but was removed from office in 1843, partly because of his attempts to reform the penal colony there. The exploration of the Arctic coastal mainland since Franklin's last Arctic expedition had left less than 300 miles of unexplored Arctic coastline. It was decided that a well-equipped Arctic expedition would be sent to finally chart the Northwest Passage. Franklin was eager to lead the expedition, and was given command on February 7, 1845. He set off with a party of 129 men on May 1845, in two ships, HMS Erebus and HMS Terror. The ships were sturdily built, and were outfitted with steam heating for the comfort of the crew, large amounts of reading and educational material, and three years' worth of preserved food supplies. Despite the better preparations, Franklin and the men were never seen again. It was not until 1859 that evidence emerged as to the Fate of the explorers in an expedition led by Francis Leopold McClintock.

them at high wages, as hunters, guides &c. Besides these they obtained a large party of Canadian voyagers, as boatmen, interpreters &c., as also two Esquimaux interpreters. Having made these arrangements, they advanced as far as the season would admit, when they made a halt for the winter, erecting log houses for their shelter, (Fort Enterprise), ~~provided~~ collected provisions for immediate use & future stores, ~~collected~~ with supplies of clothing, ammunition &c From this point they proceeded, when Spring returned, through difficulties always increasing to the Mouth of the Copper Mine River, where they dismissed the majority of their attendants, & embarked in two feeble canoes with a party of Canadian Voyagers, including one Iroquois Indian, to trace the Northern Sea Coast. This they did for a considerable distance, amid imminent danger from rough seas, ice, rocks &c. never able to leave the coast, which was indented by large bays, till at length the approach of wintry weather, & starvation staring them in the face, dictated the measure of retracing their path. |85 On their arrival at the bottom of one of the gulphs, they had explored, and from whence they hoped most easily to reach in a pretty direct line their station at Fort ~~James~~ Enterprize, where they expected to find provisions, clothing & comfort, they proceeded partly by Canoes, partly on foot; the weather grew unusually bad, winter was unusually early, the reindeer & musk oxen were migrating southward, & the chance of getting provisions daily lessened. Want and fatigue reduced the strength of the party, and the Canadians, prompt & useful, when well fed, became dejected, thoughtless, murmured and well nigh mutinous. Then comes a narrative of most thrilling horror: no narrative of starvation and despair, that I ever read, is more harrowing; yet the consolations of the Christian never deserted the admirable English, they never lost their temper, their self command or their judgment. Obliged to separate, Mr. Back went forward to seek for relief among the Indians, Mr. Franklin advanced to Fort Enterprize, where, through unfortunate mismanagement & unforeseen |86 events, he found nothing but desolation. Dr. Richardson, Mr. Hood & Hepburn remained behind in the desert: Mr. Hood was in the last stage of debility from fatigue & famine, and his few hours of life were cut short by the villainous Iroquois comrade, whose natural baseness & cruelty, untutored by any principles of religion, raged forth under the concurring stimulants of famine & love of plunder. Dr. Richardson was in self defence compelled to anticipate by a pistol shot through the head the murderous purpose of this furious savage, & at length with the faithful Hepburn reached his Commander, with little other prospect than that of lingering death by starvation. Reduced to feed on the most unwholesome herbs, & the grossest offal, their strength both of body & mind decayed rapidly, their Canadian attendants died one after another, & a few days more of destitution would have numbered them with the dead; had not Mr. Back discovered the Indians, & forwarded them food in the last extremity. Such were the difficulties, which terminated the enterprize; and what has been gained? Correct information of the internal water communica- |87 -tion, general information as to the Inhabitants, customs, productions &c of those Arctic regions, and a knowledge of the embouchures of several rivers in the Polar Sea, with correct charts of the sterile coast & ice bound Islands. It has been again proved, that British courage & discipline will surmount the greatest difficulties, & that these qualities combined with good judgment then shine most, when aided by sound religious principles, & that those principles are most consolatory in the deepest extremity of human misery & accumulated horror.

———

Wednesday Oct 27.

I accepted the office of Trustee to a Settlement made by Mr. Reade of Bath in favour of his children with his eldest son & a Mr. Batchellor of Bath. Though not highly valuing the father, by whom the request was made, yet I was anxious to serve his wife & family, who have suffered in many respects from the want of sense and prudence, which is but too notorious in him. Besides I am already in trust for his eldest daughter Mrs. Irvine, who married a relation of the Chamberlaynes of Maugers- |87 -bury, a Commander in the Royal Navy. Mr. Reade is the surviving brother of the late Sir John Reade, & uncle of the present Baronet.

Monday Nov. 1.

I went to Stanway by Lady Elcho's invitation to meet some of her neighbours at dinner. I found there as Guests, Genl. & Mrs. Fuller, who after staying some time at Cheltenham are again visiting Lady E. on their return to London, Mrs. C. Keysall, my Mother & Miss Church. The addition to the dinner party consisted of Mrs. Tracy with many of the younger branches of the Toddington family, Miss Smith, their inmate, Mrs. R. Wynniatt and her eldest daughter & Mr. T. Wynniatt.

Tuesday Nov. 2.

In the forenoon I went to Wood Stanway, called at the Vicarage, and overlooked some building on the farm, which is now nearly completed. It consists of commodious feeding Halls for twelve oxen. Since I have had the living, I have spent several hundred pounds in fencing, building and draining; I am not yet at all repaid, but I have placed the temporalities of my Vicarage |89 in a very different and far better state than I found them. Sir Thomas and Lady Phillipps, from Middle Hill, Mr. & Mrs. S. Gist, two Miss Gists, & Mr. W. Gist, & Mr. Wynniatt joined the dinner party. Sir T.P. was lately created a Baronet; he cannot boast of being an hereditary gentleman; his father, the first owner of Middle Hill of his name, raised himself from menial employments to considerable wealth by successful enterprize in the most money making times of the cotton manufactory.[13] He retired to his native parish, Broadway, where & in the adjacent villages he had realized his property, when he left his Lancashire speculations to others, & the present Baronet is the offspring of an illegitimate union. His wife is daughter of a Genl. Molyneux, who has now for some years lived at Cheltenham, of Irish extraction & possessing

---

13. Sir Thomas Phillipps, (1792-1872). Phillipps was an antiquary and bibliophile extraordinary. He quite obviously irritated Francis Witts with his unbusinesslike attitudes (see diary 20 June 1828), but his services to scholarship and the saving of manuscripts for the nation are remarkable. Vellum manuscripts, then not held in great esteem, were used in great number by goldbeaters, tailors and glue makers. Phillipps could not bear to see this waste and spent vast fortunes and a great deal of time in finding them, buying them and saving them from destruction. In Gloucestershire, in particular, great thanks should be made for his publishing of the continuations to Ralph Bigland's *Gloucestershire*. Phillipps entered into the baronetcy and the estate at Middle Hill near Broadway on the death of his father in 1818. From this point on he bought lavishly, on the Continent as well as in England, amassing many thousands of highly valuable manuscripts. His wealth was considerable, but his buying always seemed to outstrip his income, resulting in mortgages and other irritating digressions from his collecting passion. He set up a printing press at Middle Hill, but eventually moved this facility, and enlarged it at Thirlestane House, Cheltenham. At his death in 1872, his collection of books and manuscripts was one of the greatest ever amassed, and the sale of the bulk of the collection took many days. Some of the purchasers were agents for the Dutch, German and Belgian governments, who bought back important manuscripts relating to their countries.

many of the characteristics of his country, not very rich, not very prudent, not very select in his society. The Lady of Middle Hill has no greater pretensions to legitimacy than her spouse, and is a boisterous dame strongly contrasting with her |*90* Lord's reserve. He is an Antiquary, book collector; who has yet perhaps still more experience to buy than he has yet paid for, but report says, much trash has already been foisted upon him. He has lately been unfortunate in this neighbourhood by contesting a very immaterial point with the Country Gentlemen, acting as Commissioners on the Worcester road: maintaining a wrong cause with much obstinacy & rudeness, and finally reduced to an apology, when measures were pursued to compel his assent to certain matters required by course of law. In the transaction of these concerns I have been necessarily a party, as were also Lord Redesdale & Mr. Ford; the correspondence having chiefly been conducted by us. The Baronet, however, behaves as he ought to do, by abstaining from all reference to the matters litigated; not so his Lady, who was betrayed into some strong and ill timed comments to her husband's dismay and the amusement of the hearers, who were less interested than himself. The Mr. Gist, who dined at Stanway to-day, and is eldest son of the riche parvenu residing at Wormington Grange |*91* in this vicinity, has recently been married to Mary Anne Westenra, daughter of Lord Rossmore, an amiable young person, but possessed neither of talent nor beauty. She seems happy, and he and his family appear attached to her. The acquaintance was formed at Stanway in the Autumn of last year: fostered by the able diplomacy of my cousin Augusta of Rossmore, and her ~~able~~ skilful chargé d'affaires at London, the young lady's brother, John Westenra, an officer in the Guards.—

Tuesday Nov. 9.

We dined at Mr. E. Leigh's at Broadwell, meeting Mr. Penyston of Cornwell, Oxon, his son & daughter, Mr. Hall of Batsford, Lady & Miss Reade, Mr. Twisleton, and Miss Chabuzet.

Tuesday Nov. 16.

Mrs. Backhouse left us to return to Gloucester. We shall regret her absence; so sensible a person is she, & so judicious; so well principled, and so warmly attached to Margaret and myself and her grandson. I cannot speak too highly of her openness and liberality in all money matters.

Mr. F. Aston came to pass two or three days with us.

--- |92

Wednesday Nov. 17.

The principal farmers of Upper Slaughter, Messrs. Cook, Collett, E. Lea, & Davis, dined with us.

Friday Nov. 19.

Frederick Aston left us for Stanway.

Monday Nov. 22.

"The Book of the Church. By Robert Southey Esqr. LLD, &c. 2 Vols. Lond. 1824."[14] Mr.

14. Robert Southey, (1774-1843). Southey was one of the Lake poets, but his fame was eclipsed by his colleagues, William Wordsworth and Samuel Taylor Coleridge. He was born at Bristol and educated at Westminster (from

Southey, to whose excellent writings, both in prose and verse, the State, the Church, and sound in principles in general, are as much indebted as the cause of literature itself, has here performed a very great service to the public, in presenting a compendious, spirited and accurate manual of the ecclesiastical history of England. The book is extremely well written, and at this juncture most valuable for refreshing the recollections of members of the established Church, and giving a right impression to the young or ill informed. Commencing with the dawn of Christianity in England, it closes with the Revolution of 1688. It is to be regretted, that the author has not accompanied his narrative with a running chronology |[93] he might also advantageously have appended to each chapter a reference to the works, which are the basis of his relation, as also to those books, which might most profitably be consulted by those, who are desirous of extending their researches by resorting to contemporary or other the best authorities. The style, feeling & principles of the work are alike admirable.

Thursday Dec. 2.

"Extracts from a Journal written on the coasts of Chili, Peru, and Mexico in the years 1820, 1821, 1822 by Captain Basil Hall R.N. author of a Voyage to Loo Choo. 2 Vols 8vo 3d. Edit. 1824."[15] Captain Hall commanded the Conway frigate on the South American Station, and had many favourable opportunities of watching the progress of the cause of independence in the Countries, which he visited. The present state of the ancient Spanish Colonies in South America, now working out their independence, is a very important and curious subject of enquiry, particularly to the commercial interest of this country, as a very extensive and hitherto closely forbidden market is afforded for the sale of our commodities, and the purchase of metals and other produce, which we require. The exclusive system of the old Spaniards has in every instance been succeeded by an |[94] open trade, of which British Merchants have largely and rapidly availed themselves by their capital, activity, and information. In the absence of accredited consuls, for the protection of British commerce, and settlement of disputes between the ~~ship~~ merchants, captains of Merchant vessels &c. on the one hand, and the new governments, their agents, the native merchants &c. on the other, the Commanders of men of war on the Station had a heavy and important as well as delicate duty to discharge, which otherwise would have fallen on civil functionaries. Such, indeed, are now stationed in these countries. Captain Hall visited all the principal ports on the Pacific, and was in intercourse with most of the constituted authorities, whether Spanish or Patriot: and his excursions into the interior on public business enable him to give an interesting account of scenery, manners, customs, society &c. both as to the higher and lower classes. He makes out of his materials a very amusing and instructive book; he writes with spirit, cheerfully and intelligibly. Much as the South American Patriots have been talked of and written about in the Newspapers, we

---

where he was expelled for writing a magazine article condemning flogging), and Balliol College, Oxford. Southey published his first collection of poems in 1794. The same year, he, Coleridge and a few others discussed setting up an idealistic community in America, but nothing came of it. Southey's later writings were extensive and he became Poet Laureate in 1813.

15. Basil Hall, (1788-1844). Hall was born in Edinburgh and joined the Royal Navy in 1802, and eventually rose to be captain. He was one of the first to visit Korea, and wrote *Voyage of Discovery to Corea* (1818), also *Travels in North America* in 1827-28, a lively work which gave some offence in the U.S. due to his criticims of native mores. His best work was *Fragments of Voyages and Travels* (1831-40).

have, generally speaking, a very confused notion of the principles, pretensions, characters, political views &c. of the leaders in the struggle, as to Chili, Peru, & Mexico Captn. Hall's book |95 supplies in a great measure this desideratum, and puts us in possession of the characters & exploits of Lord Cochrane, San Martin, Bolivar, Iturbidé & others. Capt. Hall may have a strong bias in favour of San Martin & Iturbidé, and many of his observations may have been founded on false data, but still we rise from the perusal with much clearer notions than we before had of the progress and importance of the great political convulsion, which is rending and probably regenerating the whole System of civilized America in the South, and of Mexico in the northern division of the new continent. British heads & hearts and hands have been very much engaged on the side of independence in Colombia & Chili; both on land & by sea; the Colombian army being full of British adventurers, & the Chilian navy chiefly manned & commanded by English & North American Officers & Sailors. Most of their ships of war were commanded by English Captains. Captn. Guise, brother of Sir B. W. Guise, the Member for Gloucestershire, has for several years been serving under the Chilian Government, first with Lord Cochrane; but his Lordship had a feud with one of the most eminent Independent chiefs, San Martin, and quitted that service, in which he had |96 created a navy, & performed some very daring and gallant exploits, and is now fighting on the side of the new authorities in Brazil. Captain Hall's book was quoted with much approbation by Sir James Macintosh in a speech in Parliament on the subject of the recognition of South American Independence. He evidently is what is called a man of liberal statements; he is also possessed of high scientific attainments. Undoubtedly he merits the praise of being an amusing writer, and has kept up in this publication the credit, which he obtained by a former narrative of a voyage to the Loo Choo Islands in the Chinese Seas.

Saturday Dec. 4.

"An historical ~~Re~~View of the rise and Progress of infidelity, with a refutation if its principles and reasonings. In a series of Sermons preached for the Lecture founded by the Hon. Robert Boyle, in the parish church of St. Mary le Bow London 1802–1805—By the Right Revd. William Van Mildert D.D. Lord Bishop of Llandaff. 3d. Edit. 2 Vols 8vo Lond. 1820." A must valuable work by a very learned divine. The first Volume is devoted to the historical view of the rise and progress of infidelity from the earliest ages to the present time, the second |97 to a refutation of the principles and reasonings of unbelievers. Thus Paganism, Mahometanism, the delusions of the dark ages, Scepticism in all its forms, and free thinking in all its shiftings are traced, examined and confuted. Copious notes & illustrations are added, containing extracts from the ablest defenders of revealed truth, and pointing out those ~~able~~ valuable works, in which more elaborate arguments & refutations may be found by the Student. The whole gives evidence of the very extensive Theological learning of the author, who is a great living ornament of the Church of England, and of the University of Oxford. He was originally of Queen's College, &, not very long ago, Canon of Xt Church and Regius Professor of Divinity. He now holds the Deanery of St. Paul's in commendam with the Bishopric of Landaff.

Tuesday Dec. 14.

"Letters to and from Henrietta, Countess of Suffolk and her second husband, the Hon. Geo. Berkeley. From 1712 to 1776. With historical, biographical and explanatory notes. 2 Vols.

8vo. Lond. 1824." The publication of private correspondence, whether of literary, political, |98 or fashionable personages, meets with great encouragement in these days, nor is the taste for such reading to be wondered at. The present contribution to our stock of letters by eminent characters is derived from the stores of Emily Marchioness of Londonderry, who is a descendant of the ~~Howards~~ Hobarts Earls of Buckinghamshire, of which family Lady Suffolk sprung. She was better known as the Hon. Mrs. Howard, for many years bed chamberwoman & mistress of the robes to Queen Caroline, both when she was Princess of Wales & when she was consort of Geo. 2: and it is generally presumed, that she was Mistress to that prince. Hor. Walpole asserts it roundly; and altho' the present correspondence contain nothing in confirmation of the alledged connection, nor is any document to be found in the Suffolk papers, from which it can be certainly inferred, yet there is little doubt, that such a connection probably subsisted, at which the politic and judicious Queen connived, as being well convinced of the discretion, decorum and moderation of her rival, qualities, which might not so readily have been found in another. The queen and |99 Mrs. Howard were in fact persons of excellent sense and judgment, and to this must be ascribed the singular fact of the latter being for so many years the favourite both of her royal Master & Mistress. She was unhappy in her first marriage, with a younger brother of the Earls of Suffolk, which title her husband at last inherited. When she retired from Court, she married at the age of forty five a sensible and agreeable brother of the then ~~of~~ Earl of Berkley, and died in advanced age at Marble Hill, the elegant Villa, in the Twickenham Meadows, opposite Richmond Hill, which she had purchased with the assistance of her royal Master and mistress, & improved with the aid of Pope & the Earl of Burlington. The correspondence is very multifarious; the correspondents of all classes and calibres; nobles both male & female, Statesmen, Members of Parliament, intriguers, candidates for court favours, wits and literati, family connections, courtiers, bed chamber women & maids of honour, gossiping old maids & bachelors, the idle and the busy, the designing and the simple hearted. We have Dean Swift, Pope, Dr. Arbuthnot & |*100* Gay; the great Duke of Argyll, Mr. Pitt, afterwards Lord Chatham, George Grenville, the Earl of Bath, the Duke & Duchess of Queensbury, Lord Temple, Lord Buckinghamshire &c.—The fair Bellenden & Lepel, the twin beauties of the Court, afterwards Mrs. Campbell & Lady Hervey; and a host of others. We have little addition to the secret history of the times & parties, but abundance of amusing anecdote & views, how people of fashion lived and thought and conversed eighty or a hundred years ago. There is much levity and coarseness; indeed, people of fashion used language and indulged in allusions highly unbecoming their rank in those golden days: there is also a lamentable lack of religious principle; it is hard to conceive, that so many confidential letters should be found with so little reference to sound Christian principle. Lady Suffolk was evidently the object of warm esteem; moderate in her pretensions; though a favourite, neither ambitious, nor greedy of show or gain; warmly attached to her friends; judicious, amiable; unhappy as to her first husband, and as it |*101* would seem, having little affectionate intercourse with her son, the Earl of Suffolk, whom she long survived: the friend of Hor. Walpole, who though very partial to her, had no scruple in his Reminiscences & Memoirs of putting the worst colour on her supposed station of royal concubine, and distorting facts and dates to prove things to her disadvantage in order to gratify political spleen; for Lady Suffolk in early life had been opposed in party politics to Sir R. Walpole. But I must not give her Ladyship & her correspondents more space: the

Editor, whose name is not given, has laid his readers under great obligations by his prefaces and notes, in which he gives a view of the connexions and characters of the correspondents and persons and occurrences adverted to.

Wednesday Dec. 15.

A real holiday in the return of our dear boy from school. Thank GOD, he appears in very good health Mr. Hale makes a very satisfactory report of his progress in his studies and general good behaviour.

Thursday Dec. 16.

The annual meeting and dinner of the Cope |[102] Charity at Stow. Only three Commissioners or Trustees attended: Messrs. Vavasour, Ford & myself; Mr. Bowen joined us. Thus a social dinner followed a morning occupied in public business at the Provident Bank & Justice room.—

Friday Dec. 17.

We went to Stanway to pay a visit to Lady Elcho. My mother is still her Ladyship's guest, and we had the mortification of finding her very unwell to-day. At this season of the year we always dread her being seriously indisposed, she is so liable to inflammatory attacks on the chest. Lady Elcho has also other inmates, Lady Catherine Stewart, two sons and a daughter. Her Ladyship is Lady Elcho's second surviving daughter & wife of the Hon. Edw. Stewart, Chairman of the Commissioners for auditing the public accounts. Mr. Stewart has held several official Stations of a similar nature, & is a brother of the Earl of Galloway.[16] Of his two sons here, the eldest is an Etonian, the youngest is a schoolboy rather younger than Edward. Lady Catherine in early life was a very pretty woman, & having always lived in the first circles her manner & address are peculiar- |[103] -ly elegant. The old and eccentric Countess of Cork & Orrery and Mr. Ch. Keysall are also here. Miss Church, Lady Elcho's companion, made up the home party. Mr. Tracy and Fred. Aston joined us at dinner. Mr. Tracy is now alone at Toddington, where his splendid new house is advancing to a habitable estate. He is not now in Parliament; formerly he represented the Borough of Tewkesbury, and was also a warm oppositionist, being attached to the ultra liberalism of Sir F. Burdett &c. His manners are peculiarly polished.

~~Friday~~ Saturday Dec. 18.

The family circle was diminished by the departure of Mr. C. Keysall.

Sunday Dec . 19.

Mr. F. Aston having been so kind as to volunteer to exchange duties with me, had gone yesterday afternoon to Upper Slaughter, and I this day officiated in his stead at Stanway and Cutsdean.

---

16. George Stewart, (1768-1834), 8th Earl of Galloway. M.P. for Saltash, 1790-1795; Cockermouth1805-1806 and Haslemere, 1806. George Stewart joined the Royal Navy in 1780 and distinguished himself as Captain at the taking Guadaloupe, 1794. He was at the Battle of Cape Vincent. He was Rear Admiral, 1810; Vice Admiral, 1819 and Admiral 1830.

Monday Dec. 20.

I walked to Wormington Grange to call on the Gist family. These estimable people had been very kind to my Mother, who had visited them for a fortnight or three |[104] weeks during a recent absence of Lady Elcho in Town: It is a comfortable, but not a handsome place. The younger Mr. Gist has a small museum of natural curiosities serpents, birds, insects, fossils &c. with a few articles of dress from the South Seas Islands, which afforded great amusement to my dear boy.

Wednesday Dec. 22.

My Mother still continuing very unwell, labouring under great oppression of breath, accompanied with much drowsiness, was with difficulty persuaded this day to see Mr. Bancks, the Apothecary of Winchcomb, who took from her several ounces of blood by which operation she seemed in some degree relieved.

F. Aston dined here.

Thursday Dec. 23.

Mr. W. Gist & Miss Gist, and Mr. Aston were added to the party at dinner.

Friday Dec. 24th.

Mr. Stewart and his second son, Algernon, reached Stanway from Town to breakfast. I regretted, that they had not arrived on an earlier day, Mr. S. being a very well informed and conversible man. But our visit was |[105] necessarily limited to Christmas eve, and we accordingly reached home an hour or two before dinner. It was with much anxiety and fear that I left my mother in such an uncomfortable state of health, unwilling to leave Stanway for her own house and medical friend at Cheltenham, and persisting in fighting against indisposition to the last moment. I was also disappointed by the Apothecary, Mr. Bancks, who had promised to visit her to-day before the hour fixed for our departure.

Wednesday Dec. 29.

Continued bad accounts of my poor Mother's health, coming from Stanway, carried me there to-day. I returned, however, to dinner, having with much difficulty prevailed on my Mother to see Mr. Wood, her medical friend

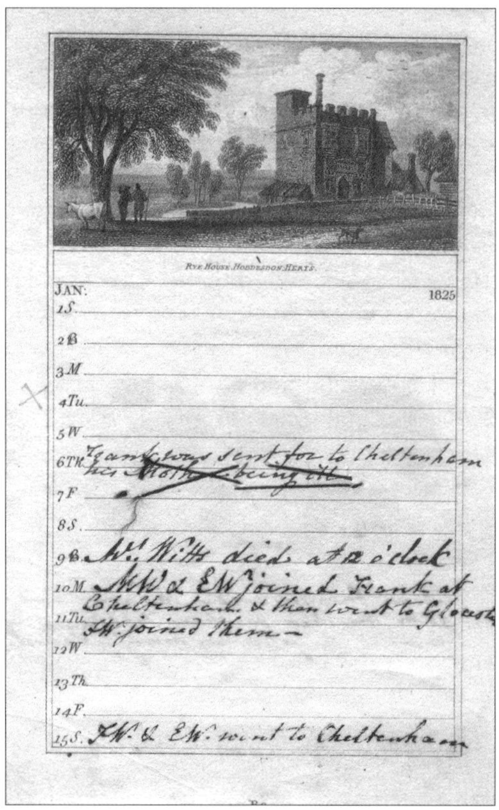

173. Page from the diary of Margaret Witts; January 1825.

from Cheltenham, to whom I wrote accordingly, and who will, doubtless, be with her to-morrow. She also promised, if Mr. Wood thought it safe for her to move, that she would return to her own home, where she may have daily visits from him, & farther medical aid, if required. Her symptoms continue the same; great drowsiness, shortness of breath, weakness &c. |[106] I was disappointed in meeting Mr. Bancks, who, however, is very desirous, that she should go to Cheltenham to her own home, & medical attendant.

The Stewarts are still at Stanway, which they leave towards the end of the week. C. Keysall was again domesticated there, as also Miss Gist, whose solicitude about my mother is very great, and who successfully aided me in prevailing on her to quit Stanway for Cheltenham.

Thursday Dec. 30.

A very melancholy event has happened to Mr. T. Welsh Hunt, late High Sheriff for Northamptonshire, and his wife, one of the Northamptonshire Ishams. Mr. T. W. Hunt is a distant relation of mine, a very respectable young man, of good fortune, and only married about half a year ago. I met him in the autumn of 1823 at his aunt's, Mrs. M. Hunt's, at Gloucester. He had been abroad before his marriage, and repaired thither immediately after his union with his bride. They were at Naples: and on the 3d. Inst. had gone with an English Party to visit the celebrated ruins of Pæstum. Returning from thence, Mr. Hunt's carriage |[107] was attacked by three brigands, to whom he surrendered an inconsiderable sum of money, protesting he had no more abut him, and even asking for some small coins back to pay necessary demands on his return to Naples. The banditti persisted, that he had more money in his possession, and required him to deliver it up, with a threat of firing at him; he rejoined, that they dared not shoot, as it was in the day light; scarcely had he uttered the words, when a shot was fired, & the contents of the piece lodged in the heart of Mr. Hunt, & in the lungs of his wife. The Banditti horror-struck, or aware of the approach of travellers, fled without rifling their victims, & some English Officers, belonging to a vessel of war in the bay of Naples, who had been on the same excursion, soon found the wounded sufferers. They were conveyed to the wretched inn at Pæstum; such poor aid, as the miserable, almost savage, country affords, was procured; an English Surgeon was brought from Naples; but all in vain, poor Mr. Hunt survived only two or three hours, and his wife died on the following day. The Brigands have not been traced. |[108] It is a most melancholy tale; & the poor Aunt at Gloucester will suffer extremely; for she was much attached to her nephew.

1825

Saturday Jan. 1.

I rode over to Stanway to breakfast in consequence of a letter from Miss Church, giving me an account of Mr. Wood's opinion of my poor Mother. He considers, that at her age, and with a habit so susceptible of inflammation, it is impossible not to entertain apprehensions, but that he had seen her worse, and if she could be prevailed on to go home, where he could daily attend on her, she might with watchfulness and proper discipline be restored. He wished me to come over to enforce her removal as to-day, but I am sorry to say, my urgent endeavours were unsuccessfully used. She promises, however, to go on Monday, when Miss Church has kindly offered to accompany her. Mr. Bancks called, when I was there; and decidedly thought her better; so, indeed, she appeared to me & others, being less lethargic. In fact depletion has partly done its work. |[109]

The Stanway party is greatly reduced by the departure of the Stewarts. C. Keysall left it this morning. I returned home to dinner.

Tuesday Jan. 4.

I received a letter from Miss Church acquainting me with my Mother's arrival at Cheltenham on Monday, whither she accompanied her, and that she was not the worse for the little journey, but on the whole as Miss Church thought, rather better.

Thursday Jan 6.

While I was attending my usual duties as a Magistrate at Stow, I received a distressing communication from Dr. Christie, whom, it appears, Mr. Wood called to his aid yesterday evening. I immediately returned home and having ordered horses to follow me from Stow, I went post to Cheltenham, where I arrived about seven o'clock. A great change for the worse had taken place & I found, that little or no hopes of my Mother's restoration were entertained. There was evidently a great tendency to dropsy, the face swelling, with a running from the eyes and mouth. The lethargic symptoms were increased, and an appearance of gout, which had thrown itself out, was now gone off. |[110] My poor Mother seemed to be much gratified at my arrival, but was so overwhelmed with drowsiness, that she could have very little conversation with me. In her medical attendants she has kind & solicitous as well as skilful friends, but alas! their skill is not likely to avail. Her servants are extremely tender and anxious in watching and waiting upon her, shewing that attachment, which their mistress's kindness towards them so well merits. I sat up with my Mother till an early hour in the morning when one of the servants took my place. She slept uninterruptedly, but not tranquilly.

Friday Jan 7.

There was no change for the better, but the difficulty of rousing my Mother seemed increased. The lethargy continued unabated, and all the unfavourable symptoms were increased. I was occupied the greater part of the morning in procuring a nurse, who came into waiting in the evening. I dined with my Aunt Travell, meeting Mrs. Whalley and her son William. On my return |[111] I found my poor Mother more roused, than at any previous time since I had arrived. She spoke of her approaching end, of which she seemed thoroughly aware from the first interview with Dr. Christie: she spoke of her everlasting hopes in her redeemer with humility, and of me & mine in the tenderest manner. She desired to be buried as my poor father had been, and by his side in the Vault at Chipping Norton Church, because it has been his wish: she gave some directions as to the distribution of her clothes, ornaments &c. particularly as regarded her own maid. Nothing could exceed the calmness and collectedness of her manner; her words were few, uttered at intervals, but well chosen; it was evident that her debility was hourly increasing, but she always assured us, that she felt no pain. Her night was restless, but her sleep uninterrupted.

Saturday Jan 8.

It was very evident, that my dear Mother was rapidly approaching her end. It was now impossible to raise her up in bed to take nourishment, and in fact it would not have been possible for her to have swallowed anything solid. Dr. Christie declared, that medicine could be of no |112 further avail, as water was rapidly forming on the brain & perhaps, also, in the cavity of the chest. From henceforth she took only wine & water, & arrow-root administered by spoons full. Yet still, when once roused, the faculties continued unimpaired, and when my aged aunt came to her bedside to say farewell to her dying sister, my mother, though hardly able to articulate, was thoroughly alive to the affecting scene, and nothing could be more solemn or interesting; the dying sister, younger by ten years, placing her hand in that of the survivor borne down by age, reduced to a shadow, shaking with ~~age~~ years & agitation, and with a voice inarticulate as that of the poor wreck extended on the bed of death, murmering out her last adieux. The only other person, whom my Mother saw, was her friend Mrs. Cooke, a kind hearted & excellent person, but to recognize her was all my Mother had the strength to do. Dr. Christie told me, death was so fast approaching, that I must remain at my post. I therefore sent back my Servant and horses, whom my dear wife had dispatched for me, and fortunately hearing, that my |113 neighbour, Mr. Hurd, the Rector of Naunton, was in the town, I had an interview with him, when he kindly promised to undertake my duty at Upper Slaughter & Lower Swell to-morrow.—The poor patient's strength both of body and mind gradually diminished as night approached, but still no pain seemed to be felt, and at midnight I retired leaving her in care of the nurse & one of the servants.—

Sunday Jan. 9.—

Death rapidly advanced during the night and morning, and at mid-day my beloved Mother breathed her last. She went off gently, & the last fearful struggle past, her features resumed the usual placidity, and lost the distortion, which for some days had disfigured them. Thus am I at length bereft of Father, Mother & Brother! GOD's will be done! GOD be thanked for the blessings still left to me, an excellent wife & promising child. Great reason have I to speak well of my departed Parent. She was a most affectionate wife & mother, a well principled Christian, warm in her friendships, |114 strong in point of judgment, well informed, had an extensive knowledge of life, and in her best days, even to a late period, shone in society & conversation. She was 76 years of age, having been born in 1748. Nov. 22. She was last survivor but one of the numerous family of John Travell Esqr. of Swerford, in Oxfordshire, her Mother being one of the many daughters of John Tracy Esqr. of Stanway. My beloved Parents had experienced much misfortune in middle life by a reverse of fortune; but activity of mind, mutual attachment, and love for their children upheld them buoyant on the waves of distress, and GOD be blessed, that it has been in my power to comfort & succour them in their declining years: this will be my consolation when I reflect on the death bed twice witnessed in this house, when I deposit the aged widow's remains by the side of the coffin containing those of her affectionate and indulgent husband.—The necessity of immediate exertion on such melancholy occasions is of advantage to the wounded spirit: the acuteness of the pang is blunted |115 by the avocations thrust upon one; thus I felt, when regulating the arrangements with the undertaker, and writing to distant friends & relations; but the still hour of night is overwhelming, and I soon found the weakness of human strength, in sleeplessness, wearing thoughts, fatigue and general indisposition.—At the request of my Aunt I repaired to her fireside for an hour to two in the evening.

Monday Jan. 10.

My dear wife and child arrived from Upper Slaughter. I had found an opportunity of communicating the mournful tidings, so that they were apprized of it before they left home. It had long been arranged, that we should visit Mrs. Backhouse at this time; and it now appeared to me particularly desirable, that Edward & his dear Mother should pursue their journey to Gloucester, for Margaret's health and strength are little equal to severe trials, and in her mother's society she would find comfort. They, therefore, left me between four and five o clock, after my wife had assisted my on many points with her useful advice, and procured mourning for the servants &c. I drank tea at Mrs. Travell's. Much of my time was taken up in |*116* writing letters to absent relations, connections & friends.

Tuesday Jan. 11.

Having made all the arrangements immediately necessary, and the remains of my dear Parent being closed down, it appeared to me unnecessary longer to remain at Cheltenham in solitude, and separated from my dear wife and child, whom, therefore, I rejoined this evening at Gloucester, and regret to say, that my dear wife, from anxiety and hurry of spirits continues to suffer sadly. It is probable, that a few tranquil days will restore her.

~~Friday~~ Saturday Jan. 15.

I returned to my melancholy duties at Cheltenham early this morning, accompanied by my dear boy. His society will be a relief to me and his presence at his Grandmother's funeral will be a proper mark of respect. We dined at Mrs. Travell's, meeting her inmate Mrs. Whalley, and one of the late Charles Whalley's sons, a schoolboy.

Monday Jan. 17.—

The mournful and last duty of attending the remains of my Mother to the grave devolved upon me. My dear boy was my companion, and the kind |*117* hearted Frederick Aston also went with me. He arrived from Stanway in time to partake of an early breakfast at Belle Vue Place, and a little after nine we departed for Chipping Norton. Mr. Newman, the Undertaker, an unobtrusive and respectable person, was the fourth in the mourning coach, which followed the hearse. We reached Stow to bait, at ½ past 2 o clock, and our final destination about 5 PM. where preparations had been made for us, and we had good accommodations and refreshment.

Tuesday Jan. 18.

A most gloomy wet morning after a stormy night was congenial to the depression of my spirits. My Mother's great nephew, William Whalley, arrived from Swerford to breakfast at nine o clock, but it was half past 10 AM. before we could reach the Church. The Service was performed by the Curate, a vulgar unfeeling man~~ner~~: his careless manner, his uncouth pronunciations, and coarse appearance were all forbidding. Crowds of curious spectators flocked round the coffin & vault; but all was curiosity, no sympathy was visible; most trying is this appearance of indifference; and equally so the suppressed voices of the assistants, as |*118* they lowered the coffin through the narrow mouth of the vault, grating against the top of the arch, and at length deposited beside the last inmate of the dark abode. At length my tender Mother reposes by the side of her beloved & indulgent husband; eight years of widowhood have been passed; now both are numbered with the dead. As to myself the burst of suppressed grief is passed, and the lassitude of sorrow remains; but I cannot and ought not to lose sight of the blessings still reserved to me by a gracious Providence, an affectionate wife, a promising child, and ample provision of earthly comforts.

We returned in the mourning coach immediately after the funeral: & reached Cheltenham at 7 P.M. Frederick Aston parted from us at Stow.

Wednesday Jan. 19.

Edward and my self repaired to Gloucester to breakfast. I had the comfort of finding my dear wife better than when I left her.

Thursday Jan. 20.

The newspaper announces the death of Ferdinand IV King of Naples, aged 73.[17] He was a very weak prince; devoted to the chace. His consort an Austrian |*119* Princess, was a woman of a very intriguing disposition; at one time supporting English, at another French Politics and connexions. In the course of the revolutionary wars these Sovereigns were obliged to abandon Naples, & fly to Sicily, in the possession of which island they were protected by the arms of Great Britain, while Bonaparte placed one of his own family on the throne of Naples. On the downfall of the French Emperor, the Queen of Naples being now dead, Ferdinand the 4th. was restored to his continental dominions, but latterly was driven from them by a new revolution originating in the political & Jacobinical faction of the Carbonari, which the Neapolitan Government was too weak to overcome single handed, but which was soon put down by an Austrian force, and the king & his authority restored.

Saturday Jan. 22.

I returned to Upper Slaughter to be ready for the duties of the following day.

---

17. Ferdinand, (1751–1825). Ferdinand had previously been king of Naples (1759-1805 and 1815-16) as Ferdinand IV and also King of Sicily (1759–1816) as Ferdinand III. A Spanish Bourbon, Ferdinand succeeded to the two kingdoms when his father became King of Spain as Charles III. His father had implemented reforms, but following Ferdinand's marriage to Marie Caroline of Austria a reactionary regime was policy was adopted. Sir John Acton was appointed prime minister. The Queen's sister was Marie Antoinette of France, and her execution in 1793 turn Ferdinand against France. In January, 1799, the French took Naples but their occupation was short-lived, and when Ferdiand returned he acted with brutality. Peace was made with France in 1801, but in 1805 Ferdinand joined the Third Coalition against Napoleon. The French reconquered Naples, and early in 1806 the royal couple again fled to Sicily where Ferdinand was under British protection. In 1812 he bowed to local political pressure, made his son regent, and had him grant Sicily a constitution. After Naples was restored to him at the end of the Napoleonic Wars, Ferdinand abolished Sicilian autonomy and proclaimed himself king of the Two Sicilies. His rule provoked an insurrection in 1820, and he was forced to grant a constitution. He reestablished his despotism with Austrian aid in 1821 and once again instituted a fierce persecution of all liberals and Carbonari. He was succeeded by his son, Francis I.

Monday Jan. 24.

I again left home, bending my course on horseback to Broadway, where I had an appointment with Mr. Averill, a Solicitor of that place, Mr. Stokes, the |[120] scientific Surveyor of the Evesham second district of Turnpike roads fully justifies by his skill in his business the confidence, which the Trustees, of whom I am one, reposed in him; the line of road being in admirable repair. Many gangs of workmen are busily employed in the alterations in the improvement of Broadway hill; the graduating which was considered by the Trustees a point of great importance, and entrusted to the management of Mr. Stokes under the direction of a Committee, of which I am a member. The funds have been procured by loan from the Commissioners for the reduction of the National debt, and when completed, the ascent of the hill will be materially eased, the road, whether to the traveller as he rises or descends, will afford the view of much picturesque scenery both near and distant, and the communication between Worcester and London ~~materially~~ greatly facilitated.

The business, which took me to Broadway, was to look over some property in that and the adjoining parish of Willersey, recently purchased by Sir Thomas Phillipps of Middle Hill, who is desirous of borrowing £6000 on Mortgage of it in |[121] part payment of the purchase money. I rode over this land with Mr. Averill, his Solicitor; the village of Willersey, near which one small farm lies, is rather more than a mile distant from Broadway, and had the day been favourable, I should have enjoyed from the eminence above the Village a fine & extensive prospect: the rest of the property is in the parish of Broadway, partly in the Village, and partly at a distance of a mile, & fronting the Baronet's mansion. Nothing can be more picturesque than the valley leading from the Village of Broadway towards Middle Hill; the Church, very inconveniently for the parishioners, is at a considerable distance from the Village, but charmingly situated, embosomed in trees, & near the scite of an ancient dismantled mansion house, of which very little trace remains. We have for some time been looking out for an investment in land or mortgage for this sum, which on a former occasion afforded me a ride to Great Washbourn, and will probably at last be advanced on the security of the property, I have |[122] this day looked over.

Sending back my horses from Broadway, I proceeded post to Cheltenham, where I arrived by tea time, and met my dear wife, who had come from Gloucester to assist in the melancholy task of looking over my poor mother's effects, with a view to ultimate arrangements.—Our dear boy was left at his grandmother's at Gloucester.—

Tuesday Jan 25.—

We drank tea at my aunt Travell's: besides Mrs. Whalley we met Mrs. Charles Whalley and her two agreeable daughters; also her eldest Son, Mr. Henry Whalley, who is a clerk in the Comptroller's Office, Whitehall, of which his Uncle Frederick is the Secretary, & also acts as private Secretary to another Uncle, Mr. Frankland Lewis, who is at the head of an important commission, which is engaged in enquiries as to the Revenue department in Ireland, with a view of consolidating some of the Offices, remodelling others, limiting the expences incident to the collection of the Revenue, and generally improving the System.—

Wednesday Jan 26.

We finished the arrangements, as far as was immediately necessary, and packed up such of my |[123] poor Mother's effects, as we did not propose leaving in the house. The lease of the house does not expire till July 1826; and we have judged, that it will be most advisable to continue the servant, who has been accustomed to let the house as lodgings in my Mother's absence, in the same charge: expecting to obtain sufficient for keeping down the rent, £105 per ann. (all taxes paid by the Landlord) and, perhaps, a per centage for the use of the furniture left, and which will be sold at the expiration of the lease. I take on myself to discharge all claims on my Mother; but I do not expect, that her assets will be sufficient; for her income was very confined: however, the amount of bills unpaid is inconsiderable. Rather more than £58 per ann. Long Annuities fall to me by the decease of my Mother; and two annuities, which I paid her, amounting to £111., cease of course. In the evening we went to Gloucester, and found our dear Edward quite well.

Friday Jan. 28.

Mrs. M. Hunt with her relations Miss C. & Miss M. Hunt dined with Mrs. Backhouse: my cousins, the Miss Witts's came to tea: they have recently returned to Glou- |[124] -cester, having passed a few weeks at Bristol.

Saturday Jan. 29.

I returned to Upper Slaughter.

Monday Jan 31.

I again went to Gloucester; by the way I called at my Aunt Travell's, and dined with her & Mrs. Whalley.

Wednesday Feb. 2.

We dined at Mrs. M. Hunt's.

Saturday Feb. 5.

I returned to Upper Slaughter, with the intention of remaining at home all next week, and repairing to Gloucester at the commencement of the week following, towards the close of which Mrs. F. Witts proposes terminating her visit to her Mother. I parted from my dear Son, who returns to School on Monday next. The melancholy cares, which have engrossed me so much of late, have prevented my paying that attention to the progress of his studies, which I should otherwise have done; and it has been a great mortification to me to have lost so much of his engaging society, and to have been so much incapacitated for relishing it, when with him. Thank GOD, his health is good, his heart pure and affectionate, his understanding sound, and his talents promising.

——— |